Adrian Rollini

American Made Music Series

Advisory Board

David Evans, General Editor
Barry Jean Ancelet
Edward A. Berlin
Joyce J. Bolden
Rob Bowman
Susan C. Cook
Curtis Ellison
William Ferris
John Edward Hasse
Kip Lornell
Bill Malone
Eddie S. Meadows
Manuel H. Peña
Wayne D. Shirley
Robert Walser

Adrian Rollini

The Life and Music of a Jazz Rambler

Ate van Delden

University Press of Mississippi / *Jackson*

The University Press of Mississippi is the scholarly publishing agency of
the Mississippi Institutions of Higher Learning: Alcorn State University,
Delta State University, Jackson State University, Mississippi State University,
Mississippi University for Women, Mississippi Valley State University,
University of Mississippi, and University of Southern Mississippi.

www.upress.state.ms.us

The University Press of Mississippi is a member
of the Association of University Presses.

All images are courtesy of the author unless otherwise noted.

Copyright © 2020 by University Press of Mississippi
All rights reserved

First printing 2020
∞

Library of Congress Cataloging-in-Publication Data available

LCCN 2019021692
ISBN 9781496825155 (hardcover)
ISBN 9781496825162 (paperback)
ISBN 9781496825179 (epub single)
ISBN 9781496825186 (epub institutional)
ISBN 9781496825193 (pdf single)
ISBN 9781496825148 (pdf institutional)

British Library Cataloging-in-Publication Data available

To Loes

CONTENTS

Acknowledgments ix
Introduction 3

Chapter 1: The First Rollini Generation Arrives in the USA 9
Chapter 2: Piano Roll Artist 20
Chapter 3: Ed Kirkeby and the California Ramblers 40
Chapter 4: The California Ramblers Taking Off 48
Chapter 5: The California Ramblers Grown Up 67
Chapter 6: The California Ramblers to the Top with Adrian Rollini 85
Chapter 7: The California Ramblers Back to Business 103
Chapter 8: Kirkeby Loses His Grip, the End of the Contracts 124
Chapter 9: Freelancer Adrian Rollini 146
Chapter 10: A Band of His Own 164
Chapter 11: With Fred Elizalde in England, 1928 177
Chapter 12: With Fred Elizalde in 1929, the Second Year 205
Chapter 13: Out of Europe and into the Depression: Bert Lown 234
Chapter 14: Adrian Rollini: Freelance 257
Chapter 15: Back to the California Ramblers and Bert Lown 274
Chapter 16: In and out of the Deepest Depression 295
Chapter 17: A Shop and a Trio 317
Chapter 18: Trio Years: Before and during the War 332
Chapter 19: Postwar Trio Years 365

Appendix 1: Adrian Rollini's Instruments 387
Appendix 2: Engagements without Definite Dates 394
Appendix 3: Filmography 395
Appendix 4: Adrian Rollini Compositions 398
Appendix 5: Adrian Rollini Recordings Issued on CD 399
Notes 401
Bibliography 473
Indexes 475

ACKNOWLEDGMENTS

This work has a long history. It started out of admiration for Adrian Rollini, whose bass saxophone was heard on many great jazz records made under the leadership of others, such as Red Nichols, Bix Beiderbecke, and Fred Elizalde, who got much attention in the form of historical research and reissues of their music—but their sidemen were usually considered just that. Around 1980 Tom Faber, a Dutchman who especially admired sideman Adrian Rollini, decided to collect material on Rollini's career. Tom not only started to collect Rollini's recordings but also decided to try and find Rollini's relatives and former colleagues. He wanted to write a book about Rollini, so he started to correspond and in many cases found an opportunity to personally meet the people who had known Rollini or worked with him. This was no easy task, because Rollini had died in the 1950s. But Tom managed to find persons who had been with Rollini from the beginnings of his career, even from his piano roll days, and he succeeded in building a great archive. He found some films, both personal and public, and many unknown recordings such as broadcasts. Finally Tom took the step of re-creating Rollini's music. He bought a fine Conn bass saxophone himself and organized a band which he called the Recreation Rhythm Kings. Tom was a busy man and hardly had time for recreation; in fact, he realized he would never start to write the Rollini book. I had helped him from the start of his project and shared his interest in Rollini. So one day he asked me to write the book and use his archive. In 2006, when Tom was seventy years old, my wife Loes and I spent a great day with Tom and his wife Willy. It was my start in the project, which should produce a biography and a discography. But only a few months later Tom suddenly passed away, and from then on I had to run the project. Willy digitized Tom's paper archive and allowed me to digitize Rollini's collection of recordings. But little did I expect that it would take me twelve years to complete the biography, while work on the discography continues.

The list of people who helped me in any way is very long. Without them the book would not have been done. One contribution might refer to a periodical while another might be a good number of obscure recordings. It has been Tom's and my luck to meet some of Adrian Rollini's relatives. When I contacted Rollini's nephew Art, he immediately invited my wife Loes and me to come and stay with him and his lovely wife Shay and their two sons. It was our starting point for a trip through Florida that brought us to the place on Key Largo where Rollini had his fishing lodge in the last ten years of his life, but also where the Deauville Casino used to be. Bruce Laue, another Rollini descendant, invited us to an unforgettable event organized by the Order of Lafayette, of which he is president. We visited Phil Sillman, Rollini's last surviving cousin, a year before he passed away at ninety-seven.

It is impossible to detail each individual contribution, but we would like to single out just a few. Marc Cantor's unique expertise in jazz films helped me make Rollini's filmography. He gave me several rare movies and identified persons on screen. Nick Dellow is probably world's greatest expert on Fred Elizalde, in whose top band Rollini worked for two years in London. His research made two chapters possible. Vince Giordano is that special personality who leads a band, plays all bass instruments including bass saxophone, and has incomparable knowledge about the years of Rollini's greatness. Frank Himpsl practically made possible the chapter on Rollini's piano rolls, by selling me an almost complete set of these rare items. Dan Morgenstern provided items from the Rutgers Institute of Jazz Studies, in particular its Kirkeby collection.

Members of the Rollini and Augenti families that were of help are Ruth Baer, Marty Berman, Esther Brumberg, Richard Greenwood, Bruce Laue, Art F. Rollini, Art N. Rollini, Mark Rubinsky, and Phil Sillman.

Persons interviewed: Sylvester Ahola, Gene Barras, Irving Brodsky, Ernest Capozzi, Nick Casti, Harry Clark, Spencer Clark, Fred Cusick, Al Duffy, Andre Eschauzier, Brick Fleagle, William Friars, Harry Gold, Gordon Griffin, Alan Hanlon, Harry Hayes, George Hurley, Jonah Jones, Max Kaminsky, Merrill Kaye (Merrill Kline), Manny Klein, Eddy Lappe, Abe Lincoln, Charlie Magnante, Hazel McKenzie, Jimmy McPartland, Peggy Michalsky, Pete Pumiglio, Jean Robert, Babe Russin, Fred Sharp, Bert Shefter, Phil Sillman, Walter Smith, Joe Tarto, Neil Waterman, and Peter Wells.

And all the others: Steve Abrams, Gerd Ahlers, Jan Wouter Alt, Mark Atnip, Jim Baldwin, Tony Baldwin, Mark Bardenwerper, Anthony Barnett, Gene Barrass, Bruce Bastin, Renee Becker, Blake Bell, Anne Behr, Mark Berresford, Bert Brandsma, Scott Black, Wim Bor, Enrico Borsetti, Bert Brandsma, Colin Bray, Michael Brooks, Ernst Bruins, Grant Cairns, Doug Caldwell, Mark Cantor, Mac Ceppos, Allison Clark, Paul Cohen, Bill Cole, Alan Cooperman, Harry Coster, Miff Crommelin, Jehangir Dalal, Marc Danval, Nick Dellow, John Dengler, Ron Dethlefson, Peter Dortmond, Robert Duis, Sherwin Dunner, Hans Eekhoff, Han Enderman, Bjoern Englund, Emrah Erken, Jop Euwijk, Jerry Fabris, Ed Farley, Sally Fee, George Ferrick, Norman Field, Maurizio Floris, Joe Giordano, Grex Goyarts, Friedrich Hachenberg, Annemarie Hadders, Chuck Haddix, Pieter Hagenaar, Albert Haim, Carl Hallstrom, Eric Hamilton, Peder Hansen, Tad Hershorn, Laurens Hertzdahl, Steve Hester, Warren Hicks, Dave Hignett,

Bob Hilbert, Brian Hills, Wolfgang Hirschenberger, Franz Hoffman, Joanna Hurst, Tomaz Jardim, Brad Kay, David Kiner, Peter Kok, Ben Kraaijenbrink, Ben Kragting, Albert Kramer, Ross Laird, Steven Lasker, Rainer Lotz, Dymitr Markiewicz, George Mazza, Mark McDaniel, Phil Melick, Gene Miller, Keith Miller, Mark Miller, Ray Mitchell, Ellen Mittelberg, Mike Montgomery, Joe Moore, John Morphew, Jan Mulder, Jaime Ferreira Muller, Peter Newbrook, John Newton, Fred Ollison, Herman Openneer, Ruud Overduin, Stephen Paget, Bill Peatman, Pio Pellizari, Agustin Perez Gasco, Al Perlis, Robert Perry, Robert Pollack, Doug Pomeroy, Ben Posthumus, Jim Prohaska, Ton Rakers, Paul Ricci, Paul Riseman, Dave Robinson, Malcolm Rockwell, "Preacher" Rollo Laylan, Rob Rothberg, Joe Rushton, Tony Russo, Stephen Ryan, Randy Sandke, Andreas Schmauder, Malcolm Shaw, Jim Shepherd, Russ Shor, Joe Showler, Frans Sjöström, Allison Sniffin, Paul Solarski, Javier Soria Laso, Merle Sprinzen, Michael Steinmann, Robert Stockdale, George Stoffer, Henk Strengers, Allan Sutton, Stephen Taylor, Mike Thomas, Matt Tolentino, Trevor Tolley, Hughie Tripp, Bill Trumbauer, Christian Van den Broek, Joop Van den Broek, Ton Vaes, Alex Van der Tuuk, Martin Van der Waals, Jacques Van Elewout, Charles Van Herbruggen, Frank Van Nus, Marc Van Nus, Guido Van Rijn, Julian Vein, Ralph Venables, Mrs. Verbunt, Jur Voorwerk, Scott Wenzel, John Wilby, Ross Wilby, Jerry Wilkinson, "K" Wilkinson, Ralph Wondraschek, and Ray Woodbine.

And my apologies to anyone who should have been listed and was forgotten....

Adrian Rollini

INTRODUCTION

New Yorker Adrian Rollini was a child prodigy, playing the piano in public before he was five years old. Twenty years later he became a celebrity for playing the bass saxophone, a musical instrument that nobody before or after him played with as much originality, artistry, and craftsmanship. Another ten years later his instrument of choice was the vibraphone, and again he had few peers. By the forties, Adrian was no longer in the limelight. He eventually followed his desire to pursue his fishing hobby, buying a property on Key Largo in Florida and exploiting it as a fishing lodge. Unlike today, the Florida Keys were undeveloped territory; Adrian's place offered little luxury, but was excellent for fishing. He continued to make music for pleasure, but only rarely would he perform for an audience that he did not know. In 1956 Adrian Rollini passed away at the age of fifty-three. At the time few noticed, not even those who knew him.

Rollini's parents loved opera (and would sing duets at home) and his piano teacher taught him to play classical music, but his heart went out to jazz. And he was at the right time in the right place. He started his professional career in 1920, at the moment that the jazz of the twenties was making a breakthrough. In 1922 he discovered the bass saxophone, an instrument impractical due to its size and without much history, but he developed it into a superb tool and became its undisputed master. Rollini had many followers, but most of them gave up quickly, like Coleman Hawkins and Joe Tarto, who would become recognized as the champions respectively on tenor saxophone and tuba.[1] The quality of Rollini's work actually discouraged competition, and as a consequence he did not create a wide tradition. Thus, when he decided to go a different way, the sound of the bass saxophone no longer was part of the mainstream of jazz and almost died out. The instrument found very limited use in the big band swing of the thirties, or in the combo jazz of the forties and what came later.[2] Only its smaller brother, the baritone saxophone, kept a place, and some of its famous users would admit being influenced by Rollini (Harry Carney, Gerry Mulligan).[3] Also Garvin Bushell, who played the bassoon in addition to his clarinet, said that he was fascinated by Adrian Rollini's style.[4] Louis Armstrong appreciated Rollini's sound too. During a blindfold test where he listened to a record by Bix Beiderbecke's Gang with Rollini, he recognized Bix immediately and added, "the bass part is especially fine on that record."[5] Others who used Rollini's advice for the bass saxophone were the great soprano saxophone player Sidney Bechet and the prominent Belgian reed player Jean Robert. Both met Rollini in 1928 and got a bass saxophone and recorded on it. In later years Rollini had other admirers, among them xylophone player Red Norvo.

When during the sixties the interest in jazz history grew and more and more literature became available, Rollini had already passed away, but most of his contemporaries were still alive. His records were cherished by many aficionados of prewar jazz and many had been reissued on long play records. However, it took another twenty years before somebody seriously started to collect data about Rollini and to interview people who had worked with him or were relatives or good friends. This person was my friend Tom Faber, who became a bass sax player out of admiration for Adrian Rollini, and the proud owner of a Conn of the same vintage as Rollini's. Tom was a successful businessman, and during the eighties he found time to make several trips to the USA to do interviews and collect material. This was at a time when Adrian's wife Dixie had also passed away, but Tom found her lady friend who guarded her scrapbooks. Elsewhere he found some of Adrian's films made in the forties, both private and professional. Also Adrian's personal record collection was found, which included some unknown test pressings, as well as many broadcast recordings. I was pleased to be able to contribute to Tom's project from its earliest days and when the years passed by and Tom started to wonder if he would ever get around to writing the Rollini book, he asked me to do it, using his material, to which I agreed. Again years passed until I could really start. That was in 2006 and then on the first day of Pentecost Tom suddenly died, at the age of seventy. His widow Willy opened Tom's Rollini archive to me and did much of the copying and scanning. The contributions of Tom and Willy Faber to the Adrian Rollini project cannot be overestimated.

Jazz collectors that I have met all like to talk about Adrian Rollini, due to his extraordinary work with the great and famous jazz players of the twenties and thirties. The list is endless. Here are just the ones that immediately come to mind: Benny Goodman, Fats Waller, Jack Teagarden, Red Nichols, Jimmy Dorsey, Tommy Dorsey, Bix Beiderbecke, Frank Trumbauer, Joe Venuti, Eddie Lang, Bunny Berigan, Jonah Jones, not to forget Fred Elizalde, the great composer he worked with in England. In no time words like "excellent" and "genius" enter the conversation, but as a person he remains largely unknown. The following pages tell his life story, but here first some words about his personality.

Adrian Rollini was born on 28 June 1903 in New York of parents who had both been born in Italy. His father made a very good living as an engraver and the family prospered. The Rollinis bought a summer home and in 1917 moved to a large house in an attractive neighborhood, one of the first Italian families in the area. One could call them an upper-middle-class family.

Adrian had unusual musical talent that was recognized by his parents, who could afford to pay a private piano teacher. He had absolute pitch and once told his brother Art in confidence that "his absolute pitch was keener than Bix's."[6] He had great admiration for Bix Beiderbecke and hired him to play in a band he organized. Adrian was the oldest of his family's American-born second-generation Italians. He was a natural leader and would lead a gang of kids, which variously consisted of his male and female cousins and his brother and sister. His cousin Phil Sillman, born in 1913 (he died in 2011, almost aged ninety-eight) gave a lively description of life with Adrian Rollini in his younger days:

> We were part of a very close family. I was the smaller of the bunch. Those Rollini cousins of mine somehow used to enjoy tripping me up as I went galloping the gravel path. . . . I'd fall on the gravel and cut my knees. I don't know why they enjoyed that. They were very active, physically active. Forever fishing, wading, swimming, and hunting. [Adrian] taught us how to build . . . cabins, how to fish and to hunt and to masturbate. He just taught us everything. He was a good older cousin. He taught us how to shoot a squirrel, how to pitch up a .22 rifle. . . . He had a good eye.

Sillman describes him as a born entertainer:

> He could [also] make a party. I remember . . . Adrian would set up an entire theatrical thing with a curtain and sound effects behind the scenes and put up the whole thing for us. I can remember that they used to dress me up in Charlie Chaplin get up, with a little moustache and a derby and a heavy prancing around with the cane and Adrian would play the piano and Vera the inevitable ukulele . . . Someone had an alto saxophone. . . . With Adrian on the stand, there was always that rapport with the audience. Adrian played for his audience.[7]

Adrian was also a good swimmer. Phil had this to say about his physique: "He had a good body for it but he was not really athletic. He had fabulous hands. I still recall the muscular structure of Adrian's hands. . . . He was a muscular guy. Yes, he could work those four mallets on the vibraphone." Spencer Clark, who admired and followed Rollini as a bass saxophone player, remembered the long fingers of his hands that allowed him to reach from C to F♯ comfortably.[8]

Figures of Adrian's height and weight are known from a 1944 document. It said that he had brown hair and brown eyes. His height was 5 feet 10 inches and his weight 174 pounds.[9] What it did not say was that Adrian was ambidextrous, an advantage when he played the vibraphone in later years.[10] Bass player Harry Clark noted Adrian's tremendous strength in his arms, which he demonstrated by lifting two chairs at arm's length, one on each side.[11]

In interviews done for this project, most of his former colleagues were full of praise for Adrian Rollini, not only as a musician but also as a person. Piano player Irving Brodsky knew Adrian even before they both joined the California Ramblers:

> He had a wonderful ear, he could hit any chord you wanted. He was talented, he had ideas, but he did not play own compositions. He was a private sort of man, a loner, somebody who is more or less himself. He did not give out information. Adrian liked cars. Once he owned a Ford, he put a body on it and made it into a racing car. Adrian was a stamp of the California Ramblers, its signature. . . . a logo. It first was an ordinary band; the bass sax was the "trade mark" of the band. The band needed no signature tune.[12]

Reed player Pete Pumiglio felt that Adrian was a very serious person and had no sense of humor: "The kind of guy you couldn't warm up to."[13] Adrian's younger brother Art disagrees and says that Adrian was no loner: "He was just the opposite! . . . Adrian had an outgoing personality and had many friends. He loved life and said to me: 'Kid, if I should die tomorrow, I could say that I had a good time!' He enjoyed being with people and mingled with some very important ones."[14]

Sylvester Ahola, who worked in Adrian's 1927 band, had a more considered and unbiased view: "He was hard to get to know, not a loner, but he was a little different. He was the big thing then."[15] Another early member of the California Ramblers, Fred Cusick said:

> Adrian didn't really seem to read the music when he was playing. . . . He imagined much better bass parts than any music had. His style was such a solid style; it was jazz but it wasn't crazy. Everything had a meaning, everything he played had a reason for it, you could feel it, you could hear it. It gave you satisfaction. When you heard it, you were satisfied because it was right.[16]

Al Duffy, Rollini's violinist in the thirties, when asked if Rollini was a good boss, said: "No, he was my buddy. He paid well, $75 always became $125 or even $150. Adrian was one of the finest musicians. I gave him preference."[17] Harry Gold, a British bass sax player, expresses his admiration as follows: "So many things: his attack, the tone quality, his tonguing ability on a cumbersome instrument like that, and the technique of combining the tongue with the fingers and doing it faultlessly and with a musical conception that was beyond belief. There were times when phrases were utterly simple but beautiful and suddenly, something unbelievably intricate would come out, so you had these two contrasts." Gold described Rollini's American humor as something you had to get used to: "He had a wonderful sense of humor. At one point I took him seriously, thinking that he was saying something which was a bit hard and then I realized that he was joking."[18]

Adrian's brother Art gave an example. It happened on April Fool's Day 1929 in London:

> I had ordered a clarinet with Lewins Music Store. When I came home one day, Adrian said: "Lewins called. Your clarinet is ready." He gave me a telephone number and I called Lewins and said: "This is Arthur Rollini. I understand my clarinet is ready." He said: "What clarinet?" "The clarinet that I ordered," I answered. He said: "We don't have any clarinets here." "Is this Lewins Music Store?" I asked and he said: "No, this is Lewins Mortuary!" That is an April Fool's joke of Adrian.

Art also describes another aspect of Adrian's personality: he was accident prone. One time in London he jumped on a bicycle and drove down a steep hill; he was not familiar the English bicycle's hand brakes and hit a row of garbage cans. He was hurt and was taken to a hospital. The doctor said: "For God's sake! Are you here again?"[19] Herb Weil, drummer with the California Ramblers from 1926, appreciated Rollini's solo and ensemble work: "The biggest musical kick I ever had was playing with Adrian Rollini. He made you want to play. His tone, intonation, attack, and creative ideas were inspiring."[20]

Merrill Kaye, a bass player with Bert Lown's band, which Adrian joined in 1930, remembers: "Adrian was in a class by himself. There are not enough words to express the opinion of Adrian. Adrian was a very quiet, subdued man. And if he had something to say he said it and let it go, just leave it go, but musically you couldn't touch him, you couldn't touch him. Because he was so far advanced...." However, Kaye sees it in the light of the time: "The musicians were not educated in those days like they are today. You discuss music today, these kids know their history, they know everything."[21]

Comments on his work usually concern his bass saxophone playing. However, Harry Clark, who worked for five years as a bass player in Rollini's trio, had this to say about his work as a vibraphone (or vibraharp, as Adrian called it) player:

> It was the way he handled those four mallets. Adrian's melody notes were on the outside hammers and he bracketed the chords in between. So when he played his hands were constantly being twisted in or out in order to be able to make the four hammers work, the melody staying on the top. Playing the way he did with four mallets was a magnificent thing and almost nobody else could do it that way and he had people come around and watch it.[22]

Gene Barras and her husband were longtime friends of the Rollinis in New York. She remembers Adrian as hot blooded, but when he would blow up, there would be his wife Dixie to calm him down.[23] Adrian Rollini may have been an extraordinary musician, but in all other aspects he was perfectly human. He liked women, whisky, and smoking. His whisky was Canadian Club and his cigarette was Camel.[24] However, his greatest hobby was fishing. To this end he bought boats. The first was when he was with the California Ramblers, and he called it the *Rambler*. Other boats were called *Rambler* with a Roman serial number. Adrian made it at least to *Rambler VIII*. The boats helped him catch some large fish, like a 323-pound swordfish thirty-five miles off Long Island and, in Florida, a 325-pound blue marlin, a local record.[25]

A great contribution to my project was made by Dan Morgenstern at Rutgers University's jazz archive. Dan let me have copies of Ed Kirkeby's notebooks in the archive. These cover the period from March 1926 until July 1931 and give dates, record labels, and the names of all participating musicians (and their pay) for all of Kirkeby's many record sessions.

Many recordings exist that allow us to hear Rollini, from his early work as a piano player and his first careful efforts on bass saxophone, to his legendary top-class work on that instrument and his later work on vibraharp. In approximate numbers, this is the number of recordings:

piano rolls	35
gramophone records	1,500 titles
of which as a leader	130 titles
pre-recorded radio shows	300 tunes
films	25 (shorts and feature films)

James Lincoln Collier, the renowned author of many books on jazz, including biographies of Louis Armstrong, Duke Ellington, and Benny Goodman, wrote: "Given his obvious musical talent and feeling for jazz, it is surprising that [Adrian Rollini] has not earned a bigger place in the history of the music. The trouble may have been that he never took himself or the music seriously."[26]

The reader is invited to draw his own conclusion.

Chapter 1

The First Rollini Generation Arrives in the USA

At the dawn of the twentieth century, Europe's layout was quite different from what it is today. Most of its peripheral areas had not found its present final shape. Norway was about to split from Sweden, Ireland from the British Empire. The Turks were about to lose the Balkans after ruling there for nearly five hundred years. And usually these changes meant war.

Italy had its share of these wars. It had gone through a long process of unification. After Napoleon had been defeated in 1815, Europe's layout was once more reshuffled and Italy was left divided. A large part was ruled by the Austrian Habsburg family. Another large part was ruled by the Pope, the Papal States with Rome as its center. It took three Wars of Independence to unify the various parts including the Papal States into one Kingdom of Italy with Rome as its capital.

Other countries were involved in Italy's growth process. France had gone through a period of revolution and Napoleonic wars, but by the middle of the nineteenth century this had stabilized. Its emperor Napoleon III kept a French garrison in Rome to protect the city and the Pope from being taken by the Italian army. However, he had to withdraw his troops during the Franco-Prussian War of 1870–71. France even asked Italy's freedom fighter Giuseppe Garibaldi to assist them against Germany. Sometime during this period one of Adrian Rollini's ancestors, a Frenchman, left his country to settle in Domodossola, in the Piedmont region in northwest Italy. He had been a member of the army of Napoleon I.[1] In Italy he used the name Rollini, derived from his French family name.[2] He was the first Rollini generation in Italy.[3]

Out of this French emigrant's marriage a son was born, Antonio. Around 1860, when he was about twenty-eight years old, Antonio married an Italian lady by the name of Amelia Grimaldi.[4] They had two daughters, Luigia, also called Gigia, and Giulia, and one son Ferdinando, the eldest child and born circa 1867 in Campobasso, about fifty miles northeast from Naples. Antonio followed in his father's footsteps in warfare. He became a member of the Italian army that took Rome (commonly called the "liberation of Rome") in 1870. For this action and thus for his contribution to the Italian unification he received medals, which in later years he would proudly show.[5]

Little is known about Antonio's family life. In addition to his military career he had artistic aspirations and became a painter.[6] Thus he was able to give his children a good upbringing. They went to school and had an English-speaking governess. However, the stories of unlimited opportunities in America became stronger and stronger. And by the end of the nineteenth century a flow of emigrants from Italy to the USA literally came under steam. Steamships had taken the place of the earlier sailing ships and presented better facilities for passengers. Son Ferdinando ("Nando" to his family) was the first to try it out.[7] In later years his sisters Giulia and Luigia would follow him to the USA and start families. They could speak English when they arrived, but it was with a British accent which they had inherited from their governess.[8]

Ferdinando Moves to the USA

Ferdinando had received formal training as an engraver and in 1895, aged about thirty, boarded the SS *Werra* and traveled to New York, to see if the stories about the New World were right. The Werra was built in 1882 in Glasgow, Scotland, and could carry 1,255 passengers.[9] During Ferdinando's trip it carried only 637, including 507 Italians who almost all traveled third class and boarded in Naples. The other nationalities mostly boarded later in Genoa and Gibraltar, *Werra*'s other ports of call. These were the happy few who nearly all had their own cabins: 107 Americans and twenty-three persons coming from Austria, Germany, Morocco, Spain, Switzerland, and Turkey. The trip offered Ferdinando a possibility to perfect his English. He arrived in New York on 2 September 1895. Like all immigrants he came through Ellis Island. He traveled as third-class passenger 498 and a clerk noted down that he was a twenty-nine-year-old single male and that he had only one piece of luggage. His profession was given as engraver. The professions given for his third-class shipmates read as those of a small village. They were barber, engineer, mason, miller, peasant, shoemaker, smith, stonebreaker, and tailor. On the other hand, the professions of the cabin passengers were generally more on the intellectual side: teachers, an architect, a physician, a lawyer, a surgeon, an artist, a musician and also a US consul.

When Ferdinando arrived in New York, he had a permanent stay in mind, a "protracted sojourn" as said on the *Werra*'s passenger list. Yet he returned to Italy, maybe for strong family ties. However, New York had convinced him of the great opportunities across the Atlantic. So he returned to the USA.

Ferdinando's second trip to the USA was on board the SS *Trojan Prince*, which left Naples on 19 November 1897 and arrived in New York on 6 December. He was passenger 26 on the passenger list, which now gave his age as thirty and his profession as "engraver" again. A special note was made that passenger 26 "is working his passage across to New York as a steward and is on the ship's articles as such."

Ferdinando could indeed find a job as an engraver. These were the days before photographic techniques had taken over the graphic side of printing. Magazines and advertising strongly relied on craftsmen to produce illustrations. Ferdinando would develop into one of the best, and the job paid well. On top of that Ferdinando had musical talent. He liked opera and played the piano. This gave him a chance to earn extra money by teaching Italian singing. He advertised as "Signor Rollini" and gave his address as 790 6th Avenue, New York.[10] He informed his family about his progress and already in 1898 he had earned enough money to pay for his 64-year old father to visit him in New York. Antonio left from Naples on 20 December 1898 with the SS *Trojan Prince* and traveled in a more luxurious style than his son had done on the same boat: as a cabin passenger.

Ferdinando Marries Adelina

Ferdinando Rollini was now over thirty years old and found himself in a position to get married and start a family. He met a young lady of Italian descent, Adelina Julia Caroline Augenti, and they married around 1902. She was the daughter of Michael Augenti, a tailor, and Mary Filomena DiLalla. Adelina's family usually called her Adeline or Adele, and like Ferdinando she was born in Campobasso, Italy, on 28 May 1878. Her family migrated to the USA in the early 1880s. Like the Rollinis they were well-to-do and owned a row of brownstone houses in addition to the house where they lived. Adelina was the eldest of five Augenti children, three of which were born in the USA.

Adelina first went to live with Ferdinando at his address on 6th Avenue, but by 1905 they had moved to a brownstone in Long Island City, Queens, at 323 W. 27th Street.[11] From here they could see the Queensboro Bridge, linking Queens and Manhattan.[12]

Music played a strong role in these families. The Augentis were all musically inclined and this matched well with Ferdinando's love for music. He sang in church and played piano and guitar. A real Italian who loved opera, he and his young wife went to New York's Metropolitan Opera to see and hear greats like Enrico Caruso. At this time, the start of the new century, music took a new direction. The Rollinis were to contribute to the new trend in a major way.

Adrian's birth certificate.

Adrian Rollini Arrives in the Family and at Age Four and a Half Gets His First Piano Lessons

Adrian Rollini was born 28 June 1903 at home, the first child of his parents. He displayed a remarkable musical talent at a tender age. This was discovered after he was given a toy piano for Christmas when he was two and a half years old. Ferdinando and Adelina would sing opera songs at home together and one day they found that little Adrian, in another room, was playing a song along with them.[13] Ferdinando detected that Adrian even played the harmony parts as correctly as he could possibly do on his toy piano. And half an hour after he had played on his piano Adrian would hum the songs in the same key. His parents decided that this should be taken seriously and found a piano teacher in New York by the name of Mary Wagner Gilbert.[14] She had received piano lessons from the Polish/German pianist Xaver Schwarwenka. In her advertisements she mentioned the basics of her training method: sight reading, ear training, and the Leschetizky Method. Theodor Leschetizky's piano education method required a thorough technical training and Miss Gilbert's sight reading and ear training were meant to reach that goal.[15] At the time, this method of musical training for

Adrian Rollini.

ITH the accompanying picture we are introducing a wonderfully gifted little boy to the readers of our "Children's Page."

Just imagine this little chap is only four years of age and already he plays a large number of solos and operatic selections in a particularly astonishing and clever manner.

So far his musical education has been entrusted to Mary Wagner Gilbert, one of our well-known local instructors, and she has every reason to be proud of the astonishing progress of her little prodigy pupil. Only recently the writer had occasion to hear the little man play some of his solos and was surprised beyond measure at the grace, fluency and command with which he performed the numbers. The most surprising part is that he has received regular instruction for only six months and only within the last three months has he shown his wonderful gifts of playing independently before strangers.

Miss Gilbert informs us that the first time he played in public was last April at her studio, and then he cried for half an hour before he could be induced to go near the piano, as he was so frightened at seeing such a number of strange people. But finally he was quieted and played splendidly.

On last May 19th he played at an entertainment given by the Gotham Club at the Waldorf-Astoria Hotel, and proved to be the sensation of the evening. He played Kuhe's "*Fra Diavolo*" fantasia and various other shorter solo numbers; he had to respond to three encores and was finally lifted on to a table in order that all the audience could get a good view of him. But while he is so very talented his teacher also informs us that he is very, very capricious, and—just imagine— sometimes very naughty and sometimes very good. He has even not hesitated to go fast asleep during a lesson, but then again, at other times he is very alert and fairly devours everything which he is told to do.

MASTER ADRIAN ROLLINI.

He plays in a most artistic, easy and natural manner, a direct result of course of his teacher's excellent methods and system.

We shall keep a watchful eye on Master Adrian and hope he will develop into a thorough and capable artist in keeping with his extraordinary promises. —G. S.

July 1908 Adrian in the *Musical Observer*. (courtesy Rob Rothberg)

children and grownups was new. Today sight reading (also called sight singing) and ear training form the start of many a musical education.[16]

In November 1907, when Adrian was four years old, Adeline gave birth to their second child, a daughter named Elvira, or Vera for short. Vera had blue eyes, was slightly cross-eyed, and as a youngster was a redhead.[17] Two months after Vera's birth Adrian Rollini got his first piano lessons from Miss Gilbert at four and a half years old. Her studio was at Room 826, Carnegie Hall, New York, but Adrian got his weekly lessons at home in Long Island City. A real piano was acquired and young Adrian still had a long way to grow. He could not reach the piano's foot pedals because of his short legs, but this problem was solved by father Ferdinando who had the pedals raised. The as yet small size of Adrian's fingers could not so easily be solved. It could only be compensated by choosing musical pieces that did not require grownup hands. Adrian turned

Adrian Rollini about five years old.

out to have absolute pitch, the rare talent that allows identifying an individual tone without the help of any tool but one's mind. His progress was such that his teacher wanted others to hear it, so she arranged a public appearance. The first occasion was in April 1908 at her studio in New York. It was no easy task for Miss Gilbert to get him to play. Later she told an editor that "he cried for half an hour" before he could be induced to go near the piano as he was so frightened at seeing "such a number of strange people." However, finally he quieted and he "played splendidly."[18]

That editor was Edith L. Winn, author of the children's page in the *Musical Observer*, who was present at Rollini's first real public performance. It took place on Tuesday 19 May 1908 and Miss Gilbert had found an excellent occasion, an evening with the Gotham Club at the Waldorf-Astoria Hotel in New York. This was a culture club, organized in the interest of philanthropy, art, literature, hygiene, music, patriotism, drama, and dancing, led by Mrs. A. Arthur Alfred Brooks, president. It would regularly organize salons at the Waldorf where members and others would present their views or talents. The audience might be about fifty and would be most pleased if an evening were both entertaining and instructive. Young Adrian did not play popular music in today's sense. His teacher had probably chosen for him and had wisely selected several short solo works. Reviews specifically mentioned the "Fra Diavolo Fantasia," a work by the German pianist and composer Wilhelm Kuhe (1823–after 1893).[19] It was based on the opera *Fra Diavolo* by the French composer Daniel François Esprit Auber (1782–1871) and consisted of a medley of its music arranged for solo piano. Adrian was the sensation of the evening and had to play three encores. "Miss Gilbert has done wonders with [Adrian] in six months' tuition."[20] Among his other pieces probably was Frédéric Chopin's well-known "Minute Waltz," which is quite suitable to display virtuoso technique.[21] After his performance, Adrian was lifted onto a table so that all present could have a good look at the young artist. Mary Gilbert also performed and played Felix Mendelssohn's "Rondo Capriccioso." The audience could furthermore listen to Frank Woelber's violin quartet and to a talk by inventor Hudson Maxim. The Gotham club reached its broad goal that night.

Now that his talent had been recognized by "such a number of strange people," Adrian would not again be hindered by his initial shyness. He would be meeting new people all his life.

Eventually Adrian Rollini would have eleven years of formal piano studies with a private teacher. At some point Mary Wagner Gilbert was probably replaced by another teacher, maybe because the trip to the Rollini home took too much of her time. Art related that Adrian's piano teacher was one Madame Negri, who would make a weekly visit for Adrian's piano lessons.[22] Thus he became a fully developed and trained musician, ready for a professional career.

The Rollinis Prosper

Those years were full of motion. Ferdinando and Adelina were the parents of two now and Ferdinando had a job as engraver with the American Tobacco Company (ATC). This company had started in 1890 and its management led it through a period of very strong growth, both autonomous and through acquisitions. They added or introduced still famous brands such as Lucky Strike and Pall Mall. ATC grew so big that the American government started an anti-trust action against it. In 1911 this resulted in a breakup into four other large tobacco companies. One of these continued to use the name of American Tobacco Company, and this one remained Ferdinando's employer. As their chief engraver he became responsible for all of ATC's engraved artwork.

The job paid well and Adrian's piano lessons could easily be afforded.[23] In February 1912 the Rollini family once more grew with the birth of Arthur Francesco, commonly called Art. He was eight and a half years Adrian's junior. Art remembered his early years quite well in his autobiography and the summer of 1915 was his earliest memory, when the family stayed at a summer home in

1912 Rollinis and Augentis at the Augenti home, Long Island. Front row from left: Adrian, his sister Vera, cousin William Laue, grandfather Michael Augenti. Second row: the ladies are Mildred and Elizabeth Augenti, sitting next to husband Phil Sillman. Third row third from left: Adrian's grandmother Mary Filomena DiLalla, Adelina Augenti, Adrian's mother with brother Art on her lap, unknown, Rose Augenti; extreme right probably Luigia Rollini sitting on lap of husband William Laue. Back row, fifth from left: Adrian's father Ferdinando Rollini.

Atlantic Highlands, New Jersey.[24] During that year he became three years old and Adrian twelve. In 1924 there was money to buy a summer home at Salt Point, about a hundred miles north of New York's heat.[25]

Adrian Is Twelve and Starts His First Orchestra

By now Adrian had had seven years of musical training, and in his elementary school environment there were others who could play an instrument well enough to play ensemble. Adrian got some of them together and started to lead a little orchestra in which he played the piano. This orchestra continued when he moved to high school. His music teacher, both at Chatsworth Avenue Grade School and at Mamaroneck High School, was Mr. Conklin, who greatly admired Adrian.[26] Conklin would eventually also give Adrian's sister Vera and brother Art musical training. Vera had both a ukulele and an alto saxophone. Adrian got Art started on the drums when he was eight and Art would accompany his brother's piano playing (Adrian was a good drummer himself, too).

No picture of Rollini's first orchestra, a trio is known to exist, but some names are known. Art Rollini never was a member since he was too young. By then the saxophone reached prominence in emerging dance bands, but while Vera played an alto saxophone, even she was too young to participate. In Rollini's small group was Arnold Brilhart on saxophone as well as flute. Brilhart would work with Rollini for many years.[27] On the drums Adrian probably used different musicians at different times. During a 1930s broadcast Adrian mentioned Joe Bohan, a white drummer who worked in Ozzie Nelson's band during the thirties.[28] Art, however, remembered that his brother used a black drummer.[29] At that time racial integration in orchestras, or anywhere at all, was rare but Adrian did not mind and simply thought that his drummer was doing a good job.[30] Sometimes a violin was added, or replaced the saxophone, or a banjo player would turn the group into a quartet, thus offering considerable melodic and rhythmic possibilities. Their earnings were small, but his group saw him as "maestro" and Rollini held out five dollars for himself on all dates.[31]

The Rollinis Move to Larchmont

Their prosperity gave Ferdinando and Adelina the financial room to consider a larger, more beautiful home than the one in Long Island City. They chose a house at 30 Summit Avenue in Larchmont, Westchester County, New York. This was a well-to-do area and the Rollinis were one of the first Italian families to move in, on 4 October 1917. Art remembered the names of the builder and the architect as Santora and Henri Cipolla, of Italian origin like the Rollinis. It was a large house with a huge living room, a dining room, five bedrooms, and several bathrooms. It had an office for Ferdinando where he could do his engraving work if he did not go to New York. Its kitchen always smelled of good Italian cooking. Phil Sillman remembered: "The living room was always bright and airy. [Adrian's mother] used olive oil like a blue ribbon cook. Garlic and olive oil. There was a lot of ground around the place. Uncle Nando had a large grape orchard at the back."[32]

Ferdinando would work long and intensive hours in this studio to get a project, a die, done. His wife would bring him lunch and after a short break he would continue to peer through his multiple magnifying glasses to see minute details. Said Sillman: "He was highly skilled, the equivalent of the top technological people of today. He had to keep working on these [dies]. He was ever at his bench.... with his magnifying glass carving away with the delicate and gifted

Rollini family home, Larchmont, NY (chauffeur's home in background).

hands of his and I assume that some of the artistic quality rubbed off on our musical genius. On Adrian."[33]

At its very end the Rollini property actually bordered on the next street, Concord Avenue. And on that side there was a second house, meant for a chauffeur. This was a small family house and it had a two-car garage. The car, a Ford Model T, came not long after the move but there was no chauffeur, no driver. Parents Ferdinando and Adelina never learned to drive, but young Adrian jumped in. You had to be sixteen to get a learner's permit, which allowed driving by daylight. Adrian had not reached this age yet, but drove his parents where they wanted to go, sitting on a cushion to look taller and with a cap on his head and a cigarette in his mouth to look older. Art described how his family became friends with the police, even with motorcycle cop Couchran, who was regarded a terrorist in Larchmont.[34] The police were invited to the Rollini home for cigarettes, brought home from his employer by Ferdinando, who did not smoke. Adrian's fine piano playing was very much appreciated by the visiting policemen and he could do no wrong.

When the family moved to Larchmont, Adrian moved into eighth grade at the Chatsworth Avenue Grade School, his sister Vera into fifth, and Art into first.[35] Adrian was about fifteen years old now, and by this time had his first girlfriend. Art remembered her as Rose Donah, who also lived in Larchmont. Adrian's parents allowed him to use the Ford to visit her and he would be back by 10:00 p.m., the agreed time.[36]

Adrian Rollini aged twelve or thirteen.

Adrian disliked high school and, after two years did not want to go there anymore. In fact, he had the feeling that he could do much better by following his drive for music. By now he had developed a taste for the trend in popular music, and at the age of sixteen he decided to make music his profession. His exceptional musical talent, combined with eleven years of fundamental piano training, three years of coaching by his music teacher at school, and even some years working with his small orchestra in public, together formed a sound basis to take the step.

Chapter 2

Piano Roll Artist

During the nineteenth century the Western world had seen major technical progress. Steam power had arrived and replaced water and wind as an industrial driver. Pneumatic systems were also in strong development, whereby air was the transmitter of power. The physics of electricity had been known for a long time in basic form, but only by the end of the century was its full potential coming to be understood. Inventors used the newly available processes and methods to realize their creative ideas. One of them was Thomas Alva Edison (1847–1931), who, in 1878, patented a device for recording and reproducing sound, called a phonograph. Eventually its most successful application would be to play recordings made in studios by professional artists, multiplied in an industrial process and widely distributed. However, it took more than ten years before such commercial recording got under way. The marketing of mass recorded entertainment began in the mid-1890s. This required major capital investments, but mass manufacturing resulted in a price decrease of Edison's economy model phonograph from $140 in 1893 to $7.50 in 1899.[1] A machine competing with Edison's phonograph was invented, the gramophone. By this last name the industry would eventually be known.

Another inventor was Edwin Scott Votey, another American, who in 1896 invented a piano-playing machine. He called it the pianola. The mechanism, housed in a large cabinet on wheels, was able to detect punched holes in a roll of paper. For each hole it would power one mechanical "finger" in a long row of fingers. The pianola had to be carefully placed in front of a normal piano so that the row of fingers would be precisely above the piano keys. The holes in the paper could be punched in such a pattern that regular music would be produced when the paper roll would run on the pianola.

Actually the pianola was the latest in a long series of mechanical musical instruments and musical automats. This development had started several hundred years earlier with automatic barrel organs and included self-playing pianos, organs, whistles, and violins.[2] The pianola's new elements were the use of air for power and of paper for containing the music. Pneumatics was easy to handle and punched paper was cheap to reproduce. Votey's pianola invention was bought by Aeolian, a company in the business of manufacturing organs and pianos. The next step was to build Votey's pianola mechanism into a normal piano. This was done by Melville Clark. His player piano was a success that Aeolian had to follow and introduce the "Pianola Piano—The First Complete Piano." Eventually this type of instrument became known as the pianola or player piano.

Creation also took place in the world of music. Black people played a new role in this. In 1898 the first musical by a black composer was performed in New York, Bob Cole's *A Trip to Coontown*. The next year, 1899, Scott Joplin's first ragtime composition, "Original Rags," was published and a few months later his best-known work, "Maple Leaf Rag." More than anything else, ragtime became the new trend in popular music, both instrumental and vocal. It was a new sound. For the public ragtime's primary source was sheet music. Selling sheet music had long been the main source of income for composers and publishers. However, now the pianola and the gramophone presented new opportunities. Both became a major factor in the market. Between 1900 and 1910 the number of pianos in American homes more than doubled from 460,000 to 1,050,000.[3] In 1919 338,000 pianos were manufactured, half of which were pianolas.[4] However, sales of gramophones were quickly catching up. During the same period annual sales by Victor, the market's largest contender, grew from zero to 107,000 in 1908 and 252,000 in 1912.[5] In 1917 Victor produced an all-time high of 573,000 Victrolas.

Both the pianola and the gramophone allowed the user to produce music without formal training. However, for piano music the gramophone was not fit yet and for its higher price the pianola offered a major extra: it was a real musical instrument.

Republic Player Roll Corporation

Ferdinando and Adelina Rollini of course had a piano for Adrian to exercise his musical lessons and also to rehearse his little orchestra. In line with the trend this probably was a pianola, which allowed everybody in the house to produce the new tunes from a roll. Certainly Adelina's family, the Augentis, had one. Adrian thus was quite familiar with piano rolls, and in early 1920 he got into contact with a piano roll company based in New York, a forty-five-minute train ride: the Republic Player Roll Corporation, which began to issue rolls in 1919.[6]

Republic was incorporated under law of the State of New York on 25 April 1918.[7] A year later, on 12 April 1919, it really started its life with a press announcement.[8] It was formed as a subsidiary of Kohler Industries, a conglomerate of companies all working in the field of piano manufacturing.[9] Kohler wanted to

Introducing Republic piano rolls.

have a major impact on the market for piano rolls and therefore hired experienced personnel. For example, Republic's president was Paul B. Klugh, who formerly was with the Imperial Roll Company, where he won a court battle about printing lyrics on a piano roll. Republic also made another major step in the piano roll market by exclusively offering hand-played rolls.[10] The April announcement furthermore mentioned that heavy investments would be made in manufacturing equipment as well as in advertising. Republic claimed that the "very best artists available" were already on their staff. No names were mentioned, except for J. Milton Delcamp. John Milton Delcamp (1892–1931) was in charge of recording and master manufacturing and was also said to be "one of the best-known recording pianists in the industry." Delcamp had worked for a company in Philadelphia, makers of DeLuxe and Unisolo piano rolls. His colleague there was Adam Carroll (1897–1974), who was five years his junior. Carroll's first professional engagement was accompanying silent movies. He cut his first piano roll in 1916 for the DeLuxe label. When in 1918 the owners of DeLuxe and Unisolo sold out to a company in New York, Delcamp and Carroll accepted an offer to come to New York and record for the new company, which became Republic. There they would play a strong role in Adrian Rollini's piano roll activities.

Republic's first monthly roll bulletin contained a handful of artists' names, which had previously been unknown to the public.[11] It announced rolls by Cal Adams, Nan Foster, Victor Lane, and Neil Shannon. What it did not say was that some of these names were pseudonyms. Manager Delcamp stimulated his artists to record under different names; thus, Victor Lane was really Adam Carroll, who was to become a prolific recorder for Republic.[12] Cal Adams was also probably Carroll. A later press release described the particular background or style of these artists: Nan Foster was said to come from "the South" and was an experienced performer of popular ballads.[13] High-class ballads were Neil Shannon's specialty. He was said to be an Englishman who had seen active service with the British army during the recent war. Victor Lane (Adam Carroll) would perform the popular show music of the day, and Cal Adams was the group's "jazz king—not long from the Barbary Coast," suggesting that he came from California. The press release continues by describing Adams's rolls as bringing home "all the 'zip' and 'zim' that is so popular to-day. 'Life,' 'pep' and 'syncopation' are the things that make [his] rolls so fascinating."

Republic showed excellent timing when it launched its first rolls. The United States had been actively involved in World War I and by November 1918 the war had ended. Now people wanted entertainment. Dancing became highly popular and new musical media found a willing public. *Music Trade Review*, a professional magazine that echoed the voices of customers and suppliers, wrote about the market for piano rolls during the spring of 1919: "we cannot get either the supply of skilled help in our factories or the manufacturing facilities which the immediate needs of business imperatively demand."[14] No wonder that Republic could issue an enthusiastic press release about its May sales, which quadrupled compared to April, its month of introduction. It carefully avoided mentioning absolute figures, however.

Republic's multitalented J. Milton Delcamp was not only an accomplished piano player but also a composer. This was announced in another press release in May.[15] Republic's roll bulletin for June 1919 contains his first five rolls, including one of his own compositions "In My Garden of Love."[16]

Republic made an impressive start, and for the next year it managed to stay in the limelight. Its promotion activities included shows, special arrangements, articles, etc. The new company was present at all major shows of pianos and pianolas, at festivals, and at conventions. In July it introduced rolls with a special effect, which it called Vodvillian rolls;[17] that same month it published an article about correct speeds in roll recording. In August there were announcements of new artists and new dealers. The news in September was that Irving Berlin supervised the recording of four of his songs. In October the company announced that the factory had to work twenty hours per day in order to satisfy the demand for Republic rolls.

This pattern of active publicity was continued the next year. In April 1920 Delcamp wrote about the high mission of the player roll: "[it] can hardly be classed in the general run of merchandise, for it represents a means of recreation. And recreation has always been recognized as one of the first essentials of a happy existence."[18] The above makes one wonder if Delcamp did not recognize the emergence of gramophone records, which would switch away piano rolls from the public's minds.

That same month of April, Republic put even more energy in its operation. First it started an advertising campaign (color, full pages) and then it announced the move to a new plant at 75th Street and Broadway "in the heart of the music belt." Every month saw the addition of more dealers, but few were the announcements of new piano stars. However, on 12 June 1920 the company announced that Adrian Rollini joined their staff.

In the meantime, Kohler, Republic's mother company, which owned several other companies in the field of pianos and player mechanisms, also increased its operations in that field. One of their companies was Auto Pneumatic Action. This company had a license from the inventor of the reproducing pianos, M. Welte & Söhne, of Freiburg, Germany. The license allowed building Welte mechanisms for American piano manufacturers under the brand name DeLuxe.[19] Such pianolas could play standard rolls as well as rolls from Welte's huge catalog of classic piano performances[20] recorded in Europe. In January 1920, Kohler and Welte had closed a contract whereby Kohler bought a Welte recorder that would allow adding American repertoire, in particular in the popular category.[21] The following September and October the first two batches of ten reproducing rolls were announced on the DeLuxe label.[22]

Sixteen-Year-Old Prodigy Records for Republic

After he had turned sixteen in June 1919, Adrian decided to make music his profession. Little is known about his first steps as a professional musician in New York. However, for piano players there were many job opportunities. In addition to playing in hotel lounges and restaurants, there were the music shops where song pluggers would demonstrate sheet music to customers. There were film theaters where silent movies had to be accompanied. Young Adrian may have done all of that, but the only thing known for certain is that he got one of the best jobs a piano player could get and that was to work for a piano roll company to record popular tunes or current hits. First he got in touch with Connorized, an established piano roll maker.[23] On the afternoon of 12 April 1920 this company offered a live concert program by their recording artists in the music salon on the eighth floor of Gimbel's department store in New York. Adrian, announced as a "Sixteen-Year-Old Prodigy," opened the program and performed "You Can't Keep a Good Man Down"[24] and "Rose of Washington Square."[25] Later that afternoon he returned to perform the tune "O"[26] in a duet with one Barnes. The three songs that Rollini performed that afternoon were recent compositions that could be performed in the new jazz style, but at this time in his musical development Adrian probably stuck close to the original melody and rhythm. Some of the tunes were said to be recent Connorized roll hits. Other artists in the program were "premier lady ragtime artiste" Eva Reeves, "prominent pianist and composer" Joseph Cirina, "Jazz King" Joe Gold, and musical director of Connorized Samuel A. Perry. A newspaper reported the concert as a great success.[27] On 25 April Adrian took part in another Connorized concert. This was at the Lafayette Theatre and the announcement mentioned that "popular numbers from Pace & Handy and other music publishers" were to be performed. Perry was now introduced as "honor graduate of the Royal Academy of Music, Vienna" and Joe Gold was again present.[28] No piano rolls by Adrian had yet been announced but it is safe to assume that Connorized's Sam Perry had such plans. However, they were not to be.

The year before, in April 1919, Republic had introduced its first rolls and, being a new company, it needed more piano talent. But since that month only two more names had been added.[29] J. Milton Delcamp, who was responsible for roll recording and reproduction at Republic, may have been among the listeners at Adrian's concert at Gimbel's. Anyway, around this time Adrian got into contact with Republic, most probably through Delcamp. A contract was signed before Adrian was even seventeen years old, presumably by one of his parents.

Republic's press release was quite detailed about his talent and experience, more so than in their earlier announcements about their artists:

> Announcement is made this week that Adrian Rollini has become a member of the recording staff of the Republic Player Roll Corporation. He is at present working on several numbers of the popular variety which will be presented to player roll buyers in the July bulletin of this corporation.
>
> Mr. Rollini is one of the youngest musicians engaged in player roll recording. He is quite young but has displayed a variety of talent which has given him immediate success and predicts an exceptional future. He has remarkable understanding of music and harmony, having devoted his entire life to the study of these subjects. His concert work began when he was five years of age and has continued unbroken until his advent with the Republic Player Roll Corporation.
>
> In addition to his activities as a concert star, Mr. Rollini conducted an orchestra with headquarters at Larchmont. He is recognized in that vicinity as a musical genius, both as an artist and as a director of his organization of musicians.[30]

When he recorded his first piano rolls, Adrian Rollini had more than ten years of experience of playing in public, had perfect pitch, and was quick to learn a new tune. And he had the physique to be a piano player. Adrian's colleague and admirer Spencer Clark (1908–1998) described it in later years: "I.... learned that he had been a concert pianist, but he could reach from C to F♯ comfortably and finger notes in between where the average person can only reach from C to E and play a tenth and not finger notes in between. He had these long, long fingers which he used with complete control and complete efficiency and accuracy."[31]

Adrian Rollini's rolls were first advertised on 26 June 1920, two days before his seventeenth birthday. It looked as if his professional career could not have a better start. Adrian Rollini's first issued piano roll concerned a tune by black composer Shelton Brooks[32] and lyric writer Chris Smith. Its title was "The Jazz Dance Repertoire" and its lyrics concerned the various "jazz dances" that were popular with the dancing public, such as Walk-The-Dog and Ball-The-Jack. Republic described it as a jazz fox trot. Adrian's first effort was a duet with Republic's experienced piano roll maker, Adam Carroll.[33] Rollini probably plays the melody part (primo), Carroll the accompaniment.[34]

"The Jazz Dance Repertoire" was quite popular as a roll tune. Other 1920 rolls of this piece are by Edythe Baker, Walter Davison, and Pete Wendling.[35] Wendling played the first part in a stiff way but then closes with a nice raggy ride-out, thus making it superior as a jazz performance to the inflexible duet version by Rollini and Carroll, but Republic's roll offered two piano players instead of one.

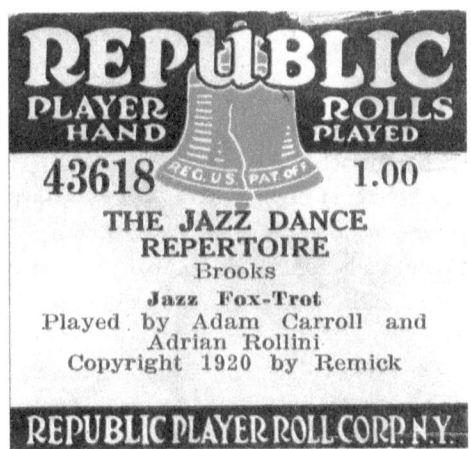

Adrian's first piano roll "The Jazz Dance Repertoire," Republic 43618.

Pete Wendling was the author of "What-Cha Gonna Do When There Ain't No Jazz," the subject of Adrian Rollini's second Republic piano roll and his first solo effort. This time, not limited by a duet arrangement, Rollini first plays the verse with several breaks in the right hand, which is followed by a straight statement of the melody. Then he plays nice variations with equivalent melodic roles for both left and right hands. This part shows jazz feeling. Republic did not know quite how to categorize the roll and described it as a Rag Fox Trot. The tune refers to the Prohibition Era that had just started ("they took away our liquor," will jazz be next?)

Obviously Rollini and Republic had a growing interest in jazz, the emerging new music. His first two rolls had "jazz" in their titles and his second roll in more than in the title. A few years earlier New York had had its first taste, and now the Jazz Age was about to begin; but for most people jazz was still regarded as a novelty and few musicians really understood the new idiom. And Rollini, talented as he was, still had much to learn and to develop.

A third roll by Adrian Rollini was announced that month. That was "Way Down Barcellona [sic] Way." There is nothing jazzy about it. It is a waltz played as a duet performance with Adam Carroll, disguised as Victor Lane.

Thirteen Rolls in Four Months

Even though the summer months traditionally showed a general sales dip, Republic announced several piano rolls played by Adrian Rollini every month for a while: three titles for July, two for August, for September another two, and for October six, a total of thirteen in four months. Republic was strongly in favor of duo performances: only five of these thirteen were solo efforts. Rollini's partners were his better-known colleagues at Republic. The August rolls were "Beautiful Stars Above" and "Don't Take Away Those Blues." No copy of the first mentioned roll has ever surfaced. The tune, a waltz, was recorded as a duet by Rollini and Adam Carroll, once more as Victor Lane. "Don't Take Away Those Blues" was the first tune recorded by Rollini with the word "blues" in the title. On this roll the left hand again contributes more than just rhythm. Phil Sillman, Adrian's younger cousin and son of his mother's sister Elizabeth, remembered:

> My family had a Player Piano and some of Adrian's rolls. I recall one that had the lyrics printed on the side of the roll. You could sing along with the music: "Don't Take Away Those Blues!" I think it went:
>
> Take away my hat, take away my shoes,
> Take away my coat and take away my booze,
> But Lordy, Lordy, Mr. Man,
> Don't take away those Blues!!![36]

During his brief career as a roll performer, Adrian would record more rolls with the word "blues" in the title. Without exception he would play them as a solo performance, not as duet. It should be noted that, for most of his audience, for his company, and most probably for himself too, until 1920 the words "blues" and "jazz" meant the same. In the title of a roll tune they were understood as recent compositions of the Tin Pan Alley type, with a fox trot tempo and possibly some careful variations on the themes. However, that year black singer Mamie Smith started to record for OKeh Records, and this would start the market for so-called "race records"[37] and change the music scene. In 1920 Smith's repertoire was a mix of popular songs and of the newer type of blues songs. At the time "blues" were not precisely defined, but in due course, the name would usually refer to a song with a twelve-bar theme with two four-bar lines of lyrics, of which the first would be sung twice, with a four-bar closing line. So when in September 1920 Adrian Rollini's next piano roll "Dreaming Blues" was announced, Republic just answered the public's request for modern popular music. The song has a sad feeling about it and Adrian's performance does the song justice.[38] Rollini's second title that month was "You're the Only Girl That Made Me Cry," a fox trot, played routinely.

By this time Kohler's management were becoming dissatisfied with the financial result of the group. Piano sales were declining. Kohler supplied piano parts to many other manufacturers, so they felt serious pain very early during the decline. In 1921 the total American production would be less than half the average annual quantity of the previous decade.[39] Republic decided to increase

Adrian Rollini on the label of a DeLuxe reproducing roll.

the prices for its new rolls from $1 (some even sold for seventy-five cents) to $1.20. All rolls introduced after 1 October 1920 went for the higher price, while older rolls still sold at one dollar, but the rate of new introductions did not decrease as yet.

October saw Adrian's name on a different roll label for the first time. This was DeLuxe, the result of Kohler's venture into the system of reproducing rolls. Rolls recorded by the Welte company in Germany had a worldwide reputation for giving a true real-life impression of the original performer. This required extra coding holes in the rolls to the left and to the right of the eighty-eight positions of the music notes. DeLuxe rolls had been introduced in September, and in October Adrian Rollini had his first roll on this label, "Yo San"; it was described as an oriental fox trot and sold for a higher price than the Republic rolls, $1.50.[40] The full effect of the real-life sound could only be heard if the roll was played on a compatible instrument, i.e. a piano with a Welte mechanism built by Kohler or Welte. On a common player piano it would sound like a standard roll. Combined with the higher price, this accounts for these rolls' rarity, which is even greater than that of Republic's rolls.

While the Kohler company had started its new DeLuxe catalog, the Republic program continued with undiminished force. Its October bulletin announced no fewer than five Rollini rolls: two fox trot solos, "I Told You So" and "Wait'n' For Me"; one fox trot duet; and two waltz duets, "Pretty Kitty Kelly" and "Tripoli." By now Rollini had settled into his own style of playing popular tunes. He played the two fox trot solos without deviating from the printed score, and Republic hardly edited his performances. "The Peacock Walk" is played as a duet with a new partner, J. Milton Delcamp, Rollini's manager at Republic and a prolific roll recorder himself. The roll's arrangement is a surprise. It opens with several breaks, which are repeated later, and both players make good contributions to the overall performance.

No copy of "Pretty Kitty Kelly" is known to collectors. It was played as a duet by Adam Carroll and Adrian Rollini and described by Republic as a waltz song. The final announcement for October was another waltz duet, "Tripoli," described as a syncopated waltz by Henry. Adrian was assisted by C.A. (C.A. was probably Cal Adams, who may have been Adam Carroll(!). For an unknown reason, Republic originally issued it as an instrumental roll, its only such Rollini roll ever. Since it was no word roll, it sold for a lower price of $0.75, the cheapest Rollini roll. The following month the same performance was issued as a word roll at the standard price of $1.20. The label said that it was played by Adrian Rollini "assisted by C.A.," probably Adam Carroll. The roll is clearly a duet.

Republic was still happy with young Adrian, and even featured him on the front page of its November bulletin which announced two more Rollini rolls.[41] They were the fox trots "It's the Way You Do It," a duet with Adam Carroll, and "Oh Gee! Say Gee!," a Rollini solo. None of these rolls is known to exist, but "Oh Gee! Say Gee!" was issued as a DeLuxe roll the following month, of which a copy is known. It has been suggested that Rollini's DeLuxe rolls are identical to his Republic rolls, with the Welte code holes added later by an editor. In that case the reproduction effect would be artificial. Making the Welte code holes ineffective would recreate the music of the Republic roll.[42] Rollini gave a fine performance of the tune and plays breaks in the right hand that enliven this otherwise straight performance.

Republic continued its Rollini program as before and issued four rolls in December 1920. One title, "In the Dusk," was a duet with Adam Carroll. The two play a long introduction and then go into the theme. The tune was also recorded for competitor QRS, but with a shorter introduction and thus more attention for the theme.[43] Since rolls were often demonstrated before they were sold, Republic realized that QRS had an advantage here with potential roll buyers who wanted to hear the main theme, the chorus. In an article the company said:

> Many possible sales are missed by dealers because the salesman must play through an introduction and verse before he reaches the chorus, which generally contains the punch of the piece. If a customer does not like anything in the intro or verse,

Adrian Rollini on the front page of Republic catalog supplement for November 1920.

he is liable to have the piece stopped right there and he never hears the best part, the chorus. The new idea of starting the roll with the chorus is making sure that the show window is in the front of the store instead of the back.[44]

Republic would change their approach to roll arranging the way QRS did. Interestingly, the choice of material for the other three rolls was different from Rollini's earlier efforts. In line with the changing public taste, Republic, or rather Delcamp, selected some recent blues titles and had Rollini play them as solos.

In "Broadway Blues" Rollini follows the written score and gives a nice performance of this tune. His solo part is supported by an accompaniment that was added by a roll editor. "The Hula Blues" received extra media attention from Republic in an article called "New developments in recording." It said:

Adrian Rollini's roll of "Singing the Blues," Republic 54428.

The latest innovation is the peculiar rhythm used in the recording of "The Hula Blues." This roll gives a unique sensation of motion through a new figure used in the bass of the recorder, Adrian Rollini, which, it is said, makes one think of the mountainous swells and daring surf riders of Hawaii. Everyone on hearing the roll the first time immediately thinks how suitable the rendition is, for it certainly draws a picture of enjoyment on tropical seas with the roll of the ocean giving rhythm for the dancing of natives on the shore.[45]

The roll itself does not sound as spectacular as one is inclined to expect after such an introduction, but Rollini's performance leaves nothing to be desired.

The last roll of the December batch was "Singing the Blues ('Till My Daddy Comes Home)," and Rollini could not have found a better way to end his first year recording piano rolls. From its opening notes one has the feeling that here is a talented piano player, a virtuoso, who has a good tune at hand.

In January 1921 Republic announced four more rolls played by Adrian Rollini, of which one is not known to exist, "Dolly, I Love You," a duet with Adam Carroll. Two more titles were duets: "Nightingale," with Adam Carroll, and "June (I Love But You)," with Victor Lane. Both are fine performances of these tunes, "June" probably being Rollini's finest duet performance so far. It demonstrates that four hands can really have added value over two, by playing variations while the melody goes on all the time. "I've Got the Blues for My Kentucky

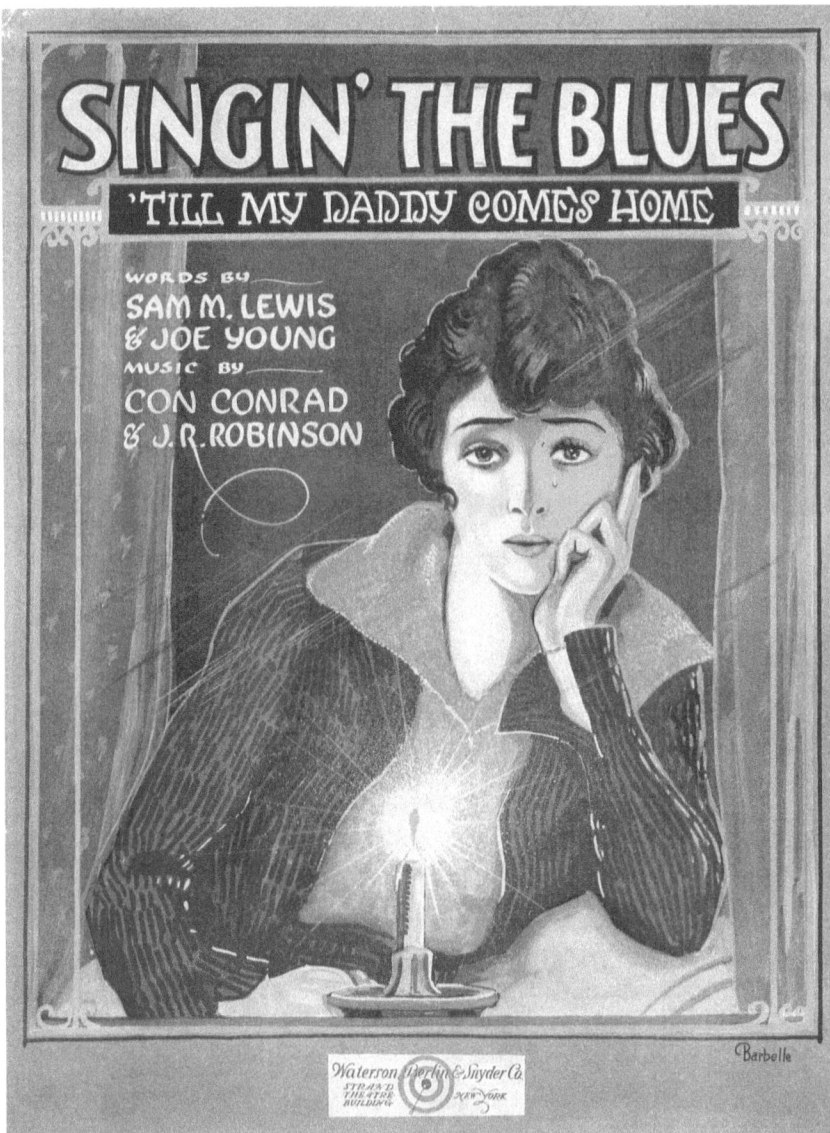

"Singin' the Blues" sheet music.

Home" is performed solo by Rollini, who sticks to the score and adds only small variations. The roll is hardly edited.

Kohler's DeLuxe label had issued two Rollini reproducing rolls so far and in February it issued three more, a Rollini solo performance and two duets. The solo performance was "Singin' the Blues ('Till My Daddy Comes Home)." No copy of this roll has been heard by the author, but it is expected to be musically identical to the earlier Republic version. The two duets were "June," with Victor Lane, and "With the Coming of Tomorrow," with Adam Carroll. These two performances are musically definitely identical to the performances on the Republic label, but with Welte codes added. "With the Coming of Tomorrow" on Republic was announced in the same month of February 1921 and it is another duet of Carroll and Rollini.

February 1921 turned out to be the top month in new Rollini rolls. Not only were three DeLuxe rolls announced but also five Republic rolls. There were two duets with Adam Carroll, the above-mentioned "With the Coming of Tomorrow," and "Isle of Paradise," of which no copy is known. The other three were solo performances. One of these was "In the Heart of Dear Old Italy," a title that Adrian and his Italian family must have liked, but again no copy is known to collectors. "No Wonder I'm Blue" is another roll with hardly any editing in the form of extra notes, unlike "Becky from Babylon (From "The Passing Show of 1920")" which could easily be taken for a duet.

The eight rolls announced in February would turn out to be Rollini's final ones on the Republic and DeLuxe labels. Republic had issued twenty-eight hand-played Rollini rolls:

14 solo performances
2 solo performances assisted by C.A. (probably Adam Carroll)
8 duets with Adam Carroll
3 duets with Victor Lane
1 duet with J. Milton Delcamp

Among these twenty-eight tunes, seven were waltzes; the others were fox trots, sometimes with the adjective "jazz," "rag," "blue," or "oriental." DeLuxe had issued five reproducing rolls, all fox trots, including one "oriental fox trot":

3 solo performances
1 duet with Adam Carroll
1 duet with Victor Lane

The End of Republic Piano Rolls

With Republic and DeLuxe rolls, the company was strictly active in the field of dance music and sentimental songs and was disappointed by its sales. Yet a December press release from Republic contained a positive message: "While public opinion everywhere seems to indicate that all business is undergoing a slump at the present time, the player roll business, so far as the Republic product is concerned, does not seem to be diminishing in the least."[46] However, Rollini's rolls did not sell so well.[47] He was not even mentioned in the press release which mentioned most of Republic's artists by name and it said that they were "working hard on special releases for January."

The company reconsidered its strategy. On the one hand it sent out messages that the holiday season was expected to be the best for several years[48] (but it had only one previous end-of-year experience!), while on the other hand it published an article saying "jazz is on the wane," thereby suggesting that it was seriously considering "the transition from jazz to classical music.... The player owner must be tactfully guided in a kind of ascending scale from the simpler things . . . to the best."[49] Their traditional customers who read this must have felt rather embarrassed. Had they been listening to inferior music all the time?

In the end Republic chose a different way. It started a sales promotion campaign that included a training program for salesmen and dealers. Arrangements for new rolls would be different so that a song's chorus, not the verse, was played first, which made the tune quicker to recognize and remember. Larger text was printed on word rolls. Advertising was intensified. In February Republic announced that its new plant, in use since last April, was at last working to capacity.

In April 1921, Republic promoted its chief recorder J. Milton Delcamp to the position of manager of the corporation. His first decision was to return to the original price of $1 a roll. However, the end was in sight for Republic piano rolls. In August Delcamp was quoted as a promoter of a piano with a Welte-Mignon mechanism (the so-called "Welte-Mignon action"), although he recorded two more rolls for Republic that same month. In October 1921 Republic announced its final piano rolls.[50]

Adrian Rollini had been a victim of Kohler's new strategy. It kept the DeLuxe label alive, but from now it would emphasize classical music. When in November 1922, Art Kahn, a piano player and orchestra leader from Chicago, became an exclusive DeLuxe artist, the company stressed the fact that Kahn was an "exponent of semi-classic music" in addition to his capabilities in syncopation.[51]

DeLuxe would continue to record and produce rolls well into the 1920s, promoting its unique Welte capabilities.

The Republic Artists Leave

When Adrian recorded his final rolls for Republic and DeLuxe, probably in December 1920 or January 1921, he was told that his contract was discontinued. So he had to look around for new income. Of course competition was ready to

Table 1. Adrian Rollini's Rollography

Artist	Announced	Issue number	Title	Type
Adam Carroll and Adrian Rollini	July 1920	Republic 43618	The Jazz Dance Repertoire	Jazz FT
Adrian Rollini	July 1920	Republic 44218	What-Cha Gonna Do When There Ain't No Jazz	Rag FT
Victor Lane and Adrian Rollini	July 1920	Republic 44618	Way Down Barcellona Way	Syncopated W
Adrian Rollini and Victor Lane	August 1920	Republic 45218	Beautiful Stars Above	W
Adrian Rollini and Delcamp	August 1920	Republic 46118	Don't Take Away Those Blues	Blue FT
Adrian Rollini	September 1920	Republic 47918	Dreaming Blues (from Midnight Frolics)	Blue FT
Adrian Rollini	September 1920	Republic 48718	You're the Only Girl That Made Me Cry	FT
Adrian Rollini	October 1920	DeLuxe B6014	Yo San	Oriental FT
Adrian Rollini	October 1920	Republic 49626	I Told You So	FT
J. Milton Delcamp and Adrian Rollini	October 1920	Republic 50326	The Peacock Walk	FT
Adrian Rollini	October 1920	Republic 50526	Wait'n' for Me	FT
Adam Carroll and Adrian Rollini	October 1920	Republic 50626	Pretty Kitty Kelly	W Song
Adrian Rollini assisted by C.A.	October 1920	Republic 50908	Tripoli	Syncopated W
Adrian Rollini assisted by C.A.	November 1920	Republic 52526	Tripoli	Syncopated W
Adam Carroll and Adrian Rollini	November 1920	Republic 52726	It's the Way You Do It	FT
Adrian Rollini	November 1920	Republic 52826	Oh Gee! Say Gee!	FT
Adrian Rollini	December 1920	DeLuxe Y6030	Oh Gee! Say Gee!	FT
Adrian Rollini	December 1920	Republic 53528	Broadway Blues	FT
Adrian Rollini	December 1920	Republic 53628	The Hula Blues	One Step
Adam Carroll and Adrian Rollini	December 1920	Republic 54028	In the Dusk	FT
Adrian Rollini	December 1920	Republic 54428	Singing the Blues ('Till My Daddy Comes Home)	FT
Adam Carroll and Adrian Rollini	January 1921	Republic 55528	Nightingale	FT
Adrian Rollini and Adam Carroll	January 1921	Republic 55928	Dolly, I Love You	FT

Artist	Announced	Issue number	Title	Type
Adrian Rollini and Victor Lane	January 1921	Republic 56328	June (I Love But You)	FT
Adrian Rollini	January 1921	Republic 56928	I've Got the Blues for My Kentucky Home	Blue FT
Adrian Rollini and Victor Lane	February 1921	DeLuxe Y6055	June (I Love But You)	FT
Adam Carroll and Adrian Rollini	February 1921	DeLuxe Y6057	With the Coming of Tomorrow	FT
Adrian Rollini	February 1921	DeLuxe Y6059	Singin' The Blues ('Till My Daddy Comes Home)	FT
Adam Carroll and Adrian Rollini	February 1921	Republic 57328	Isle of Paradise	Hawaiian W
Adrian Rollini	February 1921	Republic 57428	No Wonder I'm Blue	FT
Adam Carroll and Adrian Rollini	February 1921	Republic 57628	With the Coming of Tomorrow	Ballad FT
Adrian Rollini	February 1921	Republic 58028	In the Heart of Dear Old Italy	W Song
Adrian Rollini	February 1921	Republic 58828	Becky from Babylon (From "The Passing Show of 1920")	FT
Adrian Rollini	Mar 1921	MelOdee 4285	Two Sweet Lips	FT Key G
Adrian Rollini	Mar 1921	MelOdee 4301	Happiness (I Find My Happiness Dear with You)	FT Key G

FT = Fox Trot; W = Waltz

* All Republic rolls above are word rolls, except 50908 which was an instrumental version of 52526.
* All DeLuxe rolls above are instrumental rolls, except B6014 which is a word roll.

pick up where Republic left off and Adrian found a new employer in Aeolian, maker of several piano roll brands.[52] It had started its MelOdee label a year earlier and featured such artists as Eubie Blake, a black pioneer of ragtime and jazz, and Cliff Hess, a white piano player who had worked on the Mississippi riverboats between New Orleans and Memphis.

MelOdee's bulletin for March 1921 contained two rolls by Adrian Rollini: "Two Sweet Lips" and "Happiness," both solos. They would be Adrian's last issued piano rolls. Both rolls are impressive performances with both hands busy, even when keeping in mind that parts were added in the editing process.

With MelOdee, Rollini became a member of an impressive roster of musicians. The March bulletin announced new rolls by Blake and Hess as well as by George Gershwin, Harry Akst, and Frank Banta.

Adrian's colleagues at Republic, J. Milton Delcamp and Adam Carroll, also left. Both joined the American Piano Company, maker of Ampico rolls, Delcamp in the position of manager. They stayed many years.[53]

The new future looked bright for Adrian. He was now known by the buyers of piano rolls and his new rolls were launched into an established distribution channel. Yet for reasons unknown, MelOdee issued no further Rollini rolls after the initial two.

Still, Adrian Rollini's piano roll activity may not have been fully over yet. In interviews and letters, Irving Brodsky, who would be his colleague for many years to come, told how he met Adrian Rollini for the first time.[54] This was when both were in the Arto studio to make piano rolls. Brodsky did not remember the year, but it may have been just before Adrian joined Republic or, more likely, just after he made his last roll for this company and needed a new contract. However, no rolls by Rollini or Brodsky are known on the Arto label, but the possibility exists that they were issued under pseudonym.[55] Like Rollini, Brodsky did record for MelOdee, and some or all of Brodsky's rolls were issued under the name Irving Bradley.[56]

Were the Rolls Really Played by Adrian Rollini?

Several artist names in Republic's and DeLuxe's catalogs were pseudonyms, for which Adam Carroll was usually responsible. Republic put pictures of Victor Lane, Nan Foster, and Cal Adams (amidst various actual ones) in its 1920 catalog and they could have been real persons. However, in literature Adams and Lane are definitely called early Carroll pseudonyms and Foster could be a pseudonym, too.[57] A fact is that issues by the above after Delcamp and Carroll had left Republic, were rare. Also, unlike Delcamp's and Carroll's, their further careers cannot be followed. That they had a different status at Republic is shown by press coverage. Carroll and Delcamp got great press publicity, and Adrian Rollini as well when he started to work for Republic, but Adams, Foster, and Lane were buried in a general article.

So Republic really invested in Rollini and wanted a return. Like other roll companies, it wanted a sound that would successfully compete. When an artist had recorded a tune, the recording would be played and then an editing process started. Single notes would be added and two-handed performances could be changed into four-handed arrangements if that sounded better. In the case of reproducing rolls, the dynamics could be changed. Probably all Adrian Rollini's DeLuxe rolls were reissues of Republic rolls with Welte codes added, but there is no indication that Adrian Rollini is not heard on rolls bearing his name. On the other hand, once he became more experienced, he may have been involved in other Republic rolls that were issued under fictitious artist names.

One particular case is Rollini's roll of "Yo San," DeLuxe B6014. Its label says that it is played by Adrian Rollini but an extra harmony part was added.[58] A Republic roll of this tune was issued as by J. Milton Delcamp and Adam Carroll and it might be identical to Rollini's roll, but is has not been heard for the present research.

Collecting Adrian Rollini's Piano Rolls

All piano rolls made by Adrian Rollini are rare. Piano roll expert Michael Montgomery, who assembled the first Rollini rollography, owned fourteen, which presents less than half. After Frank Himpsl bought most of Montgomery's collection; he owned some twenty-six Rollini rolls. The author was able to acquire these rolls and integrate them with his own small collection and thus he became the owner of the largest collection of Adrian Rollini's rolls in existence. An idea of their rarity is given by noting that the highest number known of any particular roll is three (for "You're the Only Girl That Made Me Cry") and six rolls are not known to exist at all, out of a total of thirty-five different rolls.

Chapter 3

Ed Kirkeby and the California Ramblers

For many years the story of Adrian Rollini was the story of Ed Kirkeby and of the California Ramblers. This dance orchestra was to a large extent Kirkeby's creation. Adrian joined in 1922, but it had started a few years before.

Much has been written about the early days of American dance music. They were controlled by Irene and Vernon Castle, a high-flying couple who, before World War I, had already taught New York society to dance the foxtrot in a decent way, supported by a black orchestra led by James Reese Europe.[1] Vernon died during the war but dancing couples all over the world followed in the Castles' footsteps. This created a demand for dance music. A five-piece band from New Orleans, the Original Dixieland Jazz Band, came north and initially answered this demand. When in 1917 it worked in New York's Reisenweber Restaurant, its popularity with a dancing public reached great heights. However, their syncopated music had to become more danceable. Its original high tempos were lowered and its personnel was increased to six by adding a saxophone player.[2] This allowed for more variation in arrangements and for instrumental solos. Quite soon a dance band consisted of trumpet, trombone, up to three reed players, one violin (which was sometimes played by one of the other musicians), and a rhythm group of piano, banjo or guitar, bass, and drums. The free-for-all of the small jazz bands continued to be played by some bands, but larger dance bands became the rule. They played arranged music, sometimes with space for selected musicians who could play a hot solo. Although only a few of the larger orchestras were able to syncopate, the public still called the new music "jazz." Jazz bands for dancing popped up all over the United States. One of these was the California Ramblers.

The California Ramblers

The story of the California Ramblers starts around January 1921.[3] At that time a six-piece group led by banjo player Ray Kitchingman and including reed player

Jimmy Duff was working in a dancing club called Ramblers in Jackson, Michigan. The orchestra decided to use the slogan "Ramble with the Ramblers" and Kitchingman was elected manager. The following May the group used the name "Ramblers" for the first time during a trip through Pennsylvania, booked by an agent named Johnson.[4] The prefix "California" was added for the simple reason that it was the accepted idea that the West Coast produced new, interesting music, as shown by the visiting Californian bands of Art Hickman and Paul Whiteman that had made a great impression.[5] During the summer of 1921, the California Ramblers played at the Café de Paris in Atlantic City, the sea resort where Paul Whiteman had played a year earlier. And, just like in Whiteman's case, after Atlantic City the Ramblers' career really took off. In September it was announced that the California Ramblers would open on Broadway. Its personnel was given as William Borchers and Lloyd Baker, trumpet; Ray Kitchingman, banjo; Jose Torres, tuba; Fred Conrad, Jim Duff, and Francis Longon, reeds; Max McIntosh, drums; Jim Gilliland, trombone; and Preston Sargeant, piano.[6] During the fall of 1921 the band met a young, upcoming booking agent by the name of Ed Kirkeby.

Ed Kirkeby

Wallace Theodore (Ed) Kirkeby was born of Danish ancestors in Brooklyn, New York, on 10 October 1891. His musically talented father owned a store and played a five-string banjo. He also sang and gave music lessons. His son Ed played the banjo too, as well as the mandolin and the piano. The Kirkeby family were known as the "musical Kirkebys." Kirkeby senior organized a family group of two banjos and a mandolin that would perform on their front porch to their neighbors' enjoyment.[7]

One of Ed's first jobs was at Wall Street and only lasted two weeks. Another was as a soap salesman, which gave him a chance to travel. He joined the Y.M.C.A. and became a successful athlete. For the next few years he would quickly move from one activity to another. In 1913 he produced a minstrel show in which he played a part and in 1914 he joined Kirkman & Sons, makers of keyboard instruments, as the youngest member of their sales force, but playing in the family orchestra showed him what he wanted. As he said in an interview he wanted to "search a beat—the beat" and this is what led him to organize a colored jazz band, the Southern Jubilee Syncopated Orchestra. It was no success. In 1916 he got a chance to develop his commercial interest in the entertainment industry when he joined Columbia Records. The next year he was promoted to assistant manager of Columbia Recording Laboratories.[8] This gave him a good foothold in the fledgling gramophone record industry, and when in 1919

Ed Kirkeby.

he became manager of Henry Burr's Music Corporation, he was ready to launch his first recording orchestra, the Merry Melody Men, which, from March 1920 onward, cut some sixty titles for several small labels.[9] By then he had his own company and an office in the Roseland Building, which housed several music publishers targeting the black and white publics.[10] Kirkeby's company was active in many fields of music. In addition to his recording contracts, Kirkeby acted as artist representative in New York for Canadian Victor.[11] He also went into manufacturing musical instruments, in particular a special type of banjo called the Van Eps banjo. (Fred van Eps was a famous pioneer banjo player. His name sold banjos.)

Around 1 October 1921 two members of the California Ramblers walked into Kirkeby's office. They wanted to take a look at the new Van Eps banjo. Kirkeby was impressed by the quality of these men. He saw an opportunity and found that their band had been organized by reed player Jimmy Duff and banjo player Ray Kitchingman. So Kirkeby got into contact with Duff and Kitchingman and an audition of the full orchestra was arranged. It took place in the New York Recording Laboratories.[12] Ed Kirkeby agreed with Ray Kitchingman and Jimmy Duff to become manager of their orchestra and from that day on Kirkeby "handled all finances, advanced all exploitation and living expenses, rehearsed, developed and improved the band to as near first grade standards as possible. Kitchingman and Duff as originators, and Kirkeby as developer of the 'California Ramblers' orchestra, hold the absolute right to said name California Ramblers."[13]

Kirkeby took five of the band members on his payroll: Jimmy Duff, alto saxophone; Oscar Adler, violin and leader; Preston Sargeant, piano and arranger; Ray Kitchingman, banjo; and Max McIntosh, drums.[14] For a planned tour through Pennsylvania the band was augmented to nine men but the tour was canceled when not enough bookings were made. Then Kirkeby managed to book the five men into a small roadhouse, Parkway Palace in Brooklyn. For this gig saxophone player Sylvan Solomon was added.

First Recordings by the California Ramblers

Kirkeby now focused on his new band and changed his recording activities accordingly. A month after the Merry Melody Men had cut their final record, the California Ramblers cut their first, a coupling of "Georgia Rose" and "The Sheik of Araby" recorded for the Aeolian Company and issued on their Vocalion label.[15] It is revealing to compare recordings by both bands. Recordings made in the second half of 1921 by the Merry Melody Men demonstrate a style that was old-fashioned by then. A new sound on records had been introduced with great success by Paul Whiteman a year before.[16] Kirkeby's Merry Melody Men sound as disciplined as a military band but "nothing happens." "Georgia Rose" by the California Ramblers does not impress either, but their recording of "Sheik of Araby" shows a totally different mood. Ray Kitchingman's well-recorded banjo really drives the band and he solos for fifteen bars before the full band closes with a good ensemble ride-out—a step forward in arranging and playing compared to Kirkeby's earlier band.

While at the Parkway Palace, the band grew to ten pieces[17] and was heard by Sam Kessler, manager of Eva Shirley, a soprano.[18] Kessler took the band and the singer, together with dancer Al Roth, to New York's Palace Theatre,[19] a theater on the Keith circuit and America's major vaudeville house, hoping for a booking of their combined act.[20] They were indeed hired and opened for some weeks around 7 November 1921. Following this the act did a vaudeville tour along the Keith circuit for most of the rest of the year, under the name "From Syncopation to Grand Opera." Kirkeby and Kessler arranged the musical routine, Kessler selecting most of Miss Shirley's songs and Kirkeby the instrumentals. He mostly took tunes that the band had already recorded. Kirkeby also took care of Eva Shirley's big "operatic" number[21] and of her encore number "Tucky Home."[22] A few weeks later the act was engaged by Florenz Ziegfeld as part of the road company edition of his Midnight Frolic. It lasted only two weeks and was followed by a salary cut and a return to Keith time. There were short engagements in Poli's Theatre in Wilkes-Barre, Pennsylvania, and then back in New York, where they played at the Bushwick Theatre. On 8 January 1922 Shirley and her 12 California Ramblers were at the Brooklyn New Amsterdam Theatre in one of Keith's "Celebrated Sunday Concerts."[23]

The California Ramblers' contribution to the act was well-received by the press, as shown by the following quotes:[24]

> Miss Shirley . . . was one of the early jazz-band stars, and before that did singles and doubles. Now she presents the California Ramblers, and even in this jazz-jaded day the organization of nine is a sweet scent of superior syncopation. A banjo player, one of the few who uses a pick and gets true banjo music, was a revelation though never permitted to any individual work such as Paul Whiteman wisely slips into every member of his . . . outfit who can do anything more than vamp till ready. This banjoist is a find. (*Variety*, 16 December 1921)

A week later *Billboard* was even stronger in favoring the band to the singer: "Were it not for the nimble dancing of Al Roth and the rather pleasing musical effects produced by the California Ramblers [. . .] this act would have little in its favor. Totally lacking in big-time entertainment value are the moments when Miss Shirley holds the stage. . . . The California Ramblers . . . have the makings of a first rate band" (*Billboard*, 24 November 1921). The praise of the band would continue:

> Miss Shirley has a corking band to help her win . . . consisting of ten chaps who play like Orpheus. They would put pep into even a corpse and carried Miss Shirley along much further than she would be able to carry herself. (*Zit's Vaudeville Chart*, 17 December 1921)

> Eva Shirley and Company, which includes the California Ramblers, a corking nine-piece orchestra, and Al Roth, an exceptional dancer, went well. . . . The band got a wonderful sound. (*Clipper*, 4 January 1922)

> Eva Shirley has with her the California Ramblers, a dandy band. They pay strict attention to playing music splendidly. They do not attempt to be comedians. Moreover, they conduct themselves with a refreshing air of modesty. (*Billboard*, 5 January 1922)[25]

> The musicians landed solidly with their selections. Roth connected decisively with his dancing, and Miss Shirley registered with her songs, all of which totaled a conclusion that dug into the time allotted for the intermission. The act is running nicely, with no stalling and plenty of action. (*Variety*, 5 January 1922)

These reviews showed that the band was the better part of Shirley's act, and helped Kirkeby in his decision to go on with the band alone.[26] In fact he realized that, with the band, he had a potential goldmine in his hand, which he did not want to give up. He felt that the band's success would tempt other leaders or agents to hire his men away, so on 12 December 1921 he asked all band members to sign an agreement that committed them "not to consider any offer that shall come from any outside sources whatever to leave the said California Ramblers Orchestra, unless Mr. Kirkeby gives his unqualified consent in writing."[27] Kirkeby inspired great confidence, and the agreement was signed by all seven band members: Lloyd Baker, trumpet; Irving Rothwell, trombone; Jimmy Duff and Sylvan Solomon, reeds; Preston L. Sargent, piano; Ray Kitchingman, banjo; and Max McIntosh, drums.

Kirkeby continued his policy of recording for any company that was interested. From 14 December 1921 the California Ramblers were regulars in the recording studios of Arto, Columbia, Emerson, OKeh, Paramount, and Vocalion.[28] It looked like Kirkeby was in control now, but this was not the case. The band's personnel was not fixed at all and for the Keith circuit the California Ramblers were led by violinist Oscar Adler, who was not satisfied with his pay. He wanted $150 a week, which Kirkeby refused and wanted to let Adler go. He told Sam Kessler, who informed him that the Keith office would not allow any change in personnel for the engagements in Washington and Baltimore the next two weeks. Kirkeby accepted, and the original band members sacrificed to pay the high-priced leader and two new men. Kessler also felt that he did not make enough money and tried to lure the band away from Kirkeby. When the band worked in Washington and Baltimore, Kessler started to work on its members and tried to get them to sign for him, with Adler and Rothwell on his side. Although nearly all belonged to the group that had signed the above-mentioned agreement (and the others probably signed similar contracts when they joined the California Ramblers), Kessler succeeded in having all except two of them sign with him. Ray Kitchingman and Jimmy Duff, originators and co-owners of the California Ramblers, were offered $100 a week but did not accept. They had kept the band together through ups and downs and remained loyal to Kirkeby. Kessler, Eva Shirley's manager, found replacements, so he could continue her act for a while, with contracts for New Haven and Hartford. He billed the accompanying band as the California Ramblers as before, but he did not own this name; so on 3 March, Ed Kirkeby wrote to the Keith office to make them stop Kessler from using the name. Kessler and Adler obeyed, but only after a last counter action: they issued the misleading statement that the California Ramblers had changed their name to Oscar Adler's Orchestra.[29]

On Sunday 5 March 1922, Kitchingman, Duff, and Kirkeby severed all connections with Kessler. Kirkeby had a band name now, but no band. Or had he?

The California Ramblers on the sheet music cover of "Sweet California."

March 1922: A Blessing in Disguise

Ed Kirkeby had shown himself to be a person who could quickly move from one job to another and could also create new business opportunities. He was never a person to bet on only one horse. So now he had to exploit his other musical activities. In a thumbnail biography that Kirkeby wrote in the late forties, he claimed that "in 1921 he introduced the Original Memphis Five to records and from then on supervised all their records including the tune that made them famous, *Sister Kate*."[30] Kirkeby probably was a year off here, since in 1921 the five recorded as a Sam Lanin unit and it was 1922 when the name Original Memphis Five was introduced on records. Even in 1922 Kirkeby's involvement with the group may not have been more than as a contractor for some of their recordings, based on his good contacts in the gramophone record industry. He also claimed to have used their trumpet player Phil Napoleon for some of the first recordings by the California Ramblers. During the conflict between Kessler and Kirkeby in March 1922, Napoleon's salary had been an issue.[31] Other members of the Original Memphis Five may have participated in recording dates for Ed Kirkeby during the next few months, including the ones he directed by the Superior Jazz Band; in April and May this five-piece jazz band recorded for Arto.[32]

All of this allowed Ed Kirkeby to continue his recording activities even after nearly all the California Ramblers had left. During March 1922, without a working band, he was still able to organize five record sessions under the name California Ramblers, the first on 3 March, the last on 18 March. The personnel for these sessions remains largely unknown.

Kirkeby may have felt the departure of most of his men to be a blessing in disguise. It forced him to form a new band and he knew better than before what musicians to look for. He found some of the best.

Chapter 4

The California Ramblers Taking Off

In the spring of 1921, the final two piano rolls played by Adrian Rollini had been issued by the Aeolian Company on their MelOdee label. Making piano rolls allowed Adrian to continue working with orchestras. At first this was his own orchestra, in which he played piano and xylophone (his very first instrument, on which he had never been formally trained but on which he was a virtuoso almost as much as he was as a piano player). The xylophone had no formal place in a dance band. It was a typical solo instrument and had been given great popularity by the work of the Green Brothers, Joe and George Hamilton. Both had been drummers early in their careers and both were billed the country's best xylophone player at various times. Joe cut his first record in 1918 when he was twenty-six, George in 1917 when he was twenty-three. George became the more famous of the two and published an instruction course. Chances are that Adrian was self-trained as a xylophonist using George Hamilton Green's training method. No thriving xylophone player could have avoided the Green Brothers' influence, Adrian Rollini included.[1]

Arthur C. Hand was born in 1898 as the son of Joseph C. Hand. Hand Sr. was well-known as the owner of several New York hotels, such as the Vendome and Marlborough, the Majestic, the San Carlo, and the Percival. Arthur had violin lessons at a young age. During World War I he was drafted and joined the navy. After his discharge Arthur entered his father's brokerage office. He liked music more, though, and soon played the violin at private parties. He particularly enjoyed the newer jazzy style, which Joseph did not appreciate, but, there were more trends in popular music that could be followed. Around 1919 Arthur formed his own small orchestra. In the beginning he kept his day job as an insurance manager, while running his band at night.[2]

One of his musicians was saxophone player Fred Cusick, born 9 September 1902.[3] He had met Hand when he played the trumpet and saxophone with a little jazz band near Catskill, a rich New York town where the Hand family lived. Hand asked him to come to New York where he might have a job for him in his new band. Cusick accepted the invitation and with Hand he went to a hotel on

Arthur C. Hand.

Broadway commonly called the "Riding Academy." It was located between 94th and 95th streets, and there was a piano and xylophone player in its lobby by the name of Adrian Rollini.

The little band that Fred Cusick played in before he joined Hand was one of numerous similar small groups that copied the ODJB. However, the pure jazz style of these small jazz bands did not suit Hand. A current trend existed to make the ODJB's music more danceable. Most new bands did that, but Hand needed something different to really attract attention. The approach of the Six Brown Brothers did not work for him either. They had an act with six saxophones, toured the country with it, and started to record as early as 1911. Their concept was hard to copy and becoming old-fashioned. The greater popularity of the saxophone family was their contribution to the music history. Yet another

Adrian ca. 1923, before he met Dixie.

approach was the Green Brothers' act, with a strong accent on the xylophone. When Rollini's xylophone offered him the special element he was looking for, Arthur Hand found that he could follow the footwork of the Green Brothers.

Both Cusick and Rollini were hired by Hand. Cusick even came to room with him in his large apartment at 97th Street. The first place where Cusick and Rollini worked with Hand was at Rector's, where they found Irving Brodsky working.[4]

Hand now had an orchestra with possibilities and it drew attention indeed. Ed Kirkeby was always on the lookout for talent, but especially now that he needed a new band. He checked Hand's orchestra out and saw that these were the men he needed. Later he said in an interview: "In this group was a young guy playing xylophone who knocked us all out. His name was Adrian Rollini." Kirkeby described Hand as young, personable, and extremely popular with the women—but a lousy fiddle player.[5] He offered him a partnership to front the California Ramblers. Backed by his contract with Kitchingman and Duff and with their support, Kirkeby could legally take this step. From now on the California Ramblers were owned by these two musicians together with Kirkeby and Hand. On 1 April 1922 these two gentlemen started a new company by the name of Kirkeby & Hand, Inc.[6] Arthur C. Hand would front the band and pose as their musical leader.[7] Edward Wallace Kirkeby would take care of the business side of the new company.

One newspaper, looking at the process from the outside, did not mention Kirkeby's inside role and reported: "The California Ramblers under Oscar Adler have made a mutual exchange of musicians with Arthur Hand's Rector Dansant Orchestra. The Rector Dansant Orchestra is now known as the California Ramblers, led by Hand, and the Ramblers are now in vaudeville with Eva Shirley as Oscar Adler's Orchestra."[8]

April 1922: A New Band on the Scene

The reformed California Ramblers consisted of nine musicians:

Arthur Hand—leader, violin
William Henry "Bill" Moore—trumpet
Lloyd "Ole" Olsen—trombone
Jimmy Duff—clarinet, alto saxophone
Fred Cusick—clarinet, tenor saxophone
Adrian Rollini—xylophone, piano
Irving Brodsky—piano
Ray Kitchingman—banjo
Fred Henry—drums

Only Duff and Kitchingman came from the original California Ramblers. Cusick, Hand, Rollini, and a few others came from Hand's band. Trumpeter Bill Moore (1901–1964) was a colored American of mixed background and light enough to pass.[9] Irving Brodsky remembered him as an educated man who knew a lot of "big words and studied a dictionary all the time, a study guy."[10] He was said to originate from Hawaii and was sometimes billed as "the hot Hawaiian." The backgrounds of Ole Olsen and Fred Henry are unknown. Irving Brodsky had been a successful piano player for many years and may have worked for Hand, too. He knew Adrian Rollini from making piano rolls at the Arto Company. In later years he remembered how surprised he was to meet Rollini again when both joined the California Ramblers. Brodsky was obviously Jewish, so to tease him, band members called him "Brady," an Irish name![11]

Kirkeby wanted his men to read arrangements, but clearly they were not all equally able to. Fred Cusick remembered how one day, "they came with a new stock [arrangement] and they didn't have [a tenor saxophone] part.... they gave me a part that I had to transpose to tenor. So I played it. Then Duff, who was a crusty kind of a guy, wanted my part because I had melody a couple of times. So I gave him the sheet and I took his sheet. Okay, he gave a downbeat and starts off and ... he's in the wrong key. Accused of playing dirty tricks on him, I said: 'Can't you read?'"[12]

Ed Kirkeby immediately got into action when his new band was ready. He had contracts for playing in public and of course also for recording sessions. The first was a session for Emerson on Monday 3 April 1922. As the new band's recording debut it was not striking at all. A session would normally produce two or three successful recordings, but Emerson issued only one title, a long forgotten tune called "Tell Her at Twilight." Kirkeby probably did not want to run any risk and as a result the band sounds very average, playing arranged choruses all

The California Ramblers standing in front of California Ramblers Inn sign, 1923. From left: Adrian Rollini, Stan King, Lloyd "Ole" Olsen, Frank Cush, Irving Brodsky, Arthur Hand, Ray Kitchingman, Bill Moore, Fred Cusick or Orville Gibbs, Jim Duff.

over. No xylophone is audible, or a second piano (in fact no piano can be heard, due to the poor acoustic recording), so this was not Adrian Rollini's debut on gramophone records.

Later that same week, on Thursday 6 April, the band was again in a recording studio. This time it was with Kirkeby's old friends at Vocalion, but again only one tune was successfully recorded, "My Honey's Loving Arms."[13] It was waxed by several jazz-oriented dance bands and the California Ramblers' version with straight solos by tenor sax and trombone is not in the class of those others.[14] There was still no sign of xylophonist and second piano player Adrian Rollini. Many American Vocalion recordings, including "My Honey's Loving Arms," were issued in Europe on the British Aco label. However, like the United States, Europe had to wait a little longer before it could hear Adrian Rollini on a record.

Further sessions that month were with Paramount, Arto, Cameo, Vocalion, and Columbia. Adrian could be heard on record for the first time on the new Ramblers' third recording session in April. This memorable moment was on Friday 7 April 1922 with the rerecording of another almost forgotten tune, "Little Grey Sweetheart of Mine," for Paramount. Less than a month before, Kirkeby had recorded it with his previous band, and the result was issued. However, with Rollini in the band he made another try and it was more effective. Even at this early stage Kirkeby recognized Adrian's added value in the band. His xylophone work starts after the record's opening bars and ends with a break, after which the band plays the coda. The arrangement allowed Adrian to switch between soloing with band accompaniment and playing rhythm in the background, a role he would often have in the future. Rollini obviously had no written score and just did what he felt best. A real document.

The next day, 8 April, the band made its public debut, at Shanley's, on Broadway between 43rd and 44th Streets, playing during lunch, dinner, and supper.[15] They stayed for the rest of the month. On 20 April Shanley's advertised as "The Dancing Palace" and the California Ramblers provided the music. According to *Variety* magazine, Shanley's patterned its dance hall policy after the famous Roseland.[16]

The Shanley brothers had come from Ireland, and from 1890 till the end of the Prohibition era they played a major role in the restaurant business in New York and its suburbs. The Shanleys not only gave the California Ramblers their first live audience, but they were to play an even more important role for Kirkeby the following year when one of their restaurants became his home base.

In the new band, most piano work was done by Irving Brodsky. Adrian Rollini had been hired for his capabilities at the xylophone and as a second pianist.[17] Both tasks gave him less work than his colleagues and he would see that in his paycheck, but at least he got on record again, this first month. On 17 April the band recorded for Arto. Of the tunes heard by the author, "Stumbling" is the most interesting, a piece of novelty ragtime composed by Zez Confrey and one of his greatest successes in this style.[18] The arrangement used by the California Ramblers features a thirty-two-bar duet for two pianos, Rollini sharing the limelight with Brodsky and his first appearance on a gramophone record as a piano player. A week later the band cut the arrangement of "Stumbling" for the Cameo label, but with the added attraction of several choruses by Rollini ad libbing on the xylophone. This is the first of only a few instances where he is heard both on piano and on the xylophone in one record title.[19] Cameo coupled it with "On the Alamo," which features Rollini on the xylophone again. Further sessions during that month were with Columbia and Vocalion, and sometimes Rollini would contribute a xylophone part.

In May 1922 Kirkeby succeeded in booking the band for half a year, from May till 1 November at the Post Lodge, a well-known place on the old Boston Post Road, Highway 1 in Larchmont, New York. It was run by a lady, Mrs. Meyers, and her son Sunny. Though located quite far away from Manhattan, it had no lack of customers, being near the Larchmont Tennis Club. A few months before the California Ramblers arrived, the Post Lodge had been raided by prohibition agents who were successfully disguised as tennis players. A newspaper report mentioned three thousand persons at the Club and the Lodge. How the lawsuit was settled is uncertain, but in 1922 the Post Lodge was open again.[20]

The long engagement at the Post Lodge had several advantages for the band. It allowed them to really settle after a period of constant changes in locations and personnel. And for Adrian, who would have his nineteenth birthday in June, it was convenient to be close to home.

The summer of 1922 was without any extraordinary events and one Saturday, when they had nothing to do at the Post Lodge, five men decided to take a ride in Ray Kitchingman's new car. Fred Cusick, who was a house friend of the Rollinis now, thought that Ray was joined by Jimmy Duff, Ole Olsen, Adrian Rollini, and himself.

> We went up the river and wanted to visit Sing Sing, the penitentiary, just for fun. So we went up there and a guide had taken us and finally says: "Through this door this is the Death Row. You want to go through?" We said: "Sure." We went in and on a side were cells with about 4 to 5 people waiting to be electrocuted. We went through there and we went into that chamber where the chair was, the death chamber. The guide said: "Well, there it is. . . . Anyone want to sit in it?" he asked. The others said: "Oh, no, no, no, no, no!" Well, I jumped at that one. . . . I sat down, 'cause this is something to say, something to talk about. They pulled the fuse.[21]

Certainly more fun were the California Ramblers' frequent recording sessions. Kirkeby wanted to increase the band's fame and records were his best bet. He managed to get his band in the recording studio at a rate of more than once a week.[22]

Rollini Moves to the Bass Saxophone

When Adrian Rollini joined the California Ramblers on piano and xylophone in 1922, the band used two reed players. Fred Cusick's main instrument was tenor saxophone and Jimmy Duff played alto saxophone. After some months, Rollini suddenly choose the bass saxophone as his main instrument. He never gave a solid reason why he did that, so for an answer a look at the music scene seems necessary.

At the time the saxophone was a relatively new addition to the musical instruments scene. It had literally been invented in the previous century, by Belgian Adolphe Sax. Sax was born in Dinant in 1814, in what has since become the French-speaking part of Belgium.[23] His father gave him a solid training in building musical instruments and at a conservatory he became a clarinet virtuoso. He seemed to be the right person to improve reed instruments and even to invent new ones. In fact, he did, and in 1842 he traveled to Paris with his first saxophone. He was lucky to get the support of famous composers such as Hector Berlioz and Domenico Donizetti. Sax's first product was a bass saxophone and Berlioz admired it: "Its sound is of such rare quality that, to my knowledge, there is not a bass instrument in use nowadays that could be compared to the saxophone. It is full, soft vibrating, extremely powerful and easy to lower in intensity."[24] Sax soon added higher pitched members to the family and it became apparent that the saxophone was a highly versatile instrument. In half a century it conquered the music world.

In the United States, the first saxophones were manufactured by the Conn company around 1890. The designer of their first saxophone, Gus Buescher, started his own company in 1893 and became Conn's major competitor. The popularity of the saxophone received a strong boost by the work of the Six Brown Bothers, a vaudeville act with six musicians playing saxophones from alto to bass sax.[25] The period of their greatest success were the years 1910–20. Their successful tours and gramophone records made both the group and the saxophone popular. In their concept the bass sax did little more than accentuating the beat and providing an occasional break. Dance orchestras also adopted the saxophone, primarily the alto and tenor. Harry Yerkes is said to be the first to have used a bass sax as a bass instrument in his band in 1918, strictly in the "oompah" role. From 1920 the bass sax was being used by groups that played a form of jazz. Ted Lewis's Jazz Band may have been the first. Lewis had a small jazz band, styled after the ODJB. He would occasionally hire extra musicians for his recordings. In January 1920 he tried a bassoon player to enhance the bass line, but in August of that year he took an unknown bass sax player with him to the studio.[26] This unknown musician still played in the style of the Six Brown Brothers, but it would not be long before someone would use a bass sax as a solo instrument in a jazz band. This pioneer was Joseph Samuels, a violin player. In his own recording groups, he would play the clarinet and sometimes the bass sax.[27] He even soloed on the bass sax, but his solos were strictly a novelty effect, missing jazz feeling.

So the bass saxophone was a new thing in jazz, and the California Ramblers noticed. But the bass saxophone arrived in the band in a rather casual way, as Kirkeby told later: "Once during a rehearsal, we sat and talked about how we ought to add some bass instrument to the band like the tuba, bass trombone or something like that. Rollini wondered if it would be OK with a bass sax, and of course it would. The same day he got a sax and started to practice and after only a couple of weeks he had found his right place in the Orchestra."[28]

In an interview with Warren Scholl in 1934, however, Adrian told a different story:

> Ray Kitchingman played guitar and directed the orchestra. One day "Kitchy" was at Conn's buying new strings for his guitar when he noticed a reconditioned bass saxophone which was being sold at the special price of $75. When he next met Adrian he

told him to purchase it. The next day Adrian went down to Conn's and bought the $75 bass saxophone. Rollini himself does not know to this day why he bought the instrument..... The first night Adrian played on his new instrument he acquired a stiff neck, sore throat, and a tightening of the muscles of his stomach. Gradually he played sax more and more often and finally abandoned the piano entirely.[29]

Adrian's brother Arthur remembered: "Adrian was living at home when he took up playing the bass sax. Not once did he bring it home to practice, but merely mastered it in three weeks on the job with the Ramblers' early days."[30]

Once Adrian Rollini had switched to bass saxophone, he would only rarely record on the xylophone or the piano anymore. In most dance bands a tuba or a sousaphone made the band good to watch. Rollini's bass sax not only improved the sound of the band, it even improved its looks. The huge instrument was an asset in many ways. However, Rollini still had a long way to go to master it.

Thus, in 1921 the bass sax was making its appearance in the world of jazz and dance orchestras. It was not surprising that Adrian Rollini saw it as an opportunity to improve his position within the California Ramblers. Although his professional experience was with playing the piano and the xylophone, Rollini and saxophones were not strangers at all. His brother Arthur related that Adrian bought an alto and a curved soprano as well, once he had mastered the bass sax, but he gave the alto, a Conn, to his sister Vera and the soprano, a Buescher, to brother Art.[32]

Ed Kirkeby claimed that Adrian Rollini only needed a few weeks to learn to play the bass saxophone. The recordings made by the California Ramblers during the months of May to October 1922 allow us to observe Adrian's progress. This was precisely the period of the Post Lodge engagement. In April he had been featured on the xylophone and in piano duets. Recordings made the following months feature none of these. Rollini may not have participated at all in recordings made in May and early June. On 8 June, however, he can be heard playing his bass sax on a gramophone record for the first time.[33] It was for a minor label and the records appeared anonymously. This label was Little Wonder, and its records were only 5½" in diameter and sold in dime stores for five or ten cents. The records had only one tune, which played for fewer than two minutes. There was clearly no risk involved, so Kirkeby allowed Rollini to try his bass sax in the recording studio. By the time the California Ramblers recorded for Little Wonder, the label had been absorbed by Columbia. Adrian Rollini's first recorded bass efforts were not impressive. They show him simply accentuating the beat and his tone can best be described as slap-tonguing.[34]

For the California Ramblers' earlier recordings, an extra brass bass player had usually been hired. Rollini's emergence as a serious alternative did not immediately change this policy. So both in July and August a brass bass is

Advertisement for "I Wish I Could Shimmy Like My Sister Kate."

heard on some recordings and Rollini is absent. However, from September 1922 onward the change was definite. Adrian Rollini became the band's bass player. The arrangement of "I Wish I Could Shimmy Like My Sister Kate" even gave him solo space for the first time, albeit only a two-bar break near the end of the recording. It was recorded on 13 September for Vocalion and was the first time the band recorded a pure jazz tune. The public appreciated the record. It became a best-seller for Vocalion and for its publisher Clarence Williams.[35] Vocalion's European outlet also issued it.

Rollini was now quickly making progress. A few days after "Sister Kate" had been recorded, the band was in a recording studio again. This time it was Arto and one of the tunes was "I'm Always Stuttering." The first half of its arrangement has no surprises, but the second half includes a fourteen-bar trumpet solo accompanied by Kitchingman's banjo and Rollini's bass sax, who concludes with a two-bar break. For the first time on record, his playing is looser, he is not just playing on the beat, and he is adding notes. In other words, he is starting to swing and the trumpet soloist, probably Bill Moore, with him. It is as if a new spirit was released in the band. This device, a trumpet solo backed by the bass sax, would become a standard feature in many arrangements for the California Ramblers. A review in *Variety* describes how the band was growing in quality, but still below the level of the top bands. The review mentions no names, but makes clear that Rollini was playing a major role in the band. The cornet player, probably Bill Moore, also gets a positive note, but Hand as a frontman did not shine at all:

> A good dance band of 10 pieces playing several selections, with a few specialties. Whether the boys are capable of stepping into the big time theatres behind Whiteman, Lopez and Bernie is questionable. They do not sound as good as that, nor is the act as pretentious, but for the smaller policy houses this combination should be just about right. The normal routine consumes 19 minutes, but a trio of demanded encores brought the total up to 28. Six numbers are played. which includes an evolution of the modern dance music, imitations of "bands we have heard" (Whiteman, Six Brown Brothers and Sousa), a piano duet, xylaphone [sic] and banjo bits and four numbers with all the boys working in an orchestration. The bass saxaphone [sic] player is the most active, doubling on a piano, xylaphone and banjo, while one of the cornet players steps out to shake through a "hot" arrangement. It's nicely routined and there is no stalling. All the men are dressed in tuxedos, backed by blue hangings and playing under the red lights, except when all the electricity is turned on. No outstanding personality, and this is particularly true of the violinist out front. A little animation on his part would help. At present it's simply a matter of watching the title cards changed. There's nothing to look at, just to listen, following the first flash.
>
> Instrumentally the Ramblers present two cornets, two saxophones, piano. trombone, drums, violin and bass sax as the combination. This orchestra should be good for a swing around the neighborhood houses and can undoubtedly play good dance music, but there has been too much opposition ahead of them on the biggest time (signed Skig).[36]

More Engagements

The long engagement at the Post Lodge not only allowed for recording work, but also for occasional performances elsewhere in the New York area. One such occasion received much publicity, in Arthur Hand's hometown of Catskill in upstate New York, about 100 miles north of the Post Lodge. Hand's wealthy family lived there and from 10 to 23 June the town held its Old Town Week. On Friday 23 June it had its grand finale, a "Big Dance," and the California Ramblers were there to make it happen. A newspaper said "Arthur C. Hand of Catskill is director and leader, and a member of the Old Town Week Committee who recently heard the orchestra says 'Artie' has made good and that the music to be furnished will be the best ever heard in Catskill."[37]

No doubt the band worked for a friendly price, but Kirkeby refused to pay for the transportation. This problem was solved by a local company: "It was only after considerable persuasion and agreement to transport the orchestra to and from Catskill by automobile that their services were procured, and Van Cott Duncan with three cars has undertaken this part of the work." The newspaper added that "considering the expense, the price of admission was set at $1.10 . . . and the committee asks that liberal purchases of tickets be made."[38] Reviews were excellent. One comment read: "The music was all that had been promised—the best ever in Catskill."[39]

After the Post Lodge engagement ended, the California Ramblers went on a tour along the Keith circuit, doing eastern cities for the months of November, December, and January. The band became experienced and more and more successful. In November trumpeter Frank Cush joined the band. He had been a member of Jimmy Durante's jazz band with New Orleans clarinet player Achille Baquet, and thus had some firsthand experience with white New Orleans jazz.[40]

During the tour they would have a mixed audience of people who were familiar with the new music style the band was bringing and people who were not. On 16 November the band started a gig at Proctor's, a vaudeville theater in Yonkers.[41] The *Yonkers Statesman* wrote: "Jazz is popular. There is no question about that. . . . the fame of the California Ramblers has become widespread. Their coming to Yonkers will doubtless be the signal for a wonderful turnout of those who just love 'jazz' and those who can't help but be moved by its unmistakable appeal."

Kirkeby did not appreciate the trend away from straight music to jazz, to hot music. Spencer Clark, who worked with the band off and on in later years, remembered him "moaning about the band playing too much jazz and he wanted them to play stock arrangements and more waltzes. . . . but people didn't want waltzes, they wanted jazz. They came for the beat in that band, the swing."[42]

The band had tremendous success in Yonkers and returned during the following weeks. It also participated in a benefit for the local police. A review mentioned that the band played Sousa's "Stars and Stripes [Forever]" and were "recalled and recalled."

On 21 December the California Ramblers were in Montreal, Canada, to open the Mount Royal Hotel. Canada had no prohibition and the boys were tempted to drink more than ever. For Irving Brodsky, it was too much, and he got sick.

Fred Cusick: "We couldn't find him. We did not know where he was. After an hour we found him sitting in the men's room, he had thrown up all over the place. That was because we could get booze up there. We used to go and sit on the curb at 8 o'clock in the morning waiting for the liquor store to open up. That's how crazy we were."[43]

It was midwinter, ten degrees below zero, and the band had no heavy underwear, no overcoats. Because of the snow there were no taxis and they arrived at their hotel in a sleigh. Life on the road often presented such unexpected problems. Fred Cusick related one such incident:

> We were in New England somewhere, I think on our way to Boston, and we had all the instruments and the music in a small van and I was driving. We go along this road, it was a back road, narrow, gravel. I don't know why we were on it but it must have been a detour or something. Anyway we go along and all of a sudden I looked in the rear view mirror and it looked to me like the back door was open. We stopped and ran around and back and things were falling all over the place, music parts, manuscripts they were all over the road. We gathered up what we could. A guitar was gone. We backtracked and I think we found the guitar, I'm not sure, but most of the music we never did get. It was gone, falling off, blowing away into the bushes and stuff. We did the job that night, we could do without music.

They were reviewed after the performance in Boston, but the reviewer had a dilemma which was typical for that time. He liked jazz, but appreciated "more refined and sentimental music" as well. He wrote:

> One might easily imagine that the audience of Keith's last evening was largely made up of "Native Sons," judging from the enthusiasm and appreciation it displayed at the performance of the California Ramblers Orchestra, known here through their phonograph records. They well deserved the applause they received, for the organization was well balanced in its instrumentation, particularly for jazz, with saxophones sufficient to temper the crackling horns in more refined and sentimental music. The organization showed excellent training and technique, expression and rhythm and a perfect blending of tone, unusual in a band of this kind in vaudeville. It captured the audience through musicianly work rather than by monkey tricks. Its long and well-selected programme was not long enough to satisfy its hearers, and again and again it was recalled . . . and each response added to the furor it created.[44]

Notwithstanding such nice comments, the band was still struggling for more recognition, especially in New York itself. The breakthrough that they needed came when they were still at the Keith Theatre in Boston. Arthur Hand received a telegram from Paul Whiteman that read:[45]

> Offer you two weeks commencing Monday February fifth Palais Royal Stop Hours seven pm two am with ten to eleven out Stop Play dance and for Vanda Hoff providing you are willing to accept this engagement for one thousand per week Stop Looks like big opportunity for you Stop If your reply is favorable please advise just when you can get into New York to rehearse Vanda Hoff Paul Whiteman.

Vanda Hoff was the stage name of dancer Mildred Vanderhoff. She had been a dancer in Ziegfeld shows and had married Paul Whiteman shortly before, in November 1922. Whiteman had used the Palais Royal as his main location ever since his September 1920 debut in New York.[46] It had been the best place for him to start since it was the favorite spot for the rich and famous. Now he was going on a two-week tour through New England and needed a replacement, while Vanda Hoff would stay and dance at the Palais Royal. She used intricate orchestrations for her dancing. Therefore, Whiteman decided that Ernest Cutting would conduct the band at the Palais Royal. Kirkeby & Hand were eager to grab the opportunity to go to New York and agreed with Keith to end their tour. The California Ramblers were enlarged with six "symphony men," horns and violin players. Reed player Frank Cusick remembered how impressed he was:

> We went in there. They augmented the Ramblers with two horns and strings and we played for Vanda Hoff, Whiteman's future wife, she was a ballet dancer. And we had a music publisher Jack Robbins who came in and he heard us play the tune that we played for Vanda "Parade of the Wooden Soldiers." He said: "What's that?" We told him what it was. "Give me a part, give me it over!" In a matter of short time it was out as a big hit.[47] I have a picture on my mind. I was sitting there, playing.
> Whiteman conducted, he was an imposing figure this guy. We played and I found music and wind coming from my toes when he went like that. You gave your blood and without any effort. Oh, it was a real wonderful feeling. What an experience that was. All I remember is that beautiful sound and when those horns played that duet behind us, two of the finest horns in New York. Nobody in the band, nobody in the pit ever opened a book after the third day.

This short period when the band substituted for Whiteman at the Palais Royal would be used whenever the California Ramblers were being promoted.

Kirkeby & Hand had even bigger things in mind, but first the band returned to the Keith vaudeville circuit. It started at the best place, the Palace.[48] However, the band got a negative review. *Billboard* wrote: "They should go back to California and stay there. Band is overbrassed and stridently so. Rendition of part of Tannhauser was inexcusable. The Organisation is the weakest of quite a few orchestras that have played this House recently. They are mechanical, unmusical, noisy and lacking in novelty of any sort of description of other than time wasting! The Band were 4th on the bill."[49]

Good or bad reviews, the band continued its uphill battle and the next few weeks the California Ramblers toured around.[50] They were back in New York for the celebration of the National Vaudeville Week, where Sophie Tucker topped the bill at the Palace. On Friday 6 April the "monster National Vaudeville Artists' Ball and Entertainment" was held at the Terrace Garden Dance Palace. Music was provided by the bands of Ben Bernie, Paul Specht, and the California Ramblers.

The California Ramblers Inn

In 1922 the California Ramblers had been quite lucky to have a six-month contract at the Post Lodge, since it took them over the summer months, which were often a period of fewer customers, as restaurants had no air-conditioning at the time. Kirkeby did not want to run such a risk again and preferred a location of his own. In its new form the band's first engagement had been at Shanley's in New York the year before. The Shanleys were also running a place not far from the Post Lodge, at Pelham Shore Road, Pelham, New York. Originally it was a mansion built as an Italian villa for James A. Suydam, member of a rich family and a successful hobby painter. Suydam's property stretched from the shore of the Long Island Sound over to the other side of the Pelham Shore Road, over 1750 acres. It was completed between 1846 and 1848 and after Suydam's death in 1865, it had several owners until it was acquired by the city before the turn of the century.[51] By 1915 it had been converted into a roadhouse called the Pell Tree Inn. The roadhouse was bought by the Shanleys in 1918, who called it the Shanley Inn.[52] Similarly to the Post Lodge, which was located near a tennis court, the Shanley Inn got extra clientele from the Pelham Bay Golf Course across the street.[53] Kirkeby & Hand decided that this was the right spot and made a deal with Pete Shanley, who agreed to a multi-year percentage arrangement.[54] Hand may have preferred to buy the place outright and tried to get money from his wealthy father Joseph, but Joseph refused, saying he did not like the band's music and that he had disinherited his jazz leader son when his band played at Rector's.

Kirkeby & Hand called the new place the California Ramblers Inn. Saxophone player Frank Cusick remembered: "... that's the place the Ramblers built as a group effort. We cleaned the place up, we painted it and worked in it on the building. We did make it up so that we could open up."[55] The official opening was planned for 1 April 1923. This was announced by huge posters placed at strategic spots, which mentioned the music, the golf course, as well as the "delicious food—shore dinner—a la carte French cuisine." Looking back a year later, Kirkeby gave the opening date as Friday 18 May 1923 and said that it was "a tremendous success and within two weeks' time after the opening it was necessary ... to provide accommodation for two hundred more guests." Eventually the Inn could hold up to five hundred guests.[56] In an interview Spencer Clark, Rollini's successor on bass sax with the California Ramblers, described the interior: "It was a fairly large room that [the band] played in. It was an old converted house. I don't think it was constructed for the purpose [for] which it was used. It had a long room with the bandstand on one end ... and the tables spread off. It had a low ceiling and there was another room off there on one side.... There were dark drapes around the windows and on the walls. It was ornate, but it was not Rococo or anything as they generally got in that period."[57]

Neil Waterman, a college kid and a fan of the California Ramblers, would become one of Adrian's close friends.[58] He visited the Inn from about 1925 and said:

> It was a rather spacious ... building with a rather small dance area.... The stage was raised not too much, because it was easy for the boys to get up and down and sit in with them and a lot of them did.... The Inn was right on the water, in other words the Long Island Sound was right behind it. And when the parties lasted through until the morning, which they did very often, anybody who wanted to stay up and dance [could] sit in and play with the band, that was great, everybody just joined in. The first thing when the sun came up they would all go swimming in the Sound, ... go swimming and they break up. Another night the same deal. It was all very informal and wonderful and of course there was no music like that around. The place was not "dry."

According to Waterman: "You could buy alcohol, but nobody would admit it and they'd bring their own if they wanted to, but mostly you bought what the people were selling in those days and it was all under the table."[59]

Spencer Clark gave some insight on the life of a California Rambler at the time:

> Weekends were always big. Back then they played seven nights a week. The musicians did not get a day off until the early or middle thirties. If you had a day off, you were out of work! There was one clever thing that I learned. On week days when it was rather slow, everybody parked out front, musicians and everybody else. So that anybody driving along would see a lot of cars and think: "Oh, this is a good place

to go. We go in there!" And they go in and be the only people in the place. On the weekends you couldn't park [there]. You had to park in the back and hide your cars. It was not that close to the water for swimming and the water, although nearby, ended in a marsh. There was no beach or any facility for swimming. [The California Ramblers Inn] was open twelve months a year, it never closed. It was very, very popular during that period.[60]

The press reacted positively. One newspaper, with some journalistic freedom, wrote:

> The California Ramblers are making a "go" of the spacious restaurant overlooking the Sound on the Pelham shore road, formerly known as Shanley's Pell Tree Inn, which the members of this orchestra purchased about a month ago and which is directly under the management of Kirkeby & Hand. The Orchestra commercialized the name they had used in playing in various first grade vaudeville circuits and are calling the establishment the California Ramblers Inn. It is the only orchestra in existence that "owns its own home."

Three weeks later the same newspaper informed its readers that an additional room had been opened, called the Ramblers' Room, thus increasing the inn's capacity by another hundred guests.[61]

Kirkeby would claim that he had bought a partnership in the Inn, thereby suggesting that Hand was the other partner. However, it was a lease. A year after the acquisition he said that "a new lease on the property has just been negotiated and many years of substantial business is looked forward to."[62]

It was a success. Spencer Clark: "The place was frequented by primarily local people, although a lot came out from New York, but this was in the middle of a very wealthy area, Westchester County. People had the money, they had the nice cars. We'd see beautiful cars parked outside there night after night and they loved to drink and have a good time."

The various members of the band also brought their own friends to the California Ramblers Inn, and that included girlfriends, of course. The band room was on the second floor. One time Kirkeby was walking up the very dark stairs while trombone player Abe Lincoln had a "dame" there and was fooling around. "Kirkeby stepped on something and he heard 'Ouch!' and Kirkeby said 'Is that you, Abe?' 'Yes, Mr. Kirkeby!' 'Take your two weeks.'"[63]

Alcoholic beverages were indeed easily available at the California Ramblers Inn. Irving Brodsky said: "it was Prohibition, but they sold about just the same. I don't know where they used to hide it, but everybody seemed to have a lot of booze."[64] Spencer Clark adds a lively description of an evening at the California Ramblers Inn:

The California Ramblers sitting on the grass in front of California Ramblers Inn, 1923. From left: Lloyd "Ole" Olsen, Stan King, Adrian Rollini, Ray Kitchingman, Arthur Hand, Bill Moore, Frank Cush, Fred Cusick or Orville Gibbs, Jim Duff, Irving Brodsky. (courtesy Eric Hamilton, Jim Duff's grandson)

That was a great drinking place. Oh, boy, I've seen an awful lot of people drink themselves silly. Of course this is back during Prohibition when the booze that you got was not necessarily good and in fact a lot of it was just downright bad, and they'd come in because there was wide open drinking in there. The bottles were on the table. It was far enough out in the country and I suppose they paid off the local police so they leave them alone, something of that sort. No offense intended! That's been a habit here, especially during Prohibition days. There was so much money involved, it tempted everybody.

Pictures in my mind are the dancers out in front of the band, doing the Charleston with the fringes on the skirts swinging back and forth, kicking high, wearing a little hat, calotte hats they call 'm, tiny helmets, and the band drove them crazy, it did. It was a very new experience to them I presume, a unique experience to dance to a band of that persuasion, because that band could move people and it did and of course the liquor they would consume all helped to put them in the right frame of mind.

But the room would change. Early evening when it would start out before people became too inebriated it would mostly be quiet and smooth and then as the evening wore on when the tempo increased and the liquor started to flow it changed and they started jumping all over the place. The Charleston and the Black Bottom were a real popular thing at that particular point.[65]

The Inn was a remote place, but once found by the public, they kept coming.

Taking Stock

The last few months of 1922 and the first of 1923 resulted in a good number of recordings again. Most of these feature the usual Tin Pan Alley material, played in a traditional way, but there is one interesting exception, the coupling "Bees Knees"/"Teddy Bear Blues," recorded in November 1922 for Paramount.[66] The arrangements gave Rollini a striking role and the recording balance makes him audible throughout both titles. In "Bees Knees" he produced three short solo moments, only one bar each but quite effective. In both titles he played a part that went beyond the brass bass tradition. The California Ramblers were on their way to finding their individual, recognizable sound based on Rollini's bass sax.[67]

In one year the band had come a long way. The California Ramblers had worked in the Palais Royal, Paul Whiteman's home base. Thus they could be regarded as being in Whiteman's league. They had accumulated experience and stability during the long stay at the Post Lodge, all the time with hardly a change in personnel. They had made an amazing number of recordings, including several hits, for nearly all labels, both minor and major. The band now had its own home in the California Ramblers Inn. The music world was watching them.

Chapter 5

The California Ramblers Grown Up

For the weeks between the original and the actual opening dates of the California Ramblers Inn, from 1 April 1923 until 18 May 1923, Kirkeby had found enough work for his band, based on his good contacts with the Keith organization. Before and after the tour he organized four recording sessions. Two of these, for Paramount, produced demonstrations of Adrian Rollini's growth on bass sax. The first session was on 30 April 1923. The arrangement of its first title, "I Love Me," gave Rollini a sixteen-bar solo spot, which, though fully arranged, gave him a chance to shine.[1] On the second title, "Who's Sorry Now," Adrian performs three breaks, of respectively two, one, and one bars. This record is Rollini's best so far. Trumpeter Frank Cush remembers the recording as an outstanding effort from a jazz standpoint, and one that caused a mild sensation, especially among musicians.[2] The other Paramount session is almost equally interesting. On both "Keep It Under Your Hat" and "Long Lost Mama" Rollini plays several one- and two-bar breaks. On the first title he integrates these into a solo by the tenor sax player.

No doubt Kirkeby's marketing talents had much to do with the tremendous success of the California Ramblers Inn from its start. He probably was the author of the following promotional text, aimed at the growing group of people who had a car or a motorcycle and could use it for entertainment. Who wouldn't wish to make the trip to the inn after reading it?

"The Call of Spring"
   We are now reasonably sure that Spring Weather is here to stay.
   The countryside is rapidly responding to the warm sunshine, and the green will soon be with us in its full glory.
   What a joy to get out again with one's motor on the road.
   Always before the motor ride one's thought is—"where shall we go?"
   Why not motor to the California Ramblers Inn? Get an early start and enjoy the delicious food served in its famous special dinners: "California Shore," "A la carte" or "Ramblers Plate."

> The prices are very reasonable—two dollars to three dollars per plate—and NO COVER CHARGE to those having dinner no matter how late they remain.
> Enjoy to the fullest the quiet restfulness of the delightful view overlooking the Sound.
> Dance to the enchanting music of the world famed California Ramblers—and you are sure to return many times.
> Week nights are particularly pleasurable for the fastidious.
> "Come early and spend the evening."[3]

However, now the band could hardly be missed at the inn and it was poor planning (or just a friendly service to Keith) that it had to fulfill a one-week contract from 3 June, at the Palace in New York. The Palace was the top location in American vaudeville and Kirkeby had been there several times, both with the first edition of the California Ramblers back in 1920 and with his present band. So it might be worth the effort and certainly meant great publicity. The program's headliners were the Duncan Sisters, vaudeville artists, and Valeska Suratt, an actress and singer.[4] At this time the unique sound of the band was not yet generally known, and Kirkeby may even have solved his dilemma by sending a substitute band. He knew enough people in the business.

In fact, the investment paid off quickly. Columbia, the second most respected record company, now wanted the band. Back in April 1922 when the California Ramblers restarted, it had made some recordings for Columbia, Kirkeby's old employer, but the one resulting record did not make an impression and the only other recordings the Ramblers would do for Columbia that year, were for its small-priced (and -sized) label Little Wonder. Now in July and August 1923 the band recorded intensively for Columbia and almost every recording featured Adrian Rollini on the bass saxophone. On the first title from this series, "My Sweetie Went Away," he played a thirty-two-bar duet with trumpeter Bill Moore, who usually took the hot trumpet solos. Frank Cush, the band's other trumpeter, remembered this recording as its only outstanding effort from a jazz standpoint. It caused a mild sensation among musicians.[5] This was followed by "I Love Me," which uses the same arrangement as the earlier Paramount recording, with sixteen solo bars by Rollini. Each of the final three Columbia titles from this short period also features sixteen or thirty-two bars of his solo work. One of these, "That Old Gal of Mine," featured Frank Cush's first solo on record. Cush's proud father bought copies for all neighbors and relatives.[6]

The records sold well and Columbia now went a step further. It had started to sign exclusive contracts with several popular artists.[7] Among these were black artists such as trumpet star and orchestra leader Johnny Dunn and blues artists Bessie and Clara Smith. Columbia's white exclusive artists included dance band leaders Ted Lewis and Paul Specht and singer Dolly Kay. Now the company decided to add the California Ramblers to this roster. Ed Kirkeby's strategy of recording for any New York record company did not stop him from signing with Columbia.[8] In November 1923 he agreed to Columbia's exclusive use of the name California Ramblers on records.[9] It allowed Kirkeby to continue recording for other labels but from now on those companies could no longer use the artist credit California Ramblers. Instead they had to use pseudonyms.[10] The best-known of these would be the Golden Gate Orchestra, which once again suggested a California connection.[11]

In August a copyright was issued for the song "Daisie," with words by Arthur Hand and music by Adrian Rollini, probably Rollini's first copyright.[12]

The Band-within-a-Band

The band's personnel had hardly changed since its restart in April 1922, but in September 1923 the first important change took place when reed players Bobby Davis and Arnold Brilhart joined, and Jimmy Duff left.[13] Since Duff was one of the band's founding fathers, Ed Kirkeby had to buy him out. Little is known about Bobby Davis's early years. Robert P. Davis was born around 1903 in Charleston, New Hampshire, and was of Irish descent. In 1920 he worked for an insurance company, but he had enough musical experience to join the California Ramblers when he was twenty. Arnold Brilhart was born in 1904, and started playing the saxophone when he was seven and listened to the Six Brown Brothers and virtuoso Rudy Wiedoeft. He had been a member of Adrian Rollini's own small orchestra and worked with pioneer bandleader Harry Yerkes before he joined the California Ramblers.[14] Brilhart was a good reader but did not regard himself as a good arranger. Unlike Brilhart, Bobby Davis was a great improviser, and he was to brighten up many California Ramblers recordings with excellent solo work. He would soon have his first opportunity.

Kirkeby continued to find ways to get the public's attention. In September he introduced weekly feature nights at the California Ramblers Inn. Some of the themes were the Ziegfeld Follies, Variety, and Carnival. There was also a Versatile Sextet night, which suggests that a small group was selected from the full band, a new concept for Kirkeby but not his invention.[15] His colleague at Columbia, dance band leader Paul Specht, not only also had an exclusive Columbia contract for his dance band, but also for his band-within-a-band, the Georgians. This group's recordings were jazz-oriented and at least as successful as those by the larger dance orchestra.[16] Specht in turn had copied this concept from Paul Whiteman, whose reed player Ross Gorman led a jazzy recording group, the Virginians. Ed Kirkeby liked this concept and may have been looking for a similar smaller group from his California Ramblers for the same purpose, namely jazz. Adrian Rollini would play a major role in this new venture. With Rollini's bass sax, Kirkeby now had a sound that not only set them apart from any other dance orchestra, but also allowed him to make jazzier recordings. He had enough musicians in his band that could swing and produce hot solos, such as trumpeter Bill Moore and sax player Bobby Davis. With a small jazz band, they would get more space to show it. Since admiration for the new jazz music was particularly found in university circles, Kirkeby called his new group the Varsity Eight. The Cameo label had already issued some records by the full band and agreed to do the first recording session by the smaller group, which took place on 6 September 1923. Two Tin Pan Alley tunes were recorded that day, "Last Night on the Back Porch" and "Oh Joe." In both tunes Rollini is strongly featured on a sixteen-bar solo and two sixteen-bar solo duets, but the arrangements also gave newcomer Bobby Davis much freedom with two sixteen-bar solos.[17] The first tune also features two special choruses by members of the band, the first sung and the second whistled. It gives a vivid illustration of the happy-go-lucky mood that the band created evening after evening at the California Ramblers Inn.

After the Varsity Eight's session for Cameo, the California Ramblers would have another first the same day. The band would do its first radio broadcast, so it had to move to a different studio to go on the air. The station was WHN and the thirty-minute broadcast started at 3:45 p.m.[18] Radio studios used a new tool, a microphone, to capture the sound instead of the (sometimes multiple) acoustical horns used by the gramophone studios. This new technique, together with the concept of a wide audience, formed a new experience to all band members, who must have been impressed. Yet no comment by any of them is known. In hindsight it may have been just like any other recording activity for them.[19]

"Last Night on the Back Porch" became a best-seller for Cameo and the Varsity Eight quickly became a household name at that company. The 1924 Cameo catalogue featured a photo of the group with the caption "a style of their own—perfect dance rhythm—and an abundance of character to all their records."[20] In fact, a large share of these small-group recordings by contingents of the California Ramblers would have more character than those by the full band. This had to do with the way the band got its arrangements. Most top bands used staff arrangers, whose consistent styles would create a sound by which the band would be recognized. Paul Whiteman was strongly dependent on Ferde Grofé for this, and Don Redman wrote many arrangements for Fletcher Henderson. Both arrangers were also members of those bands, but the California Ramblers had no staff arranger and no single band member produced custom arrangements for the band. Instead, the band mostly relied on stock arrangements issued by the publisher of the music they played. These stocks were doctored to fit the capabilities and strengths of the band, but only when special choruses were added might the results become out of the ordinary. This doctoring was a task most band members were involved in. Piano player Irving Brodsky was one of them. When Kirkeby was asked about arrangements for the California Ramblers, he confirmed that Adrian Rollini wrote a few.[21] For the small-group sessions, special versions of these arrangements were made with more solo space. Kirkeby described the method as follows: "We did it with what we called head arrangements. We would take a stock arrangement with no orchestration whatsoever as far as special arrangements were concerned and go into a studio. Routine was the thing there by giving this man a break, another man sixteen bars and an eight-bar release. Or a duet here and duet there. Strictly head arrangement."[22] In Cameo's words: "an abundance of character." "Last Night on the Back Porch" offers an instance in which two takes survive of a particular recording. They show that it was all well under control: the two takes mainly differ in single notes played by alto sax soloist Bobby Davis. Basically he plays the same solo on both takes.

While these developments took place, Kirkeby did not neglect his usual recording work with other companies. In August the full band recorded for Arto again, and in September for Pathé/Perfect. The latter session deserves special mention. First of all, at the end of "Tell All the Folks in Kentucky," the first of three titles recorded, clarinet player Bobby Davis, embarks on a solo that results in an ending like a New Orleans–style "free-for-all." It proves that some of the band's members were listening to this type of music, that they liked it, and were able to perform it. The remaining two titles, "Easy Melody" and "Sittin' in a Corner," were the first recordings by the California Ramblers with a vocalist. The singer was called George Perry on the record labels, but his actual name was Arthur Hall.[23] A vocal chorus would from now on be a common feature on their records, although the singers were hired just for the recording sessions. Hall would often return and be followed by many other male singers. Even Ed Kirkeby himself would sing on some records, but his performances did not compare favorably with those by singers who were specially hired.[24] The California Ramblers never had an official band singer.

Kirkeby's original idea had been to have his band in the California Ramblers Inn, their own place, during summer and to get contracts for outside work for the winter season. So after the initial and successful first five months, the band moved to a different place. This was the Monte Carlo, where they opened on Wednesday 17 October, "coincident with the establishment's new show [which] will be changed weekly, says Teddy Reilly, director of Stagecraft Productions, who is in charge." The Monte Carlo's owner, William J. Gallagher, explained to a newspaper that the public wanted better music and that "dancing had been popular as a diversion for the youngest diners, but it has spread so that now persons of all ages recognize that it is a healthful, enjoyable means of exercis-

Adrian Rollini ca. 1925.

ing. Time was when even the middle-aged dancer was subject to considerable derision and condemnation, just as were the intrepid women who started the fashion of smoking cigarettes in public."[25]

The day following the opening at the Monte Carlo saw the Varsity Eight back in the Cameo studio. One of the tunes that they recorded was "Mama Loves Papa, Papa Loves Mama," which contains a solo on a kazoo, a toy instrument, blown by drummer F. Stanley (Stan) King, an early case of the use of a novelty instrument on a California Ramblers record.

By the end of that month another recording by a contingent of the band took place when it recorded for a label new to Kirkeby's list, Gennett. For this company a new pseudonym was chosen, the Vagabonds. Lewis James was hired to do a vocal chorus on the tune "Rememb'ring," but the session is mainly memorable because of the thirty-two-bar duet between the trumpet and the bass sax on "Sittin' in a Corner," the third time they recorded this tune.[26]

The final date for Pathé in October produced an exceptional number of five titles in one day, three of which were commercial. The usual arrangement for such material consisted of a statement of the melody, sometimes followed by a vocal chorus and then by one or two hot choruses before the closing. However, two tunes got a special treatment. The arrangement of "Frankie and Johnny" featured Bill Moore's trumpet work, which seems inspired by Louis Panico's work on the successful recording of the same tune with Isham Jones's band.

However, the major surprise from this session was a little-known tune called "One Week Ago." Here the statement of the melody is followed by a thirty-two-bar duet between clarinet and bass sax, then by sixteen bars of trumpet and piano, then the alto sax joins in for another sixteen bars, after which the full band closes the recording, but not without some breaks by the trumpet. This is an uncompromisingly hot record, more like a jam session than a formal recording. It may have been recorded as an afterthought: three or four commercial arrangements were recorded and time was left for one more recording, which the band used in its own way.

On 1 November 1923 the California Ramblers interrupted their work at the Monte Carlo for a special occasion. They were one of a long list of orchestras performing at the ball of the Loew-Metro Club in the Hotel Astor. This was announced as "the greatest show of its kind presented anywhere!" Tickets were $5—but included supper, dancing, and show. When the first press articles and advertisements appeared, the California Ramblers were one of only seven bands listed. The others were Jack Fox's Clover Garden Orchestra, Alex Hyde's Orchestra (under Whiteman's management), Joe Jordon's Melody Boys, Al Jockers' Serenaders, Saranoff's Wigwam Orchestra, and Paul Specht's Orchestra.[27] However, when *Talking Machine World* published its final announcement, it listed twenty-seven![28] Making a schedule when each band would play one or two numbers presented a problem. Among the many celebrities present were Victor Herbert, Al Jolson, Vincent Lopez, and Mrs. Rudolph Valentino. A newspaper review read: "Who's who in the Land of Make Believe and a couple of thousands of their relatives and friends had a real shindig at the Hotel Astor last night.... the only difference between it and a real old-fashioned barn dance was about half a billion dollars' worth of diamonds and gowns."[29]

Rudy Wiedoeft

Ed Kirkeby had contracts with his musicians that forbade them to make recordings other than with the California Ramblers. His strategy of working for any record label made this rule relatively easy to comply with. However, for Adrian Rollini it was too strict. His position in the band as the one who primarily created its distinctive sound put him in a good position to negotiate with Kirkeby. So when he got an opportunity to make a record on the side, he decided to use it. The opportunity came with with Rudy Wiedoeft.

Rudy Wiedoeft (1893–1940) really did come from the West Coast. His parents were German immigrants who settled in Los Angeles. Rudy was one of four brothers who all became music professionals; before he was ten, he played clarinet in the Wiedoeft family orchestra. When he moved to New York City in 1916 he had started playing saxophone, then still an unusual instrument. His brothers stayed on the West Coast and worked in a band formed by brother Herb. Rudy Wiedoeft's main instrument became the C-melody saxophone. He became famous as a virtuoso saxophonist and made hundreds of recordings, which saw worldwide issue. Thus he did much to popularize the saxophone as an instrument in both the United States and overseas. Wiedoeft's style was noted for very rapid runs of well-articulated notes in between long, lush, legato phrases and for being influenced by ragtime. The rapidly articulated notes were made possible by his advanced techniques of double-tonguing and triple-tonguing, similar to those used by brass (trumpet, trombone, etc.) players and flutists. He employed several other sound effects, such as slap tonguing and "laughing" through his horn, on tunes such as "Valse Vanité," "Valse Llewellyn," "Saxema," "Saxophobia," and "Sax-o-Phun."[30] Wiedoeft recorded with many different combinations (first with his Frisco Jazz Band) and developed into a saxophone virtuoso, primarily as a soloist.

The work of the Six Brown Brothers, a saxophone sextet that toured the country, also interested him. Its instrumentation consisted of two alto saxophones, two tenor saxophones, one baritone saxophone, and a bass saxophone. For some Brunswick recordings Wiedoeft assembled a similar group. The instrumentation of his Saxophone Sextet did not vary but its personnel did, and on one occasion in November 1923 the bass saxophone was played by Adrian Rollini. Only one title was recorded, "The Rosary." The tune was published as a song in 1898 and composed by Ethelbert Nevin.[31] It became a popular piano piece. The arrangement does not really feature Rudy Wiedoeft, but his beautiful tone is prominent throughout the recording. In fact, Rollini's role was to contribute the lower harmonies to the overall ensemble sound. The result is a recording that in no way compares to the dance and jazz sounds of the California Ramblers and thus formed no competition for Kirkeby. He may even have liked it. And it created more respect for Rollini's work with some older members of his family who preferred Wiedoeft's novelty work to Adrian's dance band music. Adrian Rollini himself was absolutely proud of this recording of "The Rosary." Interviewed in 1929 in Europe about his musical career, he hardly went into his great jazz recordings, but he did mention his single recording with Wiedoeft, specifically the fine organ sound created by the six saxophones.[32]

1923 Comes to a Great Close

Columbia's November announcement of fourteen new issues (announced as "New Process") was headed by two California Ramblers records.[33] Other artists in the list, such as the Georgians and Fletcher Henderson, only had one issue

Ad for Radio Ball at Roseland Ballroom, 3 December 1923.

each. On the 21st the California Ramblers were one of seventeen(!) orchestras selected to perform at the third annual dance of the Talking Machine Men, Inc., the proceeds of which were to be used for "advertising and other purposes beneficial to the association." It was claimed that all of the leading orchestras contributed their services. The list included Brunswick's Ben Bernie, Columbia's Ted Lewis, and Victor's Paul Whiteman.[34]

Clearly, the California Ramblers belonged in the top echelon now and Columbia's promotion activity would push it further. The recording industry was at that time debating the value of radio for the sales of gramophone records. Some companies saw it as competition, but Columbia took the side of the radio stations. Harry Yerkes, its assistant general manager, was quoted saying: "we have urged that our exclusive artists sing for the radio whenever possible.... I think radio ... by forcing a great deal of public attention upon music, is certainly doing the phonograph industry a good turn."[35]

Adrian Rollini about aged twenty.

Columbia realized that radio broadcasting was the next upcoming publicity medium, and made an arrangement with New York station WEAF, a subsidiary of the American Telephone & Telegraph Company, "to feature a special radio program with the artists who record for Columbia records."[36] The California Ramblers were now one of their exclusive artists, so they would go on the air under the Columbia flag. Their earlier broadcasts, for WHN in September and October, had been in the afternoon, but WEAF would feature them in the evening, when more people were listening. It also meant extra income for the band: WEAF was paying competitor Vincent Lopez $250 per evening broadcast and Kirkeby would not have settled for less.[37] The opening program took place on Tuesday evening, 4 December 1923.[38] The program was broadcast directly from the Columbia recording studio from 9:15 to 9:45 p.m. A bulletin called "Advertising by radio" had been sent out by George W. Hopkins, Columbia's vice president and general sales manager, and this opened the broadcast. Then advertising manager Lester L. Leverich introduced the organization and the band played. *Variety* wrote: "judging the enthusiastic reports . . . the broadcast was heard and enjoyed throughout the country." This seems exaggerated, but WEAF certainly was one of the most powerful stations at the time and the program could be heard by millions of radio fans.[39] One of these was Emerick N. Berger, who wrote from Bridgeport, Connecticut: "Won't you please try to arrange a program for a weekly night for one hour at least. . . . ramble on, Ramblers, you play the snappiest jazziest and most tuneful numbers we hear."[40] The program had a stimulating effect on the sales of the California Ramblers' Columbia records. That same month however, Vincent Lopez was the winner of a contest for the

Opening the Hippodrome with twenty-five-piece band directed by Julius Lenzberg. Ray Kitchingman second from left; Stan King, drums to the left of the accordion player; Adrian Rollini center, behind Irving Brodsky; Bobby Davis in front row next to piano; Ole Olsen extreme right; Bill Moore fourth from right.

most popular broadcasting orchestra, over four other orchestras including the California Ramblers.[41]

In addition to the regular work at the California Ramblers Inn and in various studios, December 1923 had even more activity. The band worked at the Monte Carlo, at Proctor's, and on the day after the broadcast contributed to a benefit performance for the New York American Christmas Fund at the Roseland Ballroom.[42] Others present were the bands of Gene Fosdick, Sam Lanin, Vincent Lopez, and Paul Whiteman.[43]

As the year's climax, the California Ramblers were selected to reopen the new Hippodrome Theatre in New York on Monday 17 December for the B.F. Keith organization. The Hippodrome had been built in 1905 and was famous for large-scale spectacles. It stretched between two corner towers from 43rd to 44th Street on 6th Avenue and seated five thousand. Keith took over the lease and converted the Hippodrome into a vaudeville theater at the cost of $600,000. For the opening, the California Ramblers were augmented from ten to twenty-four men and a conductor:

3 trumpets

2 trombones

5 alto saxophones (doubling on clarinet and baritone saxophone)

5 violins

1 accordion

2 pianos

1 bass saxophone

1 tuba

2 banjos

2 drums

A photograph of the entire group was taken that Conn, in a full-page advertisement, used to promote its catalog of musical instruments.[44] Deals whereby the name of a famous artist could be used by an instrument maker in return for a free instrument were common in the industry. No doubt the California Ramblers had been fitted with Conn instruments before the photograph. Rollini's bass saxophone looks shop new in the Hippodrome photo. The advertisement mentions the happening and says that the California Ramblers were the largest dance orchestra that ever appeared in vaudeville. Members of the band can indeed be seen in the picture, but the large orchestra on the new stage was a conglomerate of three dance bands. The other composing bands were the Golden Gate Orchestra and the Brunswick Orchestra.[45] This combination was directed by Julius Lenzberg. Fully in line was the long list of participating artists.[46]

On opening night, the California Ramblers' act was fourth of a total of eleven acts. The show was called "In Melody Land" and a review was far from flattering.[47] It mentioned the three orchestras (which mainly accompanied the singers and dancers) but said that they were conducted by Arthur Hand and under direction of Ed Kirkeby. Arrangements were by W. C. Polla and Irving Brodsky. According to the reviewer: "possibly . . . the combination has not had . . . sufficient time to get together. . . . The musicians are continuously rehearsing. The fault just now appears to be that this is too much of a band and not enough of an orchestra. . . . an orchestra of 20 piece. . . . on a stage 60 feet wide and 45 feet deep." This review gives the impression that the violins, who were sitting on stage left, simply could not hear the reeds that were far away on the right, and vice versa. The reviewer had a suggestion though, "whereby the large band would not back the singing and dancing: . . . this [band] combination should be able to hold the stage alone for 12 to 15 minutes."

While these activities took place, Ed Kirkeby also kept his men busy in New York's recording studios. In November recordings were made by Arto, Paramount, Columbia, Cameo, and in December by Columbia and Cameo. For unknown reasons all of Columbia's November recordings were rejected except

(Enlargement) Adrian Rollini at Hippodrome opening.

for the final take of "Kaintucky." This title features what had become a popular element in the California Ramblers' work, a thirty-two-bar duet between Rollini and one of his colleagues, in this case trumpeter Bill Moore.[48] Another such duet by Rollini, but now with Bobby Davis was recorded during the Paramount session this month. Davis played soprano sax on "Bit by Bit You're Breaking My Heart." In December Columbia finally managed to get some usable masters for the titles that had been rejected in November. These and the other titles recorded during December were of no jazz value.[49]

The final months of 1923 were a turning point in the musical careers of Ed Kirkeby, the California Ramblers, and particularly for Adrian Rollini. From one of many distinguished piano players he had grown into the top performer on the bass saxophone, setting an example for many, but, as it turned out, inimitable. Kirkeby realized that he now had a definite individual sound with his band, and Rollini had made it happen.

1924, the Third Year

Their first six months as "owners" of the California Ramblers Inn had been a tremendous success, so Kirkeby & Hand decided to continue the lease on the inn and extended the contract for five years, up to the end of 1928. After the New Year's festivities, the inn closed for "extensive redecoration" and the band took up a combined engagement at New York's Monte Carlo Club on Broadway and at the Hippodrome.[50] They would return to their home base on 1 April, where in the meantime their position had been filled by a substitute band, called the Intercollegians.[51]

An impressive list exists of the work done at the California Ramblers Inn during the first three months of 1924.[52] The inn was almost turned upside down.

It was totally cleaned up, both upstairs and downstairs. Downstairs drapes and carpets were taken off the restaurant and the lounging room and brought upstairs before repairs were done. The repairs included doors, heating system, the leaking water system, and electric systems. New construction included a nine-foot partition around the bar that provided a separate entrance to the men's washroom. In the cellar all bottles were assorted and stored on shelves. A mysterious item in the list mentions that "all soft stuff is moved from bar to cellar." This suggests that "hard stuff" was stored elsewhere, possibly the "stuff" that could not be sold in Prohibition days. As before, the inn was leased from Shanley, and one Peter F. Shanley went bankrupt that year. He had a $1,000 liability to Kirkeby & Hand.[53]

A newspaper article from early 1924 announced the band's imminent return to the renovated California Ramblers Inn, its summer quarters. The article repeats the misleading suggestion that the band had come from the West, much like Paul Whiteman's and Art Hickman's bands, but also lists personnel of the band at the time, early 1924. The list was clearly dictated by Kirkeby or by Hand and probably missed reed player Fred Cusick. The amount of doubling by most musicians looks exaggerated, but it was probably realistic:

- Arthur Hand, violin, director
- William Moore, trumpet
- Frank Cush, trumpet, saxophones
- Lloyd Olsen, trombone, saxophones, violin, cello
- Arnold Brilhart, family of saxophones, including reed instruments
- Robert Davis, family of saxophones, cornet, clarinet, melaphone [sic]
- Adrian Rollini, bass saxophone, piano, xylophone, banjo
- Irving Brodsky, piano, arrangements
- R. F. Kitchingman, banjo, trombone
- Stanley King, drums, tympani[54]

Even Adrian Rollini got three instruments in the list in addition to his bass sax. Piano and xylophone are no surprise, since two years before he had been hired for these instruments, but this is the only time that he is listed as playing banjo. What really surprises is Irving Brodsky's listing as an arranger, since the band was known to use stock arrangements that were doctored in order to accommodate solo work. This adaptation work was one of Brodsky's tasks, who probably used suggestions from other band members. Anyway, the band's individual sound was not the result of special arrangements, but of the personal styles of its musicians, in particular Rollini, Moore, Davis, and drummer Stan King.

One person not listed was Gilbert Kahn, son of banker Otto Kahn, who lived with his family in a "Florentine Palace" at 1100 Fifth Avenue, New York.[55] Gil-

California Ramblers, 1924. Left to right: Irving Brodsky, Adrian Rollini, Stan King, Arthur Hand, Ray Kitchingman, Frank Cush, Bill Moore, Bobby Davis, Ole Olson, Jim Duff.

bert was a student at Princeton University and loved to play saxophone, which he occasionally did with the California Ramblers. In a magazine article Arthur Hand spoke quite positively about Gilbert: "We like to have him with us. He's a prince of a boy and a good musician besides. He's full of pep."[56] Gilbert had good contacts and one of these resulted in an idea by songwriter Jerome Kern to use the band in a show, but it did not happen.[57] Gilbert, unlike his younger brother Roger, did not last long in the music field, but followed in his father's footsteps and became a banker.[58]

If this did not produce a new band member, it did produce new publicity for the California Ramblers. So did the radio broadcasts from the Columbia studio on Tuesdays and Thursdays every week. Columbia was "trying the novelty of disproving that radio hurts record sales," one newspaper said.[59] Listeners enjoyed the broadcasts and some sent messages to station WEAF at 195 Broadway. One letter from Ohio mentioned the California Ramblers' first recording, "Sheik of Araby," and said that "from then on, we have procured every record by you that we could." Columbia must have loved to read this. Other requests were for "I Found a New Baby," "Wonderful One," "Dreamy Melody," and in particular for "Two Blue Eyes."[60] This tune was composed by Irving Brodsky and Arthur Hand and reached the special milestone of being a 100 percent recorded number: "all the big recording leaders ... requested that he be allowed to record this number for their companies."[61]

Kirkeby's next effort to promote his band business was to try to get California Ramblers registered as a trademark at the patent office in Washington. A letter from Dallett H. Wilson's law office in New York to W. T. Kirkeby, 1674 Broadway, New York, mentions an amount of $60 (plus attorney fee) for registration.[62] Kirkeby had always been very protective of the name California Ramblers and may have noticed that now and then records were issued with this label credit that had not been recorded by his band. Therefore, he wanted to go a step further and have the name California Ramblers on record labels as a trademark, so he could more easily sue for infringement. However, the patent office denied his application. Kirkeby did not accept this and filed appeal. Eventually he would lose the case but he won in publicity.

In February 1924 the Columbia Phonograph Company started a strong advertising campaign, which involved all their major recording artists. In the popular genre this meant Al Jolson and a host of orchestras, including the California Ramblers. The list of classical artists was much shorter, but it included celebrity cello player Pablo Casals.[63]

During much of the winter season, the California Ramblers worked at the Monte Carlo, but during March, just before the band returned to its home base in Westchester, it took short engagements at other spots. On 1 March they furnished the music at the Ritz-Carlton Hotel for the annual tea dance of the Marymount College of Tarrytown-on-the-Hudson. Even after the inn had opened they played a benefit performance for the Red Cross at its "House on the Hill." There were other appearances of the band outside the inn, some major, some minor. One of the bigger ones took place the week of 13 April. Over three hundred theaters throughout the United States took part in N.V.A. (National Vaudeville Association) Week; the California Ramblers were at the New York Hippodrome, the largest theatre of them all. And on 30 April they played at the annual ball of the Talking Machine and Radio Men's Association at the Hotel Pennsylvania, New York. Fifteen bands, both black and white, volunteered, by courtesy of the six major gramophone record companies.[64] The white bands included the orchestras of Paul Whiteman and Paul Specht. The black bands were Fletcher Henderson's and Armand Piron's.[65] The entire entertainment was broadcast by station WJZ.

During the first months of 1924 the California Ramblers' recorded output was their standard mix of straight dance music and pure jazz recordings. In the jazz category, the January Pathé/Perfect session produced two hot titles, "Mindin' My Business" and "Lots of Mama." The latter title is a composition by Chicago bandleader/piano player Elmer Schoebel, and several great jazz recordings were made of it. The California Ramblers' version stands out because of Adrian Rollini's fine solo work (three breaks and a fifteen-bar solo). The same month the band, as the Varsity Eight, recorded "Mean Blues" for Cameo, with a twelve-bar solo by Rollini. His accompaniment to the following clarinet and trumpet solos is impressive. Even longer Rollini solos can be heard on the three ver-

California Ramblers on sheet music of "Tryin' to Keep Away from You," recorded by the Varsity Eight.

sions of "Hula Lou," recorded for Columbia, Arto, and Cameo. The Cameo version (by the Varsity Eight) has some of the finest Rollini work on record so far. The small Arto company produced a record with two jazz sides, a rarity for the full band: "Limehouse Blues" and "Tin Roof Blues." "Limehouse Blues" had first been recorded by Paul Whiteman's band only two months earlier and would become a jazz standard, as is "Tin Roof Blues." The latter had been launched by the New Orleans Rhythm Kings in 1923 and on their original recording trombone player George Brunies played a solo that became a standard feature in any performance. However, at the time the California Ramblers recorded it, this tradition had yet to be born and a sixteen-bar solo spot was filled by Adrian Rollini on his bass saxophone.

The longest Rollini solo was recorded in March. As part of the Columbia recording of "I Must Have Company," he played a thirty-two-bar solo. No doubt such a long solo was no exception when the California Ramblers played in public but it was unusual on a record, not only for the California Ramblers but for any orchestra at the time. Adrian Rollini had graduated to the position of the band's solo star. This would become more and more evident in the following months.

Chapter 6

The California Ramblers to the Top with Adrian Rollini

Finally back at the California Ramblers Inn, the Ramblers found their home base perfectly fit for the coming summer season. The invitation for the official opening on 16 April 1924 says that it had been "redecorated in true California Style—combining colors both bright and cool." It emphasizes the inn's food quality: "We are determined to have the best food—properly served—on the road, and to that end we have put our kitchen under the supervision of one of Europe's famous stewards, Carl Planker." It ends with a reference to its trademark: "be pleased with the . . . music—well—just hear the Ramblers again."

The opening was just after Paul Whiteman's first concert at New York's Aeolian Hall, billed as "An Experiment in Modern Music." It definitely put Whiteman in front of all other bandleaders and was a challenge to those colleagues to stay in the limelight, too.[1] Kirkeby used all his promotion talent to get the public from the city to the Ramblers Inn in Westchester. In June patrons could become members of the Sunday Afternoon Tea Dansant Club.[2] In July the Westchester Follies Night was organized, offering young, local talent ("and other entertainers") a chance to be heard. The same month there was a Celebrity Night featuring "many well-known entertainers." The invitation listed Rudy Wiedoeft, "The World's Greatest Saxophonist"; Frank Banta, "Internationally Known Pianist"; and others.[3] Celebrities were welcome in the audience too, of course. Fan mail kept coming in. From a gramophone record shop a letter was sent to "The Manager, The California Ramblers, New York" and it indeed got on Kirkeby's desk. The shop owner asked for a photograph of the band and showed his appreciation for their Columbia records, especially "California Here I Come," calling them "the cleverest exhibitions of syncopated music on record."

Kirkeby's entrepreneurial spirit was far from silenced. In 1924 he started the C.R. Publishing Company, to make money on musical copyrights in competition with major houses such as Feist, Mills, and Robbins. Some of the first songs it published were blues: "Rocking Chair Blues" and "Sorrowful Blues" by Bessie

Smith, "Weeping Willow Blues" by Paul Carter, and "Deep Blue Sea Blues" by Clara Smith.[4]

With C.R. Publishing, Kirkeby & Hand's enterprise now rested on four legs: income from public performances by its bands, from making gramophone records, from running the California Ramblers Inn, and from publishing. Adrian Rollini was strongly involved in the first two.

On the cost side, things could be improved. An arrangement was made with musical instrument company Conn so that the band got musical instruments at a special price or even for free. Conn advertised itself as "the world's largest manufacturer of high grade . . . instruments." The California Ramblers got top billing in a full-page Conn advertisement. The company claimed that the band were exclusively using Conn equipment and published a letter from Kirkeby with a nice testimonial for Rollini, although he was not mentioned by name: "As you know we were selected by the Keith organization to open the New York Hippodrome, New York's largest playhouse, as a vaudeville theater. This is also a wonderful tribute to your instruments and we attribute a large measure of our success to the fact that we are all users of Conn instruments. It may interest you to know that one of the features of our Columbia records is the work of our bass saxophone player. The deep sonority and clarity of tone which is absolutely necessary in recording was found possible only through the use of a Conn bass saxophone."[5]

Mid-1924: More and Smaller Bands-within-the-Band

More steps were taken to get the band on records. The recordings by the Varsity Eight and the Vagabonds had been successful, both commercially and musically. These groups had been only slightly smaller than the full band. The idea was worth being developed. "San," a recent recording by the Varsity Eight, was pure jazz in which Adrian Rollini had recorded on the goofus for the first time.

"Goofus" was the name used by musicians for a toy instrument that was introduced by the French company Couesnon. This company had been started in 1882 by Amédée Auguste Couesnon. It saw great growth and in 1890 it called itself world's most important maker of musical instruments. In 1911 Couesnon had a thousand employees. In 1924 the company introduced what it called the "couesnophone" and it added the name "goofus." The goofus was to be blown via a rubber tube and featured a bell like a saxophone, but it worked like a harmonica. It had 25 keys and could produce 2 octaves. Rollini played it without the bell and blew into it from a simple mouthpiece rather than via a rubber tube.[6]

Rollini's thirty-two-bar solo on this novelty instrument proved that he understood its possibilities (swing and tone) and limitations (only two octaves). It was swinging indeed and it made something special out of this jazz standard.

Little Ramblers. Left to right: Irving Brodsky, Ray Kitchingman, Stan King, Bill Moore, Adrian Rollini.

Fred Cusick remembered how Rollini's pianistic abilities allowed him to play certain things on this instrument: "The funny part of it was, he had to go backwards with one hand 'cause he held one hand this way and the other hand this way. He came out crosshanded and he had to change one hand entirely with the other one. The most adaptable musician I've ever known."[7]

Kirkeby got the idea that a small jazz band using the goofus would sell. In an interview he remembered: "Using novelty instruments came fundamentally from the negro, street bands. The idea was to get a novelty in the [gramophone] record. [We] might use it only for sixteen bars as, say, what we would call a break chorus—sixteen, eight and eight."[8] Within a period of six weeks in July and August, recordings were made under four different names for four different labels by a group of five men from the band. The group consisted of Bill Moore, Adrian Rollini, Irving Brodsky, Ray Kitchingman, and Stan King. The first label was Columbia and the band was called the Little Ramblers. The tunes were "Them Rambling Blues," composed by Irving Brodsky and Bill Moore, and "Arkansas Blues" by Anton Lada and Spencer Williams, two New Orleans men. "Arkansas Blues" was a best seller on the Brunswick label by a novelty group from St. Louis called the Mound City Blue Blowers. They were two men blowing a kazoo and a comb, accompanied by a banjo. Their sound caught on and was frequently copied. The Little Ramblers, however, replaced the kazoo duets with a duet between Rollini's goofus and Stan King's kazoo for both blues. Columbia made no secret about the band's origin, when it advertised the Little Ramblers' first record: "Here's a new dance organization assembled from the famous California Ramblers, who play exclusively for Columbia. Of course the Little Ramblers have a style of their own, but when you hear them you'll only say: 'They're a chip off the old block!'"[9] Both titles mixed twelve-bar and sixteen-bar themes and Rollini did not play the bass saxophone on either title, as he had sufficient experience on the goofus now to play it throughout both titles. Another reason to leave out the bass sax may have been that Kirkeby wanted a different sound with the new band name. And after all, the main reason may have been that he wanted jazz and, unlike the bass saxophone, in Adrian's hands the goofus could not really be used for anything else.

Three weeks later the same group recorded for Pathé/Perfect and was called the Five Birmingham Babies, as before without the bass sax but with the goofus. They recorded "Arkansas" again, in a hotter version than the previous one by the Little Ramblers. A week later the same five men entered the New York Gennett studios, where before they had recorded under the Vagabonds name, but now they came in a reduced number and were to be called the Kentucky Blowers.[10] "Rambling Blues" was rerecorded and again more exciting than the Little Ramblers' version. This title, as well as the record's reverse side "Charley, My Boy," featured a sixteen-bar duet between two kazoos, one played by drummer Stan King and the other probably by Rollini, displaying yet another of his capabilities. Another ten days later the group recorded for OKeh. By calling themselves the Goofus Five, their feature instrument, the goofus, was fully emphasized. Again on this first session they recorded "Them Rambling Blues," this time together with "Tessie, Stop Teasing Me." "Tessie" centers on two thirty-eight-bar duets, the first with Rollini and Stan King on kazoos, the second with Rollini on the goofus and Bill Moore on trumpet.[11] Recordings like "Charley, My Boy" and "Tessie" are among the band's most exciting, early recordings. It is fair to state that these small groups consistently produced jazz records, rather than the wide variety of styles between straight dance music and hot jazz as recorded by the larger band.

Personnel changes in the band had been minimal so far. The few exceptions were the addition of trumpeter Frank Cush in November 1922 and the replacement of founding father and reed player Jimmy Duff by Bobby Davis and Arnold Brilhart in August 1923.[12] However, in the fall of 1924 two of the players were replaced. Jimmy Duff's colleague from the first days of the California Ramblers, banjo player, and founding member Ray Kitchingman left. He was succeeded by Thomas (Tommy) Felline.[13] Kitchingman had been a stable factor in the rhythm group and his work was often well recorded. The loss had little or no influence, however, and Felline would fill the banjo and guitar spot adequately for many years. The other change had more effect on the band's sound. Reed player Bobby Davis was replaced by the upcoming Jimmy Dorsey (1904–1957), who joined Arnold Brilhart on reeds. Dorsey's career had already been moving along nicely, together with his brother Tommy's. It had started in 1921 with the Scranton Sirens, a band from their home state, Pennsylvania. They moved to the new Jean Goldkette Orchestra in Detroit, and from there Jimmy joined the California Ramblers. The contact was made at the initiative of the Dorsey brothers' father, who thought that they deserved to be introduced to the best musicians New York could offer at the time. He got in touch with Arnold Brilhart, who set up an audition in July 1924. They were both asked to join the band. Jimmy accepted; Tommy declined but eventually joined half a year after his brother.[14] Bobby Davis had been a great soloist in the band and Dorsey was a great successor with a style of his own, having superb technique and excellent jazz feeling.

The personnel change happened after the summer season of 1924, which the band spent at the California Ramblers Inn. It was foreseen that this would be followed by an engagement at one of the New York locations, and Kirkeby actually advertised to get a good offer, but in the end he found it more attractive to stay at the Inn longer. Thus, as late as November, on Thanksgiving Day's Eve, they could be heard in their own place.

In December the band went on a short tour again. On Monday 1 December they opened in a special show at the Hippodrome. It was special because W. C. Fields was the headliner and he did not often do vaudeville work, going into a new Ziegfeld show shortly. The California Ramblers accompanied dancer Florence Walton to the enjoyment of a reviewer: "[it] proved the value of a good dance orchestra to that kind of act. Miss Walton was excellent, as was the band...."[15] As usual, *Variety* gave more details of the band's actual performance. No musicians' names were mentioned, but Rollini's work was highly appreciated, as were the hot solos by Bill Moore and Hand's fronting the band: "In one spot, the doubling discloses a saxophone sextet among the 10 ... musicians.... Four saxes are ordinarily in the line-up, the bass reed balancing the other three on the opposite side.... What they did was worthy. Occasionally, snatches of that deep sax which has gotten to be a trade mark of their disk work, asserted itself, but only for comparative flashes. A nice effect was the bass sax doubling at the piano for a two-piano interlude. A "hot" cornet also sizzled effectively. Hand personally adds considerably to the effect with his debonair 'front' and precise conducting."[16]

At this time it was tried to get a contract for the band with the Ziegfeld Follies, but without success.[17] The reason may have been the band's orientation toward jazz. There were places where this was highly appreciated, like the Strand, a movie theater in Yonkers. They worked here for five days and Arthur Hand would announce a novelty. A local newspaper proudly mentioned that their citizen Arnold Brilhart "of 10, Cornell Avenue" was a band member, and complimented the Strand's management for this program in the weeks that are "the deadest of the year in the small-town theater business."[18] The newspaper's reviewer, who called himself "The Theatregoer," showed an unusual interest in detail, which makes his review quite interesting. The band gave two one-hour shows each day.[19] The Theatregoer was not much pleased by the band's opening number "Tea for Two," which he considered "quite dry" for the Ramblers, but when the band continued with "Follow the Swallow" and "Everybody Loves My Baby," the reviewer got what he wanted: "special variations" and "unusual solo bits." What he probably meant was "special arrangements" and "original solo performances," thus showing that the language of jazz reviews was far from established. "Everybody Loves My Baby" featured solo work by Bill Moore, Adrian Rollini, and newcomer Jimmy Dorsey. The full band finished its set with a medley of operatic airs.[20] Then Arthur Hand came with the novelty: he introduced the Little Ramblers to the audience, a five-piece group out of the large band.[21] It consisted of Moore, Dorsey, Rollini, Brodsky, and Felline and they played a tune called "In a Rendez-Vous."[22] By now it was clear that the audience went for hot tunes, and when the full band came back on stage it was to finish with "Me and the Boyfriend," "Limehouse Blues," and "Red Hot Mama." They got thunderous applause. As a result, their contract was continued for another week.

Thus the California Ramblers remained in action till the year came to a close. Around the start of the New Year they worked at Proctor's in Mount Vernon. Fred Cusick remembered how, after a performance on New Year's Eve, he and Adrian Rollini ended up in jail. Because they had done "a little drinking," they went to the local police headquarters in Larchmont (well-known territory for Adrian) and said that they could not drive home. The police knew Adrian, and they slept in the jail that night.[23] Of course, alcohol played a major role in their lives. On another occasion Rollini had just bought a "souped-up" Ford, a model with a racing body. He could outrun anything on the road in those days. One night the federal agents checked where the liquor was stored and when they could not find it, they followed him and he got away. His car could do eighty miles an hour, while the police could only do sixty. Rollini had another car one day when Paul Whiteman visited the California Ramblers Inn. He lived in Pelham, where he had an estate in close proximity to the California Ramblers Inn. That night he and Adrian had a few drinks and Whiteman walked Adrian out to his car. Whiteman said to Adrian: "Say, that's a nice car you have!" Whiteman, who had about six or seven cars of his own, said: "I like that car. I'd like to buy it." So Adrian said: "OK, I'll sell it to you." "How much do you want for it?" Paul asked. "Seven hundred dollars," Adrian said. Whiteman had his checkbook with him, wrote out a check for $700, and gave it to Adrian. Whiteman drove the car and dropped off Rollini in Larchmont, then (after answering the call of nature on the curb) drove home to Pelham. The next morning at 10:00

a.m., Adrian's brother Art received a call from Whiteman's first wife. She said: "Is Adrian there?" "No, Adrian is sleeping," Art answered. "Well, tell Adrian to get this goddamned car off my lawn!" So Adrian, in the afternoon, returned the check and retrieved his car.[24]

1924 Comes to an End with Hotter Recordings

The public's reaction in Yonkers, and other places too, was confirmed by the statistics of their record sales. The effort to launch several bands-within-the-band paid off from the start. The number of record sessions in the second half of 1924 practically doubled compared to the first half (see Table 2). Not only had the total recorded output increased significantly, so had its jazz content. The newly launched Five Birmingham Babies, Goofus Five, Kentucky Blowers/Bailey's Dixie Dudes, and Little Ramblers were genuine jazz groups. "Deep Blue Sea Blues," Clara Smith's blues song published by C.R. Publishing, was recorded by the Five Birmingham Babies and the Goofus Five.[25] The full band's recorded output, as well as the work of the Vagabonds and the Varsity Eight, also appeared to be hotter than before. Duets and chase choruses with Adrian Rollini, usually on the bass sax and sometimes on the goofus, became a specialty and can be heard on many recordings from this period, such as the California Ramblers' "I'm Satisfied Beside That Sweetie of Mine" and "Too Tired" or the Varsity Eight's "A New Kind of Man," which were recorded on three consecutive days in September.

Table 2. Number of Recording Sessions		
	First half of 1924	Second half of 1924
California Ramblers	21	28
Band-within-the-band	9	31
Total	30	59

That same month produced an interesting proof of the growing influence a young cornet player from the Midwest was having on his fellow jazz musicians. Bix Beiderbecke, recordings with the Wolverines, a pure jazz band, attracted much attention. In May they had recorded "Copenhagen" and "Riverboat Shuffle." Bobby Davis used Bix's solo on "Riverboat Shuffle" as an inspiration for his own solo on the California Ramblers' recording of "She Loves Me," copying the first four bars.[26] "Copenhagen" was the Wolverines' biggest seller and a major business success for its author Charlie Davis and publisher Melrose. Melrose had a transcription made from the Wolverines' record.[27] This became the published arrangement and helped "Copenhagen" become a jazz standard, played and recorded by jazz bands throughout the world. In October and November, the California Ramblers recorded it for three different companies.[28] They used Melrose's published arrangement but, by doubling some notes, "managed to sneak a Charleston sequence into the first strain."[29] This sudden interest in Bix was certainly stimulated by the arrival of the Wolverines in New York (on the very day that the California Ramblers recorded "She Loves Me"). The Wolverines worked in the Cinderella Ballroom at 48th and Broadway, and recorded for Gennett.[30] Major bandleaders came to hear the band, such as Paul Whiteman and Nick LaRocca. Adrian Rollini or other members of the California Ramblers may have been there, too, but there is no evidence. In fact, their work at the inn, combined with a heavy recording schedule, left them little free time.[31]

In November another memorable recording was cut, "Those Panama Mamas" by the Little Ramblers. It shows that the group had fully mastered playing at breakneck speed and all the soloists (Davis alto and clarinet, Rollini bass sax, Moore trumpet, King kazoo) had developed into jazz men. It ends with a split break by clarinet, trumpet, and bass sax, concluding a masterpiece. Jimmy Dorsey was present at this session but did not play on the issued titles. His first recording session with his new employer was with the Vagabonds. The session produced only one title with jazz value, "Back Where the Daffodils Grow." It features a sixteen-bar chase chorus split between trumpet/trombone and alto saxophone, which may be played by Dorsey.

Dorsey can be heard to greater advantage on titles recorded the next day. This was for yet another company that Ed Kirkeby managed to contract, the much respected Edison company.[32] Thomas Edison himself had to approve any artist who was a candidate to record in his studios. His own musical taste played a strong role and he did not like jazz. Maybe Kirkeby let Edison hear some of their least hot recordings; anyway, the California Ramblers passed this exam with success.[33] Edison records were special. For the recordings the musicians each were put into a little isolated booth that allowed them to see and hear each other.[34] The recordings used a non-standard groove, so-called hill-and-dale or vertical cut, so that they could practically only be played on an Edison phonograph. The different groove allowed Edison recordings to have an extended playing time of about four minutes instead of the usual three. They were also known for their superior sound quality. Edison's sound engineers had made acoustic recording into an art and once they had a successful way of recording a particular artist, they were able to repeat it. This, together with the practical monopoly with their phonographs, allowed Edison to sell at a higher price than competitive labels such as Columbia and Victor. These companies would usually issue only one good take of a particular recording; but here also, Edison used a different approach. The company would use all useful masters in turn for various pressing runs; thus all good takes of a given recording might eventually be used if the market asked for enough pressings. This was the case with most of the California Ramblers' Edison sessions. For example, the second date produced the titles "I've a Garden in Sweden" and "Southern Rose." Of the first title three takes were recorded and issued; and of the second four were, a great exception for Edison. Interestingly both titles feature alto solos by Jimmy Dorsey, his first on a California Ramblers record. "Southern Rose" offers a thirty-bar solo by Adrian Rollini. The song is played at a medium tempo and Rollini takes his solo in a relaxed way staying close to the melody with minor variations between the four takes.[35]

A week later that same month of November, trumpeter Bill Moore was not available for a Goofus Five date and was replaced by Red Nichols (1905–1965). The small group recorded two hit tunes, "Everybody Loves My Baby" and "Oh! How I Love My Darling!" These were among their best. Nichols, Dorsey, and Rollini solo on both titles.

During December the various combinations from the California Ramblers hardly made any straight recording; nearly all titles recorded were hot, a clear change of policy. The development of Adrian Rollini from a classically trained musician playing music as written into a fully fledged jazz man was essential for this. Moreover, he was showing leadership and was gradually taking Hand's place as musical leader. Kirkeby & Hand certainly recognized this, but to them the musical taste of their public was the most important factor. This public consisted not only of the collegians who had little money to spend but also of the "young, urban professionals" as well as the older generation who had "made it." They bought records and paid for the public performances.

Hotel Alamac and the Congo Room

January 1925 brought a long engagement in New York at the Alamac Hotel, at the corner of Broadway and 71st Street in Manhattan. The hotel had opened in December 1923 and was famous for its rooftop Congo Room. Its interior had been designed by Winold Reiss (1886–1953), who had come from Germany in 1913 and who used cubistic elements in his work.[36] A photograph of the Congo Room shows furniture with square forms with the faces of black people painted on. From the Alamac's opening the resident orchestra had been Paul Specht, who also featured his jazz band he Georgians there. While Specht's men were at the Alamac, its drummer Chauncey Morehouse had heard the California Ramblers and wanted his colleagues to hear them. Joe Tarto, Specht's bass player, remembered how he first heard Rollini. Specht had finished working at midnight, while the California Ramblers would not stop before 2:00 a.m. This allowed enough time for a trip to the California Ramblers Inn. A group consisting of Chauncey,

Flyer promoting Congo Room engagement and suggesting a Florida background for the band.

piano player Arthur Schutt, trumpet player Frank Guarante, plus Tarto himself. "Believe me, we got a real treat!" At the time Tarto owned a bass saxophone, but "after I heard Rollini that night, the next day I took my bass sax and went down to 14th Street to Buescher and turned it in."

The Alamac had a facility for broadcasting and accommodated several radio stations.[37] Specht had orchestras at the Alamac for about a year till the end of 1924, and his successors were the California Ramblers.[38] In spring the band needed to be back at the California Ramblers Inn, so the Alamac contract ended after ten weeks.

His contract with the Alamac allowed Kirkeby to play one-day gigs elsewhere. Universities presented an ongoing opportunity. In February the band played the Winter Carnival at Dartmouth, New Hampshire, and the Ivy Ball at the University of Pennsylvania in Philadelphia. At that Ivy Ball they had competition from Fred Waring's Pennsylvanians. The public danced to Waring's music, which was all arrangements. However, when the California Ramblers followed to play their set, the dancing stopped. "Nobody danced and everybody was out in front. Fifteen deep they were standing, listening and watching. And Bill Moore made a big hit that night. Waring and his musicians must have felt pretty discomforted because they were being all ignored practically."[39]

Right after the Alamac engagement, the band worked in the Rialto movie theater in Washington, D.C., for a week. According to a review the music was the best part, not the movie. The tune "Me and the Boyfriend" and the "Operatic

Medley" received special mentions. The Washington week included a broadcast for local station WCAP.[40]

Back at the California Ramblers Inn; Promotion

In March, Kirkeby & Hand announced that its staff had increased with the arrival of press agent Milt Hagen in the position of "News Editor."[41] One of the first publications Hagen sent out was about himself, stating that he was "generally credited with making internationally famous a former New York orchestra director."[42] His task was to generate publicity for the California Ramblers and really scored with one of his first items, with Arthur Hand as its subject. The previous year, on 1 July 1924, Hand's wealthy father, Joseph C. Hand, had died. Originally he did not approve of Arthur's work and he had made it known that he had disinherited his jazz bandleader son, but he had turned around and in his last year had even become a regular visitor of the band. One month before he died he had rewritten his will, he had reinstating his son Arthur as principal beneficiary. So Arthur, at twenty-six, inherited almost half a million dollars, a very large sum at the time.[43] Hagen worked on this and the press picked it up. Arthur's portrait was all over the newspapers. He was quoted as saying that he "intended to keep on working—or playing."

The next few promotion actions were probably also Hagen's work.[44] On 18 March 1925, *Variety* reported that a tennis event would be organized on a tennis court adjoining the California Ramblers Inn. The event would be under the auspices of Vincent Richards, who would personally supervise the building of the court. "Richards and Arthur Hand, director of the California Ramblers, are fast friends."[45]

Having a golf course nearby and a tennis court coming, Kirkeby & Hand started to bet heavily on sports. In April they announced that they challenged all theatrical baseball teams. "Arthur Hand captains a team comprised of players recruited from his orchestra and keeps his team in practice on a field adjoining the California Ramblers Inn."[46]

However, their corporation's main product was music, so its next stunt had to be in this field. They reached the newspapers again with an idea that, today, would probably be declared humbug beforehand, but at a time when radio was still hardly understood was taken seriously. The idea was that one night station WGBS would broadcast the music of the California Ramblers in thought only. In front of a microphone Arthur Hand would read the music score and waive his baton and the radio audience was supposed to actually hear the band in their minds. Dr. Hereward Herrington took care of the scientific side. No record of the actual result seems to exist.

Hagen had the idea to let the band do a radio program of hymns. This raised more public attention than anything before. The press statement said that the broadcast would be over station WGBS (Gimbels Brothers Store) during Easter week of 1925 and that special "symphonic versions" of the hymns would be played.[47] To stay on the safe side it was added that "the hymnal music, however, will not be played for dancing purposes" and "in orthodox fashion, without any injection of syncopation." However, the seed had been sown, and discussion did not stop until after the broadcast was done on Easter Sunday. One newspaper did not appreciate the idea at all and published a persiflage of a conversation between the orchestra's publicity man and its leader.[48] Ed Kirkeby wrote a reaction, accusing the paper of narrow-mindedness. The concert took place on Sunday 12 April 1925 at 2:30 p.m.[49] After the event Hagen announced that the California Ramblers were considering another broadcast of hymns, but this idea was dropped.

Hagen got the corporation's publicity machine in gear in no time. The next step was the installation of a "wire" in the California Ramblers Inn, a facility for broadcasting. Contract partner was Gimbel Brothers at Broadway and 33rd Street, who got exclusive rights.[50] Kirkeby agreed to pay an amount of $375 for the first month including installation and $325 per month thereafter, for a minimum of two hours of broadcast per week. It was announced in April 1925 and the station was again WGBS. From then on the band was heard for one hour every Thursday from half past seven and Saturday from half past ten in the evening and with 4,879 votes they scored fourth place in a radio popularity poll a few months later.[51]

The band was kept very busy. That same week it had recording dates on Monday and Tuesday with Pathé/Perfect, on Wednesday it performed at the annual dance of the Talking Machine and Radio Men Association in a program with about thirty other prominent artists, and on Saturday it did a benefit at the Hippodrome.

As if this was not enough, Hagen kept sending out press information that was not always the full truth. In April, Arthur Hand appeared in the newspapers saying he was organizing a number of jazz bands and was "scouring the neighboring colleges and prep schools for talent, adding that we are on the look-out for personnel to form several collegiate combinations for different types of dance work and the Ramblers band is comprised chiefly of university men, which accounts for their popularity with the various educational institutions."[52] Nothing was heard any more about this initiative. A few days after the band recorded the tune "The Flapper Wife" for Edison and during a three-day engagement at Yonkers' Strand Theatre, a local newspaper published an article about the tune, which was based on a character in a serial story written for that paper.[53] Even old news like Adrian Rollini's work with his goofus and the

California Ramblers Inn as the band's new home base was recycled.[54] Anything exclusive could become good publicity.

Artistic Highs and Financial Lows

If 1924 had been a year of relative stability for the California Ramblers personnel roster, 1925 would bring continuous change. A difference of opinion appeared between Kirkeby, who judged his activities primarily as a business, and Hand, who was more interested in the musical side. Hand came from a background where money was not a problem but an opportunity. Supported by some band members, he suggested that a "super-organization" be built, which, it was thought, would be much in demand and pay well financially. What he meant was to hire musicians with experience in other major orchestras and with fresh ideas about dance music. These were the early years of the Jazz Age and dance music had to be hot, it had to be jazz. The step was taken at the time the California Ramblers returned to the Inn for the summer season. Some "higher-priced men were hired": trumpeter Red Nichols and trombone player Tommy Dorsey.[55] Nichols had already recorded with the Goofus Five, with great result.[56] He had worked in New York from 1923 onward and in December of that year started to record regularly for Sam Lanin. When Nichols joined the band he had already recorded more than a hundred titles with various Lanin groups and was firmly established in the New York music scene.[57] Tommy Dorsey had already auditioned half a year before, had been offered a job and declined at the time, but now accepted. With the California Ramblers the Dorsey brothers were united again.

The arrival of Red Nichols and Tommy Dorsey meant the departure of two old hands, trumpeter Bill Moore and trombone player Ole Olsen. Moore eventually joined Ben Bernie's Hotel Roosevelt orchestra and would continue to play a major role in the New York music scene, making many records with Bernie's band and its derivates.[58] He would later return to the California Ramblers. Unlike Moore's, Ole Olsen's career went unnoticed after leaving Kirkeby. He had only one more known recording session. It was under his own name, in 1926.

So the band got two new men on board, but this also created a complication. Red Nichols understandably did not want to give up his lucrative studio work, and in the following months continued his recording sessions with Lanin, without Kirkeby & Hand's approval. They were sticking to the original policy that no member of the California Ramblers was allowed to record for others without their consent. This is evident from the contract that Tommy Dorsey signed on 4 June 1925. It meant a commitment from both sides and read:

It is understood that I am to play for no other individual, company, partnership or corporation on any date or occasion, private or public, unless said phonograph date or occasion is designated and booked by Kirkeby & Hand, Inc. It is agreed that my salary shall be one hundred dollars weekly. I also agree to deport myself at all times as a gentleman should, and be governed by whatever rules and regulations Kirkeby & Hand, Inc., may make concerning the conduct of the orchestra and the members of it. It is agreed that Kirkeby & Hand, Inc., shall pay me an additional fee for all phonograph records made by me.[59]

The contract was for six months with an option for an extension of one year at the same salary. but Tommy Dorsey also yielded to Lanin's money and four days after he had signed, he and Red Nichols played a recording session with Sam Lanin.[60] This was not appreciated by Kirkeby & Hand and eventually they would stop it; but for the time, Nichols and the Dorseys, the modernists in the organization, had what they wanted. During the next half year, the band would consist of the following musicians, listed here with their primary instruments:

Arthur Hand, violin, director
Red Nichols, trumpet
Frank Cush, trumpet
Tommy Dorsey, trombone
Jimmy Dorsey, clarinet
Bobby Davis, saxophones
Adrian Rollini, bass saxophone
Irving Brodsky, piano
Tommy Felline, banjo
Stanley King, drums

It may have been due to Red Nichols's presence that during March the band had an up-and-coming visitor sitting in for a few nights. Bix Beiderbecke had not made many recordings but he had been in New York with the Wolverines, and at the time he had moved in with Red. Red had also used a Beiderbecke solo when he recorded with George Olsen's band almost a year earlier, and they had met not long after.[61] Beiderbecke stayed for a week with the California Ramblers and sat in with them. Fred Cusick was a member of the band and remembered how he watched Bix's fingers and more: "All thumbs. . . . It did seem like he did more with his thumbs than with the other fingers. . . . He played about five choruses in a row of one tune, just kept on improvising one after another. . . . [Bix] had feet trouble, he had 'oily' feet He sat there a couple of hours playing and in fact it went through his shoes and there were spots on the band platform where he was sitting. He left his footprints."[62] Bix had known the Dorseys for a long time and he and Tommy had even recorded together two months before.[63] Sitting in with the California Ramblers meant Bix's first opportunity to play alongside Adrian Rollini, who had developed into a much stronger bass saxophone player than Min Leibrook of Bix's Wolverines days.[64] Beiderbecke moved in with Red Nichols, who was staying at the Pasadena Hotel, 60th and Broadway, on 14 March. The two showed each other their "false fingering" and exchanged musical ideas.[65]

The Dorseys did not take a hotel. They rented a house on City Island, the largest of the Pelham Islands in the western Long Island Sound. Red and Bix had dinner there with Jimmy and Tommy, which their mother Tess cooked.[66] Later Red subleased a room at the Dorsey house.[67] During the week that Beiderbecke was in New York, the Goofus Five with Nichols had one record session, but Bix did not participate.

The character of the new organization can today be judged from its recorded output. As before, the small groups were making jazz records including hot versions of popular tunes, and the full band moved between straight dance music on the one hand and excellent hot recordings on the other. An Edison session in early April was typical. It produced two titles, "Charleston" and "On the Oregon Trail," the former nicely swinging, the latter rather stiff. Interestingly, both titles feature sixteen bars of solo piano. It has been stated that Irving Brodsky, the band's piano player, and Adrian Rollini recorded a solo duet on "Charleston." In an interview Brodsky confirmed such duet solo recordings and added that they did it on a single piano, but he did not specifically remember any tune.[68]

The best two titles from this period were recorded at a Pathé/Perfect session in May 1925, "Dustin' the Donkey" and "Tiger Rag."[69] "Dustin' the Donkey" is a composition by Howdy Quicksell, who had been the banjo player on the recording date with Bix and Tommy Dorsey, so Dorsey may have remembered it when the band wanted to record hot tunes.[70] Adrian Rollini played a major role in this recording and produced one of his greatest solos on any record so far. It opens with a glissando and ends with a series of double tones, produced by controlled overblowing of notes, thus demonstrating the superior technique he had by now developed.[71] "Tiger Rag" is even hotter. Rollini's solo work is limited to a few breaks, but his drive pushes the soloists. The Dorseys play the traditional solo parts for trombone and clarinet, but Red Nichols's solo is the great surprise. He plays thirty-two bars that are basically identical to the solo played by Bix Beiderbecke on the Wolverines' recording of the tune. This is amazing because it had not even been issued at the time.[72] It is more than likely that Bix had shown Red how to play it during his stay with the California Ramblers. It may have been in Red's hotel or during after-hours jam sessions at the California Ramblers Inn.[73]

Interestingly, the California Ramblers recorded two more titles during this Pathé session. They were "Techland" and "Tech Triumph." For a long time, they

Superior 105, a special issue and one of the rarest Rollini recordings.

were known only from a note in Ed Kirkeby's notebooks, but a copy of the record with both tunes was found during the present research period. The tunes were custom-recorded at the request of Virginia Tech, in Blacksburg, Virginia. Therefore, Pathé/Perfect issued them on its special Superior label as a private issue. It was pressed in small numbers only, possibly fewer than fifty. Both recordings are fully instrumental, with several solos, including one by Rollini on "Tech Triumph," Virginia Tech's official song, written by Wilfred Pete Maddux and Mattie W. Epes.[74]

The first half of 1925 saw a major change in recording technology. Ever since sound recording had been possible, it was done by channeling the sound via a horn mechanically to a mechanism that cut a groove in a surface. The groove represented the recorded sound. Experiments with different techniques had started around 1920, whereby the sound was collected via a microphone and then brought to a similar cutting mechanism, via an electrical amplifier. By 1925 these developments had resulted in a superior system. One of its great features was the wide dynamic range, but the overwhelming advantage of the new system was its frequency spectrum, which for the first time allowed recording notes from the deepest bass to the highest violin. Two companies introduced the new system simultaneously, Victor and Columbia. Columbia had started in-house experiments in January, but it took them till March 1925 before electrical recording was done on a regular basis.[75] The California Ramblers were not included in the experiments and Columbia records from this period by them or by the Little Ramblers were recorded the old way.[76] The first electrically recorded titles by the California Ramblers were "Ev'rything Is Hotsy Totsy Now" and "Sweet Georgia Brown," recorded 14 May 1925.[77] Irving Brodsky remembered this event: "I walked into that studio and there were wires all over the studio. . . . I said, what the hell is going on here and I find out that it was the microphone, the first of the microphones they used. . . . the Columbia studios were at the [Columbus] Circle at 59th Street."[78] Even playing such a new recording on a traditional mechanical record player revealed much of its full, glorious sound, and it meant strong competition for all other labels. Rollini had an opportunity to display his talent on the piano as well as his bass saxophone. On the first tune he plays a piano duet with Irving Brodsky, while on "Sweet Georgia Brown" he plays an eight-bar solo, the first time the sound of his bass saxophone is heard to full advantage.[79]

Kirkeby & Hand tried vigorously to keep their men from recording outside the framework of the California Ramblers and its small groups. Rollini had made one exception to this, probably with the consent of his managers, when he recorded on the bass saxophone in Rudy Wiedoeft's Saxophone Sextette in 1923, but his individual sound could not then be heard. He may also have been the piano player on an early recording date by singer/ukulele player Cliff Edwards, best known as Ukulele Ike. This was in April 1924. However, such cases had been rare and far between. However, in 1925 things became difficult to control. Red Nichols, who arrived in March, did not stop his recording work for Sam Lanin, and both Dorseys joined him. Adrian Rollini, who was now openly regarded as the band's star, also felt that he could do more. So, in February, Adrian Rollini did a recording date with Cliff Edwards in which his bass saxophone is clearly audible. Cliff Edwards had had a recording career for almost five years and usually recorded with just his ukulele. Maybe he wanted some variation in his accompaniment and maybe Pathé/Perfect, his record company, chose for him. The company knew Rollini from his work with the California Ramblers and Kirkeby agreed to let Adrian do it. Thus, for the first time his bass sax could be recognized outside the California Ramblers. Rollini's sax is only audible on one title, "That's All There Is, There Ain't No More," as he played two breaks in the intro. On the session mate, "Let Me Linger Longer in Your Arms," Rollini played the piano and celeste, thus adding another rare instrument to his growing repertory.[80]

The California Ramblers were better than ever, but taking a look at the financial side Kirkeby was getting nervous.[81] At the first of the year the band were given salary increases, but the long engagement at the Alamac in New York had caused a financial loss. Private money had to be loaned to the corporation (Kirkeby & Hand) to compensate. Back at the inn with higher-priced men added to the payroll, he feared that it would become impossible to recuperate these losses. Also the new musical quality was not appreciated by everybody. A letter tells the story:

> A super-jazz orchestra was created which to musicians was "the height" but our customers and more important still the phonograph companies began to complain that the orchestra was going backward—that it could not compare to the music we had the previous years. Internal fights in the band developed, phonograph understandings were violated and the morale of the organization ran low. The climax came when the highest priced man in the outfit was let go. This was followed shortly by another radical accepting another offer; by notice being served on J. Dorsey that it was "a matter of exclusive recording or get out," with the result that we took his two weeks' notice. And finally T. Dorsey violated his contract after becoming abusive and offensive to Arthur on more than one occasion.[82]

Although the letter does not name him, "the highest priced man" should be Red Nichols. The letter continues: "During the first few weeks at the Inn business soon began to show that either one or two things had to be done—expenses cut or income increased. That meant cutting down the band or increasing income by means of a fifty-cents increase on Saturday night cover charge." It was a difficult dilemma for the two directors. Kirkeby wrote, "For an hour Arthur and I argued the matter." Hand did not want any change, neither in personnel nor in cover charge. Kirkeby wanted to change both. The compromise was reached that there would be no personnel changes and the cover would go to two dollars. "The increase soon made itself felt. The younger crowd thinned out and went to the Post Lodge, whereas our business was supported by a new crowd of older people who by rights should have formed our normal increase in business over last year."

The income at the inn decreased to less than half of what it was in 1924. More measures were to be taken.

Chapter 7

The California Ramblers Back to Business

For Adrian Rollini, the year 1925 would become special in several ways. During the summer Adrian would meet a young lady who would change his life. She was Dorothy Van Wagoner Remer. Later she called herself Dixie Reemer. Dixie was born 10 June 1905 in Goshen, New York, and was two years younger than Adrian. She had graduated from Bay Ridge High School in Brooklyn and won a college course, but took a job as a secretary. In 1922 she took part in a large shorthand contest with excellent result. She found work with the Metropolitan Trust company, but to please her mother she stopped this job in 1925 to be with her at home. Her employer sent her a letter of appreciation ("no task was too troublesome"). Her mother and father were Orinda Swezey (1888–1955) and Joseph Coates Remer (1883–1937). Joseph Remer was a cart maker by profession. Dixie had one younger brother, George Minot. In an interview with *Down Beat* magazine, Dixie said that the occasion of her first meeting with Adrian was a yachting party in Larchmont, where Adrian invited her on his boat.[1] Her parents' marriage had ended in divorce and Orinda had remarried in 1923. Her second husband was Benjamin Howe Van Keegan Jr., who had a major career in New York's financial world. In 1939 he would become president of the Security Traders Association of New York.

Dixie and Adrian never said what attracted them to each other, but it is easy to guess. Both came from well-to-do families and lived in the same upper-middle-class Larchmont neighborhood. Adrian had less school training than Dixie, but this was compensated for by his sophisticated lifestyle. He lived in the world of the rich, of exceptional cars, expensive night clubs. As a person Dixie was the prototype of the young twenties girl, the flapper. She had a pretty face, dressed in a fashionable way, and had her hair done in the latest style. On top of that she was an excellent dancer of the Charleston, the dance that conquered the world in 1925.[2] To her, Adrian must have been the personification of the Latin lover, the masculine man. Their parents approved their relationship from the start.

Adrian must have felt like a winner all over. His rise to stardom in the world of dance music of course influenced others. One of these was Coleman

Dixie and Adrian ca. 1925.

Hawkins, who held a major position in Fletcher Henderson's orchestra, the top black band at the time. He was one of three reed players in the band and his special instrument was the tenor saxophone. Eventually he would be regarded as the major tenor sax player in any jazz or dance band for most of the twenties, but for Hawkins this was not enough, and one day, having heard Rollini, he decided to get a bass sax and record with it. Rex Stewart gave a vivid account of what happened.[3] Hawkins was proud of his fully paid acquisition. On the morning of a recording session and being one of Henderson's star musicians, he was prepared to play a solo to the dismay of his colleagues. According to Stewart, a "pandemonium broke loose, but Hawkins continued until Henderson broke down and stopped the band." Hawkins did in fact record on the bass sax with Henderson quite often, in particular in 1925, but on this instrument he never reached the greatness of his tenor sax playing.[4]

There were probably hardly any striving musicians who did not notice the California Ramblers and its prominent bass sax player. Their fame was spread by the recordings, broadcasts, and public performances as well as by publicity. Many must have tried to play like Rollini, and this had a positive influence on Conn's and Buescher's sales of the bass sax.[5] Only a few of these cases are documented like that of Coleman Hawkins. One other is Joe Tarto's story. Tarto played the tuba in Paul Specht's Orchestra when he heard Adrian Rollini on bass sax. Specht's band recorded frequently and, with the California Ramblers, belonged among Columbia's top bands. So Joe bought a bass saxophone and proudly posed with it for an early photograph. In a letter he wrote that he did it "after hearing Adrian play all those beautiful solos and good bass lines. [However] I knew I would never be able to play all those nice musical notes. . . . so I decided to sell my bass sax, and put all my ideas in my tuba."[6] It turned out to be a wise decision. Tarto would become a star tuba player and participate in countless recordings from small jazz bands to large, hot (and not so hot) dance bands.

One other well-known musician who never bought a bass saxophone but admitted Rollini's influence on his work was Harry Carney, of Duke Ellington's band. His instrument of choice was the baritone saxophone, an instrument with a slightly higher range than the bass sax. He joined Ellington's band in mid-1927 and his low notes gave additional color to the sound of that band. In a 1966 interview Carney said: "I actually tried to get a sound as big as Adrian Rollini . . . so I suppose whatever sound I get goes back to that."[7] In another interview he stated that he "tried to make the upper register sound like Coleman Hawkins and the lower register like Adrian Rollini."[8] Ellington would sometimes feature a bass saxophone on the bandstand, but Dixie, Adrian's wife, had this to say about the Duke: "When we go to the Cotton Club, as soon as they see Adrian, they hide the bass sax."[9]

Rollini's influence was stretching out even further than his bass sax playing. By 1925 Paul Whiteman was looking for a trumpeter to play hot solos, an important position in his large band in the years to follow. The first man to fill this chair would be Ted Bartell. He had been called to replace Red Nichols with the California Ramblers on a recording date for Plaza.[10] In an interview Bartell said how it happened that he joined Whiteman. Paul visited the California Ramblers Inn on the day of the recording. He said, "I need a touch of jazz in my band. But he's got to be a real musician to play with me." Bartell: "Well, Adrian Rollini—God bless him—recommended me."[11]

Adrian Rollini Becomes Bandleader

The musical acclaim did not stop the band's management from worrying about the financial state of affairs. The California Ramblers may have been at the top musically speaking, but they were owned by a corporation, Kirkeby & Hand, that wanted profit. The problems in the band had led to the departure of Red Nichols and the Dorseys, but new men came in to replace them. On trumpet this was Roy Johnston; Bobby Davis returned in his alto sax chair; and on trombone several replacements were tried out, the first being Abe Lincoln.[12] Although their salaries were lower, Kirkeby did not see the personnel cost sufficiently reduced and suggested laying off the second trumpet. Before this was announced, reed

California Ramblers in 1925 before the Deauville adventure. Left to right: Irving Brodsky, Tom Felline, Roy Johnston, Stan King, Arthur Hand, Adrian Rollini, Frank Cush, Fud Livingston (standing), Bobby Davis (seated), Eddy Stannard, Herb Winfield.

player Fred Cusick resigned and no further personnel reduction took place for a while.[13] However, forward-looking Kirkeby saw a loss for 1925 and kept trying to avoid this. Accordingly, on 1 October he produced a plan to replace the California Ramblers at the inn with a small orchestra led by trumpeter Bill Moore. His foresight proved right. In October, with the band still at the inn, the corporation lost $1,500 in one month. On 2 November Bill Moore came in with a six-piece combination, doing better than the full band had done. New Year's Eve was a financial success again.

So once more the California Ramblers had to go on a vaudeville tour, but vaudeville programs had to be set up well in advance and time was limited now. Therefore, Kirkeby did not contact Keith for a tour, but instead sent a telegram to his friend Cork O'Keefe, who had a fledgling booking agency.[14] He managed to get the California Ramblers on the road at short notice. New photographs were made on Tuesday 31 October, and the next day the band opened at the Grand Theatre, a movie house in Pittsburgh. The band was described as "not only exceptional in their music but [it] offers as well a variety of unique specialties, all of which are decidedly entertaining."[15]

Other short engagements during that month were in Springfield's Butterfly Ballroom from 16 to 18 November and on the evening of 25 November, Thanksgiving Eve, in Auburn's Armory for the annual Elks' Ball. During the weeks before the Elk's ball, the ball and the band got almost daily publicity in the local newspaper. It was agreed that the California Ramblers would do a broadcast from Auburn's Strand Theatre on the day of the ball. And the press unsuspectingly had a "first," too: as a side remark in one article it said that "these famous musicians will be under the direction of Adrian Rollini, noted saxophonist."[16] It was the first time that Adrian's name was mentioned in the press as leader of the band. Adrian Rollini had been the foundation of the success of the California Ramblers, by his major musical talent and his highly personal sound, but also as an inspiration for his colleagues.[17] As a former orchestra leader, he had the ambition to front his own group again. Kirkeby understood this and had noted his musical talent and natural leadership, so it was no more than logical that Rollini would become musical leader of the California Ramblers. Even before the tour, at the California Ramblers Inn, Neil Waterman had observed it: "Arthur Hand was, what we call, a dilettante. He had a fiddle, a violin, which he purported to play, but nobody ever heard it and he would take it out of the case and he had a handkerchief and he would dust the violin off. Everybody figured he was about to play something and he would put it back in the case again and Adrian would run the band."[18] The publicity in Auburn may have led to expectations that even the California Ramblers could not meet: afterward a reviewer said that they "did not quite come to their usual high standard of syncopators featured on similar past occasions."[19] There are no signs that the poor review was a handicap for Rollini.

Back at the California Ramblers Inn, there also were celebrations on Thanksgiving's Eve, but without the famous band. The invitation said that the California Ramblers Inn would "resound with festive gayety" but, unlike before, the music and the band were not mentioned. The band's final engagements during December were in Ohio, for two weeks at the Moonlight Ballroom, Meyers Lake, Canton, and in New York's Monte Carlo on Broadway.[20] Before the Ohio gig, Nusbaum, a local shop with musical instruments, promoted its offerings:

> Adrian Rollini, Leader of the Ramblers, endorses Conn Instruments. And the Majority of His Players Endorse Them, Too. They've Been Columbia Recording Players For the Last 3 Years—Hear Them Next Week at Moonlight Ballroom. . . . Read what Rollini says. Adrian Rollini, leader of the California Ramblers, plays a Conn Bass Saxophone. He says "I've been playing a 'Sax' for years. Three years ago I decided—because of its superiority over all other makes—to change to the Conn. So for the last 3 years I've played the Conn exclusively. In my opinion it's the BEST."[21]

The Deauville Disaster

During November and December some press announcements for the band mentioned that the California Ramblers were going to Florida for a short engagement.[22] This was the first time that a new Kirkeby & Hand enterprise was mentioned in the press, an enterprise that came about at the last minute. It went along with one of the biggest business explosions in American history and was named after the state where it happened: The Florida Boom. In the fall of 1925 it was at its height and the public was exposed to "the most delirious fever of real-estate speculation which had attacked the United States in ninety years." The boom started in the early twenties when Florida was underdeveloped and ground prices were low, but prices went up steadily at an increasing speed. During the memorable summer and autumn of 1925 Miami had become "one frenzied real-estate exchange. There were said to be 2,000 real estate offices and 25,000 agents marketing house-lots or acreage."[23] The town had grown from 30,000 inhabitants in 1920 to 75,000 in 1925. And it was predicted that this would grow further to one million in ten years. By 1925 the public was buying any real estate as long as it was in Florida. Prices increased at an incredible rate and money was quickly made. One day in the summer the *Miami Daily News* printed an issue of 504 pages, the largest in newspaper history. The mayors of Miami, Miami Beach, Hialeah, and Coral Gables decided that on New Year's Eve and during the following two days, major festivities would take place all over their four towns.

However, some people started to feel that the number of new buyers of real estate would decrease and that more and more owners would want to realize their profit. In the spring and summer of 1926 the system collapsed. And whatever remained of the Florida Boom was destroyed by a huge hurricane that hit the coast on 18 September 1926.

Kirkeby & Hand were typical victims of the Florida Boom. The musicians preferred to work in a fixed location such as the California Ramblers Inn rather than play short engagements here and there, but if the full band worked at the inn it would result in another financial loss to Kirkeby & Hand. Their first priority was to find a place for the band to work during a large part of the winter season. No doubt K&H had heard about the great real estate business in Florida, so they got in touch with one of Miami's many men working in real estate, Joseph Elsener. Elsener had started his own business after gaining experience as a salesman for the real estate company of Carl Fisher, probably the largest in the business.[24] He was now the president of Beach Properties, Inc. Elsener's story was so convincing and Kirkeby & Hand were so much in a hurry that they closed a deal with him without investigating the conditions. As Kirkeby admitted later, it was closed "not as business men closing a deal, as we did not even see the property."[25]

In the deal with Elsener, a Deauville company was set up of which he would own one third and Kirkeby & Hand two thirds. Also K&H received a share in Elsener's corporation Beach Properties. The new company would lease property from this corporation. This had to be newly built on the North beach, some six

Artist's impression of Club Deauville.

miles north of Miami's center.[26] The property measured 550 by 300 feet. It would be called the Deauville Casino and would have 142 hotel rooms. Its centerpiece would be a large, elliptic swimming pool with a large deck with cabana units around it. The pool would be 165 feet long and 100 feet wide and be filled with sea water via pipes. Bathing facilities would include private rooms "furnished en suite to include a living room, dressing room and bath."[27]

Kirkeby & Hand were now operating in three locations: the California Ramblers Inn, the project in Miami, and on the road with the large band. Each of these needed a leader. It was decided that Arthur Hand would go to Florida, Ed Kirkeby would manage the inn, and Adrian Rollini got the daily leadership of the California Ramblers. Trumpeter Frank Cush did not stay with the new setup and left.

The Deauville lease was signed around 1 November and that same month Kirkeby, after having put Bill Moore and his Varsity Eight into the California Ramblers Inn, traveled to Miami to see the new place. He was shocked. The work on the swimming pool had only just begun and construction of the restaurant areas had not even started, but Elsener had no doubt and said that opening on New Year's Eve was not in danger. He would even be glad to let K&H out of the deal, but said that he would be going through with it. A few weeks later, a crew of hotel and band personnel, a total of forty-four people, was ready in New York and about to sail to Florida when Arthur Hand arrived in Miami.[28] What he saw made him believe that it would be a fallacy to open at that time and he wanted to telegraph to New York not to sail, but again Elsener convinced his partners that all would be ready in time. So the crew sailed and that included the California Ramblers.[29]

Adrian Rollini at Club Deauville, Miami.

Before the band left, a multiple-day record session had been arranged with Columbia. It started on 1 December with three titles for its Harmony branch. This was followed two days later by a Little Ramblers session (two titles) and the day after that by the full band (three titles). Both the small and large groups recorded again the following day (four titles). Harmony thus had a reserve of three titles and Columbia of nine, enough for some months.

Elsener gave news to the newspapers that several well-known swimmers would be at Deauville Casino.[30] Indeed the Deauville opened on the chosen date—but with construction work still going on all over the place and without kitchen equipment or freezers. So it had to close the next day, and it took a full month to bring the Deauville into a minimum condition to receive guests in a proper way. Hand realized that the Miami public went elsewhere and saw business slipping away.[31]

In addition to all personnel, the weekly payroll of the operation now included a dancing team of $1,500, two bands costing $2,000, and a maître d' at $300.[32] At one moment Hand personally deposited $5,000 and asked Elsener for his contribution, but Elsener was reaching his bottom dollar.

On Monday 25 January, a dinner room at the South end of the casino could at last be opened. It was still temporary, waiting for the formal opening of a supper room the following week, but at least the band could start their work. The program included the dancing couple of Basil Durant and Kay Durban, who were hired to demonstrate "unusual dances," so the invitation said. It also mentioned

Pool of Club Deauville on day of opening.

that there would be two orchestras for the dancers. In addition to the California Ramblers there would be a band by the name of the Varsity Six.[33]

Even on 3 February, when Hand had agreed to open the place, the electric power failed when the guests were halfway through their dinners, but at last also the pools could be formally opened that day.

In March the financial situation finally looked better and K&H figured that they could pay all outstanding bills if Elsener and Beach Properties would pay their debts. However, Elsener told them that he was broke. K&H then decided to let one orchestra go. On 4 March, Adrian sent a telegram to Dixie saying that he would leave Miami on Sunday 7 March and arrive in New York two days later. Thus the California Ramblers returned to New York and on 18 March they were back in the Columbia recording studio.

For the California Ramblers, the Deauville adventure was over now, but not for Kirkeby & Hand. They had decided to supply the Deauville Casino with a supper club. The newspapers were not quite clear about it, but the casino would be a place for gambling and the restaurant a place to eat. To enter one had to be a club member. Special events were organized as before, so on Wednesday night 24 March it was Carnival Night at Club Deauville. The dancing couple was still there and there were more artists. The California Ramblers were also said to be present, although the band had left a few weeks before. Kirkeby & Hand owned the name and knew its drawing power. Presumably they had simply renamed the Varsity Six or a local band.

It is said that Elsener paid generous weekly contributions to the local police retirement funds and "the casino resounded to the collision of dice. Neither the sheriff nor the police ever raided the place."[34]

In his thumbnail biography, Kirkeby wrote that the lease sum on the two restaurants was $2 million (presumably for a full year) and the weekly expense for 110 employees was $14,000.[35] The Deauville adventure was a major financial loss to Kirkeby & Hand.

The emerging feeling that the Florida Boom was coming to an end only made the situation worse. The Deauville adventure had to stop. Sometime during 1926 Kirkeby & Hand were able to give up their lease, but Elsener kept it going for a while, and eventually he sold out too. The Casino was demolished in 1956 to make place for a new building, the Deauville Beach Resort.[36]

Lawsuits

Rollini's stay in Florida was like a holiday for him. During December and January, the band had little else to do other than rehearse, so he could enjoy the surroundings and the climate, even when the place was not ready. Irving Brodsky enjoyed it, too: "We had a wonderful time one winter season. We played only night time, till midnight. It was nice to play there."[37]

On the other hand, for Ed Kirkeby the Florida adventure was a quite unexpected disaster. By the end of 1925 Ed Kirkeby had a history of ten years with one success after another, and his greatest success were the California Ramblers. However, Deauville ended in problems and those troubles were not over yet. Kirkeby got involved in lawsuits. The first one was minor. The term "California Ramblers" had become a brand name, well-known with the public, not only around New York but nationwide due to Columbia's success in selling their records. The idea of putting the name on the inn outside New York had worked. It sold the inn as well as the band. Kirkeby realized that this brand name had become a valuable asset. Today the public is used to this marketing concept of "merchandising," but in the twenties it was new. Kirkeby picked it up and got the idea to make his brand name a trademark. It has to be guessed what his real purpose was with the use of the name California Ramblers as a trademark. He may have wanted to start a record label under that name, but then he would have to use a different name as an artist credit, since Columbia had exclusive rights to the actual artist credit. Instead of a record with a Columbia label and a California Ramblers recording, the public could buy one with a California Ramblers label as well as a recording.[38] Or maybe he wanted to bypass the Columbia rights and be able to apply the name not as an artist credit but as a trademark on other record labels. Trademarks had to be approved by the Patent Office in Washington, D.C. Kirkeby had applied for it in 1924 but had been denied. However, now he was determined and started an appeal. That process took almost two years. While Kirkeby & Hand were trying to get the Deauville under control, the trademark process continued and finally resulted in a decision by the Commissioner of Patents. In February 1926 the decision was published that the name of an orchestra "may not be used as a trademark for music industries products." The only benefit Kirkeby had was publicity: the decision was published in the *Music Trade Review*.[39]

Kirkeby's second lawsuit provided more drama. This time it was Wallace T. Kirkeby versus Arthur C. Hand "et al."[40] At various occasions the two owners of the California Ramblers had disagreed about the direction of their business, whereby Kirkeby showed his business mind and Hand his feeling for the musical side. Since each owned half the company, a decision would often be a compromise and satisfy neither Kirkeby nor Hand. After the disastrous adventure of the Deauville Casino, Kirkeby had had enough of this and decided that their existing relationship had to change or end. He took Hand to court, but it did not come to a verdict. In March a judge in Dade County, of which Miami is the seat, wrote an order of restraint. It said that Hand, "individually and as an officer of Kirkeby & Hand, Inc., is . . . restrained from operating or conducting . . . the restaurant and supper club . . . known as the Deauville Casino, and from disbursing any funds in connection with the operation of said restaurant and supper club and from incurring or imposing upon said corporation Kirkeby & Hand any further obligations, financial or of any other kind." On 29 May 1926 the order would have become effective, but the two partners settled out of court and Kirkeby ended the procedure.[41] The case was dismissed and Kirkeby had to pay all costs, a total of five dollars. No document about their new agreement exists, but it may be assumed that in practice it was described by the judge's concept order.

This eventually meant the end of the partnership of Wallace T. Kirkeby and Arthur C. Hand. Its complete unbundling took some time, and in his thumbnail biography Kirkeby dated the split in 1927. About Arthur Hand, the band's piano player Irving Brodsky had this to say: "He was a partner of Ed Kirkeby. He was the front man . . . a violin player. He was a handsome guy and the women liked him a lot and they used to come in to see him, but eventually the liquor got him!"[42]

Recordings by the Replacement Bands

When the real California Ramblers were in Florida, a replacement band worked in New York. During this period there were a few recording sessions under the name California Ramblers or its derivates. The final one in that year, on 21 December, may still have been by the original band.[43] The following January a group recorded for Cameo and its resulting two titles, "T.N.T." and "In My Gondola," were issued under the normal Cameo pseudonym of Varsity Eight.

These titles were hot recordings, but by a partially different band, most probably the replacement band led by Bill Moore.[44] It had to have a California Ramblers sound so a bass sax player was needed and found. He is distinguishable from Adrian Rollini because, unlike Rollini, he only plays in a slap-tongue style throughout on these recordings.

Around the end of January there were recordings for Pathé/Perfect as the Five Birmingham Babies. For these sessions another bass sax player was found. This was Spencer Clark, whose lifelong idol was Rollini. For several years Clark would be the only serious alternative on bass sax for Rollini, and he would be his replacement with the California Ramblers more than once, eventually becoming his successor.[45] In an interview Clark remembered these recordings: "I think my first sub for Adrian was that date in which we recorded Down By The Vinegar Woiks.[46] [Rollini] was always alert for extra work and was ambitious for having his own band. And I was the only bass sax player available at the time. Plus that, he knew that I would be no competition for him and so would recommend me."[47] Spencer Clark was born 15 March 1908 and originally played the mandolin, the xylophone, and the clarinet. His admiration for Adrian Rollini, who was four years his senior, started when Spencer's friend Herb Weil took him to hear

> "a most wonderful band playing down in Pelham Heath Inn called the California Ramblers and you've got to get down and hear this band!" So we made it down there one evening and not having any money we sat outside and listened to the band through the open windows. I heard Adrian Rollini, I later learned that it was Adrian, playing xylophone. This guy playing fantastic xylophone. He was playing "Nola" using four sticks—I got up to the window and peeked at him—and ... it was only Adrian playing alone. And that was the beginning of this thing and we sat there that night. Then I heard him play the bass saxophone which I'd never heard of before, I didn't know there was such an instrument. And that started a long, long relationship in love with the bass saxophone.[48]

In 1923 Spencer had his first gig on C-melody saxophone and the next year he took up the bass sax. He got a secondhand Buescher, a very poor horn as it turned out at the time, "but to me it was a beautiful piece of brass."[49]

Coincidentally, Spencer's family lived near the Rollinis in Larchmont, New York. As a result, an acquaintance was struck, but

> Adrian was not too friendly then, or ever for that matter, though he did help with suggestions on fingering, etcetera. He was kind enough to show me quite a few things like the high-E and -F fingering and the baritone mouthpiece routine so forth and so on. It started a pleasant relationship that went on for a period of time and then I started playing with the bass saxophone and later Adrian said: "You're

getting ... along pretty good on the thing, would you care to substitute for me some time down at the Inn?" And of course I'd be delighted to do that, 'cause he would like to take off and do other jobs. I did substitute for him off and on from late 1925 up and almost through 1933 one way or another. He was a good relationship, a thoroughly professional musician.[50]

Also Dixie, Adrian's girlfriend, lived in the same neighborhood and Spencer became very friendly with her. Spencer remembered how she advised him for his style one evening, thereby giving some insight into Adrian's personality:

I was playing a little job out in the county one night and Dixie was at the job—this is before they were married—as a guest with a boy friend. And I was honking away ... and that evening her date got too drunk or something happened and she asked me if I would take her back home which I did.

We sat on her front porch for hours almost till dawn I think and talked ... and she finally even got to the point of telling me. She said: "I'm going to tell you something. I hope you'll take it the right way but I think it's for your own good. Don't try to play like Adrian!" I said: "Why not?" and this was my goal you know. She said: "Well, you're not the right kind of personality to do this. He is a very aggressive person. I don't see you as an aggressive person and it takes that to play as forceful as he does, to be as aggressive as he is on his instrument as well as he is in his personal life. He is a very aggressive person." She said, "Find some other avenue for yourself and don't set him as a goal. Think of other things." And that, in later years, actually paid off because I finally realized that she was right. I was not cut out to do as he was doing. I couldn't do, so why try? Then I became interested in, choose to think of it as, a more melodic approach to music.[51]

Clark may also be present on the next recording session by a group that was related to the California Ramblers, just a few days later. This was again for Pathé/Perfect, and went under the name of Fred Rich and his Orchestra.

Clark probably remembered these Pathé sessions correctly as his first recordings substituting for Rollini, but he was mistaken when he thought that he was the only bass sax player available. Thus the identity of the man before him, who played slap-tonguing bass sax on the OKeh and Cameo sessions from this period, remains unknown, like the names of most of the other musicians in the replacement bands.

The replacement band had outside engagements under the name California Ramblers. The California Ramblers Inn was then closed, as may have been the case for all of January and February. In February it had an engagement in Toronto, Canada, which was followed by a gig in Cleveland, Ohio.[52] Spencer Clark remembered a disastrous tour made by a smaller group, the Little Ramblers with Bill Moore as leader on the trumpet and Jack Russin on piano. They were to do some Pennsylvania mining towns. The first stop was a large ballroom in Harrisburg, but there was hardly any public and they were not paid. The next place was fifty miles up the road, but Moore and Russin found out that there was a red-light district and the next morning all money that Moore had received to cover the band's expenses was gone, "so we canceled the trip and went home."[53]

From March onward such disguising was no longer needed, since Adrian Rollini was back in New York from Florida, and with him probably all his colleagues who had worked there. The California Ramblers Inn reopened on Thursday 18 March. The band was directed by Rollini and recorded for Columbia the same day.

Broadcasts, Recordings, and Gigs

After the relatively relaxing winter months in Florida, the band had to generate money again, and Kirkeby, as before, used any possible method. So when they did not work in the California Ramblers Inn, as its regular orchestra, the band was busy with broadcasting, touring, and recording.

The previous year, during the summer its weekly broadcasts had ended and they had not restarted before the band left for Florida. Even the replacement band did no broadcasts under the California Ramblers name. Broadcasting was important to stay in the public's mind, but it only resumed when the original band went on the air again. This was on Thursday 15 April, via station WMCA. A newspaper mentioned the resumption and that the radio audience could hear the band every day at 6:30 p.m. on Tuesdays, Thursdays, and Sundays.[54] Although this schedule could not be upheld in practice, it did mean that the band could be heard more than once a week. This assumed that it was working comfortably close to the studio, since broadcasting at the time still meant a live performance before a microphone. A flowery text survives that was used to say goodnight to the radio audience. Variations of it were probably used more than once:

> The Ramblers have just played the concluding number of their program for this evening.
>
> Before saying good night, they wish to extend a cordial invitation to their many friends, who know them through the medium of their phonograph records and their Keith vaudeville appearances, to visit them at their California Ramblers Inn.
>
> Now the charm of the country is at its height. Gentle breezes—refreshing green—and the quiet countryside, afford an ideal evening's motor trip with its attended relaxation.

Then, too, these are moonlight nights at the California Ramblers Inn—and what is more peaceful, more romantic, and altogether more restful than a view of the water, the gentle sighing of the trees with a gorgeous moon over all.

The California Ramblers signing off.

GOOD NIGHT.[55]

As this invitation suggests, the band could be heard at the California Ramblers Inn and on its gramophone records. Recording still formed an important source of income. From the band's start Kirkeby had kept a precise administration of its recording activities. The notebooks that he used present a major source of information for researchers of jazz history. He would generally write down the recording date and the company, as well as the cost and income, not the titles of the tunes that were recorded. In the beginning when the band's personnel was fairly constant, he did not note the personnel, but from March 1926 he also noted the names of the participating musicians as well as their individual earnings. The first session for which such a full personnel list is known took place right after the band's return from Florida on 18 March for Columbia, a major outlet both for the full band's records as well as those by the Little Ramblers. This is how the musicians were noted and their pay (first name and instruments added by the author):

Frank Cush—trumpet	20
Bobby Davis—reeds	25
Tommy Felline—guitar	20
Roy Johnston—trumpet	25
Fud Livingston—reeds	20
F. Fabian Storey—piano	15
George Troup—trombone	20
Herb Weil—drums	15
Elmer L. "Bunny" Drown—reeds	15
Sam Fink—violin	15
Adrian Rollini—bass sax	25

In total the musicians received $215 while Columbia paid $450 to Kirkeby, who thus made a profit of $235. The next day Columbia recorded the Little Ramblers. The six men received $125 and Kirkeby's profit was $175.

This was followed by sessions at Gennett and Edison. Competitors Pathé, Cameo, and OKeh also issued new recordings by the full band and all its smaller jazz-oriented groups. At a Pathé session in April, Kirkeby made an important change in the way he administered the income and payments from each record session: he put himself on the payroll as a participant. Thus from now on he

California Ramblers directed by Adrian Rollini, with Dixie Remer dancing.

would not only receive money from a session as fifty percent partner in Kirkeby & Hand, but also as a session participant, in fact as the highest paid of them. This was caused by the fact that Arthur Hand's involvement in the activities of Kirkeby & Hand was reduced to a minimum, and probably not more than by correspondence.

There were also two Pathé sessions in which Adrian accompanied their star performer Cliff Edwards. In total he participated in twenty-three recording sessions till the end of June.

With the heavy schedules for broadcasts and gramophone records, the California Ramblers were quite occupied and touring was out, but now and then short engagements were accepted.

The most publicized of these gigs was a dance on Monday evening 21 June in the Central Park Pavilion, a week before Adrian Rollini's twenty-third birthday.[56] He directed the band and was described as "the World's Greatest Bass Sax Player," a label that he would wear for many years. By now Adrian had known Dixie Remer for just over a year and her talent at dancing the Charleston was well known, so he added her to the band as an extra attraction.[57] New photographs had been made with Dixie in the center and no other leader than Adrian (see Fig. 35).

The band, now definitely under Rollini's leadership, was as active as before the Florida adventure, but Kirkeby was not satisfied. Personnel changes in the band created discontinuity, and financially the Florida adventure was not over and had resulted in a conflict with Hand.

The Goofus Five (six men!). From left: Irving Brodsky, Bobby Davis, Adrian Rollini, Stan King, Tom Felline, Chelsea Quealey.

The Music

The three months in Florida had meant a recording hiatus for Kirkeby's men. During the second half of 1925 they had produced about eighty titles. Less than half were by the full band. The high recording rate after the band's return was not good enough to produce as much: only some fifty titles until July, evenly split over the full band and the smaller groups. Looking through these twelve months of recordings, one finds several that set the band's music apart from its competitors. Though basically dance music, there were many that could be called milestones and some are even jewels of hot jazz.

The first one that should be mentioned is "I Miss My Swiss," recorded in July 1925 for Plaza, well before the Deauville adventure—not a very hot recording but remarkable for its pure entertainment. To underline the "Swiss" element of this Tin Pan Alley hit, Rollini played the theme of the old German folk song "O, Du Lieber Augustin." Guest trumpeter Ted Bartell contributed the hot element in the form of a good sixteen-bar trumpet solo. It became a best seller like no other recording by the band before this. It was issued on at least twenty-seven(!) different labels in the United States, Canada, Australia, Germany, and Poland, maybe an all-time record. From a jazz point of view, the other two titles from this session are of greater interest. "Say Arabella" again features Bartell, followed by singer Arthur Fields and then by solos from Tommy Dorsey and Bobby Davis. The arrangement of "Oh, Say Can I See You Tonight" includes a chase chorus by Bartell and Dorsey.

As the previous titles recorded by the Goofus Five, "Are You Sorry" and "I'm Gonna Charleston Back to Charleston," recorded a week later, are jazz throughout. Rollini, who did not solo on the previous session, takes thirty-two bars on the first and sixteen bars on the second title on bass sax, not on the goofus. More long solos by Rollini are heard on "Love Me Daddy Blues" and "I Know What It Means," from July by the Five Birmingham Babies. The latter recording is also remarkable for other reasons, first for the way Rollini moves from one solo instrument to another. He had done this before, but here we have a perfect example. He starts on bass saxophone and plays a break in the introduction, then switches to goofus to accompany a trumpet solo, and then quickly back to his sax to play a break followed by a long solo. Second, but even more important to Rollini, must have been the fact that the recording of "I Know What It Means" was the first time that his name appeared on a record label. He was the composer of the tune and this meant extra income from royalties.

It is not surprising that the Pathé/Perfect company gave Rollini this opportunity. The California Ramblers had recorded in the Pathé studio in New York for three years now and the records sold well. The Five Birmingham Babies had only added to that success and Rollini was getting recognition as their musical leader (and soon would be their factual leader). What is really remarkable is that it was only Pathé/Perfect who would record his tunes in those years. The next one would be "Dixie Stomp," recorded in October with the Five Birmingham Babies. The word Dixie had long been used as a romantic nickname for the South. Rollini's romantic feelings were not for the South, however, but for his girlfriend Dorothy, who by now called herself Dixie; Rollini named the tune after her, although record buyers associated the name in the traditional way.[58] "Dixie Stomp" is pure jazz. Again Rollini moves easily between his various roles. At the start he is the bass player, and then he moves to the front and leads the group. He is back to the bass function during the alto sax solo, but halfway he stops to pick up a new instrument that record buyers would be unable to identify for some time. This was the "hot fountain pen," another exotic wind instrument that had caught his eye. It looks like a miniature clarinet or rather like a big fountain pen, hence its name, given by Rollini.[59] Accompanied by a guitar, he manages to insert a break with a run of short notes into his novelty solo after which he returns to his role as the prominent bass player. It had been Jimmy Dorsey who had introduced the hot fountain pen to the band; he had even recorded with it, but as one former band member said, "Adrian played it better and took it over."[60] The Five Birmingham Babies would record two more compositions by Adrian Rollini, "She's Not Too Hot, She's Not Too Cool" and "Remember the Night."

In September a small group under the name of the Varsity Eight recorded the first version of "Fallin' Down." This hot tune would immediately be recorded for Plaza and for Pathé/Perfect too and soon for Columbia as well as for its sublabel Harmony, each time under a different pseudonym. The Pathé session also produced "Red Hot Henry Brown," another nice hot recording.

Recordings for Harmony would become an additional outlet for the band's output, in particular for jazz. For this label a new name was added to the long list of pseudonyms for small and larger groups out of the California Ramblers: the University Six, aimed at students, who formed a major market for jazz music. Its first session produced two titles with fine solos by Rollini, "Desdemona" and "The Camel Walk."[61]

A session for Cameo, and thus as the Varsity Eight, the following October, produced "I'm Gonna Hang Around My Sugar," a little-known tune that was also recorded by an early Duke Ellington group. Abe Lincoln and Bobby Davis took the first solo choruses, Chelsea Quealey and Sam Ruby (a new addition on reeds, born 1902) followed, after which Rollini brought the matter to an end in a way that shows who is the master. The second tune from this session, "Milenberg Joys," proves this even more. It is one of the finest recordings from Rollini's career, not only because it is one of those legendary early twenties tunes that no band made a bad recording of. What sets it really apart from all those other recordings is Adrian Rollini's twenty-four-bar solo near the end of the record. He plays around with the theme, interjecting a quote from "Meditation," a popular melody from Jules Massenet's opera *Thaïs*, and produces breaks in his own solo that are unforgettably humorous and precisely fitting. Add to this some good solo work by Lincoln and Davis and you have a masterpiece.[62]

Nearly all of the above were recordings by smaller groups, but the full band would also record exceptionally pure jazz. One such case is "I Ain't Got Nobody," with solos all over, the final one as usual taken by Rollini. He recorded this only a week after "Milenberg Joys" and a day before "Clap Hands! Here Comes Charley!" with the Goofus Five, on which he was featured both on the goofus and on the bass saxophone.

From the final two months of 1925 several more important recordings can be mentioned, but at least one should be singled out. This is the University Six recording of "Dustin' the Donkey," made in December. Basically the same arrangement as the Pathé/Plaza recording of the previous May, but with differences in personnel, such as Abe Lincoln on trombone instead of Tommy Dorsey, but Rollini's role is the same and he contributes a twenty-four-bar solo. It was recorded for Harmony by the old-fashioned acoustic method on 1 December. This was the first day of the marathon session for Harmony and Columbia that took the rest of the week. All recordings made on the following days were done by Columbia's superior new electric system. They were almost Rollini's final recordings before he left for Florida.

After their return from Florida in March 1926, it was decided that the first studio to record the band would again be Columbia. Columbia was still the only label that could issue recordings under the name of California Ramblers, and its recordings were excellent. One of the finest recordings from this session is "Could I? I Certainly Could," by the Little Ramblers. The band recorded this tune a second time that same day for Gennett, as the Vagabonds.

By now Adrian Rollini had taken over Arthur Hand's position as bandleader. This would allow him to accept offers for activities outside the environment of the California Ramblers, but that remained exceptional for a while, such as two sessions with Cliff Edwards in April. By now Edwards and Rollini had done several sessions together and it had worked. Rollini accompanied Edwards on bass saxophone. He even had a few small solo spots in the form of breaks on some of the recordings.

The Edison company also wanted the California Ramblers back in the studio. The company was known for a middle-of-the-road policy in its musical output, and thus the band would have to hold back; but Rollini preferred to play jazz, and now that he led the band he was in a position to suggest an experiment and to record some hot titles. So in April 1926 Edison recorded "What a Man!" and "Shake." Both tunes have a tricky element. The first title has a male vocalist who sings a lyric that was obviously meant for a female vocalist, but probably nobody took notice at the time. The latter title presented a greater risk. It was composed by black blues singer/entertainer "Papa" Charlie Jackson, who had recorded it a year before under its real title "Shake That Thing."[63] The title's erotic suggestion may have been the reason for Edison to change it to "Shake." The tune is taken at a medium tempo, which gives ample opportunity to soloists Abe Lincoln, Roy Johnston, Bobby Davis, Rollini, and even drummer Herb Weil on kazoo. A further Edison session, the following month, also produced two good hot sides, "I Wonder What's Become of Joe" and in particular "Hard to Get Gertie," Tin Pan Alley tunes that the band turned into undiluted jazz.

However, for jazz fans the best was yet to come. It happened the day after the Edison session, when the University Six came to the Harmony studio. This time no pop tunes, but two titles that are counted among a small number of early jazz standards and that are loved by jazz fans for the many great versions that exist. The first one that day was "Tiger Rag," on which Rollini's push is felt from the start. His accompaniment to trumpeter Chelsea Quealey's solo makes it more of a duet. Rollini takes a long solo on the second title of the session, "San." Two takes were issued of all three titles from this session; this allows insight into Rollini's approach to a solo. The first time a listener hears his solo on either take, it is a striking experience. It is well-constructed, logical, and highly original. And as the final solo, it brings the arrangements to a climactic ending. It is often thought that such solos are improvised on the spot, but any such thought disappears in this case when the alternative take is heard. Rollini plays the same solo.⁶⁴ After having played "San" for several years, the band had developed a fitting arrangement with a major role for Rollini, who had developed a perfect solo and would play it anytime the tune was on the program. He approached his solo as a professional and did not want to take a risk.⁶⁵

For a full year now Columbia had been the only company that made electrical recordings of the band, but during June 1926 their competition became more serious when Cameo started to use the new technology, too. The first trials with the band, as the Varsity Eight, were done on 11 June and all recordings were rejected, but the remakes, done two weeks later and including the title "Static Strut," were approved and issued.

A few days later the final session that month took place. This was by the Goofus Five for OKeh, who still used the old acoustical recording method, but the two resulting pop tunes were played as hot as could be expected, and on "Where'd You Get Those Eyes?" Rollini contributed a long solo.

Between the remake Cameo session and the OKeh session, Adrian Rollini celebrated his twenty-third birthday. He was the official leader of the California Ramblers now and his girlfriend Dixie had become a regular member of the team. The band was considered one of the two best dance bands in New York.⁶⁶ Life was smiling at Adrian Rollini, but Kirkeby was in for another debacle within a year.

Chapter 8

Kirkeby Loses His Grip, the End of the Contracts

During New York's hot summer, Ed Kirkeby was probably considering how to recover from the financial losses made in Florida, while members of the California Ramblers were thinking of that state's comfortable winter climate. The summer of 1926 looked much like the one of the year before as the maximum temperature in July, the hottest month, varied largely between 70° and 90°F and peaked much higher. One day it went to 108°F, a new record.[1] Yet the location of the inn, so near the waters of the Long Island Sound, was a good one in order to escape from the heat of the city. However, business was not as it used to be and it was decided that the California Ramblers would go on tour again, led by Adrian Rollini and with Dixie in the act. In all advertisements this was the band that was promoted as the California Ramblers. but by this time Kirkeby had ample experience running two or more bands in parallel, so that the work at the inn could be continued. There he could use a different name for the band, such as the Golden Gate Orchestra (from many of the band's record labels and probably also the name of an existing band) or the Intercollegians, a band that had replaced the full band before. The financially very rewarding recording activities also continued under the proven artist credits.

Rollini's tour was probably organized by the Keith vaudeville organization. It led the band out of New York state into Pennsylvania. During the week of 18 July the band under Rollini's direction performed at the Willows, a resort in Oakmont, near Pittsburgh.[2] Newspapers showed the latest band photographs and announced Dixie as a dancer and Adrian as a saxophone soloist. Donald Gaffney was featured as a xylophonist, not Adrian, although he had made his start with the California Ramblers in that capacity (and as a second pianist).[3] On the following day the band did a one-hour broadcast via local radio station KDKA, a proven method to get the public to a dance hall. They stayed around Pittsburgh for the next days, and two weeks later performed at the Vanderbilt Hotel in Oakdale, still in Pennsylvania, and at Kennywood Park, West Mifflin.

California Ramblers directed by Adrian Rollini with Dixie Remer sitting on the piano. (courtesy Dave Hignett)

During that same week the band worked at the Sunset near Altoona and at the Triangle, a dance pavilion in Bald Eagle. By the end of the week they were at Alfarata Park, Huntingdon. This dance, on Saturday 7 August, was very well promoted with articles in the *Huntingdon Daily News*, the local newspaper on three different days. The first was on 4 August, when it said that the band "is reputed to be the "greatest "big hot band" in the country," adding that "a unique feature of the orchestra is its extreme progressiveness, accounted for through the initiative of the managers." In present-day language this would mean that the band featured musically advanced arrangements and up-to-date solo work. The next two days, the band was called the "world's greatest hot band" in ads and both Adrian and Dixie were mentioned. On the day before the dance the following article appeared:

> Dance lovers and local musicians will have the opportunity August 7th of seeing and hearing the world's greatest bass saxophonist in action. Adrian Rollini is the product of the famous California Ramblers which is being brought to Alfarata Park for a special engagement on Saturday night.
>
> He has been with this organization of talented musicians for nearly five years, and has been featured on their records and in their dance engagements on account of his marvelous technique and style on what was formerly looked upon as a cumbersome oom-pah instrument.

Adrian plays many instruments, and was the first professional to bring into prominence, thru his solos on the Little Ramblers Columbia records, the instrument known as the Couesnophone.

His knowledge of harmony comes through his familiarity of the piano, which instrument he plays in a manner almost equal to his bass saxophone. He plays all the saxophones, xylophone, banjo and his ukulele playing is a revelation.

Coupled with his musical ability, Rollini was endowed with a "good head on his shoulders," which is shown by his being intrusted [sic] with the leadership of the Ramblers, known as the world's greatest hot band. . . . In addition, the Ramblers are bringing with them the latest sensation in Charleston dancing, Miss Dixie Remer, during the recent Charleston craze which has swept the country, has been acclaimed winner, time and again in every contest of the many which she entered in and around New York City.[4]

The series of articles in Huntingdon's newspaper continued until the day of the dance. It emphasized Rollini's importance by claiming that "the selling power of the band is in the name of the leader and not in the name of the band."[5] After this engagement the band may have had a few days off and Adrian traveled back to New York so that he could contribute to recording sessions for Edison and Columbia. Then the tour was resumed and the week starting Sunday 22 August the California Ramblers worked as part of a vaudeville company in the Lafayette film theater in Buffalo. The feature picture was *One Way Street* and the band were "proving as good as their reputation, which is national. Dixie herself is so good that she is practically stopping the show."[6] Others on the bill were V. Lamphis, with a comedy magic show, Fiedler-Mann with a sketch, and the dancing revue of Stan Hughes and his Girls. During the band's engagement at the Lafayette some Columbia record dealers "took advantage of the exclusive Columbia dance orchestra's appearance in their midst and co-operated with the theater in running a smashing three-quarter page advertisement in the *Buffalo Evening Times*."[7] The same week advertisements in the *Niagara Falls Gazette* announced that the band would also perform at the Homestead, a roadhouse near Buffalo, with Grey Siebert as an added attraction.[8] Dixie Remer's popularity was strongly growing and Tuesday was proclaimed Dixie Night at the Homestead.

From Buffalo and Niagara, the band traveled back toward Pittsburgh and worked for a week in the town of Aspinwall. "A feature of the appearance of the Ramblers will be the inclusion of a female entertainer in the personnel." On the opening day the band went on the air again via station WCAE.[9]

The band had now been on the road for about two months and the tour continued. In September they started in the Golden Pheasant, a restaurant in Cleveland, Ohio. It was announced as their first engagement in Cleveland, and they provided music for dancing and for entertainment, from noon till 2:00

Advertisement for Lafayette Theatre show in Buffalo, NY.

p.m., again from 6:00 till 8:00 p.m., and finally from 10:00 p.m. till 1:00 a.m. The tour's final known engagement was by mid-September in another dance hall and restaurant, Pulakos-on-the-Lake in Erie, Pennsylvania.[10] Here the band worked on Friday, Saturday, and Sunday only. On other evenings the hall could be rented by private parties, with the band or a part of it as an option.

Who were the musicians in Rollini's band during the tour of nearly three months? Some nice pictures exist of this band, which was probably formed especially for this tour and may have included some men who made the trip to Florida the previous winter. Two of the participants were trumpet player Bill Moore and trombone player Abe Lincoln. Lincoln remembered the tour and Dixie's dancing. He mentioned a problem that Adrian had at the time. He would often have a bad headache, which Lincoln thought was caused by Adrian's biting on the hard rubber of the mouthpiece, which would produce strong vibrations for the low notes. He used to take aspirins and all kinds of stuff and his colleagues were sorry for him. They would tell him that he did not have to play so loud, as long as they got that bass feel, but Adrian wanted to be heard. His bass sound made the California Ramblers. Rollini's headache problem may have been only for the period when Lincoln worked in the band. They have not been mentioned by anyone else and Rollini probably found a solution later.

Some more musicians' names can be mentioned but the full touring personnel remains a question. Although trombone player Abe Lincoln certainly toured with Rollini, Ed Kirkeby wrote that Herb Winfield played trombone during the tour.[11] Judging from the photos, reed player Danny Polo may have been present, and drummer Herb Weil also has been mentioned, but he was on some recordings made in New York at the time.

The band traveled by train and one day their next destination was Wilkes-Barre. Rollini was getting the tickets. There was a delay and while Rollini was away, a porter closed the door to the compartment where the instruments were stored, including Rollini's bass saxophone. Rollini did not carry it in a heavy box, but preferred a black velvet bag to hold it. When the porter closed the door, he banged it into the saxophone, which got so badly damaged that Rollini could not use it anymore. When Rollini got on the train, he was told what happened and his colleagues became worried how to get another saxophone for Rollini, because without it the band could not play certain arrangements. However, when they arrived a good, silver-plated bass saxophone was borrowed from a high school and Rollini was able to use it with his own mouthpiece.[12]

Names of musicians who did not go on the tour are known in detail. While Rollini toured, Ed Kirkeby organized fifteen record sessions using a kernel of personnel, plus a few extras for some sessions. Kirkeby's notebook gives the musicians' names, which leads to the conclusion that nearly all "name" California Ramblers stayed behind in New York:

Trumpet: Roy Johnston
Trombone: George Troup (in September replaced by Max Taub, Ivan Johnston, and Abe Lincoln)
Reeds: Bobby Davis, Sam Ruby
Bass saxophone: Art Pugliese or Spencer Clark
Piano: Jack Russin
Banjo: Tommy Felline
Drums: Herb Weil
For various sessions Kirkeby added one or more of the following men:
Trumpet: Frank Cush, Chelsea Quealey, Bill Moore
Reeds: Fred Cusick, Pete Pumiglio
Tuba: Art Campbell

After his return Rollini went right into the recording studios again. The first occasion was on 24 September, and it would be a busy day. On that Friday the Goofus Five recorded for OKeh in the morning and the Varsity Eight made records for Cameo in the afternoon. To complete this well-spent day, the full band had a broadcast via WMCA at 11:10 p.m.

Work at the California Ramblers Inn continued too. In the week of 10 October the North End Democratic Club of the Bronx organized a private party, a dinner, with three candidates for the position of Justice of the Supreme Court.[13]

Around this time Rollini was probably not working at the California Ramblers Inn but at the Monte Carlo on Broadway, and somehow this resulted in a financial deficit. Kirkeby supplied the money and, according to his notebook Adrian earned it back with the income from a few recording sessions. In November the Monte Carlo again announced that it had the "Fastest and Best Revue" in New York, with shows "twice nightly at 7:30 and 12:00 p.m.—informal at all time—dinner $2.25 from 6 to 9 and no cover charge." All this was musically accompanied by the California Ramblers.

Maybe the California Ramblers Inn was not such a safe place after all. In October a thief managed to walk away with two saxophones and a banjo. He was caught.[14]

The Lido Venice and Taking Stock Again

Kirkeby had done another thing. He was still trying to recover some of the losses resulting from the Florida adventure, so he started another venture, now in New York City. In his thumbnail biography he wrote that he opened a club on 53rd Street. It was called the Lido Venice and its opening on 18 November was brilliant.[15] In Kirkeby's own words "society, royalty, glamour and wonderful press" were present. He did not exaggerate. One press publication said that the

Lido Venice had been closed for the last year and that several large parties had been coming from the theater and opera for the dancing on the opening night. The newspaper continued by listing the names of fifty-nine guests, including those of an Italian prince and princess.[16]

As good as publicity had been before opening night, just as poor was the follow-up. It must have been wrong from the start. With his experience at the California Ramblers Inn and in Florida, both far away from the New York anti-alcohol patrols, Kirkeby may have underestimated their effectiveness in the city. As a result, the Lido Venice closed again three weeks later. Kirkeby had to add a $28,000 loss to his somber financial state of affairs. He wrote that it was "due to inability to handle the liquor account" when there was "great 'Dry Agent' activity."

While the California Ramblers worked at the Lido Venice, a replacement band worked at the California Ramblers Inn. It was called the Little Ramblers and consisted of Pete Pumiglio, reeds, Al Duffy, violin, Carl Kress, guitar, and Lennie Hayton, piano, who was followed by Walter Gross. The band that Kirkeby had at the Lido Venice had to be his best combination, and included Rollini. The others may have been some of the men he used for recording work during Adrian's tour. During the few weeks that the Lido Venice was in operation, the band did broadcasts via WMCA. The club closed around 9 December 1926 and at that moment the band was without a job. So they went back to the inn, knowing that business there would not be sufficient to afford a full band. Advertisements said that the California Ramblers, playing at the "smart, rural restaurant California Ramblers Inn were available for a limited number of engagements 1926–1927."

Only one such engagement is known. On Tuesday 14 December the *New York American and Evening Journal* organized a large Radio Ball at the famous Roseland Ballroom. It was a benefit affair and all receipts were donated, so the advertisement said. The California Ramblers' popularity was undiminished, so they were one of sixteen bands that provided the dance music. Among the other bands were Paul Specht, Fletcher Henderson and his Orchestra, as well as the Mound City Blue Blowers.[17]

Thus the year was approaching its end. Work at the California Ramblers Inn continued with a small group. Bass sax player and Rollini-follower Spencer Clark organized one of these bands, most probably in this winter of 1926–27:

> I put a band in there one winter when the big band went on the road. I had very memorable men as a matter of fact. I had Lenny Hayton on piano, Carl Kress on guitar but he was playing banjo then and I had Pete Pumiglio on clarinet and (Walter) "Kidsy" Drewhurst on trumpet and Charlie Bush on drums. It was a very fine little six-piece band. I could play muted cornet and we played two cornets muted and clarinet. Little free wave things we'd work up and cute little things and had a lot of fun doing them.[18] Clark particularly liked Pumiglio, a lovable, little guy, a good technician.... who would spark things, give things a punch.[19]

For New Year's Eve, invitations were handed out that announced an "elaborate supper" to be served from 10:00 p.m. "Reservations at Ten Dollars per person" and "fifty per cent deposit required with all reservations."

Business at the California Ramblers Inn had indeed been falling off lately and the high price for New Year's Eve and the down payment were illustrative of Kirkeby's poor financial state. In his thumbnail biography Kirkeby would write "Season at C.R. Inn fell off [on] account of terrific competition nearer city."[20]

He had not been able to pay out his men in full and in his notebook he wrote what Kirkeby & Hand owed them. "Recapitulation—Balance Due Boys—1926—One half to be paid by W.T.K.—One half to be paid by A.C.H." The list shows that half of the men waited for more than one hundred dollars. Even band leader Rollini had to wait for money, though for a smaller amount:

Herb Weil	$195.00
Bob Davis	$192.00
Abe Lincoln	$60.00
Adrian Rollini	$33.65
Tom Felline	$220.00
Jack Russin	$150.00
Roy Johnston	$187.00
Sam Ruby	$8.30
W.T. Kirkeby	$338.00
F.S. King	$15.00
Jos. La Faro	$15.00
Pete Pumiglio	$15.00

This meant a grand total of $1,428, $714 by each of the partners. Kirkeby's clever way of bookkeeping becomes visible when the amount is noted that he had to receive himself: $338. This was the result of giving himself a good salary from each record session that he organized from 22 April 1926 on, when he realized that Arthur Hand would no longer contribute to the musical side.[21] Thus he had only to contribute $376 to the total, and Hand more than a thousand.

During 1926 Adrian Rollini had proven to be able to run a band. While he must have known about the sad state of Kirkeby's main business, there are no signs that he felt any urgency to leave his old boss and mentor; but change was in the cards.

Intermezzo: The Music of the Second Half of 1926

The musical heritage from the second half of 1926 is as varied as before. Adrian Rollini was on tour for most of July, August, and September. To keep the California Ramblers sound on their records, Kirkeby could choose between bass saxophonists Spencer Clark and Art Pugliese or even tuba player Arthur Campbell. On a Goofus Five session in July, it was Pugliese. The group recorded hot versions of pop tunes "Mary Lou" and "Someone Is Losin' Susan," but Rollini's absence was felt, and Pugliese played no goofus. Even the Columbia session a few days later, which produced "She Belongs to Me" and "Me Too," was quite routine, though benefiting from the electric recording. "What-Cha-Ma-Call-It," recorded the next day for Pathé/Perfect, fared a little better, with solos on trumpet, alto saxophone, and piano.

However, Pugliese shows himself a better replacement for Rollini on "Oh! If I Only Had You" by the University Six. He has the right attack, but plays in a slap-tongue style throughout. This title and its companion "I Ain't Got Nobody" are nice hot recordings almost up to the normal level of this group. Yet the best feeling got back into the band when a week later Adrian himself was in New York for a few days and available when the full band recorded for Edison. Three titles were the result: "Up and At 'Em" (where Rollini solos for fifteen bars), "Looking at the World Through Rose Colored Glasses" (4-bar Rollini solo), and "Me Too."[22] The short break in the tour also allowed Rollini to take part in a recording date for Columbia; the band was the Little Ramblers and the tunes were "And Then I Forget" and "My Cutie's Due at Two-to-Two Today." The effect of his presence is impressive; he drives the band in an incomparable way. Columbia added its magnificent recording technique to make it all into a technical and musical product of the highest level.

Although the focus here is on Rollini's work, it should be noted that some of the dates without him contain excellent work by his colleagues. Spencer Clark usually was a better replacement than Art Pugliese and he was growing in this role along the way. Clark solos for the first time on the Columbia version of "She Knows Her Onions." A recording such as "Wait'll You See" allows trombone player Abe Lincoln to show his class in a good solo of sixteen bars followed by another eight bars.

By 24 September Adrian was definitely back, so he took the bass saxophone position again. On that day two recording sessions were scheduled. In the morning seven men recorded as the Goofus Five for OKeh and in the afternoon two men (trumpet and reeds) were added for a Varsity Eight date at Cameo. The Goofus Five produced an interesting cover version of Louis Armstrong's famous hit "Heebee Jeebies," recorded earlier that year by Armstrong's Hot Five in Chicago for the same label. The Goofus Five's version uses the arrangement of Armstrong's record including the vocal, now done by Ernest Hare, who ends it with a scat chorus as did Armstrong. OKeh issued Armstrong's original version in its race series, which had less general distribution than their dance music series in which the Goofus Fives were issued, but the fact that this was one of

OKeh's last acoustic recordings certainly did not help sales. The Harmony and Edison labels would continue to use this old recording method for a few more years; Harmony sold cheaply, but Edisons were expensive. "It Takes a Good Woman," by the University Six for Harmony, is one of their finest recordings from this period. The tune is taken at a relaxed, medium tempo and features solos by clarinet, trombone, alto saxophone, and finally Adrian Rollini's bass saxophone. The finest and hottest recordings were done by the full band at an Edison date in December. No Tin Pan Alley fare this time, but compositions by jazzmen like Jack Pettis and Jelly Roll Morton. The titles were "Stockholm Stomp" and "Sidewalk Blues." Three takes were issued of each of these two titles. This, plus Edison's longer playing time of over four minutes, creates a unique opportunity to hear the California Ramblers at their best.

During the final week of the year two more important sessions took place. The first one produced the first electric recordings by the Goofus Five. On the titles "I Need Lovin'" and "I've Got the Girl," Rollini soloed on the bass saxophone and, in line with the band name, on the goofus. However, a few days later it was back to acoustic, with the University Six, when they did two compositions by black composers, "I Wish I Could Shimmy Like My Sister Kate" (by Clarence Williams and Armand Piron) and "Beale Street Blues" (by W. C. Handy).[23]

The final week of 1926 ended with more recordings, but all were rejected. And 1927 was to bring more trouble for the California Ramblers.

1927 Gets Off to a Careful Start

With the exception of Ed Kirkeby, nobody could have expected that 1927 would develop so differently from the previous years. However, the signs were there. Though Kirkeby & Hand as a corporation was in name still owned and directed by the partners, Arthur Hand did not actively contribute anymore and Kirkeby ran his business alone.[24] The California Ramblers Inn made less money than before and it would not really pick up. It could not support the full band, which therefore had to tour.

Broadcasting also went downhill. After a long period of regular broadcasting via station WMCA, this was discontinued in December. Kirkeby sent a letter out "regarding broadcasting of the California Ramblers Orchestra," probably to several stations, with little response, but in the first week of January he received a reaction from station WOR, in Newark, New Jersey. Assistant Director C. Feland Gannon liked the idea and invited Kirkeby to discuss this "by telephone. . . . I think perhaps we can arrive at some definite understanding, more quickly than if we confine ourselves to correspondence." Kirkeby moved carefully this time. He wrote on this letter: "Investigate status of WOR. Frank Walker believes this station not to be compared with WMCA or WRNZ prestige. Believes either of latter, preferably WMCA. Take time to investigate further."[25] That was the end of it. During 1927 the California Ramblers were not on the airwaves.

The company's financial situation did not have much room for a new year salary raise for the band members, with the exception of Adrian Rollini, since he would be paid as the musical leader. On the first page of his 1927 notebook, Kirkeby wrote a note that Adrian Rollini was to receive an additional five dollars for each recording session. He had received $20–25 per California Ramblers session in 1926; this moved up to $27–35 in 1927.[26] In 1926 he and Bobby Davis had been the highest paid men in the band; in 1927 Rollini was the highest paid. The different amounts per session depended on negotiations with the record company.

Table 3. Rollini's Income per Session in Dollars		
Company	In 1926	In 1927
Banner[1]	—	30, 27
Cameo	25, later 22	20
Columbia	25	30, 27
Edison	20	25
OKeh	25	27, 30, 35, 30
Pathé	22	27, later 30, 27
Starr[2]	—	30

[1] Kirkeby called the company Banner after its best-known label; its actual name was Plaza.
[2] Starr was the company behind Gennett Records, who issued records by the Vagabonds.

In October 1926 a major shakeup took place in the world of record companies when the Columbia Phonograph Company, maker of Columbia records, bought the OKeh division of the General Phonograph Company.[27] As long as it had been using Western Electric's superior electric recording system, Columbia had had a great commercial advantage over any competitor that stayed technically behind. And that included OKeh, which had used a different electric system called Truetone, starting in November 1925. It missed the sound quality of the Western Electric system and collectors have long doubted that it really was electric. A month after its absorption by Columbia, OKeh was using Western Electric's system too. They were quickly approaching Columbia in recording fidelity.[28]

Columbia had yet another advantage over OKeh and its competitors. From the end of 1923 it held the exclusive right to the use of the name "California Ramblers" on its record labels. Other companies had to go by "Golden Gate Orchestra" or another pseudonym. However, now that it was owned by Columbia, the OKeh label was in a position to produce records under the full "California Ramblers" name, too. And the name "Little Ramblers" would also be available, for the small group recordings that had gone under the name of Goofus Five on the OKeh label, but giving up brand names was not Kirkeby's idea of doing business. He preferred to repeat his earlier successes and decided to introduce a new orchestra to the record-buying public. This was "Ted Wallace and His Orchestra." His given name was Wallace Theodore Kirkeby and he simply took his first names and used them for a band name.

The first session by Ted Wallace and His Orchestra took place on 3 January 1927. For a Goofus Five session, the previous December, OKeh had paid $300 to Ed Kirkeby, who paid his seven musicians $150, out of which Rollini received $25. The surplus was for Kirkeby and his company. For this first Ted Wallace session OKeh was not willing to pay more than for a Goofus Five session, $300, but now there were eleven musicians to be paid. Kirkeby gave 165 dollars to his boys, as he liked to call his men by then. Rollini received only $15, the lowest he had received in a long time. The following OKeh session, on 21 January, was not better for most band members, but Rollini received $27, in line with his new status.

However, most band members were starting to feel the new financial constraints. Moreover, there were fewer recording dates than before and a smaller band was working at the California Ramblers Inn. It was winter and, from the start three years before, the rationale for the inn had been to give the band a spot in the summer, when New York City was not the place to be. So the life of moving from one engagement to another started again, while the good news was that Adrian Rollini had become an experienced orchestra leader by now. The week ending 16 January they were at Scranton (Wilkes-Barre Theater) and the following week Rollini led eleven pieces at Maso on Broadway. For this and the next few weeks, the musicians and their salaries, known for each engagement, are shown in Table 4.

The performance in Syracuse went into the newspapers because of something of local interest: the band's trumpeter Roy Johnston had gone to high school there and had left the town to join Paul Whiteman's Collegians. The papers said that he had "had a wonderful success in the orchestra circle . . . having played in every phonograph recording station in New York City."[29] Johnston was one of the best paid men in the band, but he left soon after, while his brother Ivan stayed on. The men were paid by Rollini. Johnston may not have liked the new hierarchy in the band. He joined a smaller group that included Spencer Clark and Lennie Hayton. This may have been the group that worked at the California Ramblers Inn, but it also took outside engagements.[30]

The vacancy resulting from Roy Johnston's departure was filled by Sylvester "Hooley" Ahola (1902–1995). He had joined Paul Specht a year before and was looking for a new opportunity. This came when Ed Kirkeby called him, offer-

Table 4. Musicians' Weekly Pay in Dollars

week ending		23 Jan	28/29 Jan	5 Feb	12 Feb	18 Feb	22 Feb	4 Mar
		Maso Broadway	Syracuse	Lexington, Colgate	Bethlehem, State College	Unknown location	Unknown location	Branford, Newark
Adrian Rollini	Leader, bass sax	125	125	150	175	125	60	150
Roy Johnston	Trumpet	110	45	90	—	—	—	—
Chelsea Quealey	Trumpet	85	35	100	100	65	35	85
Sylvester Ahola	Trumpet	—	—	—	—	—	—	100
Ivan Johnston	Trombone	105	40	80	125	104	45	100
Bobby Davis	Reeds	125	60	125	125	80	40	125
Fred Cusick	Reeds	100	35	80	70	75	40	85
Sam Ruby	Reeds	75	35	70	75	80	35	75
Joe La Faro	Violin	60	—	—	—	—	—	60
Jack Russin	Piano	70	50	90	85	60	35	70
Tommy Felline	Guitar, banjo	85	55	100	100	65	40	85
Herb Weil	Drums	70	50	90	85	60	35	—
B. Busig	Drums	—	—	—	—	—	—	70
Part week			2 days			4 days	2 days	
Ed Kirkeby	Royalties	70	120	190	50	—	—	unknown

At Branford Theatre, Newark, NJ. Adrian serenading Tommy Felline with Tommy's guitar.

ing $100 a week for four weeks at the Branford Theatre in Newark, New Jersey. Just before that engagement started, Ahola took part in a California Ramblers recording date for Edison on 24 January.

To Dick Hill, writer of his life story, Ahola gave a description of Adrian Rollini:

> He was a hard guy to understand. He was hard to get to know, not a loner, but he was a little different. He was the big thing then, because he could do so many things. He had made those piano rolls as a boy, could play the "Hot Fountain Pen" and all those odd-ball things. . . . . but it was the bass-sax—he was the pioneer on that, and he knew what he was doing. He was a good musician—very good. I liked Adrian and got along with him very well, as I did with his brother Arthur who was also a nice guy.[31]

The California Ramblers were part of a show at the Branford Theatre, which was emceed by Don Alvin. It included a musical chorus, a pit band, and a ballet

Adrian with Tommy Felline and Sylvester Ahola (holding camera) at Branford Theatre, Newark.

chorus, and Alvin called it the Merry Mad Gang.[32] The band had to dress up in uniforms, a different outfit every week. For a show called Canadian Capers they dressed as the Canadian Mounted Police. Pictures and even some 16 mm film of this exist, made by Hooley.[33] At another occasion they were dressed as pirates. Hooley had positive memories of the band:

> Abe Lincoln played a lot of trombone with the band. I've heard a lot of his records, and in my opinion he was an unsung hero. . . . Bobby Davis was good for the time, having a nice tone and he played good lead alto sax. Chelsea Quealey played good trumpet and played all the jazz solos. But the stuff that they turned out! Ed Kirkeby booked them on every record label there was. They'd knock off those stock arrangements, and someone would take a chorus and as long as you didn't make any mistakes, they would let them go through for issue. They didn't have many arrangements, they would take "stocks "and Adrian usually fixed them up. That was a good, loose band, and easy to go with.[34]

Ahola stayed with the California Ramblers only for a few weeks, but Rollini would not forget him when, later in the year, he had to form a band. Another musician who worked with the California Ramblers when they were at the Branford Theatre was Nick Casti, who played lead trumpet.[35]

Behind the scenes, Kirkeby was still very much in control. Contrary to what he had done during Rollini's 1926 tours, Kirkeby administered every dollar earned from engagements in his notebooks, between pages with recording dates. Moreover, he would charge a royalty for the use of the name California Ramblers so that his company would also make a good result on these engagements.

However, the winner was Adrian Rollini, who received $910 for seven engagements in a period of seven weeks, followed by his mate Bobby Davis with $680 and by another old hand, Sam Ruby, who got $445. During those weeks there were days without an engagement; on these days recording dates were scheduled, which yielded an additional $99 for Rollini. On another day he recorded with singer Cliff Edwards. Engagements and recording dates with and without the California Ramblers had brought Adrian Rollini's weekly income to an average of over $150.[36] For a young man (he was twenty-three) that was a good salary, but comparing this to Paul Whiteman's payroll, one might get the feeling that Kirkeby's boys were underpaid. Whiteman's highest paid musician received $350, the lowest $150.[37]

However, there was no room for higher salaries. Kirkeby's financial prospects were not improving and this came into the open early February when *Variety* published the outcome of a judgment whereby Kirkeby & Hand were forced to pay a bill.[38]

By the end of that month Kirkeby saw no solution but to file for bankruptcy. His notebooks show that he had always paid his "boys" in full. They were his greatest asset and musical entertainment was his home base. He would pay in cash or by check and sometimes, if one of the boys needed it, he would give a salary advance, but Kirkeby had considerable debts and they were listed in his bankruptcy application. Under the heading "Kirkeby 'In' for $438,889," *Variety* of 2 March 1927 had the following story:

> Cafe and restaurant season is not so good, according to a quartet of voluntary and involuntary bankruptcy petitions filed during the past week. All of the alleged bankrupts are engaged in the café business. They include Wallace T. Kirkeby..... Kirkeby is involved through having unsuccessfully operated the Deauville Casino, Inc. at Miami, Fla., and the Lido-Venice restaurant, 35 E. 53d street, New York, in partnership with Arthur Hand, leader of the California Ramblers orchestra, which Kirkeby & Hand managed....
>
> The Kirkeby petition involves the greatest amount of money. He lists liabilities of $438,889.78; assets $22,142.05 of which the latter included money loaned to Kirkhand, Inc., and Kirkeby & Hand, Inc., two holding corporations in which Wallace T. Kirkeby and Arthur Hand were vitally interested. Another item included

in the assets is $3,333.33 due from Joseph C. Elsener who allegedly agreed to pay $15,000 for a one-third interest in the Deauville Casino, Inc., towards which he paid $6,666.37. Insurance policies of no immediate cash value, aggregating $71,500, are part of the paper assets.

The liabilities incurred in the Lido-Venice venture are for salaries due Guerrino Gregory, 117 W. 71st street, the head waiter and his large crew of waiters, busboys, kitchen staff, etc.; also moneys due musicians for salaries and their share of income from recording dates.

Of the liabilities Georgia Shaw, entertainer, has two judgments for $2,531.45 and $1,050.32; Eddie Davis, orchestra leader, $900; Basil Durant, the dancer, now at the Club Lido, $6,600 on an employment contract; Arthur C. Hand, Woodward Hotel, $125,000; Kirkeby & Hand, Inc., $12,200; Joseph C. Elsener $25,000 due on the lease of the Club Deauville; Beach Properties, Inc., $200,000 due on a two-year lease; Dan Hennessy, $10,000, due for moneys loaned as advance for stock in Kirkeby's corporations.[39]

This article reveals that the unwinding of the Florida adventure had not happened. There were several companies owned by three partners, Elsener, Hand and Kirkeby. First of all, Beach Properties, owned by the three together, and furthermore Hand and Kirkeby owned two holding companies Kirkhand, Inc., and Kirkeby & Hand, Inc. These companies owed moneys between them as well as to individuals. As a result, Elsener could be found in the list of debtors as well as among the creditors.

The article also shows that the Lido Venice eventually had its own orchestra and entertainers. Eddie Davis led an orchestra and entertainment was provided by Georgia Shaw and Basil Durant, a dancer who had worked for Kirkeby in Miami.[40]

From the beginning in 1922 Ed Kirkeby may have looked like the perfect boss to work for in the eyes of young Adrian Rollini. At that time Kirkeby was already experienced in the business and had created an excellent network in the world of gramophone records, but now, five years later, Kirkeby's image was damaged. Adrian no longer felt in any way obliged to Kirkeby and would be looking for greener pastures.

However, for a while Adrian Rollini and his colleagues remained loyal to Kirkeby. Since he kept them busy with short engagements, often one-day affairs and recording sessions, Kirkeby meant income. For the following months Ed Kirkeby's notebooks mention several short engagements and not all gigs came into the newspapers. One that did, but was not listed by Kirkeby, was a performance by a band called the Golden Gate Orchestra, at a piano show in Pennsylvania on 17 March. This must have been without Rollini who, that same day, in the morning recorded for OKeh in New York and in the evening worked at the

California Ramblers Inn, which reopened that week. In fact, it may have been Jimmy Carr's band that was called the Golden Gate Orchestra.[41]

From mid-March till mid-April, Rollini worked at the California Ramblers Inn with Chelsea Quealey trumpet, Bobby Davis and Sam Ruby, reeds, Jack Russin, piano, Tommy Felline, banjo and guitar, and Herb Weil, drums. During the first week two men were added, one Robison, who probably played the trombone, and reed player Bob Fallon. A fifth week at the Inn was planned for this group but Kirkeby crossed it out in his notebook, adding that he discontinued the weekly payroll at the inn. This had everything to do with his poor financial state and it had great symbolic meaning.[42] From now on "his boys" would only be hired for individual occasions and there could be long idle periods. On the other hand, they were no longer bound by a contract and could work for any other leader.

So ended the last known live performance of the California Ramblers with Adrian Rollini—however, not of the California Ramblers per se. During May Kirkeby arranged several engagements around New York for a smaller band that consisted mostly of different musicians. Of the group that worked at the inn, only Tommy Felline remained. Others in this group were Roy Johnston, Spencer Clark, and Jack Russin, or Irving Brodsky.

The California Ramblers Inn may have been open during the summer months of 1927 but Kirkeby's notebooks contain no data about this and there are hardly any press clippings mentioning the inn at all. It looks like the above small touring group was about all that was left from the heyday, but there was one thing more and that was recordings. Adrian Rollini would now work on a freelance basis for Kirkeby, who hired him for no fewer than twenty-five recording dates between mid-April and the end of August, averaging six sessions per month. On 31 August 1927 Adrian Rollini would make his final records with the California Ramblers.

Recordings: Early 1927 Vintage

The first four months of 1927 were the last months that Ed Kirkeby had all his "boys" on his payroll. The new year had hardly begun when they had their first recording date. This was on 3 January, for OKeh. The new pseudonym of "Ted Wallace" was introduced on three titles, all with the same concept and without interest as jazz—straight performances with vocals by Irving Kaufman or Kirkeby himself. The best moments are near the end of each recording when Bobby Davis takes a short alto sax solo. Rollini's only solo contribution is eight straight bars on one title.

About two weeks later a remake session took place for the Columbia titles that were rejected in December: "Stockholm Stomp" and "I Love the College

Girls," of which the first is the most memorable. It moves along nicely and features solos on trumpet, violin, piano, and finally a well-structured sixteen-bar solo by Rollini.

The new Ted Wallace identity needed quick promotion, and therefore a second OKeh session under that name took place in January. With thirteen or fourteen participants, it was the biggest group that Ed Kirkeby had ever assembled for a recording date, with the following personnel:

Roy Johnston and Chelsea Quealey—trumpet
Ivan Johnston—trombone
Bobby Davis, Fred Cusick, and Sam Ruby—reeds
Joe La Faro—violin
Jack Russin—piano
Tommy Felline—banjo, guitar
Herb Weil—drums
Adrian Rollini—bass saxophone
Ed Kirkeby and Hal White—vocal
B. Busig (listed in Kirkeby's notebook, role unknown[43])

Unlike the first Ted Wallace session, the second one produced cover versions of hits. "Ain't She Sweet" is memorable only for a short solo on the goofus by Rollini. The other two titles from this session, "There Ain't No Maybe in My Baby's Eyes" and "Crazy Words Crazy Tune," have a little more to offer: both feature Rollini on bass saxophone. A week later the same large group recorded a similar set of tunes of the day for Pathé, the first time that company used the new electric recording system for Kirkeby's band. He had brought even more vocalists, who mostly produced comedy vocals so that there was little room for jazz. The best moment is Rollini's solo on "Crazy Words, Crazy Tune." Kirkeby judged this the right type of material for recordings by the California Ramblers, also under his new nom deplume of Ted Wallace, but for a University Six session a few days later slightly hotter material was selected. Cusick, Ruby, and La Faro dropped out. Thus the group was reduced in size, not to six, but to ten. The best title from the session, "Nobody But My Baby," was composed and published by the black team of Clarence Williams and Andy Razaf. Main soloists on this title are Bobby Davis, both on alto saxophone and clarinet, and Adrian Rollini, with sixteen bars of bass saxophone, resulting in a nice, hot performance of the tune. Two further titles from this date, "Oh Lizzie" and "The Cat," were both quite restrained, but on the final title, "It's O.K., Katy, with Me," the band really moves. The next day the group was smaller again when, as the Goofus Five, they went to the OKeh studio to record three jazz standards, "Farewell Blues," "Sister Kate," and "Some of These Days." Now Chelsea Quealey also dropped out and there was no singer, so that the Goofus Five were eight men this time. It is sad that no trace exists of the third title, since the first two are among the band's finest recordings. The front line consists of the two Johnston brothers plus Bobby Davis, but Rollini adds his bass saxophone to create a sound almost as big as from the previous larger combinations. Both tunes are taken at a relaxed tempo, which allows the soloists, Davis and Rollini to shine. It is amazing to hear how perfectly these musicians switched from playing straight dance music for popular entertainment to the latest form of jazz fit for a smaller public. OKeh must be thanked for their wisdom to keep the Goofus Five alive after they had started the Ted Wallace orchestra. Thanks did come to OKeh, indeed: some of the electrically recorded titles by the Goofus Five sold in very good numbers on a wide scale, and would stay in catalog for years to come.

After this Goofus Five date Rollini took several short engagements with a California Ramblers group, so he missed a few sessions at Cameo and OKeh. For the Cameo session Kirkeby hired an outside band and for the OKeh (Ted Wallace) session his own men were used, including Spencer Clark on bass saxophone.[44] Clark shows that he had managed Rollini's style of accompaniment by now; Kirkeby did not allow him to solo yet but knew he would have an excellent replacement ready as soon as Rollini was no longer available.

In March, Rollini took part in a Cliff Edwards session for Pathé/Perfect. Cliff had gathered a small jazz band around himself with remarkable instrumentation, which he called his Hot Combination. In addition to Rollini's bass saxophone, there were valve trombone, alto and tenor saxophone, piano, violin, and guitar. With the exception of the latter two (who may have been Joe Venuti and Eddie Lang), no names are known. Rollini is very active and pushes the jazz band on both titles, "Oh, Baby! Don't We Get Along" and "Side by Side." A new element is evident in his playing: he frequently injects notes in between bars just after the band, or a soloist, finishes a bar and starts another. This is demonstrated on "Ain't She Sweet," a recording made the same month for Edison by the California Ramblers. It remained unissued at the time.

Still in March, Rollini took part in sessions under the new Ted Wallace flag (OKeh) as well as under the names California Ramblers (Columbia) and Golden Gate Orchestra (Perfect). They produced little of jazz value with the exception of the final Perfect title, "Leave My Baby Alone," which features hot solos by violinist Joe La Faro, trumpeter Chelsea Quealey, Rollini, and Davis. The company's electric recording system made the result even more enjoyable, but Columbia was still the winner in recording quality, as proven a week later when the full band recorded Howdy Quicksell's tune "Pardon the Glove," with good solos by Rollini and Davis.

The following month saw another Goofus Five session. Four titles were recorded: the recent Tin Pan Alley hit "Muddy Water"; two old jazz/blues standards, "The Wang Wang Blues" and "Arkansas Blues"; and a novelty tune, "The Whisper Song." All tunes feature advanced jazz arrangements, and solos abound. Rollini takes solos on goofus and bass saxophone on the first three titles, and on "The Whisper Song" produces a piano duet with Jack Russin. This was another sign that Rollini was considering adding more instruments to his repertoire, instruments he had played before he discovered the bass saxophone. The following month he recorded further examples of this trend in the Gennett studio, during a session that stands out in experiments. "I'm Back in Love Again" features Rollini on bass saxophone in the intro and later on a solo on xylophone and in another piano duet. The next tune recorded at this session, "Yes, She Do, No She Don't," got an exceptionally hot treatment; Rollini starts his bass saxophone solo before Kirkeby finishes his vocal. On "S-L-U-E Foot," the final tune from this session, he again plays xylophone. He would be using it frequently during the next few months, but not on prestigious labels such as Edison and Columbia, for which he recorded that same month. On one day near the end of the month, a morning session at Columbia produced beautiful recordings of "Lazy Weather" and "Vo-Do-Do-De-O Blues," while in the afternoon a smaller group at Pathé/Perfect recorded two tunes that belong to American folklore, "Casey Jones" and "Steamboat Bill." Each concerns the story of a legendary engineer, Casey Jones driving a railroad train and Steamboat Bill a riverboat.[45] A month earlier Charlie Troutt, a relatively unknown orchestra leader from Atlanta, Georgia, had recorded these tunes for Columbia under the title "Transportation Blues Parts 1 and 2," and the record was a tremendous success. Troutt's arrangement consisted largely of the recitation of the complete ballads, with orchestral accompaniment. The California Ramblers' version shows the same approach with the multi-verse ballads done by the Collegiate Rollickers, whose identities remain unknown. During the few instrumental moments Rollini's bass saxophone produces a few breaks, and at the end of "Steamboat Bill" the sound of a ship horn.

Rollini can be heard on the xylophone again on the results of the sessions for Plaza and Harmony, but his solo work on the bass saxophone on "Zulu Wail," the third Plaza title, is the most memorable. The tunes were hits of the day, but even these could be given a hot treatment, as shown by "Beedle-Um-Bo," recorded for Edison a few days later. Though including a silly vocal, several instruments are heard soloing, including eighteen bars by Rollini. Even better from a jazz point of view were the results of an OKeh session that same week. The first tune was "Lazy Weather," which they had recorded two weeks earlier as the University Six, with Rollini on xylophone. Now as the Goofus Five, Rollini soloed on bass saxophone and goofus, which, in addition to the superior recording, resulted in a top performance. "Vo-Do-Do-De-O Blues," done next, was almost as good, with the band and its soloists moving along with great momentum and Rollini producing one of his finest goofus solos.

With the exceptions of one (non-jazz) recording with Rudy Wiedoeft and a few sessions accompanying Cliff Edwards, Adrian Rollini had so far strictly adhered to Ed Kirkeby's ruling only to make records with groups he managed. Rollini had occasionally sat in with other bands, which, together with late-night jam sessions with jazz greats, resulted in his growth as a jazz man. The time had come to spread out.

Chapter 9

Freelancer Adrian Rollini

Being away from Kirkeby's heavy schedule of live performances mixed with recording dates, benefits, and tours gave Rollini a free hand to make serious work of a career as a freelancer. His first opportunity was with Red Nichols. He had worked with Red Nichols, and Red had made some of his hottest records with Rollini in the band.

The Sixth of the Five Pennies

The California Ramblers were essentially a dance band and its recordings were a mix of sweet and hot. However, the records that Adrian Rollini made with Red Nichols's small jazz band were exclusively meant for a public of jazz devotees. They were milestones in his career and turned Rollini from a well-known dance band musician and orchestra leader into a full-blown jazzman that could hold his best in an environment of jazz professionals.

As a young boy, Ernest Loring Nichols lived in Ogden, Utah, where he was born on 8 May 1905. His father was a music professor and a conductor at a local college. He was his son's first music teacher and started him on violin. Ernest, who preferred to use his middle name Loring, had red hair, hence his nickname. By the time Red was six he had become a capable cornet player, too, and eventually and inevitably for a young boy at the time, he was attracted to the sound of the Original Dixieland Jazz Band. He practiced the style of cornetist Nick LaRocca, their leader, and in 1922, when he was seventeen, he joined a small jazz and dance band, the Syncopating Five. This band soon had seven members and Red made his first gramophone records with them.[1] A year later Red worked in Atlantic City, New Jersey, in Johnny Johnson's Orchestra.[2] In Atlantic City he heard three musicians for the first time, who together with Red would have a major influence in the developing jazz scene: trombone player Irving Milford "Miff" Mole, violinist Joe Venuti, and his friend, guitar player Eddie Lang. Red was by now making a name for himself and when Johnny Johnson's Orchestra moved to New York, he had many new job opportunities. In 1924 he joined Sam Lanin's orchestra. Lanin used a strategy toward the gramophone companies similar to Ed Kirkeby's. Like Ed, Sam Lanin would record the same tune for as many record labels as he could, thus giving his musicians extra income. For many years he had a steady position at the Roseland Ballroom, which had a policy of using two bands. In July 1924 the second band became Fletcher Henderson's, which gave Red a chance to hear Louis Armstrong, who arrived in October.[3]

During his stay with Sam Lanin's dance band, Red started a career as a jazz musician, next to his work as a dance band musician.[4] In November 1925 Nichols made the first record in a series that would bring him international fame. This was with a small group called the Red Heads [sic] and Miff Mole was his trombone player.[5] Miff Mole (1898-1961) was born on Long Island, New York, and joined the Original Memphis Five in 1922, the most successful five-piece jazz band at the time. A tour took him to California, where he worked for a few months. He returned to New York and worked with Sam Lanin, and then joined Ray Miller's band, in which Frank Trumbauer was one of his colleagues. From Miller he moved to Ross Gorman's band, where he met Red Nichols, who selected him for his jazz band.

In addition to his major musical talent, Nichols had a great sense for business and built a network of contacts that could provide paid work. His network included leaders of dance bands, managers of recording companies, contractors of musical shows, and of course musicians. Thus the Red Heads' success led to invitations from other companies for Nichols to come that made him a leader in the jazz scene and his band, the Five Pennies, one of the best known jazz bands ever.[6]

Nichols's first recordings with his Five Pennies were indeed done with a five-piece group, consisting of himself plus Jimmy Dorsey (reeds), Arthur Schutt (piano), Eddie Lang (guitar), and Vic Berton (drums). Each of them was a pioneer in his own right, but particular mention should be made of drummer Vic Berton. He was co-composer of the early jazz standard "Sobbin' Blues," which was played by all jazz and dance bands in 1923. The bands that he played with before he joined Nichols included Bix Beiderbecke's Wolverines. Berton made several innovations to the hardware of the drum set. One of these was what today is called the "hi-hat," a contraption of two cymbals mounted on a vertical rod and facing each other. It is operated by the foot and allows the drummer to sharply give accents. However, Berton's best-known contribution to jazz drumming is his use of tuned tympani.[7] He was able to change a tympano's pitch while playing and thus could play bass line harmony by using two tympani, one for each hand. He called it "hot tympani."[8]

After the first session, Miff Mole was added on trombone, thus creating a formidable front line of Nichols, Mole, and Dorsey. Add to this that the rhythm men were at least in their class, and you had a bunch of creative, energetic young musicians who had no equals. Richard Sudhalter, jazz historian and cornet player, wrote about Nichols and his music: "He was a cornetist, an excellent one, and a strong and positive force in producing and disseminating a body of music which can still astonish with its subtlety, ingenuity, harmonic and technical brilliance." Sudhalter added that much of what later became "modern" jazz can already be found in Nichols's work in the twenties. "These men were deft, accurate players who could compose, arrange, read anything at sight and toss off coherent improvised solos with almost contemptuous ease."[9]

Rollini's talent would flower in their company. The first session in which he took part was on 20 June 1927.[10] Two tunes were recorded, of which one, "Cornfed," was issued immediately and the other, "Five Pennies," several months later. From the first notes of "Cornfed" it is clear that Adrian Rollini feels at home in this environment. He and Vic Berton play the intro, a never-heard combination of bass saxophone and tympani. Rollini plays several breaks and does the coda together with Lang. "Five Pennies" is taken at a very slow tempo and Rollini has a sixteen-bar solo.

The perfect cooperation shown by these recordings was primarily the result of great musicianship of all participants, but also of repeatedly playing together and having a common idea about the music. The fine arrangements added much to the overall results. Definite identification of the authors of these arrangements is not available and they may have been made up during rehearsals. Red Nichols must have had a strong hand in them. Within the California Ramblers, Rollini had been working in an environment in which arrangements were of secondary importance, usually with publisher's stocks that were adapted to the band by its members, including Rollini himself. However, for its small spin-off groups, special arrangements were made, which relied on the solo performances of the musicians. The work with Red Nichols came close to this, but its arrangements were more elaborate.

A Busy Week of Freelancing

Now Rollini belonged to a large group of New York freelance musicians, who were available to do short-term studio work playing in large orchestras or accompanying singers. They could also work in one of many bands that played in shows, hotels, ballrooms, or on tour. In Rollini's case, nothing is known of such engagements in the spring and summer of 1927. His main interest seems to have been making jazz records. A heavy recording schedule by the end of June illustrates this, as shown in Table 5.

On 20 June, Rollini had recorded two tunes with Red Nichols, but Red's contract required a third title and this was set up on a date five days later that same

Table 5. Two Weeks Day-to-day

Date	What	Group	Label
Monday 20 June		Red Nichols	Brunswick
Wednesday 22 June	Rehearsal for 27 June	Ed Kirkeby	
Friday 24 June	Morning	Varsity Eight	Cameo
Friday 24 June	Afternoon	California Ramblers	Pathé/Perfect
Saturday 25 June		Red Nichols	Brunswick
Saturday 25 June	(or Monday 27 June)	Annette Hanshaw	Pathé/Perfect
Sunday 26 June	Rehearsal for 27 June	Ed Kirkeby	
Monday 27 June	Ted Wallace & his Orch.	Ed Kirkeby	OKeh
Tuesday 28 June	[24th birthday]	Joe Venuti	OKeh
Friday 8 July		Little Ramblers	Columbia

week. However, before Rollini recorded again with Nichols, he did two sessions with his former colleagues from the California Ramblers. On the morning of 24 June, he recorded with eight men for Cameo as the Varsity Eight, and in the afternoon with seven for Pathé as the California Ramblers. The choice of tunes for these dates suggests that the musicians wanted to deviate from the traditional California Ramblers approach and produce some out-and-out jazz.

The Cameo session produced only two titles, a new version of the old success "Arkansas Blues" and a recent piece "Vo-Do-Do-De-O Blues," both fully instrumental. It was planned to do more and when this did not happen, Kirkeby reduced the individual pay. Rollini got $20 instead of $25. However, what was recorded was fine; "Arkansas" has a nice, light feeling about it and freelancer Rollini plays a sixteen-bar solo as well as a coda. He also solos for sixteen bars on the second title, but on the goofus.

For the afternoon session at Pathé, the trombone was dropped.[11] The first tune recorded was another version of "Vo-Do-Do-De-O Blues." The Cameo version had featured a trombone solo, which had to be replaced now and the choice was a vocal, which Ed Kirkeby did. According to the plan, Pathé recorded a total of four tunes during the session, an exceptionally high number, including one instrumental. The second Pathé title that day was a composition by Adrian Rollini, "Heartbreakin' Baby." The intro is played by trumpet, alto saxophone, bass saxophone, and drums in quick succession and this perfectly leads into the melody, stated by alto saxophone and trumpet. After the vocal, Rollini takes the lion's share of solo space in his own piece (and probably his own arrangement), soloing for a total of thirty-four bars, the most he ever had on a record so far. Though less spectacular, the next title, "Goin' Home Blues," also has much to offer, with another intricate intro, played by trumpet and piano. There are solos by trumpet and alto saxophone and another long one by Rollini. The fourth title recorded at this session would become an icon of twenties New York jazz: the old tune "After You've Gone."[12] The performance is a complete departure from the California Ramblers' tradition of straight dance music in a simple arrangement with some solo space. "After You've Gone" is taken at a high tempo. An opening statement of the melody and the verse is followed by a solo from trumpeter Chelsea Quealey, who ends it with the most amazing four-bar break ever heard on a Rollini record. Without accompaniment, he blows more than twenty short notes and manages to keep the swing and the tempo going. It was not improvised: on the two existing takes of this recording he plays the same break. This was not the case for Sam Ruby's clarinet solo, which follows. On one take he gets badly lost, the alternate take is a little better. The next solo is a surprise. One of the musicians shows himself to be a capable whistler, doing a sixteen-bar solo. Kirkeby's notebook offers no identification. Judging the phrasing and his known interest in exotic instrumentation, one can easily imagine Adrian Rollini here in another surprise appearance. However, in view of a later recording, where he accompanies the same whistler, it cannot be him. A moment later Rollini is back for a twenty-four-bar goofus solo, after which he returns to his bass saxophone for the final ensemble chorus and plays a wonderful break before the recording ends.[13]

The next day, 25 June, Adrian was back at Brunswick to record one more title with Red Nichols's Five Pennies, "Mean Dog Blues." Rollini proved his versatility by again perfectly fitting in this environment, as if he had not been back with the California Ramblers the day before. Four takes were recorded, in order to get one that was judged good enough for issue. The tune's arrangement, made by Red Nichols, gave Rollini an opportunity to solo, but his presence is heard and felt throughout. The recording was probably done with one microphone. Modern mixing consoles were still many years away, so a good recording balance depended to a large extent on the musicians, who had to move to the microphone to be heard loudly, and then move back again. Rollini knew how to treat this. After he had played a break at full strength, he is heard accompanying Eddie Lang's guitar solo at a low level, never getting in Eddie's way. He consistently drove the band's performance by his well-placed bass notes, both following the beat and filling in holes between his colleague's musical phrases at unexpected moments. The other musicians' performances are of an equally high standard.

Adrian Rollini's next assignment was at the Pathé studios again, with singer Annette Hanshaw.[14] Hanshaw had made her recording debut with Pathé the year before and her popularity was rising.

Catherine Annette Hanshaw was born in New York on 18 October 1901. She was the second child of Frank Wayne Hanshaw, a salesman, and Mary McCoy, a middle-class family. She had no formal musical training but at a young age she showed she could sing.

She wanted to study art and turned two offers down for a musical scholarship before she was fifteen. Eventually she sufficiently learned to play the piano and the ukulele to accompany her own singing. Her father helped her grow in her fledgling career. He was involved in some roadhouses in upstate New York, where she would sing for guests during their parties. He also got her to work in a record shop, of which it is said that she was the owner. Here she could listen to the songs of the day. At one party, when Hanshaw was twenty-five, she was discovered by an executive of Pathé records, Herman "Wally" Rose. Rose heard her singing and convinced her she had talent.[15] And talent she had. She could not only sing, but she could also act a tune in front of a public and cooperate well with her accompanists, who loved to work with her.

At the instigation of Herman Rose, she made a test recording for Pathé in July 1926. The company judged it good enough to let her make her first commercial recording and decided that she should be backed by their hot unit, the Red Heads with Red Nichols. Previously, Pathé had used the same successful approach with their male singing stars Cliff Edwards and Jay C. Flippen.

As a personality, Annette Hanshaw was shy; in an interview she calls herself an introvert. In that same interview Annette describes how, with little preparation, she would come to a recording session:

> I used to walk in, scared, all the musicians were there, there were some excellent ones. . . . I had magnificent musicians but the trouble was I didn't have an awful lot of arrangements. They were usually head arrangements. We'd come in . . . and they would make up an introduction and sometimes, you know, if it isn't all worked out ahead of time it could be a bit of a shambles and I was always so nervous and bad. . . . I had such respect for the musicians that I would know it wasn't right, it wasn't the way I wanted it but I wouldn't want to do it over again and make the musicians stay.[16]

Cliff Edwards and other Pathé artists used various accompaniments in their recordings, and the company now wanted the same with Annette. During her first year with Pathé she had fourteen recording sessions, not only with Nichols's hot group but also backed by smaller combinations, such as piano and violin or piano only, sometimes even her own. In June 1927 the company grouped her with Adrian Rollini and three other musicians. This time the company unconsciously created a jazz combo that would make some of the greatest small-band jazz of the twenties. Annette's accompaniment would be done by Adrian Rollini, bass saxophone, Joe Venuti, violin, Eddie Lang, guitar, and Vic Berton, drums. Rollini and Berton brought their individual collections of extra instruments along, too. Rollini took his goofus, his hot fountain pen, and his celeste. Berton brought not only his tympani but also a new instrument called a harpaphone.[17]

The titles for this session were all fit for a singer, so that Annette could have her way with them.[18] The first two recorded were "I'm Somebody's Somebody Now" and "I Like What You Like," and by a strange quirk they were issued not as by Annette Hanshaw but with the artist credit Four Instrumental Stars, with Annette's name added in small print (still better than the four stars, who remained anonymous). The first title opens with a demonstration of things to come. Venuti and Lang had often recorded together before, but the addition of Rollini's bass saxophone brought an extra sparkle to their music, which must have been a pleasant surprise to them and which they wanted to keep having. Rollini kicks off with a rousing break and then, in his usual way, moves to help create the great ensemble sound. Solos follow by all participants, including Vic Berton, who shows his control of the tympani with a sixteen-bar solo. Interestingly, just before Hanshaw does her vocal contribution, Rollini plays a modulation to a key that was more comfortable to her. He does the same in the second title, "I Like What You Like," of which he was co-composer.[19] The arrangement features a piano solo, which probably was not played by Rollini.[20]

The six-bar intro of "Ain't That a Grand and Glorious Feeling?" is the strangest mix of instruments and sound colors one can imagine. First the duo Venuti and Lang is heard, then Vic Berton follows with a few notes on his harpaphone, and finally Rollini with his hot fountain pen. Hanshaw then starts to sing as if to say, "this is my record," and indeed she returns after an instrumental chorus. She finishes the piece together with the quartet.

"Who-Oo? You-Oo, That's Who!" gives the impression that it was recorded as a straightforward performance by the group, without any form of arrangement, just a sequence of vocal and ensemble choruses. In the interview mentioned above, Hanshaw related that her accompanists would come to the studio and fix the arrangements there. This is an example where they kept it simple.

The final recording from this session was titled "Under the Moon."[21] Hanshaw sings in falsetto, which has a comic effect. She is probably also the person who plays a two-bar piano break. After Eddie Lang slows the tempo down (and Annette is heard almost starting too early with her next chorus), Rollini on celeste and Eddie accompany Annette on her final chorus. This ended another memorable session.[22]

On Monday 27 June, Adrian Rollini's old boss, Ed Kirkeby, had another recording date for his new OKeh group, Ted Wallace and his Orchestra. This meant a large group that had to be rehearsed; and when piano player Jack Russin arrived late at rehearsals on the Wednesday and the Sunday before the OKeh date, he was fined, as is revealed by Kirkeby's notebook. The third title recorded at this session, "Pleading," contains a thirty-two-bar piano duet of Russin and second piano player Ted(?) Black. For Rollini there was a huge contrast between this session and the previous ones. This OKeh date missed almost all jazz feeling and his only role was to accentuate the beat and not to play fantasies around it. The other three tunes were "Bless Your Little Heart," "Who-Oo? You-Oo, That's Who!," and "Love and Kisses," all straight performances with little solo work.

On 28 June, Adrian Rollini celebrated his twenty-fourth birthday. That did not stop him from recording, and on that particular day he continued the cooperation with the violin/guitar duo of Joe Venuti and Eddie Lang that had begun on the Annette Hanshaw date.

Giuseppe Joseph "Joe" Venuti was born in Philadelphia on 16 September 1903, in an Italian neighborhood. He was one of seven children of Giacomo Venuti and Rosa LaMacchia, who had migrated from Sicily. He got his first violin lessons when he entered primary school and showed great talent. He could have become a great concert violinist had he not been so attracted to jazz. He would become the most important violin player in early jazz and inspired many. His numerous recordings made him a pioneer. His sense of humor is legendary and no musician was safe from his practical jokes. Joe Venuti was one of the greatest personalities in jazz in the twenties.[23]

Eddie Lang's parents had also come from southern Italy to Philadelphia. He was born on 25 October 1902, as Salvatore Massaro, one of seven children of Domenico Massaro and Carmela Tamburo. Domenico had been a guitar maker and made a simple instrument for his son when he was not even two years old. However, Salvatore's first serious instrument was a violin. He and Joe Venuti went to the same primary school, but they became friends only in their teens. They started to work together in a small local orchestra and from then on developed a duet style that had no equal. Interestingly, their personalities were totally different. Venuti was a born leader and would speak loud; Salvatore, who adopted the name Eddie Lang around 1919, was quiet and a man of few words. However, they realized that their ideas about music were complementary and together they would come further than individually. Indeed, they remained close friends as long as both lived. Their professional careers started with different orchestras, but after a few years they got together again.

When working in Atlantic City, New Jersey, in 1926, their duet work was captured on record for the first time. The company was Columbia and the tunes were "Stringing the Blues" and "Black and Blue Bottom."[24] Then suddenly they were all over the place, being featured on recordings by the orchestras of Jean Goldkette, Roger Wolfe Kahn, and Jack Pettis and making more records under their own name. In December 1926, when Red Nichols started his series of recordings by the Five Pennies, Eddie Lang was one of them, and in March 1927 Joe Venuti joined them on one session, reuniting the duo. Their first recording date with Adrian Rollini was the above Annette Hanshaw session. The chemistry between the three Italian Americans had been obvious on that date, and just a few days later the opportunity arrived to bring it to the next level. The duo of

Venuti and Lang had had three recording dates under their own name so far. On the third Arthur Schutt had been added on piano; now, a few days after the Annette Hanshaw date, another Venuti/Lang session was planned and the good feeling of the Annette Hanshaw session was still in the air, so Rollini was added, complete with all his instruments.

The duo did not try to become popular by recording hit tunes. They were the authors of all tunes they had recorded under their own name, and the session with Rollini was to be no exception. The titles expressed little respect for animals: "Kickin' the Cat" and "Beatin' the Dog." On the first tune, Lang on guitar and Rollini on goofus play the intro. Rollini takes his hot fountain pen for a thirty-two-bar solo with Lang's accompaniment. Then Venuti joins the ensemble and during his following solo Rollini takes his bass saxophone and solos again. A well-balanced ensemble closes the recording. Venuti and Lang would have the basic ideas for such arrangements the day before the session and the following day men like Rollini and Schutt would contribute to the final form. "Beatin' the Dog" opens with an intro by Rollini, bass saxophone, and Schutt, piano. Then Venuti leads the ensemble chorus which ends with breaks by Rollini, who continues with a thirty-two-bar solo, one of his finest. Then he immediately returns to the background to accompany Joe Venuti's solo, showing his perfect fit for this kind of string-group jazz, pushing the beat and playing fills.

Actually, when Joe Venuti and Eddie Lang decided to invite a bass instrument for their recordings, they had a choice of several musicians and various instruments, including a tuba or a string bass. They were smart enough to find the best there was, Adrian Rollini and his bass saxophone. When Rollini was no longer available, they invited another musician to fill his role. A bass saxophone player of Rollini's quality could not be found, so a baritone might have to do, and at various moments they recorded with Don Murray and Jimmy Dorsey. Even Frank Trumbauer came in one day to play bassoon, an instrument he rarely played on records.

Thus a busy week ended, in which Rollini had done a Ted Wallace date in the same week that he produced monumental jazz pieces such as "After You've Gone" by the California Ramblers, "Arkansas Blues" and "Vo-Do-Do-De-O Blues" by the Varsity Eight, Red Nichols's "Mean Dog Blues," as well as the five titles with Annette Hanshaw that led to the Venuti Blue Four recordings of "Kickin' the Cat" and "Beatin' the Dog." He was at the top of his game.

Still Working for Kirkeby

Ed Kirkeby was not out of his financial and legal problems but was able to continue what he did best, and that was organizing recording sessions. So in July and August he had ten band sessions, and Rollini participated in all but one. He would also return to organizing recording sessions for other artists.[25]

In July Kirkeby recorded for Columbia, Edison, Harmony, and Plaza. The Columbia session turned out to be the last one by the Little Ramblers.[26] The previous Little Ramblers session had been a year ago and this shows in the music. The first title, "Play It Red," reminds the listener of Rollini's recordings with Red Nichols, made the month before.[27] Trumpeter Chelsea Quealey's style is directly linked to Nichols's. Rollini plays a sixteen-bar solo on goofus and two four-bar breaks on saxophone. Four takes were recorded of the next title, "Lazy Weather," but none was accepted for issue. The final title recorded by the Little Ramblers was "Swamp Blues." One of its themes is twelve bars long, thus justifying the "blues" title. In addition to solo work on goofus and bass saxophone, Rollini plays a duet with Quealey in which he demonstrates the range of his reed instrument in the upper register, playing some of his highest notes ever.

After this session, Adrian Rollini may have taken time to relax with Dixie. However, it is more likely that he needed time to work on his old idea of having a band of his own again. This dream had never left him and now was the time to make it happen. He would need a contract with a financial backer and with musicians, a location, arrangements. No small wonder that he could not make it to all of Kirkeby's sessions. He missed the next one, which was for Edison, and his replacement was tuba player Jack Albin.[28] Of course, as long as no further details are known, any other reason is possible for Rollini's absence, including the possibility that Kirkeby simply decided not to select Rollini for this session.

Rollini was back in the studio for Kirkeby's third July session in 1927. This was for Harmony and three titles were recorded and issued under the usual University Six pseudonym. Rollini brought his xylophone to the studio and used it in solos on all three: "Roam On My Little Gypsy Sweetheart," "Pastafazoola," and "Swanee Shore." The second title is memorable for Rollini's thirty-two-bar xylophone solo, one of his longest so far, but even more for the comedy vocal, probably done by two band members.[29] The arrangement for "Swanee Shore" features a sixteen-bar solo by an unidentified human whistler. This reminds the listener of "After You've Gone," recorded the previous month by the same personnel and with a whistle solo by the same musician. The whistler on "Swanee Shore" is accompanied by Rollini's bass saxophone, so it cannot be him.

The same mysterious whistler returns on one take from the California Ramblers' final July session. This date only produced undiluted jazz, so it is questionable if Ed Kirkeby had anything to do with it other than giving the band its name. The musicians were the same as for the last Harmony session, the company was Plaza, and the choice of the three titles was left to the band, who picked "Beale Street Blues," "Delirium," and "Farewell Blues." Rollini had recorded a nice version of W. C. Handy's "Beale Street Blues" the year before for Harmony, but that recording was restrained, its arrangement tame, and the musicians were paid to hold back in order to satisfy Kirkeby. However, now no longer: this was an occasion for an out-and-out jazz session. The arrangement features hot playing throughout and during its first part, Rollini plays a two-bar break, which ends in a glissando that suggested that it would end in the wrong key, but it did not. "Delirium" was a composition by piano player Arthur Schutt and quite popular among New York musicians at the time and thus often recorded. The tune did not have a pleasing melody. Its attraction rather was that it had a different sound, a new sound to the listener's ears. Composer Schutt participated in most recordings of his tune, but the twelve-bar piano solo in this version by the California Ramblers is played by Jack Russin. "Farewell Blues," a composition stemming from the New Orleans Rhythm Kings, has a surprise. As is often the case with these Plaza recordings, more than one take survives. However, it is uncommon that between takes an arrangement is changed, and such is the case here. Take 1 features a sixteen-bar solo by a human whistler, which ends in a quote from "Chopin's Marche Funèbre"; take 2 has a kazoo solo, ending in the same quote.[30]

Rollini's agenda would again be crowded in August. The first recording session was organized by Ed Kirkeby, with male singer Jay C. Flippen (1899–1971). Flippen had made his first record for Columbia in 1924. In 1926 he had his first of several bookings at the Palace in New York, America's major vaudeville house, and for recordings he then moved to Pathé. Like they had done for Cliff Edwards and Annette Hanshaw, Pathé chose a jazz band for his accompaniment, and the combination was called Jay C. Flippen and His Gang. The Gang's personnel was taken from bands such as Harry Reser's and Red Nichols's. But now that Kirkeby managed this Flippen session, he selected musicians that he had regularly employed for his recordings. So this time Flippen's Gang consisted of Adrian Rollini, plus Chelsea Quealey, Bobby Davis, Jack Russin, and Tommy Felline. With this group four titles were recorded: "Clementine," "And Furthermore," "You Don't Like It Not Much," and "I Ain't Got Nobody." The cooperation between singer and band worked well and the result was a swinging sound. Flippen, a vaudeville artist, had a talent for handling a text and takes the major share of each performance, but the band gets its moments, too. On "You Don't Like It Not Much," Flippen is about to start to sing another chorus, when he says: "Oh, boys, you play it and I listen" after which we hear Davis in a rare clarinet solo. On "I Ain't Got Nobody," the band starts its chorus with a group vocal, is then interrupted by Flippen, who says "Oh, play it, boys, play it!" after which an instrumental chorus follows, as well as an eight-bar solo by Rollini. The records sold well and were issued in Europe, too.[31]

The following week, Kirkeby brought the Goofus Five back to the OKeh studio. Lately such sessions had resulted in three titles. For this new occasion the choice was "Clementine," "Nothin' Does-Does Like It Used to Do-Do-Do," and

"I Left My Sugar Standing in the Rain." Beth Challis did the vocals.[32] Although the band was in magnificent form, only the first two titles were successfully recorded. However, Kirkeby had another studio session later that same week with a vocal group called the Palm Beach Boys, and he squeezed the third Goofus Five title in on that date.[33] The three titles stand out in the recorded legacy of the Goofus Five. All musicians have great individual contributions and take solos. On "Clementine" Rollini solos on goofus and bass saxophone, and when Challis sings about Clementine's castanet playing, drummer Herb Weil produces a castanet sound on a rim of his drum set. "Nothin' Does-Does Like It Used to Do-Do-Do" opens with the same intro as was used on "I Ain't Got Nobody," recorded the week before with Jay C. Flippen (and soon to be used again). Also heard again is a solo by a whistler, probably drummer Herb Weil. Rollini's solo contribution consists of a chase chorus on goofus with clarinet player Bobby Davis, and a two-bar break on his saxophone. However, his finest work came with the third title, "I Left My Sugar Standing in the Rain." Uncharacteristically, he plays in a slap-tongue style while accompanying Bobby Davis's alto solo. After Challis's vocal, he returns with a magnificent solo, one of his finest ever. He is totally in control of his instrument and seems to say, "This is my record."

After they had recorded one tune for OKeh in the morning, the same group got together again in the Plaza studio in the afternoon, where they had recorded three jazz standards two weeks earlier. The idea was to add three more titles in the same vein, and the choice was "Someday Sweetheart," "Jelly Roll Blues," and "I Ain't Got Nobody." Kirkeby, who had apparently finished the job at OKeh, sang on the first and last titles, those that had a clear melody. He most certainly was no jazz singer, not even a vaudevillian, and just recited the lyrics. However, the musicians used their opportunities to play great jazz around his vocals and in particular had their way with "Jelly Roll Blues." The California Ramblers had their own fine, intricate arrangement for this jazz standard, with solo spots for all. Their recording only occasionally reminds one of the classical version by its composer Jelly Roll Morton.

Jazz collectors were and still are amazed at the consistent output of so many masterpieces by Adrian Rollini and his fellow musicians during the summer of 1927. The week after the previous Plaza session was no exception. This was the week of the next Red Nichols session. It brought the largest Nichols band so far to the studio and, after a full day of hard work, would result in four great jazz titles.[34]

Compared to the previous edition of his Five Pennies, Nichols brought several new players to the studio. The session took place in what Brunswick called its Room #1 and was spread over the morning and afternoon.[35] For the morning session Nichols brought ten musicians, more than he had done before.[36] In addition to some original Pennies (Nichols, Miff Mole, Adrian Rollini, and Vic

Brunswick advertisement for a Red Nichols record Rollini appears on. (courtesy Mark Berresford)

Berton), two more trumpet players arrived (Leo McConville and Manny Klein), two more reed players (Fud Livingston, tenor saxophone, and Pee Wee Russell, clarinet), piano (Lennie Hayton), and guitar (Dick McDonough). A total of ten musicians required well-prepared arrangements.[37] Newcomer Livingston provided the arrangements for the two tunes to be recorded in the morning, "Riverboat Shuffle" and "Eccentric." "Riverboat Shuffle" offers a first chance to hear Pee Wee Russell (1906–1969). He had been a member of Frank Trumbauer's band with Bix Beiderbecke, which worked in St. Louis in 1925, and Russell continued working with this fabulous duo until mid-1926. When Red Nichols needed new men for his Five Pennies, he heard of Pee Wee Russell. The Trumbauer band had become a legend among musicians and Russell's role was known to Nichols, so he sent him a wire. Russell arrived in New York on 14 August 1927, the day before this Brunswick session. At his hotel, he received a note, which asked him to come directly to a particular speakeasy. There he found Nichols, Mole, Berton, and Lang. He recalled: "I got panicky again. They told me there would be a recording date at Brunswick the next morning at nine, and don't be late. I got there at 8:15. The place was empty except for a handyman. Mole arrived first. He said: 'You look peaked, kid' and opened his trombone case and took out a quart. Everybody had quarts."[38]

Pee Wee Russell was trying to find a different sound from his clarinet, which he eventually would and on which he would build a reputation and a following. More importantly, he experimented with uncommon, futuristic harmonies. However, in these recordings he plays in a style that is still in line with the fluent reed playing of the territory bands that he had worked in.

Both Russell and another newcomer, piano player Lennie Hayton, can be heard in solos on "Eccentric." Livingston's arrangement features choruses for Russell, Rollini, and an amazing thirty-two-bar chorus for the three trumpets.

Piano player Leonard George "Lennie" Hayton (1908–1971) had been a member of the Little Ramblers with Spencer Clark. Before he got on records with Red Nichols and other New York jazzmen, he worked with Cass Hagan and later with Paul Whiteman. During the thirties he would be Bing Crosby's musical director and still later he worked for MGM. He married singer Lena Horne. Hayton was the arranger for the third title recorded that day, the first title of the afternoon session, "Ida! Sweet as Apple Cider," which opens with a long straight chorus by Rollini.

Reed player Fud Livingston (1906–1957) had the exceptional talent to have a great career, but it never happened, mainly due to his alcohol habit. He was lucky enough to join Ben Pollack's band in Chicago in 1924, and by then was writing arrangements for the bands of Roger Wolfe Kahn and Jean Goldkette. In 1927 he was a member of a circle of advanced New York jazz musicians and wrote several important arrangements, such as the one for "Feelin' No Pain," his own composition.³⁹ It features Rollini in a major way: first in twenty-four solo bars on bass saxophone and then in a thirty-two-bar duet with Miff Mole. However, the first solo spot was for Pee Wee Russell, who had not forgotten his work with Bix. When in later years the record was played for him, he said: "They were a smart group in some ways, but if it hadn't been for Bix they would probably have never happened."⁴⁰ Red Nichols's recording of "Ida! Sweet as Apple Cider" became a bestseller, reportedly selling over a million copies.⁴¹

The day following the long session organized by Nichols, Rollini was working for Ed Kirkeby once again. This meant less jazz and more straight dance music. Four titles were recorded at Pathé by the usual California Ramblers personnel, with the addition of Bob Fallon on trombone and vocalist Harold Sandeman, who on the record labels was called "Banjo Buddy." Three titles have been heard by the author, of which "Marvelous," a hit of the day, is the finest. Soloists are Adrian Rollini and Jack Russin, who succeed in bringing life to the music.

However, by now Rollini's thoughts centered more on forming his own band than on making records. He had found a location and the opening was about a month away. The location he had in mind was to be called the Club New Yorker, at 1600 Broadway at the corner of 48th Street. It had an interesting history. On its first floor Paul Whiteman had had his unsuccessful Paul Whiteman Club just a few months earlier and before that it was called the Cinderella Ballroom, where Gene Fosdick worked with his Hoosiers in 1923 and Bix Beiderbecke with the Wolverines in 1924.⁴²

The last few days of that August month were filled with memorable recording sessions. Jean Goldkette's orchestra, commonly called the Victor Orchestra, had fulfilled several engagements in and around New York since January and had had a recording contract with Victor since 1924. The newly formed booking agency of Tommy Rockwell and Francis "Cork" O'Keefe got him a contract in Atlantic City for one month. This would allow Goldkette to continue making records for Victor and a contingent from the band would also do so. After that, Rockwell-O'Keefe planned to have the band in New York's famous Roseland Ballroom and then aimed at getting it into the Club New Yorker, the same new location that Rollini had in mind.

At this time Jean Goldkette was having financial problems. The Victor Orchestra, which had resided in the Graystone Ballroom in Detroit for years, had gone on tour because the Graystone could no longer financially support it.⁴³ However, the tour did not bring sufficient income to compensate for Goldkette's losses. A rumor started in the band that it might be dissolved. On the other hand, there also was a rumor in the New York musical scene that Adrian Rollini was trying to put a band together. Rollini even visited Jean Goldkette's band in Atlantic City in the first week after the opening. With the possible end of the Goldkette band in mind, he must have made a pick list of men that he wanted in his band. No doubt he discussed this with those men, but he was also invited by Frank Trumbauer to record with members of the Goldkette band.

Rollini had more on his "wants list" than several Goldkette men. High on that list was trumpet player Sylvester Ahola, who had worked with the California Ramblers earlier that year. Ahola was not only an excellent reader but also could produce a hot solo when this was asked for. Of him, Spiegle Wilcox, another California Ramblers alumnus said: "I never met Ahola, but he must have been the best, the very best, to hold down the job with Rollini, because Rollini would only have the best."[44] Rollini called Ahola on 23 August and they met the next day at what was to be the Club New Yorker. Ahola was working with Peter Van Steeden's band and needed time for his decision.

So several decisions were pending at this moment in time. Would Jean Goldkette's band really break up? And where would his musicians go? Who would get the contract for the Club New Yorker?

Paul Whiteman also went to Atlantic City to show his interest in several of Goldkette's men, including Bix, Tram, and Bill Challis, who all hesitated. It is said that Bix brought up the subject of the Club New Yorker and who might land the job, Goldkette or Rollini. Whiteman, who had only recently run a club there himself, reacted negatively and said that it had poor backing and that no band would stay there for long.[45]

Amidst all this uncertainty, recording activity only increased. On the very day that Rollini talked to Ahola, a large section of the Goldkette band went to the Edison studio and recorded two tunes under the name of piano player Joe Herlihy. The group included Tram but not Bix, who was replaced.[46] Tunes were "Bye-Bye," "Pretty Baby," and "Gold Digger Stomp," which remained unissued. The next day was for Frank Trumbauer, who earlier that year had recorded for OKeh with a small group including Bix. Tram's first session had produced the masterpiece "Singing the Blues," and Tommy Rockwell, who not only ran the new booking agency but also held a major position at OKeh, thought that he could sell more by the same group. In August the Goldkette band worked in Atlantic City, which gave Tram another opportunity to make records, so on 25 August he had a session planned. Although the Goldkette band had one of the finest string bass players in its personnel with Steve Brown, Trumbauer had not used a bass instrument on his first OKeh-sessions. However, by now he had heard Adrian Rollini, who could provide a bass line but was also a superb soloist.[47] On this date, Tram led a band that consisted of all-Goldkette personnel, with the addition of Adrian Rollini. The Goldkette men were Bix Beiderbecke, cornet; Bill Rank, trombone; Don Murray, clarinet and baritone saxophone; Doc Ryker, alto saxophone; Itzy Riskin, piano; Eddie Lang, guitar; and Chauncey Morehouse, drums.[48] This team of great musicians recorded three titles: "Three Blind Mice," "Blue River," and "There's a Cradle in Caroline." They were the first Trumbauer OKeh titles with a bass instrument and Rollini's first recordings with Bix and Tram. The most memorable of the three titles is "Three Blind Mice," a tune by Chauncey Morehouse, arranged by Tram and Goldkette's main arranger Bill Challis. After Bix and Lang solo, Rollini plays a sixteen-bar solo, of which arranger Challis said that it was one of the best he had ever heard him do. "Blue River" also benefited from a Challis arrangement, yet does not have the quality of "Three Blind Mice."

However much Rollini may have enjoyed the Trumbauer session, the following day he was in the Edison studio again to record with the California Ramblers. The standard personnel had been slightly changed. Nick Casti had been added on trumpet, Eddie Lappe took the often-changed trombone position, and Pete Pumiglio joined Sam Ruby and Bobby Davis on reeds. Two tunes were recorded, "At Dawning" and "You Don't Like It Not Much." The first title was not issued and Rollini's solo sounds uninspired.[49] "You Don't Like It Not Much" was much better; its arrangement nicely fills the four minutes of the Edison record, with solo space for Quealey, a duet between a human whistler (Weil?) and a clarinet player (Pumiglio?), then Russin, a chase chorus between Quealey and Rollini, and finally for Davis. It would be Rollini's last recording with the California Ramblers for a long time.

In the meantime, Red Nichols still had the successful recordings with Pee Wee Russell, Fud Livingston, and Adrian Rollini fresh in his mind, and thus they were invited to participate in his next session. For Rollini it meant back to the OKeh studio, now to record under the name and nominal leadership of Miff Mole. Red wanted to record more of Livingston's material and in addition to "Feeling No Pain," the group recorded Fud's "Imagination." The numerous key changes in this recording have been pointed out; however, they are not distracting and help creating a happy feeling, "no pain."[50] Pee Wee Russell is heard in a short solo on tenor saxophone. Fud Livingston's presence is felt on the strengths of the recorded material, but he does not solo.

The next day formed some kind of a milestone, though it may have gone unnoticed at the time: it marked Adrian Rollini's final recording in a long series of studio sessions organized by Ed Kirkeby, which had started five years before. Present were Quealey, Davis, Ruby, Russin, Felline, and Weil, Rollini's colleagues from many Kirkeby sessions. The tunes were "Who's That Knocking at My Door?," "Oh Doris! Where Do You Live?," and finally "Zulu Wail." Rollini took solos on the bass saxophone on all three titles, a symbolic farewell.

There is still more to Adrian Rollini's freelance work from this period. The following story is an example. It concerns a recording date organized by Ed Kirkeby. On this occasion Rollini met Merrill Kaye, who remembered that he was one of ten violin players on the date. Kaye, who used to call himself Merrill

Kaye at the time, started as a violin player and then became a bass player too, playing bass fiddle, tuba, and bass saxophone.[51] The story was told to Tom Faber by Kaye:

> I met Adrian through Ed Kirkeby of the old California Ramblers. We were on a recording date, I played the violin. . . . this band for this purpose had to add violins, I really don't understand why because the California Ramblers, with their arrangements, we would not need it but they wanted something more beautifying, sort of a concert orchestra. [Adrian and I] were talking, I told Adrian [that] I played wooden bass and [that] I played a little bass sax. He says, "Play something [on your bass sax] for me." I played the scale and so forth, and he said, "Why don't you hold your lower jaw a little bit lowered so you can grab on to the reed. And you know it's a heavy reed, you may get that cane effect in there, would give it a reedy tone. . . . You want more of a bass tone."
>
> To be very explicit. The mouth, I used to grab the whole jaw onto the mouthpiece instead of lowering my lower jaw and my upper lip a little looser. So the vibration going into the reed wouldn't catch the reedy sound and he would say "When you get to the low notes, just relax and it will flow right out. It will surprise your ears what you're going to hear." He says, "Sit down and I'll show you." He played it and he showed me just what he meant by the lower jaw. "Now you sit down and you do the same thing." I did it the first time. He says, "A little lower." I said, "Well, it's hard for me to feel the intonation coming out of the horn because I'm trying to get the bass part and I don't hear." He said, "Try it again." Which I did. Tried again and again. I did it for about 25 times and before you know, it just blended in. He said, "That's what I want! Just remember!." And I practiced that. Well, then we had to go back into our recording session. Intermission was *over*.

Chapter 10

A Band of His Own

Now, August 1927, things were falling into place, one by one. Just before the Miff Mole OKeh date, Rollini had won the contract for the Club New Yorker, and he immediately checked with Bix, Tram, Bill Rank, and Chauncey Morehouse, who all accepted.¹ Bill Challis was asked to play third alto, but preferred to join Paul Whiteman as a staff arranger.

Before the new band would have its first rehearsal, Rollini would have another two recording sessions. The first one was with Red Nichols, again under Miff Mole's name and with the same personnel used. The titles were "My Gal Sal," "Honolulu Blues," and "The New Twister," and Rollini solos on all three titles.

A week later Adrian was contracted to record with Annette Hanshaw. Just like the previous session with Rollini, her other accompanists were Venuti, Lang, and Berton. However, Rollini only made the second half of the session and missed the first title "It Was Only a Sun Shower," probably due to his extra activities. Annette and her three musicians nevertheless made a memorable, relaxed recording of the tune. However, when it was time to do "Who's That Knocking At My Door?" the tempo went up and the little band had more to do. Rollini compensates for his earlier absence by playing several breaks on his saxophone and a long goofus solo. Trumpeter Sylvester Ahola was present during this session and told Rollini that he accepted his invitation and would join the Club New Yorker band. The duo of Eddie Lang and Joe Venuti also joined the new band, as did piano player Frank Signorelli and former California Rambler Bobby Davis. Thus Rollini had completed his band. Seven (*) of the eleven members had worked for Jean Goldkette. This included trombone player Bill Rank, who was not Adrian's first choice. His brother Art recalled that Adrian preferred Miff Mole as a trombone player to Bill Rank and did not appreciate whatever talent Rank had.² A stronger opinion on Bill Rank was given by Adrian to Andre Eschauzier, a Dutch jazz collector and jazz musician, who was his host in 1929: "Do you know what 'rank' means? Rank means rotten! Bill Rank is rotten!"³

Adrian Rollini—leader, bass saxophone, chimes[4]
Sylvester Ahola—trumpet
Bix Beiderbecke*—trumpet
Bill Rank*—trombone
Frank Trumbauer*—C-melody saxophone
Bobby Davis—alto saxophone
Don Murray*—clarinet
Joe Venuti*—violin, fronting the band
Frank Signorelli—piano
Eddie Lang*—guitar
Chauncey Morehouse*—drums

According to Ahola's diary, Rollini had negotiated a weekly sum of $1,750 for his band.[5] Since this was for eleven persons, it seems higher than what Goldkette paid his band ($1,923 for sixteen persons), but it was far less than the $6,400 weekly that Whiteman had been guaranteed by the club owners.[6] Meanwhile, Goldkette had tried everything in his power to keep his band going, but he had to give up and would start another Victor band.

Rollini's band got together for its first rehearsal on the day after Annette Hanshaw's session.[7] For Goldkette's men, this meant working at the Roseland in the evening and rehearsing with Rollini at the Club New Yorker during the day. On this day, 9 September, Ahola, or Hooley as he was commonly called, met Bix for the first time in his life. In 1963 he wrote to Phil Evans about this event:

> The following is not in [my] diary: Bix . . . shook hands with me and said "I'm only a musical degenerate" (smiling). He was embarrassed by his [limited] reading ability. He was modest and unassuming. Not a trace of egotism. Later he confided to me he wished he could play and read as well I could.[8] Later Ahola stated: We used some of Bill Challis' arrangements from the Goldkette library. I had to sight read them, while most of the others had lived with those arrangements.[9]

The rehearsals continued on the three days starting 12 September, but on the morning of the third day, Rollini, Venuti, and Lang managed to include a recording session in their busy schedule. It was at OKeh, a follow-up to their successful June session, with piano player Rube Bloom instead of Arthur Schutt. Like that earlier session, it went under the flag of Joe Venuti's Blue Four and no other names were mentioned on the OKeh labels.[10] Venuti and Lang signed for ownership of the tunes, "Cheese and Crackers" and "A Mug of Ale." The arrangements sounded perfectly balanced for all four instruments and they were probably finalized in the studio. From its opening onward, the first title swings along

The New Yorkers, directed by Adrian Rollini. From left: Sylvester Ahola, Eddie Lang, Bill Rank, Chauncey Morehouse, Bix Beiderbecke, Adrian Rollini, Frank Trumbauer, Bobby Davis, Don Murray, Joe Venuti, Frank Signorelli.

smoothly. Rollini plays a high-register solo on his sax and a break on his goofus. "A Mug of Ale" is at least as good. There is solo space for all of the Blue Four and Rollini surpasses himself with two excellent solos, first thirty-two bars on the bass saxophone, then sixteen bars on goofus. The coda is a jewel of understanding between the musicians.[11]

Rehearsals were interrupted on Thursday 15 September, when the Goldkette band would record for the last time with its stellar personnel. And they were in for a masterpiece. Seven of Rollini's band were involved. The exceptions were Rollini himself, plus Ahola, Davis and Signorelli. The tunes recorded on this farewell party were "Blue River" and "Clementine," the latter rightfully being the most famous of all recordings by this band.

On the following day, Rollini led again, which meant more rehearsing. He took his band to the Apeda studio, New York's best-known studio for photographs of musicians. Several years later, showing the resulting photograph to a music journalist, Rollini said: "See that baton? Well, I didn't have one, so for the picture, I posed with a clothes hanger!" Joe Venuti said that he would front the band during performances, since the public would normally accept the violinist as director.¹² On the day of the photograph, the band tested broadcasting from its new club.¹³ And that was not all. The Joe Herlihy session of a few weeks earlier had not produced satisfactory results, and most of Goldkette's band had to show up again. This time it worked and two titles were issued, "Bye-Bye, Pretty Baby" and "Rolling Around in the Roses."¹⁴

The following weekend there were no rehearsals, but both days would become historical milestones. On Saturday three band members, Tram, Bix, and Lang, did a memorable recording session at OKeh. With Bix at the piano, and Tram and Lang in their normal roles, they recorded "Wringin' and Twistin'," a tune by Trumbauer and Fats Waller.¹⁵ And the following Sunday was the day of the final performance of Jean Goldkette's Victor band at the Roseland Ballroom. It ended in a riot and the management had to call in the police to let the band off the bandstand and leave the hall.

The Club New Yorker

The Club New Yorker was to open on Thursday 22 September, and that last week Rollini intensified the rehearsals. Sylvester Ahola would finish working with Peter Van Steeden's band at the Half Moon Hotel that week, but still had to fill in a few nights. On Monday 19 September Rollini telephoned him for a rehearsal and it filled the day till 5:00 p.m. The next days the band rehearsed from 11:00 a.m. till 5:00 p.m., but on Wednesday, the day before the opening, Rollini thought that even this was not sufficient. Ahola had to be back with Van Steeden for the evening, but Rollini asked him to return to the club for a last rehearsal from midnight till 5:00 a.m. on the day of the opening.

Newspaper publicity had been limited. *Variety* of 31 August had a small item which mentioned the opening date of Thursday 22 September. It also mentioned the band and its leader, Adrian Rollini, calling them "a 5-in-1 band, composed of star recording instrumentalists, who, in different combinations, comprise five recording orchestras." However, most newspapers announced it on the day itself:

> The latest of Broadway night clubs, the New Yorker, will open tonight at 11 at Broadway and 48th St. in the rendezvous formerly known as Paul Whiteman. The decoration and arrangement will reflect the romance and color of Spain's beautiful patios. Frank Fay, "the Aristocratic Vagabond," will be the featured entertainer. Robert M. Langdon is owner and Jack Figel is general manager.¹⁶

A daily night club guide in a newspaper called it "Last year's Whiteman's Club smaller and smarter."¹⁷ The club had been reduced in size compared to the days when it was Whiteman's Club and could now hold up to a thousand guests.¹⁸

Advertisement for Club New Yorker.

Guiding principle for the interior decoration was the choice of a Spanish patio. In an advertisement for the opening, a De Luxe Dinner from 5:30 p.m. was offered at a price of $2.50 "No Cover Charge."

Robert Langdon and Jack Figel were the people with whom Rollini had had to negotiate. Both had a history at the club. Langdon had been one of the owners of the Paul Whiteman Club. Whiteman had sold his share to his co-owners when the club folded. Langdon then bought the others out, so by the time Rollini opened, he was listed as the sole owner. Figel probably had an even longer history with the club. Four years earlier, in 1923, it had opened as the Cinderella Dancing and an advertisement mentioned that it was under Figel's personal direction. Another person Rollini had to deal with was actress Bea Palmer. She was scheduled to work at the place and may have been the person who suggested to Langdon to invest again in the club. All had to be convinced that an all-star band at the Club New Yorker was a wise investment.[19] Palmer decided to leave New York and go to Chicago.

Frank Fay (1891–1961) was an experienced vaudevillian and had great popularity.[20] In the months before the Club New Yorker opened, he worked around New York, and after it closed he easily found new jobs in the city's theaters, such as Shubert's.[21]

Behind the scenes there was another party with a financial interest: the Waterman family, owners of the well-known fountain pen company. Their twenty-year-old son Neil Waterman had become a close friend of Adrian, and his family invested in Adrian's venture.[22]

The opening night could easily have ended in disaster. In an interview Ahola talked about the last day before the opening.[23] He was married and lived on Coney Island. After that day's rehearsals, he decided not to take the long ride home on the subway, but to have dinner with Bill Rank, who was single and stayed at a hotel. After dinner it was still well before opening time, but Ahola went back to the club. Ahola was early and the personnel was still making preparations when at about 10:00 p.m. suddenly a fire broke out in the papier maché decorations, which were not fireproof in those days. The personnel managed to put the fire out in time, by quickly beating it with towels. This happened before the Fire Department was called, who would have stopped the proceedings.

The rehearsals had been to build a band book, which, on the opening day, consisted of several charts from the Goldkette band, plus a few adapted stock arrangements and some material for the floor show. One of the Goldkette tunes was "Clementine" and at the club Bix played his solo into a four- or five-foot-long horn, which stood on the floor.[24] Of course most of the band members were familiar with the Goldkette material and for the others it was no problem to sight read (Ahola and probably Davis, Signorelli, and Rollini, too). In an interview Ahola said that Rollini's band featured a jazz group in which he (Ahola) did not participate. It would perform one or two sets each evening and did not use full arrangements, but outlines only, which allowed for an abundance of solos. "It was largely the Goldkette sound as it sounded in the Roseland. I feel the jazz was over people's heads."[25]

Joe Venuti had a reputation as a special character and his working in Rollini's band offered him new opportunities, one of which led to a clash with Bix. Venuti had dark brown eyes and Ahola remembered how "he would look right through you, as though he was mad at you, but he didn't mean that, you see. One night Venuti looked at Bix, and Bix said 'I can't play when you look at me like that.'" He told Joe not to look at him while he was taking a solo. Ahola thought that Venuti then really was mad at Bix.[26]

On the opening night the band played till 5:00 a.m. the next morning, for which it had a special permit. Ahola wrote in his diary that it was "going sad."[27] So intensive rehearsing did not yet have the desired result. However, the star personnel attracted much attention from colleagues and on the first three nights, visitors were orchestra leaders Jacques Renard and Paul Specht and members of Art Landry's orchestra.[28] Public interest remained low, in particular the dinner show. So that show was soon to be dropped. Ahola had his worries about the band's payments, but at the end of the first week he was satisfied when he got paid for the three days of work at the club.

Recording Continues

While the Club New Yorker struggled for continuity, recording activity continued as before. The late hours at the club allowed recording during the day. Within the two weeks after the opening, Bix was involved in four sessions, three for OKeh and one for Harmony. Rollini participated in the three OKeh sessions. The first was led by Trumbauer and produced three titles: "Humpty Dumpty," "Krazy Kat," and "Baltimore." The second OKeh session was again under Trumbauer's leadership and resulted in two more titles: "Just an Hour of Love" and "I'm Wonderin' Who." "Humpty Dumpty" was composed and arranged by Fud Livingston and was far from easy on ears that were used to traditional dance music.[29] Such compositions caused discussions among musicians and public. Some listeners did not appreciate its ingenious structure and surprising harmonic elements; others regarded this music as advanced jazz music and just the right thing. The same was true for "Krazy Kat," which was composed by Chauncey Morehouse and Frank Trumbauer. Today, in hindsight, they do sound totally different from contemporary popular dance music, even from hot dance music, but perfectly fitting in the musical idiom of the best New York jazz musicians at the time and for a long time after. In his liner notes to a compact disc, Brad Kay, a present-day jazz collector, wrote of "Humpty Dumpty" and similar Livingston compositions: "The miracle is that none of this modernistic, revolutionary stuff sounds the least bit jarring and out of place."[30] Rollini did not solo on either title, but he did on the last one of the first session, the popular tune "Baltimore." Its arrangement allowed for more easygoing jazz and for numerous solos and breaks.

The second OKeh session took place two days later. "Just an Hour of Love" and "I'm Wondering Who," both from the musical *Burlesque*, had vocals by Irving Kaufman.[31] The arrangements were not as futuristic as at the previous session. They presented a more commercial approach and might be examples of how the band played for dancers. To distinguish them further from the previous Trumbauer recordings, they were issued as by Benny Meroff, who had once recorded for this label. On the evening of this day, Friday 30 September, Roger Wolfe Kahn and Nat Shilkret came to the club, and although the recording at OKeh had gone well, the evening performance did not, as Ahola noted in his diary. Shilkret was an official of the Victor company and of course he did not just come for pleasure, but rather with the idea of a potentially new Victor orchestra. Thus Rollini may have missed an important business opportunity.

On the day between the two OKeh sessions, Rollini planned another rehearsal. More than half of his band (Bix, Rank, Murray, Tram, Davis, Signorelli, and Venuti) had to combine it with an additional recording session. The session was organized by Sam Lanin and was for Harmony, one of the last labels to stick to the old acoustic recording method. Harmony used the name Broadway Bellhops for this studio combination. The tunes were two popular songs, "There Ain't No Land Like Dixieland" and "There's a Cradle in Caroline."[32]

The Club New Yorker had been in operation now for one full week, and Rollini's band had done well in terms of recordings but poorly in public.[33] The second week would be more extreme, although there were a few memorable moments.

Ahola noted the visit of Phil Wall, his friend and former colleague from Paul Specht's band on Monday; and two days later there was another recording session at OKeh, with a difference. Each evening at the Club New Yorker a small contingent from the full band would give a short performance. Participants remembered by Sylvester Ahola were Bix Beiderbecke and Adrian Rollini, plus Don Murray and probably Bill Rank. This group would "take numbers without any music at all. 'Sensation Rag,' 'Riverboat Shuffle,' and those things."[34] Inspired by this small group, OKeh's recording manager Tommy Rockwell decided that he wanted to get them on record. Since the previous February, Bix Beiderbecke had been recording for OKeh in groups that were led by Frank Trumbauer, but this time it was to be with a small jazz band led by himself and with the classic frontline of cornet/trombone/clarinet. It would go under Bix's name and be called his "Gang." The group consisted of Bix, Rank, Murray, Rollini, Signorelli, and Morehouse only. No second trumpet, no saxophone, no bass other than Rollini's bass saxophone, no violin, and no guitar or banjo. Small jazz bands had been popular in the first half of the twenties, but by 1927 they were regarded as old-fashioned by a part of the public. To underpin the link with jazz beginnings even more, tunes were chosen that had been recorded by the Original Dixieland Jazz Band as far back as ten years before: "At the Jazz Band Ball," "Royal Garden Blues," and "Jazz Me Blues."[35] No effort was done to include any futuristic elements in the arrangements.[36] Bix's fresh and uninhibited blowing is reflected by the exuberance of his colleagues' work. The result was a set of recordings that are unequalled in the history of recorded jazz, and this date stands out as a milestone in the life of all Gang members. OKeh did not immediately understand what to do with them. Would they not be too hot for their catalog of dance music? Indeed, it coupled "At the Jazz Band Ball" and "Jazz Me Blues" and issued it in the popular series, but it kept "Royal Garden Blues" in store.

More than anything else, the recordings by Bix Beiderbecke and his Gang brought international fame to its members. Eventually, this would more than outweigh the short-term poor results at the Club New Yorker.[37]

Winning the War, While Losing the Battle

It was becoming clear, that business would not become any better and so the Club New Yorker management decided to drop the dinner show. Rollini had to find more work and succeeded. From Saturday 8 October, Rollini's band with Frank Fay doubled in a show at the Mark Strand Theatre at Broadway and 47th Street. The program said:

> The Aristocratic Vagabond
> FRANK FAY
> presenting for the first time on stage
> "Midnight at the New Yorker"
> with original
> New Yorker Orchestra
> Patsy Kelly
> Lew Mann
> Olive McClure
> Arthur Franklin
> and Frank Fay (himself)
> Direct from the Club New Yorker
> (Kramer Miniature Grand Piano used by New Yorkers) [38]

The piano (not a celeste) was played by Bix.

On the two days before the opening, Rollini rehearsed his band. In the opening number, the boys gave a hot accompaniment to Frank Fay. Later in the show, they played three instrumental numbers without Fay.[39] The Strand was a movie theater and Rollini's band played before the picture started. A movie magazine gave it a positive review, but also commented that a comedy number by the band had been too long and so was boring.[40]

Discontinuing the dinner show at the Club New Yorker was the beginning of the end. Ahola's diary is illustrative of what happened: "Sunday 9 October: No business tonight—Monday 10 October: Business was very sad." On Thursday 13 October, Adrian had to tell his boys that the club would close on Saturday 15 October. Ahola wondered if he would get his money and it is not known if he did. The management at The Strand also thought it wiser not to continue with the band, so that ended, too.[41] However, Adrian did not give up and agreed with the band to give him a week to find work again. In the meantime, Ahola accepted another recording date with his former band leader Peter Van Steeden.[42]

Again Rollini succeeded in getting a new contract and on the day the Club New Yorker closed, the entertainment magazine *Variety* reported that Rollini's musicians were hired by comedian Jack Benny, who worked at the Audubon Theater on 14th Street.[43] They would do an act with Benny, whereby the show would open with Venuti directing the band; then Jack would come on stage and take the baton from Joe; the result would be a band that seemed in total confusion.[44] Jack would give the baton back to Joe, take his violin and ask the band to accompany him on some recent popular songs, but he would be playing off-key throughout so that the band could not follow him. The thing would end with the whole audience and the band bursting into laughter.[45] Jack would do this act for years to come, but for Rollini's band it was of short duration and on 26 October *Variety* reported that the job with Benny was over.[46]

However, the boys hardly had time to be sad, because studio work kept them very busy. First of all, there was a Pathé date that was issued under the name of Willard Robison, who may have organized the session, under the pseudonym of Chicago Loopers. The date of this session is uncertain, but it was around the closing date at the Club New Yorker. Rollini, who may have been too busy finding work, did not participate, but for the next recording date he was present. This was a combination of a follow-up on the first OKeh session under Bix's name and of a Trumbauer session. The personnel of Bix's Gang was six pieces as before. In addition to Bix and Adrian were Bill Rank, trombone; Don Murray, clarinet; Frank Signorelli, piano; and Chauncey Morehouse, drums. The tunes were "Goose Pimples," "Sorry," and, recorded the same day but after the Trumbauer session, "Since My Best Gal Turned Me Down." The spirit of the Gang session of three weeks earlier resurfaced. Again each of the titles marks a milestone in recorded jazz. One of the high spots is the clarinet solo with which Don Murray opens "Sorry," Howdy Quicksell's tune and arrangement. Rollini's presence colors the music from start to finish and he solos on the last title recorded that day, "Since My Best Gal Turned Me Down." It was pointed out that the idea of temporarily halving the tempo during this tune was brought by Bix from Bill Challis's arrangement for the Goldkette band and that the long glissando at its start came via Rollini from "Tiger Rag" by the University Six.[47] "Goose Pimples" and "Royal Garden Blues," from the first Gang session, were tunes by black composers.[48] This may have led OKeh to couple these two titles and issue the coupling in its race series, as by the New Orleans Lucky Seven, which suggested a black band from New Orleans. Bix told his friend Esten Spurrier about this session, the session where he recorded "Sorry": "I never felt better on a recording date."[49]

Bix's remark certainly counted as well for the two titles that the group recorded under Trumbauer's name, "Cryin' All Day" and "A Good Man Is Hard to Find." Four musicians were added to the six of the Gang. In addition to Trumbauer were Pee Wee Russell on clarinet and tenor sax and the duo of Eddie Lang and Joe Venuti. "Cryin' All Day" is a composition by Trumbauer and Morehouse, who were inspired by the opening of "Singin' the Blues," probably Tram's most successful OKeh record. Clarinet solos on both titles were not by Don Murray but by Russell, who plays in a totally different style. Murray played in the fluent style that was brought up the river from New Orleans, but Russell was trying to find a new sound on his clarinet, which, in 1927 he had not yet fully developed. In line with their titles, the two tunes were performed in a slower tempo than the three titles by the Gang. "A Good Man Is Hard to Find" featured several nice solos including an unforgettable twenty-four-bar duet of Venuti and Rollini. It featured tempo changes, by doubling, which was exceptional at the time, but "Since My Best Gal Turned Me Down" by the Gang, also featured tempo changes, in that case by halving.

Now that Rollini's band was all but finished, the men were happy to have so much recording work at hand. The day after the successful OKeh session that resulted in recordings under Bix's name and under his own name, Tram fixed yet another session at OKeh. However, this time there was a difference. He had met Red Nichols and proposed a partnership deal, whereby he and Red would pick a tune and record it for two companies, one chosen by Red and one by Tram. The benefit would be, that both leaders, as well as a number of their sidemen, would participate in two recording sessions. Red did not want to use his lucrative Brunswick contract for this, and he found Victor interested. So on the morning of 26 October, Red and Tram were in the Victor studio to record the chosen tune, which was "Sugar," as arranged by Arthur Schutt.[50] The Victor files give an extraordinary instrumentation of twelve men, not counting the two vocalists, the biggest group that Red had brought to the studio so far. In addition to Bill Rank, there was Glenn Miller on the trombone, who wrote the arrangement for the second title, "Make My Cot Where the Cot-Cot-Cotton Grows." Rollini took long solos on both tunes. In addition to the issued takes (take 1 for both tunes), one more take of each tune was marked "hold indefinitely," which may mean that Victor would keep it in store till the present day.

However, Nichols and Trumbauer had more to do on this day—Trumbauer's OKeh session, scheduled for the afternoon. So most of Nichols's group hurried to OKeh's studio to find Tommy Rockwell there, who did not want Red on the recording. Bix had not been invited and a story circulating in the jazz world is that he was found in a nearby bar after a quick search. The trumpet solo on this record, certainly is not up to Bix's usual high level, but this might have been caused by the booze. Thus the trumpet player could be Bix on an "off day," one day after his top day. This legend cannot be substantiated; but fact is that some of his colleagues, who were present, recognized him as the soloist on the single issued title from this session, which was "Sugar."[51] It is tantalizing to know that a test pressing of the second title recorded by Tram's group, "Did You Mean It?" was sent to the UK, but did not survive World War II.

The Break-up

This Trumbauer date had been the last one when Rollini and a part of his orchestra recorded together. It really fell apart now. Rollini had failed to find a new job for his band after the week with Jack Benny and he had no other recording dates coming. His old boss Ed Kirkeby continued making records just as before, but Rollini's successor on the bass saxophone, Spencer Clark, had grown and replaced his idol almost to perfection.[52]

The last few months had been a far-reaching experience for Adrian Rollini. He had proven to be a good negotiator and to be able to pick a good band. However, he had not been able to bring discipline into his band and thus the music was often bad. It did not become great to dance to and its music was often above the heads of its public. Also, the work of Frank Fay was not appreciated by many. Frank Trumbauer noted that the public did not take to Fay.[53] John Steiner asked two of Rollini's associates who both heard the band, Frank Cush and Bill Priestley, why the club closed so soon after it had opened. They felt that "Rollini must have overlooked the glaring lack of personal and musical discipline, which was clearly evident from the audience viewpoint. Indeed, it was a lusty band of stars and the solos were fine. However, it was also a band of temperamental drinkers who, in the distracting atmosphere of New York nightlife, had little time for rehearsal or enthusiasm for arrangements. The band did not appeal to the average businessman dancer. Rollini was not a firm director and Bea Palmer was too hip, too amused with the band's antics, to advise them of their weakness."[54]

Adrian's friend Neil Waterman believed that he was disappointed that support by the public was so low. His type of music was associated with small intimate places in New York, low ceilings and lots of noise, that were packed when they had 100 people. The visitors at the Club New Yorker were not sophisticated enough to know what they were listening to. The cover charge was high, which discouraged a number of people from coming, and those who did come expected a big show for their money.[55]

Two months after Adrian got the Club New Yorker contract, his band ceased to exist. The day after the recordings of "Sugar," Bix and Tram took a plane to join Paul Whiteman in Indianapolis. At the time of the break-up of the Goldkette Victor band, Whiteman had tried to hire them, but they preferred to go with Rollini. Now the two did not hesitate and accepted. Trombone player Bill Rank also would soon take a job with Whiteman.

Sylvester Ahola, who had been thinking about going to Europe for a while, found work immediately and worked in quick succession for Peter Van Steeden, Paul Specht, Cass Hagan, and Sam Lanin, recording with Van Steeden and Lanin. Then he was tipped that Reggie Batten, leader of the Savoy Orpheans, a British band, was in New York looking for a first trumpet player. The Savoy Orpheans were the house band at the Savoy, one of London's best hotels. Ahola signed on 12 November 1927 and left for the UK on 14 December 1927.[56] As a memory to his days with Bix and Rollini, he kept some home movies, made with his 16mm camera on 14 October and showing the entrances of the Club New Yorker and the Strand.

Don Murray also found new work immediately. He worked for a while with Cass Hagan and in February 1928 joined Ted Lewis, with whom he would work alongside a colleague from the days of the New Orleans Rhythm Kings, trombone player George Brunies.

Joe Venuti and Eddie Lang stayed together, did much freelancing, and recorded under many names, including their own(!). By the end of 1928 they had opened and closed another club and then joined Whiteman. Frank Signorelli was a successful composer and would work with the reformed Original Dixieland Jazz Band, with Paul Whiteman, and with New York Dixieland bands. Chauncey Morehouse joined Don Voorhees's orchestra and later worked as a studio musician. The Club New Yorker reopened the following year as the Jardin Royal with an orchestra directed by Paul Specht.

So what happened to Adrian Rollini? After the two days of recording for OKeh, under Bix's and Tram's names, he had no more recording dates. There is no evidence that Whiteman made him an offer. Maybe he did, but more than likely he did not. Whiteman had known about Rollini from the days that the California Ramblers replaced his band at the Palais Royal in 1923 and could not have missed his rise to fame and leadership. However, Whiteman may have had several reasons for not asking Rollini to join. First of all, Rollini's salary conditions may have been too heavy or maybe Whiteman was afraid that Rollini would not be satisfied with the role of a sideman anymore. Also Whiteman did not need a bass saxophone player in his band, since he had a top bass player with Steve Brown.[57]

However, in all likelihood Rollini was not in the mood for another New York engagement anyway and, like Ahola, got the idea to go to Europe. During November, Ahola had agreed with Reggie Batten to join his band at the Savoy in London. Rollini got an offer from Fred Elizalde, who had a contract to lead the second band at the Savoy from 1 January 1928. It appeared that he wanted some Americans to fill important chairs. Rollini would be one of them. Bobby Davis was also included in the deal.[58]

And thus all members of Adrian Rollini's Club New Yorker band were employed again. Adrian Rollini looked forward to a new start in the Old World.

Chapter 11

With Fred Elizalde in England, 1928

When Adrian Rollini made the trip to England, it was to join Fred Elizalde's dance orchestra in London. Elizalde had a contract to provide the music at one of London's top hotels, the Savoy. Elizalde came from a wealthy family that had its roots in the Basque region of Spain but had made its fortune running sugar plantations in the Philippines. Basques have wanted independence for ages and the movement for an independent Basque nation is ongoing.

Fred Elizalde's great-grandfather was Joaquin Marcelino, who was born in 1833 in a town by the name of Elizondo in the Bazian valley in Navarre. He used the family name Elizalde, which in the Basque language means churchyard. Joaquin left his parental village and Europe for an uncertain future on the other side of the globe when he was only thirteen. When he took this big step, he was not alone in doing so. Young Basque boys were obliged to join the army, which they disliked because it defended Spain, the enemy. They were migrating to escape military service.[1]

Joaquin Elizalde found a job in a company in which he soon acquired a minority share. He became more and more important in Manila, and by the time he was middle aged he had become a respectable businessman. He married and they had one son, José Joaquin, who inherited and continued his father's business. José Joaquin married Carmen Diaz Monreau, a girl from Spain.[2] They had six children, five sons by the names of Joaquin Miguel ("Mike"), Juan Miguel, Angel, Manuel ("Manolo"), Federico ("Fred"), and a daughter, Carmenchu. Their dates of birth and death have not been published, with the exception of Federico, who lived from 12 December 1907 till 16 January 1979.

The education of the children was very important to their parents, and being wealthy, they could afford to give them an international training. They were sent to schools in Spain, England, the United States, and Switzerland. It is said that mother Carmen stimulated them to study music, and thus it was discovered that son Federico had an exceptional musical talent. He played piano and it is said that he had composed a minuet by the age of four and a symphony when he was eleven.[3] As Fred Elizalde, he would become the leader of a major dance orchestra in the late twenties in England.

Federico studied music in Madrid, where at the age of fourteen he won a first piano prize at Madrid Royal Conservatory. Then he went to London, for further studies at St. Joseph's College. From there he went to Stanford University in what is today Silicon Valley near San Francisco, California, to study law.[4] This may have been around 1924, when he was 17. In that year his elder brother Manuel, who was called Manolo back home and later would receive the nickname "Lizz," started his studies in Cambridge, England. Both brothers immediately started to work with local orchestras, Manuel in Cambridge, Fred in California. Manuel, a reed player, became a member of a student band called the Quinquaginta band. Federico, who by then was called Fred, became a band leader in California. In July 1926, by the end of the academic year, Manuel left Cambridge for California and joined his brother. When the two brothers got together, Federico already had a local reputation as a leader of a dance band. Most probably he was already leading an orchestra while at Stanford University, but his break came when he followed the well-known Herb Wiedoeft Orchestra at the Cinderella Roof Ballroom on top of the Los Angeles Biltmore Hotel.[5] In June 1926, just before Manuel's arrival, Fred's band even made several records for the rare Hollywood label, which allow us to hear his highly individual piano style today.[6] The final title recorded was "Siam Blues," Fred's own composition, played as a piano solo.

Manuel told his brother about musical life in Cambridge and the quality of some university musicians, and Fred decided to go back to England. He understood well that this was against his father's will and that he was by now banished from the family home in Manila.[7] Apparently he was not cut off from his parents' financial allowance, since he continued to have plenty of money at his disposal. It is said that he then told his father that he wanted to study law under Manuel's supervision in Cambridge.

Fred arrived in Cambridge on 1 September 1926, at the start of the 1926–27 academic year. He probably traveled together with Manuel. In Cambridge his interest once more drifted toward music and he became piano player and musical director of the Quinquaginta band. Manuel continued as reed player with the band and also became its general and stage manager. In October 1926 the band gave its first public performance. Fred had renamed it Quinquaginta Ramblers, after the California Ramblers, whom he greatly respected. The band's quality was such that both Brunswick and His Master's Voice gave Fred a contract to record. The sessions took place in spring and summer of 1927, a year after the recordings in California.[8] They show that Elizalde could assemble bands that were disciplined and with capable musicians, including some good soloists.[9] The recordings also show that Fred could write arrangements that inspired musicians, and he was asked to arrange for other dance bands, too.[10]

Fred stayed in Cambridge for less than a year. In June 1927 he left for London, soon to be followed by his brother. To quote British music journalist Nick Dellow: "With Fred in town, the London dance band scene would never be quite the same again."[11]

The management of the Savoy Hotel, then and now a top hotel, had the policy of always having the best in dance bands.[12] In 1921 they had the Savoy Havana Band and two years later they had added the Savoy Orpheans. Both bands were managed by William J. de Mornys; when his contract ended by the end of 1927, it was not renewed. The reason that the Savoy's management gave was that the bands did not vary their program sufficiently, and on 25 September it wrote to De Mornys that "other arrangements were to be made in regard to dance bands at the end of the year." In fact, the Savoy had received complaints that the bands had been too "noisy" and "old-fashioned." Both bands had to leave and the Savoy wanted two new bands. Reg Batten was asked to form a new Savoy Orpheans for 1928. He went to New York to find musicians for his band. He returned with trumpeter Sylvester Ahola, fresh from Adrian Rollini's New Yorker band, and with pianist/arranger Irving Brodsky, who had been with the California Ramblers until the year before.

For the other band the Savoy wanted something special, with a modern style of its own, that would make the Savoy the place to enjoy one's evening.[13] They gave the contract to Fred Elizalde. He offered a combination of a personal and a bit exotic style, a great musical talent and a remarkable track record, a Cambridge background, and last but not least, he came from a wealthy family. This set of assets helped convince Richard Collett, the Savoy's director who handled the music policy, that Fred Elizalde was the right person for this job. However, Elizalde had no band and little time to assemble one. America was the answer, and Fred sent his brother Manuel to New York with the names of several musicians and probably with some of his own recordings, too. Manuel really delivered. He managed to contract three former members of the California Ramblers: trumpet player Chelsea Quealey,[14] clarinet and alto saxophone player Bobby Davis, and Adrian Rollini. Like Ahola, who joined the Orpheans, Davis and Rollini had just finished the adventure with the latter's New Yorker band. To show what quality Manuel Elizalde picked up, listen to one of the California Ramblers' finest recording sessions, which produced "After You've Gone" in June. Quealey, Bobby Davis and Rollini were the main soloists on these great sides. These Americans were well known to British jazz enthusiasts, whose main source of information was music magazine *Melody Maker*. Its writing about them could not have been more enthusiastic.

British work permits were granted on 12 December. A day later Rollini got a copy of his birth certificate to get a passport. On 17 December he left the harbor of New York; he arrived in Liverpool, England on 26 December.[15] His colleagues traveled with him, as well as Irving Brodsky. They were met by Manuel Elizalde.

While Fred Elizalde was filling in names for his band, the Savoy was thinking about recordings. Both the Savoy and record company His Master's Voice had benefited from the long series of recordings by the Savoy Havana Band and the Savoy Orpheans, and the Savoy wanted to continue this. His Master's Voice was a highly respected label, but it seemed to have no interest in continuing, although it had done a successful recording of Elizalde's student band. The Savoy gave them until 14 January 1928 to decide. However, the new Brunswick company was a serious alternative; it had also recorded Fred Elizalde's bands.[16] And in early December, with perfect timing, Brunswick wrote to the Savoy about further recordings by Elizalde. The Savoy answered by offering Brunswick "the full benefit of our Publicity Department and to broadcast the Elizalde band on our broadcasting nights, if in return . . . you are prepared to pay us a royalty on the sale of records made by the Elizalde Band." The letter added that "records made by the Elizalde band . . . must not bear the name of the Savoy unless we arrange with you to do all the recording; but when broadcasting we can use 'The Elizalde band at the Savoy' if that is considered desirable."

Fred Elizalde's Savoy Band

By the end of December Fred Elizalde had filled all positions. To the press he said that he had "an entirely new combination of instruments thought at present to be irreconcilable. . . . There will be a completely new rhythm which may set a new fashion for ball-rooms."[17] His new band consisted of nine musicians and a vocalist:

Chelsea Quealey, first trumpet
Norman Payne, second trumpet
Bobby Davis, first alto saxophone, clarinet
Harry Hayes, second alto saxophone
Rex Owen, tenor saxophone
Adrian Rollini, bass saxophone
Fred Elizalde, leader, piano
Len Fillis, banjo, guitar
Ronnie Gubertini, drums
Richard Maxwell, vocals

Len Fillis had come from South Africa; the others, except the three Americans, were British. Elizalde had to turn this group of musicians into a well-oiled music machine in no time, since the Savoy targeted for New Year's Eve to present the new bands for the first time. Its publicity department created some flowery text for a colorful folder:

With Fred Elizalde in England, 1928

Fred Elizalde's Savoy Hotel Orchestra, 1928. From left: Dickie Maxwell, Len Fillis, Adrian Rollini, Ronnie Gubertini, Rex Owen, Norman Payne, Chelsea Quealey, Harry Hayes, Bobby Davis. Elizalde at piano.

> HELP! we are all dancing and cannot stop. Yes, and you, too, will dance when you hear the Fierce Exultation of Syncopated Music leap into life as the New Dance Bands at the Savoy play. Their Rhythm gets in your blood—into your brain—into your very being.... Come and Dance to them! Just you Come and Dance to them! They've gripped the heart of London.... We have brought together three bands which are out and out the finest in the world. New York has nothing to touch them.[18]

Of Elizalde, they exclaimed:

> Fred Elizalde and his Music is a Newcomer. Called to play before the King of Spain when Elizalde was only 12 years old, this Amazing Genius will thrill you with his band. We sent him round the world with carte-blanche to pick his band from amongst the Finest Players that money and the prestige of the Savoy could secure. Now he is playing every night and making musical history. You simply can't sit still when he begins—you have to dance.

Melody Maker, which had given great support to the white New York jazzmen, immediately got into the new Savoy picture. Its January 1928 issue devoted a

SAVOY HOTEL

To complete your Evening—
DANCE AT THE SAVOY
From 11 p.m. to 2 a.m.
FRED ELIZALDE *and his Music*
and the SAVOY ORPHEANS

Supper and Dance in the Restaurant at an Inclusive charge of 12'6; or À la Carte in the Grillroom

THE MOST PERFECT DANCE FLOOR & THE BEST BANDS IN LONDON

Savoy Hotel advertisement.

page to Elizalde and the Savoy Orpheans, headed "The New Savoy Bands" with lists of the personnel. It commented:

> Fred Elizalde himself is too well-known to Melody Maker readers to need any further introduction from me. The American contingent of his band comprises three of the world's most famous musicians. I write the words "world's most famous" with some diffidence, not because they are not true, but because so many have laid claim to a similar distinction, only to prove they had no title to it. Such is not the case this time. Adrian Rollini is not only considered a star by the American public, but also

by his brother musicians, which means much more. One has to be something very out of the ordinary to gain such standing with them as Rollini has won on nothing but his originality of style put into practice via his undoubted musicianship. Little less can be said of Bobby Davis, who has been the first saxophone of the Goofus Five and the Goofus Washboards for many months.[19] Quealey is on a par with Red Nichols and Bix Beiderbeck [sic]. He was first trumpet with the Californian Ramblers [sic], which band, under the leadership of Rollini, not so long ago was considered by musicians as the most up-to-date dance combination in the States.

The Savoy organized "Tea Dances" every day from 4:00 p.m. until 6:00 p.m. The Elizalde band would alternate each week with the Orpheans, while the tango band would be there every week. Every evening all three bands appeared, each playing two sets of half an hour. While one band was on the set, two bands could relax and use the Savoy's excellent facilities for its musicians: recreation rooms some floors below the main ballroom, where they had free beer and could have dinner.[20] After the final set the musicians often went over to nearby Lyon's Corner House for a breakfast.[21] At other occasions they would go for a late drink to a nightclub on Gerrard Street, the 43 Club.[22] George Hurley remembered:

> this club started at eleven and went on till the early morning. Drinking was illegal there but it used to go on. [The men] could take their instruments along and play and enjoy themselves, ... they could let themselves go there. I remember one occasion ... the Vincent Lopez band was at the Kit Kat and they came down and the entire band brought their instruments and lined up chairs alongside the dance floor and played.[23]

The Savoy believed in publicity. Its management presented the new bands for the first time on Friday 30 December and used every opportunity for promotion. On Monday 2 January a private cocktail party was given in the ballroom for the cream of London society, who could hear the new Savoy bands for themselves. Three days later, on Thursday, both the Savoy Orpheans and Elizalde's band did a broadcast for the BBC from 10:30 p.m. till midnight.[24] Each band played twelve tunes. The bands did not have to travel to a studio: The BBC installed its equipment in the Savoy's own ballroom. Due to the short time for rehearsals, the selection of tunes played by Elizalde's band must have been close to the repertoire during the band's introduction on New Year's Eve. They were, in order of performance (Fred recorded tunes indicated with a * as a piano solo for Brunswick, those with ** with his band).

Bye Bye Pretty Baby
Shy Anna**

I Ain't Got Nobody*
Musical Moonlight**
Hallelujah
The Blue Room
Just Another Day
Sirens Dream
Blue Heaven
Charmaine
Rhythm Step**

These titles form a set of popular tunes of the day and do not suggest a particular accent on jazz. However, for the musicians in the band this was a well-known pattern and certainly the Americans were used to this from their work with the California Ramblers. They were able to throw in a good, hot solo when asked for.

"Rhythm Step" was a composition of Fred and his brother Manuel Elizalde. Fred recorded it both with his band and as a piano solo. The tune had been marketed as a new dance and its sheet music gave all needed information and showed the prescribed steps. By publishing a transcription of a chorus for the goofus by Rollini, *Melody Maker* underlined Adrian's prominence in the band.[25]

The Savoy and the BBC had a contract, valid till April 1928, for two broadcasts a week, on Thursday and Saturday nights and sometimes an extra broadcast on Saturday afternoon at the Savoy's request. The BBC had no other cost than to provide an announcer and an engineer. They got the bands completely free of charge.

Promotion activities continued. On 3 February the *Savoy* gave a cocktail party to introduce its new bands to the members of the press. The band played Elizalde's symphony "Heart of a Coon." The press found it difficult to judge. The *Daily News* said: "Jazz is a purely physical form of music, impossible to listen to seated.... Yet jazz and its weirdly noisy instruments may be musical, as was illustrated by Mr. Elizalde's symphony, 'The Heart of a Coon,' in which the blatancy was partly eliminated...." The *Daily Sketch* was more critical: "Though there is much that is colorful and exuberantly youthful in it, most people agree that [Fred Elizalde] has some way to go before he becomes a second Gershwin."[26]

However, the general public liked him and in no time the orchestra became very popular with London society and the radio public. One admirer was the Prince of Wales, heir to the British throne. One night he came in and asked to sit in on drums and Ronnie Gubertini relinquished his drum seat to the prince. Art Rollini remembered that he was not a good drummer, but he sent the band two cases of champagne that night.[27] After one radio show Elizalde received over 100 telegrams from admirers, which was a surprise to him.[28] The Savoy treated him with care, but one evening his orchestra was obliged to work longer than his contract said, which annoyed Fred. However, director Collett wrote him a letter complimenting him and his band for their fine spirit and he promised precautions to avoid similar experiences in the future.

Of course, Fred enjoyed the success he had. His career was going upward with the speed of lightning. However, he was having a dilemma. First of all, he was not really interested in producing sweet dance music, but this was a major part of his job. Second, he had some of the best jazzmen in his band, but most of the time they had to play straight dance music. And finally, even hot jazz was not what Fred was striving for. He wanted to be composing and playing advanced modern music in the forefront of twentieth-century composers. An article from his hand gives some insight in his feelings and ideas:

> You dancers don't take kindly to new-fangled ideas, and for my part I am content to introduce variation by novel orchestration.... Now for dance music, so far as the orchestra is concerned; and spare me a little sympathy, for I don't think you appreciate all the difficulties. The chief trouble is that we leaders have to please the tastes of so many. If you play "straight" you are termed uninteresting, while if your orchestration is elaborate or curious, you are dubbed a creator of cacophony. "Cheap," "cacophonous," "puerile," "barbarous," these are some of the terms we get from our almost unknown contributors and correspondents who class all syncopated music as "jazz." It is my opinion that old-fashioned "hot" methods of playing have given way to more melodious, but still highly rhythmic presentation. This is what the wireless listeners and dancers want....[29]

Fred Elizalde's Savoy Band on Records

HMV's option to continue recording the Savoy bands ended without being picked up. So the road was open for the Savoy to close a deal with Brunswick. One of the Savoy's conditions was that it would receive a ha'penny (half a penny) for every record sold. Another was that the labels of Fred Elizalde's Brunswick records would not mention the Savoy Hotel, unless Brunswick did all recordings of Savoy bands. Since the contract only concerned Fred Elizalde's band, the "Savoy" name was omitted from the Brunswick labels.[30]

One day after HMV's option ended, on Sunday 15 January 1928, Fred Elizalde had the first recording session with his new band. The studio was located above the Cavour Restaurant at Leicester Square. Due to the noise of heavy traffic on working days, recording could only take place here on Sunday mornings.[31]

Elizalde tried to cover a wide spectrum of tastes at this first occasion to present his band on records. Six tunes were to be recorded, four by the full band (two waltzes and two foxtrots, including a hot tune) and two tunes by a small jazz group.

The first two tunes were "Under the Moon" and "Diane." Brunswick decided to issue these titles before the other four. The record was issued the following month and reviewed by *Melody Maker*. It is doubtful if the magazine knew the tunes that had been recorded, but it was familiar with the band's work at the Savoy and probably expected jazz from the band on its first record. Therefore, it was surprised by Elizalde's new debut. Elizalde could do no wrong in their opinion, so the record got an enthusiastic write-up anyway:

> Under The Moon is a sweet melody number and young Fred has been far too clever to use it as a vehicle for showing off all the "hot" and trick stuff this band can do. He has given an ideal "melody" interpretation, for the most part the performance is by the ensemble.... Elizalde has done the one thing for which we have all been waiting for years.... He has incorporated the most modern of what have been considered only as "hot" rhythms without making his performance hot in itself.[32]

Indeed, the one thing that was new to listeners' ears was the rhythm. This was in no small part due to Rollini, who managed to be heard consistently blowing well-placed bass notes that made the band swing. Solos, by Quealey and Elizalde, were short, and Rollini played a break. The second title, "Diane," has nothing to offer in terms of modern music. Elizalde plays an intro, which is followed by Rollini playing the theme. As if to feature all of his Americans on this first record, Elizalde had Bobby Davis doing one of his imitations of a Hawaiian guitar on his alto saxophone.[33]

However, for record buyers who wanted to hear the jazz side of the band, its second release was all they hoped for. For the third and fourth titles recorded on 15 January, Fred Elizalde decided to work with a small unit from his band. On the record label the group was called "Fred Elizalde and his Hot Music" and the musicians were the three Americans plus Elizalde, piano; Fillis, guitar; and Gubertini, drums. The tunes were "Dixie" and "Tiger Rag" and the recordings are among the best jazz sides made in England. "Dixie" is a composition by Adrian Rollini, the second one named after his girlfriend Dixie, who had stayed in New York when Adrian went to England.[34] He and Elizalde probably both had a hand in the simple arrangement and solos are by Elizalde and the Americans, Rollini doing the intro, a short solo, and the coda. *Melody Maker* liked the result and particularly praised the piano chorus with the saxophones working "organ chords" as a background.[35] "Tiger Rag" starts with the traditional approach to the tune, with clarinet breaks in the beginning and, after a solo by Elizalde, Davis copying a saxophone solo that had been Jimmy Dorsey's trademark for years. Then Quealey and Rollini get their chance to shine, which they do in style.[36] The record, Brunswick 143, was released around 1 April with the names of the three Americans on the label, the second time Rollini's name got on a

Fred Elizalde's Hot Music. From left: Chelsea Quealey, Ronnie Gubertini, Bobby Davis, Adrian Rollini, Fred Elizalde, Len Fillis.

record label.[37] Subsequent records by Elizalde's Hot Music would be similarly released. Rollini got even more publicity with the latest monthly announcement of records by Brunswick's competitor Parlophone and from the British music magazine *Melody Maker*. Parlophone's catalog supplement for February 1928 featured Adrian Rollini's portrait on its front page.[38] In March *Melody Maker* had the first of what eventually would become a series of articles by Adrian Rollini about the proper use of some of his instruments.[39] This first article was called "The Goofus & How To Play It."[40]

Elizalde's first recording session with his new band was not finished yet. After the intermezzo with Fred Elizalde and his Hot His Music, there were two more titles to be recorded. They were "Again" and "Sugar," and their arrangements required the full band. "Again" is a waltz, composed by Elizalde, who, just as with the previous waltz "Diane," had Bobby Davis doing his Hawaiian guitar imitation on the saxophone.[41] The arrangement of "Sugar" sounds familiar if one knows Paul Whiteman's recording of the tune, which he recorded for Victor.[42] Elizalde and Whiteman recorded an arrangement based on the same original, Bill Challis's work for Jean Goldkette's orchestra. Elizalde was the first to record it, a few weeks before Whiteman. It presents an echo of Rollini's short-lived New Yorkers band: Rollini probably got it from the ex-Goldkette men he had had in his New Yorker band, just three months earlier. According to Norman Payne, Elizalde's band used several Challis scores in 1928.[43]

Before he went to London, Adrian Rollini had never met Fred Elizalde, but now that he had worked for him for some weeks, he must have felt that he had made the right decision. In addition to his talent as a soloist and a rhythm player, Rollini had brought new music to the band. He could record one of his own compositions during its first recording session and a recent tune from Rollini's New Yorkers repertoire had also been recorded. No musician had played such a major role in Elizalde's earlier bands. Rollini's exceptional qualities were recognized by Elizalde. Also, working with Elizalde was relaxed, compared to New York's fever. Few trips to recording studios and no trips to radio broadcasters at all, since the band would broadcast from the hotel. No freelancing, but a fixed salary. Rollini earned seventy-five pounds a week, the equivalent of about $360.[44] The musicians were all sent to a tailor in Savile Row and their expensive suits were all paid for, probably by Elizalde, so that they could look as smart as any customer. In this positive mood Adrian decided to buy another sports car. He chose a 1928 Model Austin Swallow Sports Two Seater which sold for £175. It had a special body, built by the Swallow Coachbuilding Company in Blackpool.[45] Art remembered that Adrian and Dixie had a sumptuous flat in London and two addresses are known, 28 Inverness Street, London W8 and 118 Long Acre, London WC2. The first was about three miles away from where Fred Elizalde lived on Jermyn Street[46] (the same street where Bobby Davis and Chelsea Quealey rented an apartment). The second was closer to Elizalde and to the Savoy. "To live on Jermyn Street in those days, was quite something, it was a very smart area."[47] Adrian's first car in London had been an Essex, an affordable American salon car.[48]

Rollini was not alone in his feeling that he had made the right decision to join Fred Elizalde. Elizalde too, must have thought that he had done the right thing by hiring such talent. However, for him it was only a step forward to his personal goal and that was to compose and play modernistic music, ahead of its time. This interested him more than appealing to his public or his management.

In February and March there were two more recording dates. The first was for the full band and produced four titles. All four demonstrate Elizalde's elegant style of arranging, but only two are of jazz interest: "You Can't Have My Sugar for Tea" (from the show *Lady Mary*) and "Shy Anna," the latter in particular, since it featured a rare chase chorus by Bobby Davis on alto saxophone and Adrian Rollini on hot fountain pen.

For the March date a different approach was taken. Four titles were recorded, two by Fred Elizalde and his Hot Music and two piano solos by Elizalde. The first band title was "Arkansas," the tune that Rollini had recorded four times with different small units from the California Ramblers. The last time had been less than a year ago with the Varsity Eight, when Quealey and Davis also were present. Elizalde's version compares favorably with the Varsity Eight's, with a faster tempo, Elizalde's intriguing piano solo, and Rollini's work both on hot fountain pen and the bass saxophone. "Sugar Step" is a composition of Fred Elizalde and basically consists of a series of solos by the front line plus Elizalde. Surprisingly, Quealey blows his solo into a mute and Davis plays solos both on the alto saxophone and on the clarinet.

Around this time Adrian Rollini received a message from his mother, which said that his father was terminally ill. He decided to return to New York and stay there for about one month. Before his departure, his normal work with Elizalde continued. One example about which information is available, was a broadcast on Saturday 17 March 1928. The program featured some of the tunes that had recently been recorded.[49] The program was opened by the Savoy Orpheans and closed by the Savoy Tango Band.

On 28 March Adrian Rollini left England for New York. He traveled on the SS *Olympic* from Southampton. Among his papers was a promise of marriage. It is quite likely that he also took along a recording of "Dixie" by Elizalde's orchestra and maybe his bass saxophone, but most certainly his mouthpiece. Dixie and he had decided to take the step and she would join Adrian on his return trip to London.

Family Moments in New York

Adrian's voyage took six days. He arrived on Tuesday 3 April and then there was no time to lose. His father was dying from stomach cancer, but Adrian could still ask him for permission to marry Dixie. Dixie had just returned from a two-month vacation with her mother Orinda Swezey to Miami Beach and Havana. Adrian picked her up and they drove back to his parents' house. Ferdinando had been in bed since last Christmas and he was in poor condition. After Adrian and Dixie entered his room, Adrian asked "Dad, can you hear me?" When Ferdinando nodded affirmatively, Adrian said "Dad, this is Dixie. I want to marry her; do I have your blessing?" Ferdinando put out his hand. Adrian bent down and Ferdinando brushed his face and nodded in the affirmative again. Adrian kissed his father on the cheek and departed with Dixie.[50]

On the afternoon of Friday 6 April, Adrian Rollini and Dorothy Remer (Dixie's real name) were "united in Holy Matrimony" by Frederic Wamsley, rector of St. Paul's Episcopal Church in New Rochelle, New York. The ceremony took place at Orinda's home, 59 Stuyvesant Avenue in Larchmont. Newspapers wrote that "the wedding was a very quiet affair, attended only by the members of the two immediate families, owing to the illness of Mr. Rollini's father."[51] Wit-

With Fred Elizalde in England, 1928

Adrian and Dixie, at the time of their wedding.

nesses who signed the wedding booklet included the parents; even Ferdinando signed. Ferdinando died on Sunday 15 April 1928.

No doubt Adrian's family was impressed by his stories about his London activities, the grandeur of the Savoy Hotel, Elizalde's wealth, and his luxurious life. Dixie loved the idea of joining him there. However, before they went, Adrian still had some work to do.

Life in New York goes fast, but Adrian had not been forgotten by his former colleagues. Two of them were Jimmy and Tommy Dorsey. The last time the brothers worked together with Adrian was with the California Ramblers. From then on both had been with various orchestras and had freelanced in the New York recording studios. During 1927 they worked with Paul Whiteman, but by November Tommy had left and in 1928 Jimmy left, too. However, now they were recognized as some of New York's top musicians and the OKeh company gave them a chance to make records as the Dorsey Brothers Orchestra. There had been recording sessions in February and March, but the results had been tame. On 17 April another one was planned and the brothers remembered the effect that Adrian Rollini had on the bands he worked with. No doubt Rollini could use the pocket money and so he took part in the third Dorsey Brothers recording date, replacing tuba player Hank Stern. "Indian Cradle Song" and "My

With Fred Elizalde in England, 1928

Adrian and Dixie honeymooning to Europe.

Melancholy Baby" were the titles, and from the first note of the first title one can hear what difference it made. Rollini pushes the band and the result is a nice recording even without solos. "My Melancholy Baby," probably in an arrangement by Fud Livingston, is even better. In Adrian's hands the bass saxophone is not just an accompanying instrument, but it contributes a prominent voice in the ensemble, so that the band gets a new, individual sound. In this role it is logical that he plays solos and the second title's arrangement gave him two opportunities.[52]

This recording date with the Dorsey brothers may have been the only one that Rollini took part in during his thirty-one-day stay in New York. However, there were more sessions in which it is tempting to assume that he was in the personnel. The first one was on 10 April, a Frank Trumbauer date for OKeh. The titles were "Borneo" and "My Pet." It was four days after Adrian's wedding, but at a moment in time when his father Ferdinando was about to die. It is therefore unlikely that Adrian was on this Trumbauer date. In fact, Min Leibrook's presence on the bass saxophone is not contested in this case. There is a slightly better chance for another Rollini recording with the Bix Beiderbecke session for OKeh, which took place on 17 April. The titles were "Somebody Stole My Gal" and "Thou Swell," and a bass saxophone is featured prominently. Again it is generally assumed that this the work of Min Leibrook.

Frank Trumbauer owed Rollini some money from the OKeh recording dates under Frank's name. Now that he was back in New York Rollini asked Frank for ten arrangements to settle the debt. Frank noted this on 19 April but his note does not say if the deal was made.[53] On Friday 4 May Mr. and Mrs. Adrian Rollini left New York on the SS *Homeric* and, after a trip of eight days, arrived in Southampton, England.

Elizalde Expands His Orchestra and Expands It Again

While Adrian Rollini was traveling, Elizalde continued to work on his longer-term plans with his orchestra. The expectations of the Savoy Hotel were never precisely formulated, but its management closely watched Elizalde's music and the effect it had on its listeners, the dancing public in the hotel and the radio audience via the BBC. Fred was probably aware of this, but he moved ahead with his own plan. Hiring the American jazzmen had resulted in the first phase, where he could make some of the finest jazz records. In April he took the next visible step. He hired two more musicians, violin player George Hurley and bass player Tiny Stock, who both joined on 1 April 1928. Till the end of 1927 they had worked at the Savoy in the Savoy Orpheans, followed by a tour through European countries with that band, which was then called the Original Orpheans. The addition by these men would eventually allow Fred Elizalde to experiment with two top-class orchestras. Moreover, the presence of a bass player freed Adrian Rollini from his work as part of the rhythm section and gave him more freedom to be a soloist and to play a part in the ensemble. The new men recorded with the band before Rollini returned. Trombone player Ben Oakley replaced him for the occasion.

On 17 April 1928 the Savoy agreed with the BBC on a new contract, whereby the Savoy's dance bands would again broadcast twice a week, for one and a half hours on Thursdays and Saturdays. The contract stipulated that no song-plugging would be allowed.[54]

Adrian and Dixie arrived in England on 12 May; shortly after Rollini's return, the band went to the Brunswick recording studio again. A total of eight titles were recorded during two sessions. At the first session Fred recorded two piano solos and, since Rollini was available again, between these two titles new recordings were done by Elizalde's Hot Music.[55] They were two old favorites, "The Dark Town Strutters Ball" and "Somebody Stole My Gal." Both titles came out well, in particular the second one, which features Rollini on all his current instruments, hot fountain pen, goofus, and bass saxophone, in an amazing total of sixty-six bars, which may have been the highest number on any orchestra record until then.

The second session in May was for the full band. It produced four titles: "Chanson," "My Pet," "A Room with a View," and "Dance Little Lady," the last two from a popular revue by Noel Coward.[56] "My Pet" is based on the Bill Challis

Adrian in his Austin Swallow.

arrangement, which Rollini had taken to London. It is therefore not surprising that he plays the same break in its intro used on the recording of this tune by Frank Trumbauer's Orchestra, which was made during Rollini's weeks in New York but without his participation. On Trumbauer's recording, the break is played by Min Leibrook. Rollini's is clearly superior.[57]

"Dance Little Lady" presents a very special case. With a series of solos, it has even more to offer the jazz fan than its fellow show tune, "My Pet." Except for a break, Rollini is not among the soloists. However, an alternate take of "Dance Little Lady" survives in the form of a test pressing. This allows us to hear how the band struggled to create a perfect take and, more remarkable, how Fred Elizalde worked on an arrangement, even in the recording studio. On the issued take the intro is played faultlessly, while he chose alto saxophone player Bobby Davis to do an eight-bar bridge, interrupting Chelsea Quealey's trumpet solo. On the rejected take, the way the intro is played can still be improved and the bridge is played by Adrian Rollini.

In early July there was another recording session at Brunswick. It produced six titles, of which four were done by the band and two as piano solos. The arrangements were mostly straight performances, except "Blue Baby," the single jazz title from this session. One of the other titles was "Chopinata," a medley by Jean Wiener and Clement Doucet, consisting of Chopin themes. Wiener and Doucet formed a popular piano duo in Europe at the time.

Elizalde continued working on his greater ideas and as a next move he managed to get a contract to work in Paris for a few weeks, starting 28 July. The location was Les Ambassadeurs, a luxury theater on the fashionable Champs Elysées. Fred's following step was to hire even more men, and in July 1928 there were no

Fred Elizalde's enlarged Savoy Hotel Orchestra. From left, front row: Ronnie Gubertini, Al Bowlly, Fred Elizalde, Len Lee, Ben Frankel. Back row: George Hurley, Nobbi Knight, Len Fillis, Norman Payne, Mario "Harp" Lorenzi, Tiny Stock, Chelsea Quealey, Jack Miranda, Rex Owen, Phil Cardew, Bobby Davis, Harry Hayes, Adrian Rollini.

fewer than seven new additions. Five of them were British: "Nobby" Knight, third trumpet; Jack Miranda, sax and clarinet; Ben Frankel and Len Lee, violins; and Mario Lorenzi, harp. Then arrived singer and guitar player Al Bowlly.[58] He came from South Africa via Berlin, where he had recorded with several bands.[59] The final, but probably most important addition, was piano player Jack Russin. He was not only a great piano player but also a highly talented arranger. He was familiar with the American musicians in the band, since he had been with the California Ramblers from 1926 till the end of 1927, a few months after Rollini had left. Russin arrived in Plymouth, England, on 26 July 1928 and brought along his seventeen-year-old brother Babe, a talented tenor sax player. During the trip, on SS *Ile de France*, both had been working with George Carhart's New Yorkers.[60] Babe had a contract with Carhart to go to Paris. In New York Carhart had also asked Jack to join his band, but he had already signed with Elizalde, who had even sent the money for the trip. Jack saved it by working in Carhart's band on the boat.[61]

Now Fred Elizalde's band would consist of eighteen men, including himself: three trumpets, four reeds, Rollini on multiple instruments, three violins, harp, two pianos, two guitars, tuba, drums. Al Bowlly, one of the guitar players, also sang. With such a large orchestra it would become increasingly difficult to play swinging jazz, and it has been suggested that this was in line with what the Savoy management desired; however, it was Elizalde's own strategy. As the Brit-

Elizalde men on board crossing the Channel. Al Bowlly in center, Phil Cardew behind him.

ish author Nick Dellow wrote: "As time went on, Elizalde veered away from jazz, and eventually left it altogether. It is true that he was annoyed with the listening public and their lack of acceptance of 'hot' music, but the reasons for his leaving jazz have more to do with a natural progression towards achieving a deeper musical satisfaction."

By mid-1928 Elizalde's goal was still far away. In fact, just before the full band left for the continent, it had one more recording session at Brunswick, with interesting results for his jazz-oriented public. There was hardly time left for rehearsing, and the Brunswick recording studio and its personnel had to adapt to the large group. Therefore, rehearsals may have taken place in the studio itself, and it is not surprising that although four titles were recorded, only two were issued. Those two were "Just Imagine" and "Wherever You Are." These titles mark Bowlly's British recording debut, but the recording balance does not favor him.

The following day, Thursday 26 July 1928, the band traveled from London by train to Dover and then by ferry to Ostend in Belgium. Many photos were taken during the boat trip and the musicians had the feeling that they were going on a holiday. Of course, Dixie came along with her mother Orinda, who was generally known as Peggy and who had come to London to see her daughter and son-in-law.

The group probably stayed overnight in Ostend and then traveled via Brussels by train to arrive in Paris at Gare du Nord on Friday. That was well-planned, since on Saturday 28 July 1928 Fred Elizalde and his orchestra played their first concert at Les Ambassadeurs in Paris.

With Fred Elizalde in England, 1928

Fred Elizalde, Adrian Rollini, and Bobby Davis aboard ship to Ostende.

Fred Elizalde, Manuel's wife, Manuel Elizalde.

Dixie and Adrian drinking Belgian beer in Ostende.

During the band's absence from the Savoy, dance music would be supplied by the Savoy Orpheans led by Reg Batten and by Al Collins's Dance Orchestra. In Paris, Adrian and Dixie Rollini would have time for sightseeing, and visited the Eiffel Tower.

Les Ambassadeurs, Paris, and Hotels in Ostend

The Revue Nègre, which arrived in Paris in 1925, gave Parisians (and Europe) a show made in America and full of jazz music. It made Josephine Baker a star and for her musicians it was a milestone in their careers. When the public asked for more, the entertainment world reacted. One man on the scene was Edmond Sayag, who decided to rebuild Les Ambassadeurs, a traditional place for Parisians to eat, drink, and meet. Sayag's new Les Ambassadeurs was located at the entrance of the Champs Elysées, near Place de la Concorde, where the old Les Ambassadeurs had been ever since 1764. It had started as an open-air bar, which grew step by step to become a famous "café concert," a place with music. Sayag gave it a new interior design, so that guests could eat and enjoy a show at the same time. The program said: "In a well-lit garden in the middle of scented cascades one can dine and take supper while listening to the leading American stars! . . . At the side of the stage a staircase leads to the floor situated in the hall. . . . All around this floor space are armchairs and tables." On either side of the dance floor there was a space for an orchestra, one providing tangos and one providing jazz. Les Ambassadeurs reopened in 1926 with "Blackbirds of 1926," an all-black production produced by Lew Leslie. The 1928 show, which opened on 10 May, was simply called "Vingt-huit" ("Twenty-Eight"). It featured eighteen songs, all specially composed by Cole Porter. The program said that all artists had been contracted by the William Morris Agency in New York. This included Fred Waring's Pennsylvanians for the stage show, which was a success and was regarded as one of Paris's best.[62] However, Sayag was not satisfied, and after eight weeks many contracts with the artists were not renewed.[63] Noble Sissle had been at Les Ambassadeurs to entertain the guests during intermissions of Waring's band. Now that Waring was leaving, Sissle was asked to supply an orchestra.[64] He did not have an orchestra and quickly assembled a band with black and white musicians, some directly from the United States and some working in Paris. Sayag wanted to avoid the contractual problems he had had with Waring (and the resulting urgency) in the future. Therefore, in August, Sayag closed a booking contract with the large American William Morris booking agency.[65]

When Fred Elizalde's orchestra started to work at Les Ambassadeurs, Noble Sissle's band was the attraction and did Cole Porter's show. At the time, the great soprano saxophone player Sidney Bechet was a member of Sissle's band and made a lasting impression on several of Elizalde's men. The admiration went both ways. Sissle liked the sound of the bass saxophone and bought Bechet a bass saxophone.[66] Bechet soon mastered it and would record on it during the thirties.

It was Elizalde's task to provide the dance music, which the public called "jazz," and he had the personnel to provide just that. It has been said that his band was warmly received by the Parisians, but it was totally ignored by the press.[67]

While in Paris, Elizalde's quest for additional orchestra members continued. One day this developed into a bad scene, when Elizalde and Rollini visited a band called the New Yorkers. The year before, the band had been taken to Europe by George Carhart and it had made several fine records. Carhart had since returned to New York, but without him the New Yorkers still consisted of mostly American musicians, such as reed player Danny Polo, piano player Jack O'Brien, and drummer Dave Tough. The New Yorkers were working at the Abbaye de Thélème in Montmartre, Paris's popular entertainment section. Adrian was impressed by the quality of their work and asked them to join Elizalde's orchestra in London. However, Polo ridiculed the offer and told Adrian that he did not think Elizalde was playing enough jazz. Rollini became quite angry at this criticism and told Danny sarcastically that the money was better with Elizalde and to prove that playing with Elizalde offered surprising possibilities, he got on the stand at the L'Abbaye and started to play his hot fountain pen. This did not have the desired effect. The whole band ridiculed him now with sarcastic and obscene remarks. In a later interview with Leonard Feather, Danny Polo commented on this episode: "Fred Elizalde came across and heard us. He made me an offer to join him in London. I refused him, and I believe that to this day he begrudges me that refusal. I guess, in the light of common sense now, it may seem to have been a crazy thing to do, but I was so happy working with a bunch of men I liked and most of all working with Dave, that I just wouldn't quit."[68]

Melody Maker, in its August 1928 issue, had given all available information about Elizalde's continental trip. As described above, the band's first engagement was Les Ambassadeurs. However, there were also plans to work at L'Empire, a luxury hotel, and to do private parties, no fewer than six having been booked for one particular week. However, no further information has been found about such activities. They may have happened, but in the case of L'Empire the plan may have fallen through because the hotel was renovated in 1928. And private parties are not publicly advertised.

Edmond Sayag, the owner of Les Ambassadeurs, also owned one of the casinos in Ostend on the Belgian North Sea coast. Together with the William Morris Agency, he would arrange for acts who performed at Les Ambassadeurs to perform in Ostend as well. So from Paris, Fred Elizalde's Orchestra traveled to Ostend.

The SS *Ile de France* took not only George Carhart with the Russin brothers to Le Havre but also the complete Ted Lewis Orchestra, under a contract with

Adrian posing a walking cane in Ostende.

Dixie with her new hat in Ostende.

Sayag and Morris.[69] In that band were great jazz musicians such as trombone player George Brunies and clarinet player Don Murray. During the trip they performed for first-class passengers, thus earning the money for the trip. Lewis himself was regarded as a top entertainer, not so much a great jazz musician as a major orchestra leader and comedian. A newspaper wrote: "Who didn't see him singing, dancing, juggling with his hat, his cane, go from the highest comedy to the most catching tragedy, can say about himself that he does not know what is a great artist and incredible animator."[70]

After its arrival, Lewis's band went not to Paris but to Ostend, where they worked for about two weeks at the Royal Palace Hotel and at the Kursaal Casino.[71] Reading this, one realizes that there could be no greater difference between orchestra leaders than between Ted Lewis and Fred Elizalde. After Ted Lewis's performance at Ostend, Fred Elizalde could only be a negative surprise for a public that wanted entertainment. The fact that, like Lewis, Elizalde had some excellent jazzmen in the band, did not help enough. No actor, juggler, or clown fronted the band, but a serious conductor.[72]

The Belgian monthly magazine *Music* had a correspondent in Ostend who reported that Elizalde was working at the Kursaal.[73] However, the orchestra had no great effect on its public. The correspondent thought that the cause of this was its limited band book. He wrote that it "only had eight pieces and these were too old."[74] Of course the band knew more than eight tunes, but with the new men on board, Fred may have decided to only play arrangements for the bigger band and then only after they were well rehearsed. That might have limited his choice. However, the story still sounds unlikely. On the positive side, *Music*'s correspondent specifically mentioned two of Elizalde's top musicians: "the famous Andrien Rolini [sic], the American bass saxophone player who is well-known from his gramophone records," and "Jack Rusen [sic], freshly arrived from America where he was solo piano player of the famous orchestra California Ramblers." Another Belgian visitor was writer Robert Goffin. He had a taste for jazz and had great appreciation for the band. In his view Elizalde's band had a fully new formula that was founded on the solid web woven by the brilliant Rollini, who would now and then leave his saxophone for the goofus or the [hot] fountain pen.[75]

Rollini made an unforgettable impression on at least one more Belgian: saxophone player Jean Robert (1908–1981).[76] At the time Robert worked with Gus Deloof's orchestra playing the clarinet and the tenor saxophone. From Rollini's recordings he was familiar with his work on the bass saxophone and silently dreamed about playing one himself. He introduced himself to Rollini and would accompany him during many daily promenades on the Ostend Boulevard and beach, Rollini always carrying along a hip flask of American bourbon. Robert got a lot of information about bass saxophone playing. Rollini used the latest Conn production version, allowing him to play high E and high F. He did not play this heavy saxophone while it stood on a stand, but he used a wide carrying belt around his neck and body. For a solo, he would play it standing up. Rollini used a baritone mouthpiece and reeds.[77] He showed Robert that he would insert a piece of ivory from a piano key between the reed and the side rails of the mouthpiece. When he played he would bow the reed down and thus have greater tension in the reed. His reeds were light or medium weight and by bowing it he would reach a full, beautiful tone in the lower range of the bass saxophone, without sacrificing brightness in the upper range. He would insert the reed every time before he played a solo. Rollini also explained to Robert how he played a glissando on his saxophone. He would almost fully stretch out his right hand's fingers and in one fluent, controlled movement, would slowly open one or more keys. The quality and duration of the glissando depend on the speed of this action, while breathing is unchanged. Inspired by Rollini, Jean Robert bought a bass saxophone a little later. A Conn was too expensive, so he settled for a Buffet Crampon.[78] He mastered it quickly and managed to play in Rollini's style. His bass saxophone playing can be heard on the first recordings made by Gus Deloof's band, for Pathé in 1931.

Back to London and the Savoy

During the stay at Ostend, the Rollinis made numerous photographs of themselves, Dixie's mother, and band members. They demonstrate a holiday feeling. Apparently the band did not suffer from any negative public response, but preferred to regard the adventure as a holiday trip. Ostend's café terraces, the beach, and its boulevard were popular with the band. In fact, several excursions were made and some band members crossed the Belgian-Dutch border and visited the southern part of the Dutch province Zeeland. However, in September it came to an end and the band returned to its home base, the Savoy. Some took train and boat; others, including Bobby Davis and Manuel Elizalde, went by plane.

While Elizalde's orchestra returned, the New Savoy Orpheans had to leave the Savoy. Its leader, Reg Batten, had been so long at the Savoy that he thought he had privileges and so he was often absent and thus his band members lost discipline and had more fun, taking solos and talking to the female guests. The Savoy management was far from pleased with this and decided not to renew the band's contract when it expired on 30 September. This meant that its American members and Rollini's former colleagues with the California Ramblers, Sylvester Ahola and Irving Brodsky, had to find new jobs or return to New York.[79] Elizalde had probably been informed about the plans with the Orpheans before he went to Paris, and hiring some more men for greater flexibility looks like a clever reaction.

Fred Elizalde started again in London at the Savoy on 1 October, and that month *Melody Maker* paid much attention to the many changes at the Savoy. The greatest news was that Fred could split his eighteen-piece band in two now, at certain hours. "It will of course be impossible for one band to play continuously throughout all the hours during which there is dancing at the Savoy, as this would mean unceasing work every afternoon." Each of Fred's two bands would work the afternoons and Sundays on alternate weeks, and also play in turn during periods of the evenings before and after the "rush" hours. The larger of the two bands could be called a "melody combination," the smaller unit would be a "hot affair."

Adrian Rollini became leader of the "hot affair," Bobby Davis of the other. Thus Elizalde confirmed their exceptional contribution to his music. It also demonstrates the strong influence the Americans had over their leader. In an interview with Nick Dellow, Harry Hayes pointed out: "Although [Elizalde] was the bandleader, the three Americans were the governors." In fact, Elizalde left far too much to the Americans, and in doing so undermined his own position as a leader. This worried the Savoy's directors, who eventually started questioning his suitability for the task.

Table 6. Fred Elizalde's Personnel March 1928–April 1929

	Original band	From March '28	From July '28	From Oct '28 "melody"	From Oct '28 "hot"	From Apr '29
Chelsea Quealey, first trumpet	y	y	y		y	y
Norman Payne, second trumpet	y	y	y	y		y
"Nobby" Knight, third trumpet			y	y		y
Frank Coughlan, trombone						y
Bobby Davis, first alto sax, clarinet	y	y	y	leader		y
Harry Hayes, second alto sax	y	y	y	y		
Max Farley, reed instruments, arrangements						y
Rex Owen, tenor sax	y	y	y		y	
Fud Livingston, tenor sax, arrangements						y
Jack Miranda, sax, clarinet			y	y		y
Phil Cardew, (relief) saxes, arrangements						y
Adrian Rollini, bass sax	y	y	y		leader	y
George Hurley, violin		y	y		y	y
Ben Frankel, violin			y	y		y
Len Lees, violin			y	y		y
Mario Lorenzi, harp			y	y		y
Fred Elizalde, leader, piano	leader	leader	leader			leader
Jack Russin, piano, arrangements			y	y	y	
Billy Masson, piano						y
Len Fillis, banjo, guitar	y	y	y		y	
Tiny Stock, bass		y	y	y		y
Ronnie Gubertini, drums	y	y	y	y	y	y
Richard Maxwell, vocals[1]	y	y				
Al Bowlly, vocals, guitar			y	y		y
Jack Hill, guitar						y
Total size of Elizalde's Orchestra	10	12	17	12	7	20

[1] Sometime during the spring of 1928, Maxwell left and was succeeded by Eddie Sheldon, who in turn left when Al Bowlly joined.

Others did not doubt his talent at all. One of these was Mrs. Louis Oppenheimer, a Savoy shareholder[80] who hired the Savoy's Pinafore Room for the early morning of 2 October at 2:00 a.m., the day after Fred's opening night. The Rollinis were invited and probably the full band.

Melody Maker appreciated his article on the goofus, which had been published in its March issue, and wanted more of his writing. So it agreed with Rollini on a series of articles about the details of his main instrument, the bass saxophone. In December it published the first, titled "The When, Why and How of the Bass Saxophone." Eventually there would be nine articles, published at an almost monthly rate.[81]

Elizalde knew that he could advance dance music and said in a newspaper interview: "Dance bands—if they are to survive, must have better methods and better music every day. That is why I recently introduced a new style of band, incorporating a harp and two pianos. . . . That, I think, is the reason why I have succeeded." And reactions were positive. One newspaper wrote:

> Dancing men in London are naturally discussing Fred Elizalde's new 18-strong combination at the Savoy. It was a daring experiment this band which includes three [sic] pianos, a harp, and other unusual instruments in addition to the more orthodox ones. Of its success there is, however, no doubt at all. Dancers have been thirsting for something really new for some time, and as no one seemed to provide them with a new step they have naturally leapt at the band with alacrity.[82]

However, the Savoy management was not so pleased. On 12 November Elizalde received their letter commenting on the previous Saturday's broadcast. They had noticed a "lack of tone in several numbers." According to the letter, One tune in particular was poorly performed, "Chirp, Chirp," where the violins were "palpably out of tune."[83] On the technical side there was progress: The BBC had had difficulties, mainly due to the Savoy's poor acoustics, but apparently they were overcoming them.

The Savoy did not leave the matter alone, reconsidered their musical situation, and sent Fred another letter only two days later, after the Monday broadcast. It said:

> There are one or two points I would like to mention:
> Musical Comedy Numbers: The public adore these numbers and we are not playing enough of them. You should be ready to play any popular number from the latest Musical Comedy on the night that these Musical Comedies are produced.
> Sunday Nights: It is understood that there shall be not less than twelve players in the orchestra for Sunday nights, and l think it is essential that Davis should always be here. You can give him an evening off on other occasions.

Orchestra's change over: Will you please instruct the gentlemen of your Orchestra that they must not take their places on the stand during the time the other Band are still playing. This looks very bad. It would be much better if your entire Band did not come into the room to take over their positions on the stand until the definite change-over was taking place.

Orchestra Times: I think it is essential that you yourself and the Full Orchestra continue playing until the end of the session. You will please do this tonight and we can discuss the matter tomorrow.

Medleys: These have been a great success but you must be careful that they are played as written. I noticed on Monday there was a distinct tendency on the part of the trumpets to put in their own rendering.

I must impress upon you once again the absolute necessity of keeping the band down. At the early part of your session last night you were much too loud, and it was quite impossible to talk in comfort at those tables on the edge of the floor.

The Savoy linked the renewal of Fred's contract to this set of rules. It would expire in July 1929 and no doubt Fred and Manuel promised to take measures, but Fred's personality and his interest were in the way. He was thinking of a further increase of his personnel. At the same time, he let the Savoy know that Rollini was to leave his orchestra. He may have had the false idea that without Rollini the Savoy would more easily accept the hiring of more Americans. However, Rollini never left the orchestra (except for return trips to New York), and Fred asked the Savoy for financial backing to bring more Americans over but this was refused.

The writing was on the wall.

Chapter 12

With Fred Elizalde in 1929, the Second Year

Controversial feelings about Fred Elizalde were building up and becoming more extreme. *Melody Maker*, who had supported Fred from his first performances two years earlier, was getting more and more involved. In its November 1928 issue the magazine had another article in defense of the maestro. It knew that the Savoy management had given Elizalde strict rules and that renewal of his contract depended on them. The BBC had also received some negative letters and Fred challenged the Savoy to have a BBC team come and listen to a live performance at the hotel. The article is worth reading in full:

> The style adopted by Fred Elizalde and his band has been, and probably always will be, the center of divergent views. He is usually thinking a year or two ahead of anybody else, and in consequence his ideas require a good deal of consideration and understanding before they can be fully appreciated. His broadcasts, from the general public point of view, are not always popular at the moment, despite the fact that my recent ballot proved him to be the favorite with the profession. When the listening public dislikes a thing, it usually finds an outlet for its grievances by letters to the B.B.C. Apparently, some such letters have been arriving there, protesting against Elizalde's broadcasting on the grounds that the tunes he plays cannot be recognized, and that, in any case, his music sounds like a mere hotchpotch of noise. And so the officials concerned informed Fred that his services were not quite suitable and might no longer be required. I understand Fred's reply was to the effect that they could please themselves, but that he was willing to submit his playing to any body of competent critics for an impartial verdict. The Savoy Hotel, moreover, have a contract with the B.B.C., which obligates the Corporation to broadcast the dance music from the hotel.

In the end, the BBC apparently fell in with Fred's suggestion, and sent some of their musical experts to hear the band in the flesh, when Fred trotted out some of his representative music. The committee of inspection appeared to enjoy itself thoroughly, and reported that, far from the music being unsuitable, it was truly magnificent, and that the complaints must be attributable to bad transmission.

> I am delighted to acknowledge the care taken by the B.B.C. to avoid panicky action in this case, because it may well turn out to be all for the good. If the B.B.C. engineers can improve the reception for their listeners then so much the better, but in any case the music is ingenious enough, and well played enough in all conscience, to enthrall quite a large percentage of those who certainly understand enough about modem rhythm music to be able to assert with coincidence that in due course the masses too will clamor for it, even in the futuristic style as employed by Elizalde to-day.

Nevertheless, the BBC would stop broadcasting Fred Elizalde's music when the contract it had with the Savoy expired in February 1929. The reasons were not Fred's music but (1) the Savoy felt that the BBC had no properly structured dance music program, (2) the Savoy disagreed with the BBC's absolute ban on song-plugging and wanted their singers to be heard, (3) the Savoy's restaurant was acoustically not suited for broadcasting, and (4) the Savoy felt that broadcasting was an intrusion on the dinner dance routine, especially as the band had to play loudly. The *Daily Herald*, however, thought that "what lies behind this is . . . the unpopularity of the pioneer. Other bands have concentrated on melody, but Elizalde's has experimented in fresh fields. Its unusual and elaborate orchestrations are much admired by experts but the finer points are often lost in reception. Refinement of technique is wasted on many wireless sets. In fact, listeners prefer tunes."[1]

While broadcasting thus seemed to be on its way out for him, Elizalde was getting involved in a new medium, sound film. Already in 1928, probably in the spring, he made a short. That first one was *The Sugar Step*. A couple demonstrates the new dance and the band accompanies them on screen, Quealey taking a solo.[2]

In November Fred had three more sessions at Brunswick, two with the band and one to record two piano solos, his own composition "Grown Up Baby" and "She's a Great, Great Girl," the latter being one of his finest. At the first of the two orchestra sessions Elizalde tried a novelty tune, "Laughing Marionette," during which Rollini picks up his original instrument once more, the xylophone, as well as its successor, the vibraphone.[3] His virtuoso xylophone confirmed to Rollini's colleagues, particularly, the British players, that he was a genius. He plays two breaks on the vibraphone, his first recorded work on this instrument.[4] Mario Lorenzi's harp also can be heard. From a jazz standpoint, the second title recorded, "Crazy Rhythm," is more interesting. It uses an arrangement by Jack Russin that gave Rollini freedom for some exceptionally fine solo work.

For many years, collectors knew only one title from the band's next Brunswick session: "If I Had You," with a vocal by Al Bowlly and issued in Brunswick's 3000 series, in which the company normally issued American recordings. However, as might be expected, Brunswick recorded more than one title during this session. Recently a test pressing of a second title, "I'm Glad," surfaced and was issued on a compact disc.[5] It gives the listener a chance to hear Rollini both on vibraphone and on bass saxophone.

In December Dixie returned to New York; the same month brought another recording session with Brunswick, which turned out to be the final one. The full band went to the studio and Al Bowlly sang on both titles, "Misery Farm" and "I'm Sorry, Sally." "Misery Farm" has a lyric that describes a farm where everything goes wrong, a strange theme for a popular song.[6] However, it has a nice arrangement, which features Rollini and Davis, but the best moment is a thirty-two-bar solo trio of three trumpets (Quealey, Payne, and Knight) that could have been lifted out of an arrangement by Bill Challis for Jean Goldkette's band with Bix Beiderbecke.

The Brunswick company had seen declining sales of Elizalde's records, and when the contract expired by the end of the year it was not renewed. The Savoy management was not pleased with this, and certainly Fred Elizalde and his men were not. The hotel had a long history with His Master's Voice, which had issued records by the Savoy Havana Band and Savoy Orpheans for several years, until the end of the year before. So the Gramophone Company, owner of His Master's Voice, received a letter from the Savoy's Richard Collett, who wrote:

> I am wondering if the Gramophone Company would like to record exclusively Fred Elizalde and his Music. We have Elizalde under contract till the end of July and we could enter into an arrangement with you to do say a minimum of twelve sessions between now and that period. Judging from the very large number of enquiries that are received both by Elizalde himself and the hotel for gramophone records of his orchestra, I should say that the proposition would be commercially a very sound one.

Why the Gramophone Company did not pick up this offer to get London's most progressive dance band in their catalog is unknown. It may have been that the discontinuation of the previous contract was still fresh in their memory or they may have been satisfied with the way Jack Hylton was producing quality dance music for them.

As if one blow was not enough, the Savoy had to absorb another when the BBC decided not to continue the regular broadcasts of dance music from the Savoy. Their primary reasons were twofold and had hardly anything to do with Elizalde's music. The main reason was the technical difficulty involved in broad-

Adrian Rollini showing how to hold the bass saxophone for *Melody Maker* (1).

Adrian Rollini showing how to hold the bass saxophone for *Melody Maker* (2).

casting from the Savoy, which was never fully solved. Reason two was the BBC's stand against any form of what it regarded as song plugging. The Savoy did not support the BBC and sent them a letter with its thoughts: "Personally I do not think that the BBC will ever put down plugging until they have complete control over the programmes that the various dance bands broadcast."[7] It did not make a difference, and the last broadcast by Fred Elizalde and his Savoy Hotel band took place on 28 February 1929.[8]

By this time the publication of Rollini's how-to articles in *Melody Maker* had come on steam. His article on the goofus, back in March 1928, had been a finger exercise both for Adrian and for the magazine. However, in December 1929 his first article on the bass saxophone appeared and two more installments followed in January and February.[9] Also in January the magazine published the first of several "hot" choruses written by Rollini to recent dance tunes. His first was for "Because My Baby Don't Mean Maybe Now," a popular foxtrot by American Walter Donaldson. Rollini wrote it for trumpet, which was explained by the magazine by saying that "the bass saxophone was only one of many instruments on which Rollini is not merely a performer, but an artist held in highest esteem by . . . musicians who appreciate the very latest developments of modern dance music." In February this was followed by a "hot" chorus for "Back in Your Backyard," this time for saxophones. Time and time again *Melody Maker* underlined Rollini's undisputed position as the leading bass saxophone player and as a creative artist.[10] It only contributed to his popularity.[11]

While all this happened to him and around him, Fred Elizalde did not deviate from the target he had in mind with his band, which was to play his own kind of music and not take direction from nonmusical people. His wealth allowed him not to worry at all, but to continue working on his ideas.

Although his orchestra was already larger than most dance bands, Elizalde's foremost idea now was to expand his orchestra further. And what he wanted were American reed players.

Hunting Reed Players in New York

Elizalde's first step to get more musicians was to ask the Savoy for financial support. The Savoy refused to pay their passage but its management agreed to an increase of the monthly payment.[12] Had the Savoy fully refused, Fred might have paid for them out of his own pocket. However, apparently the Savoy still had good hopes and once more gave him the benefit of the doubt.

Rollini's prominent position in Elizalde's organization is illustrated by the fact that Fred decided to send him over the ocean to contract musicians and work his network in the New York music scene. For the financial side, brother Manuel went along. Adrian left on Wednesday 30 January with the SS *Majestic* from Southampton and arrived a week later. Manuel traveled separately. Like Dixie, Adrian traveled second class. He probably did not take his bass saxophone along, since he wanted to buy a new one.[13]

Reunited with his wife Dixie, Adrian probably spent much time with their families and in fact would live with his or her mother most of the time. Unlike his previous trip, there were no particular activities in Adrian's social environment, so he could concentrate on his task of finding musicians—and on making records. Knowing this before he left London, no doubt he contacted his former leaders Ed Kirkeby and Red Nichols, trying to get recording dates. Within a week after his arrival in New York, Rollini had the first one, probably through Kirkeby. This was with up-and-coming orchestra leader Bert Lown.[14] By this time Lown ran a booking office, but he did not yet have a regular band. So for this recording session, his first, he hired musicians from other bands, such as Frank Cush, trumpet; Chauncey Gray, piano; and Tommy Felline, banjo, from the California Ramblers. Also trombone player Miff Mole, who had recently found work with that band, was hired by Lown. Ed Kirkeby, still owner of the California Ramblers, certainly knew about Lown's initial session and may have tipped off Rollini. If Rollini played this date on a new bass saxophone, then it must have been waiting for him when he arrived in New York less than a week before; and if this Lown session presented the first music he heard when he was back in New York, then he was probably shocked. It was as if time had stood still. The arrangements used compared unfavorably to Elizalde's and the recordings were made for Harmony, by this time the only major American company still recording with the old acoustic system. Moreover singer Irving Kaufman had an archaic style that had been popular in the early twenties. Most of the music was straight dance music, but in one of three titles recorded that day Rollini had a short solo, "My Castle in Spain Is a Shack in the Lane." Nevertheless, Rollini saw a future in working with Bert Lown, so the musical press was informed about their agreement that Rollini would work for Lown's office "after his return this summer for permanent stay."[15]

Red Nichols was busy with his regular recording sessions and got his Five Pennies together at Brunswick a few days after the Lown session. As usual, Nichols had an all-star group in the studio. Along with himself and Manny Klein on trumpet were Miff Mole on trombone, mellophone player Dudley Fosdick, Fud Livingston and Jimmy Dorsey on clarinet and alto saxophone, and a rhythm section of Arthur Schutt, Carl Kress, and Vic Berton. Nichols, of course, remembered how well Adrian Rollini had fit in this group of top jazzmen two years earlier, so he not only added him but decided to strongly feature him as well. Three titles were recorded, "Alice Blue Gown," "Allah's Holiday," and "Roses of Picardy."

During his recording career Nichols consistently tried to bring new elements and new styles to his recorded output. Thus he led recording groups of varying sizes (yet often calling them Five Pennies) with varying styles. When Eddie Condon arrived in New York, Red started to record with the Chicagoans, but now with Rollini in the team the Pennies were all New Yorkers again and the result was a success. For his last two sessions Nichols had done without any bass instrument, and Rollini's bass work seems to have inspired the band to some of the most joyful recordings that Red made at the time. "Alice Blue Gown" features Rollini in a two-bar break, followed by a fluent sixteen-bar solo and he opens "Allah's Holiday" with a thirty-two-bar statement of the melody. "Roses of Picardy" closes the session excellently with great ensemble work and beautiful solos, including a break by Rollini and thirty-six bars of his hot fountain pen. Four days later Red Nichols started to record under a new name, the Louisiana Rhythm Kings.[16] For a while he would use this name for his "hot" recordings and reserve the name Five Pennies for larger groups playing more and more heavy arrangements. For the first session by the Louisiana Rhythm Kings, Red decided to go back to his small format and did not use a bass instrument, although Rollini had not yet returned to London and was available. However, as before in the development of the original Five Pennies, Red would develop his new band and Rollini would become a fixture.

Adrian's relationship with Ed Kirkeby may have resulted in the Bert Lown session, but it certainly was the cause for Rollini's last two recording dates during his stay in New York. It also brought him a one-night gig with the California Ramblers at the Penn Hotel, where the first recording session could be talked over. That first one was for Edison and was with the full band, including some of the men from the Bert Lown session. Rollini had been away from the California Ramblers for a year and a half, and during that period they had had more than forty recording dates. Kirkeby had used several successors for Rollini. The best fit had been Spencer Clark on the bass saxophone; when he left for Europe, Hank Stern or Jack Hansen filled the bass position on tuba. The last few months the band had even recorded without a bass. With Rollini in the band only one tune was recorded, "Guess Who?" (on 19 February, the same date as the Bert Lown session), and he received $15 for playing. Ward Lay would be the California Ramblers' next bass player.

A non-standard recording session was the final one Ed Kirkeby invited Rollini for. It took place only three days before his return to England. Kirkeby brought six instrumentalists to the Harmony studio and one singer. The singer, Smith Ballew, and Kirkeby would duet with Ballew as the Singing Boys. The records were issued on the Harmony label, some of this label's first electrical recordings There was a happy-go-lucky atmosphere in the studio and the tunes came out well, with Rollini soloing both on bass saxophone and on hot fountain pen.

Moving around in musicians' circles was the best way for Rollini to reach his main target of finding additional men for Fred Elizalde's band. Fred's brother Manuel was on hand as a support, mainly to fix the contractual details. Most of all Adrian and Manuel tried to find three reed players. However, Adrian had other ideas, too. In an interview with Nick Dellow, Norman Payne said that Adrian tried to hire Bix Beiderbecke and even Bing Crosby for the Elizalde band, but Bix was recovering from an alcohol-related illness at the time, and Bing was with Whiteman in Hollywood and thus also unavailable.[17] Reed player Pete Pumiglio, who had been Bobby Davis's successor with the California Ramblers and played on the Singing Boys session, was also approached by Adrian, but his wife persuaded him not to go. Another one who said no was former California Ramblers sideman Fred Cusick.[18]

Two of the three reed players that Adrian and Manuel found were Fud Livingston (1906–1957) and Max Farley (1896–1953).[19] Farley played ten different instruments and had worked with Paul Whiteman from August 1926 till September 1927. In addition to his work as a musician in the sax section, Farley contributed several arrangements to the Whiteman band.[20] Fud Livingston had similar talents, and on top of that was the author of several jazz standards.[21] He had worked for such top bands as those of Jean Goldkette, Ben Pollack, and Nat Shilkret.[22] In addition, both Farley and Livingston had worked with the

California Ramblers with Adrian Rollini, and Livingston had also participated in Rollini's recent recording date with Red Nichols. With these two men Rollini would bring over so much talent and experience that any third reed player could be less experienced as long as he had talent. That third reed player turned out to be Adrian Rollini's younger brother Art. Adrian was eight years senior to Art, who, in April 1929, had only just turned seventeen and had not finished high school yet. Art had been practicing tenor saxophone for many years and had even played alto saxophone at the California Ramblers Inn with a small group consisting of Bill Moore or Frank Cush, trumpet; sixteen-year-old Babe Russin on tenor saxophone; Pee Wee Russell, also on reeds; Herb Weil, drums; and possibly Jack Russin, piano.[23] At the time of his visit Adrian had never thought of his younger brother as a candidate for Elizalde's band. However, one day Manuel heard Art playing his horn somewhere in the Rollini house and remarked, "The kid's good," and then to Adrian, "Why not try to get him to go along?"[24] Adrian replied that he was going to school. However, they asked Art if he would like to go to England and this presented Art with a dilemma. On the one hand he was about to graduate from high school and wanted to go to Columbia University in New York. He had already gone to N.Y.U. to enroll for a B.A. On the other hand, he was offered $100 a week now to work in London.[25] His mother and sister encouraged him, and with mixed feelings Art stopped his unfinished high school education. One consideration he had was that he could financially help his mother Adelina, who was looking at a stack of doctor's bills without having had a steady income for some time. She would rent both Larchmont houses during the summer and live in the upstate summer house. Art would send $60 home every month.[26]

Thus, within just over a month Adrian Rollini, with the support of Manuel Elizalde, had managed to complete his task of contracting three excellent reed players, with the added attraction that two of them were great arrangers. He had also left another legacy of some recordings, the finest being with Red Nichols's Five Pennies. He had telegraphed Fred in London to get approval for their salaries. Fred approved, sent the tickets and instructed Adrian to engage them. With arrangers of the quality of Farley and Livingston, the band would have even more to offer than Bill Challis's arrangements used the previous year.[27]

On 8 March the group of four saxophone players, Farley, Livingston and the Rollini brothers, left New York on the *Berengaria*. Dixie traveled with her husband as well. Manuel Elizalde did not travel with the group and may have stayed in New York. On board Art met comedian George Burns, on his way to a vaudeville tour in England. When a show was arranged on board, George volunteered to be the emcee. In daytime Adrian and his three colleagues had taken out their horns and made and rehearsed a head arrangement of the tune "Nobody's Sweetheart" in four-part harmony. They contributed to Burns's show by performing it on their quartet of saxophones.

Adrian, Max Farley, Fud Livingston, and Arthur Rollini aboard the *Berengaria*.

In Europe the *Berengaria* first went to Le Havre, France, where they were met by Hal Fillis, Elizalde's manager.[28] Then it sailed on to Southampton, where it arrived on 15 March 1929. A train took them to London.

Back in London

Elizalde lost no time setting up a rehearsal for his enlarged band, and so the boys went directly to work. Art stayed with Adrian and Dixie for some weeks, but eventually moved to the Sherbourne, a residential hotel where he could stay for $18 per week, room and board included.

When the three arriving musicians joined the band, two other reed players left, Harry Hayes and Rex Owen. By April Jack Russin and Len Fillis also left, and there were several new additions to the band: Australian Frank Coughlan, trombone; and Brits Phil Cardew, relief saxophone and arrangements; Jack Hill, guitar; and Billy Mason, piano.[29] Coughlan had joined the band on a temporary basis, to fill in while Rollini was in New York, but Elizalde found him so good that he decided to keep him, though this required re-orchestrating most of the band's numbers.[30]

Despite all these changes, it appears that the management of the Savoy Hotel was coming to a decision not to renew Elizalde's contract when it expired.[31] After all they did not appreciate Fred's absolute lack of showmanship and his talent for creating controversy among his listeners, one group liking his advanced sounds and the other hating it. However, there was another reason for the Savoy to end with Elizalde: broadcasts from the hotel had stopped, so the hotel did not need a broadcasting type of dance band and could go for simpler music, strictly geared to (to quote Nick Dellow) the "ordinary middle-aged hotel frequenter who likes the occasional dance after dinner"—music such as provided by Al Collins's Orchestra at Claridges Hotel, also within the Savoy Group. Collins would be Elizalde's successor at the Savoy and he featured some top British talent such as Max Goldberg (born in London, though raised in Canada), trumpet, and Eric Siday, violin.

Elizalde may not have been aware of this, being occupied with his new band and the new musicians, several of whom were good arrangers too. Today the most tangible result is a recording session for the Parlophone company, four weeks after Rollini and his three new colleagues arrived in London.[32] Two titles were recorded, "Singapore Sorrows" and "Nobody's Sweetheart." "Singapore Sorrows" was an arrangement for the full band by Fud Livingston.[33] Fud's arrangement had been recorded before, by Ben Pollack's band in New York in 1928. It opened with a mock Chinese intro and solos were by Farley (clarinet), Coughlan (trombone), and Norman Payne (trumpet). The arrangement of "Nobody's Sweetheart" opens with the four-saxophone chorus written and played on board the *Berengaria* by Farley, Livingston, and the Rollinis. This is followed by a string of solos by Quealey (trumpet), Farley (clarinet), Davis (alto saxophone), Livingston (tenor saxophone), a piano duet by Elizalde and Mason, and the climax, as so often before, a final solo by Adrian Rollini.[34] The resulting record, Parlophone R1201, is a strong candidate for being the finest British prewar jazz record. The company did not issue these recordings until 1932, three years after they had been recorded. In that year Elizalde was making some new records, resulting in new publicity, and perhaps this was the reason for Parlophone to release these unissued masterpieces at that time.

By the end of that same month, Fred Elizalde's band could be heard in England in public outside the Savoy Hotel for the first time. Fred had obtained permission from the Savoy to appear in music halls and thus, from 29 April the band was engaged in a vaudeville show at the London Palladium, under a contract arranged by Elizalde's agent Henry Shrek. Shows started every day at 6:10 and 8:45 p.m., with matinees on Tuesday and Thursday at 2:30 p.m. One of the participating artists was George Burns, whom Rollini knew from the voyage on the *Berengaria*. Since the work at the Savoy continued as before (a tea session and a late-evening session), the band were good customers of London taxis.[35]

The band's first performance at the Palladium was a success, which may have led Fred to believe that his concept of advanced arrangements played by top (mostly Americans) musicians would definitely work. However, he was wrong. At that first occasion the hall was filled with a large number of his fans from Cambridge University, who reacted enthusiastically. They had sent him a large

With Fred Elizalde in 1929, the Second Year

Fred Elizalde's Savoy Music as staged at the London Palladium

Reading Left to Right—
FRONT ROW
Wm. Mason (piano), Len Lee, Ben Frankel and Geo. Hurley (Violins), Fred Elizalde (Director), Robert Davis, Max Farley (Saxophones and Flute), Phil Cardew (Saxophones)

SECOND ROW
Al Bowley (Vocalist and Guitar), W. Powell (Viola), Jack Hill (Banjo and Guitar), Arthur Rollini, Fud Livingston (Saxophones and Clarinets), Adrian Rollini (Bass Saxophone, Xylophone, Piano, etc.)

BACK ROW
Mario Lorenzi (Harp), H. Stock and Wm. Busby (String Basses and Sousaphones), Ronald Gubertini (Drums, etc.), Leonardo Gubertini (Tympani), Chelsea Quealey, Norman Payne and E. Knight (Trumpets), Frank Coughlan (Trombone)

Fred Elizalde's Orchestra at the Palladium.

tribute in the form of flowers at the Palladium. Later that night, at suppertime, the band had to move to the Savoy; these fans wanted to continue the happy occasion and followed them there.

However, the next day, 30 April, a different view surfaced when *The Times*, London's leading newspaper, published a review. It mentioned the "frenzied plaudits which Mr. Elizalde's jazz band and his two spectacular dancers . . . evoked." Trying to understand what happened it added:

> If this is a rather better jazz band than most, it is mainly because in composition it is nearer to a serious orchestra, with strings, brass, and percussion in sufficient strength to give something of the color and sonority which the usual assemblage of saxophones [unreadable] and motor horns so signally lacks. Mr. Elizalde and his men spent most of their time in producing the most extravagant cacophony that the jazz band has at its command; and what nursery stuff it is! In its darkened trench on the other side of the footlights the permanent orchestra of the theater listened for half an hour to these noises, and then filled in the "intermission" with tunes from The Student Prince, played honestly and well.

The Times was much happier with a group of black artists:

> They were mostly Americans this week at the Palladium, and easily the most satisfying of these are the nine negroes who appear together in [the sketch] "Dixie Rebels."

> There is nothing especially new about them, but their dancing is brilliant in its humor, lightness, end speed, and their singing displays not only first rate voices. but a sense of humor—a combination too rarely met. They are probably the cleverest party of comedians the United States has lent to us for some time past.

Obviously *The Times*' reviewer was not prepared for Elizalde's work, even though it had been broadcast by the BBC for more than a year on end. Reactions from most of the normal music hall crowd were similar.

Christopher Stone, BBC's well-known deejay "avant la lettre," was quite knowledgeable about Elizalde's work.[36] He wrote a revealing review after there had been several performances:

> As a student of modern dance music who has worked for two years under Maurice Ravel, the French composer, and as one who on his own admission often listens to a whole evening of Bach and sit[s] up most of the night reading the score, Elizalde has an obvious pull over most of his competitors. However, when it comes to putting a show across to a music hall audience, he suffers from the same sort of disadvantage as a senior wrangler starting work in a city office. He is an amazingly clever and intrepid pioneer, but has much to learn from others with inferior equipment but more flair for showmanship; and no amount of spotlights and brilliant intricacies of orchestration could conceal the fact that on the occasion when I heard it, his turn at the Palladium only roused the audience to anything approaching rapture when his orchestra was accompanying the incomparable dancing of Jean Barry and her partner.[37]

Finally, *Melody Maker* wrote a review and did it with more detail, giving some constructive comment.[38] It quoted Elizalde as saying that he "presented the act in full consciousness that his Savoy status made it imperative to maintain a Savoy atmosphere; that is something different, something superior and something entirely dignified." The magazine wondered if Elizalde was trying to sit on too many stools, "for the act was in the end neither a dance band, concert nor cabaret turn." The band had been augmented with tympani player Leonardo Gubertini and was twenty-three men strong. In a photograph three grand pianos are shown on the stage and there the count is twenty-four. The band accompanied the dancing team of Jean Barry and Dave Fitzgibbons, but in order to give room to the dancers, it was placed too much at the back of the stage. As a result, its sound was too weak and individual solos tended to get lost. The dancers got most of the applause. Thus during the first week, Max Farley's wonderful arrangement of "Glad Rag Doll" had gone fully unnoticed, since all attention had been for dancer Fitzgibbons. The second week this worked better because more music was played before the dancer made his entrance. *Melody Maker* enjoyed the arrangement of "Spread a Little Happiness," which included a clever hot chorus for the brass with certain notes accentuated by the contrast between muted and unmuted brass instruments. Fud Livingston's arrangement of "Lover Come Back to Me" gave the magazine's reviewer his biggest thrill: "It was mainly on 'symphonic concert' style, but tone color, instrumentation and vocal effects are exclusively of dance band character and beautiful at that. The rhythmic atmosphere is also enhanced by a hot trumpet chorus, which was excellently played by Chelsea Quealey." The review praised Al Bowlly's vocal solo, which was backed by harmonized vocal effects by the whole band: "The machine-like raising and lowering of 20 and more megaphones was the only piece of obviously attempted and successful showmanship indulged in."

Adrian Rollini played a prominent role in the performance. He not only played his bass saxophone but had at least two more instruments at hand, a xylophone and what could be a harpohone.[39] Further in the program Elizalde and Rollini played a piano duet. During the first week this piece had been "too intricate to be appreciated by any but the smallest minority." Therefore, in the second week, Elizalde gave something less involved, but then "he seemed out of his element." He simply was no showman and even played his piano almost with his back to the audience.

With such opinions in London newspapers, it is no surprise that the band's participation in the Palladium show was not continued after the contracted two or three weeks. Elizalde was convinced now that some of his men needed a vacation and he persuaded Dixie Rollini to let Adrian go to Brussels, Belgium's capital, together with his brother Art, Manuel Elizalde, and Hal Fillis, Elizalde's manager. They went by plane, a Fokker. For Art it meant his first flying experience and a tough one too: due to heavy fog the plane had to return before they finally managed to reach Brussels. They stayed at a top hotel, the Astoria, visited some nightclubs, saw a revue, and Adrian met some old friends. One time, Art drank too much and his evening ended in a brothel.[40]

There is a story about a trip of Adrian Rollini to Berlin that might be fitting here. Mike Danzi was a white American banjo player who had recorded in New York with Wilbur Sweatman's black band. Danzi had come to Berlin in 1924 with Alex Hyde's band and stayed when Hyde went back to the USA. What followed was a remarkable dance band career, Danzi making hundreds of recordings. In 1929 he was working with Teddy Kline at Les Ambassadeurs in Berlin. Danzi remembered that one day, in the middle of May 1929, Adrian and Dixie showed up in Berlin. Rollini came to see Kline's band, which consisted mainly of Americans. Danzi told Rainer Lotz, his biographer, that he recognized him immediately and Rollini, who had his mouthpiece with him, asked to sit in with the band. He played the whole afternoon. News passed around quickly in the music scene and that evening the club was filled to capacity, with many leaders present.[41]

Invitation Concert for Musicians

Melody Maker had been published starting in 1926 and had developed into the leading magazine for the jazz, dance, and light music sectors. Its readers were not only found on the British Isles; its reputation had quickly spread to the European continent and to English-language areas in the rest of the world. English was the language of jazz and *Melody Maker* usually was first with up-to-date news about it, although it was most often called "hot music" at the time. The magazine had supported Fred Elizalde and his music from the beginning and he was often the subject of articles. It recognized and supported Adrian Rollini as one of the greatest exponents of modern dance and hot music. In 1928–29 it even ran a series of ten articles written by Adrian Rollini about the use of the goofus and the bass saxophone. However, for a long period the band could only be heard at the Savoy or via the BBC, and when the broadcasts stopped, hearing the Elizalde band was a privilege for the few who could afford to dine at the Savoy. In 1929 *Melody Maker* had a great idea to promote Elizalde's music, while at the same time creating publicity for itself. This idea was to organize a concert which was to be visited strictly on invitation and then by musicians only.

Elizalde's band would work for free, but tickets could only be obtained through *Melody Maker*'s office. Application for tickets was opened with the magazine's June issue. Within a day after it had been put on sale, applications were received for 1,000 tickets. A supplement to its July issue gave a full account. First it was thought that a medium-sized West End theatre, holding some 1,200, would be large enough. With the overwhelming response a search started for a larger hall and the Shepherd's Bush Pavilion was found, a cinema theater which could seat 2,777 visitors and had standing room for another 500 to 600. "Still applications were rained upon us," the magazine wrote. Eventually there was an audience of 3,200, but it could have been 2,000 more if there had been sufficient seats.[42] In addition to visitors from all over England and Scotland, there were guests from Belgium, Denmark, and France. Each found a nice souvenir booklet waiting on his chair.

After the return of some of his men from their continental trip, Fred started to rehearse for the concert, which would take place on 23 June. At the very last moment Fred had a problem that could have led to disaster, but didn't. Chelsea Quealey and Fud Livingston had done the rehearsals, but without any warning they quit only a few days before the concert.[43] The public was told that they had returned to New York because of sudden serious illness in their families. Actually, problems with the tax authorities were more likely.[44] Their roles were taken over by two youngsters, Norman Payne on trumpet and Art Rollini on tenor saxophone. To everybody's surprise and delight, both did an excellent job and their reputation among musicians was made.

Concert program given at *Melody Maker*'s Invitation Concert. (courtesy Nick Dellow)

The concert was introduced by Edgar Jackson, *Melody Maker*'s editor. After introducing Fred Elizalde, the first number he announced was "Singapore Sorrows," one of the titles that the band had recorded for Parlophone two months earlier, in an arrangement by Fud Livingston.

The souvenir booklet program contained a program, but there were some last-minute changes, as shown by the review in *Melody Maker* of the following month. The most striking was the inclusion of what could be called a jam session as the next item. This was introduced as "The Boys Will Do Their Stuff." It was arranged by Adrian Rollini and was meant to feature individual members and sections of the band in the form of choruses of popular tunes. Rollini's choice of tunes and soloists remains unknown, but he probably chose tunes recorded for Brunswick.

Item three consisted of four popular tunes arranged by Fud Livingston and Phil Cardew. Fud had arranged "She's One Sweet Show Girl." Probably the same arrangement as had been recorded by Ben Pollack's band the year before, just like in the case of "Singapore Sorrows." The next three tunes were "A Precious Little Thing Called Love," "Let's Do It," and "The Broadway Melody," all arranged by Phil Cardew. Following this, the band made a change of rhythm and performed a waltz, possibly an unknown Elizalde composition, called "Mistakes."[45]

Next were two tunes performed by a small unit from the full band simply called "The Jazz Band," probably more or less the hot unit set up in the fall of the previous year and led by Adrian Rollini. Their first tune was "Savoy Stomp," a collaboration of Rollini and Livingston as composers/arrangers. Unfortunately no recording or score of the tune exists, unlike their second tune, "Nobody's Sweetheart," which had recently been recorded. That recording was made with Quealey and Livingston, and with them gone, some changes had to be made. Norman Payne took Quealey's place and for the four-part sax intro Bobby Davis may have taken Fud's place. The public loved it. *Melody Maker* wrote: "These performances were hot—about as hot as anything ever heard—and to say they brought the house down, would be to put it mildly. . . . Anyone who thinks hot playing is not appreciated, ought to have heard the thunderous applause which followed this."

As a final piece before the intermission, Livingston's concert arrangement of "Lover Come Back to Me" was played, which had made such a great impression during the Palladium performances. Al Bowlly sang the chorus, backed by a vocal by the whole band. During the first part of the concert, about half of the tunes listed had been arranged by Fud Livingston. Elizalde could hardly do without him, but he had to.

After the intermission it was Elizalde's turn as a composer. The first title was "At the Turn of the Tide." After this number Fred took over from the band and played some piano solos. He opened with "Pianotrope," which he had recorded as a solo for Brunswick even before his Savoy contract. Fred probably played more of his own titles, but only his closing choice is known, Bix Beiderbecke's "In a Mist."[46] For this tune he was accompanied by his full orchestra, for which Max Farley had written a score. *Melody Maker*: "If the audience had had its way, it would probably still be listening to Elizalde playing piano."

As a grand finale, Elizalde had a special, longer composition to be premiered at this concert: *Bataclan*, a symphonic work in three movements. No score or recording survives. All we have is a description in the souvenir program and a comment in *Melody Maker*. Its story concerns a person, Bataclan, who wakes up to the noise of El Carnaval, the annual Spanish National festivities. He joins the crowd and suddenly sees a woman and falls in love. The second movement begins when a year has passed and Bataclan and the woman are living blissfully together. However, jealousy creeps in and Bataclan's fears are confirmed. She is unfaithful. In the third movement Bataclan walks empty streets asking himself the meaning of life, searching in vain for truth.

For the performance of *Bataclan* some extra musicians had been engaged. Three of them came from London symphony orchestras: Jack Thurston (clarinet), James Harker (oboe), and Harry Wild (trumpet). From his colleagues' dance bands came A. Richardson (trumpet, formerly with the Savoy Orpheans) and Herbert Powell (viola, from Jack Payne).

Elizalde and *Melody Maker*, who after all organized the concert, had considered not to present *Bataclan*. However, they decided that the audience was extraordinary and consisted entirely of music lovers and musically educated and "that it will be appreciated and hailed as a work of a genius." There was little coverage in the press, since the concert was for musicians only and few journalists had been invited. One of these few was the reviewer of the *Gramophone*. He wrote:

> Bataclan was different. It would be foolish to judge it at a first hearing, but it was good enough to make one forget the performers and listen to the music for its own sake. I should like to hear it performed by a really large orchestra where due prominence could be given to the strings. Mr. Elizalde, at the age of twenty-one, is undoubtedly quite exceptional in the dance world. Here is an opportunity for the recording companies. We get far too few records from Brunswick.

How the audience actually reacted is not in the magazine. However, they were enthusiastic enough to applaud for encores, and they got two, "Sweet Sue" and "Tiger Rag." "Again everyone was given a chance to shine and hot choruses of the most marvelous kind . . . tumbled over each other." Adrian Rollini added color with his goofus.

Melody Maker expressed its satisfaction with the concert in loud terms in its July issue, and Fred Elizalde knew for sure that there was a public for his work. However, in the long run it would not be large enough to support his full orchestra. He would soon find out, but for the time he was fully occupied.

After the Savoy: Trip to the Continent

1928 had been a year with more opportunities for Fred Elizalde than he could handle. With a recording contract with Brunswick, a broadcast arrangement with the BBC, and a Savoy management that had shown great patience and tolerance, Elizalde could not have fared better. However, as long as Elizalde's Savoy contract had existed, the hotel had put question marks about his musical approach, stimulated by letters of complaint that it received. As long as those complaints came in, the Savoy was never fully satisfied with his work, and Fred must have felt that.

The Savoy's managing director George Reeves-Smith sent Elizalde a letter on 3 July 1929, which said that his contract would not be renewed after 31 July 1929. The Savoy's customers' desire to change was given as a reason, but basically it was Fred's character as a talented composer who wanted to go his own way and who could afford to do so, even if others did not want to absorb the cost.

What Fred said to the Savoy is unknown, but certainly the Savoy remained friendly to him. The following day Fred received a letter that confirmed that, till the contract's end, it would continue to pay the additional £500 a week extra for the Americans who arrived in March, even though Quealey and Livingston had left.

What Fred said to the press is known, however, and it was typical. In *Melody Maker* of August 1929 he is quoted as saying:

> I have received a wonderful letter from the directors thanking me for, as they put it, all I have done, and stating that in their opinion the band has been a great success. All of which doesn't alter the fact that the contract has not been renewed. . . . that I wasn't asked to [renew my contract] is the best thing that could have happened to me. . . . my scope of really getting much further was always limited by being confined within the four walls of the Savoy, and since it ceased to broadcast there was no chance of enlarging my sphere of action.

He had plans for a show in a West End theater that would open around 1 October. He had an agent, Henry Sherek, who was organizing it, and a financial backing of £20,000. Fred and his band were to be featured and "the show was also to be made into a talkie."

However, what the public thought was expressed by a newspaper: "Elizalde and his orchestra conclude their long engagement at the Savoy at the end of this month. They will be missed. There are not so many dance bands of such quality."[47]

So from 1 August 1929 Fred Elizalde was not bound by any contract, free to make new plans.[48] As a parting present he gave Adrian Rollini, and probably other band members, a silver sliding-action cigarette case, but Adrian lost it before he arrived home in his apartment that night.

The band now had a month off. Art Rollini borrowed his brother's car, a new American Essex and, together with Norman Payne, went to the south coast. When they returned to London after two weeks, they found that they would not have to work for another two weeks. Art picked up his check and returned to England's south coast.

Adrian and Dixie decided to visit places on the continent they had not been before. They started in the Netherlands, and for a reason. The previous month, two Dutch fans of Adrian Rollini, students at Wageningen University for Agriculture and amateur jazz musicians, decided to travel to London to see some nice shows, but particularly to visit their idol Adrian Rollini. André Eschauzier and Eppo Doeve were readers of *Melody Maker* and may have been familiar with Elizalde's Brunswick recordings, but certainly with Rollini's milestone recordings with Bix Beiderbecke, Eddie Lang, Red Nichols, Frank Trumbauer, and Joe Venuti. It was only a few days before Elizalde's contract ended, when

Rollini caricatures by Eppo Doeve, sketch and final result.
(courtesy Doeve family and Andre Eschauzier)

they arrived at the Savoy, where they met Rollini during his intermission. He was surprised that they knew all of his great jazz records. However, the two fans would feel the same controversy that ended Elizalde's contract, when, later that day, they were sitting in the Savoy with Dixie to listen to the band. They were greatly disappointed with what they heard: "They only played very fine straight ballroom music and that's not what we came for.... Only a few times during an evening they would play a swing piece. We called that 'playing hot,' with solos. Then Rollini would get going on that bass and we would be silent."[49]

Adrian and Dixie were living in an apartment and invited André and Eppo to visit them after the performance. Rollini told them that the band was working for film company British Gaumont at the time and that the Savoy contract would end shortly. The two fans had dinner with the Rollinis several times. André remembered her as a typically American lady, who dressed showily and used her makeup well. Dixie turned out to be a great cook, especially for chicken dinners. Sometimes they would spend a part of the day at Rollini's apartment and then went to the Savoy, where Adrian would take his seat on the stage and they would take a table with Dixie and sometimes dance.[50]

Eppo Doeve would eventually become a very well-known illustrator. During the trip he tried his art by drawing Rollini. A preliminary sketch and the final result are shown on the previous page.

The Rollinis told the boys about their plan for a holiday and André used the occasion to invite them to come over to the Netherlands and be his guest. Adrian and Dixie accepted and decided to visit Germany as well. The final performance at the Savoy was on Wednesday 31 July and the following Monday the couple arrived in the Netherlands. They stayed with the Goyarts family. Max Goyarts, a friend of André's, was a saxophone player and owned a bass saxophone. He had been to the Savoy, too, and had met the Rollini brothers there. Max's mother worried if she could get along with her American guests, but noted in her diary on Monday 5 August: "The guests arrived in the evening at seven. Eschauzier brought them with his car. They are most charming and neat people and we had a fine evening. Rollini I find an exceptionally nice fellow. I am glad for Max that it turned out like this."

The following afternoon the group with Adrian and Dixie went on a tour, and when they returned Rollini used his newly bought camera to capture family and friends on film. In the evening there was music made by an improvised band consisting of Rollini (piano), Max Goyarts (bass saxophone), André Eschauzier (alto saxophone), and Emile Verbunt (drums). Max's mother wrote: "It was a very nice day and evening and there was a lot of music and much laughing with the Band.... It was a mess." For a short moment Rollini also played on Goyarts's bass saxophone, as a short demonstration. He said that his style was very simple!

Rollini with Dutch fan Andre Eschauzier at Alkmaar cheese market.

The next day after dinner, the group went out to Vught, a town nearby, first to a small lake, the IJzeren Man (Iron Man), then to the fun fair. Rollini loved it and even won a goldfish bowl by throwing rings around it. When the fair was closing, Rollini did not want to finish yet. He wanted to eat some poffertjes (typically Dutch tiny pancakes), but the owner only accepted the group after Rollini had given him some pocket money. They got the last booth in the rear of the restaurant, so that the police could not see them.

On 8 August Adrian and Dixie left the Goyarts family. André Eschauzier owned a car and took them to Amsterdam. They were typical tourists and visited the towns of Volendam and Marken with their old harbors and fishing boats. Adrian bought his wife a real Dutch costume, even to the wooden shoes, as worn at the time by the wives of the fishermen. Alkmaar and its historical cheese market were also visited. In Amsterdam they went to Tuschinsky, a beautiful film theater, where an American jazz band played in its dancing room, La Gaité. The name of the band remains unknown, but when André told its members that Adrian Rollini was in the audience they knew who he was, but could hardly believe it. In André's words: "They reacted like crazy and burst out in a vocal chorus, something like: A great man is here. Rollini is here. He is sitting here; he likes the Dutch beer." In fact, Rollini preferred whisky to beer, which he always ordered as a "double" and which André as a good host, offered him, so that he had to wire his mother for cash. A double whisky cost five guilders, and André remembered that Rollini could easily drink eight during one evening.[51]

The music at La Gaité was managed by Max Tak, who also had a music column in a leading Amsterdam newspaper and was interested in the jazz scene.

Rollini giving camera instruction to Andre Eschauzier in Scheveningen.

The American bandleader informed Max Tak that Adrian Rollini was in the audience and Tak decided to ask for an interview. He walked to Rollini and took time for a long introduction of himself. When he finished at last, Rollini had a chance to say: "And now Mr. Tak, may I introduce you to my friend Eschauzier?" Tak managed to get a good short article about Rollini's career. The article mentions Rudy Wiedoeft's "The Rosary" and Red Nichols's "Roses of Picardy," recordings Rollini was apparently most proud of. Rollini also went into the plans to go into the music halls ("all financial preparations are done") and do a talking picture.[52]

Another place André visited with the Rollinis was Scheveningen, The Hague's sea resort, where the best Dutch dance band of the moment worked, the Original Ramblers, directed by Theo Uden Masman. In the past Frank Guarante and his Georgians as well as Paul Whiteman and his Orchestra had worked at the Kurhaus and its associated dancing Palais De Danse. The Original Ramblers[53] were on their way up, had made their first recordings, and used a bass saxophone as their bass instrument. The evening of Rollini's visit became unforgettable for the band when Rollini took out his mouthpiece and sat in with them for half an hour, using Maurits Dreese's Conn bass saxophone. Masman's

Rollini with Dutch dance band the Original Ramblers in Scheveningen. From left: Eddy Meenk, Maurits Dreese, Kees Kranenburg, Adrian Rollini, Wim Poppink, Theo Uden Masman, Gerard Spruyt, Jac Pet.

enthusiastic letter to *Melody Maker* was published in September, together with a photograph of Rollini surrounded by the band.

There was one small incident during Rollini's stay in the Netherlands that André Eschauzier did not like to remember. Driving back from Alkmaar, Dixie wanted to get some Dutch money and she asked André to stop at a bank. She gave him a green bill (André thought it was a five-pound bill) and asked him to have it changed into guilders. When André returned she thought that she should have received more. She and André went back into the bank together and the cashier showed them the bill that he received, five pounds. It gave André a bad feeling. Another of André's memories from Rollini's visit was funnier. Adrian told him about a trip that he and Dixie had made to Rome and his country of origin, Italy. In their hotel he had noted that some waiters would comment in Italian on Dixie's dress and makeup, saying things like "look at her silly hat" or "look at her painted lips" or "what a silly dress she has today," assuming the American guests didn't understand all this. Then at the time of their departure Rollini asked the manager to have an opportunity to speak to the hotel personnel to express his gratitude. The personnel came together and Rollini addressed them in fluent Italian, said that he enjoyed the stay, the friendly climate, the good food, and the pleasing remarks made by the waiters.[54]

Rollini in Berlin with members of Max Lefko's orchestra. Lefko center, looking at Rollini; Leo Mathisen is standing on left, with cane.

When their visit to the Netherlands ended, Adrian and Dixie Rollini traveled to Berlin, Germany. They may not have had any specific contacts there and just tried to find the right places.[55] At the time Berlin was a destination for several foreign bands and individual musicians who worked there for longer periods and made records, bands such as those of Americans Sam Wooding, Alex Hyde, and Lud Gluskin. One person whom they met there was Leo Mathisen, a Danish musician who was working with Max Lefko's orchestra in an intimate little restaurant at Kurfürstendamm, Berlin's center of entertainment. Mathisen wrote about his happy meeting with Rollini in a Danish jazz magazine in 1935:

> We had just finished the number "Ida Sweet as Apple Cider" in the well-known Red Nichols-arrangement, when one of the artists from that classical Brunswick-record peeped in through the door—lured by the familiar sounds. This was no less than Adrian Rollini, the most famous bass-saxophonist in the world! Just to be sure you had to ask himself, which I promptly did. The man nodded in affirmation and showed pleasure of being known so far from his homeland. It did not take many seconds before Rollini and our band were congregated over a bottle of whisky—a beverage that the dear bass saxophonist doesn't despise. Almost as soon afterwards did he produce a mouthpiece from his pocket and modestly asked if he could play a few numbers with us.[56]

Mathisen went on to describe the time he and the Rollinis spent together visiting other orchestras and specifically mentioned Lud Gluskin at the Ambassadeur.⁵⁷ Another band they visited was Billy Bartholomew's, whose sax player and trumpeter, Art Christmas and Louis de Vries respectively, excited Rollini.

In one of the nightclubs, the Künstlereck, there was a blind Italian man playing the piano, and as Rollini saw a compatriot in him, they chatted in Italian. The Italian fellow had a harmonium besides his piano, and it did not take long, before the two found each other in little Italian songs and fugues by Bach. Mathisen also took his turn with the old masters together with Rollini, and the mood was high. When Rollini at the piano went into "Futuristic Rhythm," the Italian guy and everybody else screamed with joy. "We were sorry when the Master had to leave us to go back to London."

Another musician who remembered Adrian's August trip to Berlin was banjo player Mike Danzi. In his biography he describes his first meeting with Rollini, which had been in May. Danzi remembered the blind piano player, mentioned by Leo Mathisen, who duetted with Rollini, specifically noting that the pianist played popular numbers, such as "Sweet Sue," while Rollini improvised hot choruses.

By 20 August Adrian and Dixie were back in London. Dixie wrote thankful letters to Theo Uden Masman and André Eschauzier and Adrian signed them, too. She mentioned that they took about six hundred feet of film: "Now we will have to buy a projector."⁵⁸

Final Months in Europe

Melody Maker never let Fred Elizalde down, but it was too late to announce the tour that his orchestra was making in September. After the holidays the band had to rehearse for its trip and the first performances were at Plaza Palace in Glasgow on 18 and 19 September. In quick succession this was followed by concerts in Aberdeen's Palais De Danse, in Edinburgh's Dunedin Palais De Danse, and finally in Newcastle-Upon-Tyne's Oxford Galleries.

For this tour the band had a new bass player, A. Axford, who replaced both Bill Busby and Tiny Stock. Chelsea Quealey had no successor, but Norman Payne played first trumpet (including all the jazz work) and Nobby Knight second trumpet.

The tour was a partial artistic success and a financial loss. The initial reception in Scotland was enthusiastic, due to the presence of Scottish musicians who wanted to hear the latest in dance music. Usually, however, the halls were only half filled. Elizalde's stage performance lacked any feeling for show business and public interest dwindled as a result. Norman Payne said that a tour of

Fred Elizalde's Orchestra on northern tour. From left, front row: Billy Mason, Mario "Harp" Lorenzi, Fred Elizalde, Bobby Davis, Jack Hill, Arthur Rollini. Middle row: Nobby Knight, Jack Collins, Ben Frankel, unknown, Adrian Rollini, Al Bowlly. Top row: Unknown (probably not a band member), Max Farley, Tiny Stock, Phil Cardew(?), Ronnie Gubertini, Bill Busby, Norman Payne. (identification Nick Dellow)

Scotland was the common thing to do by such bands as Jack Hylton's and Billy Cotton's, but those leaders were stage personalities, which Elizalde never was.[59] One musician wrote: "The Elizalde performance was spoiled by Elizalde himself. A grand piano was taken to the center of the ballroom floor for Elizalde to do a solo spot. The dancers were making too much noise, so he banged down the piano lid and walked off. Rollini was on his feet at once and got the band playing without a pianist."[60] Max Farley could play any woodwind instrument and he demonstrated it in Scotland. One day he went into a shop and bought bagpipes and played them.

Back in London, Fred concentrated on work for a movie soundtrack. A contract to provide the music for the film *The Woman He Scorned* had been signed by him before he left the Savoy. This film had been made in the late spring and summer of 1929 as a silent film, starring Pola Negri.[61] The main work was done at the Elstree Studios, Borehamwood, Hertfordshire, and most outdoor scenes were filmed in Cornwall. Before it was released, it was decided to add sound to

Fred Elizalde's Orchestra on northern tour. From left: Ronnie Gubertini, Nobby Knight, Max Farley, Ben Frankel, Tiny Stock, Billy Mason, Dixie Rollini, unknown, Bobby Davis, Mario Lorenzi, Jack Hill, Al Bowlly, Art Rollini, Adrian Rollini, Fred Elizalde, unknown, unknown. (identification Nick Dellow)

it. The film is also known as *The Way of Lost Souls*. Music was recorded by late November.[62] Art remembered that Adrian played the bass saxophone on the soundtrack and that the band was working from 10 o'clock in the morning till 4 the next morning, for three weeks. After the band had finished each night, Elizalde would continue to write on the score all night long.[63]

This film project almost led to another. Producer Rex Ingram invited Elizalde to produce the soundtrack for a large-budget production that was to be made in Nice, France, with Lionel Barrymore and his wife, Dolores Costello, but the project was canceled.[64]

In addition to this film work, Elizalde worked on another theater production, to be called *The Intimate Revue* and to be staged at a West End theater. Rollini knew about all these activities and mentioned them when he was interviewed during his European vacation.

All this time Fred Elizalde kept the full band on his payroll, which did not seem to worry him in the least. However, he did not realize that no theater might be financially strong enough to afford such a large band.

Since the Brunswick recording contract had been discontinued, the band had been in a recording studio only once. That had been back in April to record two titles for Parlophone. Now at last, on 4 December 1929, they would record again, for a small company called Metropole.⁶⁵ Unlike the Parlophone recordings, the results were meager from a jazz standpoint. The titles may have been selected by the company. One was a waltz and one a foxtrot, "After the Sun Kissed the World Goodbye." Elizalde was preparing the band's second Scotland tour at the time of this recording, so he could not be present and the band was under Adrian Rollini's direction. On the record labels, the artist is listed as Fred Elizalde's Rhythmusicians and Rollini is mentioned. The foxtrot side has its merits, with several solos including Rollini's last solo recorded in London and an excellent Bixian solo by young Norman Payne, already regarded as one of the best British trumpeters in the Bix Beiderbecke style.

The day after the recording session the band traveled to Scotland again, but the Rollinis did not join this time and stayed in London. Adrian was to handle some of Fred's affairs while he was away. The first performance was in Dundee and it went well. The second, however, a dance and concert on 6 December in Edinburgh, was badly received by a rowdy audience. When Fred gave a few piano solos, a noise broke out and he could not silence his public anymore. Fred walked off. His band lacked interest in calming the hall and they gave over to the resident band. In a similar situation, Adrian Rollini had shown his special ability to keep the performance going, but without him Elizalde had no solution.

The tour continued with performances in Aberdeen, but a planned concert in Brighton had to be canceled due to a poor railway connection, as reported in *Melody Maker*.

By mid-December Elizalde was back in London and his band had no plans other than the *Intimate Revue*, the stage show Fred had worked on for several months. However, at this time the Ministry of Labour started to bother him with questions about his need for so many Americans in his band. To add to his problems, the Wall Street Crash started to be felt in London too, some two months after it happened. This was particularly felt by people with a bank account, and this included Fred Elizalde. His funds were frozen by the bank and thus he could not pay his musicians. On one particular day, Adrian went to the bank to cash a check. He was in time, but his brother Art arrived a little later and was too late. Adrian took this as a signal to return to New York.⁶⁶

On Tuesday 17 December 1929, Adrian and Dixie, together with brother Art, sailed off on the SS *Leviathan*.⁶⁷ After a six-day trip they arrived in New York, just before Christmas. They had left fellow Americans Max Farley and Bobby Davis behind and would find a country that was getting deeper and deeper into the economic depression.⁶⁸ Eventually Farley would work in Germany and then return to London, where he recorded with Spike Hughes, after which he traveled back home. Bobby Davis also went back to the United States.⁶⁹ To keep the band together, Fred Elizalde had spent thousands of British pounds of his own money.⁷⁰

Fred Elizalde's Further Career

Fred Elizalde made an effort to get back into the Savoy in the New Year, but a letter from the hotel dated 18 December made it clear that that was no option. This did not discourage him and so he assembled a new band for the *Intimate Revue*, which opened in March 1930. However, it closed within three weeks and recordings of its tunes were not issued. This was Elizalde's last project with a band. He turned away from dance music and would spend his time composing. The results were three compositions in 1930, "Spirituel," the tone poem "Moods," and a Spanish dance called "Jota." These compositions brought new success to him in Spain, where he would study under Manuel De Falla. Fred found a new future and would compose more pieces in this field.

As a kind of intermission, he would occasionally get back to dance music. Thus he would record some piano solos for Decca during the winter of 1931–32. For the same company he recorded his ideas of the history of jazz, on two twelve-inch discs, the first as a piano solo, the second with a studio orchestra.

British Brunswick did not archive its recordings by Elizalde's band, so the company had a problem, when in the mid-thirties it wanted to satisfy the requests from jazz fans to reissue the best jazz titles. This was solved by dubbing original issues: good copies were played on a gramophone and the signal used to cut a new master. An album with four records was issued with a leaflet written by an enthusiastic H. G. Penniket, who wondered why such excellent Elizalde arrangements as "I Can't Give You Anything but Love," "I Ain't Got Nobody," and "Chloe" had never been recorded.

In 1936 Fred was in Spain and got involved in its civil war. He became a member of the Basque Regiment, the Requetes, fighting against the reds. He even got wounded but recovered quickly. In 1946 Fred was living in Santa Monica, California, and later returned to Manila in the Philippines, where he worked at his family's broadcasting company.

Federico "Fred" Elizalde died in Manila in 1979, aged seventy-one years old.

Chapter 13

Out of Europe and into the Depression: Bert Lown

When, just before Christmas 1929, the three Rollinis stepped off the boat in New York, it was a step from the Old World into the New. In Europe Adrian had been treated as a famous personality from the day of his arrival. He had been socializing with the rich and famous who came to the Savoy to entertain and be entertained. He had led a life of earning and spending much money, had lived in the best parts of London and could comfortably travel around Europe from what he earned. The fact that Europe had no Prohibition further helped create a feeling of luxury. The Depression had hardly been felt.

Life for a musician in New York was quite different. There was still much work all around, but competition between musicians was getting stronger. This was a time when talent and personality would survive. What was Adrian's position? His many years of playing the bass saxophone in New York had not created a large following. Rollini's unique style of playing a solid but refined bass part, alternating with a special accompaniment or a solo, set him apart from any competition and several would-be followers had already given up. His uniqueness made him part of a musical world in which the bass saxophone was still a rare instrument and not a regular element in an arrangement.

The first recordings Adrian made after his return from Europe were with Bert Lown's dance orchestra. He had participated in the first recording session under Lown's name in February of the previous year, when he was in New York to find additional musicians for Elizalde's orchestra. That Bert Lown band was a pick-up group, mainly consisting of members of Ed Kirkeby's California Ramblers, and Kirkeby may have had a hand in Rollini's participation. At the time, Rollini agreed with Lown that he would work for his office once he returned to New York. And now, almost a year later, the time was ripe. Bert Lown had a band of his own. It had a spot for Rollini.

Bert Lown.

Bert Lown, a New Name on the Block?

Bert Lown was born on 6 November 1903 in White Plains, New York. While still in high school, he assembled a group of musicians when he could not even play an instrument yet. His group attracted the attention of Frank Munson, head of Munson Steamship Lines, who subtly suggested that they might sail for South America on one of his steamers. Lown and his friends arrived at the ship the next morning and indeed sailed off. They played at clubs in Buenos Aires.[1] A short biographical article, published in 1931, mentions that Lown later on became a cash register salesman, in which position he won a gold watch for setting a national sales record.[2] However, Lown had learned to play the violin and found out that he preferred music. In 1925 he was a member of Fred Hamm's orchestra, with which he may have made his first recordings. Together with Hamm and piano player Chauncey Gray he authored the Tin Pan Alley hit tune "Bye Bye Blues," which the band recorded in April or May 1925 and which eventually became a jazz standard.[3] However, as early as 1922 he led an orchestra of his own, which he called Bert Lown's Country Club Orchestra.[4] He found that his real talent was not in playing the violin, but primarily in the organization of musical activities. During the following years newspapers would report about his further steps in music management.[5]

In December 1927, Bert Lown met Rudy Vallée, the start of an interesting relationship. Lown was not quick enough to realize that Vallée was his biggest prize catch so far. In his autobiography, Vallée describes how it happened:

> I bumped into a good-looking fellow named Bert Lown, who had been doing society work with small orchestras for coming-out parties and social affairs in Westchester society. We discussed my taking a steady job. "I would," I said, "if I could lead the band." "That's possible," Lown informed me. Then I learned that I was to lead a small orchestra at the Heigh Ho Club.[6]

At the time Vallée was a saxophone player, but this engagement meant his debut as a singer, a profession that would eventually make him one of the most popular American male singers and a celebrity.[7] For a while his relationship with Lown blossomed. Vallée took a share in Lown's booking office, which was then called the Bert Lown–Rudy Vallée office and its orchestras were labeled Lown–Vallée Orchestra. However, this situation did not last long. Lown did not understand Vallée's potential drawing power and wanted more money from him immediately. In August 1929 he started a lawsuit. He claimed that in 1928 he and Vallée had made an agreement under which they were to pool all earnings. Some newspapers now said that he wanted 50 percent of Vallée's earnings, but a sum of $50,000 was also mentioned.[8] The suit was quickly settled out of court. Vallée assigned his shares in the corporation to Lown and paid the legal fees.[9]

Lown now still had his booking office, which allowed him to supply orchestras at short notice.[10] Earlier that year, he had shown his flexibility when, in February 1929, he had an opportunity to make records for Harmony and he used men from the California Ramblers, including their former colleague Adrian Rollini, who happened to be in New York. A second opportunity with Harmony came in April, for nearly the same personnel, but without Rollini, who was back in London.[11]

October 1929 was the month of the Wall Street Crash, which deeply hurt the holders of company shares. Bert Lown may have been one of them, and this problem came on top of losing his star performer, Rudy Vallée. However, fortune once more smiled on him. As he told it himself a few years later, he was sitting in the lobby of the Biltmore Hotel, when he overheard two men talking. They were not satisfied with the current hotel band. "I jumped up and grabbed the two men. I said, 'I don't know who you are, but I agree the orchestra could be better. And I'm the fellow who can give you a better one.'" One of the men was the Biltmore manager and he said that Lown could have an audition the following day. Lown had no orchestra, but he had ten twenty-dollar-a-night musicians and explained the situation to them. Lown did not know much about music, but they did. They rehearsed all night long and the next day they got the job.[12] A slightly different story was told by Hawley Ades, a musician who sometimes worked for Lown in a Rudy Vallée band. One day Lown took Ades to the Biltmore to hear Don Bigelow's band. Ades liked the band, but Lown said it was "nothing" and told him that he was about to organize his own band to play at the

Biltmore. According to Ades, Lown had a reputation as the biggest bragger in the business, so Ades laughed it off. However, to Ades's amazement Lown did it.[13]

Bert Lown's orchestra opened at the Biltmore on 3 December (succeeding Don Bigelow's Orchestra), and would play in the Supper Room during dinner and supper.[14]

By the end of that month Adrian Rollini showed up in New York again. Lown's Biltmore contract presented an excellent opportunity to honor the agreement he and Lown had. Lown with his limited musical knowledge would certainly benefit from the deal. Rollini would push the band forward. Lown was happy to hire him.[15]

Bert Lown's contract for an orchestra at the Biltmore may be regarded as a great success for someone who had previously struggled to find work via his booking office. Certainly this was true at a time when Wall Street had crashed and dark clouds were appearing over the economy. *Radio Revue*, a monthly, published an interview in which Bert claimed that his orchestras had been heard in Paris, London, and South America. "Bert has turned musical notes into bank notes with surprising celerity." After listing Bert's successes, the article mentioned singer Jack Carey ("hailed as a second Rudy Vallée") and closes with Bert's remark that his ultimate ambition was "a million dollars—and no encores."[16]

Rollini Joins Bert Lown

Having an orchestra at a prestigious place like the Biltmore put Bert Lown on the map. He had to be present in the hotel to direct the orchestra, but he also kept his booking office going and thus could continue to have several orchestras to offer. However, his top orchestra was what he installed at the Biltmore; it opened the new year there. Its precise personnel is unknown, but a week later, on 8 January 1930, Lown recorded for Harmony again and the personnel on that session has been identified from the recordings:

Frank Cush—trumpet
Ed Farley—trumpet
Al Philburn—trombone
Lou Bode—clarinet, alto saxophone
Mace Irish—clarinet, alto saxophone
Paul Mason—clarinet, tenor saxophone
Adrian Rollini—bass saxophone, vibraphone
Mac Ceppos—violin
Chauncey Gray—piano
Tommy Felline—banjo, guitar

Bert Lown's Orchestra. Front row, left to right: Mace Irish, Paul Mason, Fletcher Hereford, Adrian Rollini, Bert Lown, Mac Ceppos, Tom Felline. Back row: Al Philburn, Ed Farley, Frank Cush, Stan King, Ward Lay, Chauncey Gray.

Ward Lay—bass
Stan King—drums[17]

Ward Lay played bass, so Rollini's primary role was as a reed player and not as bass player, and as an added attraction he could do a vibraphone solo. This was also how he had worked with Elizalde in the final period.

Lown's Biltmore orchestra had a strong California Ramblers content. Cush, Felline, and King had been with the band when Rollini was a member. Philburn, Mason, Gray, and Lay had been with the California Ramblers after Rollini left. Only Farley, Bode, Irish, and Ceppos did not share such history.[18]

At the time of Lown's previous Harmony recording dates, the company was still using the old acoustic recording system, but by 1930 it had moved up to electric recording at last. The three titles recorded that day were meant for dancing, not for a jazz public. However, the second title, "Under a Texas Moon," allowed for some solo work by one of the alto saxophone players and by Adrian Rollini, his first solo on a record after his return.

It was still January when Lown went to a recording studio again. This was at a brand new company by the name of Durium, that wanted to launch a record made by a new production process and sell it at an ultra-low price of fifteen cents, under the name of Hit-of-the-Week. The records were not pressed of shellac but were paper-based and single-sided. On this paper base a resin layer, called durium, was spread. Disks that were coated and dried could be manufactured in large quantities and kept in store without a time limit. To make the disk into a sellable record, the next step was to press it against a die which represented the recording. After the resin had taken the shape of the die, it would harden instantly and could immediately be played (and sold) as a normal record. Six records could be pressed simultaneously on one machine and thus Hit-of-the-Week's production rate was far higher than their competition's.

During the first half of February 1930, the company issued its first Hit-of-the-Week record, numbered 1019. This was a demonstration record that was given away free from newsstands in New York City. On 13 February the first regular Hit-of-the-Week was issued. This was number 1020 and its title was "Through" by Bert Lown's Biltmore Orchestra. The next weekly issue was another Bert Lown recording, "Hello Baby." These two titles were probably recorded on the same date as Lown's third title on Hit-of-the-Week, "Congratulations," which was on the newsstands on 3 April. However, before "Congratulations" was released, the label showed that it had more artists to offer, with releases of recordings by Vincent Lopez and Ben Pollack. Although the Depression was setting in, Durium's strategy was a success. Distribution became better and better and each week the volume grew. By the summer quantities had risen to 500,000 a week.[19] The connection between Lown and Hit-of-the-Week was strengthened further, when in April Lown appeared on *The Durium Hour*, a broadcast sponsored by the new record label.

Rollini could be heard on these cheap Bert Lown records, even taking short solos, but just like the Harmony session, none of these had very much to offer to his fans. Had it not been for his freelance recordings, the subject of the next chapter, his return might have gone largely unnoticed.

Working for Bert Lown

January was typical of working for Bert Lown. It meant steady work, but it was not very challenging. Therefore, Rollini was happy to do freelance recording dates with his old colleagues. Those will be discussed in the next chapter. With Lown he could not rise to prominence. The band played in the Biltmore's Supper Room during the evenings, providing music for dinner and supper. More important to raising its popularity were the regular broadcasts from the hotel, which started on Saturday 1 February 1930 at midnight from station WABC. The announcement said: "The program will have special arrangements and novel instrumental and vocal effects."[20] This suggests that Rollini was present, since the special instrumental effects probably included his work on the goofus, hot fountain pen, vibraphone, or xylophone, instruments that Lown's band was not known for. However, for a following broadcast a few weeks later, on 21 February, no special instruments were announced. Maybe Lown did not like it, or Rollini was not present.

There were more recordings for Harmony and Hit-of-the-Week, followed by two for ARC, the American Record Corporation, a company that had resulted from the merger of several record companies. Those companies included Cameo (which had the Pathé/Perfect labels) and Regal (which produced such labels as Banner and Romeo).[21] Most of ARC's products were sold at low prices via so-called "dime stores," where articles were priced at five or ten cents. The first of these recording dates with ARC was on 23 January and it produced two titles of straight dance music only. A week later, Lown had another date at ARC. Again titles were recorded which were nice to dance to, but this time one of the three, "The One I Love Can't Be Bothered with Me," got an attractive arrangement with solo spots for trombone and clarinet; Rollini played two breaks and an eight-bar solo.

The Biltmore Orchestra was Lown's flagship now, but he managed to continue his booking office, too, and kept the newspapers informed about activities of his orchestras. One typical occasion was a supper dance at the Bossert Hotel in Brooklyn on 4 February 1930. The organizers were the Colony House. The guests first enjoyed a show, the Colony House Capers, and could then participate in a supper dance for which "Bert Lown, musical director of the Biltmore Hotel, furnished the orchestra."[22] Lown did not bring his Biltmore band but had assembled another group for the evening. A similar occasion was a so-called "senior dance" of the Sarah Lawrence School in Bronxville, on 1 March.[23] The announcement mentioned Bert Lown and the Biltmore and that he "will make a personal appearance ... directing his orchestra and also singing several of his own numbers." Lown's personal appearance was part of the contract. He tried out his singing talent but had no success. No other singing performances by Bert Lown are known.

Bert Lown Had Talents but Not as a Musician

Bert Lown's talents were in organizing bands and contracts, not as a musician himself. Ernest Capozzi, a guitar player, who did club work for Lown in a band that included Adrian Rollini on the bass sax, remembered that Lown could only play one tune on a piano, "The World Is Waiting for the Sunrise."[24] Reed player Pete Pumiglio, who worked with Lown in 1932 or 1933, had similar memories. At this time some of the other men in Lown's band were Ed Farley and Frank Cush, trumpets; Al Philburn, trombone; Larry Tice, alto saxophone and clarinet; Mac Ceppos, violin; and Chauncey Gray, piano. According to Pumiglio:

> Bert Lown was a nice guy, but not a good musician. He didn't play anything. Originally he was a cash register salesman! That's a fact. But he was a good businessman. He could lie with a straight face... but he didn't know much about music. So the guys in the band liked to put him on sometimes. When they would get a new arrangement Bert Lown of course would get a conductor sheet.... Well, they could as well have put a page of the journal in front of him. To him that was the same thing. Trumpeter Ed Farley was a funny guy. So he stopped the band and said: "Hey Bert, I've got here an A-flat instead of a G-sharp." It's of course the same note. Another guy then said very seriously: "Well I think you better play the G-sharp." Bert Lown wouldn't understand the joke, ha, ha![25]

Eventually Lown made publicity out of his handicap. He had publications in several papers that would say, with sufficient exaggeration, that he could not write a note of music and yet had composed three successful songs in a year.[26] One interview quoted him saying that he did not know the first thing about music. "I can't even play by ear," he said, and clarified this by explaining that he used a sort of "plus and minus" system. As a boy he would watch pianists and note the course of their fingers, recording their movements by what he referred to as "arithmetic." With one key designated as "one," those on either side are numbered in order. Plus numbers go up the scale, and minus downward. He composed using this system of music writing.[27] The numbers would be transcribed to notes by his pianist Chauncey Gray and thus into finished songs.[28] Earl Sparling, who was considered an ace interviewer, is said to have wrangled Lown's system from him. Lown demonstrated to Sparling how he did it. He sat at a piano and beat it with one finger, jotting down figures on a sheet. He wrote "plus 1, 5, 3 (11), minus 4, plus 1, 3, 5."

"Now you see," he told Sparling, "that is the first part of the chorus of 'Bye Bye Blues.' I take middle 'C' on the keyboard as my number one. A note with parenthesis around means that it runs into the next octave. A note with a little degree sign above it is a half note."[29] During a broadcast Lown would fill his conductor's stand with a sheaf of papers, lettered with strange hieroglyphics, his substitute for conventional music notation.[30]

Lown's next recording date was for ARC. Three titles were recorded with singer Smith Ballew and with arrangements that were void of any jazz element or jazz feeling.[31] As a compensation Adrian Rollini was making freelance recordings in the jazz vein at this time (of which more later). Those outside jobs challenged his talent as a jazz musician, but not these recordings with Bert Lown.

To Bert Lown recording dates were not as important as his daily job at the Biltmore. Since his name was on the label, and connected to the Biltmore, they spread his fame among the general public, but even more so did his broadcasts. As a result, he got more and more engagements for outside performances of orchestras under his name. One of these orchestras was under the leadership of Tom Clines.

Tom Clines, a Paradigm Shift

On 14 February 1930, Rollini had two recording dates at Brunswick. The first was under the direction of Red Nichols and it will be discussed in the next chapter. The second session was done with an orchestra led by Tom Clines.[32] Clines was the leader of one of the orchestras run from Bert Lown's booking office. He was born as Thomas in Washington Heights, a part of Manhattan, in 1905. The family was of Scottish descent and had a tradition of producing good violin players, and Thomas followed in the footsteps. He went to Fordham University and his violin study gave him enough musical knowledge to lead the college band. This early success made him choose a career in music, but after some disappointments, he went a different way and for some time he did newspaper work and was a truck salesman. However, Clines tried again in music and his second time was more successful. Eventually he would have several engagements at major hotels.[33] His first known engagement was at the Milton Point Casino for the summer of 1929. A newspaper announcement said that a Bert Lown orchestra would be conducted by Tom Clines.[34] Clines made his first recordings for Harmony in May 1929, but the same year he moved to Brunswick. Eventually he would record twenty-four titles for that company. A picture of a Tom Clines band shows ten men who, judging the instruments spread out on the floor, play fourteen reed instruments, three violins, two banjos, a piano, a string bass, and drums. A personnel lineup for Clines's band, published at the time of Rollini's first recordings with Clines, lists no well-known names, but of course Bert Lown had a hand in this.[35] Anyway, Adrian Rollini is heard on most if not all of Clines's 1930 Brunswick dates, and in fact Clines may well have used Lown's top personnel for his recordings, rather than the band he filled his gigs with. The only brass instrument in Clines's first recording band was a tuba and the suggestion that Clines had no jazz pretension, is confirmed by his first recordings with Adrian Rollini. Clines produced straight dance music for the same markets as Bert Lown: debutantes' balls, club parties, dinners, and hotel ballrooms. His first title with Rollini, "So Sympathetic," is typical, a syrupy arrangement with a major role for singer Jack Carney. The few vibraphone notes are not by Rollini, whose bass saxophone is heard in the

Tom Clines' Orchestra in 1930. Clines center with Bert Lown to left of him.

ensemble. The second title by Clines's band, "Until Love Comes Along," gave Rollini more exposure. He plays a break and a coda, supported by a drummer who uses the occasion for what almost becomes a solo. The third and last title of this session, "Alone with My Dreams," goes back to the syrup of the first, but it has a short spot for Rollini.

The music by Lown and Clines was worlds apart from Rollini's earlier jazz work. But for pure jazz music he found continuation in new freelance work (see next chapter). His flexibility allowed him to satisfy his employers without hesitation and he had no problem with the repeated paradigm shift.

Managed from Bert Lown's booking office, Tom Clines's orchestra had various short engagements, but only a few are known. In May 1930 he worked with a nine-piece band in Mamaroneck, New York, at the Oriental Beach Club and during the summer his band was at the Milton Point Casino in Rye (where he had been the year before, too).

Tom Clines's recording career had started in 1929, some months before the Wall Street Crash. The resulting economic crisis ended many careers and, although he was able to continue in music, Clines's recording career would end in 1930. After his February recording date, the first with Rollini, he would return to the Brunswick recording studio six more times. The first two dates were in April and each produced two titles that were issued. Rollini can be heard on all four and one even features him, "The 'Free and Easy.'" He plays four breaks, a ten-bar solo, and closes the recording with a nice coda.

The month of May produced another four titles from two dates at Brunswick. This time the arrangements, written by an unknown arranger, were generally more interesting than those of the earlier Clines sessions. On these recordings Rollini's role was mainly as a rhythm man, but it is safe to assume that Clines used him as an assistant bandleader. From a jazz viewpoint the most interesting title is "You Darlin," with an arrangement that gives Rollini two eight-bar solos.

In July Tom Clines took his band to Brunswick again, this time to record three titles. Again the arrangements were slightly more interesting than before, due to the addition of a trombone player, who made himself heard from the first title onward, "Just a Little Closer." This title is of particular interest, first because it features Rollini in a sixteen-bar solo, and second because two different takes were issued in the USA and another take by Brunswick's branch in Argentina, where the vocal chorus was replaced by a saxophone chorus. Thus three versions of Rollini's solo survive. The second title was Bert Lown's composition "Bye Bye Blues" and the third "I'm Needin' You," where Rollini plays no significant role.

Another two months later Clines had his final recording date. It was for Brunswick again and produced three titles. The trombone player plays a major role, which gives the result more jazz feeling than most earlier Clines recordings. Rollini plays short solos on "What's the Use of Living Without Love" and "Passing Time with Me."

After Tom Clines's recording career ended, he did not immediately disappear from the music scene. A news item from 1931 mentions him as a singer.[36] His link with Bert Lown had become a close friendship, and in 1932 Lown was invited on Clines's daughter's birthday party at the Clines home in Sunnyside.[37] That same year Clines was usher at Lown's wedding party and his band got an "indefinite contract" to work at Pavilion Royal at Valley Stream, Long Island.[38] Although "indefinite," it ended and in June 1933. Tom Clines's orchestra, announced as his National Broadcasting Company orchestra, provided the music at the reopening of the Hunter Island Inn, Pelham Bay Park, in June 1933. The list of participants shows that this was a big event.[39] The following year Clines was back at the Pavilion Royal and then he got out of the limelight.

Bert Lown's Career Flowers

Lown's work at the Biltmore had become a steady job. During the winter season his orchestra was at the Biltmore's Supper Room and for the summer Lown got a contract to work at the Biltmore Cascades, the restaurant at the top on the nineteenth floor. It opened with a dinner dance on 11 June. At the Cascades Lown would again be playing for supper and probably during dinner, too. Biltmore's management had invested in a renovation "far more attractive than ever

Out of Europe and into the Depression: Bert Lown

Bert Lown's Orchestra. Front row, left to right: Mace Irish, Paul Mason, Fletcher Hereford, Adrian Rollini, Bert Lown, Mac Ceppos, Tom Felline. Back row: Al Philburn, Ed Farley, Frank Cush, Stan King (with his chimes behind him), Ward Lay, Chauncey Gray. (courtesy Vince Giordano)

Adrian Rollini playing his bass saxophone with Bert Lown.

before . . . the cascade is still there, however."[40] The Supper Room had a hand-cranked sliding roof which gave the guests the opportunity to gaze at the stars while having dinner.

Lown's regular broadcasts continued via WABC, the CBS chain.[41] Often the station would fill a full evening with dance bands. One such program might start with Bernard Levitow's Commodore orchestra, followed by Sleepy Hall, Ted Fiorito, and then, at half past ten, Bert Lown and his Biltmore orchestra for half an hour. The evening would end with an hour by the Cotton Club Band.[42] Lown claimed that he would never broadcast a new tune until it had been danced to five times, but he knew that his broadcasts were an excellent medium for plugging and by announcing the song in the newspapers the publicity would be doubled.[43] The song "I'd Be in a Fairway with You" was thus announced and played on a Saturday night over WABC.[44] It did not help; the song was not recorded by Lown and is now forgotten.

The orchestra's repertory contained many old-time tunes, some from before 1920. A newspaper article signaled that the older songs were most popular, quoting dance orchestra leader Fred Rich, whose music was heard on seventeen programs a week over WABC and the Columbia Broadcasting network:

> "Songs that had their first wave of popularity before the advent of radio as a plugging medium have met with a hearty response from radio listeners." As a reason Rich mentioned "without casting any aspersions on the popular songs of today, it is generally accepted that their predecessors possessed more merit. They were written with more care by the same composers, who must now go in for quantity production."

Tunes mentioned by Rich included "Limehouse Blues," "Poor Butterfly," and "Whispering." The article said that a check of some orchestra leaders revealed that the old songs most consistently played were "Avalon," "Dinah," "Japanese Sandman," "June Night," and "Whispering," as well as medleys of past musical comedies.[45] Some of these surviving hits had been among Paul Whiteman's first recordings. Bert Lown had his own tune to return to, "Bye Bye Blues," recorded by Fred Hamm's band in 1925 when Lown was a member. Lown was not its only composer. For Merrill Kaye, Lown's bass player, it was the first tune he recorded with Lown. Kaye remembered:

> There was a lawsuit. . . . ASCAP was brought in, BMI was brought in. . . . [ASCAP's] lawyers were better than BMI's and the judge ruled that Fred Hamm should be paid compensatory value. So they made some kind of a deal and the whole thing was settled . . . but on the sheets it was written by Bert Lown, Chauncey Gray and Al Philburn. Ed Farley wanted a piece of it too, you know, everybody wanted a part of the act.

"Bye Bye Blues": sheet music.

Kaye was in the band when the tune was first played on a Bert Lown broadcast. It became a special event.

> We made "Bye Bye Blues" on our first radio date from the Biltmore Hotel. We played that for one hour ... One song. You know how we played it. First we played it as a ballad, then we played it as a waltz, we played it as a tango, we played it as a jazz group, then we played it as a full orchestra and then we played it just as is. One song one hour.[46]

During the first four months of 1930, Lown had had three recording sessions for the ARC labels (Banner, etc.) and one for Hit-of-the-Week. Now, in July, he recorded "Bye Bye Blues" for Columbia and for Hit-of-the-Week. Together with the broadcast this meant a tremendous popularity boost for the tune. From now on Lown would forever be linked to "Bye Bye Blues." The Hit-of-the-Week issue was launched on 7 September 1930. The press release called the tune Broadway's greatest hit of the season.⁴⁷ Its arrangement was slightly changed between the two recordings. Both versions feature Al Philburn's trombone and he is nicely accompanied by single-string guitar player Tommy Felline. The Hit-of-the-Week version ends with a vocal by Scrappy Lambert, the Columbia version with a vocal quartet accompanied by Adrian Rollini on vibraphone. The Columbia backed it with "Under the Sun," one of the finest arrangements recorded by Lown so far, with Rollini on vibes and bass saxophone. In September Lown had another recording date with Columbia which produced another interesting title, "I'll Be Blue Just Thinking of You," which featured Rollini at the intro, the coda, and in two short solo moments in between.⁴⁸

The same month a message was given to the press that Bert Lown was using a new signature song, "You're the One I Care For," and that his orchestra was going on a sixteen-week Keith tour.⁴⁹ The tune was a composition by Lown and his piano player Chauncey Gray. It is doubtful that Rollini took part in the tour, since another message that month said that Lown's orchestra would return to its winter spot, the Biltmore Supper Room, on 8 September.⁵⁰ It would also play for tea dances.⁵¹

During October Bert Lown's Biltmore Orchestra supplied the music at a campaign ball for the Republican Party. The ball took place on 21 October at the Westchester County Center under the auspices of the Westchester County Woman's Republican Club. Charles H. Tuttle and his wife were guests of honor. The month before Tuttle had won the Republican nomination for the election of governor of New York State. Promotion for the campaign ball started three weeks before the event. It was described as one of the social highlights of the coming winter season and it was the biggest ball ever organized in the large auditorium, setting a precedent in social entertainment of this type. Bert Lown's Biltmore Recording Orchestra was said to consist of twenty-eight pieces. To give it a local flavor, Lown was said to be "of Pelham." As a climax to the evening, Charles Tuttle would head what the organizing committee called "an old-fashioned Republican grand march," together with the committee's chairman. The event did not bring Tuttle what he had hoped for. The election took place two weeks later. Tuttle's Democratic opponent was Franklin D. Roosevelt, who won with the largest majority in the state's history. Roosevelt's victory was based on his position on Prohibition. Tuttle was regarded as "dry," Roosevelt as "wet." Two years later Roosevelt won the American presidency and the following year he ended Prohibition.

Most often such activities only took half a day, so that the orchestra could be back at the Biltmore for its daily work. On occasion Lown would organize a short tour. The following story, told by bass player Merrill Kaye, illustrates Lown's management style:

> One day he told his men: "Boys, we're gonna take two days off, because the room is gonna be closed for repairs.... Louis Lilienfeld, he's gonna take over. I have booked

four, five days. The first stop will be a one-nighter in Bridgeport, Connecticut. The second will be the Winter Carnival for Dartmouth College. The third will be in Washington and the fourth will be in Philadelphia and then we come back to New York and we go right back to the Biltmore." He wanted me to take care of the band because he would be busy talking to people. . . . I want you to take full charge." I said, "It's gonna be a little rough for me because I'm the bass player in the band." Bert answered, "Well, we'll have Adrian play the bass notes." [I added] "But I want you to be very explicit to the manager of the house that I am committed to do all the business." . . . [Lown] never did one nighters. He only did club jobs in NY where you send a band to the hotel and that was it.

When it came in the middle of our date [we had] an intermission of a half hour. That is the time when . . . you collect your money on the guarantee that you're supposed to get. I did. I went to the manager and I told him, I'd like to have my cheque. He said, "Well you got 1000 dollars guarantee." I got the cheque. And [from] then you work on a 60/40 [base]on admissions. I said, "Fine. 60 percent for me, 40 for you," which is the usual take. . . . I went back to the orchestra and he said, "What time are you coming back?" I said, "Well, I'll be back, it's intermission now, in one hour." He said "OK." . . . but I didn't come back in an hour. I came back in about 20 minutes, because I happened to [see] the admission cashier closed. So I went into the office and I said, "Here I am, sir." And he said," What's the routine." And I said, . . . "I wanna know the correct count." He says, "Don't you trust me?" I said, "Mister, I trust everybody but I want to see the cheque." We had the numbers, . . . we multiply, 60, and he said, "That's all of our money." I said, "Oh yes, I'm not finished yet." He says, you know, you're a pretty wise guy from NY. I said, "No sir, I'm not." [He said] "Call Bert Lown." I said, "You do nothing of the sort, you have got to talk to me. Either you make out a cheque right now or else . . . that band is finished and I'm gonna sue you according to my contract. Well, the fellow that was the original booker, that booked all these dance halls, I said "I'll get him on the phone and tell him." He said, "You're just a little bit too smart for me." I answered, "No, I'm no dummy, just give me my cheque." He got out the cheque. I said, "How much cash have you got? . . . Give me the cash." $1,500 in cash. Put it in my pocket, but I kept one cheque for the guarantee. So I went back and I said, Adrian, OK. I said, Adrian, keep on playing, I start packing my instruments. I let him finish, and I said to Bert, "Bert, OK. Not another word. Pack."

The following day Bert Lown's orchestra had to be in Dartmouth. Merrill Kaye continues his story:

Bert said, "Boys, don't forget tomorrow morning I want everybody on that station, not in the lobby, on the station at such and such a time because we have a special train. . . . [with] 20 cars special with all the girls from all the girls' schools in NY and around going to Dartmouth for this big carnival. It's the winter carnival and it's the most famous thing in the world where they ski and everything parties. And I want everybody on that platform. Merrill, make sure everybody is there. I will take care of the music case." Now, what happened? Everybody was on the station and it's about 8:30, 8:20. I want everybody there early and it's cold. Snow on the ground. Awful. I said "Anybody see Bert Lown?" He had a private room and so. And all of a sudden, who comes up? Bert Lown. Big fur coat. I said "Where's the music?" "I forgot the music." "How on God's earth are you gonna be playing in that big gym with no arrangements of ours?" He says, "I'll go back for the music, don't worry." Fine. [We get into the train] and I hear: "Bert Lown Orchestra?" We are the last car. I said "Come on boys." Everybody gets on. The car is almost full with girls and they have their chaperones. [One of them] said "Where's Mr. Lown?" I said "Oh, he'll be along." I didn't want to say anything because I thought she was the one that booked the orchestra. I said "Don't worry about him, he'll be along." We all are on the train ... and before you know ... off. I said "Boys, I'm gonna tell you something, he elected me to be the boss, you have to take orders from me, just relax. This train is a special with all these girls going up to the carnival. We have to stop way up in Massachusetts, you know, for water." And the boys said "Hey look!" We were playing our instruments in the train, entertaining the girls, trying to flirt with all the girls, you know, beautiful ... but I'm with the chaperone to get her mind off Bert Lown. ... So everybody said "Come on Merrill we're going to get some fresh air." They're watering at this station and while standing there, all of us, we see a plane coming down and all of a sudden ... sure enough ... who gets out? Bert Lown! With the big fur coat, carrying the music and all of a sudden the conductor is hollering "Let's go!" ... We quick grabbed a hold of Bert Lown. He couldn't walk anymore in the snow. Deep snow. And here we are ... but we said "Did you pay this guy for the plane?" [Bert] said: "It cost me a fortune. I begged and did everything for this guy. It's a private plane. I took a chance. He said: "All I can do is follow the railroad tracks." He didn't know where we were." ... Now, we get on the train and I went to the chaperone. I said: "Bert you better not come into the last car, you better go into the car up front and then walk back and say: 'Hey,' as if you have been on that train all the time." ... I made him come back with the whole band.

Now. We land into Dartmouth, Howard Junction. There is about ten fellers and they see only the band; and the rest, fifteen cars, all girls. They say "Hey, hey, here, Bert Lown, Bert Lown." Well they took the instruments, put them in the cars, they took us up to a fraternity house. And we didn't have to play the affair until that night so we come into the fraternity house and the boys say "What would you like to do?" So Ed Farley, the trumpet player that wrote "The Music Goes Round And Round," ... said: "You know, it would be a good idea if we all went skiing." So the guy says "We have got plenty of skis here, right outside the door, you can ski right down." We were up on top of the hill and "we will all go down." Well, everybody put their skis on and everybody was falling flat on their face.

Out of Europe and into the Depression: Bert Lown 251

They didn't know how to ski, but just for fun. I put the skis on and I knew how to ski and I went down and when I get to the bottom of the hill, a truck comes in front of me and I am going down full blast as I quick tricked around and I made a stop and everybody is hollering "Merrill, Merrill, you don't . . ." I finally get back and believe me I was shaking when I took a look at that truck. I would have been killed.

Well after dinner we all went down. We get the band all set up and all of a sudden Bert Lown said: "You know, these guys have no microphones here. They didn't prepare." So, Bert Lown is smart. He said: "Well, let us start the job." I remember starting and standing there in that band as if all this happened yesterday. The place is packed, you couldn't get in, thousands. And all of a sudden Bert gets a megaphone and he makes a speech. You know he and Rudy Vallée were partners. We all knew Rudy very well so Bert gets an idea and he says: "Will you please come forward. . . . Can you hear me?" And then the pack said: "Yes, we hear you, Bert." He says "I just want to let you know, it's a pleasure being here. It's our first trip leaving the Biltmore Hotel, just for this special occasion; the Winter Carnival for Dartmouth College." He says "I must let you in on a secret. You see the decorations in the center? We are doing something new. There are ten microphones up there that are going to record this whole program. We have no microphones here, but that is picking up through the whole auditorium. Something new." And everybody is looking up, they don't see a damn thing. They all thought it was behind the bunting of the flags. And then, all of a sudden Al Philburn gets up and he starts playing. They whistled, they shouted, they stamped their feet. It was so great. We went into a program, we played. When we finished they said "You can't, you can't go home. You got to stay here and play again." Lown says: "I cannot, because tomorrow morning we have a special Sikorsky plane meeting us here to take us to Washington." They said: "What does it cost." One kid comes up he says: "My father will pay for anything that I want." . . . [but Lown answered] "I am sorry but we have a signed contract, we must be in Washington at noon time. We have to roll off, we are here in Dartmouth, a kind of a junction, and this plane is special just for us." . . . We get on the plane and half of the band [gets] sick, sick, they just go wobbly, hazy, you know? We finally get to Washington, Bert Lown calls an ambulance [but] how could we put the whole band, twelve to fifteen guys in one ambulance? So he says "Call another, call a truck." We get back to the hotel and we play another big college dance . . . but he called in a doctor, and the doctor gave everybody something and he says "Just go to bed."[52]

For his recordings Bert Lown had moved up from the minor league with Harmony and ARC to the middle league when he recorded for Columbia. However, now he would move up even further: The Victor Talking Machine Company had discovered his orchestra. In 1928 the company had lost Paul Whiteman to Columbia, a company that already had a major band like Ted Lewis's under contract. Victor tried to fill the gap that Whiteman left behind by taking

Leo Reisman's orchestra from Columbia, but Reisman was no Whiteman, so Victor also took Bert Lown. His first recording date with Victor was on 25 September 1930, and within the next twelve months Lown recorded forty-two titles for his new company, more than half with Adrian Rollini in his band. The first date produced two titles, "I'm Yours" and "Here Comes the Sun." At the time Lown had a twelve-man band:

Frank Cush—first trumpet
Ed Farley—second trumpet
Al Philburn—trombone
Elmer Feldkamp—clarinet, second alto saxophone, vocal
Paul Mason—tenor saxophone
Larry Tice—first alto saxophone
Adrian Rollini—bass saxophone
Mac Ceppos—violin
Chauncey "Judd" Gray—piano
Tom Felline—banjo
Merrill Kaye—bass
Stan King—drums[53]

Rollini is featured on bass saxophone on the first two titles, the first of which with only two bars during the intro, but the second title with a total of eighteen solo bars, the most he had done on any Lown record so far. The record was announced in newspaper advertisements.[54] The Victor publicity called the music "as full of unique effects as bread is full of flour." Victor's catalog supplement for December, had most words for the first title, the record's "A" side, which typically was the least jazzy:

> Another dance orchestra added to the Victor roster . . . one that plays afternoons and nights at a fashionable New York hotel where the smart set drops in to dance to the fascinating music which Bert Lown and his men play. You can dance to it also . . . on a Victor Record . . . and enjoy repeatedly the rhythmic features and the unusually interesting and clever instrumental effects which this leader employs in his orchestrations. The fox trot on the "A" side of the record is in slow tempo . . . but so dance-compelling that it will be utterly impossible to remain still while the music is playing. The other one moves in faster time, and is equally fine. When you hear these selections it will be easy to understand just why this young leader is so busy, for in addition to his appearances at the Biltmore, he has been engaged to play both senior and junior "proms" at a prominent university. And if the college crowd is no criterion, we miss our guess! Better not put off listening to this record.

Out of Europe and into the Depression: Bert Lown   253

Bert Lown's Orchestra in Victor studio, Rollini's vibraphone in front. From left: Elmer Feldkamp(?), Al Philburn, Tom Felline, Merrill Kline (Kaye), Paul Mason(?), Stan King, Bert Lown, Frank Cush(?), Larry Tice(?), Adrian Rollini, Ed Farley(?), Chauncey Gray, Mac Ceppos.

By the time Bert Lown's first Victor record came on the market he had already done more recording, and it was reported that Victor wanted to extend Lown's one-year contract to five years.[55] His second date came the following month, October, and produced two more titles, "Loving You the Way I Do" and "The Penalty of Love," from the musical show *Hot Rhythm*.[56] However, by the time Lown recorded these two titles the show was closing, after about seventy performances. Yet Victor issued Lown's record even when it had another coupling of the two tunes in its catalog.[57] That was one by Bubber Miley, formerly Duke Ellington's star trumpet player, who was now leading his own orchestra. Victor had had to make a major effort to produce a satisfactory recording of the two titles by Miley's band.

At Bert Lown's third Victor date, he recorded his new signature tune "You're the One I Care For." It is a slow and sentimental song and Rollini decided that it lent itself well to his vibraphone accompaniment. On the second tune recorded that day, "You're Simply Delish," he plays several breaks on his bass saxophone.

A few days later, Rollini was in the Victor studio again, to record two more titles in Bert Lown's style, melodious, danceable well-arranged music, without great surprises and usually with a vocal chorus. Although the Victor files do not mention it, Rollini often brought his vibraphone and sometimes his celeste to the studio for a special effect (but never his goofus). On this session, Lown's last in 1930, he brought both. On "And Then Your Lips Met Mine," he played vibraphone and on "Crying Myself to Sleep" he played celeste. On both titles he also soloed on the bass saxophone.

One day after New Year, Bert Lown was back in Victor's studio to record two more tunes. The Victor files for Lown's previous sessions list twelve men, including four saxes, but for the next four sessions the presence of an additional musician playing celeste is noted. Rollini plays bass saxophone and solos. The arrangement of one tune, "To Whom It May Concern," includes an amazing break for two instruments, possibly Al Philburn's trombone and Rollini's bass saxophone.

A few days later the band returned to Victor, but the results were rejected except for one tune, "They Satisfy," which was eventually issued on Victor's new price-fighting label Timely Tunes. One of the recordings that were rejected was "My Missouri Home," which Lown "thought more like a waltz, but [Victor's] sales executives wanted it in real Hill Billy style. . . . We spent nearer nine hours than one on that record."[58] Lown won, and it was finally issued as a waltz. Still in January, a remake session for the two rejected titles was set up. The waltz was rejected again, but "Say Hello" was issued and turned out to have a nice arrangement with a Rollini solo. It was coupled with "Heartaches."[59] From this session onward, Rollini would play the vibraphone, or vibraharp as he called it, anytime he recorded with Bert Lown. It took another session to get an acceptable take of the waltz. At that session, during the last week of January, two more titles were recorded and Rollini soloed in one, six bars bars in "I'm So Afraid of You."

During two sessions in March, Rollini made his final recordings with Bert Lown. The finest of the resulting six titles was the first, "Please Don't Talk About Me When I'm Gone," where Rollini solos for eight bars and the band shows a nice balance between playing dance music and playing hot. Even on his last title with Lown, "Running Between the Raindrops," Rollini had a short solo spot.

By 1 April 1931, Adrian Rollini had left the safe haven of Bert Lown's band. His final gig with Lown may have been an afternoon dance at Stern Brothers, a department store. He was succeeded by his old colleague Spencer Clark. Clark had followed in his footsteps when Rollini left the California Ramblers in 1927. In 1928 he had gone to Europe and worked with Lud Gluskin, but by 1931 he had returned to New York and a job with Bert Lown was welcome.

There are a handful of photographs of Bert Lown's band with Adrian Rollini. Interestingly, two of these were made in the Victor recording studio, one with Rollini holding his saxophone and the other where he plays the vibraphone. Merrill Kaye remembered that musicians did not like the idea of band photographs:

> Well the only pictures that were taken were [taken] in the recording laboratory, that's at Victor. And I never received any, but I saw them. . . . but the boys in the

band had a very, very superstitious idea of taking pictures. Once you took a picture of the band, a short time after that the band broke up. They said: "no pictures." They didn't want it. Individuals, yes, we have. I have individual pictures of myself and everybody else, but they didn't like the idea of one whole big band picture.[60]

By now Lown was at the top of his popularity. Despite the Depression, which had set in the year before, Lown had a nice Victor contract, continued his work at the Biltmore and at WABC, and had several other orchestras working under his own name or that of Tommy Clines or Ben Cutler.[61] The debutante balls continued, to which Christmas parties were now added. In December Lown had announced that he would have an orchestra at the New Colonial Hotel in Nassau at the Bahamas, a British colony with an increasing number of New Yorkers who wanted to pass a holiday at its beautiful beach.[62]

Lown's orchestra had also been selected for what a newspaper called one of "the most extensive radio 'whoopee' parties ever staged."[63] On New Year's Eve it would participate in a four-hour CBS broadcast with one dance band after another. At 10:00 p.m. the first was the Plaza Hotel Orchestra of Buenos Aires, which was followed by twelve American bands, including Bert Lown's.[64]

In February Lown's band was one of two orchestras selected to launch a new radio station, WOKO in Albany, New York.[65]

Of course the press wanted to know more about Lown, and this offered him an opportunity to give them a typical success story. One afternoon at the Biltmore he told a journalist how his working schedule was during that day. It must have been exaggerated and it certainly was not typical, but it was printed anyhow:

> Take today; it's typical of most of my days. It's five-thirty now. I'm here till six, when I leave and go to my office for dictation. Then I dress and am in White Plains for a dance at eight thirty. I am in Greenwich, Connecticut, from ten to ten thirty for a debutante party. Then I'm at Ossining for fifteen minutes at a public dance. Then I'm back here at the Biltmore from twelve to twelve-thirty, when we also go on the air. I'm at another dance from one-fifteen to two. I'm at the Plainfield Country Club in New Jersey, from three to six. I get back to New York at seven. I sleep till nine-thirty and then get up in order to make my appointment at the Victor studios at ten. . . .
> I go to a doctor once a month and have him look me over. I'm careful about diet. I don't drink or smoke. It's just a question of getting used to it . . . but it doesn't leave you much leisure.

During the same interview, Lown said that it was his ambition to buy a South Sea island and make a million dollars building up a business: "In four or five years, if present conditions keep up, I'll have my million."[66] Lown was said to be in charge of seventeen orchestras in cities such as Boston, Buffalo, Detroit, Los Angeles, and outside the United States in London, Paris, and Rio de Janeiro.

Lown also became active in films. An article mentioned his success in the film *Secrets of a Secretary* and that he had a contract to make Vitaphone shorts.[67]

Bert Lown was riding high now, but when radio listeners were asked which nationally known orchestra was the best, the list was topped by Coon-Sanders and Lown, despite his many broadcasts ended in the lower category.[68]

And how about Adrian Rollini? His work with Bert Lown was his main income. However, Lown did not feature him to the extent that he had been used to with the California Ramblers or Fred Elizalde, two orchestras that he had eventually been leading. Although his musical talent was far superior to Bert Lown's, Lown was the orchestra leader to the outside world and also in practice. There is no sign that Rollini was leading any of Lown's orchestras. Fortunately, he found musical compensation (and extra income) in freelance recording with jazz musicians. The next chapter will tell the story.

Chapter 14

Adrian Rollini: Freelance

Adrian Rollini returned from Europe in December 1929. Immediately after his return he had a fixed job with Bert Lown, who had just started his Biltmore engagement. The new year was only a week old when Rollini cut his first record. This was with Lown's band for Harmony. The story of Rollini's subsequent work with Lown was told in the previous chapter.

The same month Rollini started an intensive parallel program of recordings outside the Bert Lown band. What follows is the story of this freelance work. During each of his years with Fred Elizalde, Rollini had made a trip back to New York and each time he had managed to contract a few recording dates for some extra income (Elizalde continued to pay him during his absence). Now, at the time of his definite return to New York, he did the same.

Side Jobs: Rube Bloom, Jan Garber, Red Nichols, Leo Reisman, Adrian Rollini

Most of the time that Adrian Rollini worked with the California Ramblers he had to respect a contract that did not allow him to make recordings with other bands. In the spring of 1927 that contract ended, and during the following months Rollini made some of his finest recordings, both with the California Ramblers and with others, and he could even start a band of his own. In London Rollini had not recorded outside the Elizalde band. Elizalde paid him very well, so he simply did not need the extra money there. But now with Bert Lown and the Depression becoming more and more serious, he did need the extra income. Rollini's contract with Lown allowed him to record outside the Biltmore Orchestra. In fact, two days after the Harmony session with Bert Lown, he may have taken part in a recording session with Leo Reisman, who had a history of rerecording tunes after the earlier takes had been rejected. In the morning of 10 January 1930, Leo Reisman's Orchestra came to the Victor studio to record what was to become his signature tune, "What Is This Thing Called

Love?" However, all takes were rejected and the tune had to be rerecorded ten days later. For this second session Reisman augmented his orchestra with a violin and a saxophone player. Their identity is not known. However, after three more takes Reisman still was not satisfied. And then he took an extraordinary approach and for the fourth take on that day Reisman brought in black trumpet star Bubber Miley. Miley had put his stamp on Duke Ellington's great orchestra at the Cotton Club and in 1929 had started a career as a soloist and orchestra leader.[1] Of course the arrangement was adapted to give Miley ample chance to shine. It opened with a short piano intro. Then Miley started a thirty-two-bar solo accompanied by Adrian Rollini, who may have been present on the earlier takes, too. Miley and Rollini showed full reciprocal understanding and respect. At last Reisman, who was no jazz fan, approved the take for issue.

Leo Reisman's orchestra with Bubber Miley and Adrian Rollini recorded one more title on that particular day, the memorable "Puttin' On the Ritz."[2] Dance music with a jazz element is often called "hot dance music." If this type of music needs an archetype, then Reisman's recording of "Puttin' On the Ritz" seems fit. Bubber Miley reigns supreme from start till end and does another thirty-two-bar duet with Rollini, who closes it with a nice break.

In these two Reisman recordings Rollini played a major role, but on the same day that he made them at the Victor studio, he would return to pure jazz work too, at the Brunswick studio. This was at a recording session organized by Red Nichols for a group that was called the Louisiana Rhythm Kings. Like so many similar band names, its geographical connection was imaginary. The band name had been used for some pick-up sessions for the Vocalion label, involving the bands of Guy Lombardo and Coon-Sanders. However, when in 1929 Red Nichols negotiated a new contract with Brunswick, owners of the Vocalion label, its management decided to use the name exclusively for recordings by their star artist. By the end of the year, however, Nichols had not at all fulfilled his side of the contract, which called for twenty-four titles in one year.[3] He still had twelve titles to do, so urgently two recording dates were set up, with the challenging plan to cut six titles on each date. Nichols liked the deep sound of a bass saxophone, and now that Rollini was back in New York Nichols wanted him on this date.[4] However, it coincided with Rollini's session with Leo Reisman. They found a solution for this dilemma, which satisfied all parties.[5] The Reisman session ended at 1:15 p.m. and Rollini did not participate in the final tune recorded, in order to be at Brunswick and with Nichols in time.

Red Nichols's Louisiana Rhythm Kings consisted of men who had been associated with Nichols for some time. The group included the Russin brothers—Babe, tenor saxophone, and Jack, piano—with whom Rollini had become acquainted in Europe. Red shared the cornet/trumpet work with Tommy Thunen.

The group managed to record the six tunes in one afternoon, an amazing number for any band, but certainly for one that had hardly worked together as a group before. Rollini soloed in two medium tempo pieces, "Squeeze Me" and "Meanest Kind o' Blues."

Rollini's first freelance record date had been a few days before the above double date with Leo Reisman and Red Nichols. That date was organized by Rube Bloom (1902–1955), a piano player and composer. Long before, Bloom had been a member of Ray Miller's band when it featured Frank Trumbauer and Miff Mole. He had already recorded an impressive number of titles as a band member, soloist, and accompanist to various singers and, in 1928, he became winner in Victor Records' song contest. His first great success as a songwriter had been the year before with "Soliloquy." Its experimental harmonies inspired such recordings as Duke Ellington's and Don Voorhees's. His winning composition at the 1928 contest was called "Song of the Bayou." Bloom did not record it, but the contest gave him much publicity, and when he got a record contract he capitalized on the song's name by calling his band the Bayou Boys.[6] He assembled a typical New York all-star group. Its front line consisted of Manny Klein, trumpet, Tommy Dorsey, trombone, and Benny Goodman, clarinet. In his usual way, Rollini not only soloed but also added power to Bloom's small rhythm group, which only consisted of himself and drummer Stan King. Their first recording session produced two excellent titles. "The Man from the South" was Bloom's own best-selling composition and the men obviously enjoyed playing it. They attack the piece like a hot jazz tune, both in the arranged parts and in the numerous solos. The fabulous drumming by Stan King should especially be mentioned. He and Rollini had been colleagues in the early days of the California Ramblers. The quality of his drumming could not really be heard on those records, but here it can. He plays a leading role in "The Man from the South" and actually solos, a rarity for a drummer in those days, especially on record. Other good solos are by Klein on trumpet, Goodman on clarinet, and of course Adrian Rollini. Roy Evans and Rube Bloom each do a vocal chorus, which was important enough to be mentioned on the Columbia label. Rollini clearly felt at home again in this group and produced a fourteen-bar solo of great beauty, which started with some long, slow notes and suddenly accelerated. The second tune recorded that day, was the well-known ballad "St. James Infirmary." Taken at a fitting medium tempo, the arrangement of this traditional tune offered solo space for another round of solos for the front men, including Rollini. On the same day and in the same studio, most of Bloom's musicians accompanied singer Lee Morse, but Rollini had to leave.

Rollini's next freelance date was another dual recording date. The one with Leo Reisman and Red Nichols on Monday 20 January had worked well. With eight accepted masters on one day, Rollini had set a personal record and the two bandleaders as well as the record companies must have been pleased with the results. So when, on Friday of that same week, Rollini had another dual date, he must have had full confidence that it would work once more. This one was a combination of Red Nichols and Jan Garber.

On the morning of Friday 24 January 1930, an orchestra assembled by Jan Garber, came together in the Columbia studio. On the record label the band was to be called "his Greater Columbia Recording Orchestra." Garber had led regular dance bands for more than ten years and recorded for Victor and Columbia. However, now he no longer had his regular orchestra and still owed Columbia a recording. He assembled an orchestra that only existed for this recording date. With the exception of Rollini and cornet player Jimmy McPartland, Garber's personnel for this session is uncertain.[7] Two tunes were recorded, "Puttin' On the Ritz" and "When a Woman Loves a Man." As may be expected from an experienced leader like Garber, "Puttin' On the Ritz" reveals a well-rehearsed and disciplined band, but the arrangement is less attractive than Reisman's and offers hardly any solo space. Only McPartland has a few notes, and Rollini is hardly heard. "When a Woman Loves a Man" is slightly more interesting. It features solos on trumpet, clarinet, and finally Rollini on bass saxophone. This Columbia date was Garber's last for that label. Except for one Hit-of-the-Week date, Garber would not record again for more than two years.

Adrian Rollini was in time for his second record date that Friday. This was a regular Five Pennies session with Red Nichols. Including himself, Red's Pennies had grown to ten players by this date. Red had hired one trumpeter, two trombone players, three reed players, plus a three-man rhythm section. The tunes were "Sometimes I'm Happy" and "Hallelujah!" The arrangements were written by Glenn Miller, one of the trombone players, who must have been thinking of the Pennies' recording of "Japanese Sandman" of three years earlier; it had been played at an amazingly slow tempo and this might have contributed to its excellent sales. So for both titles Miller chose a low tempo. The resulting music is less exciting than many earlier Nichols recordings, but again the record sold well.

Nichols was still under pressure to complete his Brunswick contract for twenty-four titles by the Louisiana Rhythm Kings. He still needed to produce six more titles, and they were all recorded on the following Monday. Rollini contributed from the first recorded notes: he plays a sixteen-bar solo at the intro of the obscure tune "O'er the Billowy Sea." And he would produce two of his longest solos on any record so far. The first, on "Karavan," is thirty-two bars long and Rollini plays the first half close to the melody and the second half around it. The ensemble finish is an unforgettable free-for-all, driven by Gene Krupa's great drum work. Rollini plays an even longer solo on "Tell Me," thirty-five bars close to the melody, which accounts for nearly a third of the record's length. The last of the six titles recorded that day was another obscure tune called "There's Egypt in Your Dreamy Eyes," which, unlike its title suggests, was played as a hot tune. With it Nichols had delivered the twenty-four tunes that he promised to Brunswick. However, he continued under his Five Pennies flag and a week later he was back at Brunswick to record two tunes, "I'm Just Wild About Harry" and

"After You've Gone." However, but for a few notes at the end of the second tune, Rollini is hardly heard and all attention goes to trombone player Jack Teagarden, who was taking over the important position with Nichols that Miff Mole and Glenn Miller had had before.[8] The first title, a happy tune by ragtimer Eubie Blake, is almost turned into a blues by Teagarden, who plays a great solo. "After You've Gone" is even more for Teagarden, who sings the lyrics and solos on trombone in his own way, which would become his trademark.

January 1930 could have ended with a milestone, but it did not. On 31 January, Adrian Rollini had his very first recording date as a leader, almost nine years after he had made his recording debut with the California Ramblers. The idea was to record as a trio, consisting of himself on the bass saxophone and hot fountain pen, accompanied by Frank Froeba, piano, and Teddy Bunn, guitar, who together got the artist credit "Snake and Teddy."[9] Three titles were in fact recorded, but none of these were ever issued and tests never surfaced. However sad this may seem, the reason for this may have been that this was a racially mixed session, Teddy Bunn being colored. Drummer Herb Weil talked about the session in *Melody Maker* of March 1930:

> Adrian Rollini just recorded some of his own numbers in a novelty trio for Brunswick. Using his bass sax and his little clarinet (or hot fountain pen), Adrian is accompanied by guitar and piano. I understand the trio is to be called "Adrian Rollini with Snake and Teddy" and one of the forthcoming records is to be titled Clam House, backed by Round Town.[10]

A third title was "Black and Blue," written by Fats Waller for the 1929 show *Hot Chocolates*, and there may have been more titles.[11] The negative result of this recording date meant a setback for Rollini. The next recording under his own name would not occur for three more years.

However, Rollini hardly had time to think about such things. His return to New York had meant that he had to speed up again to its rapid heartbeat and he had stood the test. Working with Bert Lown's band and as a freelancer, he had done at least eleven recording sessions, from which thirty-one titles were issued. This was more than he had done in England during the whole of 1928 and almost as much as he had done in 1928 and 1929 together.

More Side Jobs: Miff Mole, Red Nichols, Cornell Smelser

Adrian Rollini fully picked up the role that he had played in New York in 1927, before he left for London. His first month back in New York had set him fully on steam. His side jobs were not conflicting with his work for Bert Lown and they had worked out well for all parties, so the requests for more studio dates kept coming in.

The first one was with trombone player Miff Mole. Mole was a jazz pioneer if ever there was one. He started recording jazz in April 1922 with the Original Memphis Five, a five-piece jazz band (around the same month that Adrian Rollini made his debut with the California Ramblers).[12] Mole became the prime example for many white trombone players in jazz. He was a capable technician, able to produce solos that were tough to copy. In 1924 he made his first record with Red Nichols and they became a strong team. Mole was on all the Five Pennies records until 1929. Reciprocally, Nichols was on the recordings that Miff Mole made for the OKeh label from January 1927 until November 1928. From then on Mole used other trumpet players and in February 1930 he had Phil Napoleon, his old mate from the Original Memphis Five.

None of Mole's earlier OKeh records had featured a vocal, but the company now required a vocal chorus. However, non-vocal takes were recorded as well, probably for release in non–English-speaking countries.[13] The first of the two tunes recorded was "Navy Blues," with a vocal by Scrappy Lambert and played as a hot tune, not as a blues. Napoleon shows that his lead is as strong as Nichols's and the solo work is excellent, particularly from Mole himself. He was known for his staccato style and in each of the takes he plays an unforgettable glissando, but instead of sliding, he plays short, single notes, as if to show that he did not need a valve instrument like a mellophone or a valve trombone to do this. During the second title, "Lucky Little Devil," Rollini plays a long solo, thirty-two bars, the first half straight, with variations in the background played by Napoleon. Then Napoleon stops and Rollini plays variations during the second sixteen bars.

For the non-vocal takes, the arrangements were adapted. Instead of the vocal on "Navy Blues," a thirty-two-bar duet of Mole and Rollini is inserted, Mole playing the melody straight with a mute and Rollini playing around it on his hot fountain pen. On "Lucky Little Devil" the vocal is replaced by solos on muted trumpet and tenor saxophone. Rollini solos again on hot fountain pen, sixteen bars in duet with Napoleon and sixteen bars alone.[14]

A day after his successful session with Miff Mole's Molers, Adrian Rollini was again in the OKeh studio, now for a date under the leadership of Cornell Smelser.[15] Smelser played piano but was also one of the few major accordion players in jazz.[16] He was born in Hungary in 1902, studied at the Budapest conservatory, and migrated to New York in 1920. He worked in the New York area and probably made his first record in 1929.[17] Smelser's OKeh recording date with Adrian Rollini was the first under his name, and for this occasion his band was called Cornell and his Orchestra.

The first title, "Collegiate Love," was obviously aimed at the college crowd and it is a top example of hot white New York jazz. Rollini plays a four bar intro, followed by the full band of eleven men. He also plays the eight-bar bridge in Jimmy Dorsey's alto saxophone solo. This is followed by a solo from his old mate Irving Brodsky, also back from London, in which the bridge is played by Smelser. It was Rollini's second recording date together with trombone player Jack Teagarden, who plays a short but exciting solo.

Cornell Smelser himself was one of the authors of the second tune recorded that day, "Accordion Joe." This is primarily a vehicle for Smelser to demonstrate his swinging style, but Rollini and Teagarden also have short solos. The session ended with "I Was Made to Love You," a sweet tune without jazz interest but with a straight trombone solo by Teagarden.

Two months later, Smelser would record his own tune "Accordion Joe" in good company once more: with Duke Ellington's band, a rare mixed-race session. He also recorded with Ben Selvin, Fred Rich, and Irving Mills. In 1939 Smelser had tuberculosis, but he recovered and lived till 1993.

A week after the OKeh dates, Adrian Rollini was in Brunswick's New York studio for another date with Red Nichols, with the same personnel as on the previous Nichols session. It produced two titles, "I Want to Be Happy" and "Tea for Two." Both tunes were well trodden, but got special new arrangements by Glenn Miller.[18] "I Want to Be Happy" is played in a hot style and sounds fresh with solos by Teagarden, Dorsey, and Babe Russin. "Tea for Two" was another return to the success formula of "Ida Sweet as Apple Cider," recorded three years earlier. Rollini wrote the introduction and opens the record with a slow thirty-two-bar solo, but the recording never gets exciting.[19] However, since it featured popular tunes, it may have sold well. Rollini had another recording session with Brunswick on this date with Tom Clines, who directed a Bert Lown orchestra, as discussed in the previous chapter.

Singers in a Row: Jack Miller, Lee Morse, Buddy Rogers, and Eddie Walters

Who was responsible for Rollini's next studio assignment? Probably Ben Selvin, who had been involved with Columbia in management roles since 1927, leading orchestras and organizing recording dates.[20] On 27 February 1930 he brought seven musicians to the studio and three singers, one lady and two men. The seven were Tommy and Jimmy Dorsey, trumpet and clarinet; Charlie Butterfield, trombone; Frank Signorelli, piano; Carl Kress, guitar; an unknown violin player (probably Selvin himself); and Adrian Rollini on bass saxophone. The lady singer was Lee Morse; the male voices were Charles "Buddy" Rogers and Eddie Walters.

Rogers (1904–1999) went first and sang two tunes.[21] The first, "I'd Like to Be a Bee in Your Boudoir," demonstrates that Rogers was no great singer, but the ensemble chorus that starts halfway through the recording is excellent. Three takes of the second title, called "My Future Just Passed," were recorded, but remained unissued. The title was rerecorded a few days a later, together with two more titles, but without Rollini.

The next singer, Eddie Walters, sang two comedy numbers, "'Leven Thirty Saturday Night" and "Me and the Girl Next Door." Walters was a good singer in the style of Eddie Cantor, and his drive combined favorably with the jazz musicians who accompanied him to create a swinging record. *Variety* magazine wrote that Walters had "excellent style, clear diction and vocal personality for comedy numbers."[22] The date ended with singer Lee Morse,[23] the most experienced of the three singers with a recording career that had started in 1924 with Pathé/Perfect. In 1927 she moved to Columbia, where she became one of their most successful vocalists. She sang two tunes, "'T Ain't No Sin" and "I'm Following You," that allowed her to display her natural swing and her wide vocal range. The first title featured a good chorus for the jazz band. Rollini was present only for Morse's first title.

Two days later, Adrian Rollini was in a Columbia studio again with yet another male singer, Jack Miller, who would record four titles to be issued on Columbia's bargain Harmony label.[24] Miller made his first record in August 1928, the same month that Rudy Vallée made his vocal debut on Harmony records. Their styles were very similar and in fact Miller and Vallée may sometimes have used the same accompanying orchestra and in a few instances they were on both sides of the same record. Miller was Dutch born and bred, but if he had any accent, then it was New England, like Vallée. In February 1929 their competition was over, when Vallée started a Victor contract. In line with his image as a romantic crooner, Miller recorded four slow titles with the group, first two waltzes, then a slow foxtrot, all of which had little to offer to the jazzmen in the accompaniment. However, the fourth title, "The Moon Is Low," was hotter and had short solos by Tommy Dorsey and Adrian Rollini.

Dates with Ben Selvin, Irving Kaufman, and Jack Purvis for Columbia and OKeh

Ben Selvin, who probably organized all of Rollini's 1930 Columbia recording dates, had been leading his own orchestras on records since 1919 and during the 1930s he continued. Thus, two days after the Jack Miller date, on 3 March 1930 Rollini recorded with Ben Selvin again. The plan was to record two titles, "Looking at You Across the Breakfast Table" and "Let Me Sing and I'm Happy." Of each title both a vocal version and a non-vocal version were planned, the latter probably for distribution in Asia and Middle and South America. Selvin brought

Smith Ballew in for the vocals, an experienced singer, but all his takes were rejected and had to be remade on a later date. The non-vocal takes fared slightly better and what may be a South American issue is known.[25] Columbia decided to sell these recordings on its Harmony label under one of Selvin's pseudonyms. "Let Me Sing and I'm Happy" is an excellent recording with solos by Rollini, Rube Bloom (piano), and Jimmy Dorsey (clarinet and alto saxophone).

By the end of the month, "Let Me Sing and I'm Happy" was recorded by Rollini and colleagues once more, with Irving Kaufman, another old-timer. For Kaufman's comfort, the song was taken at a slower tempo and his singing hardly left space for his accompanists, but Rollini and Jimmy Dorsey each managed to squeeze in a short solo.

In early April Rollini was selected by Jack Purvis to take part in the first of two memorable OKeh record sessions under Purvis's leadership. Unlike most other white trumpet players, Jack Purvis (1906–1962) was influenced by Louis Armstrong, and indeed he managed to play in a way that was reminiscent of the jazz great. Not only could Purvis technically play in Armstrong's style, but his tone also communicated emotion like Armstrong's. Purvis would go to Harlem, where he succeeded in sitting in with black bands. Fletcher Henderson's trumpet player, Rex Stewart, called Purvis one of the "swingingest white trumpet player I ever heard." He certainly was one of the greatest musical talents in the early years of jazz, but his talent for pulling a leg was at least as great.[26] With Jack Purvis we have one of the most picturesque figures in the history of jazz.

Purvis came from a middle-class family in Kokomo, Indiana, and by 1923 he had mastered both trumpet and trombone. During the twenties several orchestra leaders wanted him for his musical capabilities and were glad when he left, once they experienced his behavior. Those leaders included Whitey Kaufman, Paul Specht, Hal Kemp, and Arnold Johnson. Purvis went to Europe as a member of George Carhart's band and after his return, returned to Kemp and then, in 1930, he started working for Ed Kirkeby. Purvis can be heard on several records by the California Ramblers from this period. At the time he shared an apartment with Bob Stephens, who had a job at OKeh as assistant A&R manager.[27] Through Stephens's inside contacts, Purvis got a recording contract with OKeh.[28] His first was a solo performance recorded in December 1929 and it shows Purvis as an Armstrong stylist, one title even being called "Copyin' Louis." During the following months Purvis continued to record with various combinations, mostly for OKeh, and in April and May he recorded the titles that would give him a firm place in jazz history.

Jack Purvis had two recording sessions with his own orchestra, which together resulted in six titles. Fully in line with Purvis's surprising personality, OKeh decided to issue most results from the two sessions in its race series, not in the normal popular catalog between singers and dance bands.[29] The sessions were remarkable in another way; they were interracial. For any record company this was rare.[30] However, for Purvis it was a most natural thing and an opportunity for a return service to his colleagues in Harlem. For Rollini, working with black musicians was not new either. In his early days he sometimes worked with a black drummer and, with the California Ramblers, his colleague Bill Moore certainly was not white. After his recent return from London, Rollini had recorded with black trumpeter Bubber Miley and guitar player Teddy Bunn, the latter participating in the first recording date under Rollini's own name. At the first session, Purvis's group consisted of four white musicians and three blacks. For the white musicians this kind of freelance work was normal, but for the black musicians it was exceptional to be in a recording studio other than with their own bands, the Luis Russell band and the Mills Blue Rhythm Band. Purvis's recording group consisted of:

Jack Purvis—trumpet, leader
J. C. Higginbotham—trombone (from Luis Russell)
Castor McCord—tenor saxophone (from Mills' Blue Rhythm Band)
Adrian Rollini—bass saxophone
Frank Froeba—piano
Will Johnson—guitar, vocal (from Luis Russell)
Charles Kegley—drums

The first tune recorded, "Dismal Dan," opens with Purvis playing a strong and daring lead and it is immediately clear that Purvis has it all under control. Adrian Rollini has two solo moments, the first as the bridge in Purvis's introductory solo. the second as a duet with McCord. Other solos are by Froeba, McCord, and by J. C. Higginbotham who clearly feels at home in this strange company. However, Purvis is the hero of the performance and leads the group to a perfect finale, playing high notes like his idol could.

The next tune, "Poor Richard," uses the same introduction as "Aase's Death," a part of Edward Grieg's *Peer Gynt Suite*, which suggests that Purvis knew about European classical music. Its medium tempo gives it a bluesy atmosphere, not unlike that of a tune like "St. James Infirmary." This is enhanced by Higginbotham's solo. The tune's arrangement limits Rollini's solo contribution to a break, and that is still more than in the final tune recorded that day, "Down Georgia Way." As Richard Sudhalter, author of *Lost Chords*, wrote about this recording: "Purvis achieves a real sense of drama, even majesty, the quality most sought after—and hardest to capture—in this brand of trumpet playing." His stop-time solo and the way he leads the group in the final ensemble make it an unforgettable performance.

The second session took place a few weeks after the first, with the same instrumentation, but Purvis had to make a few changes in his personnel. Tenor sax player Greeley Walton replaced McCord and guitarist Dick McDonough replaced Will Johnson. The session produced another three titles and again all compositions were by Purvis, but this time Bob Stephens got a share. "What's the Use of Crying," the first title from this session, has a solo by Adrian Rollini, but as before, Purvis is the star of the session, playing a long solo.[31] OKeh decided to issue this title and the next one, "When You're Feeling Blue," on its subsidiary label Odeon. It had a very small distribution and consequently these recordings are rare in their original form.[32] On this title Rollini's role is limited to playing a bass accompaniment, but on the final tune, "Be Bo Bo," he is back in the limelight with a swinging solo and interesting question-and-answer work with Higginbotham's vocal work. The six titles by Jack Purvis's orchestra are monuments in the history of jazz and belong to the best work recorded in the Depression era.

Follow-up Dates with Rube Bloom, Annette Hanshaw, and Joe Venuti

During the week after his first recording date with Jack Purvis, Rollini had a follow-up date with Rube Bloom's Bayou Boys. The first date with Bloom had been in January and had been a success both musically and commercially. Now, three months later, Bloom managed to get the same group together, augmented by Babe Russin on tenor saxophone and an unknown banjoist/guitar player. They recorded two tunes, "Mysterious Mose" and "Bessie Could Not Help It," typical novelty material that required a vocal chorus, which was provided by Roy Evans. Bloom's intricate arrangements offer solo space for the whole front line. In "Mysterious Mose" nobody gets more than eight bars, but "Bessie Could Not Help It" has several longer solos, including sixteen bars by Rollini on goofus.

Bloom's team had shown to be good professionals and thus it is no surprise that they tried to stick together. An opportunity came when in early May the nucleus (Manny Klein, Tommy Dorsey, Rollini, and Bloom) would record with Annette Hanshaw, together with unknown clarinet and violin. Since Rollini's last record session with Hanshaw, she had moved from the Pathé/Perfect label to Columbia. Some of her records were issued under her real name on Columbia and Harmony, but most of them pseudonymous on Columbia' budget label Harmony. Thus on this session she appeared as "Gay Ellis," the pseudonym used for her romantic songs, and her band as "her Sizzling Syncopators." Fortunately, Harmony records were electrically recorded by now.

Two tunes were recorded: "Telling It to the Daisies" and "I've Got 'It.'" On the first, Hanshaw starts with the song's verse; during her following chorus Rollini softly accompanies her on the goofus. The second title is similarly arranged, but opens with a hot intro. Rollini plays an accompanying role in the short instrumental chorus.

Back in 1927 on his first recording date with Annette Hanshaw, Rollini had added his sound to the great duo of Joe Venuti and Eddie Lang and only a few days later these three, with piano player Arthur Schutt, recorded two instrumentals. Thus Joe Venuti's Blue Four was born, which was to be hugely successful. This Blue Four with Rollini would have one more recording date before Adrian left for England and Fred Elizalde. Venuti had missed the deep sound of his bass saxophone and tried to emulate it with other competent musicians: Don Murray, Jimmy Dorsey, and Pete Pumiglio, who played baritone saxophone, and even Frank Trumbauer who occasionally recorded on the bassoon. However, now that Rollini himself was available again, Venuti invited him to the studio. With Itzy Riskin at the piano, the first tune that the new Blue Four recorded was "Ragging the Scale," a ragtime piece from 1915. This tune had been a hit at the time and Rollini may already have played it with his first little group at home in Larchmont. However, not in the way the Blue Four played it: Venuti takes the lion share of the solo space but Riskin and Rollini also play solos. This is fully grown-up jazz, played with great swing by some of New York's top musicians. "Put and Take," the second tune recorded that day, exceptionally survives in two issued takes, and it gives an excellent opportunity to judge Rollini's solo work. He opens the piece on hot fountain pen, exchanging short notes with Venuti, then proceeds on this instrument with a thirty-two-bar solo. While Lang plays an introduction to Venuti's following solo, Rollini switches to bass saxophone to accompany the others and plays two solos and two breaks.

Now, about half a year after the stock market crash, the Depression started to be felt. Recording dates were becoming less frequent. However, Rollini still had a few freelance sessions lined up. The first was another date for Columbia as a member of Rube Bloom's Bayou Boys, which was to be their final recording. It produced "On Revival Day," a pseudo-spiritual (its label says "A Rhythmic Spiritual"), and "There's a Wah-Wah Girl in Agua Caliente."[33] The session meant another meeting for Rollini with Jack Purvis, with whom he had recently recorded on two occasions, resulting in some of the greatest jazz of the period. Bloom's arrangements gave both men new solo opportunities. While Purvis's playing usually reminds of the influence that Louis Armstrong's style had on him, on "On Revival Day" it seems inspired by another great black trumpeter, Henry Allen, playing with Luis Russell's band on, yes, "On Revival Day."[34]

Breaking the Race Barrier: Ethel Waters

Ten days later Rollini was back in the Columbia studio for another memorable date. This was to accompany black singer Ethel Waters (1896–1977). Waters had been one of the first black female singers appearing on records. That was in 1921 after the market for vocal blues had been opened up by Mamie Smith and OKeh records. For some years Waters recorded for small labels that were aimed at the race market, until in 1925 Columbia gave her a contract. She continued to make race records for Columbia, but this company also gave her a chance to record for its popular catalog. She did so with great success and it paved her way for a further career and to a wider audience. From 1928 on, she mainly recorded popular songs and in 1929 she cut her last race record. Thereafter on records she usually worked with white accompanists. At the June 1930 recording date with Adrian Rollini, the other men were some of Ben Selvin's group of standard studio musicians: Manny Klein, trumpet; Tommy Dorsey, trombone; Benny Goodman, clarinet; possibly Rube Bloom, piano; and Ben Selvin himself on violin. The new media of sound pictures brought new popular hits and two of these were taken, "My Kind of a Man" (from MGM's *The Floradora Girl*) and "You Brought a New Kind of Love to Me" (from Paramount's *The Big Pond*). Their arrangements gave the band little else to do than to play an accompaniment. Rollini plays a break and Goodman two short solos. In the first tune Waters includes a scat chorus.

Transcription Discs and More with Red Nichols: The "Heat" Programs

It would be at least a month and a half before Rollini earned extra money again from a recording date, once more with Annette Hanshaw. The record label was Harmony, Columbia's budget label, and the musicians were most likely all from Bert Lown's Biltmore Orchestra. Its personnel is anyone's guess and if Rollini is present, it is as the piano player. However, it might be Lown's usual man, Chauncey Gray, at the piano. Hanshaw recorded four tunes, two hot and two sweet. The two hot tunes, "I Want a Good Man" and "The Way I Feel Today," were issued on Clarion, Columbia's new Depression label, and are rare in their original form. However, on all four titles Annette has left her shyness behind and produces some great vocal work, with the band backing her perfectly and cutting loose on the hot tunes.

Rollini fulfilled one more side job before his freelance recording work dried up. In the first and last weeks of August, Red Nichols had jobs with his exclusive employer Brunswick. In 1929 Red had started to record broadcasts for Brunswick. These broadcast programs were called Brunswick Brevities and these so-called transcription discs were used by radio stations across the country. This type of disc was not meant for public distribution and they usually were in a format that could only be played with special equipment, rotating at 33 rpm or having a diameter larger than twelve inches. In August 1930, after almost a year, Red recorded a second batch of broadcast discs, to be issued under the flag of National Radio Advertising, Inc., in their series of "Heat" Programs. These broadcast discs are rare and research is continuing. The fact that Brunswick studio books from this period are missing does not help either. Not all have been found by collectors and not even all titles are known.[35]

The first session was on 2 August and produced the striking number of eight recorded titles.[36] At present five of these are known (and available on CD), and three remain to be found. Nichols brought a large band to the studio, consisting of two trumpets, trombone, four reeds, two violins, piano, banjo, and drums. The four reeds were Benny Goodman, Sid Stoneburn, Babe Russin, and Adrian Rollini, the last one in his usual dual role in the reed and rhythm sections. All available recordings are long for the time, sometimes lasting more than four minutes. This is partly due to the fact that some recordings are medleys of two tunes, as shown by the first theme that can be heard, "My Future Just Passed." The recording continues with "Oh, Baby!" after which the first theme returns. Rollini does not solo, but his bass sound is heard all over the recording. In fact, his sound here is not much different from the sound of a tuba. He does solo, however, in the following recording, "After You've Gone," where his bass saxophone is heard in a thirty-six-bar solo. On the next title, "St. Louis Blues," Rollini's role is again little more than supplying bass notes. The trumpet player, who produces the final trumpet solo, shows the influence of Louis Armstrong. He could be Manny Klein, who was known for his talent to play like other trumpeters. "Call of the Freaks" is known from interpretations by black bands and Nichols uses the same arrangement, including the staccato rhythm. It is Rollini's turn to solo, and in eleven bars he puts his stamp on the performance. One more title from this transcription session is available, "The Sheik of Araby." Red had recorded this before for a normal release by Brunswick and on that occasion Jack Teagarden had sung an impressive introductory chorus. This time Teagarden was not present and Nichols decided to play Jack's bluesy chorus on his trumpet. On the whole this performance is lackluster but for the solos by Benny Goodman and Babe Russin. This was the seventh tune recorded that day. The men were getting tired and it is possible that the eighth and final were not even issued for that reason. They probably did not survive.

The following day ten more titles were to be recorded. Only four of these are available to collectors for the reasons mentioned above; even titles of the others are not known. Three of the four survivors are medleys, in which one theme opens and sometimes a different second theme closes the performance. The first two medleys were "Strike Up the Band"/"Alexander's Ragtime Band" and "Black and Blue"/"Ain't Misbehavin'." Rollini is not heard in either, and a tuba (probably Joe Tarto) supplies the bass notes. In the other two surviving recordings from that session, Rollini did have solo features. The arrangement of a medley consisting of "Sweet Georgia Brown" and "I Ain't Got Nobody" allowed him an exceptional thirty-one-bar solo, excellently executed at a very high tempo, and during the fourth surviving performance, "Some of These Days," he solos for sixteen bars.

Later that same month, Nichols had another transcription date with Brunswick, for National Advertising's "Heat" programs. Four recordings were produced, of which two are available. They are medleys again, respectively "Ballin' the Jack"/"Walkin' the Dog" and "I Lost My Gal from Memphis"/"Here Comes Emily Brown." Nichols used the same personnel except for Goodman and Russin, who were replaced by Jimmy Dorsey and Bud Freeman. The first medley is kicked off by Rollini with a sixteen-bar solo.

Only days after the second set of transcriptions had been waxed, Nichols got his Five Pennies back in the studio, this time numbering nine musicians including Red. It was to be Rollini's final recording date with Nichols and also his final freelance jazz job for some time. Glenn Miller provided the arrangements and the first, for "Carolina in the Morning," is quite surprising, not in the least for the boogie-woogie style rhythm that was used in part, but also for its intriguing intro in which nearly all instruments are heard in solos. A second tune remained unissued, but the third, "Who?" gave Rollini a chance to play a thirty-two-bar solo. The session ended with "By the Shalimar," with another arrangement in the style on Nichols's early Brunswick success of "Ida." To Rollini it meant one of his first opportunities to display his talent on vibraphone, although the instrument that he used had no strong vibration.

This ended August 1930. In addition to his fixed job with Bert Lown at the Biltmore Hotel, he had had a steady income from side jobs, studio jobs for Columbia, Harmony, OKeh, and Brunswick. Losing this work meant less income. The Depression was being felt at last.

Freelance Recordings with Other Bands: George Posnack and Jacques Renard

Adrian Rollini may have recorded with at least two more bands and there may be more. It has been suggested that they were from Bert Lown's booking office but this has not been documented. Information about the two bands is scarce; however, Rollini's presence is suggested by some of their recordings.

The first band that should be mentioned is George Posnack's orchestra. Posnack was born around 1905 and in 1921 graduated from Boys High School in Brooklyn, New York. He played piano and chose a career in music. In 1925 he worked with Ben Glaser's Orchestra at the Beaux Arts, New York.[37] Around March 1927 he went to Europe, and he and some more Americans worked in Bert Ambrose's Orchestra at the Mayfair Hotel in London.[38] In September Ambrose's Americans returned to New York. In March and April 1930 Posnack cut some titles for the QRS label with his orchestra. Posnack's band had a standard instrumentation of trumpet, trombone, two clarinets/alto saxophones, violin, piano, banjo, drums, plus bass saxophone.

The QRS company had a long history of issuing piano rolls, and by 1930 it was one of the few survivors of that industry. However, it saw the writing on the wall and sought to expand its business by going into gramophone records. Its launching moment was badly chosen, just at the time of the Wall Street Crash, so its records sold poorly and are rare today. The two Posnack titles are therefore among the last discovered Rollini titles. The first is "Black Horse," a composition by Joe Tarto, tuba player on countless white New York jazz recordings. The second is "Minor Gaff," by Dick George and Harold Arluck, who were the two piano players of the Buffalodians, a territory band from Buffalo, New York.[39] Both tunes were meant to be played by jazz-oriented groups, and indeed they got good arrangements with much solo space. Rollini solos on both titles. On "Black Horse" he is heard playing goofus behind the trombone solo. George Posnack himself only solos on "Minor Gaff." Posnack is known to have worked as a studio musician for Warner Bros in 1934, but after that he stayed out of the limelight.[40]

The other band in this category is Jacques Renard's. Renard started to record for Brunswick in the second half of 1930. His relation with the company would eventually last five years. Renard was born in 1898 in Russia and his family migrated via Romania to the USA, where they landed in Boston. Renard had musical talent and showed fast progress when his father bought him a violin. He was offered a job with a symphony orchestra but was more attracted to dance music. He had a job with Meyer Davis's orchestra, then got an orchestra of his own. He had several engagements at Boston clubs and started to make records for Victor in 1927. In 1930 he opened a supper club of his own, Renard's Mayfair, and a year later he rose to fame when, in 1931, he became leader of a sponsored radio show, the *Camel Quarter Hour*.[41]

The standard discographies mention that Adrian Rollini is present on some of Renard's Brunswick titles. There is a solo by him on bass saxophone on "A Girl Friend of a Boy Friend of Mine" from October 1930. Moreover, the band had an agile tuba player whose sound might be confused with that of a bass saxophone in a rhythm role. The ending of the fifth title from this session, "Readin', Rittin',

Rhythm" may suggest a bass saxophone.[42] However, this session was done not by Renard's regular orchestra but by the Brunswick House Orchestra, directed by Bob Haring, as pointed out by Ross Laird.[43] Thus its personnel was selected from New York's large number of white freelancing musicians. Rollini may have been one of them.

Listening to all of Jacques Renard's other 1931 Brunswick recordings reveals no bass saxophone, but all have a tuba or a string bass in the rhythm section.[44]

Looking for a Change of Environment

The steady flow of freelance work that Rollini enjoyed during the first eight months of 1930 ended with his final Red Nichols session in August. Rollini must have been thinking about a change of environment. One opportunity is mentioned by tenor sax player Bud Freeman.[45] According to Freeman, a band was rehearsing at the Roseland Ballroom in New York for a ten-week European tour by the end of 1930. The band was formed after the ten titles that Freeman had recorded with Bix Beiderbecke and Hoagy Carmichael in that year. It consisted of Bix Beiderbecke, cornet; Tommy and Jimmy Dorsey, trombone and clarinet; Bud Freeman, tenor saxophone; Joe Sullivan, piano; Gene Krupa, drums; Dick McDonough, guitar; and Adrian Rollini, bass saxophone. However, Bix became ill and the plan was over. But the next opportunity came soon.

Chapter 15

Back to the California Ramblers and Bert Lown

After Adrian Rollini had left the California Ramblers in 1927, Ed Kirkeby kept his business going as before and hired musicians on the basis of contracts he had to fill. There were regular broadcasts, recording dates, and tours for the California Ramblers, and there still was the California Ramblers Inn. The name Little Ramblers would also occasionally pop up.[1]

Kirkeby and Hand had decided to extend the initial lease contract to five years, till the end of 1928. In January 1928 Kirkeby played his old trick again and added yet another name to his recording groups, when Edison started issuing records by a subset of the California Ramblers under the name of the Seven Blue Babies. In the beginning of 1929 Columbia lost its exclusive rights to the name California Ramblers on its records and Kirkeby became the sole owner to the name.[2] "Golden Gate Orchestra" could now be replaced by the real thing, as Edison did that year.[3]

Kirkeby knew that the name California Ramblers was his biggest asset, and kept struggling against unauthorized use. But there was one bandleader who continued to give him trouble: Joe Tenner continued to perform as Joe Tenner and his California Ramblers into 1929, claiming that he paid Kirkeby commission.[4]

When the five-year term of Kirkeby's lease on the California Ramblers Inn ended, he did not lease it for another period. In May 1930 newspapers brought the news that "the place on Pelham Road that was formerly the California Ramblers" was taken over and that the new owners were spending a quarter of a million on it. By the end of the month it was to reopen as the Hollywood Gardens, featuring Paul Whiteman and his band.[5] It would "seat 3,200 people and turn out one of the best dinners extant for $1.50 and no cover charge! There'll be a 40-girl show, a forty-cent minimum lunch (outdoors) and a 65 by 75-foot dance floor."[6] The Hollywood Gardens would exist until October 1932, when it burned to the ground.[7]

In April 1931 Kirkeby and his California Ramblers did the first of a series of broadcasts sponsored by the Scholl Manufacturing Company, makers of Dr. Scholl's Foot Appliances and Remedies.

For about four years Ed Kirkeby had now done both the business management and the musical leadership of the California Ramblers. He had survived, but with the increasing effect of the economic depression, he felt that he wanted to share his responsibilities again. He found Adrian Rollini again, who was ready for a change. They decided that they would lead together and they found a place to do it: Will Oakland's Hunter Island Inn.

The Original California Ramblers Orchestra at Will Oakland's Hunter Island Inn

At his return to New York in December 1929, Adrian's brother Art Rollini moved in with his family, when he found that his mother and his sister Vera had rented both Larchmont houses and moved to an uncle's apartment in Lafayette.[8] To get a job he called Ed Kirkeby, who gave him work with his California Ramblers. The work consisted at first of a commercial radio show and club dates.[9] Then, in the fall of 1930, Kirkeby booked his band in Will Oakland's Terrace.

Will Oakland (1880–1956) was an experienced vaudeville and recording artist when, in the early twenties, he became a club manager. He was from German descent and his real name was Herman Hinrichs. He became well known as a countertenor, a male singer with a range like a (female) alto. In 1923 he was in a revue at the Chateau Shanley, a Shanley-owned restaurant off Broadway in New York, and the same year he was its manager.[10] In the following years he became owner of another New York club, the Terrace, on 51 St. between Broadway and 7th Avenue. In the fall of 1930 Ed Kirkeby booked his California Ramblers there.

At Will Oakland's Terrace, Art received $70 a week, working six nights from 6:00 p.m. until 3:00 a.m. He took a hotel room near the Terrace, which he shared with the band's drummer Herb Weil. Kirkeby's personnel was:

Jack Wechsler—musical leader, violin
Chelsea Quealey—trumpet
Bobby Davis—1st alto saxophone
Johnny Rude—3rd alto saxophone
Art Rollini—tenor saxophone
Lew Cobey—piano
Noel Kilgen—guitar
Carl Smith—bass
Herb Weil—drums

Adrian Rollini's band at Hunter Island. From left Carl Smith, Johnny Rude, Herb Weil, Art Rollini, Noel Kilgen, Adrian, Lew Coby, Chelsea Quealey, Bobby Davis, Jack Wechsler.

The year before, Quealey, Davis, and Art Rollini had been members of Fred Elizalde's band in London; all three had returned to New York, Davis being the last.

Will Oakland's name as a former recording star still had great drawing power and his shows were no disappointment, so his business grew. He seems to have lost much money due to the Depression, but in 1931 he had sufficiently recovered to be able to also take over the old Hunter Island Inn on Pelham Parkway, not far from the former California Ramblers Inn. In summer it would have the same climatic advantage over the city as the California Ramblers Inn.

From 1 April till Will Oakland's opening date at Hunter Island Inn, Art Rollini did club dates for Bert Lown.[11] After the opening, Art lived with his mother again, who had moved back to Larchmont. Adrian and Dixie probably had a room at the inn and may also have used Adrian's boat, the *Rambler IV*, to live in for the summer.

For the opening night on Saturday 16 May 1931, Oakland brought the California Ramblers to the Hunter Island Inn. On the invitation they were called "The Original California Ramblers Orchestra ... with Adrian Rollini." Guests paid $4 per person for the entire evening, including an eight-course dinner. Oakland brought many guests at his expense, by taxis from the Terrace to the Inn. Several well-known radio and stage personalities were there to celebrate the opening, including Jimmy Durante; Buddy Kennedy was master of ceremonies. A newspaper gave an enthusiastic description of the event:

We thought we had been to some nice places before, but this—ah, this! A tremendous country house with none other than the genial Will . . . Oakland out by the front door to welcome you with a hearty handshake. Grouped around the steps are numerous songbirds, perched on trees, taking lessons in singing from superlatively sweet Lois Ravelle, Molly (Personality) O'Doherty and the Grenadine—pardon, Grenadiers Quartet. Not to mention Mayor Will himself.

The article described the place: "as though it had been designed by Cecil B. De Mille, what with knives and forks being used as anchors for colored balloons, and with Anna Korina there. Oh, Anna Korina! A blonde, and what a blonde! Oooooh!"[12] At the end, the public became so enthusiastic that Oakland was nominated "Mayor of Hunter Island." After the opening night prices would be from $2 up.[13]

The opening night was a success. From half past eight, it could be heard via station WMCA. A newspaper said that the inn had been filled to capacity and more than 300 people had been turned away at the door, due to lack of sufficient seating space. Two weeks later, Oakland solved this by opening the inn's Summer Garden, which almost tripled the inn's capacity. The garden was located at the side of the inn and had a platform for Adrian Rollini and his California Ramblers. Adrian had his bass saxophone in front of the bandstand.[14]

His beautiful inn, its garden, and the band were not Oakland's only source of publicity. There were regular broadcasts from the inn via WMCA, WPCH, and WOR.[15] By the end of June, Oakland was in the newspapers again with an early-warning system for storms. He was an experienced electronics hobbyist and had designed a radio detector that would ring a bell when a storm was approaching.[16]

Adrian Rollini got his share of publicity too, due to his yacht. After he had returned from London, he had bought another boat, which he moored on a dock at 78th Street. He called it *Rambler IV*. In July he rescued three people from drowning in the Long Island Sound. And then, a few days later, he slipped when he stepped from his boat onto a slippery rock. He fell on his face, lost two teeth, and cut his lower lip, a newspaper reported and added that he had to give up saxophone for at least a month.[17] He may have fully switched to the xylophone/vibraphone for a while, as suggested by a newspaper that mentioned the inn's new marimba band. In May a newspaper mentioned that Rollini's orchestra played rhumbas and Adrian's accident may have given an extra impulse to the band to embrace the new South American rhythms, which were growing in popularity.[18] The band stayed in the limelight, but sometimes negatively, as in a newspaper that complained that Rollini's orchestra should enlarge its repertoire, instead of playing the same tune, "Dancing in the Dark," four times in an hour.[19]

The California Ramblers worked full weeks at the inn till 18 October, and then one more month on weekends only until 15 November, when Will Oakland took them back to his Terrace in New York.[20] However, Adrian Rollini did not join them there and violin player Jack Wechsler took over the band's leadership.

Recordings in 1931

In 1931, after his final recordings with Bert Lown's orchestra in April, Rollini made only a handful of records. 1931 is the final year from which Ed Kirkeby's payment books are available; they end in July 1931. For 1931 they list twenty-two recording dates and Rollini (without a first name) is mentioned only twice.

All sessions are for full dance bands, with one exception, a recording date for ARC on 22 May for a five-man group consisting of Jack Purvis, trumpet; Bobby Davis, reeds; Lew Cobey, piano; Jack Powers, drums; and Rollini, with two vocalists whose names are hard to read. Chances are that this was Adrian in his old role of supplying the bass rhythm on his saxophone, as well as soloing and supporting his old pal Bobby Davis as a reed player. On that date ARC only recorded two matrices, by Billy Murray and Walter Van Brunt. The recordings were issued under the names Billy Murray and Walter Scanlan "with Orchestra," but have not been heard by the author.

The second date on which a Rollini is listed is a Ted Wallace date for Columbia on 29 May. No bass saxophone or vibraphone is heard on the resulting record, the personnel of which consisted of Jack Purvis and Fred Van Eps, trumpets; Carl Loeffler, trombone; Bobby Davis; Elmer Feldkamp; Paul Mason and Frank Sax, reeds; Ed Sexton, guitar; Ward Lay, bass; Jack Powers; drums; plus Rollini. Since Kirkeby used Lew Cobey on piano on almost all other sessions at the time, it is safe to assume that this is a rare occasion where Adrian Rollini plays piano throughout.

Rollini may or may not have been on these Kirkeby dates, but he was on two of the hottest dates of the year under the leadership of trombone player Jack Teagarden. Teagarden was born in Texas in 1905 and arrived in New York in 1927. He immediately made a deep impression on his fellow musicians. His style was totally different from Miff Mole's, which had been the example for all New York trombone players in the years before. Mole's style was shaped in the years of the small hot jazz bands of the early twenties, which became popular with the Original Dixieland Jazz Band and just after ragtime. It has been described as cool, precise, and academic but highly creative and fitting in the jazz bands of the time. However, Teagarden played in a more relaxed style, which fit better in the larger bands of the mid-twenties. Moreover, Teagarden proved to be one of the best jazz singers of the time, which was a major asset when the trend toward a vocal chorus in a band arrangement became strong in the late twenties. From 1929 Red Nichols had used him regularly in his Five Pennies recordings, and thus he had recorded with Adrian Rollini in February 1930.

In 1928 Teagarden had joined Ben Pollack's band, which included Chicagoans Jimmy McPartland and Benny Goodman. In 1931 he was still with Pollack, but in September the band had no work and Teagarden joined a Dorsey brothers pit band in a Broadway show. The day after the opening of the show on 13 October 1931, Jack had to get up early for a recording date at the Columbia studios with no one from the Dorsey pit band but with two of his Pollack colleagues, trumpeter Stirling Bose and guitar player Nappy Lamare. Others were Jack's brother Charlie, reed player Pee Wee Russell, and Adrian Rollini, who was there to solo and to play the low saxophone parts, since Artie Bernstein was the bass player. However, the hero of the group was piano player Fats Waller. Waller had used Teagarden on some of his recording dates in 1929 and now Teagarden returned the service. Both are strongly featured on each of the four titles, with some hilarious duet vocals on the first two. Rollini seems to have missed the start of the session and carefully plays an introduction to the second title, "That's What I Like About You." He is even less audible in the third title, "Chances Are," but he takes a fine solo on the fourth, "I Got the Ritz from the One I Love," which remained unissued until the LP era.[21]

Teagarden's career as a leader at recording dates had started the year before and in 1931 it began to take off. A month after the successful date for Columbia, he was able to contract another and this was for Plaza. The idea was to form a background band for singer Gene Austin. This time Teagarden not only took Bose and Lamare from Pollack's band, but also reed players Matty Matlock and Eddie Miller, as well as Gil Bowers, piano; Harry Goodman, bass; and Ray Bauduc, drums. Four more players were held over from the Columbia date: Jack's brother Charlie, Pee Wee Russell, Fats Waller, and Adrian Rollini. Four titles were recorded and Gene Austin sang on two, "Lies" and "I'm Sorry Dear." The band provided a straight and subdued accompaniment for Austin, with Bowers on piano. The two recordings present only a suggestion of what potential the band had. This full potential was shown the same day, when the men were allowed to make some hot recordings. It was decided to do "China Boy" and "Tiger Rag," two tunes that they would have played at almost any after-hours session. "China Boy" is opened by Waller and then the band gets loose in the theme, followed by several solo choruses, including one by Rollini. "Tiger Rag" is played as hot and in fact is a Rollini recording. The intro was changed from the standard arrangement so that Rollini could play an impressive series of short breaks that are unequaled. Then the band goes into the classic "Tiger Rag" themes, followed by more solos, including by Teagarden and Waller. Typically for the record company's commercial strategy, the Austin sides were released but not the hot sides.[22]

One day later the California Ramblers, directed by Ed Kirkeby, recorded two sugary tunes, without any suggestion that Rollini could be present. Kirkeby made no further recordings under the names of the California Ramblers and Ted Wallace Orchestra after January 1932, but he continued to record as one of the orchestra leaders for ARC-Brunswick.[23] Adrian Rollini may have participated in a few of these Kirkeby sessions.

The two Teagarden sessions were a welcome change from the disciplined dance music produced by the bands that Rollini had been working and recording with since his return from London. However, his best work from these dates remained unissued until the LP era, Teagarden's "Tiger Rag."

Kirkeby's payment books for this period demonstrate that the musicians that he used for his recordings basically formed a different group from those he used at Will Hunter's Terrace and the Hunter Island Inn.

The New California Ramblers Inn

Except for the second recording date with Jack Teagarden, no definite information is available about Adrian's activities between November 1931 and June 1932, when he became leader of the New California Ramblers.

There is a possibility that Will Oakland asked him to stay at the Hunter Island Inn. Oakland was quoted saying that he planned to keep the inn open all winter.[24] With his capabilities as a multi-instrumentalist and as a leader, Rollini would be the right person to provide the music. Another possibility is that he was playing engagements with his old friend Red Nichols. Peter Wells studied at Yale University during the years 1931–34 and remembered a fraternity dance where Red played for dancing and had Rollini on bass saxophone and Arthur Schutt on piano.[25]

Meanwhile Ed Kirkeby had the band at Will Oakland's Terrace in New York City. The band was directed by violinist Jack Wechsler, included Adrian's brother Art, and worked there until late spring of 1932.

Both Kirkeby and Rollini were thinking back on the early years of their cooperation when they had their own place, the California Ramblers Inn, only a few miles from Hunter Island. Some of their most successful years had been when Kirkeby took care of the business side and Rollini directed the band. So it is logical that they set up a plan to repeat that success and looked for a place. In 1930 the former California Ramblers Inn had been enlarged and had become the Hollywood Gardens; it was not an option for Kirkeby and Rollini.[26] They found another place, on Pelham Parkway a little further from the shore of Long Island Sound, and called it the New California Ramblers Inn. It had been known as the Castilian Royal, a restaurant that featured dance bands and acts, and

> **NOW OPEN**
> Offering A Startling New Price Policy with
> No Cover Charge . No Minimu[m]
> AT THE NEW
> **California Ramblers Inn**
> ON PELHAM PARKWAY
> (on the site of the old Castillian Royal)
> The first Road Restaurant to meet present day conditions by putting its prices within reach of all
>
> **Special Feature every**
> Sunday Night. Prominent Radio Stars.
>
> Music By The Famous California Ramblers Orchestra
> Under the Direction of Adrian Rollini
>
> **Full Course Dinner $1.50**
>
> Banquets and Parties of all Kinds   Tel. TAlmadge 2-9160-8836

Advertisement for the New California Ramblers Inn.

before that as the Pelham Heath Inn, which was made into a success by Harry Susskind, who still was its manager when Kirkeby and Rollini appeared.

A contract was made up between Kirkeby, Rollini, and Susskind, and the Castilian Royal was renamed New California Ramblers Inn. Adrian got a new band together and his brother Art was a member again, as were several men from the band at the Hunter Island Inn.[27] Salaries were low and Art called it "the deep depression." When in 1930 he had started with Kirkeby at the Terrace, Art received $70 a week; this was later reduced to $65. Now at the New California Ramblers Inn he got only $40, and it would even get worse.[28]

The New California Ramblers Inn opened on Thursday 2 June 1932.[29] The drapes and matching table cloths were Dixie's work. The band book contained their own arrangements and some that were stocks with adaptations. The food was good and advertisements announced a "Startling New Price Policy with No Cover Charge ... No Minimum." However, despite the low prices, there was little business and Art remembered that their opening night was dismal.[30] This was partly due to strong competition from across the street, where Isham Jones's fourteen-piece band did tremendous business in the new Pelham Heath Inn.[31]

To get more business and publicity, Kirkeby hired extra acts for the Sundays in June. So on 12 June he had the Pickens Sisters and on 26 June Frances Langford. Kirkeby recognized their talent in an early phase of their careers. The Pickens Sisters, Jane, Patti, and Helen, were led by Jane, who had the best musical training. They recorded for Columbia in 1931 and had just moved to Victor, when they worked for Kirkeby. They were Victor's answer to Brunswick's Boswell Sisters.[32] Frances Langford (1914–2005) was starting an impressive career in 1931, which would include many films and records and bring her great popularity as an entertainer for the military during World War II.

In 1930 ARC had started a program of recordings of dance music, which the company issued under various names of orchestra leaders, who were usually involved in name only. Ed Kirkeby had allowed ARC to put his name on some of those labels almost from the start of the program. Exceptionally, in July 1932, Kirkeby personally directed a five-title session. One of his musicians was Sylvester Ahola. Others were from the band at the New California Ramblers Inn, and Adrian may have been one of them.[33] However, some weeks after the opening of the New California Ramblers Inn, Adrian became seriously ill. A doctor Martin was consulted and his diagnosis was gonorrhea, a sexually transmitted infection.[34] At the time penicillin had not yet been found as a very effective medicine, and with the available drugs it took several weeks to cure. Doctor Martin did not want to create marriage problems and told Dixie that Adrian had a kidney infection. Adrian and Dixie were living upstairs in the inn and Adrian had to stay in bed for a while. By the end of the first month Kirkeby made Art the temporary leader of the band. He wrote a few new arrangements to spark things up, but without great success.

Yet there were good moments, too. Despite the depressed economy there were still society parties with dining and dancing and there were the local Elks who, on 20 July, held their annual "shore dinner" with 300 participants. And there were some pleasant side effects. One evening, Art met his future wife Ena here, who was fifteen and the daughter of May Kelsall, the lady who had the concessions for the coat room and the ladies room. Also Vera, sister of Adrian and Art, met her partner here: George Hnida, who played string bass with the band. George was twenty-four years old and good-looking, but he made a bad impression on Art, who described him as smoking pot, with rotten teeth, and drinking too much alcohol. George would go around the tables and drink unfinished drinks of people who had left.[35]

However, all this did not pay enough. Adrian was still in bed recovering from his illness, while Art was running the band. "Business was so bad, I didn't get paid," Art wrote later. Art got no salary and "the boys got a few coins which they jingled in their pockets." He was getting more and more problems getting them back on the bandstand. When trumpet player Teddy Sandow refused to get on the bandstand, a fist fight was narrowly avoided.[36]

Kirkeby had more interests to take care of and only came to the inn once a week, usually on Friday night. By September he and Adrian gave up and decided to sell the club. Early September he sold out to a gangster boss called Jimmy Baker. Baker took over quickly. The waiters and the chef were replaced by new men, who all had guns bulging in their clothes. However, the band could stay and received its $40 a week again.

The new situation was short lived. Two weeks after the takeover, the police raided the inn, looking for Jimmy Baker and for liquor. However, they did not find Baker, who had fled in time. They did not find the booze either. It was hidden upstairs under a trap door under Adrian's bed, with a rug over it. While this was going on, the band had stopped playing, but they did not get bothered.[37]

The waiters and the chef were rounded up and the police padlocked the place. However, they respected Adrian's illness and Dixie and he were allowed to stay with one access door. The boys from the band were all gone. Years later Jimmy Baker was shot by the mob.

So the end of the New California Ramblers Inn came three months after it opened. While Adrian and Dixie stayed until Adrian's full recovery, Art went home to Larchmont.[38]

Back to the Studio, Freelancer Adrian Rollini and His Orchestra

No definite information is available about Rollini's activities between August 1932, when the New California Ramblers Inn closed, and the end of the year. However, in January 1933 he was in a recording studio again, for the first time in half a year.

Recovering from his disease and getting his full energy back would have taken several weeks, but this does not account for five months of silence. He and Dixie may have lived at the Larchmont home to relax and recover. Also in the depth of the Depression it was not easy to get a steady job and when he could work again, Rollini may have had to accept club dates and party dates, such as Bert Lown continued to contract.[39]

At the end of the year, Rollini's situation was finally improving. He had kept himself in shape and when he was asked for a recording date by orchestra leader Freddie Martin, he was ready. Martin was embarking on a recording career with his society dance band and in 1933, his top year, he would be in a studio every month, producing more than 100 titles for ARC. The jazz age was over and Martin was not interested in jazz. His music was peppy or sweet dance music with a pleasant vocal, so that buyers could remember the name of the tune. In January 1933, at his third recording date, the band would record six titles, none of them jazzy. Rollini only took part in one, "When the Morning Rolls Around." Its arrangement gave him several short solos, which he played in his usual self-assured way.[40]

Freddie Martin's recordings mostly present straight dance music and only a few have been heard by the author. Thus there may be more with Rollini.[41]

Slowly Rollini was getting back into the groove now. He even managed to close a deal with ARC, owner of several low-priced record labels, some of which were sold via dime stores. The first date was on 14 February 1933, when he recorded the first titles that would be issued under the name of Adrian Rollini and his Orchestra, a milestone in his career. Rollini selected musicians with years of experience in the world of dance music and who were able to give any recording a jazz flavor: Manny Klein, trumpet; Tommy Dorsey, trombone; Tommy's brother Jimmy, clarinet and alto saxophone; his own brother Art on tenor; Fulton McGrath, piano; Eddie Lang, guitar; Art Miller, string bass; and an unknown drummer. To give the band an individual sound, there were violin player Joe Venuti and accordionist Charles Magnante, not to forget Adrian himself, who would play on an unsurpassed number of four different instruments at this session, bass saxophone, goofus, vibraphone, and xylophone.

The first title, "Have You Ever Been Lonely?" opens with Rollini's notes on the vibraphone, then he switches to his bass saxophone, then back to the vibraphone to accompany singer Dick Robertson and at the end of the recording he plays his bass saxophone again. However, there is no solo for the leader. On "You've Got Me Crying Again," Adrian is again all over the place without soloing: he starts on bass saxophone, moves to vibraphone, after a solo by brother Art moves to xylophone, then back to bass saxophone, and ends with some notes on his vibraphone. "Hustlin' and Bustlin' for Baby," the third title recorded that day, is taken at a brisk tempo and has solo space for Art's tenor, then for a chase chorus for Adrian and Jimmy Dorsey, and finally for Joe Venuti's violin. The fourth title, "You Must Believe Me," goes back to the sweet style of the first two and has little to offer in terms of jazz, although Eddie Lang takes a short solo.

Recording contracts were hard to get and jazz was out. So it is a miracle that Joe Venuti was asked to make some pure jazz records, just two weeks after Rollini's first own session. These recordings were at the request of the British branch of Columbia Records. Back in 1927 and again in 1930, Lang, Rollini, and Venuti had recorded some of the finest small-group jazz ever and now, as an anachronism, they did it again. Those early recordings by Joe Venuti's Blue Four had given both Venuti and Rollini great popularity among British jazz fans and Rollini's two-year stay in London had only added to this. This was reason enough for the Brits to ask for more. Four titles were to be recorded, of which two were not released in the USA at the time. On the British label the group was called Joe Venuti and Eddie Lang's Blue Five, the five being Venuti and Lang plus Jimmy Dorsey, Adrian Rollini, and Phil Wall. It worked. They started out with an old standard from ragtime days, "Raggin' the Scale," which they had done in 1930, too. Comparison with that earlier version is useless, because both deserve the highest praise. No sign of any Depression, but the old spirit and jazzmanship that these men would demonstrate at their most creative and swinging moments. The second title recorded by the Joe Venuti–Eddie Lang Blue Five was "Hey! Young Fella," which presents Adrian Rollini as a swinging vibraphone player and Jimmy Dorsey as a trumpeter, both in addition to their usual instruments. Joe Venuti can be heard playing string bass during Rollini's first solo. When Joe heard this recording decades after he made it, he recognized the tune after Dorsey's first notes and said "I got fifty potatoes for recording that" (potatoes meaning dollars).[42] Next was an original composition by the Blue Five called "Jig Saw Puzzle Blues." Eddie Lang was quite accomplished in playing blues tunes and produced a typical twelve-bar solo. Rollini played bass saxophone and vibraphone again and Jimmy Dorsey trumpet, clarinet, and alto saxophone. The session was completed with "Pink Elephants," a popular tune of the day. It swings from starts to finish and has solos by Dorsey, Venuti, Wall, and even one on goofus by Rollini.

Rollini's first recording session as a leader had been a milestone for him. And now, two weeks later, he had another breakthrough, his first session where his vibraphone work was as important as his bass saxophone work.

The session presented another milestone, a sad one. It turned out to be Eddie Lang's last. The following month he would not survive an operation on his tonsils. He passed away when he was thirty.

Back to Bert Lown

Adrian may have tried to start another dance band of his own, but his latest adventure had been a disaster due to the combination of his illness and the bad economic conditions. And when in February 1933 Bert Lown asked him to join his band again, he said "yes." Lown had successfully continued his career after Rollini left, but his contract at the Biltmore had ended in January 1932, after two years.[43] During those years he had many recording dates and simultaneously ran a booking office. Both were continued after he finished at the Biltmore. In 1931 Lown had closed a contract with MCA, the Music Corporation of America, and just like Whiteman and Kirkeby had done before him, he hired a press agent.[44] Her name was Carlyne Miller.[45] Lown continued to record for Victor, but the labels now said Bert Lown and his Orchestra, without reference to the Biltmore.[46]

In 1932 Lown and his band went on tour. On 15 March 1932 he was in St. Paul, Minnesota, where his band did a remote broadcast over the nationwide NBC network from the Lowry Hotel. The following month Lown had an engagement in Kansas City, Missouri. In April Lown married Carlyne Miller, his press agent, and at their marriage Tom Clines acted as master of ceremonies. Broadcasting continued to support his popularity, but when a radio magazine did a "Jazz King" contest in early 1933, Ben Bernie, Guy Lombardo, and Wayne King were among the winners (and even finished ahead of "King of Jazz" Paul Whiteman himself). Lown was almost invisible in the results.[47]

The engagement Bert Lown asked Rollini for in 1933 was at the Cocoanut Grove, a dinner and supper club at the Park Central Hotel at 870 7th Avenue in Midtown Manhattan.[48] Lown could quickly assemble an orchestra for one-day engagements, but for this occasion he assembled a special band and contacted Adrian Rollini for his leadership and instrumental versatility.[49] Adrian thought that his brother was a good candidate for the tenor saxophone chair. He called Art and asked: "How would you like to go with Bert Lown?" Art asked "How much does it pay?" Adrian answered, "Fifty bucks."[50] Art took the job and opened with Bert Lown on 2 March.[51] Adrian was playing bass saxophone and vibraphone. Art remembered it as an uneventful six months, but the band was good. Its full personnel was:

Eddie Petrovitz—1st trumpet
Eddie Farley—2nd trumpet
Al Philburn—trombone
Larry Tice—1st alto saxophone
Bernie Gluckman—2nd or 3rd alto saxophone
Art Rollini—tenor saxophone
Adrian Rollini—bass saxophone and more
Mac Ceppos—violin
Fulton "Fidgey" McGrath—piano
Tommy Felline—guitar
Stan King—drums
Merrill Kaye—string bass, later succeeded by Spencer Clark—bass saxophone[52]

Art Rollini often soloed and Al Philburn was one of the arrangers. As a bass saxophone player, Adrian had to play solo on that instrument and a fourth saxophone part or a second trombone part. He also played vibraphone and added another exotic instrument to his repertoire, the chimes.[53] Nobody realized it at the time, but in later years Rollini would make his living, only playing the latter two instruments.

Bert Lown must have been fond of the sound of bass saxophone. Thus when Merrill Kaye left, he decided to ask Spencer Clark back, just like he had asked Adrian Rollini to return to his band. This resulted in a unique instrumentation of a band with two bass saxophones. Phil Sillman heard this band and thought that Clark played the bass part and Rollini the fourth saxophone or trombone parts. However, it was not to Rollini's satisfaction. Art remembered that Adrian was annoyed by Clark, because he played the bass notes with vibrato. Spencer annoyed him terribly.[54]

The Depression dictated that hotels keep their prices low, in order to tempt the public to spend money. So the Park Central management decided to offer a seven-course dinner for $1 and no cover charge. From 10:00 p.m. the cover charge was $1 ($2 on Saturdays and holiday eves) and this paid for all the (non-alcoholic) drinks "that you may desire." During that month the first signs that Prohibition might eventually come to an end became visible, when it became legal to drink beer of 3.2 percent alcohol. The hotel immediately included beer in its offering of free drinks.[55]

To further stimulate the public, the Park Central engaged extra stars to perform with the orchestra. In the opening week it presented a floor show with Frances Langford; in the following weeks there were singers Ted Holt and Kate Smith, piano player Eddie Duchin, and musical comedy star Verna Burke.[56] On Sunday evenings Lown was broadcasting from the hotel and he could show a report where thirty-one stations requested his music via the WEAF network. In June his band would broadcast every night from the Cocoanut Grove, via WJZ, WOR, and WEAK. Lown also managed to get publicity once more by getting his method and codes for directing his band during broadcasts into the newspapers. He used them to adapt a tune's arrangement while it was being played, for instance to shorten it.[57] That he used seven vocalists with his Cocoanut orchestra also got into newspapers, as well as his theory that playwright Shakespeare was familiar with cars, (almost) quoting from several of his plays, such as *The Merry Wives of Windsor*: "Which of you know Ford of this town?"[58]

In June, a contest started for writing the best advertisement for one of twenty-eight participating concerns. *The Cocoanut Grove* was one of these twenty-eight and offered an extra prize if it was the winner's subject. This meant regular news in the papers until the end of July. One contender wrote a text under the heading "By By Blues" [sic]. He did not win. The winner wrote about Bert Lown:

> Soft lights and sweet music. Dinner above the clouds. Where? In the cool, soothing atmosphere of the Cocoanut Grove Roof Garden where one may eat the finest of foods, cooked by a master chef. Where one may dance to the smooth, swaying rhythms of Bert Lown and his orchestra. Good dining and good dancing at a moderate price. Eat, drink and be merry at the Cocoanut Grove Roof Garden. We offer you an excellent cuisine, a world-famous orchestra and an enjoyable time. Can you refuse?[59]

Bert Lown worked at the Park Central Cocoanut Grove until the end of September 1933, nearly seven months. He was succeeded by Ozzie Nelson and his orchestra. It was announced that "Lown and his famous band" went into a New

York theater for several months. In December Lown returned to vaudeville as headliner at Broadway's Palace Theatre, where the movie *The Invisible Man* was shown.[60]

Recording with Bert Lown

The period where Bert Lown had one recording date after another was followed by a year with only two, the last one in August 1932. That was again for Victor, the company that had helped build up Lown's reputation as a leader of top bands. One reason for Victor to reduce Lown's recording activity was the return of Paul Whiteman's band to their catalog. In September 1931 Whiteman had his first date with Victor, after he had signed their contract. After that date Lown had only two more dates with Victor and nothing after mid-1932.[61]

Another reason for Victor to lower its profile was the competition the label experienced from several cheap record labels, like ARC's. Victor decided to start its own budget label. This had some false starts, but in March 1933 the second start of the Bluebird label became a commercial success. The company reissued some recordings that had originally appeared on the Victor label, but original material quickly appeared on Bluebird, too. Here Bert Lown got a new chance and on 18 May 1933 he had his first session for Bluebird.[62] Judging from the seven titles recorded on that one day, Lown's music had not changed. The orchestra produced a steady rhythm, fit for dancing, and the arrangements included a vocal chorus and allowed a solo now and then. The best of the group is "We'll Have a Honeymoon Sunday," which featured solos by Fulton McGrath, piano; Mac Ceppos, violin; and probably the best solo by Adrian Rollini from all of his recordings with Bert Lown. Adrian solos again in "I'll Build a Nest," but this title is of greater importance for a solo by Art Rollini on tenor saxophone, probably his first recorded solo after he returned from England.

One month later Bert Lown had his second recording date for Bluebird. With eight titles, this date even surpassed the first. Adrian can be heard playing celeste on "Moonstruck" and he takes a short solo on bass saxophone in "Here You Come with Love." Art, too, solos on one title, "Charlie's Home." "Black Panther" has Rollini's celeste intro, but its "Casa Loma"–styled arrangement featured no vocal or other solo.

These were Bert Lown's final recordings. He continued his band booking business and would assemble bands for engagements in vaudeville and do party and club dates. One such gig was on 3 February 1934 in White Plains, the town where Lown had gone to high school, a fact that was proudly reported by a newspaper.[63] This was the annual ball of the Westchester local of the International Association of Theatrical Stage Employees. Lown provided continuous dance music alternating with Chick Webb and his Harlem Orchestra.[64] Tom Clines also continued to have engagements. However, Lown did not keep the needed discipline in his band. Reed player Pete Pumiglio remembered how it ended one day:

> Up in St Paul we had a short lunch session . . . but guys just came late when they were due for this lunch session. It got to a point that Bert Lown said: "You're gonna be fined a dollar a minute that you're late." And Chauncey [Gray] was appointed to collect the money . . . but Chauncey was my roommate and we could come late every day, and nobody collected, ha, ha. The tour was disastrous. Bert Lown had made a lot of money, but going on a tour like that was not a good thing to do. Bert Lown couldn't make it anymore, and he was losing money hand over fist. Then at one point he couldn't pay the salaries anymore. He still owes me 50 dollars. Somewhere the band broke up, but I had my car with me, so I took Chauncey Gray back with me. Bert Lown had to pay me for that, but he wanted to lower the travelling scale to save money. We even went to Petrillo in Chicago, he was the head of the union in Chicago and a tough man. You better do what he said. We went right to his office, sat down, and told him about it. He said: "No way, wait a minute" and he got on the phone and called Jules Stein of MCA who booked us. Petrillo said: "Jules, I think you screwed." He was more explicit but I don't want to be. That hurt Bert Lown, because he was losing all this money. He went broke and that was the end of the Bert Lown band.

In November 1934 "Albert Lown, also known as Bert Lown, an unemployed musician of Bronxville" filed for bankruptcy, listing liabilities of $9,318.18 and assets of $3,271." The Depression had stopped his plan to quickly make a million dollars. For some years he did not run an orchestra and in 1937 it was reported that he worked for his old protégé and opponent Rudy Vallée.[65] However, in 1939 he started an orchestra again, using his original theme song "Bye Bye Blues."[66] In later years he worked for radio stations and for Muzak and in 1951 joined CBS, where he became western manager of CBS-TV affiliate relations, until he died on 20 November 1962 in Portland, Oregon, aged 59.

Freelancing as a Steady Source of Income

Back in 1927 Rollini had taken the step to become his own boss. He became a freelancer and had plenty of work, but then his first shot at a band of his own missed the target. He had to look for cover again and in London he became a sideman once more. He knew both sides of a musician's life when he came back to New York a married man with a responsibility toward his wife. However, this was Depression time and jobs were scarce. He took the job with Bert Lown, which allowed him to take other engagements on the side. Bass player Merrill Kaye remembered what they were:

> What we called club jobs, casuals. . . . Here in New York, you can be a contractor one day, a leader the next day, a player the next day. You are a freelance musician. . . . take Banner records at that time. They would ask me. "Hey look, you know you used to work with a fellow who played bass sax. Can you get him?" "Sure." [I would] call Adrian. "Come on Adrian, I got a date for you." If he wasn't working, we did dates for everybody and anybody. . . . I booked individuals . . . I even wanted Arthur to join us but he didn't know the tunes.[67]

After Lown's band had settled at the Park Central, Adrian Rollini had a few freelance recording dates again. The first was on 2 May with Leo Reisman. Rollini was hired for just one title, "Happy As the Day Is Long." This song was composed by Harold Arlen, who also took the vocal chorus. Arlen had sung his most famous composition "Stormy Weather" at Reisman's previous session and here he was back. Both songs had been written for the 22nd Cotton Club Parade in 1933. Arlen's collaborator was Ted Koehler. Arlen's vocal work on "Happy As the Day Is Long" is a demonstration of excellent timing, and his cooperation with Rollini is perfect, saxophone player and singer as equivalent partners in a duet. Rollini's saxophone really pushes Arlen in a strong, swinging way and then he plays a striking solo. Working with a singer in this way was something Rollini had never done before on a record. The arrangement included a vibraphone chorus that also may have been played by Rollini.[68]

A few days after this date with Leo Reisman, Adrian again took off long enough from his Lown job to make a few records. This time it was Joe Venuti, in a follow-up to the recordings made in February. Like before the target was to record four titles, and also like before the session was at the request of the British branch of Columbia. The concept of the first two titles was similar to that of the February session, with the difference that Eddie Lang had passed away and had to be replaced. This task was in the capable hands of Dick McDonough. Jimmy Dorsey was there again to play both his reed instruments and trumpet. Singer Smith Ballew was asked to contribute and was featured on two titles. The first of these was the opening number "Hiawatha's Lullaby," where the introductory notes by Venuti and Dorsey seem to suggest a romantic tune, but then the men swing into a hot groove. At the previous session Rollini premiered the idea that his vibraphone work was as important as his saxophone work. On the second tune he pushes this idea further. It was his own composition and he called it "Vibraphonia."[69] He plays saxophone but his solos and coda are on vibraphone. Piano player Phil Wall has told that Venuti asked a visiting fan to play the kazoo solo and then gave Rollini some other noise-making tools to finish the chorus, before Dorsey took his cornet solo.[70] Lacking Rollini now to take up the bass notes, Venuti himself played the string bass most of the time. The final two titles recorded at this session were greatly different. The small-group idea was canceled in the middle of the session and to Venuti's men were added two trumpets, a trombone, two alto saxophones, and a tenor saxophone, thus creating a full orchestra of eleven men and a vocalist. The two titles produced by this big band are "Isn't It Heavenly?" and "My Gypsy Rhapsody." The only jazzy element here is a good tenor saxophone solo in the first of these. It could be by Art Rollini. Adrian is not heard on the bass saxophone, but a bass player was added.

Rollini's next freelance recording date was on 12 June and again it was commissioned by the British branch of Columbia. This time Rollini was session leader himself and as before Columbia wanted four tunes. He assembled a full band with Manny Klein, trumpet; Tommy Dorsey, trombone; Jimmy Dorsey, clarinet and alto saxophone; Art Rollini, tenor saxophone; Fulton McGrath, piano; Dick McDonough, guitar; Art Miller, string bass; and Herb Weil, drums.[71] There were two singers on this session; on the first title, "Blue Prelude," it was Howard Phillips. Adrian opens this slow, bluesy tune on his vibraphone, then switches to his bass saxophone and he and Dorsey give the singer a nice accompaniment. On this and other titles from this session, Art Rollini shows himself several times as a fully developed tenor saxophone player. "Mississippi Basin," with a vocal by Irene Beasley, gets a different arrangement here from the version Rollini recorded a few weeks earlier with Bert Lown. In both Rollini takes an eight-bar solo, but on this second recording he plays in a ballad style that reminds one of tenor saxophone player Coleman Hawkins's work of the thirties. "Charlie's Home" was not issued at the time, but its master was kept in storage and later issued on LP. It is an uptempo tune with a funny vocal and Rollini plays a total of thirty-six solo bars on bass saxophone and vibraphone. His vibraphone solo is followed by Art's tenor saxophone, which allows Adrian to switch back to his bass saxophone. Adrian would again record "Charlie's Home" two days later, with Bert Lown, but in a different arrangement and he would not solo. The final title recorded for Columbia that day was "Happy As the Day Is Long," which Rollini had recorded the previous month with Leo Reisman and vocalist Harold Arlen. Were it not for that excellent recording, Rollini's own version would have the highest praise, but it lacks the perfect duet between Rollini and the vocalist, which makes Reisman's version superior.

Adrian's first freelance recording date with a band of his own had been for ARC and, despite the low sales in these depression years, that company wanted him back and for the rest of the year Adrian would practically have a date every month with ARC. In July he brought a band again to ARC. It had a different front line from the first ARC session in February and the June Columbia session. It consisted of Al Philburn, trombone; an unknown trumpet player; and Pee Wee Russell, clarinet.[72] Vocalist Howard Phillips is joined by Red McKenzie, years before a Mound City Blue Blower. The four resulting sides are nice dance music, but most of the time they lack jazz spirit. Pee Wee Russell's clarinet often breaks through the monotony, but he cannot heat it up. Russell's finest solo is on "I've Got to Get Up and Go to Work," which swings and features more solos and is also brightened by McKenzie's vocal.

In September Rollini brought the same group to ARC for his third session with that company. It produced four titles with even less jazz content than the second. Rollini is busiest on the last side of the session, "Beloved," where he takes some short solos on bass saxophone and closes on vibraphone.[73]

In 1931 John Hammond, a jazz fan and member of a rich family, started a remarkable career in recording and promoting bands that he personally liked and, despite the Depression, was successful enough to be asked to do more. He had the feeling that the British public was fonder of jazz than the American and in the summer of 1933 he went to London with the idea to get a contract to organize jazz recording dates for British record companies. When he came back, he had an order from British Columbia to record the bands of Bennie Carter, Benny Goodman, Fletcher Henderson, and Joe Venuti. These leaders may not even have known that such a contract had been made. Anyway, Goodman could not believe it, but when Hammond said that British Columbia paid the dates, he cooperated. In October 1933 Hammond recorded a group led by Joe Venuti. He wanted Chicagoans Benny Goodman, Bud Freeman, and Joe Sullivan on the date and Venuti agreed. Venuti wanted Rollini on bass saxophone, but Hammond preferred a normal bass, played by Artie Bernstein, because he thought that bass saxophone was outdated.[74] However, Venuti did not agree and insisted that Adrian Rollini be on bass saxophone. Well-known musician Marty Grosz wrote in a review: "It's a good thing he did, for Rollini's bass sax work proved to be crucial to the success of the date."[75] Grosz notes that the intro of the first title, "Sweet Lorraine," looks forward to the style of Benny Goodman's Sextet of 1939 and points to Bud Freeman's solo, which is followed by Rollini, who "plays one of his brilliant modulations, in this case back to the original key, F-major." Later on in the recording Rollini is "playing a riff. He has the distinction of finding a riff to fix the ever-shifting chord structure of the tune. I dare say, he's one of the few musicians to pull off this device. It's almost unique in all of the hundreds of recordings of the tune." Such praise is deserved by the other musicians as well and the remaining three titles are as good. "Doin' the Uptown Lowdown" has a fifteen-bar solo by Rollini on bass saxophone. "The Jazz Me Blues" has him playing some beautiful breaks, as well as a duet part to the second half of Goodman's great solo. Venuti himself produces one of his four-string solos, for which he was nicknamed Four String Joe. The last title from this great Venuti session was

"In the Ruff," a retitling of King Oliver's "Dippermouth Blues," where one hears Oliver's well-known solo chorus played on clarinet by Benny Goodman. Two takes survive of this recording and Columbia may have had difficulty choosing which to issue.

Musically speaking, Joe Venuti's recording date organized by John Hammond for British Columbia had been a tremendous success. As most recordings under Venuti's name, they were distributed internationally, but initially only "Doin' the Uptown Lowdown" was issued in the United States. Hammond did not like bass saxophone, while his influence in the jazz scene would only increase. So for Rollini the writing was on the wall. To make a living in the years to come, he had to make himself more and more independent from bass saxophone. However, his friend Venuti never lost his taste for the sound of a low saxophone in duet with his violin. In 1934 he would make a European tour and asked Rollini to join him. Adrian did not accept the invitation, probably due to tax reasons.[76] So in Europe Venuti recorded with tenor saxophone player Don Barrigo. In 1935 Venuti would use Rollini on a recording date again.

There were still three months to go in that year 1933 and they were good for three more ARC recording dates. The record companies and most leaders and their musicians felt that the public no longer wanted hot music but popular tunes instead, played in a danceable and recognizable way. And this is how ARC approached its business.

In October Rollini brought almost the same group to the studio as for the July session. There were two major differences, however: Bunny Berigan replaces the unknown trumpeter and Benny Goodman plays clarinet instead of Pee Wee Russell. The four tunes recorded that day, show that ARC followed the rule of avoiding hot jazz, but they contain several solos by Berigan, Goodman, and Rollini, the uptempo "Sweet Madness" being the best of the set.[77]

The following month ARC once more had an Adrian Rollini orchestra in its studio; who they were has not been identified, but for Rollini himself playing vibraphone and bass saxophone. None of the musicians that had been on his recent recording dates can be heard in this big band of eleven pieces, yet ARC entered the session in their books as directed by Rollini. The four titles from the session were issued as by Gene Kardos's Orchestra, which suggests that Rollini may have been sitting in with Kardos's band. Kardos recording career started in 1931 with Victor and ended in 1938 with ARC. He recorded prolifically and in 1932 moved to ARC doing one, sometimes two sessions a month of dance music, although he made an occasional jazz record like "Milenberg Joys" in 1932. Rollini's recordings with this band show him as a member of a dance band and have little to offer as jazz.

Adrian Rollini's final recordings in 1933 were again for ARC, in November 1933. He used much the same men as before, including his brother Art. He also had Berigan and Philburn again but on the clarinet was Artie Shaw. The first title recorded that day was a waltz, "Song of Surrender," without any jazz value. It only proved that these men could handle dance music perfectly, too. They felt more at home with "Coffee in the Morning," recorded next, which has some nice work by Shaw and Berigan as well as solos by both Rollinis. "Sittin' on a Log" is even better and is swinging throughout, with solos and great work by Berigan, who even manages to get some fire into the otherwise lackluster last title of the session, "I Raised My Hat."

End of Prohibition

In March 1933, President Roosevelt legalized the drinking of beer. This was the overture for a full repeal of the Eighteenth Amendment, which had forbidden all consumption of alcoholic beverages. That final step was taken on 5 December 1933. It was a major step on the way to repair the country's economy, which still needed more time.

Adrian Rollini was still trying to find his way in the world of jazz. He once reigned supreme as the undisputed master of the bass saxophone. However, the scene was changing. The public was turning to radio for entertainment and record sales were at a low.[78] Gramophone records did not sell well.[79] In dance bands, the guitar had taken over from the banjo as a rhythm instrument. And the string bass was taking over from the tuba as well as from the bass saxophone. The bass saxophone could still play an individual role in a band's reed section, but there were easier ways to fill a chord on the low end. Fortunately, multi-instrumentalist Rollini had a good line of defense, but it needed to be developed. In 1933 he had used his vibraphone more often than before and knew it could be his future.

Chapter 16

In and out of the Deepest Depression

Unemployment was almost negligible before the United States (and the rest of the world) got into economic depression. The rate was around 2 percent, which meant that practically everybody had a job if they wanted. However, the depression would make itself immediately felt in the increasing unemployment rate, which in three years climbed to 25 percent. It stabilized around that level for a while.

Adrian Rollini had nicely survived the years of the deepest Depression as a member of Bert Lown's orchestra, as leader of the California Ramblers, and finally with Bob Grant's Society Dance Orchestra. Grant, whose real name was Bob Glaser, had been an orchestra leader since 1921. At that time, he worked for Texas Guinan, a singer/actress, who opened a famous club in New York in 1920. In the first half of 1933, Grant worked at New York's Embassy Club, but during the summer its owners sent the band to Saratoga's Piping Rock Club to work there during the horse racing season. Rollini went to Saratoga with Grant and in September returned with him to New York, where the band returned to the Embassy Club.[1]

Rollini's work with Grant probably ended by New Year 1934, but then he had no steady job. It took some time before the effect of Roosevelt's economic program, called the New Deal, became visible in a decrease of the unemployment rate. In 1934 it would still be 22 percent. Rollini did as he had done before between contracts: he used any opportunity to earn a dollar.

American society had been based on a structure in which wives took care of the household while their husbands worked on their jobs. The Depression was changing this establishment and wives were taking outside jobs. Although both Adrian and Dixie came from families which adhered to the old culture, Dixie had been working as a dancer with the band some years back and she was certainly willing to take another job. However, their financial situation probably was not bad enough to make this a necessity and there is no evidence that she did. However, Adrian took any job that he could get and eventually Dixie would follow.

Adrian's first documented engagement in 1934 was his final recording date for the group of ARC labels that had started him as an orchestra leader a year earlier. He used the same men as on the previous ARC session, except for Artie Shaw, who was replaced by Benny Goodman. After recording two titles of straight dance music, the band introduced more hot elements in the arrangements and Rollini solos in nice versions of "Who Walks In When I Walk Out?" and particularly in "Got the Jitters."

By that time ARC was also issuing recordings on its higher-priced Brunswick label. The company decided to move Rollini to Brunswick, and he assembled a different group to record for this label, a group that had little in common with his previous orchestras. On the record labels it was called Adrian's Ramblers, a wink to Rollini's old band. More importantly, the music tended to be different, with less accent on danceability and more on the jazz talents of the performers. "Keep On Doin' What You're Doin'" has Rollini on bass saxophone and he even takes his goofus for eight bars after Jimmy Dorsey's clarinet solo. On "Get Goin'" he solos on bass saxophone and accompanies singer Chick Bullock on vibraphone. The personnel for this session included an excellent, but very obscure trumpet player by the name of Pasquale "Pat" Ciricillo (1907–1978), whose only recording date this may have been. Ciricillo worked with such different leaders as Rudy Vallée and Arturo Toscanini. Another band member was Rollini's first cousin Phil Sillman on drums. Sillman was born in 1913. His mother and Adrian's were sisters. Sillman got a drum set when he was about fifteen, and had a musical career of about thirty years.[2] He died in 2011, aged 97.

Richard Himber

Sometime in 1934, Adrian Rollini got involved with bandleader Richard Himber, with whom he would work off and on for at least three years. Richard Himber was born in 1900 as Herbert Richard Imber in Newark, New Jersey. His parents gave him a violin and at the age of fifteen he left home for New York, where he was heard by Sophie Tucker. She offered him a job in the form of a novelty act with her and her Five Kings of Syncopation. Himber was the highlight of Tucker's cabaret act. A 1918 advertisement shows that, as Dick Himber, he became one of the Five Kings. The others were Julius Berken, cornet; Frank Machan, cello; Al Siegel, piano; and Al Levine, drums.[3] In 1919, Bee Palmer took over Sophie Tucker's jazz band, which then had six members.[4] Again Himber had a special role in the act: he would sing with Palmer and then the band would "blue the blues," as one newspaper wrote. Himber kept moving quickly. His jazz violin playing, as well as his solo dancing ("he is a graceful stepper") were popular. In fact, he was one of the first to play violin in a jazz style. In 1920 he did a duo act with singer Helen Patterson and the following years he worked in vaudeville with dancer Corinne, his sister.[5] In 1923 he toured the Orpheum circuit, which took him as far as New Orleans. Reviews were not always positive; in 1925 *Variety* wrote: "Dick Himber is a violinist, adept chiefly at the jazz stuff, although offering a fairly satisfactory classical solo. He also assists his sister in her dances, but adds little in the way of grace to them as he is inclined to be rather heavy . . . a barely adequate act for the smaller houses."[6]

The message was taken and by the end of 1925, the Keith-Albee circuit advertised that Corinne and Dick were preparing a new act, which involved Yerkes Happy Six Orchestra.[7] However, Corinne announced her marriage and this would eventually lead to the break-up of the duo act.[8] Himber had to go a different way and decided to work with an orchestra. He got a contract from Meyer Davis and worked in several of his orchestras.[9] He also played lead violin with Rudy Vallée's band, but what he wanted was a band of his own. Vallée gave him $2,000 to get started. Himber believed that only airtime could build a dance band into a marquee attraction.[10] He had seen Rudy Vallée's band rise to fame by broadcasting from a small Greenwich Village nightclub. His association with Vallée gave him an open door to important executives at NBC. His ideas for a program would be based on relaxed listening and would include harp interludes, one chorus of a song, a vocal, and slow tunes. It would not be interrupted by announcements, other than at the start and the end of a program. This gave the band an identity of its own. At that time most broadcasts were not yet sponsored by companies; this was the time of sustained broadcasting.

Variety helped build him up and in 1932 called him a "society maestro on his own," managing his own orchestra as well as others such as Rudy Vallée's and Jolly Colburn's.[11] The following year, Himber got his break with a contract for a small band at the Essex House Hotel and in August of that year he made his first recordings, for which he augmented his orchestra.[12] The Essex contract allowed him to take lucrative outside society work. By the end of the year Himber had moved his orchestra to the Ritz-Carlton Hotel, which allowed him to do recordings and broadcasts. He was allowed to use the prestigious Oval Room of the hotel for his NBC broadcasts. Himber increased his personnel for these broadcasts to twenty-two men and used some of the best New York freelance musicians. His payroll grew to $4,000 a week, a very high sum for those days. Himber's singer Joey Nash remembered that they were on the air seven nights a week and for thirty-nine weeks on two NBC shows, the *Pure Oil Hour* with banjo virtuoso Eddie Peabody and the *Spartan Radio Show* with singer Frances Langford.[13]

Through the years Himber got extra publicity for two reasons outside music. He had a constant battle with overweight (in 1934 he shed thirty pounds in thirty days), and he was a successful amateur magician.[14] In one of his tricks he would ask a guest to pull a card. Then the guest had to call any music publisher and ask for a particular person. Whoever picked up the phone, would correctly mention the card in the guest's hand. For this trick Himber had developed an elaborate code and planted it with each music publisher. The man he told to be asked for did not exist, but his initials were the key to the card in the guest's pocket.[15]

Just like Ed Kirkeby and Bert Lown, Rollini's previous orchestra leaders in New York, Himber wanted his music to be played straight, including solos. Ernest Capozzi, Himber's banjo and guitar player for about ten years, told an illustrating story. It happened in October 1933, when the band was to record the tune "Gather Lip Rouge While You May" for Vocalion. According to Capozzi, Himber never had a set band. For his recordings Himber always tried to assemble a band of top New York musicians and for this occasion he had no fewer than five orchestra leaders in the studio, including himself. The others were Will Bradley on trombone; Benny Goodman and Artie Shaw on clarinet and alto saxophone; and trumpeter Sammy Spear, who would lead Jackie Gleason's TV pit band after World War II. The arrangement required Tommy Dorsey to play a sixteen-bar solo, and on the test Dorsey noodled around the melody. Himber did not like that, but Dorsey said: "'I'm a trombone player. I play the way I wanna play.' Himber says 'I'm the guy that's paying you! Now play the way I want you to play.' Tommy Dorsey got a hold of him. There was a closet. He pushed him in the closet, locked the door, and we made the record without Himber directing the band."[16]

The following year Himber started to record for Victor and called his band the Ritz-Carlton Orchestra. The first recordings were made in March and were issued on the Bluebird label. According to Joey Nash, the band was an all-star group with:

Charlie Margulis and Bunny Berigan—trumpet
Tommy Dorsey—trombone
Artie Shaw, Benny Goodman, Arnold Brilhart, and Henry Wade—reeds
Lou Raderman, Murray Kellner, and Jack Zadye—violin
Eddie Steinberg—piano
Ernest Capozzi—guitar
Jack Kimmel—bass
Nat Levine—drums

In line with Himber's strategy, the band played good music, but without any jazz content. The top musicians who were present could only show their reading talent, and had no chance to demonstrate their improvisatory capabilities at all. A vibraphone is heard accompanying the singer on several titles, apparently ad libbing, and he may be Rollini.

Himber's next recording dates were in June and July. These results were issued on the Victor label. Joey Nash remembered that Freddie Fradkin had

Richard Himber's orchestra in the 1935 film *The Magic of Music*. From left Richard Himber, Eddie Steinberg, Morey Samuel, unknown (singer?), unknown trumpet, Kal Katz, Harry Patent, Sugar Kane, unknown trumpet, Ernest Capozzi (who identified the others), Isodore Zir, Nat Levine, Gene Van Hallberg, unknown violin, Adrian Rollini, unknown reed player, unknown violin, unknown harp player, two unknown reed players.

been added on violin and that Herman Wolfson replaced Goodman. The records reveal another major change in personnel. This was the addition of a harp player, which supported the romantic mood created by Nash's singing. Himber allowed a solo on two of the eight titles recorded, a muted trumpet on "Let's Take a Walk Around the Block" and a tenor saxophone on "You're a Builder Upper." His career on gramophone records flowered. In the final months of the year he recorded a total of eighteen titles and Rollini's vibraphone can be heard on most of them, fitting in well in this environment of straight dance music.

1934 would be a top year for Himber. During that year he made his first film. It featured his Ritz-Carlton Orchestra and was shot by Vitaphone in its Brooklyn studio as one of their "Melody Masters" series of thirteen one-reelers.[17] It was simply called "Richard Himber and his Orchestra" and featured a violin special by Himber, vocal work by Joey Nash, and a hot rhumba dance.[18]

In 1934 Himber was broadcasting for the two big networks, NBC and CBS, and did the first of his radio shows sponsored by Studebaker cars. The Studebaker broadcasts started in the summer and were recorded on transcription discs. The band did three transcription shows a week. In 1935 these Studebaker shows practically meant the end for Nash's radio work with Himber, the reason being that his name was mentioned often during each show and it happened to be the name of a competing car manufacturer! Nash refused to change his name, since it was his trademark.[19] His successor was Stuart Allen. That same year, Himber started a series of radio programs for Lucky Strike and had a monthly feature for RCA Victor, doing guest shots along with other Victor artists.

All the while, "Richard Himber orchestras" were appearing in vaudeville and as a supporting act in movie theaters, but often these orchestras were not his radio or film orchestras. They performed under Himber's name and were using his arrangements and sometimes Himber directed in person. One such occasion was at the Paramount Theatre in March 1936. It was important enough to be reviewed by Abel Green in *Variety*. The public enjoyed both a movie (*The Milky Way* with Harold Lloyd) and a performance by Richard Himber's seventeen-piece band, which included a female harpist. Special features included tenor singer Stuart Allen, violin virtuoso Wladimir Selinsky, and Louis "King" Garcia, "crack trumpet specialist who swings it pretty."[20] Himber performed some of his card tricks and had so much success that he reportedly considered becoming a professional magician.

Later that year, Himber opened again at the Essex House and his Studebaker Champions provided music for another transcription disc campaign.[21] It was directed at thirty-one radio stations and included three fifteen-minute programs a week.[22] By the end of the year Himber hit the papers again, with a claim that world peace could be stimulated by making peaceful music instead of martial music.[23] And for Christmas 1936 he promoted his special dinner in the press and gave all his men a watch with the note "If you don't use this and get to rehearsal on time, you're fired."[24]

No Regular Work?

In 1934 and 1935 Adrian participated in many of Himber's major activities, but it meant uncertain, fluctuating money. Therefore, he tried and managed to find other income and one source was recording.

In March 1934 Rollini had a recording date under his own name with Vocalion within one week after Himber's Bluebird date. He used Himber's singer Joey Nash for all vocals. Nash's recording career had started together with Himber's less than a year before and his recordings with Rollini were his first on a jazz date. Rollini's group included Artie Shaw and Al Philburn, who were good for several solos. "Waitin' at the Gate for Katy" is the liveliest of the five titles recorded that day. Times were still tough and it must have pleased Rollini to give some work to two of his relatives on this date, his brother Art on tenor saxophone and his cousin Phil Sillman on drums.

Although Nash claimed that the first title that day, "A Thousand Good Nights," was a big hit, his romantic style did not fit in this band.[25] He quickly returned to the safe environment of the Himber band, and on Rollini's next recording date in May, old hand Chick Bullock and newcomer Ella Logan (1913–1969) did the vocal work. Logan sings on the only real swinger of the session, "I Wish That I Were Twins." Logan was from Scotland and the session was early in her career. She adapted nicely to her new American environment. Adrian had almost consistently used his brother on recordings, but now Art had accepted an offer from Benny Goodman, for whom he would work for five years as his primary tenor saxophone player. Bud Freeman now filled the tenor saxophone position, but Adrian would use Art again whenever it would fit.

In October 1934 Rollini contracted a recording date with Decca, a relative newcomer in the business. Ella Logan was present once again and sang on "It Had to Be You." Rollini had assembled a top group with his brother Art, Benny Goodman, and Jack Teagarden. Benny was asked by Art to join and was not pleased when he only received $25, which was union scale, for the three-hour session. On the trumpet the work was split between Manny Klein and Bunny Berigan, who both had other commitments that day.[26] Rollini only played bass saxophone on this session, but, as he explained to his brother, he had not played it for three months, playing the vibraphone instead.[27] When he opened the instrument case, he noted that the reed was warped, but he straightened it and after the band had done a rundown of "Sugar," which opened with Rollini playing the melody, they were ready to record. The other titles were "Davenport Blues," "Somebody Loves Me," and "Riverboat Shuffle," all references to the twenties, when these men had made their first recordings. Looking backward may have been compensation for the type of music that some of them were regularly recording at the time, and that included Rollini. His choice to play exclusively bass saxophone that day may have been a case in point. These recordings show that Art Rollini had developed into a great tenor saxophone player and it is understandable that Goodman would keep him for many years. John Hammond referred to the band as a "small collection of superior music makers" and specifically mentioned Jack Teagarden's trombone playing, "which has been termed the most natural and finished in the world."[28] The arrangements were by Fred Van Eps.[29]

A few months later, in March 1935, Adrian had another recording date at Decca contracted by Joe Venuti. He had both Rollinis and a rhythm group with Fulton McGrath, piano; Frank Victor (who had been Eddie Lang's successor with Venuti, sometime after Lang died), guitar; and Victor Engle, drums.[30] The group recorded six titles, four of which were composed by Rollini. Rollini wrote "Mello as a 'Cello," "Vibraphonia No. 2," "Nothing But Notes," and "Tap Room Blues." A fifth title, "Send Me," was by Venuti, while for the sixth title, "Mystery," no composer was given on record labels (pun intended?). Working with Venuti had always inspired Adrian and the group really went swinging from the first title. Rollini plays both bass saxophone and vibraphone on most titles. "Tap Room Blues" refers to the club that Adrian was running at the time of this Venuti session, about which more later. Venuti had a reputation as a practical joker and saw this recording date as an excellent opportunity to play another one. So he made two special recordings. Art Rollini wrote about it: "The Italian record was recorded together with Stick Out Your Can on the very same date of the six Venuti recordings. . . . Frank Victor was of Italian origin and . . . spoke to Venuti on that record. Venuti had a fine aptitude in writing scripts while in bed the night before a recording session."[31] The "Italian record" has dialogue in an Italian dialect between Venuti and Victor, with Rollini blowing low notes. In "Stick Out Your Can" Brother Joe's 167th birthday is celebrated. Brother Adrian is asked to confirm, but cannot, since he is only 110 himself. Brother Joe belongs to the Salvation Army and he is happy to announce that three young ladies have just been reformed, Agnes, Sarah, and Peggy. Their names happened to be those of three well-known preservatives at the time.[32]

With his broadcasts and his hotel contract, Himber had enough work. Adrian Rollini also had opportunities galore and continuous, though irregular, employment. When Bert Lown wanted to make a tour to South America, his bass player Merrill Kaye left him to join Vincent Lopez, taking Rollini with him.[33] With Rollini he did radio advertising for Pabst Malt Beer. Kaye also remembered that he got Rollini into Ben Bernie's band as a featured artist.[34]

Art Rollini remembered that Adrian did eight radio shows a week in 1934. One of these was called *40 Flying Fingers*, a show with four pianos. With his bass saxophone he was a featured guest on Norman Claudier's show and on singer James Melton's show he played tympani, vibraphone, chimes, and bells. One day Melton's drummer did not show up, so Adrian sat in. After the show Melton said: "From now on you are my drummer!" Art met his brother on 49th Street carrying a snare drum case and said: "Where in hell are you going with that?" and Adrian answered: "I'm playing drums now, kid!"[35] Rollini's cousin Phil Sillman added another engagement to Adrian's list for 1934, an engagement at the Waldorf Astoria hotel.[36] Phil did not remember the orchestra's name, or whether he himself was the drummer with the band.

However, this type of work did not satisfy Adrian Rollini. He wanted to become his own employer again. His solution was to have a club of his own.

A Club of His Own Again

Adrian had led a band in a club of his own club twice before. The first time was the short-lived Club New Yorker in 1927. Although he had assembled a band of top musicians with great respect for each other, it was quickly over when the public stayed away. His second shot at a place of his own had been the New California Ramblers Inn in 1932, where he shared responsibilities with his former boss Ed Kirkeby. However, the Depression took its toll, and once again there was little business; and while Adrian was ill, Kirkeby sold out.

In 1934 Adrian Rollini was ready again to start a new business venture. The economy was at last making an upturn and record companies were issuing jazz records again. However, Rollini did not think of assembling another band of his own. Just a club would do, where he could sell drinks at late hours and where musicians would have an opportunity to play their instruments. He found a good place. This was the Whitby Grill at the Whitby Hotel, at 325 W. 45th Street, between 8th and 9th Avenues. 45th Street had many Broadway theaters and having a club there was a good choice. Its clientele consisted primarily of musicians "on a busman's holiday." In a Fats Waller biography, the Whitby is called a favorite musician's "hand-out" and a stopping-off point for entertainers of all type.[37] The club has been said to have opened at Easter 1933 and closed after eighteen months, but an opening at Easter 1934 seems more likely. Willie "The Lion" Smith could often be found at the piano. Timme Rosenkrantz, a visiting jazz aficionado from Denmark, met Rollini at a Broadway bar. Rollini invited him to his Whitby Grill, which he opened "a few days ago." Before they were at the Whitby, where Kirby Walker was playing the piano that night, some more bars were checked. It turned out to be Rollini's method to round up customers.[38] Adrian's venture hardly got publicity in the press. The place was a success, but when Rollini's lease on the Whitby ended, he did not renew it. One reason given was the proximity of a Catholic school, which objected to the club, but Rollini had probably simply found a better place.

Rollini called this new place Adrian's Tap Room and it was located in the basement of the President Hotel at 234 W. 48th Street, a musicians' hotel just one block away from the Whitby.[39] The club was a little niche on the right of the hotel and could hold about 150 people.[40] When Adrian first saw the place, it looked bad.[41] It was filled with junk, but by hard work he got the place ready in time for the opening, which was Friday 12 October 1934. By ten o'clock, many notables in the music world were on the club floor, talking and drinking. Adrian had asked Willie "The Lion" Smith again to be the piano player, but he did not show up. This was not much of a problem, since many of Adrian's guests were only too happy to make music. Then, as midnight was approaching, in strode the unmistakable form of Fats Waller. In 1934 Fats had returned to New York

Flyer for Adrian's Tap Room: "Dance to hot Harlem music."

from a tour and in May he started on a long series of recordings for Victor with a small band, which he called his Rhythm. Eventually this would make Fats Waller world famous. However, at the time of Rollini's opening, Fats was still only the Harlem piano player that he had been for more than ten years.[42] Fats looked around with a big grin and noticed Adrian, who was quite upset. He asked what was wrong and Adrian answered that Willie the Lion had let him down on this opening night. As if he had not expected anything else, Fats jumped in right away. Thus he became the Tap Room's regular piano player and remained there for six months. Kirkeby's Waller biography says:

> He never made it a full-time job, but he did manage to spend some parts of his nights there, playing the piano and jamming with the many musicians who nightly came in flocks, eager to have a blow. Fats would pick up about $65 a week and tips—a sum Rollini blushed to mention, for Fats was rated well above this amount for a single fifteen-minute broadcast in those days. But the Tap Room needed a piano tuner's continual attendance, for Fats gave the "box" a real work-out.

A flyer for Adrian's Tap Room ("Just West of Broadway"), probably from 1935, promotes the music ("Harlem on Broadway"), its food ("American and Chinese Dishes"), its wines ("Imported Wines and Liquors"), and even its singing waiters. Guitar player Danny Barker, who worked there at the time, remembered that Rollini had one bartender, two waiters, and a Chinese cook in the back cooking the food.[43]

Another flyer announced an addition to the Tap Room, called the Cubby Hole. It was located at 242 W. 48th Street.[44] It said that it had "a new bar . . . serving the finest imported wines and choice liquors . . . beer on tap . . . drawn from the wood."

Business at Adrian's Tap Room was good from the start and Adrian worked seven nights a week and loved it. He needed a lady for the coat room and to sell cigarettes. He called Ena Kelsall, who was his brother Art's seventeen-year-old girlfriend. When she arrived, it was getting winter in New York and there were plenty of coats and hats to be guarded, so she got good tips which she shared with Adrian.[45]

Martha Raye (1916–1994) and Ella Logan (1913–1969), two up-and-coming young singers, had a series of song battles between them at Adrian's Tap Room, taking turns singing against each other. Their scat duels delighted the customers. Both would have major careers on records, film, and television. Small items would get the Tap Room regularly in the press. One such item involved Ella Logan. One night she was singing "Ain't Misbehavin'." At the moment when she came to the line "I'm savin' all my love for you," she looked at the ceiling and her fingers trembled. The reason was that her husband, from whom she was being divorced, was entering the Tap Room.[46] Others who entertained the customers were Tommy Dorsey and Edythe Wright. During the late hours, musicians from all over town would get together at Rollini's Tap Room. It became a living Who's Who of music.[47]

Seeing the famous and less famous musicians was not the only reason for the Tap Room's fame. It had a talented group of waiters who "would switch from table service to the shim-sham at a moment's notice and would lead gay lines of patrons and musicians in and around the tables and out into the street and back again in a dance which forecast the later, more famous conga."[48] Adrian's cousin, Phil Sillman, also remembered that those waiters had an act of weaving through the crowded tables when they served the food and that they used to tap dance, too. A review confirms this and adds a few details. Reviewer Louis Sobol relates that

> quite by accident Thursday night I wander into a cellar rendezvous known as Adrian's Tap Room and I hesitate, almost, in mentioning the place, for here is an old-time, speakeasy-era atmosphere that used to kill the boredom of post-midnight hours in days before repeal. . . . The owner is a musician, Adrian Rollini, and here after their night's work, you find the Whitemans, the Lombardos, the Duchins and others at ease. . . . On this night, Fats Waller is at the piano and Ella Logan chants . . . Four thinnish Senegambians who wait on you furnish most of the paid entertain-

Adrian's business card for his Tap Room.

ment.... They wail weird blues, they dance, they moan, but they deliver your mug of beer at the same time.... Incidentally, they won't let you in unless Adrian knows you.... "Why spoil the place?" is his theory....[49]

The final remark seems strange, but it is explained in a 1935 article in *Melody Maker*, by the American author Warren Scholl. The British magazine had never given up on Rollini. Scholl noted that another club, the Onyx, had lost its position as a favorite spot for musicians. It had received so much publicity that it lost much of its professional trade. Scholl described a typical night at the *Tap Room*: "About 3 a.m. the Rollini Band begins to take on the appearance of an all-star orchestra when the old gang (Venuti, Berigan, Dorseys, etc.) arrives and sits in for a jam session. Then you hear some real 'gut-bucketing' as you would say in England, or 'going to town' as we would say here in New York."[50]

One British jazz collector/writer who managed to come to New York at this time, was Leonard Feather. He arrived in July 1935 and directly checked in at the President Hotel, for the simple reason that its basement club was Adrian's Tap Room. He knew Rollini from records with Bix Beiderbecke and Joe Venuti. "Where else in New York could you stay, at $12.50 a week, with music of that calibre just an elevator trip away?"[51] Feather would settle in the United States and become a major jazz critic.

By this time, Fats Waller had a steady radio program on CBS and after a few months that company stopped him from performing at the Tap Room. His successor was Putney Dandridge, who worked with a small band from March 1935. When Waller's Victor records started to break sales records, competing companies had to find a soundalike and only Decca managed to find a real one and he was Louis "Putney" Dandridge (1902–1946). In 1934, after working for years with bands, Dandridge had decided on a solo career. His engagement at the Tap

In front of Adrian's Tap Room. From left: Joe Marsala, Rollini, Wingy Manone, Jeanne Burns, Sid Weiss, Carmen Mastren, Putney Dandridge. (courtesy Joseph Rushton)

Room was one of many similar club jobs, maybe his first. Dandridge was almost a Waller duplicate as a pianist/entertainer (but not in size). However, Rollini complained that Dandridge would fall asleep on the job and that he had to then wake him up. Dandridge and his band made their first records around the time he started at the Tap Room.

Sometime during the winter of 1934–35, Adrian Rollini hired Wingy Manone. Manone's career had started in New Orleans and stretched back to the early 1920s. For many years he had consistently been working with small groups, and thus he was a logical choice for Adrian's club. He joined Adrian's little band, which had his brother Art on reeds, Dandridge on piano, and Adrian himself on vibraphone.[52] Manone:

> Man, that was probably the first real jam session stuff in New York.... Martha Raye used to come in and sing with us free, just because she liked our way of playing.... Adrian had a colored waiter who was nuts about our music.... his favorite number was Honeysuckle Rose and we played it four or five times a night. When the band got to swingin' he shook all over, and gave the people a laugh by bouncing his bottom up against the wall, while serving water.

During 1935 Manone would score an enormous hit with his version of "Isle of Capri." However, Manone got an offer to have a band of his own at the Hickory

House, after he left the Tap Room.⁵³ Following Manone was a black group consisting of clarinet player Albert Nicholas; Freddie Jenkins, trumpet; Joe Watts, bass; and Bernard Addison, guitar.⁵⁴ Addison was later replaced by Danny Barker, who remembered that he worked there for about half a year, from 9:00 in the evening till around 3:00 or 3.30 in the morning.⁵⁵ Barker also remembered a somewhat darker side of the Tap Room: "Most hotels closed round 1 or 1.30. The swinging musicians came to the Tap Room, the ones who boozed and smoked. And there I saw and heard about reefers. . . . At the Tap Room they had a secret thing going for musicians." Barker discovered a dark corner of the hotel basement used by musicians to relax while smoking reefers. "All you could see was a flashing, the rising of the red light that diminished when they were drawing a cigarette." Barker didn't take part, he said.

Timme Rosenkrantz heard Freddie Jenkins at Adrian's club and called him a brilliant showman and his quartet "top shelf."⁵⁶ Jenkins had come from Duke Ellington's band and even during his time with the Duke he had had health problems. They got worse when he worked with Nicholas at the Tap Room and he had to stop playing trumpet. Nicholas then hired Ward Pinkett in his place. However, Pinkett was, as Barker calls it, a chronic alcoholic. Nicholas became impatient and fired him.

By the end of 1935 Adrian's Tap Room experienced increasing competition from clubs on 52nd Street. *Variety* reported that its "quality of swing had slumped" and that "music boys have wandered to the Famous Door and the Onyx where they could hear Red Norvo, Roy Eldridge or Mike Reilly."⁵⁷

Ed Kirkeby and Recordings for Victor

Ed Kirkeby continued his remarkable career after he had sold the New California Ramblers Inn when Adrian was ill and in bed in 1932. To Kirkeby, one positive thing remained from that adventure. One day at the Inn, the Pickens Sisters came to perform and Kirkeby kept an interest in this vocal group. With his help their career took off, with recordings for Victor and broadcasts for NBC. Spencer Clark once replaced Adrian at a Pickens Sisters recording date. This was on 4 May 1934, when Adrian had booked two dates and preferred to do the other one, which was under his own name for Brunswick.

> Adrian said: The date is at 8:30 at RCA-Victor's. . . . and take your vibe hammers along. There might be a note or two to play. . . . I got there a little early, about a quarter after eight. . . . and I'd had only a couple of hours sleep so my tongue was about as big as a watermelon. First of all, they started at 8 o'clock, which I found out he knew and so I was off to a bad start. There they all stood and waited for me.

The first tune up was Meet The Beat In My Heart and they opened with the bass saxophone.... and I could not get [those first notes] out with a fat tongue.... Then they did a thing that had a xylophone solo in it and I didn't even have a xylophone stick but the studio had some.... The point is [Rollini] deliberately did this 'cause he knew what was in the charts ... and he had me come late to kick me off at the wrong foot so that I wouldn't look too good in case they wanted to hire me again. So he was protecting his own interests in that matter.[58]

Kirkeby was doing well. He made his relation with Victor stronger and became their artists and repertoire (A&R) manager. In 1935 he met Fats Waller, who had been working at Adrian's Tap Room since it opened. By that time, Fats had a regular radio show at CBS, his fame increased, and Victor became interested in giving him a recording contract. In June Kirkeby supervised his first recording date with Waller.[59]

Adrian had been recording at Victor with Richard Himber many times, but his old relationship with Kirkeby helped him a step further. That step was a Victor date with a band of his own, which he called his Tap Room Gang. Most, if not all of its personnel, were working in his club at the time. In addition to Rollini on bass saxophone and vibraphone, there were:

Wingy Manone—trumpet
Joe Marsala—clarinet, alto saxophone
Putney Dandridge—piano
Carmen Mastren—guitar
Sid Weiss—bass
Sam Weiss—drums

Vocals were by Manone and Dandridge, as well as by Jeanne Burns. Unlike Rollini's previous session, for Decca, the tunes were all new. The first, the instrumental "Bouncin' in Rhythm" by Wingy Manone, has Rollini on bass saxophone. He has solo spots at the intro and at the coda as well as a sixteen-bar solo, with a break in the middle shared with Joe Marsala on the clarinet. The second tune was by Jeanne Burns, who sings it herself.[60] In a comic duet with Wingy Manone, Burns sings "Got a Need for You" and Manone reacts, saying "I wish you had a weed for me!" "Weather Man" has another comic vocal duet by Manone, now with Dandridge, which shows that both were great entertainers. Rollini is silent on this title, which features a guitar solo by Mastren. "Honeysuckle Rose" and the hit tune "Nagasaki" are feature pieces for Putney Dandridge, showing his talent at impersonating Fats Waller. The last piece, "Jazz O' Jazz," was another composition by Jeanne Burns, who sings it with some chatting, probably by Dandridge and Rollini. These six sides give an idea of how the music at Adrian's Tap Room may have sounded.

Within a few months after Kirkeby's start as Victor's A&R man, he organized several sessions in which Adrian participated. One of these came a month after the Tap Room Gang's session. Kirkeby still owned the right to the names California Ramblers and Little Ramblers and thought they still had drawing power. First he revived the Little Ramblers, in July 1935. This session is very important in Rollini's discography because it shows him as an accomplished piano player late in his career.[61] His piano style is swinging and prominent. He does not limit himself to simply playing harmony, but finds his own role in the ensemble, playing a melody part as well, just like he could do on bass saxophone or vibraphone. Adrian was the only representative from earlier Little Ramblers sessions. The new Little Ramblers recorded five titles, of which one remained unissued. As the issued titles show, the arrangements allowed for as much freedom to play as if the men were in a jam session, which was becoming all the rage in New York at the time. The first two titles were co-composed by piano player Rube Bloom, but Rollini was sitting on the piano stool. Gordon Griffin (1915–2005) played the trumpet and Sid Stoneburn the clarinet; other musicians are unknown. Rollini had a major contribution to the first title, "Truckin'," a tune that promoted a new dance. He plays the intro, follows with a rousing accompaniment to singer Fred McElmurry, and ends with three short swinging solos. The second title, "Cotton," is mainly vocal, but again Rollini is prominent. "Streamlined Greta Green" is another vehicle for the band to produce some swinging music. The final title was Handy's "Loveless Love," which gets a good treatment with interesting piano work again by Rollini and solos and breaks by the others.

A month after this session, Ed Kirkeby made a recording of a band he called the California Ramblers, the first after almost four years.[62] Adrian Rollini did not participate. However, less than two weeks later Rollini was in the Victor studio again. Six titles were recorded by a group under shared leadership of trumpeter Freddie and guitar player Bernard Addison. This was probably the group working at the Tap Room at the time. Three titles were issued under Jenkins's name and three under Addison's. Other band members were Albert Nicholas, clarinet; Joe Turner, piano; and Joe Watts, bass. The previous year Rollini had been playing drums in public and now he decided to do it on records. As a result, this session offers the unique opportunity to hear Adrian on drums. At the time, Jenkins was in poor health and this may have been the reason why he used a second trumpeter, presumably an Egyptian whose name is not remembered. The first title, Freddie Jenkins's composition "Swingin' 'em Down," features a hot chorus by the two trumpets. Rollini's part in this session is under-recorded in all but the last tune, "Lovely Liza Jane," where he produces a short drum break. Like the previous session, these sides display an easygoing jam session mood, like one could find in Rollini's club on late hours.

Ed Kirkeby had recorded Fats Waller and His Rhythm in June for the first time and the records sold very well. The market for swinging small-band jazz was definitely growing and Kirkeby decided to get a large share.[63] Not to compete directly with Waller's output, he chose to use Victor's cheaper Bluebird label for his action. For his next date in October he again selected men who worked in Rollini's Tap Room; Adrian would play vibraphone, making this into a group of mixed color. The others were Ward Pinkett, trumpet and vocal; Albert Nicholas, clarinet; Jack Russin, piano; Danny Barker, guitar; Joe Watts, bass; and Sam Weiss, drums. Rollini comes in with a solo on the second title from this session, "I'm on a See-Saw." Ward Pinkett takes vocals on most titles and he, Nicholas, and Russin all solo. Nicholas's sound no longer has the typical New Orleans fluency it had before, but his solos still are a pleasure to be heard. The titles were all Tin Pan Alley material with one exception, the final title. This was called "Tap Room Special," a tune that was popular at Adrian's club. It was nothing but a retitled version of that famous New Orleans standard "Panama." To avoid copyright trouble, the Bluebird issue showed no composer credit.

The following month, on 26 November, Kirkeby organized a double date. First, four titles were recorded as by the California Ramblers. This probably was a group led by Tommy Dorsey. A vibraphone is briefly heard on two titles and may have been played by Rollini. This session was followed by four titles recorded as by the Little Ramblers, possibly with Rollini on piano.

Ed Kirkeby's first year at Victor could hardly have been better. By the end of 1935, he had done five sessions with Fats Waller, nine with Tommy Dorsey, and five more where he used Dorsey's men. Including Rollini's Victor session in June, he organized five or six sessions with Adrian. Five were with men who worked in his Tap Room. One more was with men from Dorsey's band and probably Rollini. Just before the year was over, he did the last of these, with personnel much like the October session. The only change was the replacement of Ward Pinkett on trumpet by Bill Dillard (1911–1995). Rollini was on vibraphone again and the tunes were Tin Pan Alley products, including "The Music Goes 'Round and Around," a hit by Mike Riley and Eddie Farley.

During the first week of the new year, on 6 January 1936, Kirkeby organized another double date. Five titles were issued as by the California Ramblers and three by the Little Ramblers. A vibraphone is heard on some titles, but this does not suggest Rollini. The same is true for a session organized by Kirkeby in the same months that produced no fewer than eight titles, four of which were issued as by the California Ramblers. The other four were issued under the name Ted Wallace, one of Kirkeby's old pseudonyms. He called the band his Swing Kings, and in line with this band name the arrangements featured more solo spots than other recent recordings by the California Ramblers; in fact, most titles were quite hot. This suggests that Kirkeby was feeding a trend toward more swinging music, which may have been stimulated by working with Fats Waller, who could not be stopped from swinging. By January 1936, the days of the California Ramblers and even the Little Ramblers were practically over.[64]

Adrian Rollini had one more recording date with a jazz group at Victor's in February 1936, under the leadership of Louis Garcia, who had the nickname "King."[65] In April Garcia was a member of Richard Himber's orchestra and *Variety* identified him as Himber's "ride" trumpeter and as a player of high notes.[66] Garcia's recordings under his own name confirm his Armstrong-influenced hot trumpet playing. The most obvious example is his coda to the last title, "Love Is Like a Cigarette." Rollini was again playing piano and contributed an interesting harmony part instead of simply playing rhythm. The recording balance was in his favor and his solo piano can be heard on all five titles.

Toward the Depression's End

With all the action at his Tap Room and various recording dates with its musicians, Rollini was still a regular and so was Richard Himber. Himber's public was different from the Tap Room's clientele and his music originally had had nothing to do with jazz. Rollini had worked in such an environment before and it had presented no problem to him. But the music scene was changing. Big band swing, with Benny Goodman as its foremost representative, became the new thing. Himber reacted and from mid-1934 until the end of 1937, his style gradually moved away from straight dance music to a looser form of arranged music. This must have pleased Adrian Rollini. Himber emphasized his full orchestra sound, but he would give more room to some of his musicians. In his Victor session of October 1934, Rollini's vibraphone is heard prominently. On "Autumn in New York," from Himber's December Victor date, Rollini plays celeste accompanying Joey Nash. "I'm Going to Dance at Clancy's," from the following February session even shows Himber's try at swing with fine but short clarinet solo work and Nash's scatting.[67] Himber then replaced Nash with Stuart Allen, who would do a vocal chorus on each Himber recording just like his predecessor but who did not have Nash's velvet sound. Himber's remaining recording dates in 1935, all with Allen, did not yield anything of jazz value, but in January 1936 his recording of "This Is Heaven" featured a trumpet soloist, possibly Louis "King" Garcia, who was a member of his orchestra by this time. This was only a hint of what Himber's next session, in April, had to offer. Each of the six titles, even one waltz, featured soloists on trumpet, clarinet, or trombone. It must have been an experiment, for Himber did not repeat it for the rest of the year. Only "Wintertime Dreams" from October featured several solos again.

The Swing Music Concert of 24 May 1936. Adrian playing goofus; George Hnida bass.

Still, for playing jazz Rollini had to look elsewhere. Jazz was definitely returning into the public interest now and in 1936 Rollini had his share. In March he had another date with Decca with a new group, for some purely instrumental recordings. At the drums he had hired his cousin Phil Sillman again and on bass there was George Hnida, who had married Adrian's sister Elvira. All titles were Rollini compositions. The first, "Tap Room Swing," referred to his Tap Room. As was his rule on all recent recordings under his own name, he played both vibraphone and bass saxophone. He used the saxophone mostly for ensemble work and soloed on vibraphone. The same month Adrian's band took part in NBC broadcast *Is Swing the Thing?* another sign that there was money in jazz music again at last.

On 24 May 1936, the first Swing Music Concert took place.[68] Its location was the Imperial Theatre and the announcement listed some fifteen bands, including some black musicians, from Bunny Berigan to Paul Whiteman, including Adrian Rollini and his Tap Room Gang.[69] It was sponsored by the Onyx Club, another popular New York jazz club and a competitor with Adrian's Tap Room.

Only weeks later and fully in line with this new wave, CBS started a series of radio programs that would become classics. These thirty-minute programs were called the Saturday Night Swing Club and the first took place on 13 June 1936. Adrian Rollini did not participate in this particular concert, but recordings survive from two other broadcasts in which he did, and he may have been on more broadcasts in this series. On the broadcast of 10 October he first played "Honeysuckle Rose" as a vibraphone solo, accompanied by a drummer and by the studio band in the coda. His second tune was his own "Tap Room Swing," played with a small swing band. There are solos on piano, trumpet, and tenor saxophone, and finally Rollini himself on bass saxophone. The following month, on 28 November, he was back to play two compositions of his own, one that was as yet unnamed, as well as "Swing Low," accompanied by guitar player Frank Victor. The public was asked to give the first tune a name, thus it became "Vibrollini." On "Swing Low" Rollini not only played bass saxophone, but also a thirty-two-bar chorus on his hot fountain pen, after which he duets with the trumpet soloist, probably Bunny Berigan. Interestingly, Rollini came to these broadcasts as a soloist, not as leader of an orchestra. It illustrates his spreading fame as a musician.

In 1936 he recorded as a sideman, too. In June 1936 guitar player Dick McDonough began a series of recordings under his name, assembling small swing groups from the vast number of New York musicians. Adrian Rollini participated on the second and third of these dates, playing both his main instruments. The first recordings from these sessions sound like a return to the sweet dance music of the earlier thirties, but then the session heats up and all instruments are heard soloistically, including Rollini's bass saxophone.[70] The recordings from the next session were all good jazz recordings, with Rollini soloing on both bass saxophone and vibraphone. Trumpet on these sessions was Bunny Berigan, who was in great form.

Rollini's final recordings in 1936 may have been in December for ARC, with a band directed by Jack Shilkret. They are among his most unlikely recordings. On the first three, he is not audible, unless he does not play his usual instruments. Only on the fourth title, the most swinging of this session, a short solo by a bass saxophone player is heard, who may have been Rollini.

Adrian's Tap Room had been prominent among New York's jazz clubs from its start. Looking back on these formative years, one writer even thought that swing really started there. He wrote: "Swing was played on 52nd Street in small, dark basements for people who drank watered whisky, inhaled bad air, and considered themselves the patrons of a fresh fad. It began in Adrian's Tap Room on 48th Street near Eighth Avenue where Wingy Manone played Isle Of Capri. It spread to the Onyx on 52nd Street."[71] However, sometimes the news was negative too. In the eye of some competitors, what tap rooms like Rollini's did was feature a floor show without having a license from the state. This was considered unfair competition and in February 1935 representatives from the world of restaurants, hotels, and theaters got together to start an action. It was said that tap rooms only charged 5 or 10 cents for a beer and thus would be unable to pay

In and out of the Deepest Depression 315

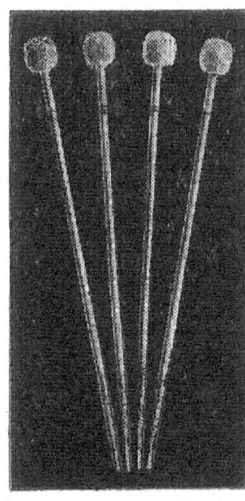

ADRIAN ROLLINI
Vibe Mallets
Marimba Mallets
ONE PAIR ...$2.00
SET OF 4...... 3.75
Send for our bargain list on drum equipment
White Way
Musical Products
1587 Broadway
New York City

Advertisement for Adrian's White Way Musical Products shop.

the $500 license fee. If the action were successful, tap rooms would have been compelled to discontinue their shows.[72]

The outcome of this action is not known, but in 1936, after two unforgettable years, the end came for Adrian's Tap Room. Clubs like the Onyx and Hickory House were strong competition and Adrian's clientele had many places to choose from. What helped end his club was Rollini's habit of giving free drinks to his friends. "Adrian gave me the impression that he owns the place. He pays for this; he pays for that. Why, you know, everybody wants to be a big man."[73]

More negative news came as 1936 was coming to an end. One Franklyn Frank, writing for the Associated Negro Press in a California newspaper, quoted Leonard Feather who had a discussion with Nick LaRocca, trumpet player of the Original Dixieland Jazz Band. LaRocca had told him that "every worthwhile jazz musician got his education from [his] records, and not from colored musicians." And more of this stuff. Feather went on to say that this "warped standpoint [was] shared . . . with other distinguished Italo-American swing artists and mentioned Wingy Manone, Adrian Rollini and Joe Venuti." No reaction from Rollini is known, but if he read it, he might have reacted by saying that he used a black musician in his first band, that the trumpet player in the California Ramblers was of mixed race, and that he used and recently recorded with black performers who worked in his Tap Room.[74]

Due to his old relationship with Ed Kirkeby and his steady work with Richard Himber, 1936 had had mostly ups and only a few downs for Adrian Rollini,

He was developing a fishing hobby and would take friends, like Manny and Dave Klein and Fred Rich, out on his latest boat, *Rambler IV*.

Rollini saw new opportunities laying ahead and by the end of the year he made new starts with two ventures. He opened a shop for musical instruments and he made the first recordings with his trio.

Chapter 17

A Shop and a Trio

The period from the fall of 1936 to the spring of 1937 can be regarded as a time of fundamental change in Adrian and Dixie Rollini's lives. In 1936 Rollini had seen his thirty-third birthday and Dixie her thirty-first. For all his professional years their income had been almost fully dependent on Adrian's employers—Kirkeby, Elizalde, Lown, and Himber—and with each of them he knew, and sometimes experienced, that he could do better. Although he was a happy-go-lucky type, it is safe to assume that he was looking for an opportunity to become his own boss once and for all. Now this opportunity came around. In fact, there were two opportunities and Rollini did not have to choose. He took both.

The White Way Music Shop

In September 1936 Adrian Rollini opened a shop for musical instruments. It was located at 1587 Broadway and was called White Way Musical Products, after Broadway's nickname. Its specialty was percussion and its letterhead mentioned that it catered to drum corps and to orchestras. The shop offered repairs and supplies as well. Apparently it was Rollini himself who handled the daily affairs at the start, but when it became clear that he could not combine this with his work as a performing musician, it was decided that Dixie should be involved. This turned out to be a success. She developed into an expert in winding mallets for vibraphones and similar instruments. The following promotion text, written by an unknown author, appeared in part or in full in several periodicals:

> White Way Musical Products, specialists in modern drum equipment, vibes, etc. having as its President Adrian Rollini, number one vibraharpist and director of America's biggest little band, is located at 1587 Broadway, in the heart of New York City.
> While devoting a great deal of his spare time to White Way Musical Products, Adrian soon found out that he needed a partner, so who better than his wife. Thus it was that Dixie stepped into the picture.

Adrian's sixth *Rambler*.

In a field held exclusively by men, it required great ability and plenty of grit for women to make good. Dixie has made good and if you know drums or drummers you have heard of her—and the reports are favorable. She is the only drum expert of her sex in the country, to our knowledge. If you have a problem concerning the drum business—sticks, heads, cymbals—in fact anything at all—you can put your troubles before Dixie and rest easy. If she doesn't know the answer, you can bet that no answer so far has been given.

This busy lady is hostess to the famous, the near famous, the little known and the unknown, with equal charm and equal interest. That, if anything, is the secret of her success; that and the ability to know the likes and dislikes of each of her customers concerning drum equipment. The autograph hound will gladly pay an entrance fee to stand at the door of her office, for the certainty of meeting the great names in music who call daily.

A brief talk with Dixie would amaze many men who boast of how much detail they have to attend to in their own line. From early morning until late—even for Broadway—you will find the active Dixie Rollini clearing a mass of detail sufficient to swamp a score of mere men.

In addition to the usual daily rush, Dixie finds time to develop new ideas for business. She and Adrian are responsible for the Adrian Rollini vibe and marimba mallets, which are acclaimed by all who have used them to be absolutely "tops." The skins used for drumheads also have been specially selected by her from a source remote from Broadway. The result of this was a torrent of mail from drum men begging Dixie to get these skins for them.

The office is a complete factory run by a Rollini trained technician. Everything necessary for making, repairing, adjusting and inventing equipment is right there. Speed, thoroughness and reliability are passwords. If Dixie makes a promise—you

Adrian and Bill West on the roof of the instrument shop.

can count on that promise being kept! Next you visit New York's White Way—remember the name Dixie. Just ask the nearest drummer—if you can spare the time to a lengthy speech on Mrs. Rollini—he'll probably be glad of the excuse to visit with you![1]

Adrian's cousin Phil Sillman, a drummer himself, remembered that Dixie was running the shop, but that the in-house drumming expert was Bill West, an English guy who was acknowledged for his work as a drummer. White Way also had a mechanic, Bill Mather.[2] Dixie used to pick the drum heads. "She knew how to pick good calve skin heads. She also knew how to get good cymbals out of Zildjian [who were then] up in Quincy, Massachusetts. And she wound the mallets. She was always busy up there."[3] Phil thought that Adrian and Dixie were rather frugal and remembered how his father, who liked carpentry, was asked to make drum practice pads for White Way. He did so until Adrian started to hedge on the agreed-upon price, cutting by some five cents.[4] Art Rollini confirmed that:

Adrian's wife did not play drums but ran [the shop].[5] She wound vibraphone mallets constantly, day and night, even at home.... she got $7 for a pair of mallets and she [would] be winding these mallets for all the vibraphone players. She had a drum teacher there, Bill West was his name, and she'd also prepare a lunch. She had a little stove in the back, [where] she'd cook up a pot of spaghetti and meat balls. The place smelled like an Italian restaurant sometimes.... but everybody came up there, including Buddy Rich. Buddy Rich was a young lad at the time and he came up and Adrian recognized his tremendous talent and he was instrumental in getting Buddy Rich a job on 52nd Street for the jazz group.

Red Norvo was also a client there. He got a lot of knowledge from Adrian, he admired Adrian's talents. As a matter of fact, he was on "The Prime of Your Life" [a TV show]. It's on every Sunday in this country and he was on one night and they asked him: "What interested you in the vibraphone?" and he said: "I was first interested in the instrument when I heard Adrian Rollini play!"[6]

Norvo originally was a marimba and xylophone player. Both instruments use a hardwood keyboard, while the vibraphone is all metal. Both may feature metal tubes hanging down below the keys, for resonation. Compared with the wooden keys of these instruments, the metal keys of the vibraphone ring longer, thus giving the player additional options. Moreover, it featured a mechanism in each resonator tube, that allowed the player to produce a vibrato. Manufacturer Deagan called it "vibraharp," but its common name became vibraphone, "vibes" for short.

In 1930 Norvo was an experienced xylophone player and as such he was quite unique, with a repertoire that included Bix Beiderbecke's composition "In a Mist." In 1932 he arrived in New York as a feature with Paul Whiteman's orchestra. By this time Norvo already had a great reputation among musicians and Adrian Rollini became interested in him. So Adrian took Red up to Harlem. Rex Stewart wrote that the two "made the rounds of Harlem at least once a week. However, we never had a chance to hear Red play, because there were no xylophones in Harlem."[7] It is no surprise that Norvo became Dixie's customer after the White Way Shop opened.

As Art Rollini mentioned, another famous customer was Buddy Rich (1917–1987). At the time that Adrian Rollini opened the White Way Shop, Rich was twenty. His career had started as a child and he had always wanted to be a drummer. Adrian's cousin Phil Sillman, a drummer himself, brought him into contact with Adrian Rollini, who recognized his great talent and who, in 1937, recommended him to Joe Marsala for his band at the Hickory House.

Rich made his first records in January 1938 with a studio band led by Rollini, who, on 26 March 1938, introduced him to the radio public during a *Swing Session* broadcast. Rollini predicted that "this boy will be on top very soon."[8] Harry Clark, who would closely work with Adrian Rollini, remembered that Adrian became Rich's agent for a year:

He talked him in signing a contract with him. So first thing he did . . . was trying to find him a room at the Piccadilly Hotel where we were playing and he decided a good place would be on the roof and there he opened with a four-piece band up on the top of the hotel, probably 22 stories high and they made room around there for a rooftop nightclub. Buddy was so loud that they closed immediately. He was playing for the whole Times Square area. . . . He had that feel for rhythm [that Adrian had too.] [This] impressed Adrian. You know Buddy is a good tap dancer, just like Sammy Davis is a good drummer and tap dancer.[9]

As a matter of fact, Rich often owed money to White Way, a reason for Dixie to complain to Phil Sillman, who had recommended Buddy.[10]

The Adrian Rollini Trio Shapes Up

On 28 November 1936 radio listeners could enjoy another *Saturday Night Swing Session* via WABC. Paul Douglas announced Bunny Berigan's band and the guests were singer Shirley Howard, piano player Mary Lou Williams, and vibraphone player Adrian Rollini. Douglas announced him in the then typical announcer's style as "genius of swing, the master of the bass sax, vibraphone, goofus and any other instrument you care to mention, the one and only Adrian Rollini."[11] He had been on an earlier broadcast and this had resulted in letters from shortwave swing fans from Europe and even Australia.[12] Rollini's first tune was a new composition, which was as yet unnamed. The public was asked to suggest a name and this had to happen quickly, since the tune was shortly to be recorded. On the broadcast, Rollini mentioned guitar player Frank Victor (1900–1970), who accompanied him.[13] Victor had been working with Joe Venuti in 1934 and 1935, including a trip to Europe, and had recorded some guitar duets in 1936. Adrian's second tune during this broadcast was "Swing Low," another recent composition. Accompanied by Bunny Berigan's band, he first played bass saxophone, followed by a chorus on hot fountain pen accompanied by guitar only, ending with the full band as before, with a trumpet chorus by Berigan.

At such broadcasts Rollini was featured as the major jazz personality he was, but his role had mostly been as a sideman for prominent leaders, or as leader of studio groups. This was about to change now.

At the recording date the following week, Rollini brought a new group to the studio. He called it the Adrian Rollini Trio. Its instrumentation consisted of vibraphone, guitar, and bass. Adrian would sometimes play a chorus on a different instrument, but the vibraphone formed the foundation of the format, which would become a success. Rollini would stick to the trio format for the rest of his life. At the time of the recording date, the unnamed tune had indeed received its

The first Trio in the film *Himber Harmonies*. Adrian with Haig Stephens, left, and Frank Victor. (courtesy Mark Cantor)

name. It was recorded as "Vibrollini," with a shorter arrangement than for the broadcast. Its session mate was another recent composition by Rollini, "Driftin."

Adrian brought Frank Victor to the Trio's first recording date. The date was at Decca and Victor had been a regular studio musician there. Harry Clark, bass player in a later Rollini Trio, remembered that Victor and Rollini each hired space in the same building, the Tango Palace Building at 48th Street and Broadway, Adrian for his White Way Music Shop on the third floor and Frank for an office on the fourth, where he gave guitar lessons.[14] They would get together there for little jam sessions before they made records. The third trio member, bass player Haig Stephens, was an experienced house musician at Decca's studio.

According to Clark, Victor could not read, preferred playing chords, and would only reluctantly play melody. These trio recordings confirm this. Rollini almost plays a solo act and Victor plays a subdued rhythm guitar, only adding embellishment notes, no solo notes. Only in the second tune, "Driftin," he can be heard playing some interesting guitar runs. However, Victor was quickly finding his new role. The following month, on 11 January 1937, the same trio set foot in the studio to record two more Rollini compositions, "Rebound" and "Jitters." On "Jitters" Victor can be heard continuously adding an individual voice to the arrangement.[15] The Trio records sold well and Rollini decided to get more out of the idea.

Richard Himber had continued to use Rollini on his recording dates. In 1937 he asked Rollini to return to his orchestra for further recordings and another engagement at the Essex House, in its Casino-on-the-Park room, where Himber followed Nat Brandwynne. Rollini only wanted to accept if Himber would hire his full Trio, and the deal was closed. Himber premiered his band on 15 October in a program for dealers, followed by special evenings for "cash customers" and music publishers. Abel Green reviewed them in *Variety* and called the Rollini Trio a "snappy swing combo." He thought that Himber could well produce "Whitemanesque" music, but found him too young to come close to looking like Whiteman, having permitted "that extra poundage."[16]

It looked like the Trio had arrived, but then Rollini had a problem: Frank Victor stayed on, but Stephens preferred his regular daily studio work and eventually refused the job. So now Rollini had to find a replacement. This was Harry Clark.

Clark was born as Harrison Sniffin and had already known Frank Victor in 1933, when he became a member of the New York musicians' union. Victor formed a trio with another guitar player, Harry Volpe, and violin player Al Duffy. The three invited Harry Sniffin, who had good musical training, to join them. However, as a quartet they did only one engagement, on a Hudson riverboat. Then, in 1934, Victor went to Europe with Joe Venuti. He tried to convince Venuti to take Sniffin as well, but Venuti wanted Rollini, who said no.[17] Sniffin then helped Volpe, who could not read or write music, assemble a guitar instruction book. Next he worked in Florida and in New York in various orchestras, until he got a message from his old pal Frank Victor, who asked him to come to the Essex. When he arrived there, he found Victor with Richard Himber's band, which was rehearsing for its new engagement at the Essex. Victor introduced him to Rollini. Later Sniffin found out why Victor wanted him in the band so much: Frank could not read music. With Sniffin

> he might be able to sneak away and this would allow him to have an advanced reading of a song, so that, when he heard it the first time with Adrian, he would not have to fumble his way. . . . I just had to play the piano parts. . . . I had an offer to go with another orchestra but Adrian talked me out of it. . . . I had known him only as a bass saxophone player. I didn't even know that he played the vibraphone.[18]

Thus Harry Sniffin joined Richard Himber's Orchestra and the Adrian Rollini Trio at the same moment. It was Thanksgiving Day, 25 November 1937. Frank Victor's recommendation had been strong enough. The Trio rehearsed at Rollini's home.

> Some of the things we did later, developed right there. There was a little trick of playing melody on the bass with a vibraphone mallet. That came up just while I was

With Harry Clark on bass, the Trio has its definite form.

sitting there waiting for an idea to come and tapping on the strings. And he says, heh, let's put that in and he gave me the notes to play. It could have been Diga Diga Doo. We got a tremendous hand in the theatres for doing that, stupid thing to do.[19]

The Adrian Rollini Trio was featured for an hour when Himber's full band was off. During their act, Adrian would announce the names of the Trio members. This meant great publicity, but Rollini did not like to announce his bass player as Harry Sniffin. Frank's real name was Vigiano and Adrian said: "How would it sound if I said Adrian Rollini at the vibraharp, Frank Vigiano on guitar and Harry Sniffin on bass. Do you mind if I change your name?" Sniffin easily agreed and believes that Adrian picked Clark because singer Buddy Clark was in the room, one of the Trio's great fans.[20] At this time Rollini did not yet realize his Trio's market value, and Clark remembered how one night they were asked to play for one hour for Doris Duke in her 5th Avenue apartment. Adrian did not know that she was one of the wealthiest women in the world and probably only asked fifty dollars for the trio.[21]

Freelancing Again: Recording for Master/Variety and Victor

Adrian Rollini always managed to find time for extra jobs to increase his income. The first half of 1937 saw an impressive series of recording dates, broadcasts, and films. The recording dates produced commercial recordings as before, but also transcription program discs meant for radio stations.

Rollini's first recording date in 1937 had been with his Trio for Decca in January. Here he played vibraharp exclusively, just like he did on Richard Himber's next Victor session the following month.

During the first months of the year, Irving Mills was starting a new record company. Mills had been a great force in the music business since the early twenties and had several major bands under contract. He saw a possibility of expanding his business by producing records and his new company was Master. Mills not only used his own artists, but also freelancers like Rollini and artists under contract with Herbert Yates. Yates worked for ARC and took a financial interest in Master. ARC was to manufacture and distribute the records, which were to be sold under the Master and Variety labels, Master selling for seventy-five cents and Variety for thirty-five. The first recordings were made mid-February. Mills wanted to move fast and built up a large inventory of recordings. By the end of March, a total of 245 titles had been recorded.[22] Some of these were not issued at the time, and many were never issued at all. However, many metal masters were stored in archives and some appeared on CDs decades later.

Adrian Rollini entered the new studio for the first time on 4 March for a recording session with Willard Robison's orchestra. The press was invited and pictures got into the news. Four tunes were recorded; two were issued, "My Melancholy Baby" and "Memphis Blues." Rollini's role was to play accents on vibraharp. Less than two weeks and thirty master numbers later, Rollini recorded for Master again, this time with Lew White's orchestra, who led from the keyboard of an electronic organ. His orchestra was a small swing group with abundant solo work. Again four titles were recorded and only three were issued, "Seventh Heaven," "Was It Rain?" and "Did Your Mother Come from Ireland?" with vocals by Sonny Schuyler. The fourth title survived in the form of a test pressing, "Farewell Blues," an instrumental.

Rollini's first true jazz session at Master came another week later. He had assembled a competent team of black and white musicians, consisting of Jonah Jones on trumpet; Sid Stoneburn and Art Rollini, reeds; Fulton McGrath, piano; Dick McDonough, guitar; George Hnida, bass; and Al Sidell, drums. On two titles Red McKenzie took a vocal, and these were the only titles issued at the time. However, masters of the two instrumental titles survived and were issued on CD.[23] Rollini played bass saxophone (and a sixteen-bar solo), a rarity by then, on the first title, "Bugle Call Rag." On McKenzie's first title, "I Cried for You," Rollini opens on bass saxophone, then accompanies McKenzie on vibraharp and follows this with a straight sixteen-bar chorus on bass saxophone. McKenzie's other title, "The Trouble with Me Is You," is a swinging recording with several solos. The next and final title, "Careless Love," an instrumental, might be the best of the four. Rollini plays one of his finest vibraharp solos so far and Jonah Jones produces some spectacular trumpet work, but in fact each musician's contribution is noteworthy.

A few days later Rollini was back at Master, now to record two arrangements with what sounds like a large dance band and an unknown male singer. The titles were "I Don't Know Where I'm Going" and "Slap That Bass," neither of which was issued at the time. Rollini recorded "Slap That Bass" for Master again a few days later, this time with a smaller unit. This second version is the better of the two, a swinging recording. At least two of the other three titles from that session, "The Love Bug Will Bite You" and "Let's Call the Whole Thing Off," were equally swinging; the third was not available for listening.

Altogether Rollini had five recording dates with Master during the month of March 1937, at which he recorded sixteen titles. Only half of these were issued at the time, in line with Irving Mills's policy to first build a large music inventory. Mills's next step was to go to Europe to organize worldwide distribution of his Master catalog. He left New York in June, but returned without a deal. The reason may have been that he would only accept a deal on the complete catalog, no cherry picking. The negative result of his trip contributed to Mills's sudden decision in July to stop issuing records on the Master label. In October this was followed by stopping Variety. The labels were gone, but recording in the Master studio would continue and the results were later issued on other ARC labels.

One leader with whom Rollini would record again at Master was Bert Shefter (1902–1999). Shefter was a concert pianist, composer, and conductor. During the thirties he experimented with a type of jazz-influenced concert music, similar to what Raymond Scott and Reginald Forsythe were doing.[24] Such music required great technical ability from its performers, as well as jazz talent. Rollini combined these and became a member of Shefter's Rhythm Octet. Others were reed players Toots Mondello and Paul Ricci. The group's first recordings were for Victor and all tunes were composed by Shefter. Rollini played vibraharp throughout. The theme of the first title, "S.O.S.," was based on the international "help" alarm signal. It demonstrates Shefter's approach, to what he considered modern music. It was fully arranged and full of little surprises, and it had space for swinging solos by both reed players. The other title from this session, "Chopin's Ghost," is similar. Shefter used a Chopin theme, and gave a solo to Rollini. A third title was recorded, "Locomotive," but its master was rejected and it was rerecorded a few days later. Its arrangement asked for the band to imitate the start of a steam train (the drummer using tympani) and it included a xylophone solo, probably played by Rollini. On "Burglar's Revenge," the final title, Rollini went back to vibraphone. These records were quite successful and got worldwide distribution, which led to another opportunity for Bert Shefter to record some of his work. After Master and Variety had stopped, ARC continued to record in the Master studio, using Master's original M series of matrix numbers.

In December ARC recorded two titles there by Bert Shefter's Rhythm Octet, "The Aeroplane and the Bee" and "Taming the Devil," titles that adequately describe the music.

Another representative of this school of jazz music was Larry Wagner (1907–2002). Wagner worked as a trumpeter on the West Coast before moving east and becoming a freelance arranger. He worked for several orchestra leaders, including Clarence Williams, and in 1937 the Victor company gave him an opportunity to record some of his own compositions. To get the sound he wanted, he hired Adrian Rollini and bass player Lou Shoobe, who brought in their experience working with Bert Shefter and Raymond Scott, respectively. With Wagner, Rollini recorded "Autopsy on Schubert," based on a Schubert theme, and "Two Dukes on a Pier." With his big band background, Wagner's music understandably tended to swing more than Shefter's. Both titles are showcases for Rollini's vibraphone playing, straight as well as in swinging solos. Lou Shoobe had not liked the work with Raymond Scott and when he found out what Larry Wagner was doing, he felt back at Scott. After the first recording date, Rollini and Shoobe did not return to Wagner.[25]

Rollini participated in at least one more recording date at Master, again with a different leader. This was a pick-up date with Charlie Barnet's swing band. In May 1937, Barnet had recorded for Master as the California Ramblers, without any original Rambler in the band. However, in August he was back to record under his own name. In addition to Rollini, Barnet's band included Frank Newton, a black trumpeter. As seemed to be the standard pattern at Master, four titles were recorded and only two were issued at the time. Rollini played vibraharp and is heard only on the fourth title recorded, "Admiration," a composition by Duke Ellington's trombone player Juan Tizol.[26]

Rollini's work with Richard Himber was not over yet. His final recording dates in 1937 were with Himber and may have been more to his liking than anything the band did before. The August session produced four titles. Rollini soloed on vibraphone on three of the four and some, such as "My Campfire Dream," are close to true swing records. In October Himber spread the news that, after three years, he was back at the Essex House to direct the house orchestra and that he would feature the Adrian Rollini Trio.[27]

Himber had agreed to hire the complete Trio and integrate it into his band, in order to fill engagements from October at the Essex, including broadcasting.[28] In November Haig Stephens, who had decided not to participate in Rollini's Trio, had been replaced by Harry Clark. In December, Rollini had his final recording date with Richard Himber. With the full Rollini Trio in the band, a record was produced that showed its versatility. It was called *The Parade of the Bands* and on its two sides the sound and mannerisms of six different bands were imitated. The first is Paul Whiteman's band playing "Hot Lips" with a muted trumpet solo à la Henry Busse. The second is an imitation of Wayne King on the tune "Vilia"; and the side ended with "Dinah" as played by the Benny Goodman Trio, with Rollini playing vibraphone à la Lionel Hampton and Paul Ricci in the Goodman role. Side two opens with a trombone player who imitates Tommy Dorsey's "Marie" solo, followed by "Sugar Blues" as made famous by Clyde McCoy, and ending with "Can I Forget You?" in Guy Lombardo's style. The *New York Sun* identified all six bands, but commented on the Lombardo part: "However, only two saxophones are out of tune . . . instead of the usual four."[29]

Himber decided to put a special label on the two final sides recorded at this session. They were recorded by a small group from his large dance band, which he called his Seven Stylists. The seven included the full Adrian Rollini Trio, consisting of Rollini, Frank Victor, and Harry Clark; the others were Johnny McGhee, trumpet; Milt Yaner, reeds; Eddie Steinberg, piano; and Nat Levine, drums. Vocals were by Stuart Allen, who sang on both tunes, "There's a Goldmine in the Sky" and "Sail Along Silv'ry Moon." Both titles were attractive sidesteps from Himber's traditional fare and gave Rollini and his Trio an important chance to get heard.

More Freelancing: Broadcasts, Transcriptions, and Films

By 1937 Adrian Rollini was a broadcasting pioneer, having been on the air since 1923, the year of his first broadcast with the California Ramblers. In the thirties Rollini was frequently on the air again, first in the setting of a dance band like Bert Lown's or Richard Himber's, later with his own groups. Lown's band did over a hundred broadcasts during 1930 alone. At that time, home recording equipment was just becoming available, so some of these broadcasts may have been recorded, but none has come to the author's attention. However, it is certain that from 1936 onward, home recordings of Rollini's broadcasts were made and some survive, in particular with his Trio. A rough count for the years 1938–39 shows over 200 Rollini broadcasts in two years. At the time Harry Clark joined Rollini with Richard Himber at the Essex, the definite start of the Trio, the small group was on the air twice a week with NBC/WOR, on top of his two broadcasts a day with Himber at the Essex. Daytime broadcasts were from Bamberger's store in Newark and evenings from Macy's in Manhattan.[30]

Only a few of these broadcasts survive, and even fewer have even been issued on LP or CD. Those that are known to have survived are mentioned below. Most of what survives was found in Rollini's private record collection. The oldest is from October 1936, when he used his two main instruments for two titles during a *Saturday Night Swing Club* program.[31] The program also featured piano player Teddy Wilson and vocal group the Blue Flames. Rollini played vibraphone on "Honeysuckle Rose" backed by members of the studio orchestra. This was followed by "Tap Room Swing," played on bass saxophone with Johnny Williams, drums; Ward Lay, bass; and Frankie Worrell, guitar. Another surviving broadcast is from 28 November 1936 and is mentioned in a previous paragraph. During broadcasts from the Hickory House from January 1937 Rollini is heard only on vibraphone, with Frank Victor on guitar.[32] On 13 June 1937 Rollini was a guest on the first anniversary broadcast of the *Saturday Night Swing Club*, together with eleven other groups.[33] The ninety-minute show was not aired as usual from a CBS studio, but from a theater that seated over fifteen hundred. Rollini played one tune with his Trio, his own "Rebound."

One more Rollini broadcast survives from 1937. On 18 October he was a guest on a broadcast by Lloyd Shafer's orchestra. Rollini played both bass saxophone and vibraharp on his own tune "Preparation," accompanied by a full orchestra.

Direct broadcasts like this were still normal at the time, but many broadcasts were already prerecorded on transcription discs. Adrian had made such recordings back in 1930 for Brunswick, in a band directed by Red Nichols. Originally they were made for distribution to radio stations across the country, but a new market opened up when they were used to entertain people shopping or doing factory work. During the thirties making transcription discs became a source of extra income for many New York musicians. New companies appeared that specialized in this field.[34] The first of these may have been Associated Music Publishers, which issued discs beginning in 1934. The company soon combined forces with another company, Muzak, which was formed in 1934 and started by distributing music via cable and a few years later expanded into transcription discs. Ben Selvin (1898–1980) became Muzak's vice-president in charge of programming and recording.[35] Many recordings appeared on both labels. Muzak issued a total of about twelve hundred records between 1938–53; Associated, during the years 1934–42, made about three thousand.

For Adrian Rollini, making transcription discs meant a new business opportunity. His first sessions may have been with Richard Himber's orchestra. In October 1935 Himber completed a series of twelve quarter-hour transcriptions for WBS in Chicago, to be used by about seventy radio stations. The broadcasts were from 4 till 30 November, advertising a new Studebaker car model. For this job Himber called his band the Studebaker Champions. A year later, on 15 September 1936, the Studebaker Champions started another prerecorded broadcast campaign over thirty-one stations with three fifteen-minute broadcasts per week. WBS estimated the total market for transcription placements to be larger than $10 million that year.[36] In 1938 Himber started a long association with Associated.

No information is available on Rollini's presence on any of these Himber recordings. If they contain any vibraphone work, this may be assumed to be handled by Rollini. However, from 1937 on he is definitely present on transcription discs. His earliest known transcription is from 23 April as a sideman in an orchestra led by Ben Selvin, Muzak's vice-president. At that time Muzak distributed music by cable and were not yet making transcriptions. Muzak's good relations with Associated allowed Selvin to work for them as well. The session produced twenty-three titles, but only fifteen of these were actually issued. Two of the unissued titles, actually the last titles recorded by Ben Selvin's band on this particular date, have been found in the form of a test pressing. They feature Rollini in solos on bass saxophone and vibraphone.[37] Some or all of the other titles from this date may also feature Rollini; one of them is even called "Vibraphone Interlude."

As if twenty-three titles in one day was not enough, and having Rollini in the studio, Associated continued the session with the first transcription recordings of the Adrian Rollini Novelty Trio. Although previously their Decca issues had simply been issued as by the Adrian Rollini Trio, it was decided to add the word "Novelty" for the Trio's first transcription recordings. The same happened with recordings by the Adrian Rollini Quartet, which would be called the Adrian Rollini Novelty Quartet on transcription discs.

Rollini worked for all major transcription companies. In addition to Associated, he recorded for Muzak, Standard, and World, in addition to some incidental issues on other labels.[38] Altogether, company files have yielded more than seventy transcription discs that were recorded by Rollini between 1937 (Associated) and 1953 (World). Actual records are hard to find and fewer than 25 percent have been heard by the author.

In addition to broadcasting and recording, Adrian Rollini was making films again. He had made movies with Fred Elizalde and Bert Lown, and now would with Richard Himber. He was part of a plan, published in 1934, by Vitaphone to make 130 short subjects.[39] With Richard Himber, Rollini was back in a studio. It was done by Paramount and the result was an eleven-minute short called *Himber Harmonies*. The intention was to give the public an impression of a bandleader's day: rehearsals in the morning, then broadcasting, recording, and finally working at a nightclub. It was completed on 25 October 1937. Rollini is seen as a member of Himber's large band, as well as with his Trio. A concert arrangement of "St. Louis Blues" is started by the full band; then a string quartet takes over, led by Wladimir Selinski, which is followed by Rollini, accompanied by Frank Victor on guitar and Haig Stephens on bass. Interestingly, Rollini manages to insert his own composition "Preparation" into the arrangement. Both the Rollini Trio and the Selinski Quartet were members of the Himber orchestra. The short was well-received by the press.[40]

Rollini's next work with Himber brought him to Princeton. After Count Basie had warmed up the audience, Richard Himber's band came on. A reporter wrote that "Adrian's vibe jive set a good pace for the rest of the gang, and they responded with some very nice stuff."[41] The following month, on 23 November 1937, Himber organized festivities at the Casino-on-the-Park to celebrate Adrian Rollini's fifteenth anniversary "as an outstanding virtuoso."

Altogether Adrian Rollini was a busy man again. A journalist from the British music magazine *Melody Maker* visited him in 1938 in his private room in the Essex House Hotel. Rollini had a resident job there with his Trio and with Richard Himber's orchestra.

> A guy comes in and informs Adrian that he's put his name down for a broadcast the following evening. "Listen, pal" said Adrian, "I start to-morrow morning at nine and go right till two next morning and that goes for six days a week." "But Adrian, I'm relying on the vibra." "Can't be done, pal. Sorry, boy, but I'd need a forty-eight-hour day."[42]

Chapter 18

Trio Years: Before and during the War

1938: The Adrian Rollini Trio Settles In

The year was 1938 and the jazz scene had made a definite upturn from the poor years in the early thirties. Both big bands and small swing combos found an appreciative public. Benny Goodman's break had come in the summer of 1935, as a result of his band's performance at the Palomar Ballroom in Los Angeles. In 1937 Goodman's popularity climaxed at the New York Paramount Theatre, where 4,400 people were standing in line before it opened. In 1936 Count Basie had come from Kansas City to New York and a year later his was one of the top bands there. Big band swing had arrived.

However, so had small band swing. There were several successful small groups around, such as the Mike Riley–Eddie Farley band and the groups led by John Kirby and Wingy Manone, to name just a few.

Clearly there was a public for jazz, and Adrian Rollini grabbed the opportunity. He was thirty-four and had found a new future, based on his Trio. Trios had been there as long as jazz existed and some great trio records had been made.[1] Only recently the trio format had become a standard concept in jazz. Benny Goodman had made a trio recording as early as 1928 and from 1935 work by a trio was an important part of his public performances and recordings, with himself on clarinet, Teddy Wilson on piano, and Gene Krupa on drums. In 1936 he added Lionel Hampton, vibraphone, to make a quartet; and in those two years he cut more than twenty titles with his small groups. Rollini had made his first trio recordings back in 1930, without success. In 1936 he revived the concept, using a personnel of vibraphone, guitar, and bass. By 1938, the Rollini Trio was fixed. With Harry Clark on bass and Frank Victor on guitar, Rollini had two reliable partners and with their integration in Richard Himber's band, they had some security.[2]

During the first half of 1938, Rollini would still make records with a larger group. In January he recorded for Decca with an eight-piece group, called His

Pat Hoke sang on the last record date on which Rollini played bass saxophone.

Orchestra on the labels. This recording date was to be the final recording date on which Rollini played bass saxophone. It also marked the recording debut of singer Pat Hoke.

In addition to the men from his Trio, the orchestra consisted of Johnny McGhee, trumpet; Paul Ricci, clarinet; Al Duffy, violin; and Buddy Rich, drums. McGhee and Ricci worked with Himber at the time. The group fits from the first notes of "Bill," the first tune. Rollini plays bass saxophone as masterfully as before and the idea that this would be the last time is hard to accept. Any comparison of "Singin' the Blues," the second tune, to the famous 1927 recording by Frank Trumbauer and Bix Beiderbecke is useless. That recording belonged to a different age, as did Rollini's own Republic piano roll from 1920. The magazine *Down Beat* appreciated the tune's new recording and chose Rollini's bass saxophone solo as "recommended."[3] Paul Ricci remembered that the boys would hang out after hours at a bar near Radio City, where Adrian would give orders in French to his lovely poodle dog, having him do different tricks, which used to break everybody up.[4]

Singer Pat Hoke took the vocal on "Singin' the Blues" and also on the last title from this session, "The Sweetest Story Ever Told."[5] He had a good baritone voice, somewhat similar to Bing Crosby's. He was born as Glen P. Hoke in Capron, New York, on 16 December 1910, and died in Rochester, New York on 22 January 2003. Around 1930 Pat Hoke took the stage name Warren Phillips when he worked with Jack Albin's Orchestra. In 1932 he joined Jan Campbell's Washington & Lee Orchestra and stayed with it for four years, eventually becoming its leader. In 1937 he worked at the Casa Mañana restaurant on Broadway. By 1938 he was using his own name of Pat Hoke again and was working with Richard Himber. When he was selected by Ray Noble to be his band singer in May, he was Warren Phillips again. With Noble he made a British tour during the second half of 1938. After his return to New York, he did nightclub and theater work and enlisted in the army when the war broke out. He married in 1943 and decided to follow a career outside show business, as a technician.

Hoke's contract with Ray Noble created publicity; when he was interviewed in 1938, after his recording date with Rollini, he showed his lack of experience in making records. Recording with Rollini had been "a tiring task which sometimes took more than one hour per side of a single record."[6] It may have been planned to do four tunes instead of three and it looks like Rollini's next recording date, less than two weeks later, was used to make up for the difference by doing five titles. This was Rollini's final session at Decca and he used no clarinet this time. Bobby Hackett replaced McGhee; vocals were by Sonny Schuyler. "Bei Mir Bist Du Schön" is one of Rollini's most swinging recordings. Hackett had been in New York for only a year and was already a prolific freelancer. However, the star of the recording is drummer Buddy Rich, who was at the start of a brilliant career.

About Rollini's goodbye to the bass saxophone, Richard Sudhalter, co-author of a Bix Beiderbecke biography, wrote: "Rollini, like Frank Trumbauer, was doomed by his instrument. Both men had helped create their own settings, tailor-made to suit their instrument's sounds. With the death of Bix, Trumbauer's musical days were numbered."[7] Rollini's choice of vibraphone enabled him to continue, but in a different alley.

That same month Rollini got another signal that his bass saxophone work was a thing of the past. On 14 January he participated in a Tommy Dorsey broadcast called *Evolution of Swing*. It presented the history of jazz from its beginning and included a recreation of the 1925 recording of "Sweet Georgia Brown" as played by the California Ramblers. Rollini was specifically hired to do his original solo. According to author Herb Sanford, who was there, nostalgia overwhelmed Rollini when he heard Pee Wee Erwin reproducing Bix Beiderbecke's chorus of Goldkette's "Clementine." Rollini burst into tears.[8]

Things were starting to move now for Adrian. His compositions for vibraphone were getting attention. He signed a contract with Robbins Music Corporation, which allocated exclusive rights to Robbins for all his compositions for vibraphone, as well as for piano and orchestra. The first two to be issued were "Preparation" and "Gliding Ghost."[9] The contract also gave Robbins the rights to the four compositions that Rollini had recorded more than a year before for

Decca with his first Trio.[10] An article in *Song Hits* of December 1938 mentioned that Robbins had five Rollini compositions—"Au Revoir," "Lightly and Politely," "Nonchalance," "On Edge," and "Preparation"—in addition to his instruction book for vibraharp players, the *Adrian Rollini Modern Instructor for Vibraharp*.[11]

On 26 March he was a guest on the CBS *Saturday Night Swing Club*, broadcast by WABC. He brought his Trio, expanded by Al Duffy and Buddy Rich. The quintet opened with "Toy Trumpet," with whistling, followed by Rollini playing goofus. Then the novelty tune developed into pure swinging jazz led by Rollini, Duffy, and Rich. In their next number, "Chinatown," Rich was the star and Rollini announced him as "my drummer Buddy Rich—he's only twenty years old. . . . this boy will be on top very soon." As an illustration of the amount of work Rollini could get, the next day the same quintet did almost the same program for NBC on a broadcast hosted by Norman Cloutier and aired via station WNEW.[12]

Meanwhile Rollini was trying hard to find a steady engagement for the Trio. He was still a member of Richard Himber's orchestra and the Trio was regularly featured as part of its performances. Himber came back to the Essex in 1938 and Rollini had a permanent room there. The Trio had regular radio shows and Rollini himself did guest appearances where he could. In April *Down Beat* published an article in which he talked about his present activities. He said that he controlled two recording groups, a small swing combination and a novelty "all-sax" outfit which he believed would create a stir when the records were released. The all-sax outfit was never heard of again, but the small swing combination, in other words the Trio, did break through when Rollini got a contract with the Piccadilly Hotel to play in their Circus Bar from May onward.[13]

The Piccadilly Hotel was located at 227 West 45th Street, just west of Broadway, near Times Square. It had 600 rooms and in two rooms orchestras could entertain guests, the Circus Bar (at street level) and the Georgian Room (on one of the upper floors).[14] The orchestra of Jeno Bartal had been working in both rooms and this was reduced now to the Georgian Room only.

For Rollini the final recording date with a group larger than his Trio came in June for Vocalion. The personnel was as before in January, with Hackett and Buddy Rich. Vocals were by the Tune Twisters, a good vocal trio modelled after Paul Whiteman's Rhythm Boys. It consisted of Andy Love, Bob Wacker, and guitarist Jack Lathrop. Their recording experience included working with Victor Young and Glenn Miller, and they had worked on Broadway and in movies. The Tune Twisters play such a dominant role in the arrangements that the recordings might be regarded as theirs, with accompaniment by Rollini's men. However, this would not do justice to the band's own work, like Hackett's solos, the work of a fully developed trumpet soloist. Four titles were recorded, all moving along with a smooth swing. Bass player Harry Clark particularly remembered Hackett's fine chorus on "Small Fry."[15]

Just two days later the CBS *Saturday Night Swing Club* celebrated its second anniversary and the Rollini Trio was invited.[16]

Rollini's work at the Piccadilly quickly increased. The hotel had a roof terrace, located on the twenty-fifth floor. In addition to its hours at the Circus Bar, Rollini's Trio would provide the music on the roof terrace on summer evenings from 9:30 p.m. "till curfew." It opened as Adrian's Piccadilly Roof on his thirty-fifth birthday, 28 June 1938. It was canvas-covered and could hold not more than fifty people. A press note appreciated the trio's music: Rollini's arrangement of "Three Little Words" included a few bars of "I Love You" and he would conclude Ellington's "I Let a Song Go Out of My Heart" with "Without a Song." Another press clipping noted that the Trio was broadcasting nightly from the Piccadilly.[17] The Piccadilly Roof quickly became a favorite of the after-theater crowd. Now Rollini had a luncheon job, a cocktail job, a dinner and supper job, as well as weekly radio programs and recording dates.[18] The Adrian Rollini Trio had found its place.

In June Richard Himber announced that his orchestra could be heard in the newly decorated and air-cooled Casino-on-the-Park of the Essex. He had singer Stuart Allen, the Adrian Rollini Trio, a dancing couple, and the "Southern" Tanner Sisters.[19] Himber had built his reputation with sweet music, but now he had changed his style a little. *Variety* described his music as "semi-swingo" and "to heat it up for the jitterbugs" with Rollini "sparkling on the xylophone per usual."[20] In August Himber's personnel included a new vibraphone player Godfrey Hirsch.[21] However, with a fixed contract for his Trio at the Piccadilly, it would now soon be over for Rollini with Himber. Rollini knew how to entertain his public. An example of a special event was "Gridiron Night" on 13 August, the opening of the football season. On that evening the Trio featured football songs from Eastern colleges. Rollini had invited football captains from all over and several football trophies were on display.[22]

His Trio broadcasts were highly popular, but Rollini still found time now and then to do a guest performance with other leaders. One such event took place on 10 August when he participated in Paul Whiteman's Chesterfield radio show for the Columbia Broadcasting System. It was the second time that year that Whiteman invited Rollini for a guest appearance in his show. The first time had been just before the *Piccadilly* contract started, on 29 April 1938. At that show the Trio, expanded with drummer Buddy Rich, played a new composition by Rollini called "Undercurrent." This was followed by "China Town, My China Town," on which Rich got an opportunity to shine. Rollini pushed his new image as a vibraharp player by saying that he had taken none of his other instruments to the studio, just the vibraharp. Actually, two programs were performed. One went to the stations in the Eastern and Central time zones. Hours later the repeat broadcast went to the stations in the Rocky Mountains and

The trio on *The Kate Smith Hour*.

Pacific zones.[23] The following August, when Whiteman again invited Rollini to participate in his show, the concept was the same. The program handout listed the Trio playing "Flat Foot Floogie" and "That's a Plenty" and noted that there would be two broadcasts to a total of 103 stations, the first one going to 83. The next month Paul Whiteman selected his twenty-four-piece all-America swing band and appointed Rollini for vibraharp.[24]

While appearing on Paul Whiteman's show, Rollini noted the bass that was being used by Art Miller, Whiteman's bass player. He liked the sound of the instrument, which was a Voigt Geiger made in Chicago. On the other hand, he did not like the instrument that his own bass player, Harry Clark, used, a Prescott. It was too big an instrument for a trio. To Clark he said: "I think you should have that bass, in fact, I want you to have it. 350 dollars. I will lay it down and you can pay me back"—which Clark did. Clark also remembered that Adrian thought about the appearance of the trio. He was presented with a new vibraharp by Deagan, its maker. This instrument was all white and now he insisted on having a white guitar and a white bass. The Epiphone company was willing to take the red off Clark's bass and make it white for twenty-five dollars.[25] Deagan advertised their new vibraharp with prices from $185 and with a photo of the Trio, all in black and white dress with white instruments. The photo illustrates Rollini's desire that his men should always show their cuffs.[26]

By the end of the summer, on 17 September, Rollini moved from Piccadilly's roof terrace to its Georgian Room. Here the trio played at dinnertime, succeeding Jeno Bartal. After-theater work at the Circus Bar continued, so again Rollini had a double job at the Piccadilly.[27]

Once again, Adrian Rollini must have thought that he had made it. Dixie was running the White Way Music Shop and Adrian was holding a nice position at two spots at the Piccadilly. Extra income was generated by his compositions that were published by Robbins, and the Trio was consistently welcome doing broadcasts under Rollini's name or as guests with other hosts. An example of the latter was *The Kate Smith Hour*, on which they appeared on 8 September. Kate Smith invited Rollini a second time for a broadcast on 3 December, which was recorded. Introduced by their theme tune "Preparation" and Kate Smith's announcement, the Trio went into a hot version of "Alexander's Ragtime Band." Rollini brought his new instrument to the studio: a set of chimes, on which he played a chorus, maybe his first on a broadcast.[28]

Broadcasting continued and in October the Rollini Trio added a weekly program to its roster, sponsored by Manhattan Soap, makers of Sweetheart Soap. The Trio's popularity was good for second place in *Down Beat*'s third annual All-American Band Contest in the category "Quartets and Trios." They placed after Benny Goodman's Quartet and before Milt Herth's Trio and several others.[29] To attract customers, the Piccadilly management continued to organize special events, such as the introduction of the "Soho" in November, a dance coming from Europe. Roy Moulton, Piccadilly's managing director, personally demonstrated it.[30]

During the fall and the winter months of 1938, the Rollini Trio was a fixture at Piccadilly's Circus Bar, but his place in the Georgian Room would sometimes be taken by Jeno Bartel again. In November Rollini looked for compensation and found it by doubling in a revue at a new nightclub, the Band Box at 20 West 52nd Street, opening on 9 November.[31] However, Rollini's Trio had to share a small space with a fourteen-piece band. Bass player Harry Clark and guitar player Frank Victor had to stand on the dance floor, while Rollini and his vibraphone were squeezed on the bandstand. So within a week Rollini bowed out.[32]

A bigger success came on the evening of 4 December. The Trio was that week's celebrity, to be feted and featured at Leon & Eddie's at 33 W. 52 Street.[33] It was reported that their appearance at the club topped all earlier celebrity evenings. "Every publisher in town was there, as were many of radio's biggest names. Rollini's 'Swing Chimes' stood the audience on its ear. Even Eddie Davis, hardboiled son of Swing Street, gasped at Rollini's genius."[34]

With his fame getting greater and his name getting bigger, it was no surprise that the Piccadilly could not keep Rollini exclusively on a day-to-day basis.[35] The mishap at the Band Box was soon forgotten when, just before the year ended, the Trio started at the Glass Hat, a room of the Belmont Plaza Hotel at 541 Lexington Avenue.[36] Its bar had a circular design by Jac Lessman, a successful designer of several nightclubs and supper rooms in New York and elsewhere. Lessman wanted to give the room a feeling of cheerfulness and informality and he thought that a circular bar was more intimate and would have more appeal for women.[37] At the Glass Hat, Rollini met some old colleagues. Joe Venuti, advertised as the "Swing King of the Fiddle," had his own orchestra there and Arthur Hand of California Ramblers days was host.[38] Both had been working at the Glass Hat with the Andrews Sisters for some time before Rollini arrived.

Harry Clark, who drank no alcohol at all, regarded Rollini as a very heavy drinker.[39] He remembered how Rollini would carry a small bottle in his case of hammers. This case contained two sets of vibraphone mallets and two chime hammers. Between sessions he would take a nip. However, in all his years with the Trio, he saw Rollini out of control only once and that was at the Belmont Plaza.

1939: *Swing to Chiclets*, Hollywood, and More

Rollini goes commercial! This was the news at the start of 1939. Rollini managed to get a three-month contract for his Trio for a weekly radio program. The sponsor was Adams, the maker of Chiclets chewing gum, and the first broadcast of *Swing to Chiclets* went on the air 19 January over WJZ. The Trio was augmented by singers Bob Carroll, a baritone, and Dolly Mitchell. During the shows, Mitchell's true name was kept a secret. She was said to be a fifteen-year-old girl and was called Miss Chiclet.[40]

Almost the full series of programs survives in the form of discs that were privately recorded for Rollini by ARS, Advertisers Recording Service.[41] This first program was a balanced mix of hit tunes, novelty songs, and ballads, ending with an old jazz standard. Rollini used his own tunes for opening and closing, "Preparation" and "Au Revoir." Whenever a tune allowed it, the Trio would go into a swinging performance, eventually to return to the melody. The full playlist was:

Toy Trumpet
Dodging a Divorcee
I Won't Tell a Soul—vocal by Bob Carroll

The Trio on *Swing to Chiclets*. From left: Bob Carroll, Harry Clark, Dolly Mitchell, Adrian Rollini, Edward Herlihy, Frank Victor. Dolly Mitchell dedicated the picture to Adrian: "'Keep it the same tempo, Adrian.' Love, Dolly (the cherub)."

Jeepers Creepers—chimes chorus by Rollini
April in My Heart
A Tisket a Tasket—vocal by Miss Chiclet
You Got Me—vocal by Bob Carroll
Chinatown
Small Fry—vocal by Bob Carroll
Wabash Blues

Surprisingly, "Toy Trumpet" opens with some basic drumming work. The drummer's identity is not revealed and he may have been anyone in the studio. Two possibilities are out: it is not Rollini and not Victor. Rollini was a good drummer, but his first vibraphone note is heard too close to the drumming. And although he was quoted claiming "if we want the sound of drums, the guitar strums it out," they are real drums here.[42]

Radio Daily gave it a positive review the following day:

A well-built show backed by competent talent. . . . the Trio in inimitable style provides soft but hot swing rhythms, occasionally blended with a sweet tune, while

Carroll reveals an excellent voice and delivery for ballads. . . . Miss Chiclet helped on two or more occasions with the commercials and also offered two numbers in which her voice seemed more mature. Youngster is one of great promise. . . . Ed Herlihy acted as emcee.[43]

Variety was more critical and was positive about all the talent except for Rollini. The reviewer (signed Odec) seemed to have lost his feelings for jazz when he wrote: "in his efforts to be different at all times he teeters close to overdoing it. Some of his arrangements toss the original melody completely overboard and take on the aspect of a hodge-podge of contrapuntal effects on the vibraphone or the chimes."[44]

When the three months were over, the Trio's contract was continued for another month and the final broadcast was on 18 May 1939. If Rollini read the *Variety* review, it did not cause him to change the style of the program. The tunes were a mix like the first broadcast (but all different tunes) and included a vocal version of "Tiger Rag," with Miss Chiclets taking the vocal.

The Adrian Rollini Trio with the two singers did a total of seventeen broadcasts. Rollini was constantly working on the Trio's repertoire. Sixteen broadcasts survive on discs; during these broadcasts 149 different tunes were played. Most tunes were played only once, twenty-three more than once. One of these was Rollini's new compositions "Chime Time," which was aired for the first time on 9 March 1939.

These Chiclets sessions were quite informal and squeezed in between other jobs by the Trio. This sometimes required quick improvisation. The music was put on racks for each musician in the order of the broadcast. One day something told Rollini that the music was not set and he pulled the back number up in order to correct this. Clark remembered how he had to juggle, holding his bass with one hand and pulling the correct tune up with his other.[45]

After the *Swing to Chiclets* series, Rollini received a letter of appreciation from the marketing bureau that had organized it. The programs were not continued with a different group.

Adrian was becoming well known now and the press liked to quote him. As a chimes player and endowed with perfect pitch, he felt entitled to say something about the chimes that could be heard daily on NBC broadcasts. And when he said that those chimes were out of tune, it was news.

Meanwhile, in New York the public could hear Rollini in the flesh at the Glass Hat at the Belmont-Plaza, where Joe Venuti still had a band and Rollini his Trio. In February they were joined there by the Merry Macs, a vocal quartet consisting of three men and a lady.[46] In March the vocal group left and its place was taken by Lucille Johnson, described as "blond, pretty and not at all jitterbug. Possessor of a ringing soprano that can reach high C without any noticeable difficulty." The article continued by suggesting that Venuti's band should tone down its brass while accompanying her. "Otherwise the Adrian Rollini Trio continues to display their musical monkeyshines, and the Negro waiters occasionally drop their chores long enough to do a bit of their own harmonizing on the spirituals."[47] Later in March the show at the Glass Hat was changed. All artists left except for the Rollini Trio, which became an element of a show with Ernie Holst leading his orchestra. The Belmont's black waiters were also in the show, working under the name of the Belmont Balladeers.[48] There were side jobs for the Trio, too, such as a show at Riley's, a nightclub.[49]

The Trio also remained popular at the Piccadilly, so in May it returned there and on 19 May, one day after the Chiclets show had ended, it started a series of broadcasts from the Piccadilly. NBC aired them four times a week. A newspaper added that Rollini intended to devote one program a week to what Rollini described as "swing classic concertettes." The paper concluded that the works of Chopin and Bach would receive "Tin Pan Alley transfusions."[50] Rollini knew that such a choice would be controversial. He remembered the noise around the California Ramblers' 1925 broadcast of hymns. At the time it was announced that the hymns would be played straight and were not to be danced to. And that band also had an operatic medley in its repertoire, which created no protest. At the Piccadilly he had noticed the success Lucille Johnson had, who mixed operetta and opera. So looking out of the world of modern dance music into other music scenes was nothing new. In fact, Rollini had thrown in a popular classical piece before with his Trio, like during the Chiclets broadcasts where it had performed Paderewksi's "Minuet" and Dvorak's "Humoresque." The new element was a full broadcast in this vein.

Holding several jobs at the same time had been normal for Rollini for a long time, so it was no surprise to see that on the first date of his new broadcast series, he also was the special attraction in the "In Person" show at the Strand Theatre at Broadway and 47th Street, the place where he had tried to continue working when the Club New Yorker failed in 1927. The Strand featured a film and the orchestra in the show was led by Ruby Newman.[51] It was the first time the Trio performed as a stage act in a theater. The Trio contributed four tunes to each show.[52] *Billboard* wrote: "The Adrian Rollini Trio, making more music . . . than some of the bigger bands . . . are a decided click. Their chamber music jazz leaves 'em begging for more. . . ."[53]

Some of the Trio's side jobs have been identified, but there may have been more. One was at the Troc, a new, narrow nightclub at 53 West 52nd Street. They worked there from 6 July in the company of Bobby Hackett's fourteen-piece band and the "original Boogie Woogie pianists."[54] In August the *New York Times* probably referred to this gig when it reviewed the trio at a new place at 52nd Street, where it played interludes for Bobby Hackett's band.[55]

Their frequent broadcasts for the great networks had brought them fame all over the country and Rollini had always liked traveling, so when the Trio had a chance to work in California, they moved west.[56]

Rollini had a contract to work at the Trocadero, a black-tie, French-inspired supper club.[57] It had been founded in 1934 at 8610 Sunset Boulevard in Hollywood, by William R. Wilkerson, the successful publisher of the *Hollywood Reporter*, and quickly became the best in Hollywood. While Rollini worked at the Trocadero, he met the famous orchestra director Leopold Stokowski, who told a newspaper that he was a great admirer of his work.[58]

Although the Trio had by now gained in popularity and recognition, there were no recent records that fans could buy. Brunswick decided to be there first and in April Rollini signed a contract for at least twelve titles by his Trio, to be issued on the Vocalion label.[59] The Trio's stay on the West Coast became particularly memorable because its first records were made there. There were two sessions, which took place by the end of September and at the start of October in the studio of West Coast Recorders, an independent company that was used by Columbia. Most titles recorded at these two sessions are of the sweet type and usually softly swinging. They may represent the kind of music that was expected from the Trio at the Trocadero. From a jazz standpoint, the final title of the first session, "Diga Diga Doo," is the most interesting. It is a fast and swinging performance, which features all Trio members in solos and Rollini even plays one on his chimes.

Adrian Rollini and his Trio did not stay in California much longer. Only one more engagement is known before they returned to New York, at another club, La Maze.[60]

Back in their home base, the Trio did not return to the Piccadilly, but finding jobs appeared to be easy. By now they were nicknamed the "The smallest big band in . . ." or "The biggest little band . . ." On the dots wordings of different strengths would appear, as relaxed as "radio" or as ambitious as "the world."

However, in November they were back in New York and, with the William Morris Agency now representing them, continued their busy schedule.[61] *Variety* reported on a show in Jamaica, Long Island. Five times a day Ina Ray Hutton's fifteen-piece band was the centerpiece at the Carlton, a vaudeville theater. *Variety* noted that Hutton had just changed her famous "all-femme" band for a good male group, but she had had to make further changes, much to *Variety*'s disliking. Rollini's Trio was the best part: "They tap and plunk out lively rhythms . . . and had to encore to satisfy a comfortably filled house."[62]

The following month, in December, the Trio resumed its long engagement at the Piccadilly. As before they shared duties at the Georgian Room and the Piccadilly Circus Bar with Jeno Bartal's Continental Orchestra. They were now billed as the "Biggest Little Band in America," and this was supported by little press items such as this one in a music magazine. It reported that its secretary had only one fault: she didn't stop and think. So one day she asked how many pieces there were in the Rollini Trio. She was told eleven—if you count Adrian as nine.[63]

They ended the year at the Piccadilly, but before that the Trio did one more side job. This was at the Freeport Theater, a movie theater in Freeport, where they headed the stage show. The show featured dancers and comedians and there were two movies.[64] And just before New Year's Eve, Pelham Memorial High School held its annual Father-and-Son Night, at which locally born celebrities were invited to perform. The list, which included Rollini, was headed by Gene Tunney, former heavyweight boxing champion.[65]

1940: Business as Usual Plus a Boat Trip

Roosevelt's New Deal had resulted in an upswing of the American economy. One effect was the increase to the public for all kinds of entertainment products. In music the trend had been to bigger and bigger bands. Leaders of big bands were the new pop stars and they were constantly in the news. This was a world of reborn positivism.

On the other side of the Atlantic, a continent was getting more and more into trouble. In 1939 Hitler's Germany invaded Poland and step by step more conflicts appeared until by 1940 most of Western Europe had been captured by German troops. However, for the moment it remained a regional war.

While the world around him was in a period of change, Adrian Rollini continued his activities as before. The Trio did a vaudeville show at Brooklyn's Flatbush Theatre, while its work at the Piccadilly went on as well. In March it was Shea's Buffalo Theatre, where Bing Crosby's new film *Road to Singapore* was screened. D'Artega led the show's orchestra and one element of the show was the "Eastertide Fantasy," in which around thirty artists participated, including the Trio.[66] A newspaper had an interview in which Rollini was asked how his Trio could sound like a ten-piece band.

> That's easy he said. . . . I've been working on the idea for this combination for several years. I wanted something simple, a combination that wasn't cluttered up with instruments such as drums comprise. I settled on the vibraharp, guitar and string bass and we proved that you can get as much music from three pieces as from eight or ten. We use our instruments to get numerous sound effects. For instance, if we want the sound of drums, the guitar strums it out, etcetera. In congas and things like that we mimic the sound of many other instruments. The result, over the air,

is most amusing. People write in continuously and want to know how we dare call ourselves a trio. And believe it or not, one well-known New Yorker sent us the hilarious query "How many men are in the Rollini Trio?"

This joke had started as a quote from a secretary a few months earlier and Rollini apparently had picked it up and enhanced it a bit. The interviewer also notes the astonishment of "fellow craftsmen when Rollini put aside the [bass saxophone,] the instrument on which he was the undisputed master and took the vibraharp. Results, however, have proved that this handsome Italian bandsman knew very well where he was going—and it was upwards."[67]

Work at the Piccadilly would still be combined with side jobs. Golf clubs were good customers, so in May the Trio worked at the Wyoming Valley Country Club in Pennsylvania and in July at the Apawamis Club in Westchester.

In May the Trio also had what turned out to be its last recording date for a long period. It was the final set of recordings as a result of the contract that Adrian had originally signed with Brunswick. The first eight titles had been issued on the Vocalion label and so would the last four. By then, however, CBS, the company that owned the rights to use the Brunswick and Vocalion labels since it bought the Brunswick Record Corporation in 1938, had stopped using them. Thus the Trio's recordings were issued on the OKeh label.

Another July engagement became very memorable. When Rollini was playing at a country club in Rye, New York, he was approached by a shipping executive, who offered him a job for the three days of 27 to 29 July. The job was to provide the only live music during the maiden voyage of a brand-new steamer, the SS *America*, the largest ever built in the United States.[68] The trip would start at the place where the ship was built, in Newport, Rhode Island, and end in New York. Rollini gladly accepted. The trip's program was kept in his scrapbook.

On the first day of the trip, Saturday 27 July, the Trio came into action in the evening, when the ballroom, smoking room, and cocktail lounge were open for "informal entertainment." Rollini had to compete with a new feature film, *They Drive by Night* with George Raft, Ann Sheridan, and Humphrey Bogart. The next day there were church services and sports events and in the evening another film was screened, *Turnabout* with Adolphe Menjou, Carole Landis, and Mary Astor. Rollini's Trio could be found in the rooms and also in the open, on one of the decks. On the following Monday, the *America* docked at Pier 59, North River, New York. Rollini's guitar player described how the trip with 900 prize guests went:

> Everything was on the party. You just ordered anything you wanted and there were no checks. . . . Drinks were coming up fast, because it was terribly hot on the boat. . . . Waiters were rushing up drinks to this one group and one of them kept

passing bills in tips to the boys and finally a gentleman, widely known in Washington got to his feet and pounded the table indignantly. "What I want to know is—Doesn't the house ever buy a drink on this tub?"[69]

In August the Trio had a gig at Shea's Buffalo Theater, in a program with the film *Pride and Prejudice* with Greer Garson and Laurence Olivier.[70] That same month they worked at Loew's State in New York, where Mildred Bailey had top billing and the movie was *The Ghost Breakers* with Bob Hope and Paulette Goddard. Both theaters advertised the comfort of air conditioning. September started with a gig at Atlantic City's Steel Pier. The bill included two big bands, Alex Bartha's and another that was Glenn Miller's and Little Jack Little's alternating.[71] Gigs like this would remain a nice source of extra income for Rollini and his Trio.

Adrian's brother Art remembered that by the end of 1940 the Trio's contract at the Piccadilly ended and their next engagement was in Las Vegas, Nevada. Adrian was no gambler, but he was expected to gamble there and so he tried his luck.

By now Rollini's White Way Music Shop was fully established and needed no extra publicity. His Trio was known from its broadcasts and records, as well as from live performances. Rollini even found time to relax and spend time on his hobbies. One of these was building scale models. He was good at this, so when one of his models fell into pieces, he repaired it perfectly. However, his major hobby had been boating in one of his series of Rambler boats. Around 1940 he owned two boats, a speedboat and a cruiser.[72] He would combine this with fishing, and in August 1940 Adrian became news when he had the prize catch of the season, one of the Atlantic's biggest fishes, a black marlin of about five meters. Rollini also liked home movies, although most of these may have been made by his wife. His movies from the late twenties, including his trip to Europe, are lost but some (silent) movies made on his camera in the forties survive. The earliest of these are from the second half of 1940 and show the Trio on board SS *America*. There are also clips from Loew's State and from the Steel Pier, showing the outside.

1941: Two New Guitar Players, George Van Eps and Allen Hanlon

By 1941 the United States was materially supporting Great Britain in its struggle with Nazi Germany. It was not yet actively participating in military action, but was preparing for it and mentally was on the side of the British. In 1940 a law was accepted by Congress that established conscription. From 1941 all men from eighteen to forty-five years old had to do military service for eighteen months.

So all members of the Adrian Rollini Trio were eligible for the army. However, for the time being they stayed out.

In January the Trio's vaudeville work continued with engagements at the Windsor Theatre in the Bronx and at the Capitol Theatre in Washington. A review read: "Then comes our favorite, the Adrian Rollini Trio, who swing with some real music. Just a xylophone, chimes, guitar and a bass, but listen to them tear to town with Dark Eyes."[73]

Rollini's scrapbook contains a "Souvenir of the Blackout Ball" on 4 April 1941, where the Trio probably played. It was a benefit organized for the British War Relief Society, an organization that helped the British with non-military aid such as food and clothes. The British consul and his wife were patrons. It demonstrates how close Rollini felt to the British. He must have thought back to the great years he spent with Fred Elizalde in London.

By now broadcasting and vaudeville were Rollini's best customers. His working day often combined the two. Vaudeville engagements usually were not longer than a week, but Rollini managed to keep his Trio busy. Some engagements got into the press, like one in June at Loew's State in New York. Rollini probably opened with a new composition of his own, which did not sound familiar to one reviewer, who liked to recognize tunes. He noted that the Trio "opened a little cold with some unfamiliar melody, but they scored, however, with their Amapola."[74]

While at Loew's State and for the first time since the Trio started, it saw a change in personnel. George Van Eps took Frank Victor's place. Victor, who had been with Rollini even before the Trio started, decided to leave after five years. Apparently Victor saw a chance to start a band of his own: in November he debuted with a new band in Buffalo's Peter Stuyvesant Room. To a journalist he claimed much of the success of the Adrian Rollini Trio, so the newspaper wrote: "Frank is the rhythm maestro who was responsible for most of the success of the famous Adrian Rollini Trio, radio and record stars. He ... did most of the arranging."[75]

Victor's successor was George Van Eps (1913–1997), who came from a musical family. His father, Fred Van Eps, made hundreds of records as a banjo player. George worked with Benny Goodman and Ray Noble before he joined Rollini. Harry Clark remembers Van Eps:

> An excellent melody chord man who played a lot of things on guitar.... he incorporated that 7-string guitar of his when we were together with Adrian. It was made for him by Epiphone with a seventh string an octave lower than a fifth to produce bass notes in some chords which up to that point had not been right for that chord. A very good thing if you know how to use it and George did.[76]

Van Eps was quick to learn the Trio's arrangements. Rollini brought him in between stage shows and each time Van Eps, listening to Frank Victor, would

The trio with Frank Victor's successor Allen Hanlon on guitar.

learn eight arrangements until at the end of two weeks the Trio with Van Eps had sixteen.

The Dreiers, owners of the President and of the Piccadilly in New York, also ran two hotels in Atlantic City. Rollini got an offer to work there during the summer of 1942. The Trio was to play a dinner session at Dreier's hotel at the south end of the beach and then play a nightclub affair at the other end, which probably was Hamid's Million Dollar Pier.

However, Rollini got a problem in Atlantic City. He had signed a contract for one job on two locations. Much to his surprise, the union regarded the contract for the two hotels as two jobs at two scales. Rollini's contract did not pay enough to solve this money problem. He did not take the job seriously anymore and preferred to go out with his boat. As a result, he lost the job and the Trio found itself out of work. George Van Eps used this as an excuse to leave the Trio. He joined Archie Bleyer's band for the show *Best Feet Forward*. Eventually he would return to California and do studio work. On Van Eps's proposal, Rollini accepted Allen Hanlon, Van Eps's best pupil, as the guitar player in the Trio. Hanlon was working in Claude Thornhill's band at the time.[77] Thornhill agreed to let Hanlon go. Hanlon remembered how he felt honored to be invited by Rollini, "whose Trio was the biggest at the time."[78] Although Van Eps showed him a few things, Hanlon's start in the Trio was less fluent than his more experienced teacher's, whose career had started a decade earlier. Hanlon needed more time to adapt to the Trio than Van Eps and Rollini felt dissatisfied at first, but Clark asked him to give Allen more time and it worked. Hanlon brought a new element in the Trio. He played electric guitar, which made him more prominent in the ensemble sound.[79] This meant that Rollini and Clark had to adapt to the new balance. It may have been the reason for Hanlon's unlucky start.

The following month one newspaper had the news that Rollini had agreed to work at Jack Dempsey's restaurant.[80] Before they opened there in October, the Trio worked in Boston's RKO Theatre, in a program with stripper Gypsy Rose Lee, who got mixed reactions from the high-class Boston public. However, Rollini fit and "evoked encore after encore."[81] Engagements at Shubert's in Cincinnati and the Colonial in Dayton followed before Dempsey's.

Jack Dempsey (1895–1983) was a former heavyweight boxing champion. He had stopped professional boxing in 1940 and started a restaurant on Broadway near 49th Street, which became a success. It had a bar and a cocktail lounge and was advertised as "The Meeting Place of the World." The Trio opened on 7 October and Dempsey had a special bandstand on a raised platform made for them. They "played from the cocktail hour right on through until the curfew."[82] Rollini's contract was for six months.

As before, Rollini's contract gave him freedom for side jobs. The day after the opening, the Trio was invited for a broadcast with the "Chamber Music Society of Lower Basin Street" over NBC's WJZ at 9:00 p.m. This show had become famous for its silly announcements of Henry Levine's band and its various guests. Texts were full of terminology loaned from the classical music scene and Levine and his guests were invariably announced as "Professor." So Rollini became Professor Adrian Rollini. The program notes said that he "received his early training by banging on radiators for heat" and that he would appear with his Trio "in a group of contemporary concertos for Ironworks, Gitworks and Dog House with reversible crescendos and rillerahs in between."[83] We may assume that Rollini had a hand in these wordings. That same month, the Trio had another appearance as celebrity guests at Leon & Eddie's, where Rollini had been in 1938.

The British-American Ambulance Corps was one of the groups that worked the mindset of the Americans to support the British and their allies in their fight against the German Nazis. Rollini performed during the Corps' Name Band Jubilee, which was an appeal for funds. On 26 November he received a telegram from Paul Specht, who invited him to the Waldorf Astoria the next day, to be awarded a certificate of appreciation.

It did not take long before fund raising turned into fighting. Fewer than two weeks after the Jubilee, Japan made a surprise attack on the United States and destroyed numerous navy vessels in Hawaii's Pearl Harbor. The next day the USA declared war on Japan and a few days later it entered the war with Germany.

However, the work of the Trio was not immediately affected. Just before the year ended, they had another vaudeville engagement. This was at Manhattan's Roxy Theatre, where *Remember the Day*, a film with Claudette Colbert and John Payne, was shown. The show was a success and ran for three weeks. Announced as "The Biggest Little Band in The World," the Trio did the intro and then later in the show only played two numbers, "Dark Eyes" and "Hallelujah." "Dark Eyes" was a hit tune listed by *Billboard* as on the repertoire of Tommy Dorsey, Horace Heidt, Maxine Sullivan, and Jack Teagarden.[84] Rollini's version of this old Russian melody, often called "Schwarze Augen," was performed against a background of girls in white gowns and black gloves.[85] The Roxy Theatre Orchestra was directed by Paul Ash. *Billboard* regularly published financial results of such shows. The Roxy seated over five thousand and during the first of three weeks took in almost $100,000; the second week this dropped to $80,000 and the final week to $32,000, while its average weekly income was $39,000.[86] While doing the vaudeville show at the Roxy, the Trio was still working at Dempsey's, Rollini's standard way of making dual money.

1942, 1943: After Five Years, the Curve Starts to Flatten

After the Roxy, and still at Dempsey's, the Trio moved to its next vaudeville engagement in a show with an orchestra led by Lou Calabrese, who now called himself Lou Breese. The show was staged both at the Flatbush Theatre in Brooklyn and at the Windsor in the Bronx. In May they were part of a show at Loew's State (over three thousand seats), where the film *Jungle Book* was screened. *Billboard* reported the theater's income as "passably at $21,000."[87] Next was an engagement in Washington, D.C., at the El Patio on 13th Street. Still in Washington, the El Patio was followed by a July opening of the Dubonnet Room at the Lee Sheraton Hotel. Advertisements called it the "opening of the year." The Trio played for cocktail, dinner, and supper. One newspaper expressed the wish to have the Trio on radio and the Mutual Network responded with a weekly half hour on Saturday. After one month the hotel's manager Tom Deveau was pleased to say that the Dubonnet Room had evolved into one of Washington's leading bistros, helped by the Rollini Trio, which kept answering requests far into the night. A typical request was for the "Hawaiian Medley," with the tunes "Kalua," "Song of the Islands," and "Blue Hawaii." One day, a group of baseball players came in to listen to Rollini, their favorite fan and musician. They were all members of the Yankees and included Joe DiMaggio.

In the Dubonnet Room. Rollini, Clark, and Hanlon at the rear; Dixie, front right; Joaquin Elizalde, left.

In Washington, Harry Clark started to become dissatisfied with his salary. Interviewed by Tom Faber in 1983, he remembered that he was going to earn $125 a week and that Rollini cut him down to $100. Dixie had come to Washington, too, and when Harry asked her how he could manage on this, Dixie gave him the missing $25.

Rollini had time now to exercise his boating and fishing hobbies, and he was reported to catch fifty-nine fish, twenty-seven of which were bluefish. He gave them all away. A little car accident that he had also produced some excitement. It probably happened while Rollini was driving his sleek-looking green Lagonda. His intimates called it "The Green Hornet." He recovered in a few days.[88]

While at the Dubonnet Room, Adrian celebrated his Trio's fifth anniversary. On 29 October 1942 an official photographer made pictures at the dinner. Dixie was present and other guests included Joaquin M. Elizalde and his wife. Elizalde was the resident commissioner for the Philippines and a brother of Fred Elizalde, Rollini's leader in 1928–29 in London. After the dinner in the Dubonnet Room, the group moved to the new Spotlight Club for an after-hours continuation.

Once Hanlon had fully integrated, the Trio showed stability again. Epiphone, maker of Hanlon's electric guitar, even used it for their advertising and gave

Hanlon top billing above Rollini.[89] However, Rollini was the Trio's greatest talent and taught his men much about their profession. Clark gave an example:

> He had perfect pitch himself and taught me how to get relative pitch. He taught me how you can do it between your teeth. You produce a note which is very close to A. The total range between your teeth when you whistle . . . You don't sing it, you whistle it. I cannot do it anymore, these teeth don't feel right. . . . when you hear a note playing you whistle your note and then you can get the relationship, maybe a tone, half tone, a third, right away you go up to the other note and you know where you are, you get very close. . . . Adrian would have known a quarter tone. This would only get you close enough to know whether it was G or A-flat say, which are close together, C or D-flat. . . . . I did not need it. I just had to memorize my bass line.[90]

At the time Rollini was showing a decreasing interest in his work. The previous year in Atlantic City, he had already shown the capacity to lose interest in his engagements. Harry Clark remembered that the Trio never rehearsed anymore.

> All the time we were playing on the radio he was reading that music [of a new song] at the performance. The only familiarity he had with these songs was by looking over the song copy. . . . When he looked at a piano copy he grasped the whole harmonic structure with a chord-in-key and he knew what the vibraphone would have to do to play it. So we went on the air with the only knowledge he had of a song and there were a lot of clinkers in there too because a vibraphone was not easy to play from a piano part. So I don't recall learning any tunes. . . . Five numbers would almost be enough for any stage and those were the numbers the public wanted to hear anyway.

Rollini had always been rather miserly and refused to give Harry Clark a raise. Clark remembered it well. In December 1942, they worked in the Cocoanut Grove at Boston's Copley Square.[91] At the time the Trio's heavy traveling had become too much for him. He had become a father of two and he wanted more to be with his family in New York. When he said so to Rollini, Adrian took the phone and called the William Morris office. They found a job for the Trio at the Enduro in Brooklyn at $400 a week. Adrian then asked:

> if there was anything else that would make me happy and I told him that I could use an extra five-dollar-bill. He agreed to that and I expected 95 dollars at the end of the first week, I only got 90. . . . When Adrian let Frank go, [Frank] was getting the same as I. [Van Eps] was coming out of a band where he was making 45 and Adrian was able to get him for 75 and I could see that 15 dollars' difference all going into Adrian's pocket. I asked for 5 and he could keep 10. . . . I confronted him with it . . . and he said "I cannot afford that."

Yet, according to *Billboard,* the Trio was quite well paid (and in Washington, Clark had earned more). *Billboard* reported that union scales were entirely disregarded for musicians working in cocktail lounges and mentioned the trios of Rollini and Milt Herth, quoting $215 a week as a minimum, up from a former figure of $150.[92] No doubt the Trio's intensive broadcasting contributed to its market value.[93]

On 19 January 1943 the Trio, now called the "biggest little band on radio," started at the Enduro on Flatbush Avenue in Brooklyn. A newspaper praised him, saying that "with his four hammers [Adrian Rollini] can pound more notes per measure on his vibraharp than anyone else in the business." Harry Clark's unanswered request for more money resulted in a conflict. When Rollini refused the extra five dollars, Clark said: "Well, why don't you let me go, why don't you let me find my way. I cannot go out of town with you. I don't know how much money I can make anywhere else, but I cannot manage on 90. He said: 'All right, you can go.' So I turned and walked away from him."

Rollini tried to impress Clark by telling him that he got Felix Giove, a good bass player at NBC. However, Giove did not join. So when Clark was asked by Hanlon and urged by his own wife, and when Rollini offered him the extra five dollars after all, Clark returned to the Trio. Soon enough Clark received an offer for another job, but then Rollini refused to let him go. Clark found himself out of work when the engagement was over, but not for long. He would be in and out of New York with various bands and, being a piano player too, he became a song plugger and a radio and TV studio musician.[94]

Clark looked back on his years with Rollini when interviewed in 1983. He suggested that Rollini had become a drinker from the pressure to perform and a lot of the time he was unhappy with what was going on behind him. At the time Clark left the Trio, Rollini was hardly adding new titles to his band book. When Larry Clinton introduced "Martha," Adrian did not want to play it, since his father Ferdinando liked this song too much the way it was supposed to be played. Clark said:

> He finally made one of his best recordings out of it. I just pushed him to it. . . . Adrian's feeling for music was a certain kind, you could tell from the things we actually got to record. The things he was forced to play when we were at the hotel just to keep whole evenings the entertainment going. Played from a rack in front as he tried to grasp a two-step piano chord and interpret that with four [mallets], spaced entirely different. You have to realize that this put a pressure on him that I could not see then. But[what] I missed the most about Adrian [is that] I did not know him when he played bass sax. There was a time when we were on stage trying to think to help the show. I suggested to him that he have a bass sax off stage and come back for an encore [but it didn't happen]. Why? I can see it now clearly. The guitar and bass

Trio with Allen Hanlon, left, and George Hnida

he had with him were not producing the feel that he needed to be able to play the bass sax the way he would play it. It required an instrumentation that he always had when he played it.⁹⁵

It was easy for Rollini to fill the vacancy for a bass player after Harry Clark left. This musician was George Hnida. Hnida was his brother-in-law. He had been in the 1932 edition of the California Ramblers and at that time he met Adrian's sister Elvira, usually called Vera or simply Ve. Hnida was born on 17 April 1908 in New York as son of Charles and Anna Hnida and lived with his parents in Queens in 1940. He married Vera around 1941. Vera had begged Adrian to hire George, although he was not liked by Art, Adrian's brother.

In April the Trio worked in Atlanta at the Henry Grady Hotel, followed by Baltimore's Hippodrome Theater, a vaudeville show. Hnida probably was the Trio's bass player when the William Morris office sent them there. *Billboard* reported that the Hippodrome grossed "a splendid $20,300" in the first week of March. The program included the film *They Got Me Covered*.⁹⁶ The second week brought in $17,000, also called "splendid" by *Billboard*.⁹⁷ From Baltimore the Trio moved to work at the Cove, Philadelphia's newest nightspot.⁹⁸ On 12 April they contributed to a five-hour broadcast over station WIP. The program, called *This, The American Way*, was organized in support of the Second War

Loan Drive, organized by the United States Treasury. Others who contributed to the five-hour broadcast were the orchestras of Xavier Cugat and Teddy Powell, as well as the full Philadelphia Orchestra directed by Eugene Ormandy. The station sent a car to the Cove to pick up the Trio in time for the broadcast.[99]

The Morris office kept the Trio moving around. By the end of the month the men were back in New York at Loew's State.[100] *Billboard* sent a reviewer, who wrote that they could have done more than one encore for him. Morris now advertised the Rollini Trio as "the No. 1 Trio of The Nation." In the advertisement they were side by side with another trio, Art Tatum's, promoted with a quote from Paul Whiteman, "Tatum is a genius."

The interest in Rollini's old recordings continued, if only because Bix Beiderbecke or Red Nichols was on some of them. In 1943 Brunswick issued an album with his 1927 recordings with Red Nichols's Five Pennies.

At the time, the high cost of small groups, often called cocktail units, had become a problem. As a result, it was difficult for the William Morris office to get bookings of more than two weeks for Rollini. However, in September *Billboard* wrote that this problem was over: small groups were being booked on the same salary scale as dance bands. Combos could now be booked for a longer period and Rollini's new engagement was mentioned as indicative of the new trend. Rollini had a contract to work through February at Roger's Corner in New York and in "a hotel lounge in Washington."[101] *Billboard* probably meant the El Patio restaurant in Washington, where the Trio worked during that month. On 30 September they did another benefit, this time for the WAC, the Women's Army Corps, a large organization that wanted to support the US Army in the war effort. The Trio performed at the opening of the Music Appreciation Room on 30 September.[102] Such activities were now becoming a new element in Rollini's work. Only a few days later, on 3 October, the Trio entertained an audience of 3,500 at the Engineer Replacement Training Center in Fort Belvoir, Virginia. That same month they worked at the Persian Terrace at Hotel Syracuse in Syracuse.[103] On 9 November there was another performance for the Army. This time the Trio worked at Fort Meade in Maryland, where the Army had a Special Service Branch. Thus the William Morris office took them from one engagement to another, as duly reported in *Billboard*. The Trio worked at the Dubonnet in Newark, New Jersey, the Miami Hotel in Dayton, Ohio, and then into 1944 with an engagement at Chin's, a Chinese restaurant in Cleveland, Ohio.

1944: Fred Sharp Joins the Trio; Recording for WOR Feature

Allen Hanlon, who had been with the Trio since the summer of 1941, wanted to leave. After well over two years he wanted to take a step back from the Trio's heavy work and travel schedule; he preferred to do studio work in New York.

Back to front: George Hnida, Adrian Rollini, and new guitar player Fred Sharp.

However, he knew that Rollini would not easily let him go, so he told him that he wanted to join the Navy, which Rollini simply had to accept. However, before he left, he helped Rollini find a successor: Fred Sharp.

When the Adrian Rollini Trio worked in the bar at Chin's, Sharp worked with a local trio in Chin's restaurant.[104] Hanlon suggested Rollini listen to Sharp, who was twenty-two at the time.[105] When Rollini heard him, he was convinced of his talent. Rollini asked him to come to New York to his drum shop on 1587 Broadway. Sharp remembered that he disbanded his own trio and went to New York where Rollini had an office.[106] In Cleveland, Sharp had been making about eighty dollars a week and Rollini offered him $135 a week. As big a step as this might seem to be, in New York, without a place to live, this was not easy. Sharp did not have to go into the army, because he had had a punctured eardrum since he was a child. Joining the Adrian Rollini Trio was a big event in Sharp's life. He told Tom Faber that "never in my life I dreamt that I would ever be part of them."[107] Like Hanlon, Fred Sharp played an electric guitar with a pickup on it, a Gibson L7. Sharp had to learn about seventy-five arrangements by heart, most of them without music. Sharp: "Not that I read music that well in those days, I was a self-taught jazz musician." Hanlon, who had written about ten of these arrangements, was out when Sharp first acquainted himself with the music. It took some time before Sharp actually succeeded Hanlon and then he moved with his wife and a baby into the Belvedere Hotel, where Adrian also would stay. Fred had the same facilities there as Adrian, two rooms and a kitchenette. Adrian and Dixie would use the place whenever they were in New York. When Adrian would go on the road, the Rollinis would give up the Belvedere, and Dixie would move to the Larchmont family home. Fred's wife loved the city but Fred did not, not only because of New York's cockroaches, but he felt frightened, a small fish in a big town. He never learned to like New York.

In Cleveland, the Trio contributed to the entertainment of the armed forces on 15 January.[108] From there, they went to Boston's Circus Room and then to the 35 Club in Paterson, New Jersey, a place that was quickly becoming a top show town, since the William Morris office convinced local club owners to only hire top talent. Clubs indeed grossed 50 percent more, but how much their cost went up was not revealed.[109]

Next was a return engagement at Roger's Corner in New York City, with a full show that included Harry Reser. While at Roger's, the Trio did some side jobs as usual. One was at Jerry Marsh's New Cafe Lounge in Utica, New York, and another was a return broadcast with the so-called Chamber Music Society Lower Basin Street on 9 April.

Then Rollini's old colleague Paul Whiteman called him again. Whiteman's fame as a major leader in entertainment had endured and now, some twenty-five years after he started, he was known as the Dean of Modern American Music. In 1943 NBC had been forced to sell one of its two national networks. It kept the so-called Red Network, but sold its Blue Network to ABC. Paul Whiteman became its new musical director and would lead the sixty-three-piece Blue Network Orchestra, which included Adrian's brother Art. Every Sunday from 6:00 till 7:00 p.m. a program called the *Radio Hall of Fame* was broadcast via WJZ and the Blue Network. It was sponsored by Philco, maker of electric equipment. Philco left the selection of the guests for the program to the weekly entertainment magazine *Variety*. For the broadcast of Sunday 23 April, the Adrian Rollini Trio was invited. Eddie Cantor was one of the other artists on the program. Rollini received a certificate signed by Philco's vice-president. It described the Trio as "three unique music makers, who sound like a ten-piece band.... They can get in the groove and ride.... As well as go smooth on a romantic ballad."

The following month Rollini was listed by *Billboard* with other bands that had a "network line," such as Count Basie, Tommy Dorsey, Duke Ellington, Jimmy Joy, and many others who were famous at the time. *Billboard* also signaled the trend that big-time radio was opening up for lounge and small-club acts, such as Rollini's, adding that in order to be useful in radio the performer already had to be a name, or at least a semi-name.[110]

It was normal for Adrian to be the center of attention, but a few days after his participation in the *Radio Hall of Fame*, his wife Dixie was Dorothy Day's guest, a radio lady who did a regular broadcast aimed at housewives. On Friday mornings she usually featured the wife of a celebrity and now her guest was Dixie. Dixie talked about Adrian's boat, the *Rambler VII*, where they could cook, eat, and sleep and which had a ship-to-shore telephone. However, it had been out of the water for two years because of the wartime gas situation. To Dixie, "Adrian was a wonderful cook. . . . Spadini Alla Romana is an Italian dish, made with slices of bread, putting mozzarella cheese between the bread, put it in the oven, the cheese melts. Then on top of it put a hot sauce of anchovies and butter and it's delicious." Her final remarks were that Adrian liked shopping for clothes: "He'd buy the store. I love to take him."

Some of Rollini's personal friends were Gene Barras and her husband. They were frequent guests on board the *Rambler VII*. Gene described Rollini as a good boatsman, but he had not been able to avoid a near-accident, when the bottom of the boat hit something. On a following boat trip, Rollini had the Barras couple on board with two more friends, when they suddenly discovered a foot of water above the cabin floor. The boat had been repaired, a caulking job, but apparently the caulking did not hold, thus the body had a large hole. So much water came in, that *Rambler VII*'s two pumps were unable to pump it out. Fortunately, Adrian managed to drive *Rambler VII* onto a ramp at City Island. On another occasion Adrian had gone so far out from the coast he could not get back, and the Coast Guard had to tow their boat back in. Gene Barras also remembered Adrian at parties always forming a band, which every guest had to join. He would go to the piano and everybody had to play something. Dixie would drum on anything; others might be playing a tambourine or blocks.[111]

While work at Roger's continued, Rollini had another vaudeville engagement at Loew's State, after which the Trio played return appearances at the Cove in Philadelphia and Loew's Capitol, Washington.[112] In June the Trio worked in Philadelphia, two and a half years after America had entered the war against Germany and Japan. On 6 June 1944 the US armed forces led an international invasion of occupied Europe. It would be almost a year before the war was over. Many bandleaders lost men to the army, including Rollini, who lost Hanlon, who faked the draft as an excuse to leave the Trio. However, Rollini himself had managed to stay out of the draft and to continue to work, maybe with the argument that losing one man from the Trio meant no income for the others. When they were at the Capitol in Washington, all Loew's theaters advertised that they would have the latest invasion news by wire and on screen.

In July the Trio was back on Atlantic City's Boardwalk, where they worked in the Holiday Room of Hotel Knickerbocker, which had the reputation of never being too hot for dancing. Nationwide broadcasting was via WOR. The Trio provided the dance music, alternating with Henry Daye's orchestra. Other acts were singer Lee Barrett and the vocal and instrumental duo Sally and Annette. On 25

August, Rollini had another opportunity to perform for patients in an army hospital. He received a letter from the Red Cross, who specially thanked him for bringing other entertainers along, probably his colleagues from the Knickerbocker.

In August Rollini was back in New York. It had been four years now since Rollini made his last commercial recording for the general public. This had been for Vocalion/OKeh in 1940. In May 1942, the American Federation of Musicians started a ban on recording activities for its members that lasted till November 1944, when at last Victor and Columbia gave in. Recording for various transcription services as well as broadcasting had continued, and small record companies eventually made records again. One of these was WOR, a major broadcaster, which started a new venture with its Feature gramophone record label.[113] Rollini and WOR had known each other for many years and Rollini's latest broadcasts had been via WOR's Mutual network. So the company made a logical choice, when it decided to issue the Trio on its new label. WOR also wanted to promote two singers who were known from their broadcasts, Sylvia Barry and Roy Williams.

Four tunes were recorded, probably all selected by WOR. The first two referred to the war in some way and were recorded with singer Roy Williams. Titles were "Lili Marlene" and "First Class Private Mary Brown." "Lili Marlene" is a song from German origin that became very popular with both parties during the war, after a German radio station had started broadcasting it. During the war it was recorded several times, such as in June by RCA Victor, with singer Perry Como accompanied by a studio choir. In fact, Rollini's record might be regarded as a cover version of Como's, since it also had the same backing as "First Class Private Mary Brown," a song from the film *Follow the Boys*. Roy Williams has a good baritone voice that fits both tunes well. On both titles Rollini plays a solo on chimes between Williams's two choruses. They did not come out well. The next two titles were sung by Sylvia Barry, "Hesitation Blues" and "Is You Is, Or Is You Ain't (Ma' Baby)." "Hesitation Blues" was an old song, derived from the same folk source as W. C. Handy's "The Hesitation Blues." "Is You Is" was a recent hit recording by Joe Jordan. Both songs are well delivered in a supple, swinging style. Fred Sharp is featured in the final title. *Billboard* reviewed the records. "Unfortunately, added singers monopolize the sides," it said, adding that the selections did not lend themselves best for the "instrumental variety." However, each singer received a positive remark: "Roy Williams lends his baritone voice for lyrical expression" and "Sylvia Barry's throaty and husky pipes lends blues atmosphere in song."[114] It would take another three years before the Adrian Rollini Trio would again make commercial recordings, again for a small label.

By then Fred Sharp had fully integrated into the Trio. He remembered that Rollini had perfect pitch and that he would help get the guitar in tune: "I used to tune up to him. He would whistle any note and I tuned my guitar before we even got on stage.... he was a perfectionist... but he was the only one permitted to make mistakes.... on some of the records I hear [his] clinkers where he reaches for things that just aren't there."[115] In September the Trio worked at the Copa Cocktail Lounge, upstairs from the Copacabana, a New York nightclub.[116] From mid-September, it featured a revue created by Al Siegel and with Abe Lyman leading the orchestra. Three shows a day, at 8:00 p.m., midnight, and again at 2:00 a.m.

Fred Sharp remembered that one night at the Copa, he and George had an experience with marijuana.[117] None of the Trio would ever use the stuff again.

> As drunk as you got, that was OK with Adrian but he would not condone the use of drugs at all. One night George got hold of some marijuana. He had a few drags and I had a few and he had a few. We finished a whole stick of it. I said to George, I don't feel anything from this. I feel much more from whisky. He said, that's funny, I don't feel anything either. So we got on the bandstand and I stand on one side of the vibes and George stands on the other playing the bass and we start to play a tune and unbeknownst to us the marijuana started to work because I looked to George and he looked at me and I looked at Adrian and George looked at Adrian and all of a sudden Adrian became so divorced from us. It struck as funny. The two of us started to laugh at the same time so hard that we stopped playing. And Adrian put down his mallets and he turned away from the microphone and he said, What kind of drugs have you been using? He knew it right away. We were standing there with tears in our eyes, laughing. Everything he said from then on struck us so funny, we couldn't stop laughing! We couldn't play at all.

For Rollini, having a boat was not sufficient as a hobby and November 1944 he applied for a hunting license. He got a "Special Deer License" for the State of New York for the open season of 1944. He had to confirm that he had been a New York resident for the past six months. As his address he gave the Piccadilly Hotel, where he may have stayed or may have had another engagement.

Before the year was coming to a close, the Trio would fulfill engagements at the Hotel Victoria, which featured them in its Candlelight Room. Then Rollini and his men moved to Providence, Rhode Island, where they worked at the Biltmore and would end the year.[118]

The Providence Biltmore was about twenty years old and high class. Its Garden Room was the center of big band dancing in Providence at the time. While the Rollini Trio worked in the bar, which was called the County Room, the Garden Room, across the lobby, had the Duke Ellington Orchestra.[119] The Trio would time their sets so that

> they would get off when Ellington went on. We would spend all our off time listening to Ellington.... Some of the guys came in to hear us..... Ellington and Adrian

stayed at the Biltmore Hotel where we played. Then civil rights were not what they are today.... The Ellington band was not permitted to stay at the hotel because they were black. We were, George and me, but we couldn't afford it. So George and I got a room in a rooming house again and most of the guys in Ellington's band commuted between Providence and New York City where they lived. Every night after the job they took the late train and they get home at five in the morning and come back the next day except drummer Sonny Greer... we got to be very good friends. So Sonny stayed with me the whole time. I had a room with twin beds in this rooming house.... We went trout fishing together. It was there that I met Harry Carney, who was a good friend of Adrian's because he played baritone.... Harry Carney taught me some things about chords that I played on guitar that I still play to this day, that are very unusual things in the sense of chord construction.[120]

Another time at the Biltmore Hotel, Fred Sharp played a joke on Rollini that did not work so well. He remembered:

George one day said to me, "Why don't we go fishing?" And I said, "All right." So we bought a couple of drop lines or some bamboo poles and went out to the bus. Out to the end of the line on the country and we got the line in the water and were fishing. I caught a little fish, called a roach. It's about 4 inches long and 2 inches wide and nothing thick. And that was all I had. So I wrapped it in leaves, put it in my pocket and I brought it back to the Biltmore hotel. I took it to the chef of the kitchen and I had him cook it and serve it to Adrian.... He put it on a silver plate on a server with wheels. The waiter wheeled in the tea cart with the silver platter and about 6 covers on, the last one being two feet long and a foot and a half in diameter and a foot high. As soon as it was wheeled to Adrian's table side he knew that there was something up because he didn't order anything like that. He probably ordered beef stew. So he pulled up the first cover and then when he saw the second cover he knew something was up. So he took all the covers off fast, and he just made nothing of it. He was embarrassed, he blushed, I thought he'd laugh. George and I were standing over, breaking up. That was the end of the incident. The next night George and I ate in the Garden Restaurant with Adrian and they served me the same damned fish. It had been dead for two days, just with one cover on. I don't know why, but I got the same fish. I don't think anybody would play a joke on him. He didn't have a great sense of humor. He used to tell dry humorous stories... like the story about a cab driver in London who was taken into court, hauled before the judge, on the charge of a misdemeanor, and the judge said that he had used foul language to a lady. "Oh, she was no lady, your honor, she peed in me cab and she called me a bugger. That's no lady." And the judge says: "That's a very unusual definition of a lady. I'd like to hear your definition of a gentleman." "A gentleman, sir," he says, this sounds how Adrian told it, "A gentleman, sir, he says, a gentleman got into me cab the other day, a bloke American he was too, . . . he give me a five-pound note, told me to take him to Charing Cross or Marble Arch and hove the King up my ass (????). Now that's what I call a gentleman. That was Adrian's story." Adrian used to like English stories, dry English humor. He was influenced very strongly by his English period; his basic sense of humor was English. His carriage and his bearing were English, he carried himself like English royalty.

1945: End of the War; Rollini Composes Again

In February and March, the Trio moved around again. In February they were in Buffalo working in McVan's nightclub; by the end of the month they were back in Boston, this time in the Bradford Hotel. This hotel had its own broadcasting studio, with station WBZ. Some private recordings survive, made at this studio in March.

Meanwhile, World War II was still being fought, both in Europe and in the Pacific theater. The Germans used all their tools to undermine the efforts of the Allies, including propaganda, special broadcasts in which music was played that was popular with their enemy. The music went on the air with the latest overstatements of German war successes. These broadcasts were quite popular with the Allied troops and when a Rollini record was played, this was heard by lieutenant J. C. Remer, Dixie's brother. He wrote about this to his sister; she gave it to the press.[121]

Also in March, Adrian's brother Art asked to borrow Adrian's bass saxophone to be used for his work with Paul Whiteman in *Philco's Hall of Fame*. Whiteman wanted Art to double on tenor and bass saxophones. Adrian agreed and Art used the instrument during rehearsals and shows.[122]

Before the Trio moved back to New York, the men fulfilled an engagement at the Syracuse Hotel in Syracuse. From 9:30 p.m. till midnight they provided dance music during supper; and in addition on Saturdays dinner music from 6:30 till 9:00 p.m. In its advertising, the Syracuse added that their customers were provided wired music at luncheon.

In May they were back in New York. One engagement at Roger's Corner included broadcasts. At the time Mike Danzi worked at Roger's too. He was an American guitar and banjo player who had worked in Germany for many years but had returned to New York before the war broke out. He had met Rollini in Berlin in 1929 and now renewed his acquaintance. In his autobiography, Danzi tells that Roger's had a balcony and a main floor and could hold 500 guests. Those guests could not dance to the music, only listen. There were eight musical groups and every fifteen minutes another group would perform, working on one of three separate stages, so there was no break in the music. One of these

Rollini wrote the music for "You Can't Stop Now."

groups was the Adrian Rollini Trio; another was the Herbert Ricci sextet, in which Danzi played.[123] Another engagement was in vaudeville at Loew's State, where the film *Without Love* was screened.[124] Fred Sharp remembered that it was a small show, with only about five acts, compared to earlier days when there would be ten.[125] *Billboard* gave the show a meager review, but Rollini got the usual good words: "[The Trio] do okay with their jump stuff. Best was *Tico-Tico*, bringing them some nice mitting." The magazine also noted that Fred Sharp's amplifier did not work for most of their act, "but house didn't seem to mind." As part of his act, Rollini played the vibraphone, chimes, and piano.[126] *Variety* was more positive and called it one of Loew's better bills.[127]

The following month, the Trio was back in Chin's Victory Room in Cleveland, Ohio. Just as before, they agreed to entertain the military, and this time their performance was at the Marine Hospital. That same month *Billboard* brought the news that Rollini had discontinued his contract with the William Morris Office.[128] The magazine gave no reason for this break-up. The Trio's heavy touring schedule probably was not the reason. More than likely it was the large fee that the agency took from the Trio's earnings. According to Fred Sharp, Adrian got $1,000 a week and he estimated that William Morris took 10–15 percent. Adrian always complained about how much money he had to pay to the agency. Moreover, his agent had the habit of calling him "Baby." He would say: "What do you mean, Baby? We are not paying much?" And Adrian used to resent that and once told him, "Don't call me Baby!" *Billboard* did not mention another agency, so Adrian may have decided to do the Trio's bookings himself, with a better financial deal for the Trio and for the club owners. Announcements of the Adrian Rollini Trio's engagements get scarcer from then on. Rollini's notebooks are lost, so any attempt to fully cover his activities from 1945 and later is futile.

Among Rollini's activities during the war is his renewed shot at composing, to make money on the side. He wrote a song to honor the president and called it "God Bless Our President," for which he donated all rights to the cancer fund. In 1944 Lewis Music published his composition "Honky Tonk Donkey," for which he wrote both music and lyrics. Rollini's record collection included a few recordings of the tune. Lewis published both the sheet music and an arrangement for up to seventeen instruments plus vocalists.[129] Another song of his, "You Can't Stop Now," was published in 1945 by Brown & Henderson. It had music by Rollini and lyrics by Lew Brown and Buck Ram.[130]

Chapter 19

Postwar Trio Years

Rollini's postwar years are hard to map out in detail. During those years he toured to many parts of the country and those tours were not always reported in the music magazines. He also spent more and more time with activities outside music and would replace his guitar player now and then. So this chapter has to be fragmented and in no strict chronological order. Still Rollini's life was full of action and new things.

In July 1945 a magazine announced that the Trio would have a major opening in October, but before that, in September, they worked at Ciro's in Philadelphia, and a news clipping kept in Adrian's scrapbook suggests that, during that same month, Dixie and he were in Dallas, Texas, and sponsored a turtle in that city's annual turtle race.[1] Their turtle did not win. A nice story was told by Jim Cullum Jr., son of Jim Cullum Sr., who led a band in Dallas for many years. When Rollini came to Dallas for a two-week run at the Majestic Hotel, he hired some local musicians to form a band and Cullum Sr., a reed player, was one of them. After hours the Cullum home was open for a late-night jam session and Rollini joined the party. Some years before, Cullum had bought a bass saxophone, which had been lying idly behind a living room sofa for most of those years. However, when some of Bix Beiderbecke's records were played and the bass saxophone had appeared from behind the sofa, Rollini decided to try it and actually played along with his own old recordings, to great enjoyment of the party, who were soaking it up.[2]

Then, on Saturday 20 October 1945, the Adrian Rollini Trio did the formal opening of the refurbished Candlelight Room of New York's Hotel Victoria.[3] In the morning Adrian received a telegram from his former guitar player Frank Victor. Victor wrote: "Am sure you will do as good a job there as you did in building the Piccadilly Circus Bar. Wishing you lots of success. Frank Victor." The Candlelight Room was described as "a baroque room with white leather seats against red-walled background, a blue ceiling and scattered candelabra" that could accommodate 400 patrons.[4] Rollini provided dinner music and dance music. The Trio was still there when on Thanksgiving Day, Thursday 22

November, the Victoria's management offered a seven-course dinner for a special price of two dollars, instead of the usual $1.25.

1946 Hobbies and Work

During the second half of January the Trio worked in McVan's, a nightclub located in Niagara/Hertel, New York. The club had three floor shows per day, from 9:00 p.m. onward.[5] As a famous musician, and in order to promote his Trio, Adrian guested in a broadcast presented by Ed Tucholka on WEBR. The interview concerned his music and hobbies. Adrian will have mentioned his boating hobby, which in 1946 still suffered from the gasoline shortage that had started during the war. So there still were no boat trips. This may have been a reason for Rollini to go into another hobby with boats: He started building scale models. Fred Sharp was technically inclined, too, and believed that his work may have inspired Rollini.

> Adrian got the bug and he did good work with his hands. He built the S.S. United States and the S.S. America.[6] He was building a whole fleet of things. We were in some theater someplace and we were on the bill with Bill Robinson, the dancer. Bill Robinson had the sign painted at the theatre "Adrian's American Shipyards" or something. He was always building boats. They were wooden models, [the work starting with an] unfinished hull. You had to cut out things and shape the hull and paint them and sand them and paint them again. They were works of art. And he did quite good work.[7] Rollini was very occupied with this new hobby and would even be working on one of his boat models during a long train trip that brought them to St. Louis and Dallas. Sharp remembered it well because he wanted to assist but accidentally put a knife into his finger. Another thing he remembered had to do with the quality of their hotels. Adrian got a room free with the job but not the boys in the band. It was that kind of a relationship throughout the whole thing, he was always the boss and we were always the worker beast. One time we were working in Dallas Texas and at the Palace Theatre and Adrian moved into the Baker hotel . . . and he had a very nice room and George and I, we got a room in another hotel . . . about a mile from the Baker Hotel and it was cheap. It wasn't the prettiest hotel but there was a bed and it was close to the job. We went to bed that night about 1 a.m. and during the night I was awakened by mosquito bites and as I became more and more awake I realized how the mosquitoes get under the covers and I flipped the covers back and I was covered with bed bugs and my one eye was all swollen and puffy. I couldn't see through it and George and I packed up and went down to the manager, the night clerk, about four o clock in the morning and we said we have bed bugs in our room and we want our money back and we

are not gonna pay. . . . so we are leaving. He said, you can't do that, we have no bed bugs. So I went upstairs and put a few of them in a box and brought them down and showed them to him. So we got out of there and we didn't have any place to go and it was maybe five o'clock in the morning so we went to the Baker Hotel and woke Adrian up and pulled his bed apart and George and I slept on the box spring and Adrian slept on the mattress. This was only after we had bathed for an hour, had showered for an hour to get rid of the lice. This was probably the closest any employee of Adrian ever got to him. We actually slept in the same room together in different beds of course.

Their return from Dallas to New York was done by plane, a nine-and-a-half-hour flight. For Sharp it was his first flight.

It was a DC3 and Adrian had flown. . . . before in England with Fred Elizalde . . . and he knew all about flying. Before we get on the plane I am frightened. I have never been on a plane and he is [frightened too] but he didn't want to admit it. So we stopped in a liquor store and we bought a half pint of whisky with a cork on and we put it in our inside pocket with a straw so that we could drink. Well we got up in the air and Adrian goes to uncork his and it goes BANG! The hostess came out "You're not supposed to bring liquor on this plane." And he says "I'm sorry. I apologize, I didn't know" and everything quieted down. So I figured there was something wrong with his bottle of whisky. Anyhow, it turns to night time. We're flying and he says "Take a look out there" And I said "Yeah, what? He said "That light, see that light" And I said "Yeah, I see it" And a little while later he said "Oh, you see that light out there, that red one?" And I said "Yeah, I see it" And he keeps reminding me about these lights and I said "What lights are you looking at? I'm looking at the wing tip lights" And he says "They have columns . . . so that the planes fly and where they are going. They are on big towers." And he was serious.[8]

Fred Sharp remembered another anecdote concerning his boss's character. One day he learned that Adrian had a girlfriend on the road. Her name was Dolores and she followed around and Dixie knew about her. Her second name was Algoraz, or something like that. She had black hair and looked Spanish. One day she came to New York. Fred was staying at the Belvedere and his wife was not with him, but probably in Cleveland. Dolores did not have a place to stay, but Adrian could not see her. He said:

"Dolores, go and stay with Fred, he's got room." But I only had a single bed. So she stayed with me and I couldn't get near this girl at all. She was Adrian's girlfriend. We were both in bed, nude, everything but nothing at all. She was a beautiful girl . . . but she was Adrian's girl.[9]

As before the Trio's first engagements in the new year obliged them to travel. After Buffalo they worked at the Club Belvedere in Springfield, Illinois, followed by the El Patio in Washington and Jerry Marsh's New Cafe Lounge in Utica, New York. Marsh's Cafe Lounge had a hookup to NBC's broadcast network, which allowed the Trio to do a number of midnight broadcasts via WSYR. A *Billboard* advertisement in May suggests that Rollini's method to work without William Morris worked well. The advertisement was paid by Harry Moss's agency and listed a large number of large and small orchestras, which were thanked for cooperation in servicing Moss's clients. Back in New York in May, there was another engagement at Loew's State, with the Bob Hope/Bing Crosby/Dorothy Lamour film *Road to Utopia*.

Now and then Fred Sharp would interrupt his membership in the Adrian Rollini Trio. One occasion was in 1946, and Rollini had to find a replacement. One option was to hire Allen Hanlon back, since he was familiar with the arrangements and in fact had written a few himself. It was less attractive to find another guitar player, since he would have to learn the band book, but that is what Adrian did. He found Tommy Morgan to replace Fred Sharp. He had worked with Red Nichols, Charlie Barnet, and Bunny Berigan, among others. Morgan was present on a broadcast sponsored by Camel cigarettes. On 25 July, the Rollini Trio could be heard on the *Vaughn Monroe Show for Camel*. Rollini's participation had been announced the week before in a Camel broadcast with Jack Teagarden. At a few minutes past 10:00 p.m., Monroe announced the Trio:

> After hearing the trio rehearse, I can well understand why you're called "the biggest little band in radio." How do you manage to get all that sound out of only three pieces? Rollini answers: It's a matter of tricks, Vaughn. And of course you have to have a couple of aces like Tommy Morgan on guitar and George Hnida on string bass.[10] To which Monroe adds: And another ace like Adrian Rollini on vibes. Talking of tricks, all you need is three aces and you've got "full house."

The Trio then plays "Limehouse Blues." Later in the program, they returned and performed "Blue Skies," arranged for all musicians and singers in the show, including Vaughn Monroe himself. A week later, Rollini did another show for Camel and played only one song, "The Hut Sut Song." Later Camel broadcasts featured Stan Kenton and Count Basie.

Next was a club in Atlantic City, the Hialeah, which hired some major names during the summer horse race season. In 1946 this included the Adrian Rollini Trio, Joe Candullo's band, and singer/piano player Hilda Simmons.[11] Next was an engagement in October in Boston's Hotel Bradford, where the Trio worked in its Circus Room. The hotel had a broadcast contract and took the 11:15–11:30 slot on radio WCOP for a full year, featuring the Adrian Rollini Trio.[12] Most of

In 1947 Tommy Morgan (right) played guitar with the Trio.

these must have been prerecorded shows, because the Trio worked and broadcast at New York's Mardi Gras in December and at the Normandie Restaurant in Poughkeepsie, New York, in January 1947.[13] A clipping from this period, kept by Rollini in his scrapbook, shows a private party at the home of Robert Williamson and his wife on Quaker Hill in Pawling, New York. Still in January, the Trio had an engagement in Wilber's Supper Club in Schenectady, New York.[14]

1947: Buying the Driftwood Lodge and Recording at Bullet

The first half of 1947 saw a long gap in the Trio's series of engagements. The reason was simple: Rollini had temporarily left the New York music scene for new action. Around 1940 Dixie and Adrian had spent three days fishing at a place on the ocean coast of Florida's Key Largo. Key Largo is the largest and northernmost of the Keys and the one that is easiest to reach from the mainland.

Rollini's Driftwood Lodge on Key Largo. Adrian built this T-shaped pier after the first, I-shaped, pier was destroyed by a storm.

Rollini had spent some months in Florida during the winter of 1925–26 and remembered how prices for real estate had gone through the roof in the days of the Florida boom. However, land overlooking the ocean could be bought at low prices now. He and Dixie wanted to buy property in Florida so that Adrian could exercise his hobbies of fishing and boating. When the Rollinis returned to their fishing spot in the spring of 1947, they heard that it was up for sale and bought it.[15] The Florida Keys were famous for their wealth in fish, as a result of the Gulfstream passing nearby. It was the Rollini's idea to invest in a place that would pay for itself by paying guests, people who could stay and enjoy going out on the ocean water. They found the place that fit their ideas in Tavernier on Key Largo and called it the Driftwood Lodge.[16] A highway connecting all Keys from Key Largo to Key West had been completed in 1944. Adrian kept a newspaper clipping from 1947 in his scrapbook, the year that he bought Driftwood. The paper said that provisions only recently had been developed for tourists who were en route to the Keys, but cottages, hotels, and restaurants were now vying for their business. "Fishing lodges ask for business with prices generally $10 a day, American plan. At these lodges, motorboats may be rented for $5 a half day and charter boats cost $40 for parties of four."[17] The Keys, in particular the

Upper Keys, were moving ahead at the time. In May, the Chamber of Commerce of the Upper Keys was organized.[18] Adrian's new property measured about 50 by 50 meters, with two buildings facing the ocean and a 40-meter pier for the boats. The reception was a room in the main building, while the annex was for sleeping guests.

Adrian and Dixie hired a couple for the day-to-day management of the Driftwood, Ray and Anne Maloney. Anne, whose family name was Pinder, did the cooking. The *Florida Keys Weekly News* of 7 June 1947 stated that "the dining room is now open and sea foods and Key Lime Pie are being served. Mr. Adrian Rollini, the owner will be down to meet the public on or about November 1st." For a while Raymond Maloney also owned a nearby fish camp. When the Maloneys had saved enough money, they opened Ray's Cafe, a restaurant. The Driftwood Lodge could be reached via the Keys' central highway, but sometimes Rollini's guests would arrive by seaplane, which was faster and funnier.[19] The lodge was of wooden construction and faced the ocean. It seems that at first guests had to share one single bathroom, but later Rollini's road sign said that rooms had private bathrooms.

By July Rollini had the feeling that he could leave it to the Maloneys to run the Driftwood and he returned to New York. After such trips to Florida, he had to get his Trio together again, but if it had been a long interruption, his guitar player might have taken a different job and Rollini had to find a replacement. Probably sometime in 1948, the Trio made a number of film shorts. The market for these films was no longer limited to theaters; with the advent of television a new market was developing. For this occasion, Allen Hanlon rejoined Rollini and Hnida. The films were made in the New York studio of Video Varieties Corporation and were released in 1948.[20] In the films Rollini plays not only vibraphone but piano and chimes as well. Hanlon demonstrates that he had not lost the routine of the seven arrangements the Trio played.[21]

However, in most cases the details of replacements of Rollini's guitar player are not known, like when Rollini had a double engagement at Loew's State (a vaudeville program with the film *High Barbaree*) and at Dempsey's.[22] The Trio's contribution at Loew's consisted of five numbers, in which Rollini played his three instruments. The Trio had success, but in their second week the Loew's income dropped by a third and the following week a new show started without them.[23] Rollini followed it with engagements in Hagerstown, Maryland and again at Jack Dempsey's.

After a trip to Tavernier to take care of his lodge business, the Adrian Rollini Trio, with Fred Sharp, was back in New York for another engagement at the Piccadilly.[24] Advertisements "proudly announced the re-engagement of the music that made the Circus Bar famous."[25] While there, he did more recording.

Peggy Mann, singer on Rollini's last record date.

There was urgency, because another recording ban was planned by the American Federation of Musicians. The AFM demanded that record companies pay a percentage of sales to a union fund set up to help support unemployed musicians. It would be in effect from 1 January 1948. For nearly a year, recording studios would be largely silent. So record companies were in a hurry to build up stock and once again Rollini's Trio was contracted by a small company. This was Bullet, which had started as a company in Nashville, Tennessee, in 1946.[26] In December 1947 Rollini did two recording sessions with Bullet, the final one a week before the recording ban started. Bullet hired music publisher Dave Dreyer to act as recording director.

At least thirteen titles were recorded, twelve instrumentals and one with singer Peggy Mann, an experienced band singer who had worked with several leaders from the late thirties on, such as Henry Halstead, Ben Pollack, and Gene Krupa.[27] With Rollini she sang "You're Gonna Get My Letter in the Morning." It was issued as one side of the only record that Bullet released from the session. Mann probably was the best singer on any record under Rollini's name. In fact, Bullet gave her top billing on the record label. Bullet coupled it with the instrumental "Dardanella," which was a showcase for Rollini as a multi-instrumentalist. He opens on piano, then moves to vibraphone and chimes, and returns to piano to end the recording. Eleven more titles were kept in reserve.[28]

1948, 1949: Alternating Between New York and Tavernier; Al Perlis Joins

By the end of the year, New York had more than two feet of snow and Adrian was happy to leave for Florida. He left on 4 January, but did not stay away long. On 24 January *Billboard* reported that Adrian's Trio was back in the Piccadilly Hotel's Circus Bar. The following month, BMI, publisher of "You're Gonna Get My Letter in the Morning," had the song in the first of several advertisements that listed ten more of their tunes and the various artists who recorded them. Although the Bullet record label had Peggy Mann on top, the advertisement only mentioned Rollini, thus missing a chance for extra publicity. *Billboard* listed both sides of the record in their March issue.

In April, Adrian and Dixie celebrated their twentieth wedding anniversary in the bridal suite of the President Hotel in Atlantic City. They must have recalled the days when they came to London and spent several months there, paid from Adrian's excellent income.

Little is known about the summer months. On 30 June Adrian played at the swank "21" Club at the request of Gilbert Kahn, elder brother of Roger Wolfe, both sons of banker Otto Kahn. Gilbert had followed into his father's footsteps as a banker, but in his younger days he played saxophone and had once worked with the California Ramblers. The day after the performance, Kahn's secretary sent Rollini $300 and wrote how much Mrs. Kahn enjoyed the music. In early August Rollini participated in another Paul Whiteman broadcast. This was contracted by his agent Alex Kolensky, who worked at the Columbia Entertainment Bureau.[29] Whiteman hosted a short series of shows, which he called *On Stage America*. The show was a platform to present young talent (but not only young) to the radio audience. Whiteman would soon move to television, which gave him greater opportunities.

During the 1948 hurricane season, Florida experienced its most severe hurricane since 1935. In September 1948 Adrian Rollini's Driftwood Lodge was hit, but the damage mostly concerned its pier, which practically disappeared. So a new one was built and Adrian decided to give it a T-shape instead of the original I-shape, thus allowing for more comfortable mooring.

From 10 November Adrian worked at the Town House in Utica for a few weeks, which advertised his act as usual as "The Biggest Little Band in The World." Advertising stopped at the end of the month and in January 1949 Adrian left for Florida. The Driftwood Lodge now had accommodation for sixteen people, three boats, and a boat captain. His brother Art joined him on the trip, which they made by train, in which they had a compartment for a good rest. Art remembered the good meals that were prepared by Dixie and how he would sometimes go to their wine cellar and get a bottle. He would fish off

Al Perlis completed the Trio.

Adrian's dock. A sixty-meter walkway led to it. After ten days Art returned to New York, completely relaxed.[30]

In May 1949, Adrian was back at the Town House for another engagement of a few weeks. In August he celebrated the twelfth anniversary of his Trio while working in New York's Park Sheraton, the former Park Central Hotel. Vincent Lopez's congratulations came in via a telegram. At the Park Sheraton guitar player Fred Sharp was out, so Adrian needed a replacement. It seemed that piano player Anita Palmer joined Adrian for a while, but what Adrian really needed was another guitar player.[31]

Alexander "Al" Perlis took Sharp's place. Perlis was born in 1914 and worked with Rollini off and on from 1947 until 1950, at first alternating with Sharp. He had experience from Will Bradley's big band when he gave a demonstration of his talent at Rollini's White Way Music Shop. He was hired at $140 a week.

It was now becoming noticeable that Rollini was taking his music less seriously than before. Just like his predecessors, Perlis had to learn Rollini's band book, but both he and Sharp said in interviews that Trio rehearsals were becoming rare and Rollini's drinking habit was growing. He would drink a quart a day (about one liter). "There were times when he would go on the wagon, as we should say, quit drinking . . . but he would not really stop and drink Sauterne, a white wine, instead and mix it with soda."[32] These trends had a negative effect on the Trio's work. A review that Rollini kept in his scrapbook, illustrated the downward trend. It was written by an unknown author, who had come to the Park Sheraton to hear the Trio. A customer's view: "Back in New York before the war, the Adrian Rollini Trio was producing some of the pleasanter sounds around town. These sounds were not sensational. They were just pleasant, which means commercial with a sense of decency and fitness."

For a long time, Adrian was a fixture at the Hotel Piccadilly, but then came the Three Suns and they became the fixture at the Piccadilly:

> thereby once more proving the Bagelian law that corny music drives out music which is not quite as corny. . . . Now he's back in [New York], this time at the Park Sheraton. . . . It's nice that he is still playing some of the things he did at the Piccadilly, but whether he is playing them as pleasantly is something the tricks of memory confuse. Rationality says no, for his two associates, Al Perlis on guitar and George Nyder[33] on bass, don't seem to be in the spirit of the old Rollini idiom. Perlis is just a reasonably deft guitarist and Nyder's approach to the bass is lukewarm. . . . Rollini himself retains his casual charm on the vibes and his more hectic way with the chimes although his ventures on the piano are rather ordinary. But the most dismaying fact about the trio is that it is apparently determined to show it can be as commercially corn-wise as any other trio. . . . This, of course, is the wrong attitude. If you're going to be corny you have to act glad you're corny so the listener will know he, too, is supposed to be glad.[34]

Fred Sharp:

> So, if you heard him in 1944 and 49 [it would] be exactly the same. . . . When Allen Hanlon left the Trio I had to play exactly what Allen played. You could only go so far with Adrian. . . . I might play a solo and stick in a few extra embellishments and after it was over he would say "Why did you screw that second half for?" "Well," I said, "I get tired." "Next time play it as we do." . . . It's what made it musically uninteresting towards the end because there was never any room for development. It had to be the same.[35]

However, the public kept coming to what was consistently announced as "The Famous Adrian Rollini Trio." Also the Trio's broadcasts continued. Transcription services had become a major source for radio programs. In 1948 World Transcriptions, a subsidiary of Decca Records, announced its Feature Library in a full-page advertisement.[36] The Library consisted of twelve shows of 156 broadcasts of fifteen minutes each. One of the twelve shows was called *Vibraphonia* and the performers were the trios of Dardanelle and Rollini, plus guitar player Carl Kress.[37] This suggests more than fifty broadcasts by Rollini alone.

On 23 August 1949, Adrian was working at the Park Sheraton when he was interviewed as the guest in *Luncheon at Sardi's*, a radio show. He told that he had been honored to be the musical director of the entire United States Lines.[38] Also Rollini mentioned his latest song, "God Bless Our President."

The full Trio were the guest stars on 11 December on a "Savings Bonds" broadcast sponsored by the US Treasury Department. Two tunes, "Oya Negra" and "Liza," had been prerecorded and were distributed on sixteen-inch vinylite records, with the note that they should not be played before 4 December 1949. The actual broadcasts would be announced by local newspapers like the *Cortland Tribune*.[39] Broadcasting was a major source of income for Adrian at the time. According to Dixie, he did eight broadcasts a week.[40]

1950: Mercury Releases Rollini's Last 78 rpm Record

With only two tunes issued from the 1947 recording date with Bullet Records, there were still sufficient unissued masters for a new project. This was felt by Mercury, another newcomer in the record business. In December 1947 Mercury announced that it had bought twelve titles from Bullet. The company had plans to issue them both as regular single disks and in the form of a long-playing record, a new medium at the time. In February 1950, Rollini's first Mercury disc was released. *Billboard*'s review called it cocktail music played in a relaxed way. Rollini had long left the forefront of progressive jazz.[41]

On 17 January Adrian, who was working at the Park Sheraton, got a letter from the Veterans Administration thanking him for what his Trio did for their transcription service, that went under the name *Here's to Veterans*. The show had probably been recorded in the first weeks of the year.[42] Al Perlis was on guitar and a George Hnida had been replaced by another bass player.[43]

In February Rollini may already have been in Florida again, but in June he was back for an engagement at the Community Coffee Shop in Binghamton, New York. The local press paid attention and compared Adrian to characters drawn by cartoonist Gluyas Williams: thin moustache and an apologetic facial expression. Asked about his future as a vibraphone player, Rollini told the newspaper man about his Key Largo hotel. No further questions. The interview did not say if Rollini said anything about his White Way Shop on Broadway, another source of income for Dixie and him.

However, the White Way Shop was still in operation. For the daily work at the shop, there was Bill West and whenever she had time, Dixie would be winding mallets. Bill was doing well: George Wettling, a well-known drummer, wrote about the shop's new product, steel drum sticks for drumming practice, made by West himself. Wettling tried them and thought that "they were great and not too heavy. Bill did a lot of experimenting before really putting them on the market. He hit upon an ideal weight, which is six ounces per stick." Wettling named several colleagues who were practicing using the new sticks, drummers such as Louis Bellson, Morey Feld, Gene Krupa, Dick Shanahan, and Dave Tough.[44] Dixie had an administrative task: in a letter to a friend she wrote that she made the income-tax declarations for three businesses (presumably the shop, the lodge, and Adrian's work as bandleader).[45]

During the following months Rollini hopped again from one engagement to another. Such engagements were for two or three weeks. In July he was at Riley's at Saratoga Lake, which was described as one of Northern New York's most beautiful nightclubs, with a large hall where it featured what was called a star-studded Broadway show.[46] The Trio, with Perlis and Hnida present, worked in the Vogue Lounge. Perlis not only played guitar, but now sang as well.

In August it was the Blue Note in Chicago, located at 56 Madison Street, near Dearborn Street.[47] Pay was $825 a week, probably typical at the time. The Blue Note's manager Frank Holzfeind loved jazz, in particular the traditional styles, but he also featured the newer sounds. In the months preceding Rollini, the Blue Note featured great variation in jazz styles, ranging from Art Hodes and George Brunies to Sarah Vaughan and from George Shearing to Louis Armstrong.

In September the Trio worked in Milwaukee, Wisconsin, at the Towne Room.[48] It was owned by Jimmy Fazio, who presented Rollini as his biggest scoop in Milwaukee, a famous Mercury recording artist (Remember "Jazz Me Blues"), coming directly from the Piccadilly Hotel in New York.

A letter that Adrian wrote to a friend on 30 December 1950 suggests that he had had further engagements after Milwaukee, but he complains about his health. He had been ill and out of work for three weeks: bad lungs and a throat complication, many teeth to be pulled and dentures to be made. He wanted to depart for Florida that day, but he delayed it on account of his health.

In 1950 Rollini's known engagements were no longer in New York's top clubs. He had to travel far for a quality location and no engagements in New York are known. However, he still kept his White Way Music Shop in New York as well as his apartment.

1951, 1952, 1953

Having two places to live, Adrian Rollini now followed a pattern of being in Florida in the first half of the year and in New York the second half. It may be assumed that Rollini found work in Florida if he wanted to. He may have played piano, vibraphone, or chimes and he was usually backed by a guitar and a bass. Indeed a few engagements are known, but no certainty exists about anything but piano. Thus in January 1951 he started a four-week engagement at the Miami Beach Athletic Club. It was about seventy miles from Tavernier but Rollini called it "right down near my fishing lodge."[49]

In Tavernier in 1951 the Rollinis were friends with the Wilkinson family. Mrs. K. L. ("K") Wilkinson played an instrument herself and in a letter to Tom Faber she described how she and others would have many a jam session with Adrian. The others were Lee Goodyear, who played saxophone; Mac McKenzie, banjo; and Evelyn Allen, piano.[50]

> We got together in homes as well as in the Driftwood Inn in Tavernier where Dixie and Adrian were running a hotel on the ocean. One place she remembered was the Island House Restaurant, which was run by Italian friends from New Jersey and who had an old upright piano. Many a session we had there and at times gave impromptu "shows" for the tourists who happened by for a meal or a beer.[51]

Some of the Wilkinson group may have worked as members of Rollini's Trio when he had a local engagement. Adrian had asked Allen Hanlon to be his guitar player in Florida, but Hanlon was too busy with TV and radio and stayed up north.[52]

By the summer, Rollini had returned to New York. In June the Adrian Rollini Trio could be found in the Community Coffee Shop in Binghamton, New York; the previous year's performance had been good for a return engagement. The house advertised him, mentioning his coast-to-coast broadcasts "on a nationwide hook-up over a major broadcasting network." It added that it served all legal beverages (a holdover from Prohibition days?).

One more engagement in 1951 is known, before Adrian took to Florida again. That was at the Hotel New Yorker, where the Trio worked in the Terrace Room in October and again in January, and possibly for November and December, too.[53] The hotel's biggest feature was an ice show. The show was run twice each night from Monday till Saturday with a special show for children on Saturday afternoon. Music was first provided by Tommy Reynolds's orchestra and then by Teddy Powell's. The Adrian Rollini Trio played during intermissions. A reviewer enjoyed it and said it was "fast and funny," had "great big splashes of color and enough dare-devil skating to make young and old perch on the edges of their chairs." George Hnida could not make it and was temporarily replaced by Harry Clark. Clark's career had moved along quite well after his Rollini years and he joined Rollini just for kicks. He found that the trio was playing the same songs as before.[54]

In February Adrian was back in Florida, where he enjoyed life as usual. One day he made a fake sound documentary of one of his fishing trips. Rollini kept the recording in his archive and it survives.

He stayed at his lodge for some months and then returned to New York, presumably for only a short time. In July he had a return engagement at the Hotel New Yorker, playing half an hour every night. The hotel's nightclub featured a new skating show, with several acts and most music provided by Ernie Rudy and his Orchestra. No other engagements are known for that year, nor for the first half of 1953, when, as may be assumed, he was in Florida, to be back in New York for another engagement at the Hotel New Yorker, his third.[55] This is his last known engagement in or around New York. The following January Columbia released a 45 rpm record with four 1939 recordings by the Adrian Rollini Trio on its new Epic label.[56] Columbia still had the masters and issued some alternative versions. Rollini's 1947 film shorts were also for sale.[57] Billboard gave the EP a low rating, only 60, while Dave Brubeck's quartet scored 80 points.

1953 was the year Adrian Rollini turned fifty. It was also the year he made his final recording, a transcription recording for World. However, although a New Yorker, he had decided to put his accent on Florida.

1954, 1955

Early in 1954 Rollini had been back in Florida, back at the Driftwood and out of New York's limelight, but in August he returned to New York. A photograph in Rollini's scrapbook tells why. For the first time in about twenty years Rollini was again seriously ill. He had to fight tuberculosis. He was taken into Triboro Hospital in Jamaica, Queens, New York. This was a special hospital for tuberculosis patients.[58] A photograph, said to be the last one taken of Adrian, was taken at the hospital. It is unknown if he did fully recover from his illness before he went back to Florida. At the time tuberculosis usually meant a long recovery process.

Back in Florida, life in Tavernier was not only leisure. He did have engagements in Florida, although only very little information is available. A four-week engagement at Miami's swank Eden Roc Hotel, which started in September 1955, may have been typical.[59] Rollini asked Harry Clark to be his bass player and again Harry agreed to help Adrian out. However, Adrian had another bass player by the name of Harvey Sells, and the two split the work.[60] The hotel was not even fully completed when Adrian started there. It became a favorite of dis-

The last photo of Adrian Rollini, taken at the Triboro Hospital, Jamaica, New York.

tinguished guests, from politicians to Hollywood's top stars. Adrian may have worked in the hotel's Cafe Pompeii, a supper club, or in Harry's American Bar, the hotel's nightclub.

In April 1955 Dixie's mother, Orinda "Peg" Swezey, passed away and, according to Art Rollini, left Dixie $100,000.[61] This may have given her and Adrian the idea to leave New York and make the Driftwood Lodge their permanent home. In later years Dixie stated that they planned to purchase a bar and grill in Tavernier. Indeed, about December 1955 the couple were back in their New York apartment, making preparations to move to Florida. One day they were sorting and weeding out files and tin boxes of papers and records. One of the documents they handled was Adrian's will and Dixie inadvertently tore it in half. It was taped together and put back in its tin box. However, this was to have unpleasant consequences.[62]

1956: Adrian's Death

Now luck was against them. In the first months of 1956 Dixie had tuberculosis and, like Adrian before her, she went to the Triboro Hospital. So Adrian returned to Florida alone with a firm plan to buy another place there. However, in the early summer the plan collapsed.

Adrian Rollini died on Tuesday 15 May 1956. The cause of his death has always been clear. Medical reports give all information. However, the circumstances that led to it have resulted in speculation. Being a well-known personality, his death was news, so newspapers reported about it from the day of the accident that started this sad final chapter of his story. Some official personalities gave their views on what happened, as did a few of Rollini's family members. The various stories are presented here. The reader may draw his own conclusion.

On the evening of 26 April 1956, Adrian had an appointment at the Green Turtle Inn, a restaurant on Islamorada, the first key south of Key Largo, about fifteen miles from the Driftwood.[63] According to Art Rollini, his brother went there to negotiate the purchase of a nightclub:

> He'd already given his deposit, well, he had $1,000 down there. He signed the contract, and was sitting with the owner until closing time, around 2 o'clock in the morning. Adrian stayed when everybody left, he was talking to the former owner. . . . He went out the front door, and inadvertently the former owner turned off the front lights switch and it was a flight of stairs leading out of the place. As Adrian descended the stairs he fell in the dark into a pit of coral rock and one of his legs sustained a compound fracture.[64]

Rollini was found in a car on the parking lot of on 27 April. He had borrowed the car from George Sky, then the manager of Rollini's Driftwood Lodge. A few days after the accident, a newspaper article was published under the heading "Mystery shrouds 'injury' to Rollini, lodge owner."[65] It reported that Rollini had been found sitting in a car by an employee of the Green Turtle Inn at about 5 p.m.[66] The car was covered with blood, both inside and outside and Rollini was severely wounded on his right ankle. The wound was described as "an almost severed right foot." Adrian was rushed back to Tavernier and a stop was made at the "electric building" for medical assistance.[67] Dr. Harvey W. Cohn, a local physician, ordered that Rollini be taken to James Archer Smith Hospital in Homestead, a distance of about sixty miles. He was transported in an ambulance.

Dr. John Burch, an orthopedic surgeon from Miami, performed a long and intricate operation to save Rollini's foot. He reported that Rollini came through the operation well, but that he would have to stay in the hospital for five or six weeks. The article added that no explanation of the cause of the accident had been given.

Dixie was still in New York and just out of Triboro Hospital when she was told about Adrian's accident.

"Preacher" Rollo Laylan, a well-known drummer, lived near Miami and heard the news on the radio that Adrian had been injured. He decided to drive down to the hospital, but was not let in. The police told him that Adrian was sedated. So Rollo called his friend Bill Bags, editor of the *Miami News*. At his suggestion he called the district attorney, who said that "things down there are not like up here. . . . it's a dangerous situation. I will do what I can to investigate to find out."[68]

Fred Cusick, Rollini's former colleague from the earliest California Ramblers days, also tried to find him when, purely by coincidence, he was in the Florida Keys and decided to say hello to Adrian. He found the lodge but no Rollini. Somebody in the house told him that Rollini had been taken to a hospital.[69]

In the Homestead hospital, Rollini got the necessary medical treatment. However, his case turned out to be complicated. Rollini's physician, Dr. Robert Douglas, was quoted as saying "a tremendous number of complications" set in. Dr. Douglas further said that "during the last week of his life Rollini had breathed and been fed artificially. He added that Rollini had a partial stricture of the esophagus and sustained a complete respiratory collapse. The entire chain of physical breakdown was 'triggered' by the damage done to Rollini's leg."

Joseph H. Davis, M.D., was assistant medical examiner at the time. It is the task of the medical examiner to investigate and determine the cause of death of those who die suddenly and unexpectedly or as a result of an injury. In 1987 he wrote a letter to Norman Gentieu about Rollini's death, with the following details of Rollini's hospital days and the autopsy.[70]

Rollini had suffered from tuberculosis in the past. As a result, infected lymph nodes in his mid-chest became scarred and distorted as the process healed.[71] This, in turn, caused an extrinsic narrowing of his mid-esophagus. This was an important factor in his subsequent death. So was his addiction to alcohol. Due to his prior alcoholism, he suffered from delirium tremens and some liver failure.

On Friday 4 May 1956, Rollini had a tracheotomy tube put in place, because he was unable to cough up mucous and had difficulty breathing. Tube feeding also became necessary "due to his altered mental state." This was difficult as a result of the narrowing of his esophagus. It was necessary to use a tube, then in vogue, which had a small latex bag of mercury at the end. This was designed to facilitate passage through small openings.

On Sunday 6 May the bag unfortunately broke while intubation was in progress. Rollini aspirated liquid metallic mercury into the lower lobe of his right lung. This added to his respiratory problems.

Death certificate of Adrian Rollini.

Subsequently, on Wednesday 9 May a tube gastrostomy (direct opening into the stomach) was performed in order to furnish nourishment. In the meantime, his liver was failing due to the prior alcoholic cirrhosis.

Adrian Rollini expired at 1:25 a.m. on Tuesday 15 May 1956. The autopsy was performed at 10:45 that morning. Rollini was found to have a most severe degree of cirrhosis (scarring) of the liver, which also produced a severe degree of ascites (fluid accumulation in the peritoneum). Both lungs were severely involved with bronchopneumonia (infection from inability to cough up secretions). The tuberculosis was no longer active. In the outer perimeter of the lower lobe of the right lung was found a scattering of tiny abscesses surrounding the metallic mercury aspirated some nine days previous.[72]

When he was asked what had happened at the Green Turtle Inn, Rollini had said that he had slipped on a rock, twisted his right foot and broke the ankle. Dr. Davis suspected that his foot was fixed in a hole as Rollini fell over. Reporters were not satisfied with Rollini's explanation and tried to find exactly what brought the injury. However, it was not until 11 May, two weeks after the incident that the Monroe County sheriff's office ordered an investigation. The *Miami Herald* said, "Many rumors surrounded the episode."[73]

On 15 May, the day Rollini died, Sheriff's Deputy Rene Raiole said that the incident had been checked to see if there had been criminal negligence. None was found, he said. Joe Della Sandro, bartender at the inn, had told investigators that he had escorted Rollini to a parked car that night and had walked back to the inn to close up, when he heard Rollini scream for help. The bartender said that he found Rollini beside a little used back road, moaning and screaming for help. There were various theories concerning the accident: Rollini's friends said he might have slammed a car door on his foot. Others theorized that a passing car had rolled over his foot. Based on Rollini's statements, however, Deputy Raiole had concluded that the break was caused by a fall. And he added that the investigation would not have been made normally, but had been launched in the face of rumors.[74]

Shortly after Norman Gentieu's 1988 article in *IAJRC Journal*, Bob Hilbert, another *IAJRC* member, wrote a letter to the magazine about the rumor that circulated among Miami-area musicians. Hilbert had lived in South Florida virtually all of his life. According to him, the common story was that Adrian had tried to open up a bar in the Keys and that the "mob" broke his legs to induce a cut of the profits—or to dissuade him altogether from the endeavor. Hilbert wrote that "during the 1950s, much of Monroe County, which includes the Keys, was regarded as being even more corrupt than Miami. The Keys . . . has an unsavory history (or colorful, take your pick) from Spanish galleon pirate days through wholesale rum-running during Prohibition. . . . The "mob" referred to by local musicians, did not refer to a Godfather maffia, but rather to an entrenched political family that ran Monroe county for decades."[75]

Phil Sillman, who may have been Adrian Rollini's last surviving cousin, confirmed this version of the story, adding details of the "mob." "Adrian was finished off. He carried a cheque worth $35,000 intended to buy a night club on the Keys. The same mob as active on Pelham Parkway, was connected with the mob in the Florida Keys."[76] On an earlier occasion he disagreed with Art Rollini's view and said: "Dixie, Vera, all knew there was no 'flight of stairs' or 'coral pit.'" Sillman urged both Dixie and Vera not to pursue an investigation in view of the possible link to the same bootleggers Rollini had dealt with when he had the California Ramblers Inn in Westchester.[77]

Art Rollini wrote to Norman Gentieu that Adrian's wife Dixie regained the $1,000 contract deposit and, after a thorough investigation, the insurance company awarded her double indemnity.[78]

Adrian's Funeral

According to the *Miami Herald* of 16 May 1956, the Branam Funeral Home would be in charge and Rollini's body would be at Branam Chapel from 8:00 a.m. to 5:00 p.m. that day. The list of people who paid respects to Adrian in Homestead is incomplete and contains only ten names. It shows only one name of a well-known musician and that was Phil Napoleon, who had visited Adrian in the hospital just before he died.[79] The others were local friends.

Following this, Rollini's body was taken to New York, where services were in the Walter B. Cook Funeral Home in New York. About forty people paid respects to Adrian there. From the world of music were only trumpet player Billy Butterfield and bandleader Joe Candullo and his wife. Family members both from the Rollini side and from the Augenti side were present, and, as in Florida, most visitors were friends. Rollini had a religious funeral service and visitors received a memory card.

Adrian Rollini was buried at Kensico Cemetery at Valhalla, Westchester County, New York. The precise location is Lot 8429, Section #14 (3-C-1).

Adrian's Last Will and Dixie's Final Years

After Adrian's death, his will was probated; his brother Art and sister Vera were sent waivers to sign, and both signed. However, in as much as the will had been torn in half, the court ruled that the brother and sister would have to sign a second waiver, with the knowledge that the will was torn. However, now Art and Vera refused to sign. According to Art, Vera decided to take Dixie to court and he was asked by Vera to come to the courthouse. She had an attorney by the name of Wolfe and brought in a character witness by the name of Benny Morrell, who claimed to be close to the Rollini family. The judge ruled in favor of Dixie. Vera lost her case.[80]

The White Way Music Shop was sold to Bill West. Phil Sillman went into a partnership with West, but he had to use attorney Wolfe to get out of the mess he felt West had cheated him in.[81] Sillman lost his investment money, a few thousand dollars, which was meant as West's final payment to Dixie. Wolfe felt sorry for Sillman and waived his fee.[82]

Although the life in Florida and the Driftwood Lodge had been a pleasure, it had primarily been Adrian's choice. Boating and fishing had been his life's hobby and now that he had passed, and with the memory of the accident fresh in her mind, Dixie preferred New York. She kept the apartment at 17 W. 64th Street until September 1956 and then moved in with her friend Ruth Baer at 205 Gordon Avenue in Totowa, New Jersey.[83] Baer had an upstairs apartment built by her relatives Pat and Vincent Massaro. Here Dixie stayed for twenty months. In 1958 she made a trip to Driftwood and after her return found an apartment on Long Island at 62–82 Saunders Street, Rego Park, Queens. From 1963 until 1974 Dixie worked in a thrift shop for the benefit of the church. In her final years, she could only walk with a cane and hardly left home. She could rely on friends to take her out, such as the Michalskys, Peggy and Mike. Peggy had been a fan of Adrian's Trio in the forties, and after his death she became Dixie's close friend. Another was Arthur Nando "Art" Rollini (1941), son of Adrian's brother. They would go to see various sports, like basketball and wrestling. It struck Art that she knew many well-known personalities, like Ed Sullivan and Jack Dempsey.[84] She also remained in contact with friends in Florida, such as "K" Wilkinson.

The Driftwood Lodge slowly deteriorated, until in 1960 Hurricane Donna finished it off. The property was acquired by a family from Hialeah, near Miami. In 2003 it was owned by Island Escapes LLC. The company had a 2,800-square-foot area cleared to make place for an oceanfront single-family home.[85]

In the seventies, long after she sold the drum shop, Dixie was still making mallets for a few customers. One of these was Red Norvo. She passed away, aged seventy-two years, on 13 December 1977, after she had developed diabetes, spinal arthritis, and other diseases.[86] She survived her husband Adrian by twenty-one years. Most of her heritage, including Adrian's photos and records, went to Peggy Michalsky. In 1974 both Vera and her husband George Hnida passed away.

Art Rollini survived his brother for a long time, until 1993. His first wife Ena Kelsall passed away in 1977, his second wife Elizabeth Buley in 2008. Dixie's brother, George Minot Remer, passed away in 1997, having survived his wife Noeline Rose Remer. With George Minot, the last of the brothers and sisters of Adrian and Dixie had gone. However, the Rollini dynasty continues and has produced a successful musician and author, by the name of Arthur Nando Rollini.

Appendix 1

ADRIAN ROLLINI'S INSTRUMENTS

During his life Adrian Rollini owned many instruments and this appendix presents their story, as far as known.

Alto saxophone

After Adrian had mastered the bass saxophone, he bought a Conn alto saxophone, which he gave to his sister Vera. Vera's school study was at Stamford, Connecticut, where she completed the last two years playing Adrian's Conn alto sax in the school band and at sorority dances. When Vera graduated, her brother Art had just entered high school and he received the alto sax for a short period of time, until Adrian took it back and gave him a Buescher soprano.[1]

Bass saxophone

The following is a collection of bits and pieces from several interviews. The story of Adrian Rollini's bass saxophones is one of confusion and it seems to be impossible to get the full picture.

Adrian Rollini owned at least four bass saxophones and probably five, all Conns.[2] His first one, which he bought in 1922, was secondhand and nickel-plated. This was the instrument on which he taught himself how to play bass saxophone. In a 1925 advertisement he mentioned that he moved to Conn "three years ago."[3]

How long he used it is unknown, but by the end of 1923, he used a new Conn instrument, with which he was pictured as a member of the large orchestra that opened the Hippodrome in December.

His third was a 1927 model, which he bought new in that year. It was gold-plated and he used it with the New Yorkers in 1927. It was designed to allow $E\flat$, but Rollini managed to play higher notes on it.[4] In 1928, when he met Jean Robert in Ostend, Belgium, he had "the latest Conn production version, allowing him to play high E and high F." He showed Robert that he would take an ivory piano key plate, a small, wide type, from a pocket in his jacket. He would push this piece between his reed and the rails, thus bending the reed down to give it more tension while playing. He would repeat this for every solo.[5]

When he worked with Fred Elizalde, Rollini bought a new model, his fourth, during his 1929 return to the United States.[6] This one was silver-plated with gold inside the bell.

When in 1931 his bass saxophone toppled over on the bandstand, Adrian said to his brother, "Don't worry, kid, I have a spare."[7] As Art remembered, Adrian had a nickel-plated Conn horn as a backup when his normal instrument was in a shop for repair. Its sound was dull in comparison. It may have been the second-hand bass saxophone, the first one he bought.[8]

According to his brother Art, Adrian used Vandoren reeds exclusively: "He would never try them out on his saxophone but he would put his reeds on his mouthpiece when he was in the dressing room and he would get the right pressure in his mouth, just for the mouthpiece and reed and he'd go up in the bandstand and play beautifully without the horn!"[9]

Adrian had several modifications made to his bass saxophone before he was satisfied with it. First of all, he used a Conn stock baritone saxophone mouthpiece instead of the standard bass saxophone mouthpiece. He did not rebore this and faced it himself, using emery paper. Then he had a special neck made for it, to achieve a 440 pitch, which the original neck did not give him.[10]

In a letter to Tom Faber, Art wrote that Adrian had a half-dollar silver coin soldered under the thumb key (octave key) of his saxophone to reduce wear.[11] He also used a piano wire as a spring on his high D key. Adrian claimed that without it, the high D key would open slightly and cause a leak when he played the low notes.[12] Adrian told his brother not to use the side D key on the alto saxophone when playing middle D, but to use the right-hand D an octave lower, as he himself did on the bass saxophone.[13] Art remembered that Adrian could play up to high G, but did not know if he could do high E.[14]

To hold his saxophone, Adrian Rollini used a harness, which he wore under his jacket. This allowed him to stand up for a solo. The harness was made of heavy canvas, about ten to twelve inches wide, reinforced with leather where the hook extended.[15] While he was sitting, Adrian might be seen tapping both feet simultaneously.[16]

In March 1945, Adrian's brother Art got an engagement to play with Paul Whiteman on the *Philco Hall of Fame* show. He would stay for about three years. Art was primarily a tenor saxophone player, but Whiteman wanted him to double on bass saxophone (as well as on clarinet, flute, and bass clarinet). So Art borrowed his brother's bass saxophone, but he could not work with Adrian's mouthpiece, a Conn stock baritone mouthpiece.[17] Adrian's dog had chewed a part of its tip. Art thought that it was steel that Adrian's dentist used as an inlay repair job. Therefore, Art used a long, thin Brilhart baritone mouthpiece with baritone reeds.[18]

Adrian may have had it back from his brother when, around 1953, he loaned it to Peter Wells, a famed cartoonist and member of an amateur jazz band, the Overweight Eight ("all advertising men"). Adrian's friend Neil Waterman was a member of this band and introduced Peter to Adrian.[19]

Art Rollini last used Adrian's instrument on a Patti Page TV show in 1958, and then stored it in his garage, where it stood deteriorating. The canvas bag was in shreds and the pads had mostly fallen off. Art tried to sell it locally on Long Island, but found no interest from any Long Island store. Around 1970, Vera took it to Manny's Music Store, 156 W. 48th St. in New York City, and sold it for $150. Art: "It was a silver plated instrument. He had the gold-plated one previously."[20] Tom Faber visited Manny's around 1983 and was told that this particular bass saxophone was finally sold, after repair, to Garth Hudson, a musician of The Band, a rock music group. When asked by John Morphew in August 1984, Hudson told him that he just wanted to have a bass saxophone and that he had no interest in this particular instrument. He had lent it to Howard L. Johnson, another musician. Hudson is the last person known to have played on Rollini's 1927 bass saxophone.[21] In 2014 this saxophone was in Bill Cole's repair shop for musical instruments, at 47 Phila St., Saratoga Springs, New York. Cole had it in maintenance and storage for Hudson, not for sale. In an email to the author, Cole said: "I have worked on it over the years for Garth especially when he used it for recording. However, it has remained idle in my shop for years. It is a Wurlitzer 'American' Bass Sax most likely made by Conn. Serial # is 90715."[22]

Joe Rushton received Adrian's mouthpiece, a Conn baritone ebonite "Steelay," from Dixie Rollini.[23] Rushton worked with Red Nichols's postwar Five Pennies for many years, and owned two bass saxophones, which he called "Beatrice" and "Buster." It has been suggested that Rushton bought Buster from Adrian around 1943. Before he went fully into music Joe worked for Trans World Airlines, and the story goes that Joe's widow sold Buster to a TWA pilot, a lifelong friend of Joe's, when Joe died. This pilot sold it to another person who, in turn, offered it on eBay in 2000 for $8,300 with an email address. In 2013 an email to him could not be delivered.

When Tom Faber visited player John Dengler, who lived in Fort Lauderdale, Florida, John showed him his bass saxophone. He bought it from Joe Rushton's widow Priscilla. This was the instrument that Joe had called "Beatrice." It was numbered B123388L.[24] It was a nickel-plated 1923 Conn with a gold-plated neck of a different make, which according to John, was specially designed by Adrian on Joe Rushton's request.

When Adrian was in the Netherlands in 1929, he played on Max Goyarts's bass saxophone. This may have been the instrument that was sold back to Rossmeissl later on, the shop Goyarts bought it from. Rossmeissl then sold it, a 1927 Conn, to Dutch saxophone player Frits Katee in 1978. Katee traded it to Tom Faber in 1980. It had serial number B200622L and featured a gold-plated inside bell.[25]

In such cases, Rollini used his own mouthpiece, which he had with him when he traveled. In 1931, when he traveled with Bert Lown's band, his bass saxophone was so badly damaged during a train trip that he could not use it. Fortunately, another instrument could be borrowed from a local high school and Rollini was able to use it with his own mouthpiece. Also in The Hague, the Netherlands, and in Berlin, Germany, while he was on holiday, Rollini used his own mouthpiece when he occasionally played on somebody else's bass saxophone.

There are more stories about Adrian Rollini's bass saxophones. The following one sounds authentic and suggests that Adrian had a second bass saxophone, after he had lent one to Art. Reed player Kenny Davern told a story on how he acquired a pad from Rollini's bass saxophone. This was around 1951, when Davern went to see Freddie Davis to have his clarinet repaired. Davis had an instrument repair shop at 117 West 48th Street, 7th floor, in New York City. Here Davern saw an enormous silver-plated bass saxophone. He asked whose saxophone it was. Davis told him that it was Rollini's and that he was overhauling it, since Adrian had sold it to someone from the Smithsonian Institution. Davis was replacing the pads and throwing the original pads away. They were white kid leather. Davern asked if he could have one and chose the middle G pad, "the one that really gets played." It was heated out for him with the original brown shellac on the back. That night he snuck his mother's car keys and drove to the Hotel New Yorker, where Adrian was playing with the trio. Adrian signed the pad for him: "To Kenny, sincerely, Adrian."[26]

British saxophone player Harry Gold claimed that he owned a Buescher bass saxophone that once belonged to Adrian Rollini, but later he admitted that this was a bluff.[27]

Celeste

Adrian's friend Neil Waterman bought what probably was Adrian's first celeste from him one evening in 1927 at the Club New Yorker. Adrian then bought a new one. Neil kept the old one and on 17 July 1982, he handed it over to Tom Faber (Tom's interview of that day).[28] Tom gave it to Art Rollini, the son of Adrian's brother.

Goofus

Through the years Adrian used more than one goofus. Ed Kirkeby remembered: "It kept us spending plenty of money for imports of cuesnophones from France because they'd go out of tune very quickly."[29] One goofus that Adrian had used in Europe stayed there after his return to New York. In 1983 it was owned by John Morphew.[30] The goofus that Adrian brought back from Europe may have been the last one that he bought. It was given by Dixie to Adrian's friend Neil Waterman; on 17 July 1982 he handed it over to Tom Faber (Tom's interview of that day). Waterman actually played it on Christmas Eve in 1975. In 2006 the author was pictured with it, before it was donated by Willy Faber, Tom's widow, to the Jazz Archive at Rutgers University, New Jersey, the following year.

Rollini hardly had any followers on this instrument. Fletcher Henderson's Don Redman featured it on several recordings between August 1924 and December 1925, and there is an unknown goofus player with the Original Wolverines (Chicago, 24 May 1928). British examples are "Yiddisher Charleston" by the Gilt-Edged Four (Al Starita solo, September 1927), Five Omega Collegians (George Scott-Wood solo, January/February 1928), and "Happy Feet" by Harry Hudson's Melody Men (unknown soloist, September 1930).

Harpaphone

This is a member of the large family of percussion instruments that included the vibraphone and the xylophone. Rollini may have played it while he worked with Fred Elizalde's orchestra. A picture of the band shows Rollini with two instruments, one of which might be a harpaphone or a xylophone, the other a vibraphone.

Hot fountain pen

After Adrian's death, a box with "fountain pens," as Adrian called them, was given by Dixie to Adrian's friend Neil Waterman.

> I don't think that I ever had the original "fountain pen," that was the final improvement that he made, which was much smaller than any of the ones that I had and those were given to a friend who had great interest in these small reed instruments and gradually they got out of circulation, for which I am sorry. (Waterman interview by Tom Faber on 17 July 1982)

Rollini hardly had any followers on this instrument. A rare example is the 1929 UK recording of "Deep Hollow" by the New Mayfair Dance Orchestra (His Master's Voice B5632). A solo is played by someone who could be Laurie Payne, brother of trumpet player Norman Payne, or Jack Miranda or even someone else.

Piano

Adrian's first instrument was a piano, which he played at his parents' home. In later life Adrian usually had a piano at home, both in New York and in Florida. In the early fifties in New York he sold his piano to his brother for $450 at a time when he needed money. This instrument had special strings attached, installed by Sohmer, when he bought it.[31] No pictures exist and nothing else is known about this (these) instrument(s).

Soprano saxophone

When Adrian took his alto saxophone back from Arthur, he gave him a curved Buescher soprano saxophone, which he had bought at the same time as his alto saxophone.[32]

Trombone

Adrian never owned a trombone, but he played second trombone parts with the Bert Lown band at the Park Central.[33] He played them on bass saxophone.

Vibraphone

Adrian is pictured in Fred Elizalde's band with two instruments that look like a vibraphone, but only one is. The other is a xylophone or a harpaphone, which has no vibration. On one Elizalde title, "Laughing Marionette," Rollini recorded on both instruments, probably the instruments in the photograph.

From 1930 Rollini played the vibraphone as his standard second instrument and from 1938 as his main instrument. With Bert Lown and Richard Himber he can be heard playing it on many recordings. Photographs with the orchestras of Bert Lown and Richard Himber show him with a simple instrument.

Those early vibraphones were hardly impressive, and when Adrian worked with his Trio, he wanted one that he could show off. He found it with Deagan.

The first one had a dark color. The looks of the Trio further improved when Rollini decided that all its instruments should be white.

The Deagan was a creation of Clair Omar Musser, who has been called the "Father of the modern vibraharp" (as Deagan called it).[34] The Deagan vibraharp was given to Adrian by the company.

Tom Faber thought that he had seen it in "the former apartment of Art N. Rollini, when I visited him years ago, long before he got married."[35]

Peggy Michalsky, Dixie's close friend in her final years, said that Adrian's vibraharp had been sold by Dixie after Adrian's death after it had been in storage for a while.

Xylophone

Adrian played xylophone with his junior band and when he joined the California Ramblers in 1922. His xylophone work would be recorded at various times (and probably on different instruments) over more than ten years. The only photograph might be with Fred Elizalde's orchestra, mentioned under "Vibraphone."

Appendix 2

ENGAGEMENTS WITHOUT DEFINITE DATES

Some engagements by the Adrian Rollini Trio are known without a definite date:

- * Baltimore, Doc's Cocktail Lounge
- * Boston, Eliot Lounge
- * Dallas, Texas, downtown, Majestic Theater
- * Detroit, Michigan, The Bowery
- * New York, Victoria Hotel
- * Washington, 5 O'Clock Club
- * West Springfield, Massachusetts, Wayside

The Paterson engagement was mentioned in Ruth Bear's letter to Tom Faber of 16 May 1983.

The Dallas engagement, said to be 1946, was mentioned in *The Saga of the Bass Saxophone*, by Jim Cullum Jr.

Baltimore: Doc's Cocktail Lounge at 1817 N. Charles Street. Adrian was advertised as "The King Is with Us"; others in the show, at various times, were Dolly "Cherub" Mitchell, the Owens Sisters, Slim Gaillard, and Warren Phillips.

Remainder listed in Adrian Rollini's nutshell biography.

Appendix 3

FILMOGRAPHY

February 1927: **Sylvester Ahola's silent 16mm home movies** (10:52). Locations Newark, Boston; Adrian Rollini and other California Ramblers.

October 1927: **Sylvester Ahola's silent 16mm home movies**. New York; outside Club New Yorker.

1928: **The Sugar Step** (10 min.). Phonofilm. London. Fred Elizalde and his Orchestra; Chelsea Quealey solos, two dancers demonstrate how to dance to Elizalde's composition.

1928?: **Christmas Fantasy**. London; Fred Elizalde and his Orchestra. No further information.

August 1929; **Adrian Rollini's silent home movies** (25 min.). The Hague, etc.; Ramblers Dance Orchestra? Films are lost.

May 1930: **The Woman He Scorned** (1 hr. 29 min.; 8 min. of music); dir. Paul Czinner. London; Fred Elizalde and his Orchestra off-screen. Various tunes. Starring Pola Negri who playbacks one song.

1931: **Secrets of a Secretary** (1 hr. 5 min.). Dir. George Abbott. New York; Bert Lown Orchestra. Starring Claudette Colbert. Paramount Publix.

March 1931; **Bert Lown's silent home movies**. New York; films lost?

1934: **Richard Himber and His Orchestra** (9:38). Vitaphone 1758; dir. Roy Mack (announcer introduces film as "Richard Himber and the Champions"). Brooklyn; Richard Himber Orchestra, Adrian Rollini Trio. Tunes: 1. "It Isn't Fair" (Nash vocal solo); 2. "Jig Time" (solos for tpt by Sammy Weinstock?, clt by Artie

Shaw [performed on film by Arnold Brilhart], tenor sax by Hymie Wolfson); 3. "Chanson Bohemienne" (waltz, Himber violin solo); 4. "Tea at the Ritz" (Nash vocal solo); 5. "The Cariamba" (dancing couple Miss Bernhardt and Mr. Graham). Virginia MacNaughton, ballet dancer. Trumpets from left probably Ruby Weinstein and possibly Manny Weinstock (solo); trombone probably Jack Jenney; reeds Arnold Brilhart performs clarinet solo on screen, sound is by Artie Shaw; to Brilhart's left unidentified; to his right Hymie Wolfson; unidentified piano and string bass; Gene Van Hallberg accordion; Ernie Capozzi guitar; Nat Levine drums; Verlye Miles harp; Vladimir Selinsky violin to the right, Izzy Zir violin to the right; Abe Borodin cello; Kal Katz violin.

1935: **The Magic of Music** (10:01). U.M.&M TV Corp. Dir. Fred Waller. New York; Richard Himber & his Orchestra; Eddie Steinberg, piano; unidentified, vocal; Morey Samuel, trombone; unidentified, trumpet; Harry Patent, string bass; Ernest Capozzi, guitar; Nat Levine, drums; Gene Van Hallberg, accordion; Adrian Rollini; two unidentified, reeds; Phil Cole, alto sax; violins from left Kal Katz, Isodore (Izzy) Zir, unidentified, unidentified. Vocalist Sugar Cane, above band.

August 1936: **Song Hits on Parade** (4:47). Paramount; dir. Fred Waller. New York; Fred Rich and his Orchestra, Adrian Rollini bass saxophone, Jerry Colonna, trombone; George Wettling, drums; Fanfare, segue to "Happy Days Are Here Again"; "Cross Patch" (Blue Flames vocal); "I Can't Escape From You" (Jerry Cooper, vocal), "You Can't Pull the Wool over My Eyes"; "Until Today" (Bunny Berigan, trumpet and vocal); "These Foolish Things" (Benay Venuta, vocal); "Tiger Rag" (trombone and tenor sax solo).

1938: **Star Reporter #3** (2:10). Paramount; dir. Fred Waller. (Extra material from **Song Hits on Parade**.) New York; Fred Rich and his Orchestra; "Take My Heart." Features Jerry Colonna and Bunny Berigan.

1938: **Himber Harmonies** (10:32). U.M.&M TV Corp. Dir. Leslie Roush. New York; Richard Himber & his Orchestra, Adrian Rollini Trio (Haig Stephens, bass; Frank Victor, guitar), Wladimir Selinsky String Quartet. Tunes: "Sound Your 'A'"; "This Is My My True Confessions," vocal Alice Marion; "St. Louis Blues" (orch, Wladimir Selinsky Trio, Adrian Rollini Trio inserting Rollini composition "Preparation," Quartet); "Blossoms of Broadway," Stuart Allen vocal, Jack Jenney, trombone solo.

1939: **Jerry Livingston and His Talk of the Town Music.** Vitaphone B201 Melody Masters #9; dir. Lloyd French. New York; Adrian Rollini Trio: "It's the Talk of the Town"/"I Wanna Go Back to Bali"/"It's My Night to Shine"/"Chinatown, My Chinatown"/"I'm Just a Jitterbug"/"Avalon"; unknown; Jack and Jane Boyle, Barbara Richards.

1939: Swing Styles (10:43). Vitaphone B260? Dir. Lloyd French. New York; Adrian Rollini Trio (Rollini, Harry Clark, Frank Victor); "Diga Diga Doo" (Tito and his Swingtette); "Limehouse Blues" (Adrian Rollini Trio w/Rollini vibes, chimes); "Pagan Love Song," Milt Herth Trio (Frank Froeba?, p; Jack Connor, d); "It Had to Be You" (Frazee Sisters, Ruth and Jane); "Runnin' Wild: by all plus dancing couple Charles Troy and Joe Lind and minus Frazee Sisters; Tito and his Swingtette, Milt Herth Trio, Frazee Sisters (Ruth and Jane), voc, Charles Troy & Joe Lind, dancers.

1940s: Adrian's silent home movies (25 min). New York; Adrian and Art's family, scenes of Trio, Dixie dancing, etc.

late 1948: Video Varieties. Dir. Leonard Anderson? New York; Adrian Rollini Trio (George Hnida, bass; Allen Hanlon, guitar); seven shorts about 2:40 each: "Dark Eyes"; "Minuet in Jazz"; "Girl with the Light Blue Hair" (Rollini also plays chimes); "Loch Lomond"; "Blue Danube"; "Minute Waltz" (Rollini unaccompanied piano); "Martha."

Appendix 4

ADRIAN ROLLINI COMPOSITIONS

The following compositions often were cooperative works by Adrian Rollini and one or more others.

Before 1930 Adrian Rollini only rarely made a gramophone record with a composition of his own. Those that are known are indicated with *. Some of these exist as broadcasts or on transcription records.

One early composition in this list was never recorded by Rollini: "Down by the Congo." It was recorded by Bob Haring's orchestra in May 1928.

Au Revoir
Chime Time
Daisie
Dixie*
Dixie Stomp*
Down by the Congo
Driftin'
Gliding Ghost
God Bless Our President
Heart Breaking Baby*
Honky Tonk Donkey
I Know What It Means*
I Like What You Like*
Jitters
Lessons in Love
Lightly and Politely

Mello as a 'Cello
Nonchalance
Nothing but Notes
On Edge
Preparation
Rebound
Remember the Night*
She's Not Too Hot, Not Too Cold*
Stuff, Etc.
Swing Low
Tap Room Blues
Tap Room Swing
This Lonely Night
Vibraphonia
Vibraphonia No. 2
Vibrollini

Appendix 5

ADRIAN ROLLINI RECORDINGS ISSUED ON CD

With the California Ramblers and small groups 1923–27

Columbia recordings	Timeless CBC 1-053
Edison recordings	Retrieval RTR79067, Document DOCD-1104
Pathé and Plaza labels	Timeless CBC 1-090
as by the Goofus Five	Timeless CBC 1-017, 1-042
as by the Little Ramblers	Timeless CBC 1-037
as by University Six	Retrieval RTR79047
as by the Varsity Eight	Timeless CBC 1-062

Freelance recordings 1927

with Red Nichols	Jazz Oracle BDW8062, 8063
with Joe Venuti	Mosaic MD8-213
with Bix Beiderbecke and Frank Trumbauer	Mosaic MD7-211

With Fred Elizalde 1928–29:

Retrieval RTR79011

With Bert Lown 1929–31:

TOM mb105

Freelance recordings 1929–30

with Red Nichols	Jazz Oracle BDW8062, 8063
with Cornell and Rube Bloom	Timeless CBC 1-081
with Jack Purvis	Jazz Oracle BDW8035
with Ben Selvin, Tom Clines, etc.	Jazz Oracle BDW8050, Rivermont BSW1169

With his own groups 1933–38

Adrian Rollini's Orchestra	Jazz Oracle BDW8050
leading several groups	Retrieval RTR79042, 79046

Note: A few CDs are omitted that feature only one or two Rollini recordings.

NOTES

Introduction

1. Rex Stewart (*Jazz Masters from the Thirties*, 1972) mentions Hawkins's adulation of Rollini and adds that he admired his hot bass licks whenever they would meet at one of their sessions together. From 1923 till 1928 Hawkins sometimes recorded on bass saxophone.

2. Otto Hardwick (1904–1970) continued the sound with Duke Ellington's band, but his main instrument was the alto saxophone. Boyd Raeburn played bass saxophone with his own band. Also in newer jazz styles, such as free jazz, some musicians would use the bass saxophone but not as consistently and as prominently as when Rollini started it. Some names are Hamiet Bluiett, Anthony Braxton, and Roscoe Mitchell. Presently Vince Giordano, Scott Robinson, and, in Europe, Attilla Korb, Frans Sjöstrom, and others come close to Rollini's original sound.

3. Raymond Horricks, in his Gerry Mulligan biography, quotes Mulligan: "I realized the influence later. For what Rollini did with that horn melodically was beautiful. He approached it in a linear way. . . . When I heard those records again I was stunned." Mulligan once joked about Rollini saying, "By the way, Adrian Rollini is playing baritone for me tonight." This was in 1958 at the first Monterey Jazz Festival in 1958, but Rollini had been dead for two years and Mulligan played the baritone himself.

4. Garvin Bushell's autobiography *Jazz from the Beginning*, 74. Bushell recorded with Perry Bradford, Sam Wooding, Johnny Dunn, Fats Waller, Bessie Smith, Cab Calloway, and even with John Coltrane.

5. Dutch magazine *Rhythme*, 15 November 1952.

6. Letter from Art Rollini to Tom Faber, 30 June 1981.

7. Interview by Tom Faber, 29 July 1983.

8. Interview by Tom Faber, 21 July 1982.

9. Rollini's license for deer hunting. In European measures 178 centimeters and 78.9 kilograms. In later years Adrian dyed his hair black (according to Fred Sharp, Rollini's guitar player in the late forties).

10. He could do certain hand actions equally well with the left and the right hand (letter from Phil Sillman to the author, January 2010).

11. Harry Clark interview by Tom Faber, 12 August 1983.

12. Edited from telephone interview by Tom Faber, 14 July 1982, and letter, 11 January 1983.

13. Interview by Tom Faber, 20 October 1983.

14. Letter to Tom Faber, 16 October 1982.

15. Dick Hill, *Sylvester Ahola: The Gloucester Gabriel*, Scarecrow: London and New Jersey, 1993.

16. Interview by Tom Faber, 27 July 1983.

17. Interview by Tom Faber, 31 July 1983.

18. Interview by Tom Faber, 29 July 1981.

19. Interview by Tom Faber, 11/12 July 1982.

20. Herb Sanford, *The Dorsey Years*, New York, 1972, 18.

21. Interview by Tom Faber, 28 July 1983.

22. Harry Clark interview by Tom Faber, 12 August 1983. Lionel Hampton and Red Norvo played the melody at the inside hammers or only used two hammers.

23. Gene Barras interview by Tom Faber, 11 August 1983.

24. Art Rollini interview by Tom Faber, 12 July 1982. During the war his brand might not be available and Rollini would settle for Lord Calvert, another Canadian whisky. During his years with guitar player Fred Sharp, his brands were Martins V.V.O. and Dewar's White Label.

25. Broadcast interview with Dixie Rollini by Dorothy Day, 28 April 1944.

26. James Lincoln Collier, *Benny Goodman and the Swing Era*, 115.

Chapter 1: The First Rollini Generation Arrives in the USA

1. Letter from Bruce Laue to Art N. Rollini, June 2009. This positions the Rollini migration one generation earlier than Art Rollini Sr. writes in his book *Twenty Years with the Big Bands*, 1.

2. Several French family names may have been the source: Rolin, Rollin, Rollins, Roland, Rolland, Rolins, Roslins, most of which may be preceded by "De." A search (in July 2009) on these names in the French military archive in Vincennes did not yield a potential Rollini forebear. It should be noted that Phil Sillman, a member of the Rollini family, had great doubts about its French background (letter to the author, 10 January 2010).

3. Letter from Bruce Laue to Art N. Rollini, June 2009.

4. Not related to the Grimaldi family, Princes of Monaco.

5. No evidence has been found for the claim that he received the noble title of *barone* in Italy. In a January 2010 letter to the author, Adrian's cousin Phil Sillman wrote that the story was created by Adrian's brother Art in reaction to the information that one of Sillman's ancestors was a Marquis De Lamoricière, who was guillotined at the time of the French Revolution.

6. No paintings by Antonio Rollini are known to exist, but an extensive search might give results.

7. He was not the first Rollini to travel to New York. In 1893 one Lorenzo Rollini had gone before him. Also in 1895 one Cheovolo Rollini arrived in New York. Both were probably unrelated to Ferdinando. Other Rollinis remained in Italy. In 2012 there were at least seventy-four persons by the name Rollini living in Italy (cognomix.it/mappe-dei-cognomi-italiani/).

8. Note from Bruce Laue to the author, 9 October 2011.

9. The Werra was scrapped in Italy in 1903.

10. New York *Evening Telegram*, 6 December 1901.

11. In 1905 inhabitants of New York homes were listed for voting rolls. The Rollinis are listed on page 12 of the Enumeration of the Inhabitants for Election District 16, Block A and Assembly District 27, Borough of Manhattan, County of New York, State of New York on 1 June 1905. They were living at 790 6th Avenue. Listed are:

- Ferdinand, head, aged 38, born in Italy, in the USA for ten years and a citizen, engraver,
- Adele, wife, aged 37, born in Italy, in the USA since age 23 and a citizen,

• Anthony [sic], son, aged 2, born in the USA,
• Christine DeLallo [sic], cousin, aged 30, born in Italy, in the USA for ten years and a citizen.

A family Herhais (?) is shown at the same address, consisting of father (53), mother (45), and four children.

12. Adrian's aunt Lil, on the Augenti side, won a contest to be the first woman to cross the bridge when it was opened in 1909 (Art Rollini, *Thirty Years with the Big Bands*, 2).

13. Interviews, with Art Rollini Sr. on 11–12 June 1982, and with Phil Sillman on 11 June 2005.

14. *Musical Observer*, July 1908, 22.

15. Theodor Leschetizky (1830–1915). "The method he taught was to study of the score in the minutest detail, in order to discover all the implied and hidden meanings and then find a way to their technical solution. The musical ideal for which the technical solution would be found came first. . . . Extensive study of scales, chords and double notes, including octaves, as well as etudes . . . was a prerequisite" (piano player and composer Janos Cegledy on Leschetizky, Wikipedia). Leschetizky promoted the player piano, or pianola, as a musical instrument for the home. He recorded several pieces for the German Welte-Mignon company, which produced so called reproduction rolls. See chapter 2.

16. Leschetizky's method included playing with the wrists in a higher position. Piano player Oscar Levant used it to improve his endurance (Don Rayno, *Paul Whiteman: Pioneer in American Music*, Vol. 2, 250).

17. When she was old enough to leave home, she blonded her hair and changed her name to Chuck Rollins (Phil Sillman interviews by Tom Faber, 11 July 2005 and 29 July 1983).

18. *Musical Observer*, July 1908, 22. This magazine had started in January 1907.

19. Kuhe's "Fra Diavolo Fantasia" was published in 1870. Although forgotten today, Kuhe must have been quite popular in his time, for he wrote hundreds of piano compositions. Many of these were based on well-known pieces by other composers, both earlier and contemporary. Around 1894 he published a book *My Musical Recollections*, which was reprinted in a paperback edition (2008).

20. Clipping from unknown magazine, 27 May 1908.

21. A story goes that Chopin's friend George Sand, when she noticed his great talent, said that he should write a piece for her dog. At once Chopin improvised this happy waltz, which challenges piano virtuosos to play it within a minute, hence its name. A registration exists (from much later date) in which Rollini plays an arranged version of the "Minute Waltz" on piano in two and a half minutes.

22. Art Rollini, *Twenty Years with the Big Bands*, 4. In 1929 Adrian and Art, then with the band of Fred Elizalde, worked for a sound movie with Pola Negri as its female star. Pola Negri wanted to be called Madame Negri, the same name used by Adrian Rollini's private piano teacher of many years. In a letter Art confirmed that both ladies used this name.

23. His income was $400 a week, according to Art Rollini in a letter to his son, 14 February 1986. Ferdinando had other businesses he was involved in, like a furniture polish enterprise that he set up together with his brother-in-law Philip L. Sillman.

24. Art Rollini in *Twenty Years with the Big Bands*, 2–5.

25. The Rollinis also rented a summer house in Emerson, New Jersey (as remembered by Phil Sillman in Tom Faber interview, 29 July 1983 and letter of Phil Sillman, April 1983). Sillman remembered that Rollini had a car in Emerson, a "small jalopy."

26. Art Rollini in *Twenty Years with the Big Bands*, 5.

27. In a 1993 radio interview, Brilhart said he was born in 1904 and started on the saxophone in 1911. The Six Brown Brothers, a saxophone novelty act, were his inspiration. When Spencer Clark later became a member of the California Ramblers, he at first thought that Brilhart was the only trained musician. He did not drink or smoke. Fred Cusick told a story about Brilhart as an electrical engineer. He suggested sticking a wire into a potato to make a rectifier for loading a battery. It worked.

28. "So you want to be a popular musician?" discussion with aspiring young musician Tommy Green, 30 September 1938. Also in Adrian Rollini's brief biography.

29. Interview with Art Rollini Sr. on 11–12 June 1982.

30. Black musicians in New York were still struggling for recognition by then. A breakthrough came with the success of James Reese Europe (1888–1919), a black musician and a son of slaves. His took his orchestra to Carnegie Hall in 1912, recorded for Victor in 1913, and became associated with Irene and Vernon Castle, who were white and taught New York's society to dance the foxtrot.

31. Correspondence from Art Rollini to Tom Faber, 12 April 1981, plus clippings from unknown publication, ca. 1938.

32. Phil Sillman interview by Tom Faber, 29 July 1983.

33. Phil Sillman interview by Tom Faber, 29 July 1983.

34. Letter from Art Rollini to his son, 14 February 1986.

35. Letter from Art Rollini to Tom Faber, 4 December 1981.

36. Art Rollini interview by Tom Faber, 11–12 June 1982. Recent census data mentions eight persons by the name Rose Donah living in the United States.

Chapter 2: Piano Roll Artist

1. Today's equivalent is about $150.

2. Arthur W. J. G. Ord-Hume, in his book *The Pianola* (1984), mentions a surviving Italian instrument built in 1502 and still in working condition and a Dutch instrument built even a hundred years earlier, 9.

3. Ord-Hume, 124.

4. US International Trade Commission instituted investigation No. 332–401, 1998 (cantos.org/Piano/History/marketing.html), and Q. David Bowers, *Encyclopedia of Automatic Musical Instruments*, 1972.

5. Wikipedia; victor-victrola.com/index.html.

6. It had been incorporated on 25 April 1918, but preparations for its public announcement took a year.

7. *Music Trade Review*, 4 May 1918. Capital stock was $100,000 and the incorporators were D. E. Hubner, J. M. Edelson, and B. L. Marks, who were assistants and clerks in the office of Wentworth, Lowenstein & Stern, "and the names of the real directors will be announced when the company is organized."

8. *Music Trade Review*, 12 April 1919. The same issue has a color advertisement: "Zowie! She's launched! The Republic Player Roll—A hand-played singing record." Republic had been building a library of rolls from 1918 and its first announcement concerned some twenty rolls.

9. Founded in 1896 as Kohler & Campbell, it continued manufacturing pianos until well after World War II. In a 1952 article in *Music Trade Review*, the company stated that in its top year (not given) it produced approximately 32,000 pianos and over 50,000 player actions (the roll-playing mechanism in a pianola).

10. Originally piano rolls came only in the form of "instrumental rolls." These were made by copying the notes from a piece of sheet music one by one onto a paper roll. This prototype roll would be played, edited, and corrected to get a master roll. Later, machines were developed that would record a live performance by a capable piano player. The recording would be converted into a test roll and, after correction, into a master roll. Often such actual recordings would be edited to create an even more interesting performance. Such rolls were called "hand-played." Hand-played rolls would play the notes correctly but had little or no extra automatic features such as accentuation or sustaining. When these were added, so-called "expression rolls" and "reproducing rolls" were introduced. Reproducing rolls were reputed to give a real-life impression of the performer.

11. *Music Trade Review*, 19 April 1919, Republic May 1919 releases.

12. Adam Carroll was born in Philadelphia on 19 March 1897 and started playing piano when he was seven. His first professional engagement was accompanying silent movies. From 1916 onward he recorded piano rolls and his name appeared on several labels. In 1923 Paul Whiteman asked him to join his orchestra and he participated in recording a piano duet with Ferde Grofé, Whiteman's standard piano player. The tune was "Someone Loves You After All," issued on Victor 19244. Carroll also worked with Paul Whiteman on several occasions during the 1920s; in 1924 he was a member of the Original Piano Trio consisting of himself, Edgar Fairchild, and Herbert Clare; and he led one of Whiteman's orchestras. During the day he would record rolls and in the evenings he would work for Whiteman. After their years with Republic, Carroll and Delcamp moved to the American Piano Company, maker of the Ampico reproducing roll, which they brought to great popularity. Carroll even recorded duets with Grofé for Ampico. He continued to combine playing in public and recording piano rolls until, by the early thirties, the days of the player piano were over. Carroll then worked as personal pianist for Fred Astaire, and in shows such as Ziegfeld Follies and Eddie Cantor's. He became musical director for Westinghouse doing shows for their dealers and distributors, and had other musical jobs till late in life. In his final years he wrote a short autobiography, which was first published in installments in 1988 in *Amica Bulletin*, the magazine of the International Automatic Musical Instrument Collectors' Association, and then by Amica on their internet website. Carroll died on 28 February 1974 in New York.

13. "Republic player roll artists," *Music Trade Review*, 24 May 1919.

14. "Music of the month," *Music Trade Review*, 26 April 1919.

15. "Prominent composer now a member of recording staff," *Music Trade Review*, 17 May 1919.

16. Another composition by Delcamp was "Swanee Blues," published in 1920, with words by Frank Goodman.

17. *Music Trade Review*, 5 July 1919. The first such roll, the song "Take Your Girlie to the Movies," played the music heard in emotional scenes in movies between the verses of the song.

18. "The mission of the player roll," *Music Trade Review*, 13 March 1920.

19. This was the second time that the brand name DeLuxe was used. It had been used years before by the Philadelphia company where Delcamp and Carroll cut their first rolls. The name

was also used for new rolls in Kohler's program around the Welte standard for reproducing rolls.

20. The American sales potential of Welte's classical roll catalog, available to Kohler with only a small investment, must have been quite tempting. Thus the company started to issue statements about jazz being a thing of the past in favor of classical music.

21. On the same occasion, American Piano Company, maker of Ampico reproducing rolls, agreed to pay royalties for the use of Welte's patents, as did its competitor Aeolian, maker of Duo-Art rolls. *Presto*, 5 February 1920, 8; Bowers, 321. The Welte recording machine was brought to Poughkeepsie, New York, where it was installed in a Kohler plant.

22. There had been an American company by the name Welte; its mother company, the German Welte, lost ownership during World War I. American piano players such as Ford Dabney, James Reese Europe, and George Gershwin made rolls for the American Welte company.

23. This company is famous among lovers of ragtime because it had recorded composer Scott Joplin a few years earlier.

24. There were two songs by this name, the older composed by M. F. Carey in 1900 and the later by Perry Bradford and recorded February 1920 by blues singer Mamie Smith for OKeh Records. Rollini probably performed Bradford's tune. Mamie Smith's record pushed the new market for (vaudeville) blues records.

25. By James F. Hanley and Ballard McDonald, 1919. Recorded by the Kentucky Serenaders in February 1920 for Columbia Records.

26. By Byron Gay and Arnold Johnson, 1919. Recorded by Ted Lewis's Jazz Band in November 1919.

27. Unknown newspaper, probably 13 April 1920.

28. *New York Age*, 24 April 1920.

29. In August 1919 Bernhard Hamblen and in January 1920 Irene D'Giovanni (*Music Trade Review*, 9 August 1919 and 31 January 1920).

30. *Music Trade Review*, 12 June 1920. Also *Presto*, 12 June 1920.

31. Spencer Clark interview by Tom Faber, 21 July 1982.

32. Brooks was the composer of "Some of These Days," made famous by Sophie Tucker, and of "At the Darktown Strutters Ball," played by many jazz bands and one of the first recordings by the Original Dixieland Jazz Band.

33. On 26 June 1966, Carroll dedicated a copy of this roll to collector Mike Montgomery with the words: "To Mike, I'm reminded of my old buddy Adrian Rollini when I hear this recording, Sincerely, Adam Carroll."

34. It struck piano roll expert Robert Perry that the artist mentioned second on a duet roll label usually plays the primo part and the artist mentioned first plays the second part. Also it would seem illogical to feature a new artist in an accompanying role.

35. Respectively MelOdee 3737, Vocalstyle 11719, and QRS 1155.

36. Letter to the author, January 2010, in which Phil only missed a few words. Not bad at all for a ninety-six-year-old! Incidentally this was Rollini's second roll that referred to Prohibition.

37. Records for the entertainment of black people.

38. Other roll interpretations of this song exist, including one by Edythe Baker on MelOdee 3939. She may be the composer of this tune.

39. US International Trade Commission instituted investigation No. 332–401, 1998 (cantos.org/Piano/History/marketing.html).

40. The same tune, but played by Carroll and Delcamp, had been issued in September on the Republic label (Republic 48918). As long as this has not been heard, the possibility exists that the two performances on Republic and DeLuxe are identical but for the Welte codes.

41. This was a new thing for Republic; earlier bulletins did not show portraits of their artists.

42. Charles David Smith and Richard James Howe, *The Welte-Mignon: Its Music and Musicians* (Vestal Press, 1994), 456.

43. QRS 1292 played by Ted Baxter and Max Kortlander.

44. *Music Trade Review*, 11 December 1920, 74.

45. *Presto*, 11 December 1920, 7.

46. *Presto*, 4 December 1920.

47. Actual figures are unknown, but the small number of surviving copies is a good indication. Several rolls seem to be nonexistent today. When asked to estimate the rarity of Rollini's rolls on a scale of 1 (common) to 5 (extremely rare), experienced piano roll collector and researcher Frank Himpsl guessed 4 as an average. In 2012 a total of forty-two copies altogether were known of the thirty-five different rolls Rollini made.

48. *Presto*, 18 December 1920.

49. *Presto*, 25 December 1920.

50. *Music Trade Review*, 20 August 1921, 6 and 22.

51. *Music Trade Review*, 25 November 1922, 10. A year later Art Kahn started making gramophone records with his orchestra.

52. Aeolian was wise enough to also produce gramophone records in order to be less dependent on market developments. Other roll companies did the same, such as Arto and Connorized.

53. As before, Adam Carroll had rolls issued under several pseudonyms. On the Ampico label one of these was Giuseppe Collini, which suggests a reference to Rollini. The tune was "I Hear You Calling Me."

54. Among others, from a letter to Tom Faber, 11 January 1983. Irving Brodsky was born 3 April 1902 and died 7 April 1998.

55. Arto also was in the business of gramophone records and eventually it would issue several that featured Rollini and Brodsky.

56. Two rolls by Brodsky under his Irving Bradley pseudonym were MelOdee 4946, "Pack Up Your Sins and Go to the Devil," and MelOdee 5054, "Waitin' for the Evenin' Mail."

57. Smith & Howe, 963.

58. Smith & Howe list it as played by Adrian Rollini and Nan Foster.

Chapter 3: Ed Kirkeby and the California Ramblers

1. For an account of this development on music and society, see Charters and Kunstadt, *A History of the New York Scene*, 64. Similar changes took place in other metropolises around the world.

2. It is interesting to compare the two recordings of "Tiger Rag" from 1917 (by the original band) and from 1920, when the band had grown to six by adding a saxophone player: tempo down by 15 percent and a clarinet solo added.

3. Most of the following is based on documents from the late Tom Faber's archive.

4. From the undated contract signed by Kitchingman, Duff, and Kirkeby. The idea to use the name of the dancing club "The Ramblers" came from a meeting of Kitchingman, Duff, and a person named Evans. Evans may have been the club's manager or one of the other four musicians. Incidentally, among Kirkeby's papers there is a menu from a restaurant by the name The Ramblers in Mount Pocono, Pennsylvania.

5. An undated text exists (in Kirkeby's papers at Rutgers University) that quotes Ray Kitchingman, the band's original manager, saying that the story goes back to California, where he organized a "novelty orchestra made up in the main of college men, which should compete with the finest dance bands produced on the Pacific Coast." "Striking over Eastward . . . the Ramblers were finally engaged . . . in . . . Atlantic City . . . There they made a huge success, receiving the open admiration . . . among which was [sic] Arnold Johnson's famous band and the Columbia Saxaphone [sic] Sextette." Perhaps Kitchingman or other band members came from the Pacific coast, but there is no evidence of this. The text seems to mix fact with fiction.

6. *New York Clipper*, 7 September 1921. Instruments added by the author.

7. This and further information about Kirkeby's days as a youngster from an interview by Bob Kumm for *Storyville* 13, October 1967.

8. This was the time when Columbia and Victor made the first recordings by the Original Dixieland Jazz Band. Kirkeby was involved in getting the jazz bands of Ted Lewis and Wilbur Sweatman on Columbia (Ed Kirkeby interview by John Steiner, 28 June 1961).

9. First for Emerson, then for Paramount, Arto, Olympic, Vocalion, Gennett, Pathé, and Cardinal. During the thirties Kirkeby gave a personnel list for this band: Pete Brissett and Jack McCann (trumpet), Charlie Randall (trombone), Bill O'Gorman (sax), Ed Sutton (violin), Frank Banta (piano), Paul Primavalli (banjo), Roy Haines (bass trombone), Charlie Bird (drums).

10. Joe Davis Company and his race subsidiary Triangle Music, also Richmond-Robbins and Down South Music Publishing Corporation, Jack Mills's race subsidiary. The Roseland building, located at 1658 Broadway, near 51st Street, was demolished in 1956. The famous Roseland Ballroom was nearby, at 239 W. 52nd St.

11. Some of the artists whose recording careers he steered were Marguerite Matzenauer, a contralto, and Kathleen Parlow, a Canadian violin player.

12. 1140 Broadway, New York. This was a recording location owned by the Wisconsin Chair Corporation, manufacturer of Paramount Records.

13. Undated agreement signed by Kitchingman, Duff, and Kirkeby.

14. Kirkeby also took some members of the Merry Melody Men into his earliest California Ramblers personnel.

15. Kirkeby did not stop his management of singers and continued to make records with artists.

16. To a large extent Whiteman's new sound was due to Ferde Grofé's arranging but also to the playing of Gus Mueller, a reed player who had been a member of the first white band to leave New Orleans for Chicago. Other bandleaders tried to follow Whiteman: Ray Miller and

Paul Specht hired hot players with a New Orleans background for their bands (Tom Brown and Frank Guarante respectively).

17. At some time during these months in 1920, Kirkeby hired a string bass player who was a gypsy and who played entirely by ear. He was replaced by a tuba player when the band recorded.

18. Joe Terres, string bass, has been mentioned in this context (*Record Research* 18, July/August 1958, 7). Eva Schainbaum, who used the stage name Eva Shirley, tried to keep her act classy. When in 1919 she was working with Fid Gordon's five-piece jazz band, a newspaper complimented her that she managed to keep "any rough house business out of her act" (*New York Daily Clipper*, 14 May 1919). At one time, cornet player James "Toots" Mendello was in the group that accompanied her. In February 1923, when she worked in Providence, Rhode Island, Shirley was still using the name California Ramblers for the band that accompanied her act. She died on 20 November 1982 in New York.

19. Located at 1564 Broadway at the corner of 7th Avenue and 47th Street.

20. Paul Whiteman played there from Monday 3 October until Sunday 6 November 1921.

21. It was arranged by his friend Robert Hood Bowers, musical director of the Aeolian Company.

22. Probably Stephen Foster's perennial "My Old Kentucky Home."

23. Other artists included Julius Lenzberg and his orchestra and Sophie Tucker, who was accompanied by piano player Al Siegel.

24. First quote from *Variety*, 16 December 1921. The other four quotes from Ed Kirkeby's scrapbook.

25. *Billboard* had been less positive about Shirley's part of the act at the Palace in a review of a 12 December matinee: "Al Roth and the California Ramblers who were the outstanding bit of the Eva Shirley act" (*Billboard*, 17 December 1921). *The Dramatic Mirror*, 17 December, only had this to say of the act that featured Eva Shirley and Al Roth: "The Ramblers are a nine-piece jazz orchestra that scored a hit."

26. *Billboard*, 17 December 1921: "It was Al Roth and the California Ramblers who were the outstanding hit with Eva Shirley's act, and rightfully so."

27. Agreement signed by seven band members and witness H. H. M. Claskey.

28. For some of the recordings tuba player Pierce was added (*Record Research* 18, July/August 1958, 7).

29. *Music World*, 15 April 1922.

30. The original sheet music of "Sister Kate" contains a special chorus as played by the Original Memphis Five. This little jazz band recorded regularly from August 1921 onward, using the name Original Memphis Five from May 1922.

31. In an August 2010 letter from Mark Berresford to the author, he wrote: "The OM5 story at that time (early-mid 1922) is still very mysterious; the band broke up on the West Coast in 1921 and Mole stayed there for a while, working with Abe Lyman (shame he never recorded with Lyman); Lytell replaced Larry Shields with the ODJB for a while and Jack Roth worked with Durante. It wasn't until c. April 1922 that the band sort of reformed. Prior to that (from January 24, 1922) they had recorded with Leona Williams (albeit without Mole and Lytell)."

32. Kirkeby's papers listed a session on 5 April 1922, by the Original Memphis Five for Arto. Titles were "Bugle Blues" and "Gypsy Blues." Clarinet player Jimmy Lytell and piano player

Frank Signorelli were in this group and were also to be members of the Superior Jazz Band (Brian Rust, *Jazz Records*, 6th edition). Kirkeby continued to contract recording sessions for other artists for a while. Walter C. Allen (*Hendersonia*, 1973) listed sessions for Pathé/Perfect in 1923 and Arto in 1924 in which Fletcher Henderson accompanied black singers Emma Gover, Maggie Jones, and Mattie Hite. No doubt Kirkeby did other sessions with other artists.

Chapter 4: The California Ramblers Taking Off

1. It should be noted that xylophones and banjos were the instruments that recorded best on early recording equipment.

2. *Melody Maker*, 5 December 1936.

3. Interview with Fred Cusick on 27 July 1983. He was born 9 September 1902. In 1941 he stopped playing and became an audio technician.

4. Rector's at Times Square closed down in 1919, hit by a risqué reputation and by Prohibition. Cusick referred to a different Rector's. An article from ca. 1937 mentions that Rollini joined Hand at Rector's.

5. From sleeve notes written by Michael Brooks in 1969, for a Biograph LP. Kirkeby refers to Healy's (96th and Broadway) as the first place he heard Hand's band.

6. The New York Department of State, Division of Corporations has initial DOS filing date 3 May 1923. The *New York Times*, 21 April 1921, in its list of Delaware charters, mentions Kirkeby & Hand, amusement enterprises, $100.000, and gives W. T. Kirkeby, Brooklyn, A. G. Hand, Edwin Kohl, New York as interested parties. It is presently not known who Edwin Kohl was.

7. Hand posed as a society figure and would only deal with the elite in his audience (Spencer Clark interview by Tom Faber, 21 July 1982).

8. *New York Clipper*, April 12, 1922. Adler and Shirley continued their act for a while, but in its issue of 21 July 1922 *Variety* wrote that the California Ramblers gave it extra value. In August 1922 Shirley worked in a show that included black dancer Bill Robinson.

9. Ted Bartell, in a 1973 letter to Ian Crosbie, published in *IAJRC Journal* 45, no. 2 (June 2012), wrote that he knew Moore's father from "the Post Office Band and he was black as coal." Spencer Clark interview by Tom Faber on 21 July 1982, thought that Moore was an octoroon, one-eighth black.

10. Irving Brodsky interview by Tom Faber, 16 July 1982.

11. According to Spencer Clark in an interview by Tom Faber, 21 July 1982,

12. Fred Cusick interview by Tom Faber, 1 July 1983.

13. Three takes were recorded of this tune and apparently all were issued.

14. The earliest were Levy's Trio, Ladd's Black Aces, and the Virginians in March 1922, followed by Jazzbo's Carolina Serenaders and the Original Memphis Five in April. The tune had several revivals.

15. *Variety*, 14 April 1922, reported that "Shanley's opened formally last Saturday with its new dance hall policy patterned after Roseland. The California Ramblers supply the music for the Broadway wing, which is devoted to the dance clearance."

16. 14 April 1922.

17. Paul Whiteman's band was a major example for other orchestra leaders. Whiteman sometimes used two pianos for recording purposes from 1921 on.

18. Novelty Ragtime was a form of piano music which stood between classic piano ragtime and early jazz. It demanded strong technical capabilities from a performer.

19. At least five takes of "Stumbling" were recorded, three of which three issued. They were probably the result of two sessions. For the second session the xylophone work and the piano duet were taken out of the arrangement, so Rollini did not take part.

20. *New York Times*, 19 September 1921.

21. Fred Cusick interview by Tom Faber, 27 July 1983.

22. During the Post Lodge engagement, the band recorded for Arto (5), Cameo (3), Pathé (5), and Vocalion (3).

23. From 1814 until 1830 Belgium and the Netherlands formed one state together.

24. Quoted in *Saxophone Journal*, January/February 1990, in an article by Paul Cohen, saxophone player and music teacher.

25. The full saxophone range today consists of seven instruments, being the contrabass, bass, baritone, tenor, alto, soprano, and sopranino saxophones. The two extremes, contrabass and sopranino saxophones, are rarely used.

26. The result was "The Hula Blues" (Columbia, August 1920). The Benson Orchestra of Chicago was another pioneer orchestra that recorded with bass saxophone as a bass instrument, from September 1920 onward. It was played by William Foeste, in the style of the Six Brown Brothers.

27. As a leader he recorded under his own name and also as Synco Jazz Band and Tampa Blue Jazz Band. Examples of his bass sax work are "Carolina Blues" by the Synco Jazz Band (Pathé, December 1921) and "West Texas Blues" by the Tampa Blue Jazz Band (OKeh, March 1922).

28. Ed Kirkeby interview by the Swedish jazz magazine *Estrad* when he toured Europe with the Deep River Boys, a vocal group he managed.

29. Adrian Rollini interview by Warren Scholl for *Melody Maker*, 28 July 1934.

30. Letter to Tom Faber, 30 June 1981.

31. Dave Robinson, "The Mississippi Rag," December 1991.

32. Letters to Tom Faber, 30 June 1981 and 4 December 1981.

33. Rollini may have played bass saxophone on the Columbia session of 28 April or on the Arto session of 4 May, but listening gives no certainty.

34. Not surprisingly, at this stage Rollini's tone was similar to Joseph Samuels's tone.

35. *Presto*, 25 November 1922, 21, and *Billboard*, 10 December 1922. A few months later Abe Small and His Melody Boys recorded the same arrangement.

36. *Variety*, 24 November 1922. Spelling mistakes such as "saxaphone" not corrected.

37. *Catskill Recorder*, 16 June 1922.

38. *Catskill Recorder*, 23 June 1922, five days before Rollini's nineteenth birthday.

39. *Catskill Recorder*, 30 June 1922.

40. Ed Kirkeby interview by John Steiner, 28 June 1961. Cush left music in 1944. Years of birth and death unknown.

41. On 4 December 1922, the day that the California Ramblers started another gig at Proctor's, Ed Kirkeby was in the studio of radio station WEAF, where he led a band called the Golden Gate Orchestra. The following January he did the same, but in no interview did Kirkeby ever mention his involvement with an actual band by this name. The name Golden Gate Orchestra appeared on the labels of many records made by the California Ramblers and

was, in fact, their most widely used pseudonym. Interestingly, at least from 1921 until 1925, a dance band existed called Jimmy Carr and his Golden Gate Orchestra. This may have been the same band that Kirkeby led in the WEAF studio.

42. Tom Faber's interview with Spencer Clark on 21 July 1982. Clark remembered that Kirkeby wanted musicians who could read well, even in his smaller bands. "The trumpeter Wingy Manone was working with us one time ... in the small band and Kirkeby was screaming because Wingy didn't read. He played his head off but he couldn't read. So Kirkeby came in one night and said: 'Enough of this jazz. I bought some stock arrangements that you guys are gonna play. Okay?' So we put up this stock arrangement and it was a waltz of some kind or another and it opened up with a whole note for the trumpet E in above middle C. So Wingy looked sad and we get ready to beat it off—one, two, three—and he popped(?) a high B or C or something like that, all wrong whatever it was and whoo, how he looked. ... So that put him into reading. However, Kirkeby never gave up, he always kept pushing and he tried to get us to play some pretty things."

43. Fred Cusick interview by Tom Faber, 27 July 1983.

44. *Boston Transcript*, unknown date.

45. The *New York Clipper*, 7 February 1922, reported that the California Ramblers had ended their vaudeville tour in order to work at the Side Show. They opened there on 6 January 1923, but the place burned down the next day. After they resumed their tour, the offer from Whiteman came in.

46. Located at 48 Broadway.

47. The California Ramblers had recorded the tune on 21 July 1922 for the Cameo label.

48. *Clipper*, 21 February 1922. Another newspaper, the *New York Evening Telegram*, 4 March 1923, described the band as "discovered in Los Angeles by [singer] Al Jolson."

49. *Billboard*, 10 March 1923.

50. Locations in this Keith tour were the Fordham (*New York Evening Post*, 9 March 1923), the Colonial (*New York Evening Telegram*, 25 March 1923), and the Community Film Theatre in Catskill (combined with a ball at the Elks Lodge, *Catskill Recorder*, 30 March 1923).

51. The first owner after Suydam was Dr. Richard Lewis Morris, whose grandfather had been one of the signers of the American Declaration of Independence. After he had died a group of club men organized a country club on the property, with the mansion serving as the clubhouse. Then the city acquired the grounds and eventually the mansion was acquired by John Tappin, a police captain, who dealt in real estate. He sold it to the Shanleys. (Information from Blake A. Bell, Archive of the Historic Pelham Website.)

52. A Shanley Inn had been the subject of a raid by Prohibition agents in August 1920, its owner Peter Shanley being arrested. However, this concerns a different Shanley Inn, located in Yonkers (*New York Times*, 3 August 1920).

53. The golf course was located on the grounds that formed the larger part of the property that had originally been bought by James Suydam.

54. *Variety*, 30 May 1923.

55. Fred Cusick interview by Tom Faber, 27 July 1983.

56. 1924 letter from Kirkeby to the Ardsley Club, a potential customer.

57. Spencer Clark interview by Tom Faber, 21 July 1982.

58. He was born in 1907 as a member of the wealthy Waterman family, who were makers of the well-known brand of fountain pens. He and Adrian would be close friends until Adrian

died. Waterman became a musician too, and started on guitar and banjo. Then he also wanted to play trombone and Adrian taught him. "He told me how to do it and did it himself. Until the end he stayed with me until I could do it too. It was great!" Neil Waterman died in 1983.

59. Neil Waterman interview by Tom Faber, 7 July 1982.
60. Spencer Clark interview by Tom Faber, 21 July 1982.
61. *New York Evening Telegram*, 7 and 28 July 1923.
62. A Kirkeby promotion text kept in his files, undated but probably ca. January 1924.
63. Pete Pumiglio interview by Tom Faber, 7 August 1983 (probably retelling someone else's story).
64. Telephone interview with Tom Faber, 16 July 1982.
65. Spencer Clark to Tom Faber, see above.
66. At least three takes of each title were issued, probably the result of two sessions.
67. Paramount, like other small companies, often issued more than one take of a particular recording. Of both "Bees Knees" and "Teddy Bear Blues" several takes survive. The differences between these takes are quite small, even in the solo spots, the result of many rehearsals.

Chapter 5: The California Ramblers Grown Up

1. Three takes were issued. In take 3 Rollini moves away from the arrangement and effectively improvises a few notes.
2. *Ed Kirkeby's California Ramblers*, unpublished manuscript by Woody Backensto and Perry Armagnac (New York, 1950s).
3. The year of this letter is uncertain. A different version of this letter exists, aimed at car drivers.
4. The sisters Rosetta and Vivian Duncan were experienced vaudeville artists. They were twelve and fourteen when they debuted on stage in Los Angeles in 1914. They became popular with a little-girl act that they were still doing in June 1923, the time of the *Palace* engagement with the California Ramblers. A month later, in July they were in San Francisco where they premiered their Topsy and Eva act, which would bring them fame for the rest of their career. It was based on the story of *Uncle Tom's Cabin* and one of the girls appeared in blackface. Valeska Suratt (1882–1962) was an actress and singer. She appeared in a few Broadway plays, mostly musicals. She was noted for the high-fashion clothes she wore on stage and possibly was a model for the famous Gibson girl sketchings.
5. *Record Research*, November 1962, 5.
6. *Record Research*, November 1962, 5.
7. In the past it had featured "exclusive artists" in classical music only.
8. In *Variety*, 28 January 1925, columnist Abel Green discussed the issue of exclusivity, mentioning Sam Lanin, Arthur Hand, and Ben Selvin who all recorded for more than one company. Green stated that all could earn more by not signing exclusive contracts. Kirkeby found a way out and signed with Columbia for the California Ramblers and recorded under pseudonyms with any other company. In an interview published in 1967 (by Bob Kumm, *Storyville*, October 1967), Kirkeby said: "our contract with Columbia had an 'unusual clause': we would not take royalties on our record-work on the proviso that we could record for other companies using various nom-de-plumes."

9. For such recordings Columbia would print a special banner across the blue record label with the text "exclusive artist." However, when the company started to use a different label, the colorful "flag label," it dropped the banner. Kirkeby's exclusive contract was signed only a few months before this change and no blue label Columbias by the California Ramblers have been found that showed their exclusive status with Columbia.

10. Companies had to take this seriously and may have been confused. Arto/Bell first issued records by the California Ramblers under the name of Golden Gate Orchestra, then switched to the artist credit California Ramblers and later back to Golden Gate Orchestra. At least one issue exists under both names (Bell P319).

11. The name Golden Gate Orchestra had been used on labels of records by the California Ramblers as early as December 1921 (Emerson, Regal). Even before that, Al Colombo, leader of the Golden Glades Orchestra had some Paramount records issued as by his Golden Gate Orchestra. Kirkeby had a permanent battle to stop others from using the name "California Ramblers." On 7 January *Variety* had an article about this subject that said there were four bands duplicating the name (and even seven duplicating "The Georgians").

12. According to his brother Art (in a letter to Tom Faber, 14 October 1982) Adrian wrote many songs but never bothered to copyright them.

13. Duff passed away in 1993, aged ninety-four. He retired at sixty-four from his last job, in outdoor advertising.

14. From a 1993 interview by Tom Faber and from *Saxophone Journal*, January/February 1990, 40. He stopped playing in 1950 and became president of Brilhart Musical Instrument Corp. in Carlsbad, California. In the sixties he sold his company to Selmer. He died in 1998.

15. Richard Sudhalter, in his book *Lost Chords*, mentions even more special nights: A George White's Scandals Night, a Celebrity Night, a Radio Night, two Texas Guinan Nights. On 27 September Kirkeby even organized a Blues Night with African American stars Bessie Smith, Clara Smith, Johnny Dunn, and Clarence Williams.

16. The Georgians eventually became known as the "World-known Georgians" and toured Europe for some years.

17. Nine seconds after the start of "Oh! Joe," Rollini demonstrates a unique element of his style: he inserts a note between two bars, thus filling an empty spot with music.

18. WHN began as a small station in Ridgewood, Queens, New York City, in February 1922 (Wikipedia).

The first broadcast by the California Ramblers was embedded in an all-music program that started at 9:30 a.m. Before them, soprano Daisy Neibling was featured for one hour and after the band two more sopranos followed, Dolores Royola and Peggy Davis. This was followed by the Lafayette Male Quartet, piano player Alfred Dulin, and another soprano, Frances Miller. The program ended at 11:00 p.m. with popular songs and an orchestra.

19. When talking about the many recordings they made, band members may have confused radio studios with gramophone studios as they often did several sessions in one week. WHN continued broadcasting the California Ramblers with a second broadcast one week later.

20. Cameo took the standard band photo taken on the green near the California Ramblers Inn. It showed ten men, so two were simply cut out. One of them, Arthur Hand, was not involved in the recordings of the Varsity Eight, but banjo player Ray Kitchingman actually was.

21. Herb Sanford, *The Dorsey Years*, New York, 1972, 238. Rollini wrote a small number of compositions that were recorded by the California Ramblers and probably arranged these, too.

22. Ed Kirkeby interview by John Steiner, 28 June 1961.

23. Arthur Hall made hundreds of records with bandleaders such as Lou Gold, Sam Lanin, Ben Selvin, and Mike Speciale.

24. As a singer under the name of Eddie Kirk, he would make a small number of recordings for Edison in 1928.

25. *New York Evening Telegram*, 13 October 1923. Others in the show, called "Charms," were Calver and Shane, Hazel Gladstone, and the Soltis.

26. The first time had been for Pathé/Perfect and the second for Columbia, which listed the record in December 1923 in an advertisement for their "New Process Records."

27. *Film Daily*, 31 October 1923.

28. *Talking Machine World*, 15 November 1923.

29. *New York Evening Telegram*, 2 November 1923.

30. Wiedoeft's profile is based on Wikipedia information.

31. Another popular composition by Nevin (1862–1901) was "Narcissus." This was also recorded by Wiedoeft's Saxophone Sextet, but without Rollini (Brunswick 2415).

32. Interview by Dutch journalist Max Tak in Amsterdam, published in *De Telegraaf*, 14 August 1929.

33. Columbia claimed that this process resulted in a "new and unbelievably silent surface."

34. The full list, as per *Presto*, 20 October 1923, was Ben Bernie, California Ramblers, Columbians, Emile Coleman, Dixieland Jazz Band, Carl Fenton, Bennie Krueger, Ted Lewis, Vincent Lopez, Memphis Five, Ray Miller, Gene Rodemich, Joseph C. Smith, Paul Specht, Ben Selvin, Paul Whiteman, and Harry Yerkes.

35. *Wireless Age*, June 1923.

36. Transmitting at 492 meters medium wave.

37. Undated newspaper clipping from this period in Kirkeby's scrapbook.

38. The earlier broadcasts had been 6 September, 12 September, 3 October, and 31 October, all at 3:45 p.m. Then the new contract with WEAF resulted in six broadcasts in December 1923.

39. *Music Trade Review*, 15 December 1923.

40. Letter of 6 December 1923, in Kirkeby's papers.

41. *The Sun and The Globe*, New York, 8 December 1923.

42. 239 W. 52nd St., between Broadway and 8th Avenue.

43. Don Rayno, *Paul Whiteman: Pioneer in American Music*, 2003, 389.

44. *Music Trade Review*, 8 March 1924, 26.

45. On many of their record labels the Golden Gate Orchestra was a pseudonym for the California Ramblers, but at this time Ed Kirkeby may have run another actual band under this name. A clipping from the New York *Daily Argus* of only a few days later, Thursday 20 December, also mentions both the California Ramblers and the Golden Gate Orchestra in one engagement and Kirkeby's scrapbook contained an advertisement for an engagement of the Golden Gate Orchestra on Long Island. All these references may refer to a band called Jimmy Carr and his Golden Gate Orchestra, which existed during these years. Adding to this mystery of identities, another newspaper, the *Lowell* (Massachusetts) *Sun* advertised the California Ramblers in their city on the same day as this New York engagement, but Lowell is located about 350 km north of New York.

46. *New York Evening Telegram*, 16 December 1923. The article said that the Hippodrome's policy was to have two performances daily (at 2:00 p.m. and 8:00 p.m.), seven days a week, at

Hippodrome's lowest prices. The opening program included artists from Japan and Europe in addition to Americans such as singer Miss Patricola and a circus section with dogs and baby elephants. Trombone player Abe Lincoln, later a California Rambler himself, remembered being a member of the Brunswick Orchestra (he called it Brunswick Seven) at the opening (interview by Tom Faber, 5 August 1983).

47. *Clipper*, 4 January 1924 (clipping in Kirkeby's scrapbook).

48. The tune "Arcady" required three recording sessions before a useful master was produced. When it was issued at last, Columbia coupled it with the same title sung by Al Jolson, accompanied by a studio orchestra.

49. Getting good California Ramblers recordings was not Columbia's biggest problem at this time. It was still struggling to survive after it had invested too heavily in equipment and inventory. In October 1923 it went into receivership, until March 1924.

50. The gig at the Monte Carlo may have started as early as 20 December 1923 (advertisement in *Evening Telegram*, New York, 20 December 1923).

51. Clipping from unknown newspaper, ca. January 1924. The personnel of the Intercollegians is unknown except for two members: Alfred G. Mueller, who played violin and probably was the leader; and Harry Taylor, banjo and saxophone. Spencer Clark may have been on bass sax (*Stamford Mirror*, 2 July 1924).

52. In Kirkeby's scrapbook.

53. Clipping from unknown newspaper, in Kirkeby's scrapbook.

54. Clipping from unknown newspaper, February 1924, in Kirkeby's scrapbook, partially quoted in *Record Research* 3, no. 4, issue 16, January/February 1958.

55. Otto Kahn married Adelaide Wolff. They had four children, Maud Emily (b. 1897), Margaret Dorothy (b. 1901), Gilbert (b. 1903), and Roger (b. 1907). It seems that all four used their mother's name Wolff as an additional first name. Roger changed it to Wolfe.

56. Hand even had a publicity photo made of himself and Gilbert Kahn, shown in *The Sun and The Globe*, 20 February 1922.

57. Letter in Kirkeby's archive.

58. Otto Kahn bought Arthur Lange's orchestra for his son Roger Wolfe Kahn, who was only seventeen. Roger Wolfe Kahn became a popular orchestra leader who made many recordings with famous musicians such as Red Nichols, Miff Mole, Jack Teagarden, Joe Venuti, and Eddie Lang.

59. Undated newspaper clipping from this period in Kirkeby's scrapbook.

60. Letters in Kirkeby's scrapbook. "Wonderful One" and "Dreamy Melody" were not recorded by the band. In *Billboard* Kirkeby asked for letters on the subject of "Radio or Phonograph Music." One fan, Jess Morris, leader of the Collegiate Ramblers from Gainesville, Texas, wrote on 4 July 1925: "phonograph entertainment is far superior.... because of its tonal qualities and one can appreciate the music more and have the record to play from time to time and over the Radio, one hears the artists only once and soon forgets them."

61. *Music Trade Review*, 16 February 1924, 52. The California Ramblers recorded the tune both for Pathé/Perfect and Columbia. Their arrangement features no jazz solos.

62. Letter in Kirkeby's archive.

63. A full-page ad appeared in *Music Trade Review*, 9 February 1924.

64. Brunswick, Columbia, Edison, OKeh, Victor, and Vocalion.

65. The full list of white bandleaders was as follows: Ace Brigode, Emil Coleman, Charles Dornberger, Sam Lanin, Vincent Lopez, Ray Miller, Ben Selvin, Paul Specht, and Ted Weems. The Ambassadors, the Garber-Davis Orchestra, the International Novelty Orchestra, and Keating's Ramblers also performed, as well as several individual artists.

Chapter 6: The California Ramblers to the Top with Adrian Rollini

1. Vincent Lopez was another orchestra leader who followed Whiteman's example. In November he did "Jazz at The Met," a concert at the Metropolitan Opera with special roles for harmonica player Borrah Minnevich and for blues composer W. C. Handy.

2. 1924 membership cards in Kirkeby's papers.

3. The band's alto sax player Bobby Davis could perfectly do a solo in the style of Wiedoeft's novelty work. He had done so on "Please," a recent California Ramblers recording on Columbia.

4. Some payment notes still exist in Kirkeby's papers for these songs. Examples: on 20 July 1925 the Rudolph Wurlitzer Mfg. Co. paid $1.28 for selling thirty-two music rolls. This amount was split between Bessie Smith, who received $0.32 and C.R. which got $0.96, duly penciled by E. Kirkeby on the document. And on 31 July 1926 the General Phonograph Corp. (OKeh) sent a debit note of $1.98, the result of selling thirty-eight copies of "Deep Blue Sea Blues" (so author Clara Smith got $0.19) and getting a return of 148 copies of "Weeping Willow Blues," composed by Paul Carter. C.R. Publishing later published songs by artists such as Fats Waller and Pat Flowers and continued at least into the 1940s.

5. *Music Trade Review*, 8 March 1924, 26; 23 August 1924, 37.

6. There was a tune titled "Goofus," but apparently it had no relation to this instrument.

7. Interview by Tom Faber, 27 July 1983.

8. Kirkeby interview by John Steiner, 28 June 1961.

9. *Talking Machine Journal*, August 1924.

10. Some issues had label credit to Bailey's Dixie Dudes and some were subtitled "with 'Roll' Williams (formerly the Dixie Hod Carriers)." Clearly the band was having fun here. They had not been called "The Dixie Hod Carriers" on any record label before and Gennett had called them "The Vagabonds." Who "Roll" Williams was, we may never know, but "Roll" is close to "Rollini." Did his colleagues call him "Roll" Williams at the time?

11. OKeh 40179 was reviewed by *Variety* on 15 October 1924.

12. For a short period in the spring of 1924, Gilbert Kahn, elder brother of Roger Wolfe Kahn, played saxophone with the band. This got much publicity but Gilbert did not stay long and probably cut no records in this period (Brooklyn *Daily Eagle*, 30 March 1924).

13. Before he joined the California Ramblers, Felline had worked (and recorded for Edison) with the bands of Paul Victorin and Vincent Lopez.

14. Jeff Healey in the liner notes to CD Jazz Oracle BDW8004 *The Dorsey Brothers* Volume 1, 1996. Peter J. Levinson writes in his Tommy Dorsey biography that Ed Kirkeby had already noted the Dorsey brothers' talent when they were with the Scranton Sirens.

15. *New York Evening Post*, 2 December 1924. On 29 November the *Brooklyn Daily Star* listed all performers, including dancers, a strong woman, a circus riding act, a wire artist, a clown,

pantomime, and a Lilliputian city. For a moment the band's cooperation with dancer Florence Walton and her partner Leon Leitrim seemed to go a step further when it was announced that together they were to open "their own supper club in the Times Square district." The plans failed, probably due to Prohibition issues (*Variety*, 3 December 1924).

16. *Variety*, 10 December 1924.

17. *Variety*, 10 December 1924.

18. *Yonkers Statesman*, 18 December 1924.

19. Various movies are listed at The Strand during these days: *Montmartre* with Pola Negri, *The Hurricane Kid* with Hoot Gibson, as well as *The Midnight Express* with Elaine Hammerstein.

20. The Operatic Medley was arranged by W. C. (Bill) Polla (from Fred Cusick interview by Tom Faber, 27 July 1983). The band had recorded it in June and it consisted of "My Heart at Thy Sweet Voice" (from *Samson and Delilah*), "The Pilgrims Chorus" (from *Tannhäuser*), "One Fine Day" (*Madame Butterfly*), "Quartet" (*Rigoletto*), and the "Triumphal March" (*Aida*).

21. The name Little Ramblers had been introduced on Columbia Records in July 1924, on which Rollini played goofus but not bass saxophone.

22. The recording by the band under the pseudonym the Vagabonds is a straight performance without jazz value. The five men in Yonkers must have "jazzed it up."

23. Fred Cusick interview by Tom Faber, 1 July 1983.

24. Both stories from Art Rollini interview by Tom Faber, 11 July 1982.

25. One Q. Roscoe Snowden recorded "Deep Sea Blues"; this is a different tune and his own composition.

26. Two takes survive of "She Loves Me" (recorded for Paramount on 6 September 1924). Davis plays the same solo on both.

27. The transcription was done by Joe Jordan, who added a theme not found in Bix's recording. Another difference is the clarinet solo with the Wolverines in $E\flat$. Melrose's stock arrangement features the same solo, but transposed to $B\flat$. All of Rollini's recordings (by the California Ramblers, the Five Birmingham Babies, and the Varsity Eight) have the clarinet solo in $B\flat$. (This information from Bert Brandsma.)

28. Fletcher Henderson recorded it on 30 October 1924 with Louis Armstrong on trumpet, between the various California Ramblers sessions.

29. Richard M. Sudhalter and Philip R. Evans, *Bix: Man and Legend*, 118. *Variety* of 17 December 1924 reviewed the Columbia recording: "The deep sax and the cornet in duo formation stand out and the alto sax' solo is another instrumental highlight."

30. Bix moved in with Red Nichols, who was working with Sam Lanin at the Roseland Ballroom.

31. They had thirteen recording sessions in twenty-seven days.

32. Since Columbia had exclusive rights to use the name California Ramblers on their record labels, Edison issued the band's output under the name Golden Gate Dance Orchestra or, like various other companies, Golden Gate Orchestra.

33. Thomas Alva Edison personally judged various artists. His notes still exist. Jazz-oriented artists normally did not meet his approval. In addition to the California Ramblers, one of the few other bands that did pass were the Georgia Melodians, who often recorded for the company.

34. Spencer Clark interview by Tom Faber, 21 July 1982.

35. Irving Brodsky starts his piano solo with a break that suggests it is being played by Jelly Roll Morton!

36. Winold Reiss became famous as an interior decorator but also for his other work, such as his portraits of Indians and the cover design for the book *The New Negro* by Alain Locke (1925). Together with artists such as the white author Carl van Vechten and the black photographer James Vanderzee, Reiss is considered one of the people around the Harlem Renaissance

37. The first one was station WJZ, but within a year two others were added, WEAF and WHN.

38. It may be significant that Specht's orchestra and the California Ramblers both were bestselling bands for Columbia Records.

39. Fred Cusick interview by Tom Faber, 1 July 1983

40. Washington *Daily News*, 9 March 1925, and other clippings in Kirkeby's scrapbook.

41. *Variety*, 11 March 1925. Hagen also was a songwriter. Some of his tunes were "Play Me Slow" (recorded by Jean Goldkette and Fletcher Henderson) and "Heartbroken Rose." In March 1925 the California Ramblers recorded his tune "Dromedary" for Columbia (issue number 340D).

42. *Music Trade Review*, 28 March 1925, and *Music Trade News*, April 1925. The "former New York orchestra director" was Paul Specht (*Variety*, 11 March 1925).

43. Different sources quoted different amounts. The *New York Times*, 28 January 1925, mentioned $350,000.

44. The Kirkeby collection at the Institute of Jazz Studies at Rutgers University, Newark, New Jersey, includes a comprehensive promotion plan, probably written by Hagen. It aims at publicity via all available channels: newspapers, radio, magazines, and the trade press. Instrument companies were targets, as were music publishers. Its author even suggested publicity stunts and thought of approaching the local press with stories about band members from their geographical areas.

45. Vincent Richards had won the Olympic tennis championship the year before. The California Ramblers provided the music at a party thrown in his honor on 17 October.

46. *Variety*, 22 April 1925.

47. The hymns were arranged for the band by W. C. (Bill) Polla, who also had arranged for the Hippodrome opening. Titles announced were "Abide with Me" (which probably was not played during the 12 April broadcast); "Holy, Holy, Holy"; "It Is the Blessed Easter Morn"; "Lo the Stone Is Rolled Away"; "The Lord Is Risen"; and "The Palms" (*Talking Machine World*, 15 April 1925, and *Evening World*, April 1925).

48. *Variety*, 8 April 1925, and *New York Herald*, 13 April 1925.

49. The California Ramblers were not the first orchestra to link to religion. In 1922 Bennie Krueger had agreed to play in a church service (but was rejected after all), and the Jean Goldkette Orchestra later actually played in a church for Saturday Night worship *(Storyville* 138, 230).

50. Contract signed by both parties on 20 April 1925, in Kirkeby papers. *Talking Machine World*, 15 May 1925, and 15 June 1925.

51. *Daily Mirror*, 27 May 1925; *Music Trade Review*, 23 May 1925. In 1923, after they had done only a handful of broadcasts, the band made sixth place in radio popularity poll after, among others, Vincent Lopez and Paul Specht.

52. *University of Delaware Review*, 24 April 1925; *Talking Machine World*, 15 April 1925; *Variety*, 8 April 1925.

53. *Yonkers Statesman*, 28 and 30 April 1925. The heroine of the newspaper story was Gloria Gregory. The newspaper listed the band's personnel and mentioned several tunes played, including several hot titles: "Donkey Dust" [sic, probably "Dustin' the Donkey"], "Prince of Wails," and "Alabamy Bound." The Little Ramblers played "Tiger Rag." The movie features were *Ramshackle House* with Betty Compson and *Saddle Hawk* with Hoot Gibson.

54. *Talking Machine World*, 15 April 1925; *Presto*, 21 March 1925. *Variety*, 2 September 1925, said that Arthur Hand created the goofus.

55. From a letter supposedly written by Ed Kirkeby near the end of 1925, precise date unknown.

56. Goofus Five session of 25 November 1924.

57. Stan Hester's discography of Red Nichols with Sam Lanin, *Shellack Stack* 747 through 951.

58. In June *Variety* reported that the Chicago Senators, led by Al Siegel, provided rousing music at New York's Parody Club for a short time. Their first trumpet player is not mentioned by name but was remembered as the sizzling cornetist [sic] with the California Ramblers last year. It is believed that this refers to Bill Moore.

59. Contract in Kirkeby papers.

60. That recording with Lanin was lucrative is shown by a check made out on 3 June 1925 to Jimmy Dorsey by Sam Lanin for the sum of $135.

61. "You'll Never Get to Heaven with Those Eyes," recorded for Victor on 26 June 1924, features a solo by Red Nichols that is very close to Beiderbecke's solo on "Jazz Me Blues" by the Wolverines. Red's solo had been transcribed from Bix's record by Olsen's piano player and arranger Eddie Kilfeather. Red decided to hear Bix and the Wolverines. They met a month later, only weeks after the Wolverines recorded "Tiger Rag." See Stephen Stroff, *Red Head*, 9; Evans and Evans, *Bix*, 157.

62. When interviewed by Tom Faber, 27 July 1983.

63. Bix and his Rhythm Jugglers recorded for Gennett on 26 January 1925.

64. Spencer Clark, himself a bass saxophone player, said about Min Leibrook: ". . . he didn't begin to play. . . . He just played tuba notes and very little else." This is probably unfair to Leibrook. On his recording of the tune "Lovable" with Paul Whiteman, he gives a fine swinging accompaniment to Frank Trumbauer's sax solo—and definitely plays more than tuba notes.

65. Evans and Evans, *Bix*, 184. Many musical instruments allow playing a note in more than one way. When trumpeters play a note in an unconventional way, this is called false fingering.

66. Peter J. Levinson in his Tommy Dorsey biography gives the date for this dinner as 15 March 1925.

67. Stockdale, *Jimmy Dorsey*, 9.

68. Interview with Tom Faber, October 1985.

69. The Pathé company issued one title as by the Palace Garden Orchestra, one of their pseudonyms for the California Ramblers, and the other as the Five Birmingham Babies, their name for the hot band-within-the-band. There was a Palace Garden Club in New York City.

70. The tune became popular with the band. The California Ramblers would record it again later under a different name, "The Pay-Off."

71. Analysis by bass sax player and original Rollini researcher Tom Faber.

72. It was not issued until the thirties, in England and copied ("dubbed") from a surviving test pressing.

73. As an illustration how Nichols managed to increase his income, it may be noted that he recorded on the same day, 4 May, for a different label, another boss, and in a different studio, newly equipped with electric microphones instead of the old acoustic horns—with (Sam) Lanin's Red Heads for Columbia.

74. It should be noted that Virginia Tech, a center of technology, decided to have their songs recorded in the old acoustical way and not by modern electric equipment, which was almost ready for use. "Techland" was composed by Theresa Nash Harrison.

75. Sutton and Nauck, *American Record Labels and Companies*, 51.

76. A test exists of the tune "Gotta Getta Girl," recorded by the California Ramblers, probably for Columbia. This may have been electrically recorded as early as November 1924. An acoustic recording made in October 1924 and issued, had been recorded with the traditional method.

77. Jimmy Dorsey contributed to the arrangement of "Sweet Georgia Brown" (Peter J. Levinson in his Tommy Dorsey biography). Both Dorseys solo on this title. The band received a letter dated 22 August 1925, from one A. F. Joseph, manager of the Dixonians, a band in Charlotte, North Carolina, who may have had good ears. He wanted to know if Jimmy Dorsey had ever been with the California Ramblers and who played the hot sax solos on these two titles.

78. Interview by Tom Faber, October 1985.

79. *Variety* reviewed the record in its 8 July 1925 issue but failed to mention the improved sound quality and the electric recording.

80. Some of this information is from the excellent Cliff Edwards discography by Larry Kiner (see bibliography). Kiner's son David told me that his father had several conversations for his book with Edwards to get answers to his discographical questions (emails of 18 and 30 March 2007). In the case of Edwards's April 1924 recording of "California (Here I Come)," Kiner wrote "possibly Adrian Rollini piano."

81. On 10 June 1925 *Variety*'s Abel Green wrote: "The California Ramblers is possessed of a crack sax section, one of the best in the city. Its brass work is extraordinary and the general effect is corking."

82. "Personal memorandum for W. T. Kirkeby," date unknown, written by himself.

Chapter 7: The California Ramblers Back to Business

1. Adrian always called his boats *Rambler* followed by a Roman number. The boat that he invited Dixie to may have been *Rambler* I or II (*Down Beat*, May 1939, and forties radio interview by Dorothy Day). Dixie lived in the same neighborhood as the Rollinis, about one mile from Larchmont harbor, a part of the Long Island Sound.

2. *IAJRC Bulletin* 45, no. 2, June 2012, has an in-depth article about the origins and further history of the Charleston, by Albert Haim.

3. In his book *Jazz Masters of the Twenties*, 30.

4. Could this story refer to Henderson's rejected Edison session of April 1924? Stewart joined Henderson sometime in early 1928, years after Hawkins recorded on the bass sax for

the first time, so his story is "hear-say." To hear Coleman Hawkins playing bass sax listen to "Pensacola," recorded 18 December 1925 for Columbia. He plays a thirty-two bar solo in duet with Don Redman, who plays goofus(!).

5. Around 1921 Conn's sales of reed instruments increased from an average of 10,000 to 20,000 a year (Conn website).

6. Letter to Tom Faber, 4 May 1983. In his letter Joe also mentioned a place where musicians would meet after hours: Roth's Restaurant, on Broadway between 51st and 52nd streets. He lists the Dorseys, Red Nichols, Phil Napoleon, Miff Mole, and Adrian Rollini who would have an early breakfast and talk about records that had just been released by other musicians and orchestras and about their ideas.

7. Interview by Jimmy Staples for *Crescendo*, April 1966, quoted by John Altman (jazzprofessional.com).

8. In *The World of Duke Ellington* by Stanley Dance (1970), quoted by Richard Sudhalter in *Lost Chords*, 172 (1999).

9. Quoted by Phil Sillman in a letter to Tom Faber, April 1983. Otto Hardwick, one of Ellington's reed players, can be heard with Cootie Williams's Rug Cutters recording for Vocalion in 1938.

10. 2 July 1925. The session produced the best-seller "I Miss My Swiss."

11. Don Rayno, *Paul Whiteman: Pioneer in American Music*, 2003, 115. It is interesting to see that Rollini did not recommend Nichols, who had just finished working with the California Ramblers, or Beiderbecke, who had recently visited them. Both would follow in Bartell's footsteps with Whiteman. Henry Busse, Whiteman's first trumpet, may have been present: Irving Brodsky, when interviewed by Tom Faber in 1982, remembered Whiteman and Busse visiting the inn together.

12. Leroy "Roy" Johnston came from Ray Miller's band, where he worked alongside Miff Mole and Frank Trumbauer. Before that he had worked for Paul Whiteman in a band called the Collegians. Johnston left music about 1953. Abram "Abe" Lincoln (1907–2000) came from Ace Brigode's Fourteen Virginians. When Spencer Clark was interviewed by Tom Faber (21 July 1982), he remembered Lincoln as one of many good men in the band and also remembered his "big feet, size 11 or 12, which he used to keep time, boom, boom, boom, boom, boom and you could hear him all over the place, it shaked the whole damn building." Neil Waterman (interviewed by Tom Faber, 17 July 1982) thought that Abe Lincoln was as good as or better than Miff Mole: "He is the only man who would lie down under the piano and play the trombone with his foot . . . and sounded as good as anybody standing up." Another trombone player, George Crozier, left the band in the summer of 1925 after only a short stay (*New York Morning Telegraph*, 25 August 1925, also mentions departure of "Boy" Dorsey and Arnold Brilhart).

13. In an interview on 27 July 1983, Fred Cusick told Tom Faber that it came from a disagreement: "Mr. Hand was becoming unpopular with the band. . . . there was almost an agreement that if anybody get into trouble and got fired that we would all quit. [One day] it came to me that Arthur said to me: 'Didn't you like the band?' . . . I told him to his face: 'Yeah, I like the band, I'm crazy about the band but the leader I can't go too much for.' He said: 'Well, maybe you'd better not stay.' I said: 'Okay' and in two weeks I was gone. However, nobody else opened a mouth! That was a lesson to me. Summer 1925 Eddie Stannard took my place." Eventually Cusick returned to the band.

14. O'Keefe's office, together with Tommy Rockwell, would later grow into the very successful booking agency Rockwell-O'Keefe.

15. The movie was *The Beautiful City* by Richard Barthelmess and announced as possibly the screen's first realistic story of Manhattan life. *Pittsburgh Press*, 1 November 1925.

16. *Auburn Citizen*, 21 November 1925.

17. During breaks the band members would be invited by guests to sit at their table and thus they would spread around. When they were due back on the bandstand, Rollini would play a few notes on the piano, an E followed by and A, the sign to get back to work (Fred Cusick, interview by Tom Faber, 27 July 1983).

18. Interview by Tom Faber, 17 July 1982.

19. *Auburn Citizen*, various issues 24 October 1925–27 November 1925.

20. *Massillon Evening Independent*, 8 December 1925.

21. The advertisement incorrectly used an old photograph, which showed Arthur Hand as leader.

22. *Variety*, in its issue of 21 October, was the first to pick up and spread the news.

23. Quotes from Frederick Lewis Allen, *Only Yesterday*, Harper & Brothers, New York, 1931, 270. Allen gives several reasons why the boom started and number one was the climate.

24. At one moment Fisher's worth was estimated as $100 million. He lost everything in the next few years. Many artists were attracted by Florida's growth; *Variety* in its issue of 11 November 1925 noted that Irving Berlin was talking of an exclusive nightclub on a ship, and that Isham Jones, Vincent Lopez, and Paul Whiteman had contracts for Florida.

25. This and following information from a letter in Kirkeby's archive.

26. At 66th Street and Collins Avenue.

27. An article in the *Miami Herald* of 6 December 1925 lists seven contractors for the interior and various systems at the Deauville.

28. *Variety* of 9 December 1925 noted that Hand, together with Basil Durant, would travel to Miami on 14 December 1925. Show dancer Durant and his partner Kay Durban were to be stellar attractions at the Deauville. The same news item mentioned that Maurice Fitchard's orchestra, which played concert music, would move to Florida to alternate with the California Ramblers. The January 1926 issue of *Orchestra World* noted that Fabian Storey's orchestra left for Florida to alternate with the California Ramblers, playing tangos and Cuban danzos. Both orchestra leaders were experienced men with long musical careers. Storey's five-piece band had Stanley Fink, violin; Joe Bono, cello; Al Weber, string bass; Harold Ennis, drums. After his return, Storey became a member of the California Ramblers.

29. This was shortly after 5 December 1925. On a letter from Frank Cush, Kirkeby noted that the "last big CR recording date for Columbia was on 3 and 4 December before band went to Deauville." Actually it stretched into five December days. The personnel of the band that went to Florida is not fully known. The January 1926 list of transfers from Local 802, the New York Local of the American Federation of Musicians, contains only the following few California Ramblers names: Robert Davis, Thomas Felline, Arthur C. Hand, F. Stanley King, and Adrian Rollini. In a letter of 1 April 1961, Kirkeby noted that violin player Sam Fink was also a member. Fred Cusick did not go.

30. The *Miami Herald* of 6 December 1925 listed among others Olympic short distance champion Gertrude Ederle and diving champion Aileen Riggin. During the summer of 1926, Ederle became the first woman to swim across the English Channel.

31. On New Year's Eve the Miami Beach Casino also was set to open as well as the Villa Espanola, a complex of six hotels and eight apartment buildings (*New York Sun*, 12 December 1925).

32. The California Ramblers worked nightly in the supper club, while during bathing hours music would be provided on the beach by the 7th Regimental Band from New York, directed by Lieutenant Sutherland (*Miami News*, 1 December 1925).

33. This name sounds familiar since the California Ramblers recorded under the names Varsity Eight and University Six. The identity of the Varsity Six is unknown. They may have been a local orchestra, but the following theory is more likely: perhaps they constituted a second batch of musicians from New York, brought to Miami by Kirkeby, who called them the Varsity Six as long as the California Ramblers were in Florida. When Kirkeby & Hand decided to let one orchestra go, the California Ramblers went back to New York and the Varsity Six were renamed the California Ramblers and stayed at The Deauville. Taking this theory one step further: The Varsity Six may have been the group that worked at the California Ramblers Inn from 1 November, when the band went on tour.

Indeed, names are known of an alternative group of California Ramblers working in Miami, possibly the above-mentioned men who worked under that name from March: Fletcher Hereford, clarinet and tenor sax; Norman Lanning and Phil Cowe, alto saxes; Willard Keeler, tenor sax; Joe LaFaro, violin; Walter Gross, piano; Harold "Pinkey" Friars, banjo; Al Weber, bass and tuba (information from Harold "Pinkey" Friars, via Paul Burgess in his publication *Shellack Stack*, unknown date). Also, violin player Sam Fink worked for Kirkeby in Florida.

34. J. Robert Mueller of the Deauville Beach Resort in a short history of the resort and its predecessor, the Deauville Casino.

35. Kirkeby's thumbnail biography was a two-page document he wrote ca. 1945.

36. Elsener sold the Deauville to a colorful lady by the name of Princess Lucy Cotton Thomas Magraw Eristavi Tchitcherine, a former Broadway showgirl who often married. Other owners or users were tabloid magnate Bernard MacFadden, followed by the Army, a nameless Chicago syndicate, and a holiday operator.

37. Interview by Tom Faber, 16 July 1982.

38. This concept was not entirely new. Bandleaders Earl Fuller and Harry Yerkes had issued records with their respective names as brand name. Fuller's project failed after one issue, Yerkes after a few. In later years so-called "picture labels" were also issued by some large companies, whereby the company label was kept and the artist's portrait was shown on the label as well. This came close to Kirkeby's idea.

39. 6 February 1926.

40. The official court papers mentioned Wallace T. Kirkeby as complainant and Arthur C. Hand, Kirkeby & Hand, Inc., and Beach Properties, Inc. as defendants.

41. Restraining order 12295 of the Circuit Court of the 11th Judicial Circuit in and for Dade County, Florida.

42. Interview by Tom Faber, 16 July 1982.

43. Kirkeby had stated (written on a 1960 letter from Frank Cush, in his archive) that the December recording sessions for Columbia were the last ones by the "big California Ramblers" before that band went to Florida. He may not have remembered the later OKeh session by the smaller group.

44. *Variety*, 9 December 1925.

45. Another musician who would sometimes replace Adrian Rollini in the California Ramblers in the mid-twenties was Merrill Kaye, who also used the family name Kline. In an interview with Tom Faber on 28 July 1983, he remembered: "I used to help Adrian when he worked out in Westchester. When he wanted to take off, he'd send me or he'd send Spencer Clark, whoever was available. Just for one night."

46. Interestingly, Clark only remembered the waltz that was recorded that day, not the other two titles. It may have been the only waltz he ever recorded.

47. Spencer Clark interview by Paul Burgess, published in *Shellac Stack* 745 in 1977. Apparently Clark did not know that Rollini had gone to Florida, leading the California Ramblers.

48. From Tom Faber's interview with Spencer Clark, 21 July 1982. The California Ramblers never worked at the Pelham Heath Inn. During the early thirties, the New California Ramblers would work at this location, then called the New California Ramblers Inn. Clark confused the Pelham Heath Inn with the California Ramblers Inn, which was in the same area. Clark's friend Herb Weil would join the band in 1926, replacing Stan King. Weil was a funny man, Clark remembered, and would rename a song called "Because I Love You" as "A Big Horse Love You" and "It All Depends on You" would become "It Holds the Pants on You." When asked "Can you do it?" he would say "Oh, of course, of course" which would develop into "Rimsky, course, of course." And then into "Rimsky."

49. Clark also followed Rollini in the use of goofus and xylophone. His xylophone work can be heard on a recording by Lud Gluskin's Orchestra made in Berlin in November 1930, "Sweeping the Clouds Away."

50. From interviews by Paul Burgess and Tom Faber, see above.

51. Tom Faber's interview with Spencer Clark, 21 July 1982.

52. *Union Town Morning Herald*, 15 February 1926. In Cleveland they were in an act with Miss Lanphier.

53. Interview by Tom Faber, 21 July 1982. Clark remembered another story involving Moore and Russin. Jack Russin had just bought his first automobile, a fine La Salle touring car. "So we all had to go for a ride in Jacky's new car . . . we left our cars at the Ramblers Inn and we all went down into New York and . . . to a couple of spots in Harlem and had some drinks. [In Central Park] the car stalled. . . . Bill said 'Hey, look, something is dripping out of the back of the car! . . . Maybe it's gasoline . . . no, maybe it's wine? . . . I'll tell you how you can find out. If it's gas it will burn.' So he takes a match and throws it down and . . . Wham, up went the car. A brand new car that only had 15 miles on it. I can still see Bill Moore saying it to-day: 'If it's gas it will burn!'"

54. *Alton Evening Telegraph*, 11 May 1926.

55. Probably from 1926. Kirkeby papers at Rutgers University.

56. The pavilion's manager was E. J. Ferry and the dance was organized by O'Keefe-McCoy bookers.

57. During that year the dance's popularity reached its top with the biggest Charleston contest ever: on 27 June at New York's Polo Grounds, 20,000 people attended while 100 dancers competed for $1,500 in prizes.

58. "Dixie Stomp" was also the name of a different composition by Paul(?) Tremaine and recorded in 1928 by Fess Williams's Orchestra.

59. The hot fountain pen was just over 10.5 inches long and had a ¾-inch diameter. Its range was even more limited than the goofus, a challenge that Rollini easily handled. At least two types were offered for sale, one in the key of E♭, the other in C.

60. In an interview in *Melody Maker*, 27 August 1937, Ed Kirkeby remarked that Jimmy Dorsey had actually recorded on hot fountain pen before Rollini did. Kirkeby mentioned the recording of "Dromedary," but actually it is on the other side of the record, a few notes in "Just a Little Drink," recorded for Columbia on 23 March 1925. The record was reviewed by *Variety*, 27 May 1925, without noting Jimmy's exotic instrument, but the "deep sax" was. Jimmy played on other remarkable instruments, too. Spencer Clark in an interview by Tom Faber, 21 July 1982, remembered him as a "cute little guy. He played trumpet originally and when he would get in his drinks he'd take the saxophone stand and [then] a little pipe came up with a little crook to hang your horn on and it had a large base on the bottom of the stand. . . . he would take that little thin rod out and put a trumpet mouthpiece on it, stand up, and play choruses that way, just for gags."

The remark that Adrian took it over is from William Friars during a telephone interview by Tom Faber. Friars said that he worked for Kirkeby from 1925 till 1927, "but only a little with Adrian." He may have been a member of another of Kirkeby's bands and occasionally dropped in with the California Ramblers.

61. Most Harmony recordings would also be released on its derivates Velvet Tone and Diva.

62. "Milenberg Joys" was a tune composed by Paul Mares and Leon Roppolo of the New Orleans Rhythm Kings and Jelly Roll Morton, who joined the NORK when they recorded it for Gennett in 1923. The Varsity Eight take it at a slightly faster tempo.

63. C. May 1925, for Paramount, accompanying himself on banjo. The tune became a hit and was recorded by several white orchestras.

64. The only difference being a minor error in take 2.

65. It has been said that the great trumpeter Bix Beiderbecke "never played the same solo twice." However, this is not generally true. In the book *Simon Says*, its author, *Metronome* editor George T. Simon, quotes Paul Whiteman who "claimed that Bix would never play a chorus the same way, until he got just what he wanted. Then he'd stick to that chorus and play it the same way over and over again" (335). Also Frank Trumbauer's solos were often, if not always, prearranged: his solos on the two takes of Whiteman's "The Man I Love" are note-for-note the same, despite Don Rayno's description in his Paul Whiteman biography (633). George Hurley, who played with Rollini and his American colleagues in Fred Elizalde's Orchestra, made a similar remark when interviewed by Tom Faber in 1982: "You played solos off the cuff, unless you routined something for yourself, and . . . that's something that all of them did, even the American fellows. They used to have something, a basis, for what they wanted to play, so that if they felt really good that night, they could really go to town on it, but if they didn't feel so good, they always had something to play. . . . it was a very good and professional way of approaching your work."

66. Abel Green in *Variety*, 10 June 1926.

Chapter 8: Kirkeby Loses His Grip, the End of the Contracts

1. In Troy, New York, on 22 July 1926.

2. *Pittsburgh Gazette Times* and *Pittsburgh Press*, 18 July 1926. On 26 July Bob Patterson's orchestra recorded "Minor Gaff" for Columbia, which remained unissued. When an unknown

recording of this tune showed up that featured Adrian Rollini, it was suggested that this was Bob Patterson's unissued recording. However, it is more likely that it is by George Posnack's orchestra, recorded in 1930 for QRS.

3. Gaffney probably was not a member of the band.

4. *Huntingdon Daily News*, 6 August 1926. During Adrian's absence while he was in Florida, Dixie took part in Charleston contests. The *Mount Vernon Daily Argus*, 23 February 1926, reports that she won at Proctor's the previous day.

5. *Huntingdon Daily News*, 7 August 1926.

6. Clipping from unknown Buffalo newspaper, 22 August 1926.

7. *Music Trade Review*, 18 September 1926.

8. Advertisements mention Siebert's background from Earl Carroll's shows but do not mention his contribution. The locals probably knew anyway

9. *Pittsburgh Press*, 26 August 1926. The announcement refers to an appearance of the band at a "downtown Pittsburgh theater." No further information is known about this engagement. However, an undated clipping from an unknown newspaper mentions an engagement of one week at Sanders where the band will play "each night on the outdoor Spanish patio," and broadcast from station WCAE.

10. Newspaper ads and clipping from unknown source.

11. Letter from Kirkeby to Woody Backensto, 1 April 1961.

12. Abe Lincoln interview by Tom Faber, 5 August 1983. According to Lincoln, the band used no theme song.

13. *New York Times*, 10 October 1926.

14. *Mount Vernon* (New York) *Daily Argus*, 7 October 1926.

15. It was located at 35 East 53rd Street. In his thumbnail biography, Kirkeby called it the Club Venezia, but contemporary publications mentioned it as the Lido Venice. The Lido Venice was named after an island near Venice, Italy, and known worldwide for its entertainment. Its exotic name was used in centers of tourism around the world. A Dutch publication from 1991 lists 36 Lidos but misses Kirkeby's place in New York City as well as a Lido Venice in Brooklyn, New York, on Flatbush Avenue.

16. The *New York Evening Post* of 19 November 1926 mentioned Prince and Princess Francisco Rospiglioei.

17. The others were Irving Abrams, Ben Bernie, Jimmie Carr, the Diplomats, Eddie Edwards, Eddie Elkins, Jacques Green, Roger Wolfe Kahn, Sam Lanin, Vincent Lopez, B. A. Rolfe, Duke Yellman. Among fifty stars and singers were Ruby Keeler and the Keller Sisters and Lynch. Ladies paid $1.00, gentlemen $1.50 (*New York Sun*, 10 December 1926).

18. The same group without Clark but with Al Duffy, violin, worked at the Rosemont Ballroom, Brooklyn, probably early 1925. The hall had two bandstands and a jazz band, the Original Memphis Five worked on the other. (Al Duffy interview by Tom Faber, 31 July 1983).

19. Spencer Clark interview by Tom Faber, 21 July 1982.

20. Kirkeby may have been referring to the Pelham Heath Inn, located at the junction of Eastchester Road and Pelham Parkway South, about four miles from the California Ramblers Inn and closer to the city. It had the same policy: it featured New York dance bands such as Lou Raderman's and had direct broadcasts. It has a long history and existed at least from 1917 till 1955. Around 1942 it was called the New Pelham Heath Inn and this may have been at a different location.

21. Hand may have stayed in Florida. In 1929 he was president of Colony Club in Palm Beach and that year he made a trip to Europe (*New York Times*, 16 March and 9 September 1929).

22. Several different takes were issued of all sides.

23. In later years Louis Armstrong claimed authorship of "Sister Kate." Since he never got the copyright he refused to perform it.

24. In 1926 Arthur Hand's name turned up in advertisements for Koverite instrument cases. Other well-known musicians and orchestra leaders mentioned were Ben Bernie, Jean Goldkette, Harry Reser, Paul Specht, and Mike Pingitore from Paul Whiteman's band.

25. During the twenties Frank Walker was A&R man at Columbia, and after 1930 he worked in the same capacity at RCA Victor.

26. Only Cameo could not afford to pay more. It was on its way to a massive merger which would involve Pathé and Plaza.

27. The Odeon activities were absorbed by Columbia, who, a year earlier, had already taken a major interest in the Carl Lindstrom Company, OKeh's backer.

28. OKeh had been using an electric recording system called Truetone since November 1925. It certainly was not as good sound quality as the Western Electric system used by Columbia and Victor.

29. *Syracuse Herald*, 28 January 1927.

30. One such engagement is known, on 6 March at Winder Stores. In addition to Clark, Hayton, and Johnston, the group consisted of (?) Bergh, (?) Boyd, (?) Russ, (?) Cusson, and Herb Weil.

31. Dick Hill, *Sylvester Ahola: The Gloucester Gabriel*, Scarecrow, London and New Jersey, 1993.

32. According to Ahola's wife in interview by Tom Faber, 7 October 1925.

33. A part of the program survives, handwritten by Kirkeby. It started with a trumpet call, followed by the song "Indian Love Call" by a singer. Then the band would play "Canadian Capers." Other songs in the show were "Dinah," "High-High-High" (done by Don Alvin), "Worka John," "Blue Skies," "Polly from Hollywood," "Me Too," "Thinking of You" (as an encore), and as a finale "Swanee."

34. Hill, *Sylvester Ahola*.

35. Hill, *Sylvester Ahola*.

36. According to the website of the Economic History Association, the average earnings of a skilled production worker in 1927 were $31.09 weekly. A farmer earned less.

37. From the 28 January 1928 payroll. Among the highest paid were Henry Busse, Wilbur Hall, and Chester Hazlett, who got $350; "arranger" Ferde Grofé got even more, $375.

38. *Variety*, 2 February 1927. Arthur C. Hand and W. Kirkeby versus Austin, Nichols & Co. Inc. about $833.30.

39. The other three bankruptcies mentioned by *Variety* concerned Russian Swan, Inc., Will Hurlbut, and Frank L. A. Schwartz.

40. One Eddie Davis led an orchestra that recorded for Banner, Grey Gull, and Broadway in 1922.

41. *Music Trade Review*, 26 March 1927.

42. On 6 April *Variety* noted that Hand had left for Europe after losing $80,000 on the Deauville disaster and $30,000 on the Lido Venice in New York. However, Kirkeby's losses were

even bigger: his voluntary bankruptcy petition listed some $400,000 in liabilities, including $250,000 for a lease on the Deauville premises.

43. B. Busig had been drummer with the band at the Branford in Newark, New Jersey.

44. The Cameo date is not mentioned in Kirkeby's notebooks. It may have been done by a Harry Reser group, judging from the stodgy bass saxophone player. Clark's presence on the OKeh session had been unknown until Kirkeby's notebooks were carefully studied. However, when Tom Faber, originator of the Adrian Rollini Project, heard these recordings for the first time a few years before he passed away, he directly expressed his doubts that it was Rollini.

45. John Luther ("Casey") Jones (1863—1900) was a real person. He was an American railroad engineer from Jackson, Tennessee, who worked for the Illinois Central Railroad. He lost his life when he attempted to avoid a train collision. The story got into the newspapers and Jones became a hero. Popular singer Billy Murray may have been the first with a song about Casey Jones in 1910. The song would be recorded over and over again. The public reaction was so positive that Murray followed it up with another hero: "Steamboat Bill" was a product of fantasy and his story was similar to Jones's, but the scene changed from a railroad train to a riverboat. The Steamboat Bill character remained popular and in 1928 both Buster Keaton and Walt Disney based films on it.

Chapter 9: Freelancer Adrian Rollini

1. Titles were "Chicago," "Toot-Toot-Tootsie," and "Strutting at the Strutters' Ball." The band had recorded "Lips" and "Maybe" as the Syncopating Five a month before Red joined.

2. With this band Red recorded one of his first solos, in January 1924 on "Wop Blues."

3. In May, Armand Piron's New Orleans Orchestra had worked at the Roseland. Red may have heard them, too.

4. A fine and early example of his work in this style is a recording made under the name of Lanin's Red Heads on 26 February 1925; "Jimtown Blues" and "King Porter Stomp" were issued on Columbia 327-D. Red would join the California Ramblers a few weeks later and would have Bix Beiderbecke as a companion for a few days.

5. The Red Heads recorded for Pathé/Perfect. This company had strong links to Europe, and the records by the Red Heads were widely issued on various European labels.

6. Red had made hot records before for Brunswick's Vocalion label from December 1924, at first with the Tennessee Tooters, then with the Hottentots. Red would use the band name "his Five Pennies" until he died in 1965.

7. This instrument is also known by the more descriptive name *kettle drum*.

8. Ralph Berton, *Remembering Bix*, Harper & Row, New York, 1974, 100–106.

9. Richard Sudhalter, in his book *Lost Chords* and writing about Nichols and Mole in the liner notes of *Red Nichols & Miff Mole*, Retrieval CD RTR79010.

10. Rollini may have been present on the previous Five Pennies recording session on 18 May 1927, but its results were unissued.

11. Probably this was Tommy Dorsey, and in that case it may have been due to unpleasant behavior, for which he was known.

12. Composed in 1918 by black composer Turner Layton and titled "After You're Gone" by mistake.

13. Rollini's break differs between the two existing takes of "After You've Gone." On the less common take 2, Rollini's break has a "ghost" note, a note that the listener expects and hears, but which is not actually played. As the recording shows, Rollini cleverly dissolves the problem thus created. Breaks similar to Quealey's can be heard on "After You've Gone" as recorded by the Charleston Chasers, some months earlier.

14. The Annette Hanshaw date was not organized by Ed Kirkeby, who would have listed the date in his notebook. Pathé's recording ledgers are mostly lost, so it is hard to define the exact recording date. However, the matrix numbers immediately follow the ones from the above Pathé session of 24 June. Since Rollini also recorded at Cameo that day, it is quite unlikely that the Hanshaw session, which produced at least five titles, was also on that same day. It is also unlikely that the session took place on Sunday 26 June, since Rollini had never done a recording session on a Sunday. It may therefore be concluded that it was either on Saturday 25 June, the day of the Nichols session, or on Monday 27 June, when Rollini would have a recording session with Ed Kirkeby again.

15. He became her manager and married her in 1929. Herman was nicknamed "Wally." This Wally Rose should not be confused with Wally Rose the piano player with Lu Watters's Yerba Buena Jazz Band in San Francisco in the forties.

16. Telephone interview by Jack Cullen in 1972. Cullen was a Canadian radio man who played historical recordings in his program.

17. A harpaphone looks like a small vibraphone, with horizontal parts like a xylophone, but in addition vertical resonance tubes hanging underneath. It has two-and-a-half octaves and is pitched higher than a vibraphone, but lower than a glockenspiel. A hard mallet was used to strike it, thus producing a sound like a celeste.

18. Five titles were issued. A sixth title may have been recorded (matrix 107648), but it remained unissued and no title or test pressing is known.

19. According to the record labels, the others were Keane and Rodgers.

20. Frank van Nus, a Dutch musician and orchestra leader and winner of the (American) Goldkette Award, notes that it is quite normal to give a singer a key to sing in that is comfortable for him/her. He analyzed these two recordings as follows:

> "I'm Somebody's Somebody Now" starts in the key of E, then Rollini uses two bars to modulate chromatically via E♭-D-D♭-C to F. Then Hanshaw has to wait a short moment before she can start, since the tune has an upbeat; the three syllables "Be-cause-I'm" are sung before the actual first bar and there is no room for this in the modulation. The result is a short "vamp."

In "I Like What You Like" more or less the same thing happens. Rollini modulates from the key of E♭: with a chromatic modulation, from the key of E♭ to the key of F. Rollini implicates with single notes the chords E♭-D-D♭-C. The C chord now has the "dominant function," which, as in any song, decides the key for the listener. The final note C is taken over by guitar and tympani, followed by F on guitar, tympani, and bass saxophone. This brings the tune to the new key.

About the piano solo in this tune: at the start piano and bass saxophone can be heard simultaneously, and after its end the bass saxophone follows very closely (one bar between).

However, both Joe Venuti and Annette Hanshaw could play the piano, and Brian Rust in the liner notes to *Annette Hanshaw Vol. 3*, LP Retrieval FV-205, suggests Rube Bloom as the pianist. If it is not Bloom (with a surprise appearance), then Hanshaw is most likely.

21. A sixth title may have been recorded during this session, but it remains undiscovered.

22. After Herman Rose died in 1954, Hanshaw remarried, to Herb Kurtin. She died in 1985.

23. *The New Grove Dictionary of Jazz*, ed. Barry Kernfeld, McMillan, London, 1994.

24. It was not the first violin/guitar duet in jazz. Almost half a year earlier, in April two unknown musicians had recorded a thirty-two-bar duet on an obscure Pathé recording of the tune "Hello, Aloha, How Are You?" (A. Brilhardt and his Orchestra, Pathé 14619).

25. His notebooks show dates for OKeh on 12 August ("Singing Trio"), OKeh 16 September ("Trio"), Pathé 20 October ("Mixed Quartet"), OKeh 26 October ("Mixed Quartet"), and Pathé 27 October ("Mixed Quartet").

26. Kirkeby would reintroduce the band name Little Ramblers in 1935 for the Bluebird label.

27. Its titles suggest that Harry Barris's tune "Play It, Red," was composed for Red Nichols, but there seems to be no evidence other than that Red recorded it once.

28. His first name is unknown.

29. "Pastafazoola" was a 1927 hit created by the comedy team of Van & Schenk. It tells of the masterful feats of world-leading individuals who ate the traditional Italian dish, pasta Faggioli, and must particularly have appealed to the Italian members of the band, Rollini and Felline.

30. A year before, Jelly Roll Morton had also quoted Chopin's *Marche Funèbre* in his recording of "Dead Man Blues."

As for kazoo playing, this was often usually a task for the drummer of the band. For the California Ramblers, Stan King had been well-known in this capacity. Herb Weil, present on this 1927 recording, may have had the same talent, so he may have been the kazoo player on take 3. He may also have been the whistler on take 1.

31. The Depression put an end to Jay C. Flippen's recording work, but in later life he managed to build a career on radio, film, and television. As late as 1967 he played a role in the NBC western series *The Road West*.

32. About Beth Challis hardly any information is available. She was not related to arranger Bill Challis. She had made her first record for OKeh the month before, and in the following months the company recorded her again several times. In 1928 she performed in England, where she also recorded.

33. OKeh made solo recordings of Lonnie Johnson and "Texas" Alexander that same day.

34. Alternate takes have been found of three of the four titles.

35. That day Room #2 was in use by the Colonial Club Orchestra, directed by Louis Katzman, and Room #3 by Bernie Cummins and his Orchestra.

36. Brunswick studio data mention nine men (eight plus Nichols himself) for the morning session and seven for the afternoon one, both obviously wrong.

37. Brunswick studio data mention that "Printed arrangements were used."

38. Interviewed by Whitney Balliett, quoted in *Pee Wee Russell: The Life of a Jazzman*, by Robert Hilbert (1993), 47.

39. Livingston's career never took off. He moved from one big city to another and wrote arrangements for various bands and the movie industry, but never had steady work for a long period.

40. Quoted in Hilbert, *Pee Wee Russell*.

41. This is more likely than it may sound. The recording was issued in many countries as long as 78 rpm records were produced.

42. Whiteman's club opened on 18 Feb 1927 and closed three months later. It had just barely covered its enormous cost (the weekly payroll for Whiteman's band was $6,400, the club's weekly production cost $30,000). Incidentally, on opening day Bix Beiderbecke may have been present: on 17 February he had picked up a new cornet in New York, a Vincent Bach Stradivarius. According to Albert Haim in *Mississippi Rag*, March 2005, the ballroom had had different names at different times. Before it became the Cinderella Ballroom in 1924, it had been known as Rector's, the Boardwalk, and the Café De Paris. In 1927 it became the Whiteman Club and the Club New Yorker. In 2006 it was replaced by a twenty-five-story apartment building.

43. A payroll from this period shows a total of $1,923 for the Victor band, for sixteen musicians. Bix got $123, Tram got $150. The weekly payroll at Atlantic City was even higher, $2,096. Evans and Evans, *Bix: The Leon Bix Beiderbecke Story*, 1998, 277; Evans and Kiner, *Tram: The Frank Trumbauer Story*, 1994, 76.

44. Hill, *Sylvester Ahola*, 22.

45. Sudhalter and Evans, *Bix: Man and Legend*, 208. Trumbauer was commonly known by his nickname "Tram."

46. When he was interviewed by Tom Faber on 5 August 1983, Abe Lincoln recounted that he was present at a Goldkette performance when Bix fell over and lost his two false front teeth. Bix stopped playing and went looking for his teeth and found them. The next day Bix went to a dentist, and if this was the day of the Herlihy session, it would explain Bix's absence.

47. Interestingly, Red Nichols and Joe Venuti also decided to add a bass instrument to their recording groups in these months, and both chose Rollini.

48. Lang was not a regular member of the Goldkette band, but he was on several of its records.

49. A test pressing exists of an unknown take.

50. Stephen M. Stroff, *Red Head* (1996), 80.

51. Merrill Kaye's Jewish parents migrated to the United States from Hungary. Merrill was born in the United States. He was athletic, tall (6 foot 2), and became a high school physical training teacher. This did not pay enough, so he went into music. As a musician he wanted to be "aggressive," not hesitate but push forward (interview by Tom Faber, 28 July 1983).

Chapter 10: A Band of His Own

1. Chip Deffaa, in his 1988 liner notes to a Sunbeam CD set, quotes Bix's friend Esten Spurrier, to whom Bix had said that he would never join the Whiteman band no matter what Whiteman might offer.

2. Letter from Art Rollini to Tom Faber, 31 July 1981.

3. Quoted in letter from Tom Faber to Art Rollini, 12 July 1981. On the other hand, Bix Beiderbecke has been quoted to Eddie Miller saying that "Bill Rank is still my favorite trombonist" (Evans and Evans, *Bix*, 521). When Bill Rank visited the Netherlands in 1968 and 1969, his style had matured and his work was admired.

4. Neil Waterman visited the Club New Yorker about six times and remembered Adrian playing chimes there, but not goofus.

5. Confirmed by John Steiner in *Record Research* 42, March 1962, 10.

6. During Whiteman's forty-week tour from September 1927 through July 1928, he received $16,250 weekly, of which less than half went to his musicians: A weekly payroll ledger for Whiteman's band, dated 20 January 1928, exists. It amounts to about $7,500 (Sudhalter and Evans, *Bix: Man and Legend*, 252).

7. Some discographies and biographies claim that Bix recorded his famous piano solo "In a Mist" on this Friday 9 September date, before he (and Tram) could run off to Rollini's rehearsal. However, newer information suggests that "In a Mist" was recorded on the day of the Hanshaw session (Ross Laird and Brian Rust, "Discography of OKeh Records, 1928–1934").

8. Letter from Sylvester Ahola to Phil Evans, 4 February 1963.

9. Evans and Evans, *Bix*, 281.

10. Unlike the British Parlophone, which had all the names on the label but substituted Arthur Schutt for Rube Bloom.

11. "A Mug of Ale" is based on the chord sequence of the tune "Limehouse Blues" (Mike Peters in the liner notes for Mosaic MD 8–213).

12. The quote from Rollini is from a clipping in a thirties newspaper; Venuti's remark is from Evans and Evans, *Bix*, 287. Adrian's friend Neil Waterman (the financial backer of the New Yorker Club venture, according to Ahola interview by Tom Faber) had an original copy of this photograph. It burned in a fire he had in his living room, but fortunately he had had a copy made for Tom Faber just a few weeks before (letter from Tom Faber to Art Rollini, 15 September 1982). Tom may have had a copy with Waterman's name on it, but he certainly had another copy too. Sylvester Ahola had a copy that was borrowed by Brigitte Berman in Toronto for a film on Bix Beiderbecke and was not returned (Ahola letter to Tom Faber, 21 September 1985).

13. Adrian took his younger brother Art to a rehearsal, which deeply impressed him—even more so when he heard the band over his two-tube radio set that same night. Art Rollini interview by Tom Faber, 11 July 1982.

14. Both titles had solos by clarinet player Don Murray. Bix did not participate.

15. OKeh would issue this, coupled with Bix's piano solo "In a Mist," recorded the week before. The team of Bix on piano, with Tram and Lang, had made a similar experimental recording in May, "For No Reason at All in C."

16. *Brooklyn* (New York) *Daily Eagle*, 22 September 1927.

17. *New York Evening Post*, regular listing until 18 October 1927.

18. Figures for the size vary. On Whiteman's opening night, the capacity was limited to 850 (*Variety*, 23 February 1927). The size could be adapted as the situation asked for.

19. John Steiner in *Record Research* 42, March 1962, 10: Bea Palmer "who had gathered the angels for this venture." *Variety*, 22 September 1927, had the news that Bea Palmer had left for Chicago and was not to appear at the Club New Yorker, whose "sole attraction" would be Frank Fay.

20. *Variety*, 31 August 1927, said that he was to earn $1,500 a week at the Club New Yorker. His stooge there was Patsy Kelly (Evans and Kiner, *Tram: The Frank Trumbauer Story*, 1994).

21. He made several films, starting with the 1929 *The Show of Shows*, and married actress Barbara Stanwyck, who surpassed him in his career, which led to their divorce in 1935.

22. In communication between Tom Faber and Neil Waterman (interview, letters) this subject was not mentioned. But in conversation with the author, Tom mentioned it as a natural fact. He got the information directly from Sylvester Ahola, in whose biography it is stated (Hill, *Sylvester Ahola*, 1993, 22). As a guitar player, Neil Waterman recorded with bands led by Stew Pletcher and Carl Webster.

23. Sylvester Ahola interview by Tom Faber, 7 October 1985. Ahola said that he had often wondered what the other band members thought of his story, because they were not there.

24. Sylvester Ahola interview by Tom Faber, 7 October 1985.

25. Sudhalter and Evans, *Bix*, 215.

26. During an interview with Tom Faber, Spencer Clark remembered being the victim of a similar experience. In 1974 he had a recording date with Joe Venuti, in which it was intended to duplicate the Blue Four. Clark's friend ran the studio and had said to Joe: "I know a bass sax player who can do this thing." Clark: "That was a bad session because Venuti glared at me. If he would look at me at all, he ... ferocious! And I started to get this feeling and shiver up inside. I couldn't get a deep breath and I got nervous. I thought: 'This guy hates me.'"

27. On the club's opening night, it was silent in the streets. The American public stayed at home to listen to the radio: the world championship heavyweight boxing match between Jack Dempsey and Gene Tunney took place. It was heard over seventy-four stations. Tunney won, in what was afterwards called the "long count match."

28. In a letter of 27 December 1985, Norman Strutt, a member of Landry's orchestra, confirmed that he visited the Club New Yorker with "three or four other fellows, [including] Dennis 'Dinty' Curtis [sax] and Al Rickey. The latter, who played the violin and guitar, was from Philadelphia and a friend of Eddie Lang ... who was the only one to come to our table. ... Charlie Barber (bass) may have been in our group."

29. The title of this tune refers to the well-known nursery rhyme.

30. Liner notes by Brad Kay for *The Story of Fud Livingston*, CD Jazz Oracle BDW 8060.

31. Opened on Broadway on 1 September 1927.

32. A month after the recording, a $25 check was made out to Bix by Sam Lanin. This may have been for Bix's Broadway Bellhops session. The session produced a third title, a waltz titled "Rainbow of Love," in which Bix and Bill Rank did not participate.

33. On 29 September, Ahola wrote in his diary that Deno and Rochelle were in the club. They performed (as a dancing duo?) and their names were on the marquee outside the club.

34. Interview with Tom Faber, 7 October 1985.

35. In 1924 Bix had recorded "Jazz Me Blues" and "Royal Garden Blues" with the Wolverines, too.

36. According to Charles Edward Smith, the arrangement of "Jazz Me Blues" was by Adrian Rollini (quoted in Evans and Evans, *Bix*, 524).

37. Rollini's solo on "At the Jazz Band Ball" has been called his best ever, and "Jazz Me Blues" is the author's choice to take to a desert island.

38. From a letter from Sylvester Ahola of 16 February 1963 to Phyl Evans, via Scott Black.

39. According to Sylvester Ahola's diary, Fay's act involved eggs and so Don Murray brought some eggs to the stage. Ahola: "We clown with them as it is Frank Fay's gag." On some numbers Fay was accompanied only by piano player Arthur Franklin.

40. From *Film House Reviews*, quoted in Evans and Evans, *Bix*, 1998, 292. The program at the Strand (or the Mark Strand, as it was in fact called) (from the official program and an item the *New York Daily Star* of 8 October, condensed by the author):

Notes 435

1. Joseph Plunkett's Mark Strand Frolic—ballets and music with Mark Strand Symphony Orchestra, directed by Carl Edouarde, Alois Reiser or A. Coroshansky—played the ballet fantasy "The Crystal Gazer"
2. Mark Strand Topical Review—pictorial news of the world
3. The Aristocratic Vagabond Frank Fay, presenting for the first time on any stage "Midnight at the New Yorker" with the Original New Yorker Orchestra, Patsy Kelly, Lew Mann, Olive McClure, Arthur Franklin and Frank Fay (himself) (direct from the Club New Yorker) (Kramer Miniature Grand Piano Used by The New Yorkers)
4. First National Pictures, Inc. Presents Billie Dove in "American Beauty." Another leading role was for Margaret Livingstone, who, in 1930, would become Paul Whiteman's fourth wife.
5. Organ solo by Walter Wild and Frederick Smith.

The "Kramer Miniature Grand Piano" was played by Bix Beiderbecke (according to a letter from Sylvester Ahola to Phyl Evans of 16 February 1963, who added that the instrument had erroneously been called a celeste).

41. Frank Fay continued in vaudeville. He took colleagues Patsy Kelly (his stooge) and Lew Mann to the Majestic, where they were working on 23 November 1927 (clipping from *Brooklyn Daily Eagle* of that date).

42. On 17 October he rehearsed and on 19 October 1927 recorded with Van Steeden for the Gennett label. The results remained unissued.

43. Jack Benny (1894–1974) had been on stage since ca. 1910. He started his career as a violin player, but later developed into a popular comedian who remained successful well into the days of television. Interestingly, Benny has stated that he modeled his early stage character on Frank Fay. From 16 September Benny had been master of ceremonies at The Palace in a ten-act show, which was headed by Blossom Seeley, among others, and included Arnold Johnson's Orchestra and Ethel Waters.

44. When Tom Faber interviewed Sylvester Ahola on 7 October 1985, Ahola remembered a scene at the Strand that may come from the same act. Venuti asked the men in the band to play "anything you want in any key. And we did, I played a cadenza, somebody did this, Bix tried it . . . no sense to it, no key, nothing. I don't know what the people thought, they must have thought we're going crazy."

45. Evans and Kiner, *Tram*, 1994, 78.

46. Amazingly, an announcement in the *Brooklyn Daily Eagle* of 23 November says that "Jack Benny and New Yorkers" are performing at the Hillside Theater, where the movie *Spring Fever*, with William Haines, is shown. It is unlikely that this had anything to do with Rollini's group. Benny may have found another band and used the same name.

47. Vince Giordano, quoted in Evans and Evans, *Bix*, 296.

48. "Royal Garden Blues" was composed by Clarence and Spencer Williams, "Goose Pimples" by Joe Trent and Fletcher Henderson.

49. Letter to the authors of Evans and Evans, *Bix*, 297.

50. On the same date, Victor recorded Blue Steele's orchestra in Atlanta, Georgia.

51. One of those who confirmed that it is Bix was Bill Rank, in an interview in England in the sixties (*Storyville*, September 1968, 40). Several authors agree with this, but others mention different candidates. Trumpet players Sylvester Ahola and the brothers Bo and Bob Ashford, one of whom participated in the Nichols session in the morning, denied their presence.

52. This has confused collectors to the present day. After August 1927, Rollini made no records for Kirkeby anymore. The session of 31 October 1927, in which a small group accompanied Jay C. Flippen, is illustrative. Clark played several licks that he took from Rollini, but did not solo yet.

53. Evans and Kiner, *Tram*, 78.

54. John Steiner in *Record Research* 42, March 1962, quoting Cush and Priestley.

55. Neil Waterman, interview by Tom Faber, 17 July 1982.

56. Ahola became the successor of another American trumpeter, Frank Guarante, who left on a tour through Europe with the Savoy Orpheans, under the name Original Orpheans Band. Violinist Reg Batten had taken leadership of a band at the Savoy in 1923, the Savoy Havana Band. His co-leader was reed player Rudy Vallée. With interruptions, Batten kept that position until the end of 1927. The Savoy had a policy of hiring two bands and in 1923 the second band was the Savoy Orpheans. W. de Mornys, who by 1927 managed both bands, held the contracts with the musicians, but the labor permits for the American band members were obtained through the Savoy. By 1 January 1928, de Mornys had withdrawn the Savoy Havana Band from the hotel and Batten became leader of the Savoy Orpheans. (This note is largely based on an article by Edward S. Walker in *Storyville*, issue 30, August 1970, 218–29.)

57. When Brown left in February 1928, he was succeeded by Min Leibrook, who played both tuba and bass saxophone.

58. Elizalde had tried to get Red Nichols, too; the Savoy was already seeking a work permit for him when Red decided that he had enough work and did not want to go (information from Nick Dellow, 17 March 2004).

Chapter 11: With Fred Elizalde in England, 1928

1. As explained by Marciano R. De Borja in his book *Basques in the Philippines*, 2005, 128. This book has been helpful for filling in the Elizalde family background.

2. Also called Maria del Carmen Monreau Diaz.

3. As claimed by him in an interview published in The *Newcastle Sunday Sun*, 11 November 1928 (via an article on Elizalde in *Needle Time* 3, March 1986, by Nick Dellow).

4. Much to his disgust, as he admitted in an interview (*Newcastle Sunday Sun*, 11 November 1928). In the same interview he said that he had a row with his father ("a successful sugar and hemp planter—successful enough to be a millionaire several times over") when he decided not to study, and was told by his father to "get out." In the United States he had been invited by Paul Whiteman to join his orchestra, but Elizalde wanted to be a bandleader, not a sideman.

5. The hotel, at 6th Street and Olive Street, opened in 1923. In that year Herb Wiedoeft got the contract for his band and started to make records for Brunswick, a new gramophone record company in New York (available on Timeless CD CBC 1-079). In 1969 the Biltmore Hotel was designated a Los Angeles Historic-Cultural Monument by the City of Los Angeles. It is now called the Millennium Biltmore and is part of the Millennium chain.

6. Available on Timeless CD CBC 1-061.

7. From an interview published in the *Newcastle Sunday Sun*, 11 November 1926, via an article on Elizalde in *Needle Time* 3, March 1986, by Nick Dellow.

8. In a period of about half a year, Elizalde recorded twenty titles with his own bands and fourteen piano solos.

9. Available on *Cambridge University Jazz*, Jazz Oracle CD BDW 8061. The Brunswick titles were recorded in the old-fashioned acoustic way; the HMV titles used up-to-date electrical equipment, and the difference in sound quality is striking.

10. Known Elizalde arrangements are "Me and My Shadow" for the Savoy Orpheans and "Take Your Finger Out of Your Mouth" and "Possibly" for Bert Ambrose's dance band. The latter two were recorded for Brunswick. For one recording session, Elizalde used Ambrose's band.

11. Nick Dellow wrote a series of eighteen articles about Fred Elizalde in *Needle Time*, which appeared between March 1986 and May 1989.

12. The Savoy opened on 6 August 1889. It overlooks the Thames, but its main entrance was on the other side of the building, on the Strand. It had lost nothing of its elegance when it celebrated its 100th year in 1989. By that time, it featured 202 bedrooms and suites. It closed in December 2007 for extensive renovations and reopened in October 2010 with 268 rooms.

13. Nick Dellow has mentioned (in the Bixography forum on internet, 17 March 2004) that Red Nichols had been approached by the Savoy management to join the hotel band, even before Elizalde worked there. Nichols declined because he had more than enough work in the United States.

14. Born Hartford, Connecticut, 12 March 1905. According to "Dan" Wyllie (in a 1983 or 1984 article), who worked in Elizalde's first British band in 1926, Manuel Elizalde originally wanted to contract Bix Beiderbecke, but Bix had immediately joined Paul Whiteman after the collapse of Adrian Rollini's New Yorker band.

15. The group traveled via Boston to Liverpool on the R.M.S. *Cedric*, owned by the White Star Line. It could hold 347 first-, 250 second-, and 1,000 third-class passengers. On this and his following trips, Rollini and his fellow passengers traveled second class.

16. Brunswick was an American manufacturer of gramophones and records. In 1926 it opened a pressing plant in London. In August 1928 British Brunswick was taken over by Duophone.

17. *Daily Mail*, 23 November 1927.

18. In addition to the bands of Fred Elizalde and Reg Batten, the Savoy hired a tango band, Andre Pesenti's Lulu Fado Band, that played gypsy music in addition to tangos.

19. The artist credit Goofus Washboards was used on some British issues of the Goofus Five (who used no washboard!).

20. Hill, *Sylvester Ahola*, 27.

21. Norman Payne interview by Nick Dellow: "Every night, there was not a night we missed. We just had to, . . . we came from the hotel then we had a sort of breakfast you know, including Chelsea. He wanted me to have a fried egg sandwich with a flash of raw onion on them and with tomato ketchup."

22. This club became notorious during the twenties for outrageous parties frequented by the decadent rich and famous (Wikipedia).

23. George Hurley interview by Tom Faber, 28 March 1982. Hurley's colleague and friend Harry Gold was interviewed by Tom Faber in 1981 and gave details about illegal drinking of alcoholics in the nightclub where he worked, the Melton Club: "Two a.m. was the time when

people could drink until, provided they had food with it. The nightclub carried on illegally. . . . they would serve drinks after two in the morning but in teapots and coffeepots."

24. British Broadcasting Corporation, the national broadcasting organization.

25. *Melody Maker*, March 1928.

26. 3 February 1928. Musical notables were present, such as composer William Walton, who had been arranger for the Savoy Orpheans two years before.

27. This was in 1929. Art Rollini interview by Tom Faber, 1 July 1982.

28. *Hull Evening News*, 5 January 1928.

29. *Wireless*, March 1929.

30. The New Savoy Orpheans did not get a new recording contract at this time and began recording again only in late 1928, for a minor label.

31. The year before, Elizalde had recorded for Brunswick at a studio located at their pressing plant in London's Shepherd Bush district. Those recordings were made acoustically. The new studio used electric recording equipment. In the following few years, the Brunswick recording sheets (as well as the master recordings) were discarded. Thus, company files about Elizalde's recording dates do not exist.

32. *Melody Maker*, March 1928.

33. Davis had done this on recordings by the California Ramblers, such as "Iyone," from 19 May 1926. The text of that tune refers to Hawaii.

34. Adrian's first composition named after Dixie Reemer had been "Dixie Stomp," recorded with the Five Birmingham Babies for Pathé/Perfect in 1925.

35. Rollini admirer and British sax player Harry Gold started to play bass saxophone after World War II, and made a fine recording of "Dixie" for Decca. In 1981 he was interviewed by Tom Faber, who told him that Adrian had a copy in his personal record collection. Harry was proud to hear this. He named several other British saxophone players who played bass saxophone at one time or another: Arthur Lally; Bert Larson, who sold reeds and mouthpieces; Rex Owen, Rollini's colleague in Fred Elizalde's band; Gill Port, who also played hot fountain pen and goofus(!); and Hugh Tripp, who played in Roy Fox's band.

36. *Melody Maker*, March 1928. The following month the magazine ran a competition on the drumlike sound behind Quealey's solo. The winner who identified Ronnie Gubertini's drumming sounds would win one British pound. Amazingly, there were three participants with the right answer: Gubertini was drumming on a newspaper covering an overcoat.

37. For the first time; see next note.

38. It mentioned Parlophone R3490 by the Goofus Five, but called the band "Adrian Rollini and the Goofus Washboards," although Rollini was present on only one side and no washboard was used at all!

39. These articles only concerned goofus and bass saxophone. There were no articles about piano, banjo, xylophone, or even trombone. (In *Melody Maker*, 7 July 1936, Fred Elizalde is quoted saying that he would not add a trombone player to the band: "Why should I? Adrian plays all the trombone I'm likely to want and much more.")

40. The month before, the British company Keith Prowse advertised their goofus "as featured by Adrian Rollini" for a price of three pounds.

41. On the record label it was called a "Hawaiian Saxophone chorus by Bobby Davis."

42. At the time, Elizalde's listeners were also familiar with the recording, before the Brunswick record was issued. In its April 1928 issue, *Melody Maker* pointed out that it was

played "exactly the same as the boys render it on the stand and probably many of you have heard it on radio." It continued with great praise: "The orchestration is a masterpiece."

43. Interview by Nick Dellow.

44. According to Harry Hayes in an interview, Hayes earned eighteen pounds a week ($90 at the time, according to www.measuringworth.com). George Hurley interview by Tom Faber in 1982, said that it was the equivalent of what a top executive of a big multinational company would earn at the time. Rollini was earning in one week what an average man would earn in six months.

45. Letter of 28 February 1986 from the *Austin Swallow Register* to Tom Faber. The Swallow Coachbuilding Company later achieved lasting fame as Jaguar Cars Ltd.

46. Elizalde lived at different addresses at different times. Nick Dellow noted that Elizalde had a flat off Park Lane.

47. George Hurley interview by Tom Faber, 28 March 1982.

48. The Essex became popular; in 1929 Essex was third in car sales behind Ford and Chevrolet. A few years later Essex's mother company Hudson changed the name Essex into Terraplane.

49. Titles were "Calling Me Home," "Moon of Japan," "I Call My Girl Revenge," "Did You Mean It," "Again," "The Song Is Ended," "I'll Be Lonely," "Just Another Day," "Teatime," "You Can't Have My Sugar for Tea," "Baltimore," and "Is She My Girlfriend."

50. Art Rollini, *Thirty Years with the Big Bands*, 11.

51. Among others, the *Goshen Democrat*.

52. Both titles on *Dorsey Brothers Orchestra Vol. 1*, Jazz Oracle CD BDW 8004.

53. Evans and Kiner, *Tram*, 573.

54. The program of the broadcast on 12 April 1928 is available. The titles were "How Long Has This Been Going On?," "Calling Me Home," "The Song Is Ended," "Tired Hands," "Here Am I, Broken-Hearted," "Ice Cream," "Rising Sun," "Did You Mean It?," "Sugar Step," and "Playground in the Sky." There were also a number of interesting titles in the Savoy Orpheans' program for that night, like "Baltimore" and "Sugar."

55. Elizalde's piano solos were "Can't Help Lovin' That Man" and "The Man I Love," issued on Brunswick 182.

56. The revue had music, lyrics, and a story by Noël Coward; it opened at the London Pavilion on 22 March 1928 and ran nearly ten months. In November it was taken to Broadway, New York.

57. It has been suggested that Bill Challis used the arrangement as a starting point for Paul Whiteman's recording, which was done a few weeks later (liner notes for Mosaic MD7-211 CD set).

58. *Melody Maker*, August 1928, mentions two more musicians, saxophone player George Smith and violinist Len Lee. Apparently they were considered but did not actually join.

59. In 1922 and 1923 in South Africa, Al Bowlly and Len Fillis had been members of Edgar Adeler's little band, Fillis playing guitar and banjo, Bowlly singing and playing ukulele. Fillis then left for London and eventually became a member of Elizalde's orchestra. In 1928 Bowlly worked in Berlin and received a letter from Fillis, saying that Elizalde's band had a vacancy for a singer. Bowlly sent one of his German recordings and Elizalde offered him a job at £14 a week; Al asked for more and got it.

60. Based on an article by Harold S. Kaye, published in *Storyville 1998-9*, Chigwell, UK: L. Wright, 1999.

61. Apparently Jack Russin arrived in England on Thursday 26 July, the same day that Elizalde's band departed for the continent. So he cannot have been on the recording date with Al Bowlly and may not even have made it in time for Paris. On board the *Ile de France,* other members of Carhart's band were Jack Purvis, trumpet; Bud Freeman, tenor saxophone; Spencer Clark, bass saxophone; and Vic Moore, drums. Carhart himself played banjo and guitar.

62. *Variety*, 16 and 23 May 1928, had the information. It listed the American artists: Waring's Pennsylvanians plus Buster and John West, Evelyn Hoey, Eleanor Shaler, Muriel Harrison, Frances Gershwin, Joan Wardell, Morton Downey, Katherin Ray, Three Eddies, Myrio, Desha and Barte, Brothers Pearson, and eighteen American girls. After a few weeks Sayag changed the show because it was considered too long. He cut it into three sections, presented in a rotating scheme during the week.

63. Another version of Waring's closing at Les Ambassadeurs can be found in John Chilton, *Sidney Bechet: The Wizard of Jazz*: Waring had a contractual clause for a second eight weeks, which he did not use, but returned to New York to work in a Broadway show.

64. *Variety*, 4 July 1928.

65. *Variety*, 8 August 1928.

66. He had recorded in June in London backed by Perley Breed, whose baritone saxophone style was not unlike Rollini's bass saxophone work.

67. During interviews both Harry Hayes and Norman Payne said that the band was well received. However, a thorough search of Parisian newspapers, done by the author in 2009, did not bring up even a single mention of Elizalde or his band, neither at Les Ambassadeurs nor at L'Empire, the second location where Elizalde was supposed to perform, according to *Melody Maker*, August 1928. It is striking to see the effect of promotion: in September Ted Lewis worked simultaneously at Les Ambassadeurs and at the Apollo. Press information started well before Lewis arrived by boat in Le Havre and continued after he departed from Paris, saying "we still have his records to listen to." This was the work of Columbia, Ted Lewis's record company. Elizalde recorded for Brunswick, which in France was still a small operation, not organized for such publicity.

68. Probably in *Melody Maker*, 29 May 1937. Polo thought that George Carhart then still led the band, but he had left several months earlier, and in fact was about to come back to Paris with another band.

69. "The New Yorkers," article by Horst Bergmeier in *Storyville* 145, March 1991.

70. *Le Figaro*, 15 August 1928.

71. From Ostend, Lewis planned to go to Deauville, a sea resort on the Normandy coast, and then to Paris, where his band would work at the Apollo and at Les Ambassadeurs.

72. The bands of Fred Elizalde and Ted Lewis were in Ostend simultaneously for a while. Harry Hayes remembered playing cards with some of Lewis's men, when Chelsea Quealey pulled a gun on him after Harry had won a hand (Harry Hayes interview by Nick Dellow). The story goes that Rollini's bass saxophone box was lost from his car while he was driving to Ostend. He discovered this after arrival and wanted to phone around. Then a visitor was announced: Dave Klein, who was Ted Lewis's trumpeter. Klein had found the lost box while driving along the same route and immediately understood that it had to be Rollini's (*Melody Maker*, unknown date but possibly 1936).

73. Elizalde's band worked in the Ambassador Salon. The relief was a four-piece group that included Stephane Grappelli on piano. A few years later, Grappelli would become famous as the violin player of the Quintette Du Hot Club de France.

74. This and the following two quotes from *Music*, August 1928, 4th year, no. 9.

75. In 1932 Goffin would publish *Aux Frontières de Jazz*, one of the first books about jazz.

76. Interviewed at home in Hilversum, Netherlands, by Tom Faber, 16 December 1980. It was Tom's first time meeting a musician who had received instruction on bass saxophone from Adrian Rollini.

77. Possibly an Otto Link, according to Robert. Adrian's brother Art thought he used a Vandoren mouthpiece.

78. Jean Robert interview by Tom Faber, 16 December 1980. Robert said that Elizalde's band did not make much money in Ostend, so Fred may have paid his musicians out of his own pocket.

79. *Melody Maker*, October 1928, put the blame for the Orpheans' failure fully on Reg Batten. It referred to Ahola and Brodsky as "not only wonderful musicians, but they can compete with the best in America for up-to-datedness of style, both 'hot' and 'sweet.' But how often did you hear them do anything worthwhile?" According to *Melody Maker*, for Ahola this was when he was recording outside the Orpheans and for Brodsky when he could sell a fine arrangement to other bands. Ahola stayed in England and Brodsky left.

80. According to George Hurley interview by Tom Faber, 28 March 1982.

81. Available at modernbarisax.com.

82. *Accrington Observer*, 5 October 1928.

83. None of the tunes mentioned were typical hot tunes, so this broadcast may have concerned the "melody combination" of Elizalde's crew, which featured the two violins. Titles were: "Just a Little Fond Affection"; "Come Down to Earth, Little Angel"; "Virginia"; "I Can't Give You Anything but Love"; "I Think of What You Used to Think of Me"; and "Was It a Dream?"

Chapter 12: With Fred Elizalde in 1929, the Second Year

1. 20 February 1929.

2. The copy of *The Sugar Step*, a ten-minute one-reeler, resides at the British National Film Archive. Nick Dellow has seen the film and reports to the author that Elizalde's band is clearly seen just behind the dancers. One can hear Adrian as well as see him. Before the band starts, an announcer introduces Elizalde and the camera pans closer and Fred stands up from the piano and takes a bow. The quality of the film is amazingly clear and the sound quality is also superb.

3. This may have been a harpaphone, a predecessor of the vibraphone. The xylophone has wooden keys; the harpophone has metal ones.

4. It may have been the first time that a vibraphone was heard on a record. Lionel Hampton only started to play it on record in 1930, with Louis Armstrong's Orchestra.

5. Jazz Masters CD JMS1001. The composers of this tune are unknown. It is not the same tune as "I'm Glad," recorded by the Sioux City Six with Bix Beiderbecke for Gennett in 1924, the composer of which was Frank Trumbauer.

6. Actually it was a comedy number in reaction to "Jollity Farm," a big hit at the time.

7. Letter, 13 February 1929, quoted by Nick Dellow in *Needle Time*, November 1987, part 9.

8. The broadcast of 14 February 1929 was one of Elizalde's last. Its program is known. Some of the twenty-two tunes played had been recorded by the band and allow comparison of the arrangements and jazz content; these are indicated *: "Sweet Sue"; "If I Had You"*; "Sonny

Boy"; "Misery Farm"*; "Come Down to Earth, Little Angel"; "I'm Sorry Sally"*; "Get Out and Get Under the Moon"; "Where Have You Been All My Life"; "Daybreak"; "Sarita"; "Girl of My Dreams"; "I Can't Give You Anything but Love"; "Virginia"; "Laughing Marionette"*; "Sometimes"; "Crazy Rhythm"*; "Jeannine"; "Alone in a Crowd"; "Out of the Dawn"; "Grown Up Baby"; "Falling in Love with You"; "Don't Be Like That"; and "Marvelous." Jack Payne and his BBC Dance Orchestra took Elizalde's spot on Thursday nights and Ambrose's Orchestra, from the Mayfair Hotel, on Saturday nights.

9. Titles were *The When, Why and How of the Bass Saxophone*; *Selecting the Instrument*; and *Mouthpiece Methods*.

10. Further "hot" choruses for saxophones from Rollini's hand were in *Melody Maker* of May and June 1929, respectively for "Where the Shy Little Violets Grow" and "My Blackbirds Are Bluebirds Now." In July and September, the magazine published music for bass saxophone, first the rhythmic part for "I Must Have That Man," then a "hot" chorus for "You're the Cream in My Coffee." During the same period, the magazine published scores written by Sylvester Ahola, Frank Coughlan, Fud Livingston, Norman Payne, and Frank Wilson.

11. Hot choruses by other musicians were also published by *Melody Maker* across a number of issues; the serialization of such scores lasted well into the 1930s.

12. By letter of 18 December 1928, the Savoy wrote to Elizalde that it would not pay the passage of the Americans, but it did pay the extra salaries.

13. Norman Payne interview. Adrian used his new saxophone on board, playing on the return trip.

14. See chapter 13 for more on Bert Lown.

15. *Orchestra World*, April 1929. Rollini's return would be in December 1929, at which time he started with Lown immediately.

16. The name Louisiana Rhythm Kings had been in use for other bands before.

17. Payne was interviewed by Nick Dellow and the interview was discussed by Albert Haim, moderator of the Bixography Forum on internet. Adrian may have tried in vain to hire Bix and Bing, but Bix was recovering at home in Davenport, Indiana, during the full month of February 1929 and Bing stayed with Paul Whiteman and sang with the Rhythm Boys for another year. In an article in *Melody Maker*, 5 December 1936, B. M. Lytton-Edwards, a pseudonym for the female music journalists (and Rollini fans!) Betty Edwards and Mary Litton, claim that Rollini even tried to hire the complete Whiteman's Rhythm Boys!

18. Cusick was married and said "no." Cusick interviews by Tom Faber, 9 September 1982 and 27 July 1983.

19. They would work for $150 a week, while Adrian was getting $250 a week. (Harry Hayes claimed that Adrian was paid £75 a week, about $375). In 2012 this is worth tenfold. The Savoy agreed to pay Fred an extra £500 per week for three more men.

20. These include "I'm Coming, Virginia"; "Side by Side"; and "Magnolia," all recorded when Red Nichols was a member of Whiteman's band.

21. Some of his tunes were "Feelin' No Pain," "Imagination," "Humpty Dumpty," and "Sax Appeal."

22. Fud Livingston's compositions include "Feelin' No Pain," "Imagination," and "Humpty Dumpty," which he also arranged. He clearly was one of the greatest arrangers in early jazz history. A CD is dedicated to this pioneer (Jazz Oracle BDW 8060).

23. Art Rollini interview by Tom Faber, 11 July 1982.

Notes

24. Art Rollini, *Thirty Years with the Big Bands*. By the time he was heard by Manuel Elizalde, Art could play Jimmy Dorsey's virtuoso solo piece "Oodles of Noodles."
25. In interview by Tom Faber, 12 July 1982, Art said that he earned $125 a week, and Adrian $250.
26. Art Rollini, unpublished autobiography written for his son, 1978, 3.
27. Norman Payne interview by Nick Dellow.
28. Apparently, Hal Fillis had taken over some of the tasks of Manuel Elizalde, who had taken care of most of the business aspects of Elizalde's organization. Fillis would hand the musicians their weekly paycheck. According to Norman Payne, he was Len Fillis's brother.
29. Cardew was a top arranger and impressed the Americans.
30. *Melody Maker*, March 1929, 257.
31. According to a letter of May 1929 in the Savoy Hotel archive. Nick Dellow, Fred Elizalde and his Savoy Hotel Music, part 10, *Needle Time*, January 1988.
32. Parlophon (without the final "e," but with same pronunciation) was founded in Germany in 1896 by the Lindström company, as a brand name for gramophones before making records. After World War I, Lindström set up branches in the United States (OKeh Records) and the UK (Parlophone Records). Parlophone established a master leasing arrangement with OKeh, making Parlophone a leading jazz label in the UK.
33. Rollini, *Thirty Years with the Big Bands*, 19.
34. Art Rollini claimed that he took over from Davis halfway through his chorus (Rollini, *Thirty Years with the Big Bands*, 19).
35. Other artists in this show included Barry and Fitzgibbon, Cecil Cunningham, Tom Davies Trio, Helen Ford, Four Harmony Kings, Danny Small, Three Eddies (Scott, Allen, and Lee?). The Three Eddies were a famous tap dance and singing group, who were in the 1926 *Blackbirds Revue* with Florence Mills and Johnny Dunn. The Tom Davies Trio was an act involving three men and their three motorcycles. In their review of the first show, the *Times* only mentions Elizalde's band and a group of nine negroes with the sketch "Dixie Rebels."
36. In 1927 Stone became the world's first deejay when he started a BBC radio program playing gramophone records.
37. *Daily Mirror*, 11 May 1929.
38. Quotes from *Melody Maker*, June 1929, 553 and 555.
39. A predecessor of the vibraphone. Vic Berton played it on a recording date with Red Nichols and Adrian Rollini.
40. Rollini, *Thirty Years with the Big Bands*, 18.
41. Danzi mentioned Dajos Béla, Fred Bird, Julian Fuhs, and Marek Weber. Lud Gluskin was in France at the time. He had been working in Berlin at Les Ambassadeurs until the end of March. Michael Danzi, *American Musician in Germany 1924–1939*.
42. Shepherd's Bush Pavilion was built in 1923 as a cinema theater and could hold three thousand visitors. Films were accompanied by a full orchestra, the Pavilion Symphony Orchestra. After the war this theatre was the location of the BBC's breakfast show for many years, presented by Sir Terry Wogan.
43. They sailed from Cherbourg, France, on the very day of the Shepherd's Bush concert. The SS *Columbus* delivered them at the port of New York on 1 July 1929. This may have been the end of one of Quealey's frequent trips to Paris. According to Sylvester Ahola, Quealey would take a plane and often would not get back in time. As long as Ahola was with the Savoy

Orpheans, it was easy for Elizalde to ask him to play first trumpet in Quealey's place, sight-reading the arrangements (Hill, *Sylvester Ahola*, 29). At the time of the concert, the Savoy Orpheans were no longer at the Savoy, and Elizalde asked Norman Payne.

44. Livingston actually had good reason not to leave: several of his arrangements would be played at the concert. Also, after only four months in England his tax problems must have been small compared to Quealey's, who had been in England for a year and a half.

45. The original program mentioned a waltz called "Viljah Valse," arranged by Livingston and Cardew.

46. Bix recorded it in September 1927 and Robbins Music published it in November, though there appear to be major differences between these versions. Bix's recording was issued around March 1928, so by the time of Elizalde's concert, collectors were familiar with the tune.

47. *Daily Chronicle*, 19 July 1929.

48. A letter to the Savoy of 5 July 1929 lists the expiration dates of the labor permits of Fred Elizalde and his American musicians. Fred's expired 31 July 1929, the day his Savoy contract ended. Adrian Rollini's expired on 13 August and Art's had in fact already expired on 13 June. The letter adds that this was no problem, as long as "the band were not going on after July 31st."

49. From the author's interview with André Eschauzier, published in *Doctor Jazz Magazine* 77, September 1976. In London, André and Eppo called themselves Andrew and Eppy. And thus, on 29 July 1929, they autographed a Savoy promotion card together with Dixie and Adrian. The card announced the Seven Eltzoffs ("The Dancing Whirlwinds") and Sealtiel ("The Ace of Humbugs") as entertainers during dinner and supper.

50. Dixie could entertain them with a little game in which she used her pearl necklace. She laid it out on the table in the form of a ring. You would be asked to put two fingers into the ring and then forecast if it would catch your fingers or not when she pulled it. You could make a little bet, but usually you would be wrong.

51. Compare the cost of a new bicycle: twenty-five guilders.

52. Interview published in *De Telegraaf*, 14 August 1929. Probably Rollini's first published interview. Tak forgot to send a copy to the Rollinis, but the Friedman brothers did (Amsterdam diamond dealers with whom the party had a dinner; the brothers had a large collection of jazz records).

53. The name may have been chosen out of admiration for the California Ramblers.

54. The date of Rollini's trip to Italy has not been found.

55. Rollini may have kept contact with some Americans in Berlin from his trip in May, if Mike Danzi's memory is correct (see earlier in this chapter).

56. *Jazz Revy*, June 1935.

57. This is a mistake. According to a Gluskin biography, he had been working at Les Ambassadeurs till the end of March and then had his band in France and Spain till ca. 1 October.

58. Letter of 31 August 1929, with letterhead of the Shelbourne Hotel, Upper Bedford Place, Russell Square, London. In a radio interview on 28 April 1944, Dixie said that Adrian and she visited Germany, Switzerland, France, Spain, and Italy, but did not mention Belgium and the Netherlands. The films were lost in a fire in Art Rollini's house.

59. Nick Dellow's interview.

60. Saxophonist Les Cripwell, quoted by Nick Dellow in *Needle Time* 18, September 1988.

61. She was not related to Madame Negri, Adrian's piano teacher. In the film studio, Pola Negri is addressed as Madame Negri too! The film's director was Paul Czinner, a German. The producer was an independent English producer, Charles Whittaker. *Today's Cinema News* reviewed it at the time of a tradeshow in May 1930, describing the film as a "romantic melodrama" dealing with a reformed prostitute (Negri), her pimp (played by Warwick Ward), and a taciturn lighthouse-keeper (Hans Rehmann). From a text by Kirk Bond in a pamphlet for the Theodore Huff Memorial Film Society.

62. George Hurley interview by Tom Faber in 1982, remembered that the recording was done on wire. At the time of the Pola Negri film, Fred Elizalde also wrote the music for another short movie, *Christmas Fantasy*. No copy is known to exist (Edward Walker in *Storyville* 33, February 1971).

63. Art Rollini interview by Tom Faber, 11/12 July 1982.

64. Interview with Adrian Rollini, *De Telegraaf*, 14 August 1929.

65. Both Metropole and its lower cost sub-label Piccadilly first appeared on the British market in 1928.

66. *Melody Maker*, January 1930, suggests that problems with a work permit may also have been the reason why the Rollinis returned to New York.

67. On 14 December a permit had been written for two friends of Dixie (as "Countess Rollini") to inspect "public rooms and passenger accommodations." Apparently, Dixie had wanted to show some friends around.

68. Farley went to Paris and then Berlin, where he was assisted by banjo player Mike Danzi, who got him a sax and a clarinet, some recording dates, and a place in a revue (Danzi, *American Musician in Germany 1924–1939*).

69. The British Ministry of Labor refused to extend the work permits of Farley and Davis, according to *Melody Maker*, January 1930, but in March 1930 the magazine reported that both were in the orchestra Elizalde organized for his "Intimate Revue," which opened on 11 March 1930, closed after one performance, reopened after a fortnight, and closed again after seventeen performances.

70. *Melody Maker*, January 1930.

Chapter 13: Out of Europe and into the Depression: Bert Lown

1. *What's On Air*, April 1931, and *Metronome*, October 1930 (quoted in *Record Research* 16, 8).

2. *Syracuse* (New York) *Journal*, 30 August 1930.

3. In 1925 Hamm's record company Victor went through the pains of introducing the new electrical recording process. During Victor's learning curve many recordings were rejected, and it took four recording sessions to get a master of "Bye Bye Blues" fit for issue. This was take 13, an exceptionally high number. A separate tune called "The Bye Bye Blues," composed by Paul Carter, was in the portfolio of Ed Kirkeby's company C.R. Publishing.

4. *Yonkers* (New York) *Statesman*, 10 December 1922. The orchestra played at a dance at the opening game of the basketball team of the *White Plains Daily Reporter*.

5. In 1925 he led an orchestra called Bert Lown's Novelty Orchestra (*Mount Vernon* [New York] *Daily News*, 3 April 1925); in 1926 he called it Bert Lown's Briarcliff Orchestra. In 1928

his band's name was more ambitious: His Personality Band. Lown continued as a bandleader until 1941, latterly working in South America. During the remaining war years, he worked as a leading executive in war relief organizations and then became associated with the Muzak Corporation. He died in November 1962.

6. Rudy Vallée, *Let The Chips Fall*, Stackpole Books, Harrisburg, 1975, 95. The club's manager was Don Dickerman.

7. In 1922 Vallée entered Yale University to study and took his saxophone along. In 1924 he went to Europe to join the Savoy Havana Band in London. Between September 1924 and May 1925 he recorded over forty titles with this band. In 1927 he graduated from Yale in philosophy and took up his career in music again. That same year he met Bert Lown.

8. A newspaper article gave more details of the conflict. It said that Lown "bought Vallée his first suit of evening clothes and coached him until he had achieved that certain 'sob-like tone in his voice which has since proved to one of his main sources of his present singing popularity.' . . . [Lown] wishes to have a receiver appointed for the earnings of Vallée and himself. The case is now being heard. . . . [Lown] states that he and Vallée made an agreement in 1928, under which they were to pool all their earnings and during the first year draw one hundred dollars a week, splitting the profits, two-thirds for Lown and one-third for Vallée, with a fifty-fifty division of profits effective the second year." Early in 1929, Lown alleges, Vallée refused to keep a broadcasting contract Lown had obtained for him, signed an independent vaudeville agreement of his own with Radio-Keith-Orpheum, refused to observe his partnership with Lown, and claimed all the earnings were his own. (*Scarsdale Inquirer*, 6 September 1929). Some newspapers ridiculed Lown's idea about Vallée's "sob."

9. *Brooklyn Daily Eagle*, 9 October 1929.

10. Address Bert Lown Orch., Inc., 1650 Broadway, New York, telephone CIRCLE 0686-0636.

11. Jazz lovers appreciate the April 1929 Bert Lown recording date particularly for the final title recorded, the jazz standard "Jazz Me Blues," which features a fine solo by trombone player Miff Mole.

12. *Syracuse Journal*, 30 August 1931. No doubt this is slightly exaggerated: at the time Lown was regularly advertising orchestras under his direction, which were "available for your social functions" (*Scarsdale Inquirer*, 8 November 1929).

13. "Mississippi Rag," article by Hawley Ades (unknown date). In 1930 Ades would join Bigelow's band.

14. *New York Evening Post* lists Bert Lown at the Biltmore from 4 December 1929.

15. Rudy Vallée had worked at London's Savoy Hotel, too. He probably told Lown about its high social status, so when Rollini returned fresh from London and the Savoy, it made him even more attractive to Lown.

16. *Radio Revue*, February 1930.

17. *Record Research* 16, 7, has a different personnel list, with Glenn Miller on trombone instead of Philburn, Sherry McGhee for Mace Irish, and Buddy Falce for Mac Ceppos. This personnel came from British collector Charles Waring.

18. No further recordings by Lou Bode and Mace Irish are known to the author, but both had longer careers in music. In 1930 Lou Bode was a member of a trio led by banjo player Larry Funk. Mace Irish died in 1963, aged fifty-five. Ed Farley made his name during the thirties and, when he joined forces with Mike Riley, scored an international hit with "The

Music Goes Round and Round." Mac Ceppos had the most impressive career of these four men. He became one of New York's best-known studio violinists and accompanied singers such as Perry Como and Patti Page, as well as the jazz great trumpeter Clifford Brown.

19. Sales in the start-up weeks are unknown, but they were low, judging by today's rarity of Lown's initial releases.

20. *New York Evening Post*, 1 February 1930. An article in *Radio Revue*, February 1930, said that the programs were recorded. This suggests they were not transmitted from the Biltmore (and that some of the transcription discs might still exist).

21. Allan Sutton and Kurt Nauck give details and background of this merger in their book *American Record Labels and Companies 1891–1943*.

22. *New York Evening Post*, 3 February 1930.

23. *Mount Vernon Daily Argus*, 27 February 1930.

24. Interview by Tom Faber, 5 October 1985.

25. Pete Pumiglio interview by Tom Faber, 7 August 1983.

26. *Brooklyn Standard Union*, 23 October 1931.

27. *Binghamton Press*, 21 January 1931.

28. *Syracuse Journal*, 30 August 1931; *New York Movie Magazine*, October 1931.

29. *Auburn Citizen*, 26 May 1931.

30. *Syracuse Journal*, 22 June 1931.

31. "Strike Up the Band," a Gershwin tune, followed by "I Never Dreamt" and "Blue Is the Night."

32. Clines's name was sometimes spelled Cline. He was not involved in the Brunswick recordings by Cline's Collegians, who were probably led by Durward Cline.

33. The *Brooklyn Daily Star*, 17 September 1932, listed the New Yorker, the Roosevelt, and the Waldorf hotels in New York, as well as hotels in Baltimore and Boston. The popularity of his orchestra was supported by regular broadcasts via the Columbia national network.

34. *Pelham Sun*, 21 May 1929. The year before, Rudy Vallée had another Lown band at the Milton Point casino.

35. *Billboard*, 31 May 1930.

36. *Yonkers Statesman*, 18 March 1931.

37. *Brooklyn Daily Star*, 18 February 1932.

38. *Pelham Sun*, 15 April 1932; *Brooklyn Daily Star*, 15 October 1932.

39. According to the *Mount Vernon Daily Argus*, 10 June 1933, the long list of celebrities included Fred Astaire, Belle Baker, Tallulah Bankhead, Milton Berle, Jimmy Durante, Fannie Brice, Frank Fay, Tess Gardella, Ethel Merman, Barbara Stanwyck, Lupe Velez, and many others.

40. *New York Sun*, 9 June 1930. The cascades were waterfalls.

41. The *Niagara Falls Gazette*, 13 September 1930, listed sixteen more stations on which Lown could be heard. A program on 18 September, shown in the *New York Evening Post*, opened with "Bye Bye Blues." Most tunes that followed were new and are now forgotten, but some got some popularity such as "I Don't Mind Walking in the Rain," "My Baby Just Cares for Me," and "I Like a Little Girl Like That."

42. *Syracuse Journal*, 22 August 1930. In August 1930 this was Duke Ellington's orchestra.

43. *Rochester Democrat*, 9 November 1930.

44. *Mount Vernon Daily Argus*, 18 July 1930. Lown collaborated with Harcourt Strange and Harry D. Cole on this song.

45. *Syracuse Journal*, 13 July 1930.

46. Interview with Tom Faber, 28 July 1983. Record labels of Lown's recordings of "Bye Bye Blues" carry the names Hamm–Bennett–Lown–Gray. Merrill Kaye also used the name Merrill Kline.

47. *Rochester Democrat*, 7 September 1930. In that same month the Capitol Theatre in Manhattan featured the revue *Bye Bye Blues*, with Stepin Fetchit and Ted Claire. Leo Reisman's orchestra recorded "Bye Bye Blues" for Victor around the same time.

48. According to *New Movie Magazine*, January 1931, its coupling "Maybe It's Love" was one of that month's biggest hits.

49. *Brooklyn Daily Eagle*, 9 September 1930. Newspapers announced Bert Lown's orchestra headlining at the R.K.O. 58th Street Theatre in a vaudeville program together with the film *The Bad Man*, starring Walter Huston.

50. *Hastings-on-Hudson News*, 12 September 1930.

51. *Brooklyn Daily Eagle*, 7 September 1930.

52. Interview by Tom Faber, 28 July 1983.

53. *Melody Maker*, August 1930.

54. *Auburn Citizen*, 7 November 1930; *Schenectady Gazette*, 31 October 1930. The latter advertisement also listed recordings by Bix Beiderbecke and by Duke Ellington.

55. *Motion Picture News*, 15 November 1930.

56. *Hot Rhythm*, an all-black musical, opened 21 August 1930 in the Times Square Theatre. Its subtitle was "A Sepia-Tinted Little Show." Edith Wilson was one of the singers.

57. *Schenectady Gazette*, 19 December 1930.

58. *New Movie Magazine*, October 1931. Originally both "My Missouri Home" and its session mate "Say Hello to the Folks Back Home" were accepted for mastering (coded "M" in the files), but this was changed to "Hold Conditionally" (coded "HC").

59. Ted Weems's orchestra recorded "Heartaches" for Victor on a later date, this version became a great hit.

60. Interview by Tom Faber, 28 July 1983.

61. At a Yale Alumni Dance on 3 January 1931, Lown's orchestra was directed by Ben Cutler (*Mount Vernon Daily Argus*, 30 December 1930). A few days later Cutler was the singer with Lown's orchestra at the Ritz-Carlton hotel (*New York Evening Post*, 8 January 1931).

62. *New York Evening Post*, 13 December 1930.

63. *Niagara Falls Gazette*, 27 December 1930.

64. The other leaders included Ben Bernie, Mickey Alpert, Jack Denny, Morton Downey, Fletcher Henderson, Howard Lanin, Guy Lombardo, Raymond Paige, Romanelli, Paul Tremaine, as well as the WSPD Commodores and the Musical Aviators orchestras. Columbia's competitor NBC came in strong too, with a similar program that offered Vincent Lopez, Paul Whiteman, and others.

65. *Albany Evening News*, 28 February 1931.

66. *Radio Digest*, February 1931. "Present conditions" did not keep up: in 1934 Lown would go bankrupt.

67. *New Music Magazine*, October 1931. The film has been seen by the author. It shows Bert Lown's band in a nightclub scene with Rollini in the band who is seen playing bass saxophone with his back to the camera. No information is available on Bert Lown's Vitaphone shorts.

68. *Albany Evening Journal*, 1 April 1931.

Chapter 14: Adrian Rollini: Freelance

1. Although it was then almost impossible for black and white musicians to publicly perform together, Reisman had worked with a black trumpeter before: Johnny Dunn, as a soloist in a concert in Boston in February 1928. Reisman's cooperation with Bubber Miley may have started in 1929, when he did a Vitaphone short called *Leo Reisman and His Hotel Brunswick Orchestra in "Rhythms"* (Vitaphone 770). It shows a trumpeter's silhouette during the playing of "The Mooche" and "Some of These Days." The trumpeter sounds like Miley, and by showing him in silhouette a race issue could be avoided. Reisman would hire Miley for particular recordings, as well as for occasional performances in his show. On recordings Miley worked anonymously; in shows he would appear as an usher, who would enter the hall from the back and play along with the orchestra sitting behind a curtain. The cooperation ended in mid-1931.

2. A third title was recorded, but without Miley and Rollini.

3. From Steve Smith's liner notes for *Louisiana Rhythm Kings 1929–1930*, Jazz Oracle BDW 8024.

4. With his postwar Five Pennies, Nichols used bass saxophone player Joe Rushton from 1947 till 1963.

5. Having two recording dates in a day was not entirely new for them. On 26 October 1927 Nichols and Trumbauer set up sessions at Victor in the morning and at OKeh in the afternoon. Rollini took part in both.

6. The Victor Salon Group recorded it. A jazz version was recorded by Marlow Hardy's Alabamians for Columbia.

7. Jimmy McPartland's name was made when he was selected to replace Bix Beiderbecke with the Wolverines in 1924. He belonged to the group of musicians that were commonly called "the Chicagoans," most of whom had come to New York by this time.

8. Weldon Leo "Jack" Teagarden had been the "new guy on the block" when he arrived in New York in 1927. He became well known for his individual style of singing and trombone playing. Glenn Miller followed Miff Mole in the trombone chair with Red Nichols bands, but Red hired Teagarden in April 1929 and thus he had two trombones for a while.

9. In a letter to Peter Tanner (quoted in Sinclair Traill's "Collector's Corner" in *Melody Maker*, 18 August 1951, 9), Teddy Bunn mentioned recording with Rollini for Brunswick at this time. He named Frank Froeba as the piano player. Froeba (1907–1981) was born in New Orleans and worked with Johnny Wiggs and John Tobin before moving to New York with Johnny Dedroit's band in 1924 (first records). He did not return to New Orleans, but worked around New York with various bands for many years, before retiring to Florida. Teddy Bunn (1909–1978) was born on Long Island. His recording debut had been only a few months earlier as a guest with Duke Ellington's band. During the thirties and in addition to other engagements, he was first a member of Washboard Bands and then of the Spirits of Rhythm. He remained active in music till the seventies.

10. There was a late-night spot for musicians in Harlem called Gladys' Clam House.

11. The three matrix numbers that follow Rollini's three are unknown.

12. The group played in a style that was linked to that of the Original Dixieland Jazz Band, and in fact was called thus on its first issued record. Ed Kirkeby was involved with this jazz group.

13. The OKeh company had started this policy the year before. Louis Armstrong's work is an illustration. During the fall of 1929 he recorded both vocal and non-vocal takes of his tunes.

14. Amazingly, two takes each exist of the non-vocal versions of the two tunes. The A-takes were actually issued on the rare American Parlophone and Odeon labels. The B-takes surfaced in the sixties, when collector and producer Chris Ellis discovered them in the EMI archives in England.

15. Confusion exists around Smelser's real name. He has been called Jack Cornell, Joe Cornell, and also just Cornell. In later years he called himself Charles S. Cornell (from Joe Showler's liner notes for Jazz Oracle CD BDW8053).

16. Others were Charles Magnante and Buster Moten, and in Europe, Gus Viseur (a Frenchman) and Johnny Meyer (a Dutchman).

17. As a member of a trio, the Three Blue Boys, in May 1929. One title was recorded but remained unissued.

18. Miller was on Red Nichols's payroll; in 1930 he received $125 a week when they were in a show, while union scale was only $80. In 1930 he wrote fifty-one arrangements for Nichols. Ray McKinley recalled to George T. Simon that, for Smith Ballew's band, Miller would take a printed stock arrangement, make cuts in it for a broadcast, and the next night he would take the same stock and make different cuts, which made it sound like a new arrangement.

19. In a letter of 30 December 1950 he wrote to an Australian fan: "I always like Red Nichols' Tea For Two—I wrote the intro to that."

20. Ben Selvin was one of the great pioneers of American popular music. In 1919, just twenty-one years old, he led an orchestra that recorded one of the first million-sellers, "Dardanella." His recording career lasted until 1963. He recorded for almost every major and many minor labels and made more records than any artist before him and possibly since. In 1927 he became associated with Columbia and in 1929 became their recording director (*Joslin's Jazz Journal*, August 2000). For that label he organized studio bands and performed on sponsored radio broadcasts. He was no longer so much in the public eye as a bandleader, but it was still Ben Selvin and his Orchestra on many record labels.

21. Charles "Buddy" Rogers was born in a suburb of Kansas City, Kansas, in 1904. He was a good-looking and successful silent film actor who became famous when one of his first films, *Wings*, won the first Academy Award for Best Picture in 1927. He continued his success when movies became talkies. In 1932 he signed with Victor and in 1938 with Vocalion. He recorded for these companies with his own orchestra. In 1937 he married silent film legend Mary Pickford and remarried after she died in 1979. Rogers died in 1999.

22. 16 April 1930. Eddie Walters is an enigma. He is first noted in 1927 as a radio singer who accompanied himself on his ukulele. In 1929 he is announced as Eddie Walters' Pals, which suggests that he led a band; in March 1929 he made his first Columbia recording, the slightly risqué "Makin' Whoopee," accompanied by piano and guitar. The recordings with Rollini were his third session. During 1930 he made several records, both under his own name and with Rube Bloom's Bayou Boys (with Rollini), with the Charleston Chasers, and with Ben Selvin's Orchestra. He continued broadcasting in 1931 and 1932. After 1932 he had a lower profile and all that is known are some spurious broadcasts in 1935 (as a member of the Modern Minstrels via WABC) and 1939.

23. Lee Morse was born as Lena Corinne Taylor in Kooskia, Idaho, on 30 November 1897. In 1920 she started her career and in 1922 she joined the Pantages circuit, in which reviewers

admired her extraordinary vocal range. In 1924 she started making gramophone records. During 1930, the year of her recordings with Adrian Rollini, she made several movie shorts. She continued her career into the 1950s, but it was hampered by her alcohol addiction. She died on 16 December 1954.

24. Had it not been for Dutch jazz historian Herman Openneer, Miller would have been quite enigmatic. But in the 1970s Openneer discovered that Jack Miller was a pseudonym for Jaap Mulder, a Dutchman who was born in Velzen, the Netherlands, on 16 March 1889 and then lived in Amsterdam. Before 1920 Mulder had studied music in London; he had a pleasant tenor voice, so that he could work as a singer. But his musical talent was wider, so he also worked as a musician, composer, and lyricist. Around 1920 he left for the United States and got acquainted with George Gershwin and Irving Berlin. Two years later he was back in London, where he was manager of the nightclub Blue Lagoon until 1926. In that year he led an orchestra called the New Englanders, mainly consisting of Canadians. He had some more short jobs until he left for the United States a second time in 1928. In August of that year, he had his first record on the Harmony label, using a pseudonym. Some of his first records were as by "Fred Waters," but eventually it became Jack Miller, a literal translation of his Dutch name. In 1934 Jack Miller returned to the Netherlands, where, under the name Jack Millar, he had a successful third career as a composer of operettas and music for film and theater. He died in Amsterdam on 10 August 1980. (Based on Openneer's article in the *Bulletin of the Dutch Jazz Archive*, December 1997.)

25. Odeon ONY6014.

26. Several anecdotes can be found in Richard Sudhalter's book *Lost Chords* (1999), which devotes a full chapter to Purvis, whose recordings were issued on 2002 on CD (Jazz Oracle BDW8035) with extensive liner notes by Michael Brooks.

27. One day Stephens lost his job due to the Depression. So he and Purvis sneaked out of their apartment, leaving behind a rental debt and Stephens's large collection of unissued OKeh tests pressings. "I had a room full of alternate takes by Louis, Bix, Miff, Red Nichols—everybody" (as retold by Michael Brooks, liner notes for Jazz Oracle BDW8035).

28. Stephens: "We had a little bit of money in the recording budget, nothing was selling anyway. I always thought that Jack in the right setting would really get some attention and so they let me put this band together. You know, in better times these sides would never have been made because the company would have put its money in the successful bands" (as retold by Michael Brooks, liner notes for Jazz Oracle BDW8035).

29. Rollini already had another recording in the OKeh race series, one of his three records under Bix Beiderbecke's name. His recordings with Jack Purvis made him the white artist with the second highest number of records in OKeh's race series, after Eddie Lang, who would record as Blind Willie Dunn. OKeh's race series was almost 100 percent reserved for black artists.

30. Rare, but not unique: Columbia had done it with Ted Lewis as a leader, OKeh with Louis Armstrong, and Victor with Eddie Condon, Red McKenzie, and Fats Waller.

31. Richard Sudhalter, in *Lost Chords*, 477, notes that Purvis developed his solo "sequentially," as Louis Armstrong would do it, as opposed to "compositionally," as Bix and his school of admirers did.

32. In Europe all six titles by Purvis's orchestra were widely distributed, and this made his name well known among collectors.

33. "Agua Caliente" means "warm water" in Spanish. There are several locations by this name, one being an Indian reservation in Southern California (Wikipedia).

34. Russell's version was recorded a few days later for OKeh; coincidentally, two takes survive of both Bloom's and Russell's versions. Recorded a few days later for OKeh, coincidentally two takes survive of both Bloom's and Russell's version of the tune.

35. Stan and Stephen Hester's work have been major contributions to the knowledge of these "Heat" programs. They produced a CD (IAJRC CD1011) and contributed an additional track to *Red Nichols 1926–1932*, Jazz Oracle CD set BDW8062/63/64.

36. This date and the following on 3 August are commonly quoted, but neither may be correct, since they present a Saturday and a Sunday.

37. Violinist Ben Glaser had the following personnel: Murray Deutsch and Jesse Salle, saxes; George Posnack, piano; Eddie Thomas, banjo and vocal; and Ben Weinberg, drums.

38. He is in the personnel of Ambrose's Brunswick recordings of that year, for which Fred Elizalde wrote arrangements.

39. Arluck would soon change his name to Arlen. "Minor Gaff" was one of his first published works. Harold Arlen became quite successful with later songs like "Stormy Weather."

40. Some recordings on the elusive QRS label exist that feature a talented bass saxophone player, but as a rhythm man only. Adrian Rollini is a candidate. These are:

| Carl Fenton | Shake It Down | QRS Q1023 (mx unknown, recorded January 1930) |
| New Yorkers | Fireworks | QRS Q1053 (mx 2378-2, recorded May 1930) |

41. *Radio Digest*, February 1932.

42. Five titles recorded during one session was unusual. The fifth title being by far the hottest of the five (and of all 1931 Renard's Brunswicks) suggests that it was not planned and more or less done as an afterthought when the required titles were ready and the musicians were given a free hand to play as they liked.

43. Ross Laird, *Brunswick Records: A Discography of Recordings, 1916–1931*.

44. Until at least June 1931, some titles feature a vibraphone note to end the recording, which does not suggest Rollini's presence.

45. Bud Freeman, *Crazeology*, 36. The story has elements that fit into Bix's chronology and elements that do not.

Chapter 15: Back to the California Ramblers and Bert Lown

1. *Florence Times News*, 7 December 1929, Little Ramblers at football dance.

2. In a circular letter of 7 December 1928 to warn against unauthorized use of the name California Ramblers, Kirkeby still called his band an "exclusive Columbia Record organization."

3. Amazingly, Edison used yet another artist credit for the band's output. This was as the McAlpineers, presumably after Kirkeby had gotten a contract to provide the music at the McAlpin Hotel.

4. Letter of 22 December 1928 from music publisher Bibo-Lang to Kirkeby.

5. Whiteman had just returned from California, where his band had made the movie *King of Jazz*. The film company did not use its option to do another movie with the band, so Whiteman had to find engagements quickly and accepted a small payment.

6. *Brooklyn Daily Eagle*, 2 May 1930. The opening was on 14 June.

7. *Pelham Sun*, 21 October 1932.

8. It is not known where Adrian Rollini lived when he worked with Bert Lown, but it is likely that he and Dixie had a permanent room at the Biltmore.

9. The show was for furrier I.J. Fox, via station WMCA.

10. An advertisement for the Chateau Shanley mentions "Music by Mr. Lada and his Louisiana Five." This was Anton Lada, a white drummer from New Orleans. *New York Evening Telegram*, 30 May 1923.

11. Art Rollini's unpublished autobiography, 1978.

12. A former Ziegfeld dancer and film actress, said to be of Hungarian-Austrian nobility.

13. Flyers, *Mount Vernon Daily Argus*, 16 May 1931; *Brooklyn Standard Union*, 19 May 1931.

14. Letter from Art Rollini to Tom Faber, 19 April 1983.

15. *Brooklyn Standard Union*, 25 May 1931.

16. *Niagara Falls Gazette*, 24 June 1931.

17. *Brooklyn Standard Union*, 15 July 1931. Ten years later Adrian had lost most of his original teeth and had them capped. Harry Clark interview by Tom Faber, 12 August 1983.

18. *Brooklyn Standard Union*, 19 May 1931; *Brooklyn Daily Eagle*, 25 July 1931.

19. *Brooklyn Daily Eagle*, 3 August 1931.

20. Letter from Art Rollini to Tom Faber, 19 April 1983. On another occasion Art wrote that the band finished at Hunter Island on Labor Day 1931, Monday 7 September.

21. Several copies of test pressings circulated among collectors and together they were used for a CD reissue.

22. A test pressing survived.

23. From February 1931 until March 1934, Kirkeby was involved in almost thirty recording dates for ARC, some directed by himself. The company issued the recordings as by Ed Kirkeby and Ed Lloyd. In 1935 Kirkeby would restart recording using the band names the California Ramblers, Little Ramblers, and Ted Wallace and his Orchestra.

24. *Brooklyn Daily Eagle*, 3 November 1931.

25. Wells would become a famous cartoonist and an amateur bass saxophone player. Interview by Tom Faber, 1 August 1983.

26. The Hollywood Gardens burned down on 15 October 1932 (*Pelham Sun*, 21 October 1932).

27. Rollini, *Twenty Years with the Big Bands*, 26. Violinist Jack Wechsler was out, Teddy Sandow was on trumpet instead of Chelsea Quealey, and Georg Hnida replaced Carl Smith on bass.

28. Art Rollini's unpublished autobiography, 11–14.

29. Letter from Art Rollini to Tom Faber, 19 April 1983.

30. In 1924 at the old California Ramblers Inn, the cover charge alone was $1.50. In 1932, at the new location, there was no cover charge and customers paid $1.50 for a dinner. Rollini, *Thirty Years with the Big Bands*, 26.

31. The New California Ramblers Inn had been the Pelham Heath Inn in 1926 and now, in 1931, the place across the street where Isham Jones worked carried this name. Both locations may have been owned by Susskind. *New York Sun*, 6 March 1931.

32. Later the three followed separate careers. Patti married and formed a duo with her husband. When Helen retired, Jane went into Ziegfeld.

33. The records were issued under Kirkeby's name, as well as under Ralph Bennett's, Owen Fallon's, and Art Kahn's.

34. Adrian used to bring female vocalists to his boat and audition them there. One day a guitar player bragged and told Phil Sillman about having an affair with Adrian's wife Dixie. When Phil told him that he was Adrian's cousin, the guitarist did not talk to him anymore (Phil Sillman interview by Tom Faber, 11 July 2005).

35. Art Rollini's unpublished autobiography, 15–16.

36. Rollini, *Twenty Years with the Big Bands*, 26.

37. Art Rollini in a letter to Tom Faber, 21 December 1982.

38. Art Rollini's unpublished autobiography, 16–18.

39. On various occasions, Art Rollini has suggested that Adrian called him one week after the New California Ramblers Inn had been closed by the police and asked him to join Bert Lown at the Park Central. Art's memory must have failed here; in the second half of 1932 and until March 1933, other bands worked at the Park Central.

40. The next month, February 1933, Freddie Martin would have an orchestra at the Park Central hotel. This may have been the band that recorded with Rollini in January, but when Rollini recorded for ARC again that same month, he selected an all-star group. In March Martin was succeeded at the Park Central by Bert Lown's band with Rollini.

41. One possibility is the session of 20 March 1933, on which a vibraphone is prominent in the title "Love Is a Dream."

42. Mike Peters in the liner notes for Mosaic MD8–213.

43. According to the *New York Sun*, 6 January 1932, he was succeeded by Ross Gorman's Orchestra.

44. *New York Sun*, 8 August 1931. MCA was said to have under contract about 75 percent of all "name" bands in the country.

45. *Brooklyn Daily Eagle*. She was using the name Dorothy Carlyn at the time.

46. Yet sometimes during a tour, Lown's band would still be called "His Biltmore Hotel Orchestra" (for instance, Dansville, New York, *Genesee Country Express*, 25 August 1932).

47. *Radio Guide*, 29 January 1933.

48. Today it is a thirty-one-story hotel at 56th Street and 7th Avenue. It has been downsized from 1450 rooms to 935. It was renamed several times, first to Park Sheraton, but in the 1990s it returned to its original name. In 1932 Noble Sissle led an orchestra there and he was succeeded by Harry Barris, Leon Navara, Russ Colombo, and, in February 1932, Freddie Martin. Martin's successor was Bert Lown, who worked at the Park Central from March 1933. The Cocoanut Grove was atop the hotel, twenty-six stories above street level, and overlooked the Hudson and Palisades on the West and Park Avenue and Long Island on the East.

49. Adrian may have worked at the Park Central in February with Freddie Martin's orchestra.

50. Art Rollini's unpublished autobiography, 20.

51. Lown also kept his extra bookings going and had a date with what was announced as his Biltmore Orchestra on Friday evening, 10 March at Memorial Hall, Carmel. During this performance Lown had an attack of indigestion, but quickly recovered. *Carmel* (New York) *Putnam Country Courier*, 17 March 1933.

52. Rollini, *Twenty Years with the Big Bands*, 29.

53. He had played chimes with his Club New Yorker band in 1927.

54. Art Rollini interview by Tom Faber, 11/12 July 1982; letter from Art to Tom, 25 January 1984; Phil Sillman interview by Tom Faber, 29 July 1983.

55. *Brooklyn Daily Eagle*, 5 and 7 April 1933.
56. Ted Holt was the singer on most of Bert Lown's 1933 recordings.
57. Lown's "glossary" of his radio sign language (*New York Sun*, 27 May 1933):

   1. Clenched fist—Ease from one song to another, without pause.
   2. First finger and thumb forming circle—Violin for the next eight bars.
   3. Three fingers—Heavy on piano.
   4. Four fingers up—Change of key for vocal.
   5. Elbow raised—Soften brass.
   6. Left thumb up—Skip to last chorus.
   7. Quivering hand—Add piano chorus.
   8. Fists shaken—Play whole song through.
   9. Fingertip on lips—Play one chorus only.

58. *New York Sun*, 6 June 1933; also *Brooklyn Eagle*, 17 June 1933, for more quotes.
59. *New York Sun*, 24 July 1933.
60. *New York Evening Post*, 1 December 1933.
61. During the months November 1932 till March 1933 three other name bands made their last records for Victor: those of George Olsen, Fred Waring, and Ted Weems. Like Bert Lown, Ted Weems moved to Victor's budget label Bluebird.
62. Most records were issued as by Bert Lown and his Orchestra, but some as the Park Central Orchestra.
63. *Yonkers Statesman*, 11 January 1934.
64. The greatest guest star in a program of twenty special features was former German heavyweight world boxing champion Max Schmeling, who told the press that Germany's chancellor Hitler forbade him to fight Kingfish Levinsky, because the latter was Jewish. *Mount Vernon Daily Argus*, 26 January 1934.
65. *New York Evening Post*, 51 March 1937.
66. Co-composer of "Bye Bye Blues" was Chauncey Gray, who around 1950 was said to receive $800 in royalties every two months, since the tune was played often on TV as background music for tap dancers.
67. Interview by Tom Faber, 28 July 1983. Kaye left Lown when Spencer Clark joined. During the interview, Kaye said that he joined Vincent Lopez and took Adrian Rollini with him and that, in 1933, he also introduced him in Ben Bernie's band. These engagements might account for some of Adrian's undocumented activities.
68. But not the few celeste tones heard during Rollini's sax work. Some discographies say that Rollini played drums on this Reisman session, but the drummer is heard during his sax playing.
69. The file card has the note that composer Rollini and publisher Venuti were getting one cent "on 100% if used by us."
70. Phil Wall, quoted in the liner notes for the Columbia LP *Stringing the Blues* (from Mosaic CD MD-8 213).
71. Benny Goodman has often been mentioned as the clarinet player on this session, but has denied his own presence.

72. Bunny Berigan and Max Kaminsky have been suggested for trumpet. According to his autobiography *My Life in Jazz*, Kaminsky lived in Boston in 1933 and had no work there.

73. Between the two sessions under his own name, in July and September, Rollini may have been on a recording date under Red McKenzie's name, producing "It's the Talk of the Town" and "This Time It's Love." A vibraphone is heard on both titles.

74. *John Hammond On Record*, 113. The same month Hammond recorded Goodman again for British Columbia and Bernstein was in.

75. Liner notes to Mosaic MD8–213.

76. Harry Clark interview by Tom Faber, 12 August 1983. Clark would join the Adrian Rollini Trio on bass in 1937.

77. Art Rollini's favorites were "Sweet Madness" and "Savage Serenade." Letter from Art to Tom Faber, 29 January 1985.

78. Radio had threatened record sales before: in 1925 record companies had to switch from acoustic recording to electric to recover the lost business.

79. The record industry recovered when economic circumstances improved and, from 1935, the emerging big band swing helped greatly.

Chapter 16: In and out of the Deepest Depression

1. Various clippings from the 1933 *New York Evening Post*.

2. When Sillman had "learned the 'long roll' and could make more noise than Stan King," it was Adrian who suggested that he join the musicians' union; Phil Sillman letter of April 1983 to Tom Faber. After Sillman left music, he worked in linotyping and lithography.

3. *Variety*, 23 August 1918. The following year, when Tucker worked at Reisenweber, Dave Klein replaced Berken, Howard Morrisey replaced Levine, and Frank Lhotak was added on trombone. Tucker called her group "Five Kings of Syncopation and a Joker."

4. *New York Clipper*, 17 September 1919.

5. *Variety*, 16 April 1920, 13 May 1921, and 2 September 1925.

6. *Variety*, 2 September 1925.

7. *Variety*, 18 November 1925.

8. *Variety*, 2 September 1925.

9. *Variety*, 2 March 1927, and 4 July 1928.

10. Joey Nash in the sleeve note of RCA LP PJM28066.

11. *Variety*, 30 August 1932. Rudy Vallée, *Let the Chips Fall*, 51.

12. The Essex opened in 1931 at Central Park South; today it is a Marriott hotel.

13. Writer of the sleeve notes of RCA LP PJM28066. Nash had been a saxophone player with Ben Bernie and Vincent Lopez.

14. *Radio Mirror*, August 1934.

15. *Saratogian*, 7 September 1934, and 16 May 1935.

16. Ernest Capozzi interview by Tom Faber, 5 October 1985.

17. *Film Daily*, 19 June 1934.

18. This film has not been seen by the author, and Rollini's presence has not been verified.

19. *Variety*, 6 March 1935.

20. *Variety*, 1 April 1935.

21. *Variety*, 29 September 1936.

22. *Broadcasting*, 1 October 1936.

23. *Harlem Valley Times*, 5 November 1936.

24. *Radio Mirror*, December 1936 and March 1937.

25. In a letter to Tom Faber, 10 October 1985. Nash's style of crooning was a mix of Al Bowlly's and Bing Crosby's.

26. Art Rollini, unpublished autobiography, 30. Art said that both cut two titles, but since five titles were recorded, one of them, probably Manny Klein, cut the first three and Bunny the final two. Interview by Tom Faber, 4 August 1983, Manny said that there were two trumpets because they were never sure that Berigan would show up.

27. Letter to Tom Faber, 13 July 1981.

28. *Brooklyn Daily Express*, 10 February 1935.

29. Art Rollini, interview by Tom Faber, 11 July 1982.

30. Frank Victor was of Italian descent. His real name was Frank Vigiano.

31. Letter to Tom Faber, 21 December 1982.

32. Letter from Tom Faber to Italian collector Enrico Borsetti, 23 December 1999.

33. Interview by Tom Faber, 29 July 1983.

34. Letter to Tom Faber, 23 April 1983.

35. Art Rollini's 1978 unpublished autobiography. James Melton's best known TV show was the Ford show in the early fifties, but Art Rollini remembered Adrian as a drummer with Melton in the thirties.

36. Interview by Tom Faber, 29 July 1983.

37. Ed Kirkeby, *Ain't Misbehavin': The Story of Fats Waller*, gives information about the Whitby Grill. Research for the early history in that book was done by jazz historian Duncan Schiedt, including the section on Rollini's clubs (Schiedt in the *Mississippi Rag*, September 1991). The book's author is given as Ed Kirkeby, but he only wrote the period from 1936, when he was Waller's manager. In Maurice Waller's biography of his father, the Whitby Grill is called a "hangout for unemployed musicians . . . because Rollini was always good for a *handout*." Quotes from Kirkeby are from Kirkeby, *Ain't Misbehavin'*.

38. Timme Rosenkrantz, *Harlem Jazz Adventures*, 53.

39. Adrian's brother stayed at the President from 1934–35, when he worked with Benny Goodman. Traveling bands that visited New York, such as the Casa Loma and the bands of the Dorsey brothers, would often stay at the President.

40. Danny Barker, *A Life in Jazz*, 147; trumpet player Gordon Griffin interview by Tom Faber, ca. 1983.

41. A flyer for the Tap Room gives as its address 242 West 48th Street. Apparently Adrian had considered a different place for a while, as shown by a flyer announcing the opening on 4 October of the Plymouth Grill at the Plymouth Hotel, 49th Street between 6th and 7th Avenues.

42. Kirkeby would be Waller's manager from 1938 till Fats died in 1943.

43. Barker, *A Life in Jazz*, 147.

44. Adrian Rollini's business card gave his club's address as 242 W. 48th Street. This may have been a renumbering of 234. Today 234 is the President Hotel's entrance, 242 does not exist, and 244 is the Saigon restaurant.

45. Art Rollini, unpublished autobiography, 32.

46. Louis Sobol in an unknown newspaper, December 1934.

47. Foreign musicians also visited the club and would sit in with the band, such as members of Teddy Stauffer's Original Teddies, a band from Berlin (as told by their trombone player Walter Dobschinski to Marko Paysan in 1993).

48. Kirkeby indicates that Hotfeet Club already featured this back in 1931.

49. Louis Sobol in an unknown newspaper, 24 December 1934. "Senegambians" probably are black entertainers/waiters. In a later review, Sobol called them "sepian waiters."

50. Warren Scholl in *Melody Maker*, 2 February 1935.

51. Leonard Feather, *The Jazz Years*, 12–13. Just over a year later, Feather, in an article by Franklyn Frank in the *California Eagle*, 9 October 1936, was quoted saying that "most Italian-Americans have a definite animosity towards artists of color." Feather mentioned La Rocca, Venuti, Rollini, and Manone in his article. At various times Rollini worked, employed, and recorded with black musicians, proving Feather wrong.

52. Wingy Manone said, in his autobiography *Trumpet on the Wing*, 113, that Adrian played xylophone, but this seems an error. Art played with Goodman at the time, but he stayed at the President, so it was easy for him to join his brother's band in the late hours. Through Adrian's good relationship with the President's management, Art got a nice rate of $12 per week for a room with a bath (Art Rollini's unpublished autobiography, 31). Guitar player Dave Barbour got his first break when he joined Manone at Rollini's club (*Melody Maker*, 5 September 1949).

53. Probably in February 1935. In an article in *Mississippi Rag* (May 1989), photographer Charles Peterson claims that he had the idea of a Dixieland band around Wingy Manone in 1934. A band was organized and got jobs at the Knickerbocker Hotel (renamed Wingy Manone's Jam Club, closed after a week) and the Casino De Luxe (later known as The Famous Door). Then Wingy left the band in February 1935 to form a new band of his own.

54. According to *Variety*, 27 November 1935, Nicholas worked at Adrian's Tap Room at the time. He had started there some months earlier.

55. Barker, *A Life in Jazz*, 147–48.

56. Rosenkrantz, *Harlem Jazz Adventures*, 54. Rosenkrantz gives a lively description of his first evening at the Whitby, but actually confuses it with the Tap Room. His table became an all-star affair with some twenty famous people, including Fud Livingston, Red McKenzie, Eddie Condon, Arthur Schutt, and Wingy Manone. When Adrian's wife Dixie arrived, she was the hostess and took over Adrian's duties.

57. *Variety*, 6 November 1935. The magazine continued to report changes in personnel at Adrian's Tap Room, such as the notes that Charlie Johnson was at Adrian's Tap Room in December and tenor saxophone player Art Drelinger left the following April.

58. Spencer Clark interview by Tom Faber, 21 July 1982.

59. Waller had recorded for Victor from 1926. In June 1935, Kirkeby supervised the second session of Fats Waller and his Rhythm; the first had been the month before.

60. Little more is known about Burns than that she made a few recordings in 1935 and 1939. Four days after her session with Rollini, she made a test recording for Russ Morgan, with Wingy Manone and maybe some others from the Rollini session, but Adrian himself was not present. More or less the same group recorded with her and under her name, for Decca in August. In 1939 she recorded with the Varsity Seven, a group including Coleman Hawkins, Danny Polo, and Bennie Carter.

61. Adrian's first professional work was as a xylophone and piano player and included making piano rolls. See the relevant chapters. He started with the California Ramblers in this

role and then moved to bass saxophone. He would occasionally record on the piano, though he may have played in public more often.

62. It was Tommy Dorsey's new band. Dorsey had just taken over Joe Haymes's band when Kirkeby contracted him to record for Victor /Bluebird. Kirkeby's Bluebird session took place even before Tommy Dorsey's band's first Victor session. More Bluebird sessions by this band under the California Ramblers banner took place on 19/20 October 1935 and probably again on 26 November, the latter even resulting in records by a smaller group and issued as by the Little Ramblers.

63. *Variety*, 27 November 1935, quoted Kirkeby reporting a 68 percent increase in the sale of dance records compared to the previous year. As before, university students were leading in their taste for hot music. In *Variety*, 11 March 1936, Alfred C. Butterfield wrote about Harvard that they preferred Jimmy Lunceford, Benny Goodman, or the Dorseys now to bands like those of Ben Bernie, Isham Jones, and Ozzie Nelson, who were regarded as "straight."

64. The California Ramblers would still perform in public in 1936.

65. Garcia was born in Puerto Rico, learned to play trumpet, and came to New York during the twenties. Not much is known about his life and his career. He worked with members of the Original Dixieland Jazz Band and with Emil Coleman, and recorded with the Dorsey brothers in 1930–31, with Vic Berton in 1935, and with singer Amanda Randolph in 1936. In 1936 he was a member of Richard Himber's Orchestra and may have recorded with Himber. During the thirties he worked with the bands of Nat Brandwynne and Louis Prima and then had a band of his own band for a while. During the sixties he moved to California, where he retired from music.

66. *Variety*, 1 April 1936.

67. Its arrangement was apparently too different from Himber's known style and the recording remained unissued until the LP era.

68. *New York Post*, 23 May 1936. Part of the proceeds went to the Emergency Musicians Relief Fund of New York Local 802.

69. *Down Beat*, June 1936, gave the personnel of Rollini's Tap Room Gang: in addition to Rollini on bass saxophone and vibraphone, there were Irving Goodman, trumpet; Art Dollinger (probably a misspelling for Drelinger), tenor saxophone and clarinet; Jack Russin, piano; Gwyn Hester, guitar; George Hnida, bass; and Anthony Kay, drums. Two days later Rollini did the first of a series of broadcasts with singer Barry McKinley and a small group including Dick McDonough, Carl Kress, and Artie Shaw.

70. It may be significant that all titles from these two sessions were issued in Europe, with the exception of the first two, which were straight dance music.

71. Clipping from unknown source.

72. *Independent Exhibitors Film Bulletin*, 5 February 1935.

73. Merrill Kaye (Merrill Kline) interview by Tom Faber, 28 July 1983.

74. *California Eagle*, 9 October 1936.

Chapter 17: A Shop and a Trio

1. *International Musician and Ringside Sports Weekly*, date unknown.
2. Mather later had his own shop. Sillman's letter to Tom Faber, April 1983.
3. Phil Sillman interview by Tom Faber, 29 July 1983.

4. Sillman letter to Tom Faber, April 1983.

5. Letter from Art Rollini to Tom Faber, 31 July 1981.

6. Interview by Tom Faber, 12 July 1982; Rollini, *Thirty Years with the Big Bands*. the price would change through the years: an advertisement lists $2 for a pair and $4 for a set of four (*Billboard*, 1 January 1943). The price of a set of four was later reduced to $3.75.

7. Rex Stewart, *Jazz Masters of the Thirties*, 74.

8. Broadcast, WABC, 26 March 1938. Rich would become the world's highest-paid sideman as a member of Harry James band in 1954.

9. Interview by Tom Faber, 12 August 1983.

10. Sillman letter to Tom Faber, April 1983. In that letter Sillman wrote that he would meet bebop pioneer and alto saxophone player Charlie Parker in the McGinnis clam bar downstairs from the White Way Music Shop. Phil remembered that Parker said that he was not satisfied with the way he played on a recent date. "I committed the sin of mentioning the conversation in the presence of a neophyte, who blurted, 'Man, the Bird never blows ba-a-a-ad!'"

11. From acetate recording.

12. That earlier session had been on 10 October 1936. Recordings from both broadcasts exist, as well as a photograph of the first session.

13. Rollini added that Frank Victor had been with the Blue Four. This refers to the Decca session of 20 March 1935. One of Frank Victor's first recordings had been at a Wingy Manone date in 1934, on which Jelly Roll Morton played piano.

14. Some sources say Rollini hired on the second floor.

15. Clearly the Trio sound had to settle. Red Norvo described the process in a 1968 interview. Sometime in the forties he started a trio of vibraphone, guitar, and bass. Norvo said: "I didn't have a particular conception about the trio's music. I never do. Any group has to gain its own character from the people that are in it. . . . We used to do a lot of things harmonically and used to get away with it because it was soft." Interview by Les Tomkins.

16. *Variety*, 20 October 1937.

17. In an interview for *Melody Maker* (2 April 1938), Rollini stated that Venuti's tour of England had originally been booked for the old Blue Four—Venuti, Rollini, Schutt, and Victor (instead of the late Ed Lang), but he had been unable to get released from contracts. Also, Schutt did not join, and in Europe Venuti used Don Barrigo on tenor saxophone and Doug Lees on bass, and with Frank Victor, guitar, once more called the group his Blue Four. (According to a rumor Rollini refused to return to England because he had a significant tax debt there.)

18. Harry Clark interview by Tom Faber, 12 August 1983.

19. Harry Clark interview by Tom Faber, 12 August 1983.

20. Harry Clark interview by Tom Faber, 12 August 1983.

21. Harry Clark interview by Tom Faber, 12 August 1983.

22. Jim Prohaska, "The Master and Variety Labels," an IAJRC publication from an unknown date.

23. Retrieval RTR79042 and RTR79046, which include alternate takes of all four titles as well.

24. Scott made his first records for Master in 1937. Forsythe made his first records in 1933 for Columbia.

25. Lou Shoobe interview by Tom Faber, ca. 1983.

26. Barnet remembered this session in his autobiography and mentioned Rollini and black trumpeter Frank Newton. "Admiration" remained unissued until the CD era and is available on CD Doctor Jazz DJ010.

27. At the same time, Himber hired swing harpist Adele Girard. Rollini and Girard were to "make the distinctive sound of the band even more distinctive." *Variety*, 13 October 1937). Another news clipping from Rollini's scrapbook, source and date unknown, gives the harpist's name as Elsie Graves.

28. Broadcasts were over WABC each Friday and Tuesday.

29. *New York Sun*, 22 January 1938.

30. Harry Clark interview by Tom Faber, 12 August 1983. Bamberger's Department Store, at 131 Market Street in Newark, had been the original home of WOR radio. The store and WOR were taken over by Macy's in 1929. WOR then for years had two studios, one in New York and one in Newark.

31. Available on Retrieval CD RTR79042.

32. Available on Sterling STCD 1–15–07.

33. A Duke Ellington group opened and Rollini played with his Trio. This was followed by a long list of performers and groups: Casper Reardon, Raymond Scott, Kay Thompson, Bunny Berigan, Glen Gray, Les Lieber, The Quintette of the Hot Club of France, Leith Stevens and The Saturday Night Swing Club Band, Benny Goodman, Carl Kress, and Dick McDonough. The broadcast has been issued on LP and CD (Soundcraft).

34. In the early 1930s, Bell Telephone Laboratories and Western Electric announced the total reinvention of disc recording: the Western Electric Wide Range System (see en.m.wikipedia.org/wiki/Phonograph_record).

35. From short Selvin biography, written in 1966 and sent to the author by Selvin's son Rick in 2005.

36. *Broadcasting*, 15 October 1935; and 1 October 1936.

37. Associated test A-1532 C 2, titles "Alibia Bay" and "Toodle Oo."

38. These include American Forces Radio Services (AFRS), "Here's to Veterans and Treasury Department." There may be others.

39. *Film Daily*, 19 June 1934.

40. *Motion Picture Daily* and *Film Daily*, 16 February 1938.

41. *Daily Princetonian*, 23 October 1937.

42. H.E.C. interviewing Rollini for *Melody Maker*, 2 April 1938.

Chapter 18: Trio Years: Before and during the War

1. Jazz greats from Bix Beiderbecke to Red Nichols and from Johnny Dodds to Jelly Roll Morton would sometimes make trio recordings.

2. The Milt Herth Trio, consisting of organ, piano, and drums, would soon become Rollini's most serious competitor. Herth's trio made its recording debut for Decca in November 1937, a year after Rollini, and by 1938 he had already recorded twenty-three titles.

3. *Down Beat*, October 1938. In its December issue it "recommended" Rollini's solo on "Original Dixieland One Step" by Miff Mole's Molers (1927).

4. Letter from Paul Ricci to Tom Faber, 18 May 1983.

5. A third title sung by Pat Hoke, "Nice Work If You Can Get It," exists as an acetate, with the personnel from this session and possibly from this date.

6. Information on Pat Hoke from letters to the author from his daughter Diane and grandson David, 2006–14. Also from *Utica Daily Express*, 21 April 1938.

7. *Storyville* 9, February 1967.

8. Herb Sanford, *Tommy and Jimmy: The Dorsey Years*, 100–102.

9. Rollini recorded both tunes for transcription discs.

10. *Billboard*, April 1938.

11. Although a cover for this book was in Rollini's papers and photographs meant for illustration exist, no copy of this book has so far been found and it may have been canceled before release.

12. Recordings of his part in both broadcasts survived in Rollini's private collection.

13. The *New York Enquirer* (unknown date) names Dave Dreier and Roy Moulton as the Piccadilly's management. Rollini had auditioned for Dreier. The Dreiers also had the President Hotel. When bass player Harry Clark wanted a salary raise, Rollini told him to talk to Freddy Dreier, the younger Dreier of the hotel association. When the Trio had started at the Piccadilly, he had said that they could get a raise when business picked up. Clark said to Dreier: "You have pushed the walls out and we are packed and we are on air all the time. Everything is going fine. How about it?" Dreier answered: "If Adrian wants a raise, I will give it to him, but I don't need you." And that is where the conversation ended. Harry Clark, interview by Tom Faber, 12 August 1983.

14. The Piccadilly was torn down in 1982. The interior of its Georgian Room was sold for $40,000 to a wealthy Detroit manufacturer. At its location a Marriott hotel arose.

15. Harry Clark interview by Tom Faber, 12 August 1983.

16. *Montreal Gazette*, 24 June 1938. Others were Mildred Bailey and Red Norvo, Duke Ellington, Les Leiber, the Modernaires, Caspar Reardon, Raymond Scott, and Maxine Sullivan.

17. Clippings from unknown source and date.

18. *New York Sun*, 9 July 1938.

19. Not the later Tanner Sisters who became known in the UK in the fifties.

20. Abel Green in *Variety*, 15 June 1938.

21. *Variety*, 24 August 1938. Himber died in 1966, aged fifty-nine. At the time he lived in an Essex House apartment (*Utica Observer*, 12 December 1966).

22. *New York City Telegram*, 6 August 1938.

23. Recordings of his part in both broadcasts survived in Rollini's private collection.

24. *Syracuse Journal*, 3 September 1938.

25. Harry Clark interview by Tom Faber, 12 August 1983.

26. *Down Beat*, April 1939; Fred Sharp interview by Tom Faber, 9 October 1985.

27. *Women's Wear*, 2 September 1938. The *New York Hotel Gazette* gave 17 August 1938 as starting date.

28. Chimes are a percussion instrument, consisting of multiple iron tubes, hanging free in a rack. The bars are tuned to different tones and are played with hammers. A recording of his part of the broadcast survived in Rollini's private collection.

29. *Down Beat*, November 1938.

30. *Brooklyn Daily Eagle*, 4 November 1938.

31. *New York Times*, 8 November 1938.

32. *Variety*, 16 November 1938.

33. The block of W. 52nd Street between 6th and 7th Avenues was known as Swing Street for its many jazz clubs, and later as Strip Street when the jazz clubs became striptease joints. Leon & Eddie's started in the thirties with a vaudeville show, featuring jazz music now and then. It never became a full-blown jazz club; eventually its jazz offerings became fewer. When Rollini worked at Leon & Eddie's, it was offering a full program of ten acts, compered by Eddie Davis. Leon & Eddie's closed in 1953.

34. Clipping from unknown periodical.

35. He was even asked to be a jury member in a competition for a "Great Waltz," sponsored by film maker MGM (*New York Sun*, 5 December 1938.

36. The Belmont Plaza had started in 1928 as the Montclair. During the thirties it was renamed the Belmont Plaza and a new nightclub was created, the Glass Hat, at a cost of $200,000. After the war it became the Doral Inn Hotel and now is the W New York.

37. *New York Sun*, 26 June 1940.

38. Hand had been running the Colony Club in Palm Beach, Florida, after he had dropped his connection with the California Ramblers in the late twenties. But he showed up in New York now and then (*New York Sun*, 25 May 1936).

39. Rollini drank a fifth of Scotch a day, according to an unnamed member of his Trio (about 0.7 liter) (information from the Bix Beiderbecke website on 24 May 2004).

40. She was the daughter of Al Mitchell, a well-known radio personality on station WOR. She and Carroll had further careers after their work with Rollini (Carroll with Charlie Barnet).

41. Located 113 W. 57th Street. The discs were sent to Rollini's address at the Glass Hat.

42. *Buffalo Courier*, 25 March 1940.

43. *Radio Daily*, 20 January 1939. It has been suggested that Joe and Ed Herlihy were the same person (CD Jazz Oracle BDW8052)

44. *Variety*, 25 January 1939.

45. Harry Clark interview by Tom Faber, 12 August 1983.

46. Originally from Minneapolis, Minnesota, they made their first recording in1933. With various personnel, the group had a long career, spanning some forty years.

47. *New York Times*, 26 February 1939.

48. Others were the Three Smoothies and Jane Clair and the Belmont Balladeers. The Three Smoothies were well-known radio singers; Jane Clair was a singer from New Orleans and a younger sister of Loretta Lee, singer with George Hall's orchestra.

49. *Ballston Spa Journal*, 2 February 1939.

50. *Brooklyn Daily Eagle*, 17 May 1939.

51. On 19 May 1939 the film feature was Warner Bros. *The Kid from Kokomo*, starring Pat O'Brien, Wayne Morris, and Joan Blondell. Ruby Newman's orchestra was Boston's favorite during the thirties. Others in the show were singer Bert Frohman and the Weire Brothers, comedians.

52. On the first show the tunes were "Chinatown," "Chopsticks," "Hallelujah," and "Limehouse Blues."

53. *Billboard*, 27 May 1939.

54. *New York Sun*, 7 July 1939, which does not identify the pianists, but this may refer to Albert Ammons, Pete Johnson, and/or Meade Lux Lewis, who all were in New York at the time. Other newspapers mention the Bob Hamilton Trio or the Bob Campbell Trio.

55. *New York Times*, 6 August 1939.

56. According to Harry Clark, it was an agent, Larry Golden, who took the Trio to California. Golden worked with them for about a year.

57. *Los Angeles CAL Tempo*, October 1939. The Trocadero was often just called "Troc," the name of the club in New York where Rollini worked before his trip west.

58. *Brooklyn Daily Eagle*, 23 July 1940.

59. *New York Mirror*, 26 April 1939.

60. Shortly after Rollini's stint at the Trocadero it closed, but then quickly reopened in time to host the Hollywood premiere party for *Gone with the Wind* in December 1939. The Trocadero was featured in the 1937 version of *A Star is Born*; in 1938 it was parodied in a cartoon, *Porky at The Trocadero*; and during the 1940s the Trocadero was celebrated in a film that was supposed to be about its history, but which was largely fantasy.

61. At William Morris, it was Joe Marshall who worked for Rollini. Rollini had been in bands that worked with the agency in the past and now it worked for his own band.

62. *Variety*, 15 November 1939.

63. *Swing*, December 1939.

64. The films were *Two Bright Boys* and *Tropic Fury*.

65. *Pelham Sun*, 21 December 1939.

66. *Buffalo Courier*, 22 and 23 March 1940.

67. *Buffalo Courier*, 25 March 1940.

68. The SS *America* had been built in Newport News, Virginia. It was launched on 31 August 1939 by Eleanor Roosevelt, the president's wife. It made its maiden voyage from Newport News to New York, the first of several Caribbean cruises. It had been built for transatlantic passenger travel and could hold 1,200 passengers and 600 crew. But the war changed the plans. In 1941 the ship was called into service by the US Navy. It would sail under different names, until it got into an accident in 1994 on the Canary Islands. It was abandoned and left to the elements.

69. *Buffalo Courier Express*, 18 August 1940.

70. As an added attraction the theater featured the latest *March of Time* film "Spoils of Conquest: The Dutch East Indies," which dealt with the Japanese threat to the "fabulously rich colonial empire." *Buffalo Courier Express*, 4 August 1940.

71. *Philadelphia Enquirer*, 1 September 1940.

72. Clipping from unknown newspaper and unknown 1938 date.

73. *Washington Daily News*, 20 January 1941. The Capitol featured the film *Slightly Dangerous* with Lana Turner.

74. Clipping from unknown newspaper, 12 June 1941.

75. *Buffalo Courier Express*, 5 November 1941.

76. Harry Clark interview by Tom Faber, 12 August 1983.

77. Before that he worked with Red Norvo and Mildred Bailey (recordings in 1938). After his years with Rollini, Hanlon became a studio musician and teacher, writing books on guitar playing.

78. Allen Hanlon interview by Tom Faber, 14 September 2007.

79. Allen Hanlon interview by Tom Faber, 14 September 2007.

80. *New York Sun*, 21 August 1941.

81. Clipping from unknown newspaper, 5 September 1941.

82. *New York Sun*, 8 October 1941. Official curfews did not exist before the end of the year, and then only for people with German or Italian citizenship.

83. Quoted in the *Brooklyn Daily Express*, 8 October 1941.

84. *Billboard*, 21 March 1942.

85. *Billboard*, 3 January 1942.

86. *Billboard*, 24 January 1942.

87. *Billboard*, 6 June 1942.

88. This and other Dubonnet clippings from Rollini's scrapbook. Lagonda was a British car brand and in 1935 had won the famous twenty-four-hour race of Le Mans, France, breaking Alfa Romeo's series of wins.

89. *International Musician*, February 1942.

90. Harry Clark, interview by Tom Faber, 12 August 1983. Incidentally, this quote proves that Rollini could whistle between his teeth, another element of his musicianship.

91. Information about a Cocoanut Grove in Boston has not been found, but the Trio did play in the Music Box in Boston's Copley Square Hotel.

92. Milt Herth (1902–1969), who played electronic organ, made his first recordings in 1936 as a soloist, about a year after Rollini. The first Milt Herth Trio included Willie "The Lion" Smith, piano, and O'Neil Spencer, drums. He continued to record, but by 1942 he had drifted away from swing. Another keyboard player who successfully adopted the trio formula was Nat "King" Cole. He made his first records in 1940 with Oscar Moore, guitar, and Wesley Prince, bass. Cole too, moved away from swing in the following years.

93. *Billboard*, 17 October 1942, and 28 November 1942.

94. Harry Clark interview by Tom Faber, 12 August 1983.

95. Harry Clark interview by Tom Faber, 12 August 1983.

96. *Billboard*, 27 March 1943. Others in the program were Jackie Green, the Six Grays, the Four Whitsons, and singer Ramona.

97. An undated engagement of the Adrian Rollini Trio in Baltimore is known. This was at Doc's Cocktail Lounge at 1817 N. Charles Street. Adrian was advertised as "The King Is with Us" and others in the show, at various times, were Dolly "Cherub" Mitchell, the Owens Sisters, Slim Gaillard, and Warren Phillips.

98. *Philadelphia Enquirer*, 2 April 1943. Others on the bill were Don Renaldo's Quartette, Gloria Mann, Four Men of Rhythm, Mike Pedecine and the Musicalaires, and Sally Lamar.

99. The letter from the radio station to Rollini mentions "you and the three members of your quartette," probably a simple misunderstanding. Press texts usually mentioned Adrian Rollini and his Trio, which could be understood as four men.

100. Loew's State featured the film *Reunion in France* with Joan Crawford and John Wayne.

101. *Billboard*, 4 September 1943. The war was now being felt: Roger's Corner announced that, following the new Revenue Act, it had to collect 30 percent tax on all checks for the Pan-American Room.

102. Letter, 5 October 1943.

103. *Syracuse Herald Journal*, 10 October 1943.

104. With Hank Kohout, piano, and Walter Breese, drums.

105. Sharp was born in Cleveland, Ohio, on 24 June 1922.

106. It was on the second floor with W. C. Handy's office, run by his daughter, as neighbor.

107. This and other citations from Fred Sharp interview by Tom Faber, 9 October 1985.

108. Others on the bill were George Chatterton, Three Loose Nuts, and James Oriti.

109. *Billboard*, 29 January and 26 February 1944.

110. *Billboard*, 6 May and 27 May 1944.

111. Gene Barras interview by Tom Faber, 11 August 1983.

112. At Loew's State the feature film was *Broadway Rhythm* with Tommy Dorsey's Orchestra. *Billboard*, 3 June and 24 June 1944. Interestingly, the Milt Herth Trio followed Rollini in both spots.

113. *Billboard*, 6 May 1944, noted that WOR was the third broadcaster that was related to a record company, the others being NBC/Victor and CBS/Columbia. Before the Rollini records, which had catalog numbers 1005 and 1006, the company issued records by Jan Garber's Orchestra. Its recording studio was located at 1440 Broadway, New York. The WOR studio was often used by third parties and a month after Rollini's date, Charlie Parker made his first bebop records there, issued on the Savoy label. *Billboard*, 12 August 1944, called the label Feature. It was owned by Nat Abramson. Nationwide distribution of WOR Feature Records was initially done by Modern Music Sales, exclusive distributor for the states of New York, New Jersey, and Connecticut (*Billboard*, 22 April 1944).

114. *Billboard*, 14 October 1944.

115. Fred Sharp interview by Tom Faber, 9 October 1985.

116. 10 East 60th Street.

117. Fred Sharp interview by Tom Faber, 9 October 1985.

118. *Billboard*, 23 December 1944.

119. Ellington received $6,000 per week; Rollini is said to have earned $1,000 a week at the time.

120. Fred Sharp interview by Tom Faber, 9 October 1985.

121. Clipping, 23 February 1945, from unknown source.

122. Art last played Adrian's bass saxophone in 1958. See appendix on Adrian Rollini's instruments.

123. Danzi, *American Musician in Germany 1924–1939*, 152. The six other groups were a dance band, a gypsy sextet, Harry Reser's banjo quartet, and three vocal trios with accompaniment.

124. It starred Spencer Tracy and Katherine Hepburn.

125. Fred Sharp interview by Tom Faber, 9 October 1985.

126. *Billboard*, 17 June 1945.

127. *Variety*, 13 June 1945.

128. *Billboard*, 14 July 1945.

129. 1–3 trumpets, 1–3 trombones, 1–5 saxes, violin, piano, guitar, drums, bass, vocal. The arranger may have been Roy Blakeman or Rollini himself.

130. Both were successful songwriters. In the years to follow, Ram would bring the Platters to fame.

Chapter 19: Postwar Trio Years

1. *Radio Daily*, July 1945; *Billboard*, 8 and 15 September 1945; and news clipping from unknown publication in Rollini's scrapbook, dated 15 September 1945.

2. This story was told by Jim Cullum Jr. during a broadcast and can be found on internet: http://rwj-a.stanford.edu/bonus-content/saga-bass-saxophone-jim-cullum-jr.

3. The hotel was built in 1927 and demolished in 1982. It was twenty-two stories high (eighty meters).

4. *Brooklyn Daily Eagle*, 19 October 1945 and subsequent issues.

5. Other artists on the bill were emcee Frank Marlow, Picard and his trained seal, the dance team of Georges Leon and Mirana, hillbilly musicians the Two Yokies, even a xylophone virtuoso named Dolly, as well as the McVanettes with Flo West. *Billboard*, 5 January 1946; *Buffalo Courier*, 13 and 24 January 1946.

6. Rollini had special memories of the SS *America*: his Trio had provided the music on its maiden trip in 1939.

7. Fred Sharp interview by Tom Faber, 9 October 1985.

8. Fred Sharp interview by Tom Faber, 9 October 1985.

9. Fred Sharp interview by Tom Faber, 9 October 1985.

10. Wrong spelling for "Hnida" in the original typescript.

11. *Billboard*, 17 August 1946.

12. *Radio Daily*, November 1946.

13. *Billboard*, 21 December 1946; *Kingston Daily Freeman*, 27 December 1946 and subsequent issues.

14. *Schenectady Gazette*, 22 January 1947.

15. Rollini's short biographical manuscript from 1947–48.

16. The place may date from 1935 as the Driftwood Lodge.

17. Clipping of 13 April 1947 in Rollini's scrapbook.

18. Keys historian Jerry Wilkinson on the internet.

19. After Rollini died in 1956, the Driftwood Lodge deteriorated and in 1960 Hurricane Donna destroyed the remaining buildings. A bulldozer cleared the area. The property was bought by a family from Hialeah. The new owner also owned another large property in Key Largo. Her son could choose between the two and he chose the other property to build on. The Tavernier Community Association wanted to buy the area of the former Driftwood Lodge, the last waterfront tract available, but did not have the money. A lady by the name of Joyce Frite of Homestead bought the property and built a new house on it in 2003 (historian Jerry Wilkinson on the internet).

20. The company office was at 510 W. 57th Street, New York.

21. The tunes were "Dark Eyes," "Minuet in Jazz," "Girl with the Light Blue Hair," "Loch Lomond," "Blue Danube," "Minute Waltz," and "Martha."

22. *New York Post*, 26 July 1947; *Billboard*, 2 and 9 August 1947.

23. *Billboard*, 16 August 1947.

24. Nick Kenny in the *Daily Mirror*, 5 November 1947.

25. Clipping in Rollini's scrapbook.

26. One of its owners was Jim Bulleit, who chose the artists and repertoire. The label was known for country, blues, and gospel music, but it scored a major hit with "Near You" by Francis Craig's Orchestra. In 1949 Jim Bulleit sold his interest in the company and in 1952 Bullet Records ended (Wikipedia).

27. Peggy Mann was born as Margaret Germano on 24 July 1919 in Yonkers, New York. She ended her singing career in the early fifties.

28. Two years later, in December 1949, Mercury Records announced that it had leased twelve masters by the Adrian Rollini Trio from Bullet. Mercury planned to release singles as well as a long-playing record. Eventually one 78 rpm was released and an LP with all twelve titles. The Peggy Mann recording apparently was left out of the deal (*Billboard*, 31 December 1949).

29. *Lockport Union Sun Journal*, 31 July 1948. Kolensky's office was located at 1697 Broadway, New York, and he represented such other artists as Maxine Sullivan, Art Tatum, Mary Lou Williams, John Kirby's Quartet, and Claude Hopkins Quintette.

30. Rollini, *Thirty Years with the Big Bands*, 104.

31. *Brooklyn Eagle*, 11 August 1949. While Adrian worked at the Park Central, music was also provided by Ashley Miller, an organ player. Since Rollini also played the piano, the hotel now featured two pianists and an organ player, an unusual setup.

32. Fred Sharp interview by Tom Faber, 9 October 1985.

33. George Hnida's family name was often spelled Nyder.

34. Clipping from unknown newspaper from this period, kept in Rollini's scrapbook.

35. Fred Sharp interview by Tom Faber, 9 October 1985.

36. Not related to WOR's Feature Records.

37. Dardanelle Hadley (real name Marcia Marie Mullen) played piano and vibraphone and sang with her own trio, which included guitar and bass.

38. No further evidence of this nomination has been found.

39. *Cortland Tribune*, 8 December 1949. Harry Sosnik's Orchestra played "Limehouse Blues" and "The Merry Widow Waltz." The following week, piano player Erroll Garner was the guest star.

40. Letter from Dixie to a friend, dated 13 December 1949, in which she expects Adrian to shortly leave for Florida again.

41. *Billboard*, 31 December 1949, 4, and 11 February 1950. Mercury 5359 coupled "Jazz Me Blues" with "Oya Negra." Ironically, some of Rollini's fine 1930 recordings, the days that he played advanced music with Red Nichols, were reissued around this time (*Billboard*, 10 June 1950).

42. Copies of the disc are in some record collections. The Trio played "Begin the Beguine" (supported by a drummer), "Brazil," and "Dardanella," the latter with Rollini playing piano, chimes, and vibraphone. Rollini closed with "Au Revoir," his closing theme.

43. In his closing words, Adrian seems to call him "Bert Cobb."

44. Clipping in Adrian's scrapbook from 9 September 1946 from unknown source.

45. Letter from Dixie to a friend, 13 December 1949.

46. *Saratoga Saratogian*, 29 July 1950. Lily St. Cyr with a cast of thirty did a show called the *Keynote Follies*, with music provided by Francus Murphy and Don Alfonso and their orchestras.

47. It existed from 1947 until 1960.

48. *Milwaukee Sentinel*, 10 September 1950. Singer was Kay Sterling.

49. Letter from Adrian to his friend Bill in Australia, 30 December 1950.

50. The McKenzies were pioneers on Key Largo, having arrived there in 1928. The Rollinis arrived twenty years later and lived about a quarter mile away. Through music as their common interest, they became friends. In a letter to Tom Faber, 8 June 1983, Hazel McKenzie wrote that she remained friends with Dixie till her death.

51. Letter from Mrs. K. L. Wilkinson to Tom Faber, 13 May 1983.
52. Allen Hanlon interview by Tom Faber, ca. 1983.
53. *Billboard*, 13 October 1951; *Brooklyn Daily Eagle*, 25 January 1952.
54. Harry Clark interview by Tom Faber, 12 August 1983.
55. *Brooklyn Daily Eagle*, 9 October 1953.
56. *Billboard*, 30 January 1954.
57. *Sponsor Magazine*, 2 January 1954. It lists a company called Video Pictures as producer and Sterling as distributor.
58. Triboro Hospital for Tuberculosis, Parsons Boulevard, Jamaica, Queens.
59. The Eden Roc is at 4525 Collins Avenue, Miami Beach, Florida.
60. Harry Clark interview by Tom Faber, 12 August 1983.
61. Letter from Art to his son, 14 February 1986.
62. From document apparently written by Dixie, dated 21 February 1962.
63. The Green Turtle Inn had been started in 1947 by Sid and Roxie Siderious at 81219 Overseas Highway, Islamorada. It still stands.
64. From interview by Tom Faber, 11 July 1982, at Art Rollini's home in Shirley, New York.
65. Clipping in Rollini's scrapbook, newspaper source unknown, dated 4 May 1956 by hand.
66. Joe Della Sandro, bartender at The Inn, found him (*Miami Herald*, 16 May 1956, clipping in Rollini's scrapbook).
67. Letter to Tom Faber from Mrs. K. L. Wilkinson of 13 May 1983. The Wilkinsons were friends and neighbors of the Rollinis. Mr. Wilkinson had night duty at the "electric building" and was asked for help. Later he realized that it had been for Rollini.
68. "Preacher" Rollo Laylan interview by Tom Faber, ca. 1983.
69. Fred Cusick interview by Tom Faber, 17 July 1983.
70. Reproduced in *IAJRC Journal* 21, no. 1 (January 1988), in an article about Adrian's death by Norman Gentieu, who was a member of the IAJRC (International Association of Jazz Record Collectors).
71. The original text said "dostroted," probably by error.
72. The death certificate was filled out on 16 May 1956 and mentioned bronchopneumonia as immediate cause of Rollini's death and cirrhosis of the liver as giving rise to this cause. Rollini's compound ankle fracture was mentioned as a significant condition contributing to his death. It was the result from slipping on a rock while walking along the side of a road, as Rollini claimed.
73. *Miami Herald*, 16 May 1956.
74. *Miami Herald*, 16 May 1956, clipping in Rollini's scrapbook; and Norman Gentieu's article in *IAJRC Journal* 21, no. 1 (January 1988).
75. *IAJRC Journal* 21, no. 2 (April 1988).
76. From interview by Tom Faber, 19 February 2006.
77. Letters to Tom Faber, April 1983 and January 1988.
78. Double indemnity clauses are often found in life insurance policies. In the case of accidental death of the insured, the insurance company will pay the beneficiary of the policy twice its face value.
79. Letter from Harry Clark to Tom Faber, 18 January 1984.
80. Letter from Art to his son, 14 February 1986. In this letter Art wrote that he had not seen Benny Morrell before.

81. Letter from Phil Sillman to Tom Faber, January 1991.

82. Letter from Phil Sillman to Tom Faber, April 1983.

83. After Dixie's mother had divorced, Dixie first lived with Ellea Remer, then with Ruth Baer's family (letter from Ruth Baer to Tom Faber, 16 May 1983) before she married.

84. Arthur Nando Rollini interview by Tom Faber, 11 August 1983.

85. Ann Henson in *Real Estate News*, 18 March 2003.

86. About Dixie's final years: Peggy Michalsky interview by Tom Faber, 26 September 1981. According to her, Adrian had no children because Dixie could not have them. (Author's note: However, the illness that Adrian had in 1931 may also have been a cause.)

Appendix 1: Adrian Rollini's Instruments

1. Letter from Art Rollini to Tom Faber, 4 December 1981.
2. Letter from Tom Faber to John Morphew, 15 June 1983.
3. From an unknown newspaper.
4. Letter from Tom Faber to Art Rollini, 12 July 1982.
5. Jean Robert interview by Tom Faber, December 1980.
6. Letter from Art Rollini to Tom Faber, 11 April 1984.
7. Rollini, *Thirty Years with the Big Bands*, 25.
8. Letter from Art Rollini to Tom Faber, 30 June 1981.
9. Art Rollini interview by Tom Faber, 12 July 1982.
10. From Richard DuPage and Frank Driggs's notes for Columbia's four-LP set *Thesaurus of Classic Jazz* (C4L 18): "Adrian Rollini's bass sax differed from others used in that era, because he had a special neck made for it, in order to achieve a true 440 pitch, which he couldn't get as satisfactorily on the original neck. He used a baritone mouthpiece, because the bass sax mouthpiece was too 'honky.' This was even more remarkable, because while the smaller mouthpiece gave him more control in the high register, he was still able to achieve full mastery in the bottom half of the horn, pianissimo or fortissimo, right down to the low B$\flat$. An unusual pair of lungs were necessary to fill such a huge air passage, and this neck and mouthpiece were his trade secrets for many years."
11. Art Rollini interview by Tom Faber, 12 July 1982.
12. Letter from Art Rollini to Tom Faber, 27 July 1988.
13. Letter from Tom Faber to Art Rollini, 23 November 1981.
14. In a letter to Art Rollini, 12 July 1981, Tom Faber, who was a bass saxophone player himself and owned a 1927 Conn, wrote that by trial and error he had discovered how to play high F. Tom did that by depressing the octave key, keys 1, 2, 3, and 4 together with the side B$\flat$ key. Depressing the side C key instead, brings high G. But Tom did not find high E. Tom also experimented to find how Adrian blew the double notes that he sometimes produced: when using a fairly large-chamber mouthpiece and starting to blow low B$\flat$ (A$\sharp$) but with depressed octave key, the first double note comes out very nicely, but not the remaining tones on the scale.
15. Letter from Art Rollini to Tom Faber, 31 July 1981.
16. Letter from Norman Field to the author, 23 January 2016.
17. This may have been Adrian's fourth bass saxophone.

18. Letter from Art Rollini to Tom Faber, 25 January 1984.

19. Peter Wells interview by Tom Faber, 1 August 1983.

20. Art Rollini *Unpublished Autobiography*, 171; letter from Art Rollini to Tom Faber, 12 October 1982; Art Rollini interview by Tom Faber, 12 July 1982.

21. Undated letter (probably 1985) of Tom Faber to Howard L. Johnson.

22. Email from Bill Cole to the author, 12 January 2014. The Wurlitzer brand name together with the serial number make it unlikely that this really was Rollini's Conn.

23. Art N. Rollini interview by Tom Faber, 11 August 1983, who heard it from Dixie; and detailed in letter from Tom Faber to him, 1 November 1983. This may be the mouthpiece that Art could not use when he borrowed Adrian's bass saxophone.

24. Letters from Tom Faber to Art Rollini, 1 November 1983, and to Frans Sjöström, 6 April 1998.

25. Tom owned a second Conn bass saxophone, a 1923 model with a different neck type. Experienced players such as Spencer Clark were unable to hear differences in tone quality between his two saxophones.

The neck of Tom's 1927 Conn was indeed about half an inch shorter than that of a 1929 Conn owned by another Dutch bass saxophone player. This instrument also had high E and F keys and a raised high E♯ key. Tom also mentioned another bass saxophone (a Hohlert, a German make) sold by Rossmeisl that was bought by Peter Dortmond, yet another Dutch musician. Letters from Tom Faber to André Eschauzier, 11 December 1980; to Grex Goyarts, 13 July 1981; and to Bill Peatman, 29 November 1982.

26. From an interview of Kenny Davern by Carol Sudhalter, at the New Orleans Jazz Festival, Ascona, Italy, 2003, published on the internet. Confirmation from the Smithsonian that it has this bass saxophone has not been obtained.

27. Letter from Tom Faber to Nick Dellow, 24 November 2005.

28. Letter of Tom Faber to Art Rollini, 15 September 1982.

29. Kirkeby interview by John Steiner, 28 June 1961.

30. Letter from John Morphew to Tom Faber, 19 January 1983.

31. Letter from Art Rollini to his son, 14 February 1986.

32. Letter from Art Rollini to Tom Faber, 4 December 1981.

33. Rollini, *Thirty Years with the Big Bands*, 29.

34. Letter from British vibraphone player Peter Newbrook to Tom Faber, 18 February 1998. Newbrook met Rollini in Washington in 1943. Newbrook acquired a similar white vibraphone from the Deagan factory right after the war.

35. Letter from Tom Faber to Peter Newbrook, 24 March 1998.

BIBLIOGRAPHY

Allen, Frederick Lewis. *Only Yesterday*. New York: Harper & Brothers, 1931.
Atkinson, Brooks. *Broadway*. London: Cassell, 1970.
Badger, Reid. *A Life in Ragtime*. New York: Oxford University Press. 1995.
Barker, Danny. *A Life in Jazz*. London: Macmillan, 1986.
Barnet, Charlie. *Those Swinging Years*. New York: Da Capo, 1992.
Berlin, Edward A. *King Of Ragtime*. New York: Oxford University Press, 1994.
Charters, Sam, and Leonard Kunstadt. *Jazz: A History of the New York Scene*. Garden City: Doubleday, 1962.
Chilton, John. *Who's Who of Jazz*. London: Macmillan, 1989.
Coller, Derek. *Clarinet Marmalade: The Life and Times of Tony Parenti*. New Orleans: Jazzology Press, 2003.
Collier, James Lincoln. *Benny: Goodman and the Swing Era*. New York: Oxford University Press, 1989.
Danzi, Mike. *American Musician in Germany. 1924–1939*. Schmitten, Germany: Norbert Ruecker, 1986.
Dupuis, Robert. *Bunny Berigan: Elusive Legend of Jazz*. Baton Rouge: Louisiana State University Press, 1993.
Elsenaar, E. *De Saxophone*. Hilversum, Netherlands: J. J. Lispet, 1943.
Evans, Philip R., and Linda K. Evans. *Bix: The Leon Bix Beiderbecke Story*. Bakersfield, CA: Prelilke Press, 1998.
Feather, Leonard. *The Jazz Years: Ear Witness to an Era*. London: Quartet Books Limited, 1986.
Gelatt, Roland. *The Fabulous Phonograph*. London: Cassell, 1977.
Gelder, Henk van. *De Lokroep Van het Lido*. Amsterdam: Thomas Rap, 1991.
Gilbert, Douglas. *American Vaudeville*. New York: Dover, 1940.
Goffin, Robert. *Aux Frontières De Jazz*. Paris: Sagittaire, 1932.
Goldstein, Richard. *Desperate Hours*. New York: John Wiley & Sons, 2001.
Goodman, Benny, and Irving Kolodin. *The King Of Swing*. New York: Stackpole Sons, 1939.
Hadlock, Richard. *Jazz Masters of the Twenties*. New York: Macmillan, 1965.
Hammond, John. *John Hammond on Record*. Harmondsworth, UK: Penguin Books, 1977.
Hayes, Chris. *Dance Music at the Savoy Hotel 1920–1927*. Ventner, UK: Chris Hayes, 1988.
Hilbert, Bob. *Pee Wee Russell: The Life of a Jazzman*. New York: Oxford University Press, 1993.
Hill, Dick. *Sylvester Ahola: The Gloucester Gabriel*. Metuchen, NJ, and London: Scarecrow, 1993.
Horricks, Raymond. *Gerry Mulligan*. London: Apollo Press, 1986.
Jackson, Stanley. *The Savoy: The Romance of a Great Hotel*. London: Frederick Muller, 1964.
Jones, Harold. *Bobby Hackett: A Bio-Discography*. Westport, CT: Greenwood, 1999.
Kirkeby, Ed. *Ain't Misbehavin'*. London: Peter Davies, 1966.

Kirkeby, Ed (Wallace T.). *Thumbnail Biography*. Unpublished manuscript, 1940s.
Laird, Ross, and Brian Rust. *Discography of OKeh Records, 1918–1934*. Westport, CT: Praeger, 2004.
Levinson, Peter J. *Tommy Dorsey: Livin' in a Great Big Way*. New York: Da Capo, 2005.
Lion, Jean Pierre. *Bix Beiderbecke: Une Biographie*. Paris: Outre Mesure, 2004.
Lopez, Vincent. *Lopez Speaking: My Life*. New York: Citadel Press, 1960.
Manone, Wingy. *Trumpet on the Wing*. London: Jazz Book Club, 1964.
McCarthy, Albert. *The Dance Band Era*. London: Hamlyn, 1974.
Meeker, David. *Jazz in the Movies*. London: Talisman Books, 1981.
Nelson, Stanley R. *All About Jazz*. London: Heath Cranton, 1934.
Ord-Hume, Arthur W. J. G. *Pianola: The History of the Self-playing Piano*. London: George Allen & Unwin, 1984.
Rayno, Don. *Paul Whiteman: Pioneer in American Music Vol. 1*. Scarecrow, 2003.
Rayno, Don. *Paul Whiteman: Pioneer in American Music Vol. 2*. Lanham, MD: Scarecrow, 2013.
Rollini, Arthur. Autobiography. Unpublished manuscript, 1987.
Rollini, Arthur. *Thirty Years with the Big Bands*. London: Macmillan, 1987.
Rosenkrantz, Timme. *Harlem Jazz Adventures*. Lanham, MD: Scarecrow, 2012.
Schuller, Gunther. *Early Jazz, Its Roots and Musical Development*. New York: Oxford, 1968.
Schuller, Gunther. *The Swing Era*. New York: Oxford, 1989.
Shapiro, Nat, and Nat Hentoff. *Hear Me Talkin' to Ya*. Harmondsworth, UK: Penguin, 1962.
Simon, George T. *Glenn Miller and His Orchestra*. New York: Thomas Y. Crowell, 1974.
Smith, Charles David, and Richard James Howe. *The Welte-Mignon: Its Music and Musicians*. New York: Vestal Press, 1994.
Smith, Willie "The Lion." *The Memoirs of an American Pianist*. London: MacGibbon & Kee, 1965.
Stewart, Rex. *Jazz Masters of the Thirties*. New York: Macmillan, 1972.
Sudhalter, Richard M. *Lost Chords*. New York: Oxford, 1999.
Sudhalter, Richard M., and Philip R. Evans. *Bix: Man and Legend*. New Rochelle, NY: Arlington House, 1974.
Sutton, Allan. *Recording the Twenties*. Denver: Mainspring Press, 2008.
Sutton, Allan, and Kurt Nauck. *American Record Labels and Companies: An Encyclopedia (1891–1943)*. Denver: Mainspring Press, 2000.
Tirro, Frank. *Jazz: A History*. New York: W.W. Norton, 1993.
Vermazen, Bruce. *That Moaning Saxophone*. New York: Oxford University Press, 2004.
Waller, Maurice, and Anthony Calabrese. *Fats Waller*. London: Cassell, 1977.

INDEXES

GENERAL INDEX

Abbott, George, 395
Adams, Cal, 23, 30, 38
Addison, Bernard, 308, 310
Adeler, Edgar, 439n59
Ades, Hawley, 236, 446n13
Adler, Oscar, 43, 45, 50, 410n8
Adrian's Ramblers, 296
Aeolian, 21, 37, 43, 48, 85, 406n21, 407n52
Ahola, Sylvester, 282; California Ramblers, 135, 136–38, 395; London, 201, 436n56, 441n79, 442n10, 443n43; New Yorkers, 6, 161, 164–76, 395, 433n12, 434nn22–24, 434n33, 434nn38–40, 435n44, 435n51
Akst, Harry, 37
Albin, Jack, 155, 334
Alexander, Texas, 431n33
Allen, Evelyn, 378
Allen, Frederick Lewis, 423n23
Allen, Stuart, 300, 312, 328, 336, 396
Alvin, Don, 137, 138, 428n33
Ambrose, Bert, 272, 437n10, 442n8, 452n38
American Forces Radio Services, 461n38
Ammons, Albert, 464n54
Anderson, Leonard, 397
Andrews Sisters, 339
ARC (record label), 288, 314, 325–27; Kirkeby, 278, 280, 282–84, 453n23; Lown, 240, 241, 247, 251; Rollini, 284, 288, 291–93, 295, 296, 454n40
Arlen, Harold, 290, 291, 452n39
Arluck, Harold, 272. *See also* Arlen, Harold
Armstrong, Louis, 3, 8, 418n28, 428n23, 441n4, 450n13: influence, 132, 265, 268, 270, 312, 377, 451nn30–31

Arto records and piano rolls, 38, 45, 47, 51–53, 57, 71, 78, 83, 407n52
Ash, Paul, 350
Ashford, Bob and Bo, 435n51
Astaire, Fred, 405n12, 447n39
Astor, Mary, 345
Auber, Daniel François Esprit, 15
Augenti, Adele (Adelina Julia Caroline), 11, 12, 15–18, 21, 212, 402n11
Augenti, Lil, 403n12
Augenti, Michael, 11, 16
Austin, Gene, 279
Austin Swallow (car), 188, 193, 439n45
Axford, A., 229

Bach, Johann Sebastian, 216, 229, 342
Baer, Ruth, 386, 470n83
Bags, Bill, 382
Bailey, Mildred, 346, 462n16, 464n77
Bailey's Dixie Dudes, 91, 417n10
Baker, Edythe, 26, 406n38
Baker, Jimmy, 283
Baker, Josephine, 197
Baker, Lloyd, 41, 45
Ballew, Smith, 211, 241, 265, 290, 450n18
Banner (record label), 134, 240, 247, 290, 428n40
Banta, Frank, 37, 85, 408n9
Baquet, Achille, 59
Barber, Charlie, 434n28
Barbour, Dave, 458n52
Barker, Danny, 304, 308, 311, 457n40, 458n55
Barnes (musician), 25
Barnet, Charlie, 327, 368, 461n26, 463n40
Barras, Gene, 7, 358
Barrett, Lee, 358

475

Barrigo, Don, 460n17
Barris, Harry, 431n27, 454n48
Barry, Jean, 216
Barry, Sylvia, 359
Bartal, Jeno, 335, 338, 343
Bartell, Ted (Theodore), 105, 119, 410n9
Bartha, Alex, 346
Barthelmess, Richard, 423n15
Bartholomew, Billy, 229
Basie, Count, 330, 332, 357, 368
Batten, Reg, 175, 176, 179, 197, 201, 436n56, 437n18, 441n79
Bauduc, Ray, 279
Baxter, Ted, 407n43
Bayou Boys, 259, 267, 268, 450n22
Bechet, Sidney, 4, 197, 198, 440n63
Beiderbecke, Bix, 399, 420n63, 432nn42–43, 432n46, 432n1 (chap. 10), 432n3 (chap. 10), 433n7, 434n32, 437n14, 441n5, 442n17, 444n46, 448n54, 451n27, 451n29, 452n45, 461n1; with California Ramblers, 99, 418n30, 429n4, 418n30, 429n4; with his Gang, 3–5, 191, 306, 355, 434n37; with Rollini's New Yorkers, 165–76, 433n12, 433n14, 435n40, 435n44; his style, 183, 207, 211, 220, 222, 232, 273, 320, 333, 334, 365, 418n27, 420n61, 426n65, 451n31; with Trumbauer, 159, 161, 433n15; with Wolverines, 91–92, 98, 147, 160, 418n27, 434n35, 449n7
Bela, Dajos, 443n41
Bell (record label), 414n10
Bellson, Louis, 377
Belmont Balladeers, 342, 463n48
Bennett, Ralph, 453n33
Benny, Jack, 172, 175, 435n43, 435n46
Benson Orchestra of Chicago, 411n26
Berger, Emerick N., 76
Bergh (band member), 428n30
Berigan, Bunny, 313, 314, 321, 368, 396, 456n72, 461n33; with Himber, 298; with Rollini, 4, 293, 294, 301, 306, 457n26
Berken, Julius, 296, 456n3
Berlin, Irving, 24, 423n24

Berlioz, Hector, 54, 55
Berman, Brigitte, 433n12
Bernhardt, Miss, 396
Bernie, Ben, 58, 62, 75, 97, 286, 302, 415n34, 427n17, 428n24, 448n64, 455n67, 456n13, 459n63
Bernstein, Artie, 279, 292, 456n74
Berton, Vic, 147, 148, 151, 152, 159, 164, 210, 443n39, 459n65
Bigelow, Don, 236, 237, 446n13
Bird, Charlie, 408n9
Bird, Fred, 443n41
Black, Ted (?) (piano player), 152
Blackbirds of 1926, 197, 443n35
Blake, Eubie, 37, 261
Bleyer, Archie, 348
Bloom, Rube, 165, 257, 259, 265, 267–69, 310, 399, 431n20, 433n10, 450n22, 452n34
Blue Flames, 328, 396
Blue Four, 154, 165, 166, 268, 284, 434n26, 460n13, 460n17
Bluebird (record label), 288, 298, 300, 311, 431n26, 455n61, 459n62
Bluiett, Hamiet, 401n2
Bode, Lou, 237, 238, 446n18
Bogart, Humphrey, 345
Bohan, Joe, 17
Borchers, William, 41
Borodin, Abe, 396
Bose, Sterling, 279
Boswell Sisters, 282
Bowers, Gil, 279
Bowers, Robert Hood, 409n21
Bowlly, Al, 194, 195, 202, 207, 217, 220, 230, 231, 439n59, 440n61, 457n25
Boyd (band member), 428n30
Boyle, Jack and Jane, 397
Bradford, Perry, 401n4, 406n24
Bradley, Irving, 38, 407n56
Bradley, Will, 298, 375
Brandsma, Bert, 418n27
Brandwynne, Nat, 323, 459n65
Braxton, Anthony, 401n2
Breed, Perley, 440n66

Brigode, Ace, 417n65
Brilhart, Arnold, 17, 69, 80, 88, 89, 298, 389, 396, 404n27, 414n14, 422n12, 431n24
Brissett, Pete, 408n9
Broadway (record label), 428n40
Broadway Bellhops, 170, 434n32
Brodsky, Irving, 6, 201, 263, 407n54, 419n35; California Ramblers, 50–53, 59, 64, 65, 71, 77, 78, 80, 81, 87, 90, 98, 99, 101, 106, 112, 113, 119, 141, 422n11; piano rolls, 38, 407nn55–56; with Savoy Orpheans, 179, 441n79
Brooks, Mrs. A. Arthur Alfred, 14
Brooks, Michael, 410n5, 451nn26–28
Brooks, Shelton, 26, 406n32
Brown, Lew, 364
Brown, Steve, 161, 176
Brown & Henderson, 364
Brubeck, Dave, 379
Brunies, George, 84, 176, 199, 377
Brunswick Orchestra, 78, 273, 416n46, 449n1
Brunswick (record label), 75, 87, 242–44, 280, 282, 416n64, 447n32, 452n42; Elizalde, 178, 180, 183, 185–87, 192, 193, 195, 206, 207, 210, 219–22, 228, 231, 233, 437nn9–10, 437n16, 438n31, 438n42, 439n55, 440n67, 452n38; Nichols, 149, 150, 157–59, 174, 258, 260, 263, 269–71, 355, 429n6, 431nn36–37; Rollini, 261, 263, 272, 273, 296, 308, 329, 343, 345, 449n9; Rudy and Herb Wiedoeft, 74, 415n31, 436n5
Buescher, Gus, 55, 56, 94, 104, 114, 387, 390, 392
Buffet Crampon bass saxophone, 200
Buley, Elizabeth, 386
Bullet Records, 369, 372, 373, 376, 467nn26–28
Bullock, Chick, 296, 301
Bunn, Teddy, 261, 266, 449n9
Burch, John, 381
Burke, Verna, 287
Burns, George, 212, 214
Burns, Jeanne, 307, 309, 458n60
Burr, Henry, 42
Busby, Bill, 229, 230

Bush, Charlie, 130
Bushell, Garvin, 3, 401n4
Busig, B., 136, 142, 429n43
Busse, Henry, 328, 422n11, 428n37
Butterfield, Alfred C., 459
Butterfield, Billy, 385
Butterfield, Charlie, 263

Calabress, Lou, 350
California Ramblers, 40–145 passim, 146–63 passim, 274–94 passim
Calloway, Cab, 401n4
Cameo (record label), 240, 428n26; Varsity Eight, 52, 53, 70, 71, 72, 78, 82, 83, 113, 115, 117, 121, 123, 129, 132, 134, 143, 149, 411n22, 412n47, 414n20, 429n44, 430n14
Campbell, Art, 129, 132
Campbell, Bob, 464n54
Campbell, Jan, 334
Candullo, Joe, 368, 385
Cantor, Eddie, 264, 357, 405n12
Capozzi, Ernest, 240, 298, 299, 396
Cardew, Phil, 194, 195, 202, 213, 219, 220, 230, 443n29, 444n45
Carey, Jack, 237
Carey, M. F., 406n24
Carhart, George, 194, 198, 265, 440n61, 440n68
Carlyn, Dorothy, 454n45
Carmichael, Hoagy, 273
Carney, Harry, 3, 105, 361
Carney, Jack, 242
Carr, Jimmy, 141, 412n41, 415n45
Carroll, Adam, 23, 26, 27, 28, 30, 32, 34, 36, 37, 38, 405n12, 405n19, 406n33, 407n40, 407n53
Carroll, Bob, 339–41, 463n40
Carroll, Earl, 427n8
Carter, Bennie, 292, 458n60
Carter, Paul, 86, 417n4, 445n3
Caruso, Enrico, 11
Casa Loma Orchestra, 288, 457n39
Casals, Pablo, 82
Castle, Irene, 40, 404n30

Castle, Vernon, 40, 404n30
Casti, Nick, 139, 162
Ceppos, Mac, 237, 238, 241, 245, 252, 253, 286, 288, 446n17, 447n18
Challis, Beth, 157, 431n32
Challis, Bill, 161, 162, 164, 165, 173, 187, 188, 192, 207, 212, 431n32, 439n57
Chamber Music Society of Lower Basin Street, 349, 357
Chaplin, Charlie, 5
Charleston Chasers, 430n13, 450n22
Chicago Loopers, 173
Chicago Senators, 420n58
Chiclet, 339–42
Chopin, Frédéric, 15, 156, 193, 326, 342, 403n21, 431n30
Christmas, Art, 229
Christmas Fantasy, 395, 445n62
Cipolla, Henri, 17
Cirina, Joseph, 25
Clair, Jane, 463n48
Claire, Ted, 448n47
Clare, Herbert, 405n12
Clark, Buddy, 324
Clark, Harry, 317–86 passim
Clark, Melville, 21
Clark, Spencer, 5, 26, 420n64, 440n61, 471n25; California Ramblers period, 59, 63, 64, 114, 115, 129, 130, 132, 135, 141, 143, 159, 175, 211, 404n27, 410n7, 410n9, 412n42, 416n51, 422n12, 425n45, 425n47, 425n48, 426n60; further career, 308, 434n26; Lown period, 254, 286, 455n67
Claudier, Norman, 302
Clines, Tom (Thomas), 242–44, 255, 263, 285, 289, 400, 447n32
Clinton, Larry, 353
Cloutier, Norman, 335
Cobey, Lew, 275, 278
Cohn, Harvey W., 381
Colbert, Claudette, 350, 395
Colburn, Jolly, 297
Cole, Bill, 389, 471n22
Cole, Bob, 21

Cole, Harry D., 447n44
Cole, Nat "King," 465n92
Cole, Phil, 396
Coleman, Emile, 415n34
Collegians, 135, 422n12
Collegiate Rollickers, 144
Collett, Richard, 179, 184, 207
Collier, James Lincoln, 8
Collini, Giuseppe, 407n53
Collins, Al, 197, 214
Collins, Jack, 230
Colombo, Al, 414n11
Colombo, Russ, 454n48
Colonial Club Orchestra, 431
Colonna, Jerry, 396
Coltrane, John, 401n4
Columbia (record label), 41, 153, 156, 257–94 passim, 406n25, 408n8, 411n26, 411n33, 428n25, 428nn27–28, 440n67, 450n20, 450n22, 451n30, 460n24; California Ramblers, 40–145 passim, 274, 399, 413nn8–9, 415n26, 415n33, 416nn48–49, 416n61, 416n64, 418n21, 418n29, 418n21, 418n29, 419n38, 419n41, 421n73, 421n76, 423n29, 424n43, 452n2; Lown, 247–48, 251, 252; Rollini, 291
Columbia Saxaphone Sextette, 408n5
Como, Perry, 359, 447n18
Condon, Eddie, 210, 451n30, 458n56
Conklin, Mr., 16
Conn bass saxophone, 4, 55, 56, 78, 104, 226, 387, 422n5, 470n14, 471n25; Rollini's, 56, 86, 107, 200, 387–90, 471n22
Connor, Jack, 397
Connorized (piano roll maker), 25, 407n52
Conrad, Fred, 41
Cook, Walter B., 385
Coon-Sanders, 256, 258
Cooper, Jerry, 396
Cornell. *See* Smelser, Cornell
Costello, Dolores, 231
Cotton, Billy, 230
Couchran (policeman), 18
Couesnon (instrument manufacturer), 86

Coughlan, Frank, 202, 213, 214, 442n10
Coward, Noel, 192, 439n56
Cowe, Phil, 424n33
Cripwell, Les, 444n60
Crosby, Bing, 159, 211, 333, 344, 368, 457n25
Crozier, George, 422n12
Cugat, Xavier, 355
Cullum, Jim, 365, 394, 467n2
Cummins, Bernie, 431n35
Curtis, Dennis "Dinty," 434n28
Cush, Frank: California Ramblers, 48–123 passim, 129, 175, 212, 423n29, 424n43; with Lown and further career, 209, 237, 238, 241, 245, 252, 253, 411n40
Cusick, Fred, 211, 382, 404n27, 410nn3–4, 442n18; California Ramblers, 48–145 passim, 175, 212, 422n13, 423n17, 423n29
Cusson (band member), 428n30
Cutler, Ben, 255, 448n61
Cutting, Ernest, 61
Czinner, Paul, 395, 445n61

Dabney, Ford, 406n22
Dandridge, Putney, 306, 307, 309
Danzi, Mike, 217, 229, 362, 363, 443n41, 444n55, 445n68, 466n123
D'Artega (conductor), 344
Davern, Kenny, 390, 471n26
Davis, Bobby: California Ramblers, 67–163 passim, 417n3, 418n26, 423n29, 438n33, 438n41, 443n34; Elizalde, 177–233 passim, 445n69; further career, 275, 276, 278; Rollini's New Yorkers, 164–76 passim
Davis, Charlie, 91
Davis, Eddie, 140, 339, 428n40, 463n33
Davis, Freddie, 390
Davis, Joe, 408n10
Davis, Joseph H., 382, 384
Davis, Meyer, 272, 297
Davis, Peggy, 414
Davis, Sammy, 321
Davison, Walter, 26
Day, Dorothy, 357, 402n25, 421n1
Daye, Henry, 358

De Falla, Manuel, 233
de Mornys, William J., 179, 436n56
De Vries, Louis, 229
Deagan (instrument manufacturer), 320, 337, 338, 392, 393, 471n34
Decca (record label), 233, 301, 306, 309, 313, 322, 325, 330, 332, 334, 335, 376, 438n35, 458n60, 460n13, 461n2
DeDroit, Johnnie, 449n9
Deep River Boys, 411n28
Delcamp, John Milton, 23, 24, 25, 30, 31, 34, 35, 36, 38, 39, 405n12, 405n16, 405n19, 407n40
Dellow, Nick, 177–233 passim, 436n58, 436n3 (chap. 11), 436n7, 437n11, 437n13, 437n21, 439n43, 439n46, 440n72, 441n2, 441n7, 442n17, 443n27, 443n31
Deloof, Gus, 200
Dempsey, Jack, 349, 350, 371, 386, 434n27
Dengler, John, 389
Deno and Rochelle, 434n33
Deveau, Tom, 350
D'Giovanni, Irene, 406n29
Dickerman, Don, 446n6
DiLalla, Christine (DeLallo), 403n11
DiLalla, Mary Filomena, 11, 16
Dillard, Bill, 311
DiMaggio, Joe, 350
Dixie Hod Carriers, 417n10
Dobschinski, Walter, 458n47
Dodds, Johnny, 461n1
Doeve, Eppo, 222–24
Dollinger, Art, 459n69
Donah, Rose, 404n36
Donaldson, Walter, 208
Donna (hurricane), 386, 467n19
Dorsey, Jimmy, 210, 263, 265, 268, 271, 273, 279, 420n60, 421n77, 422n6, 443n24, 457n39, 459nn62–65; California Ramblers, 85–163 passim, 186, 190, 191, 426n60
Dorsey, Tommy, 190, 191, 259, 263, 264, 267, 269, 273, 279, 298, 305, 306, 311, 328, 334, 350, 357, 422n6, 429n11, 457n39, 459nn62–65, 466n112; California Ramblers, 97–99,

101, 102, 105, 119, 121, 417n14, 420n66, 421n77; Rollini's band, 284, 291
Doucet, Clement, 193
Douglas, Paul, 321
Douglas, Robert, 382
Down South Music Publishing Corp., 408n10
Dreier, Dave, 348, 462n13
Dreier, Freddy, 348, 462n13
Drelinger, Art, 458n57, 459n69
Drewhurst, Kidsy (Walter), 130
Dreyer, Dave, 372
Drown, Bunny (Elmer L.), 117
Duchin, Eddie, 287, 305
Duff, Jimmy, 41–43, 45, 50–52, 54, 65, 69, 81, 88, 408n4, 408n13, 414n13
Duffy, Al, 6, 130, 323, 333, 335, 427n18
Duke, Doris, 324
Duncan Sisters, Rosetta and Vivian (Topsy and Eva), 68, 413n4
Dunn, Blind Willie, 451n29
Dunn, Johnny, 68, 401n4, 414n15, 443n35, 449n1
Durant, Basil, 110, 140, 423n28
Durante, Jimmy "Schnozzle," 59, 276, 409n31, 447n39
Durban, Kay, 110, 423n28

Ederle, Gertrude, 423n30
Edison (record label), 20, 415n24, 416n64, 417n13, 421n4, 452n2; California Ramblers, 92, 93, 96, 99, 117, 122, 126, 132, 133, 137, 143, 144, 155, 161, 162, 211, 274, 399, 418nn32–33
Edwards, Cliff, 101, 118, 122, 139, 143, 145, 151, 156, 264, 421n80
Edwards, Eddie, 427n17
Eldridge, Roy, 308
Elizalde, Angel, 177
Elizalde, Carmenchu, 177
Elizalde, Fred (Federico), 4, 176–224, 229–34, 238, 256, 257, 268, 276, 317, 330, 347
Elizalde, Joaquin Marcelino, 177
Elizalde, Joaquin Miguel (Mike), 177, 351
Elizalde, José Joaquin, 177
Elizalde, Juan Miguel, 177
Elizalde, Manuel (Manolo) (Lizz), 177–79, 184, 196, 201, 204, 209, 211, 212, 217, 437n14, 443n24, 443n28
Elks, 106, 282, 412n50
Ellington, Duke, 121, 259, 336, 357, 360, 361, 401n1, 447n42, 448n54, 449n9, 461n33, 462n16, 466n119; musicians, 105, 253, 258, 263, 308, 327, 357, 422n9
Ellis, Chris, 450n14
Ellis, Gay, 267
Elsener, Joseph C., 108–12, 140, 424n36
Emerson (record label), 45, 51, 408n9, 414n11
Engle, Victor, 302
Epes, Mattie W., 100
Epic (record label), 379
Epiphone, 338, 347, 351
Erwin, Pee Wee, 334
Eschauzier, André "Dries," 164, 222–27, 229, 444n49, 471n25
Essex (car), 188, 222, 439n48
Europe, James Reese, 40, 404n30, 406n22
Evans (club manager or musician), 408n4
Evans, Philip R., 165, 418n29, 420n61, 420n65, 432n43, 432n3 (chap. 10), 433n6
Evans, Roy, 259, 267

Faber, Tom, 4, 163, 351, 356, 378, 388–91, 393, 403n17, 403n25, 420n71, 429n44, 433n12, 434n22, 438n35, 441n76, 470n14
Faber, Willy, 4, 391
Fairchild, Edgar, 405n12
Falce, Buddy, 446n17
Fallon, Bob, 141, 160
Fallon, Owen, 453n33
Farley, Eddie, 237, 238, 241, 245, 246, 250, 252, 253, 286, 311, 332, 446n18
Farley, Max, 202, 211–14, 216, 220, 230–32, 445nn68–69
Fay, Frank, 167, 168, 172, 175, 433n19, 434n39, 435nn40–41, 435n43, 447n39
Fazio, Jimmy, 377

Feather, Leonard, 198, 306, 315, 458n51
Feld, Morey, 377
Feldkamp, Elmer, 252, 253, 278
Felline, Tommy: California Ramblers, 88, 90, 98, 106, 117, 119, 129, 131, 136, 137, 138, 141, 142, 156, 162, 417n13, 423n29, 431n29; Lown, 209, 237, 238, 245, 248, 252, 253, 286, 417n13
Fetchit, "Stepin," 448n47
Fiedler-Mann, 126
Fields, Arthur, 119
Fields, W. C., 89
Figel, Jack, 167, 168
Fillis, Hal, 213, 217, 443n28
Fillis, Len, 180, 181, 186, 187, 194, 202, 213, 439n59
Fink, Sam, 117, 423n29, 424n33
Fink, Stanley, 423n28
Fiorito, Ted, 246
Fitchard, Maurice, 423n28
Fitzgibbons, Dave, 216, 443n35
Five Birmingham Babies, 88, 91, 114, 120, 418n27, 420n69, 438n34
Five Harmony Kings, 443n35
Five Kings of Syncopation, 296, 456n3
Five Omega Collegians, 391
Five Pennies. *See* Nichols, Red
Flippen, Jay C., 151, 156, 157, 431n31, 436n52
Flowers, Pat, 417n4
Foeste, William, 411n26
Forsythe, Reginald, 326, 460n24
Fosdick, Dudley, 210
Fosdick, Gene, 77, 160
Foster, Nan, 23, 38, 407n58
Foster, Stephen, 409n22
Four Instrumental Stars, 152
Fox, I. J., 453n9
Fox, Jack, 73
Fox, Roy, 438n35
Fradkin, Freddie, 298
Frank, Franklyn, 315, 458n51
Frankel, Ben, 194, 202, 230, 231
Franklin, Arthur, 172, 434n39, 435n40
Frazee Sisters (Ruth and Jane), 397

Freeman, Bud, 271, 273, 292, 301, 440n61, 452n45
French, Lloyd, 396, 397
Friedman Brothers, 444n52
Froeba, Frank, 261, 266, 397, 449n9
Fuhs, Julian, 443n41
Funk, Larry, 446n18

Gaffney, Donald, 124, 427n3
Gaillard, Slim, 394, 465n97
Gallagher, William J., 71
Gannon, C. Feland, 133
Garber, Jan, 257, 259, 260, 417n65, 466n113
Garcia, Louis "King," 300, 312, 459n65
Garner, Erroll, 468n39
Garibaldi, Giuseppe, 9
Garson, Greer, 346
Gay, Byron, 406n26
Gennett (record label), 72, 88, 92, 117, 122, 134, 144, 408n9, 417n10, 420n63, 426n62, 435n42, 441n5
Gentieu, Norman, 382, 384, 385, 469n70, 469n74
George, Dick, 272
Georgia Melodians, 418n33
Georgians, 69, 74, 93, 226, 414n11, 414n16
Gershwin, George, 37, 184, 406n22, 440n62, 447n31, 451n24
Gilbert, Mary Wagner, 12, 15
Gilliland, Jim, 41
Gilt-Edged Four, 391
Giordano, Vince, 245, 401n2, 435n47
Giove, Felix, 353
Girard, Adele, 461n27
Glaser, Ben, 272, 452n37
Glaser, Bob. *See* Grant, Bob
Glass Hat, 339, 341, 342, 463n36, 463n41
Gleason, Jackie, 298
Gluckman, Bernie, 286
Gluskin, Lud, 228, 229, 254, 425n49, 443n41, 444n57
Goddard, Paulette, 346
Goffin, Robert, 200, 441n75
Gold, Harry, 6, 390, 437n23, 438n35

Gold, Joe, 25
Gold, Lou, 415n23
Goldberg, Max, 214
Golden Gate Orchestra, 69, 78, 124, 134, 140, 141, 143, 274, 411n41, 414nn10–11, 415n45, 418n32
Golden, Larry, 464n56
Goldkette, Jean, 89, 153, 159–69, 173, 175, 187, 207, 211, 334, 419n41, 419n49, 428n24, 430n20, 432n46, 432n48
Goodman, Benny, 279, 292, 298, 299, 301, 312, 328, 332, 338, 347, 455n71, 456n74, 457n39, 458n52, 461n33; with Rollini, 4, 8, 259, 269–71, 293, 296, 455n71, 456n74
Goodman, Frank, 405n16
Goodman, Harry, 279
Goodman, Irving, 459n69
Goodyear, Lee, 378
goofus, 240, 253, 267, 268, 272, 284, 285, 296, 313, 321, 335, 391, 417n6, 438n39, 418n21, 420n54, 422n4, 438n35, 438n40; California Ramblers, 86, 87, 88, 91, 96, 120, 121, 132, 133, 142, 144, 145, 149, 150, 152, 154, 155, 157; Elizalde, 184, 187, 192, 200, 203, 208, 218, 221; New Yorkers, 164, 166, 433n4
Goofus Five, 88, 91, 93, 97, 99, 119, 120, 121, 123, 129, 132, 133, 135, 142–43, 144, 156, 157, 183, 399, 420n56, 422n4, 425n49, 426n59, 433n4, 437n19, 438n38
Goofus Washboards, 437n19, 438n38
Gordon, Fid, 409n18
Gorman, Ross, 69, 147, 454n43
Gover, Emma, 410n32
Goyarts, Max, 224, 225, 390
Graham, Mr., 396
Grant, Bob, 295
Grappelli, Stephane, 440n73
Graves, Elsie, 461n27
Gray, Chauncey (Judd), 209, 235, 237, 238, 241, 245, 246, 248, 252, 253, 269, 289, 448n46, 455n66
Gray, Glen, 461n33
Green, Abel, 300, 323, 413n8, 421n81, 426n66, 462n20

Green, George Hamilton, 48
Green, Jacques/Jackie, 427n17, 465n96
Green, Tommy, 404n28
Greer, Sonny, 361
Gregory, Gloria, 420n53
Gregory, Guerrino, 140
Grenadiers Quartet, 277
Grey Gull, 428n40
Grieg, Edvard Hagerup, 266
Griffin, Gordon, 310, 457n40
Grimaldi, Amelia, 9, 402n4
Grofé, Ferde, 70, 405n12, 408n16, 428n37
Gross, Walter, 130, 424n33
Grosz, Marty, 292
Guarante, Frank, 94, 226, 409n16, 436n56
Gubertini, Leonardo, 216
Gubertini, Ronnie, 180, 181, 184, 186, 187, 194, 202, 216, 230, 231, 438n36
Guinan, Texas, 295, 414n15

Hackett, Bobby, 334, 335, 342
Hagan, Cass, 159, 175, 176
Hagen, Milton, 95, 96, 419n41, 419n44
Haines, Roy, 408n9
Hall, Arthur, 71, 415n23
Hall, Sleepy, 246
Hall, Wilbur, 428n37
Halstead, Henry, 372
Hamblen, Bernhard, 406n29
Hamm, Fred, 235, 246
Hammond, John, 292, 293, 301, 456n74
Hampton, Lionel, 328, 332, 402n22, 441n4
Hand, Arthur C., 339, 410nn4–7, 428n21, 428n24, 428n38, 428n42; California Ramblers, 48–145 passim, 274, 413n8, 414n20, 416n56, 420n54, 422n13, 423n21, 423nn28–29, 424n33, 424n40
Hand, Joseph C., 48, 62, 95
Handy, W. C., 25, 133, 155, 310, 359, 417n1, 465n106
Hanley, James F., 406n25
Hanlon, Allen, 346, 348, 349, 351–56, 358, 368, 371, 375, 378, 397, 464n77
Hansen, Jack, 211

Hanshaw, Annette (Catherine A.), 149–54, 156, 164, 165, 267–69, 430n14, 430n20, 431n22, 433n7
Hanshaw, Frank Wayne, 150
Hardwick, Otto, 401n2, 422n9
Hardy, Marlow, 449n6
Haring, Bob, 273, 398
Harker, James, 220
Harmony (record sublabel), 110, 121, 122, 133, 144, 155, 170, 210, 211, 236–40, 242, 251, 257, 264, 265, 267, 269, 271, 426n61, 451n24
Hawkins, Coleman, 3, 103–5, 291, 422n4, 458n60
Hayes, Harry, 180, 181, 194, 201, 202, 213, 439n44, 440n67, 440n72, 442n19
Haymes, Joe, 459n62
Hayton, Lennie, 130, 135, 159, 428n30
Hazlett, Chester, 428n37
Heidt, Horace, 350
Henderson, Fletcher, 70, 74, 82, 104, 130, 147, 265, 292, 391, 410n32, 418n28, 419n41, 421n4, 435n48, 448n64
Hennesy, Dan, 140
Henry, Fred, 51
Herbert, Victor, 73
Hereford, Fletcher, 238, 245, 424n33
Here's to Veterans, 376, 461n38
Herlihy, Ed, 340, 341, 463n43
Herlihy, Joe, 161, 167, 432n46
Herrington, Hereward, 95
Herth, Milt, 338, 353, 397, 461n2, 465n92, 466n112
Hess, Cliff, 37
Hester, Gwyn, 459n69
Hester, Stanley, 420n57, 452n35
Hester, Steve, 452n35
Hickman, Art, 41, 80
Higginbotham, J. C., 266, 267
Hilbert, Robert (Bob), 384
Hill, Dick, 137
Hill, Jack, 202, 213, 230, 231
Himber, Corinne, 296, 297
Himber, Richard (Dick), 296, 297, 459n65, 459n67, 461n27, 462n21; with Rollini, 298–302, 309, 312, 315, 317, 322–36, 392, 395–96
Himber Harmonies, 322, 330, 396
Himpsl, Frank, 39, 407n47
Hinrichs, Herman. *See* Oakland, Will
Hirsch, Godfrey, 336
Hite, Mattie, 410n32
Hitler, Adolf, 344, 455n64
Hit-of-the-Week, 239, 240, 247, 248, 260
Hnida, George, 282, 313, 325, 354, 356, 368, 371, 376, 377, 379, 386, 397, 453n27, 459n69, 467n10, 468n33
Hodes, Art, 377
Hoff, Vanda, 61
Hoke, Pat (Glen P.), 333, 334, 452nn5–6
Holst, Ernie, 342
Holt, Ted, 287, 455n56
Holzfeind, Frank, 377
Hope, Bob, 346, 368
Hopkins, Claude, 468n29
Hopkins, George W., 76
Horne, Lena, 159
Horricks, Raymond, 401n3
Hottentots, 429n6
Howard, Shirley, 321
Hudson, Garth, 389
Hudson, Harry, 391
Hughes, Spike, 232
Hughes, Stan, 126
Hurley, George, 183, 192, 194, 202, 426n65, 437n23, 439n44, 445n62
Huston, Walter, 448n49
Hutton, Ina Ray, 343
Hyde, Alex, 73, 217, 228
Hylton, Jack, 207, 230

Ingram, Rex, 231
Intercollegians, 79, 124, 416n51
Irish, Mace, 237, 238, 245, 446nn17–18

Jackson, Edgar, 219
Jackson, Papa Charlie, 122
James, Lewis, 72
Jenkins, Freddie, 308, 310

Jenney, Jack, 396
Johnson (agent), 41
Johnson, Arnold, 265, 406n26, 408n5, 435n43
Johnson, Charlie, 458n57
Johnson, Howard L., 389, 471n21
Johnson, Johnny, 146
Johnson, Lonnie, 431n33
Johnson, Lucille, 341, 342
Johnson, Pete, 464n54
Johnson, Will, 266, 267
Johnston, Ivan, 129, 136, 142, 143
Johnston, Leroy "Roy," 105, 106, 117, 122, 129, 131, 135, 136, 141–43, 422n12, 428n30
Jolson, Al, 73, 82, 412n48, 416n48
Jones, Isham, 72, 281, 423n24, 453n31, 459n63
Jones, John Luther (Casey), 144, 429n45
Jones, Jonah, 4, 325
Jones, Maggie, 410n32
Joplin, Scott, 21, 406n23
Jordan, Joe, 359, 418n27
Jordon, Joe, 73
Joy, Jimmy, 357

Kahn, Art, 35, 407n51, 453n33
Kahn, Gilbert, 80, 81, 373, 416nn55–56, 417n12
Kahn, Otto, 80, 416n55, 416n58
Kahn, Roger Wolfe, 81, 153, 159, 170, 373, 416n55, 416n58, 417n12, 427n17
Kaminsky, Max, 456n72
Kane, Kathryn (Sugar Cane), 396
Kardos, Gene, 293
Katee, Frits, 390
Katz, Kal, 299, 396
Katzman, Louis, 431n35
Kaufman, Irving, 141, 170, 210, 264, 265
Kaufman, Whitey, 265
Kay, Anthony, 459n69
Kay, Brad, 170, 434n30
Kay, Dolly, 68
Kaye, Harold S., 439n60
Kaye, Merrill (Kline), 7, 162, 163, 246–54, 286, 290, 302, 425n45, 432n52, 448n46, 455n67
Keeler, Ruby, 427n17
Keeler, Willard, 424n33

Kegley, Charles, 266
Keith (B. F. Keith Circuit), 43, 44, 45, 59–61, 67, 68, 77, 86, 106, 116, 124, 248, 297, 412n50, 446n8
Keith Prowse, 438n40
Kellner, Murray, 298
Kelly, Patsy, 172, 433n20, 435nn40–41
Kelsall, Ena, 282, 305, 386
Kelsall, May, 282
Kemp, Hal, 265
Kennedy, Buddy, 276
Kenton, Stan, 368
Kentucky Blowers, 88, 91
Kentucky Serenaders, 406n25
Kessler, Sam, 43
Kilfeather, Eddie, 420n61
Kilgen, Noel, 275, 276
Kimmel, Jack, 298
King, Stan (F. Stanley), 259, 425n48, 456n2; California Ramblers, 52, 65, 72, 77, 80, 81, 87, 88, 106, 119, 431n30; Lown, 238, 245, 252, 253, 286
King, Wayne, 286, 328
King of Spain, 181
Kirby, John, 332, 468n29
Kirk, Eddy. *See* Kirkeby, Ed
Kirkeby, Ed (Wallace Theodore), 265, 409n32, 430n14, 436n52, 445n3, 449n12, 453n23, 453n33, 457n37, 457n42, 458n48, 458n59, 459nn62–63; California Ramblers, 40–163 passim, 209, 211, 234, 274, 275, 278, 280–83, 285, 298, 303, 391, 408nn4–9, 408nn13–15, 409n17, 409n24, 412n42, 412n56, 413n62, 413n2, 413n8, 414nn9–11, 414n15, 415n37, 415n40, 415n45, 416n47, 416n60, 417nn2–4, 417n14, 418n44, 419n50, 420n55, 421n82, 423n29, 424n33, 424n35, 424n38, 424n40, 424n43, 426n60, 427n15, 427n20, 428n33, 428n38, 428n42, 429n44, 452nn2–4; at RCA-Victor, 304, 308, 309–11, 315, 431n26
Kirkman & Sons, 41
Kitchingman, Ray, 40–43, 45, 50–52, 54, 55, 58, 65, 77, 80, 81, 87, 88, 408nn4–5, 408n13, 414n20

Klein, Dave, 316, 440n72, 456n3
Klein, Manny, 159, 210, 259, 267, 269, 270, 284, 291, 301, 316, 457n26
Kline, Merrill (Kaye), 7, 162, 246, 248–54, 286, 290, 302, 425n45, 432n52, 448n46
Kline, Teddy, 217
Klugh, Paul B., 23
Knight, "Nobby," 194, 202, 229–31
Koehler, Ted, 290
Kohler Industries, 21, 24, 28, 29, 33, 35, 405n9, 406nn19–21
Kohlert (instrument manufacturer), 471n25
Kolensky, Alex, 373, 468n29
Korina, Anna, 277
Kortlander, Max, 407n43
Kress, Carl, 130, 210, 263, 376, 459n69, 461n33
Krueger, Bennie, 415n34, 419n49
Krupa, Gene, 260, 273, 332, 372, 377
Kuhe, Wilhelm, 15, 403n19
Kurtin, Herb, 431n22

Lada's Louisiana Five, 87, 453n10
LaFaro, Joe (Joseph), 131, 136, 142, 143, 424n33
Lagonda (car), 351, 465n88
Laird, Ross, 273, 433n7
Lally, Arthur, 438n35
LaMacchia, Rosa, 153
Lamare, Nappy, 279
Lamberts, Scrappy, 248, 262
Lamphis, V., 126
Landis, Carole, 345
Landry, Art, 169, 434n28
Lane, Victor, 23, 27, 28, 32, 34, 36, 37, 38
Lang, Eddie, 147, 290, 416n58, 432n48, 433n15, 434n28, 451n29; Rollini, 150–54, 161, 164–66, 173, 222, 268, 284, 285, 416n58; Venuti, 143, 146, 176, 301
Langdon, Robert F., 167, 168
Lange, Arthur, 416n58
Langford, Frances, 282, 287, 297
Lanin, Howard, 448n64
Lanin, Sam, 47, 77, 97, 98, 101, 147, 170, 175, 413n8, 415n23, 417n65, 418n30, 420n57, 420n60, 427n17, 429n4, 434n32

Lanin's Red Heads, 421n73, 429n4
Lanning, Norman, 424n33
Lappe, Eddy, 162
LaRocca, Nick, 92, 146, 315, 458n51
Larson, Bert, 438n35
Lathrop, Jack, 335
Laue, Bruce, 402n1
Laue, William, 16
Lay, Ward, 211, 238, 245, 278, 329
Laylan, "Preacher" Rollo, 382
Lee, Gypsy Rose, 349
Lee, Len, 194, 202, 439
Lee, Loretta, 463n48
Lees, Doug, 460n17
Lefko, Max, 228
Leibrook, Min, 99, 191, 193, 420n64, 436n57
Leitrim, Leon, 418n15
Lenzberg, Julius, 77, 78, 409n23
Leschetizky, Theodor, 12, 403nn15–16
Leslie, Lew, 197
Levant, Oscar, 403n16
Leverich, Lester L., 76
Levine, Al, 127, 296, 456n3
Levine, Henry, 349
Levine, Nat, 298, 299, 328, 396
Levitow, Bernard, 246
Lewins Music Store, 7
Lewis, Meade Lux, 464n54
Lewis, Ted, 68, 75, 176, 251, 451n30; early band incl. bass saxophone, 55, 406n26, 408n8, 415n34; Europe, 198, 199, 440n67, 440nn71–72
Lewis Music, 364
Lhotak, Frank, 456n3
Lilienfeld, Louis, 248
Lincoln, Abe, 64, 105, 121, 122, 128, 129, 131, 138, 416n46, 422n12, 427n12, 432n46
Lind, Joe, 397
Lindström Company, 428n27, 443n32
Little Ramblers, 87, 88, 90–92, 101, 110, 117, 122, 126, 130, 132, 135, 149, 155, 159, 274, 310, 311, 312, 399, 418n21, 420n53, 431n26, 452n1, 453n23, 459n62
Little Wonder (record label), 56, 68

Livingston, Fud, 106, 117, 159, 162, 170, 191, 202, 210–14, 217, 218–20, 222, 431n39, 442n10, 442n22, 444nn44–45, 458n56
Livingston, Jerry, 396
Livingstone, Margaret, 435n40
Lloyd, Ed, 453n23
Locke, Alain, 419n36
Loeffler, Carl, 278
Logan, Ella, 301, 305
Lombardo, Guy, 258, 286, 305, 328, 448n64
Longon, Francis, 41
Lopez, Vincent, 58, 73, 76, 77, 183, 239, 302, 374, 415n34, 417n65, 417n1 (chap. 6), 417n13, 419n51, 423n24, 427n17, 448n64, 455n67, 456n13
Lorenzi, Mario "Harp," 194, 202, 206, 230, 231
Lotz, Rainer E., 217
Louisiana Rhythm Kings, 210, 258, 260, 442n16, 449n3
Love, Andy, 335
Lown, Bert: later career, 446n5, 448n66, 454n46, 454n48, 454n51, 455nn56–57, 455nn61–62, 455n67; before Rollini, 237, 445n5, 446nn5–15, 447n34; with Rollini, 209–11, 234–56, 274–94, 390, 392, 395, 399, 442n15, 447n19, 447n41, 447n44, 448n46, 448n49, 448n61, 448nn66–67, 453n8, 454nn39–40
Lunceford, Jimmie, 459n63, 454n46
Lyman, Abe, 360, 409n31
Lytell, Jimmy, 409nn31–32
Lytton-Edwards, B. M., 442n17

Machan, Frank, 296
Mack, Roy, 395
Maddux, Wilfred Pete, 100
Magic of Music, The, 299, 396
Magnante, Charlie, 284, 450n16
Maloney, Ray (Raymond) and Anne, 371
Mann, Lew, 172, 435nn40–41
Mann, Peggy (Margaret Germano), 372, 373, 467n27, 468n28
Manny's Music Store, 389

Manone, Joseph "Wingy," 307–9, 314, 315, 332, 412n42, 458nn51–53, 458n56, 458n60, 460n13
Marcelino, Joaquin. *See* Elizalde, Joaquin
Mardi Gras, 369
Margulis, Charlie, 298
Marsala, Joe, 307, 309, 320
Marshall, Joe, 464n61
Martin, Dr., 282
Martin, Freddie, 283, 284, 454n40, 454nn48–49
Masman, Theo Uden, 226, 227, 229
Mason, Billy, 213, 214, 230, 231
Mason, Paul, 237, 238, 245, 252, 253, 278
Massaro, Pat and Vincent, 386
Massaro, Salvatore. *See* Lang, Eddie
Massenet, Jules, 121
Mastren, Carmen, 307, 309
Mather, Bill, 319, 459n2
Mathisen, Leo, 228, 229
Matlock, Matty, 279
Matzenauer, Marguerite, 408n11
Maxim, Hudson, 15
Maxwell, Richard (Dickie), 180, 181, 202
McAlpineers, 452n3
McCann, Jack, 408n9
McClure, Olive, 172, 435n40
McConville, Leo, 159
McCord, Castor, 266, 267
McCoy, Clyde, 328
McCoy, Mary, 150
McDonald, Ballard, 406n25
McDonough, Dick, 159, 267, 273, 290, 291, 314, 325, 459n69, 461n33
McElmurry, Fred, 310
McGhee, Johnny, 328, 333, 334
McGhee, Sherry, 446n17
McGrath, Fulton "Fidgey," 284, 286, 288, 291, 301, 325
McIntosh, Max, 41, 43, 45
McKenzie, Hazel, 468n50
McKenzie, Mac, 378
McKenzie, Red, 292, 325, 451n30, 456n73, 458n56

McKinley, Ray, 450n18
McNaughton, Virginia, 396
McPartland, Jimmy, 260, 279, 449n7
Melrose Brothers, 91, 92, 418n27
Melton, James, 302, 457n35
Mendelssohn, Felix, 15
Menjou, Adolphe, 345
Mercury Records, 376, 377, 468n28, 468n41
Meroff, Benny, 170
Merry Macs, 341
Merry Melody Men, 42, 43, 408n14
Metropole, 232, 445n65
Meyer, Johnny, 450n16
Meyers, Mrs., 53
Michalsky, Peggy, 386
Miles, Verlye, 396
Miley, Bubber, 253, 258, 266, 449n1
Miller, Art, 284, 291, 337
Miller, Ashley, 468n31
Miller, Carlyne, 285
Miller, Eddie, 279, 432n3
Miller, Frances, 414n18
Miller, Glenn, 174, 260, 261, 263, 271, 335, 346, 446n17, 449n8, 450n18
Miller, Jack (Jaap Mulder), 263, 264, 451n24
Miller, Ray, 147, 259, 408n16, 415n34, 417n65, 422n12
Mills, Florence, 443n35
Mills, Irving, 263, 325
Mills, Jack, 85, 408n10
Mills Blue Rhythm Band, 266
Minot, George, 103, 386
Miranda, Jack, 194, 202, 392
Miss Chiclet, 339. *See also* Mitchell, Dolly
Mitchell, Al, 463n40
Mitchell, Dolly, 339, 340, 394, 465n97
Mitchell, Roscoe, 401n2
Mole, Miff (Milford), 146
Mondello, James "Toots," 326
Monroe, Vaughn, 368
Monroe County sheriff, 384
Montgomery, Mike, 30, 406n33
Moore, Bill (William Henry), 48–123 passim, 128, 129, 212, 266, 410n9, 420n58, 425n53

Moore, Oscar, 465n92
Moore, Vic, 440n61
Morehouse, Chauncey, 93, 161, 162, 164–66, 170–71, 173, 176
Morgan, Russ, 458n60
Morgan, Tommy, 368, 369
Morgenstern, Dan, 8
Morphew, John, 389, 391
Morrell, Benny, 385, 469n80
Morris, Jess, 416n60
Morris, Richard Lewis, 412n51
Morris, Wayne, 463n51
Morris, William, 197–99, 343, 352, 354, 355, 357, 364, 368, 464n61
Morrisey, Howard, 456n3
Morse, Lee, 259, 263–64, 450n23
Morton, Jelly Roll, 133, 157, 419n35, 426n62, 431n30, 460n13, 461n1
Moten, Buster, 450n16
Moulton, Roy, 338, 462n13
Mound City Blue Blowers, 87, 130, 292
Mueller, Alfred G., 416n51
Mueller, J. Robert, 424n14
Mueller, Gus, 408n16
Mulder, Jaap. *See* Miller, Jack
Mulligan, Gerry, 3, 401n3
Munson, Frank, 235
Murray, Billy, 278, 429n45
Murray, Don, 154, 161, 165, 166, 170, 171, 173, 176, 199, 268, 433n14, 434n39
Musser, Clair Omar, 393
Muzak, 289, 329, 330, 446n5

Napoleon, Phil, 47, 262, 385, 422n6
Napoleon I, 9
Napoleon III, 9
Nash, Joey, 297–301, 312, 395, 396, 456n13, 457n25
Nash Harrison, Theresa, 421n74
Nauck, Kurt, 447n21
Navara, Leon, 454n48
Negri, Madame, 15, 403n22, 445n61
Negri, Pola, 230, 395, 403n22, 418n19, 445nn61–62

Nelson, Ozzie, 17, 287, 459n63
Nevin, Ethelbert, 74, 415n31
New Orleans Lucky Seven, 173
New Orleans Rhythm Kings, 84, 156, 176, 426n62
New Yorkers, 164–76 passim, 187, 188, 194, 198, 387, 435n40, 435n46, 440n69, 452n40
Newbrook, Peter, 471nn34–35
Newman, Ruby, 342, 463n51
Newton, Frank, 327, 461n26
Nicholas, Albert, 308, 310, 311, 458n54
Nichols, Red (Ernest Loring), 183, 368, 389, 416n58, 418n30, 420n57, 420n61, 421n73, 422n6, 422n11, 431n27, 435n51, 436n58, 437n13, 442n20, 449n5, 449n4, 451n27, 461n1; with Rollini, 146–60, 162, 164, 174, 209, 210, 212, 226, 228, 242, 257–63, 269–73, 279, 280, 329, 355, 399, 430n14, 450n19, 468n41; California Ramblers, 85–102 passim, 105; Five Pennies, 222, 429n9, 431n36, 432n47, 443n39, 449n8, 450n18
Noble, Ray, 334, 347
Norvo, Red, 4, 308, 320, 386, 402n22, 460n15, 462n16, 464n77

Oakland, Will, 275–78, 280
Oakley, Ben, 192
O'Brien, Jack, 198
Odec (reviewer), 341
Odeon (record label), 267, 428n27, 450n14, 451n25
O'Doherty, Molly, 277
O'Gorman, Bill, 408n9
O'Keefe, Cork (Francis), 106, 160, 423n14, 425n56
OKeh Records, 28, 165, 190, 191, 262–65, 267, 269, 271, 345, 359, 406n24, 411n27, 416n64, 417n4, 424n43, 428nn27–28, 431n25, 431nn32–33, 443n32, 450n13, 451n27, 451nn29–30, 452n34; California Ramblers, 48–163 passim, 424n43, 429–44 passim; Wallace, 135, 141, 142, 143, 149, 152, 154; Venuti, Trumbauer, Beiderbecke,

Mole, 165, 167, 170, 171, 173, 174, 176, 191, 433n7, 433n15, 449n5
Olivier, Laurence, 346
Olsen, George, 98, 420n61, 455n61
Olsen, Ole (Lloyd), 51, 52, 54, 65, 77, 80, 97
Olympic (record label), 408n9
Openneer, Herman, 451n24
Oppenheimer, Louis, 203
Ord-Hume, Arthur, 404nn2–3
Original Dixieland Jazz Band, 40, 146, 171, 176, 278, 315, 406n32, 408n8, 415n34, 449n12, 459n65
Original Memphis Five, 47, 147, 262, 409nn30–32, 410n14, 415n34, 427n18
Original Orpheans, 192, 436n56
Original Ramblers Dance Orchestra, 226, 227
Original Wolverines, 391
Ormandy, Eugene, 355
Orpheum. *See* Radio-Keith-Orpheum
Otto Link, 441n77
Overweight Eight, 389
Owen, Rex, 180, 181, 194, 202, 213, 498n35
Owens Sisters, 394, 465n97

Pace & Handy, 25
Page, Patti, 389, 447n18
Palace Garden Orchestra, 420n69
Palm Beach Boys, 157
Palmer, Anita, 374
Palmer, Bee (Bea), 168, 175, 296, 433n19
Panico, Louis, 72
Paramount, 269, 300, 330, 332, 395, 396, 426n63; California Ramblers, 40–84 passim, 408n9, 408n9, 408n12, 413n67, 414n11, 418n26
Parker, Charlie, 460n10
Parlophone (record label), 187, 214, 219, 231, 232, 433n10, 438n38, 443n32, 450n14
Parlow, Kathleen, 408n11
Patent, Harry, 299, 396
Pathé (record label), 150, 156, 173, 200, 240, 264, 267, 408n9, 410n32, 411n27, 429n5, 430n14, 431nn24–25; California Ramblers, 67–145 passim, 149, 150, 160,

399, 411n22, 415n26, 416n61, 420n69, 428n26, 438n34
Patricola, Isabella, 416n46
Patterson, Bob, 426n2
Patterson, Helen, 296
Payne, Jack, 221, 442n8
Payne, John, 350
Payne, Laurie, 392
Payne, Norman, 180, 181, 188, 194, 202, 207, 211, 214, 218, 220, 222, 229, 230, 232, 392, 437n21, 440n67
Peabody, Eddie, 297
Pelham Memorial High School, 344
Penniket, H. G., 233
Perfect (record label). See Pathé
Perlis, Al (Alexander), 373–77
Perry, George, 71
Perry, Robert, 406n34
Perry, Samuel A., 25
Pesenti, Andre, 437n18
Petrillo, James Caesar, 289
Petrovitz, Eddie, 286
Pettis, Jack, 133, 153
Philburn, Al, 237, 238, 241, 245, 246, 248, 251–54, 286, 292, 294, 300, 446n17
Phillips, Howard, 291, 292
Phillips, Warren. See Hoke, Pat
Piccadilly (record sublabel), 445n65
Pickens Sisters, 282, 308
Pickford, Mary, 450n21
Pierce (tuba player), 409n28
Pinder, Anne, 371
Pinkett, Ward, 308, 311
Piron, Armand, 82, 133, 429n3
Planker, Carl, 85
Pletcher, Stew, 434n22
Polla, W. C. (Bill), 78, 418n20, 419n47
Pollack, Ben, 159, 211, 214, 219, 239, 279, 372
Polo, Danny, 128, 198, 440n68, 458n60
Port, Gill, 438n35
Porter, Cole, 197
Posnack, George, 271, 272, 427n2, 452n37
Powell, Herbert, 221
Powell, Teddy, 355, 378

Powers, Jack, 278
Prescott bass, 337
Priestley, Bill, 175, 436n54
Prima, Louis, 459n65
Primavalli, Paul, 408n9
Prince, Wesley, 465n92
Prince of Wales, 184
Pugliese, Art, 129, 132
Pumiglio, Pete, 6, 129–31, 162, 211, 240, 241, 268, 289, 413n63
Purvis, Jack, 264–68, 278, 400, 440n61, 451nn26–29, 451nn31–32

Quealey, Chelsea, 156, 275, 453n27; California Ramblers, 103–25 passim, 150, 155, 162, 276, 430n13; Elizalde, 177–233 passim, 395, 438n36, 443nn43–44
Quicksell, Howdy, 99, 143, 173
Quinquaginta Band/Ramblers, 178

Raderman, Lou, 298, 427n20
Radio-Keith-Orpheum, 296, 446n8
Raeburn, Boyd, 401n2
Raft, George, 345
Raiole, Rene, 384
Ram, Buck, 364
Rambler I or *II*, 346, 421n1
Rambler IV, 276, 277, 316
Rambler VI, 318
Rambler VII, 358
Rambler VIII, 8
Randall, Charlie, 408n9
Randolph, Amanda, 459n65
Rank, Bill, 161, 164–67, 169–71, 173–75, 432n3, 434n32, 435n51
Ravelle, Lois, 277
Raye, Martha, 305, 307
Razaf, Andy, 142
Rector Dansant Orchestra, 50
Red Heads, 147, 151, 421n73, 429nn4–5
Redman, Don, 70, 391, 422n4
Reeves, Eva, 25
Reeves-Smith, George, 221
Rehmann, Hans, 445n61

Reilly, Mike, 308
Reilly, Teddy, 71
Reisman, Leo, 252, 257–60, 290, 291, 448n47, 449n1, 455n68
Reiss, Winold, 93, 419n36
Remer, Ellea, 83
Remer, George Minot, 103, 386
Remer, J. C., 362
Remer, Joseph Coates, 103
Remer, Noeline Rose, 386
Renard, Jacques, 169, 271–73, 452n42
Reser, Harry, 156, 357, 428n24, 429n44, 466n123
Reynolds, Tommy, 378
Ricci, Herbert, 363
Ricci, Paul, 326, 328, 333
Rich, Buddy, 320, 321, 333–36
Rich, Fred, 115, 246, 263, 316, 396
Richards, Barbara, 397
Richards, Vince, 95, 419n45
Richardson, A., 221
Richmond-Robbins (music publisher), 408n10
Rickey, Al, 434n28
Riggin, Aileen, 423n30
Riley, Mike, 311, 332, 446n18
Riskin, Itzy, 161, 268
Ritz-Carlton Orchestra, 298, 299
Robbins (music publisher), 85, 334, 335, 338, 408n10, 444n46
Robbins, Jack, 61
Robert, Jean, 4, 200, 387, 441n78
Robertson, Dick, 284
Robinson, Bill "Bojangles," 366, 410n8
Robinson, Dave, 411n31
Robinson, Scott, 401n2
Robison (band member), 141
Robison, Willard, 173, 325
Rockwell, Tommy, 160, 161, 171, 174, 423n14
Rogers, Buddy (Charles), 263, 450n21
Rollini, Adrian: bass saxophone, 52, 54–58, 65–313 passim, 387–90, 426n2, 438n39, 438n40, 441n76, 442n13, 466n122, 470n10, 470n14; California Ramblers and small groups, 48–145, 149, 152, 155, 162, 274–83, 310, 399; childhood, 4–5, 12–19, 69; composer and arranger, 69, 120, 138, 149, 186, 321, 334, 335, 398, 414n12, 434n36, 438nn34–35; Elizalde, 7, 177–232 passim, 395, 399, 403n22, 441n2, 442n19, 443n25, 444n48; final years in Florida, 369–71, 373–74, 378–81, 468n40; freelancing, 101, 141, 150–52, 156, 171, 173, 190–91, 209, 257–73, 278–79, 291, 302, 310–13, 325, 327, 399–400, 455n67; goofus, 86–88, 91, 96, 119, 187, 221, 313, 391, 438n38; Himber, 296, 299, 300, 312, 323, 327, 329, 330, 395, 396; Lown, 209–11, 234, 237–54, 285–90, 328, 395, 399, 453n8, 453n17, 454n49; multi-instrumentalist, 80, 88, 101, 120, 126, 137, 188, 217, 240, 254, 288, 302, 310, 321, 341, 347, 353, 387, 390–92, 426n60, 433n4, 457n35; music shop, 315, 317–21, 338; Nichols, 146–50, 157, 209, 258–60, 269–71, 399; own Orchestra, 16, 17, 69, 160–76, 261, 280–84, 293, 295, 300, 301, 309, 313, 333, 400, 433n13; personality and appreciation, 3, 4, 6, 8, 93, 103–5, 114, 129, 137, 138, 361, 366, 401n3, 403n9, 412n58, 422n6, 425n45, 454n34, 470n86; piano, 21, 23–39, 40, 48–51, 53, 80, 87, 101, 278, 358, 392, 406n33, 407n58, 421n80, 445n61; Trio, 321–78, 396, 397, 462n13, 468n28, 468n31; vacation trip, 224–29, 444n49, 444n58, 445n64; vibraphone (vibraharp), 206, 207, 237–38, 242, 248, 253–54, 285, 291, 293, 294, 302, 307, 311, 313, 321–93; Venuti, 153, 154, 284, 290, 301; Whitby Grill and Tap Room, 303–15, 457n41, 457n44, 458n57; xylophone, 48–54, 80, 124, 393, 458n52
Rollini, Antonio, 9–11, 402n6
Rollini, Art (Arthur Francesco), 5–7, 15–18, 184, 188, 212, 213, 217, 218, 222, 230–32, 275, 276, 281–84, 286, 288, 291, 293, 301, 302, 305, 307, 319, 320, 325, 373, 380, 381, 384–86, 388–90, 392, 402n5, 443n24, 443n34, 444n58, 454n39, 456n77, 457n26
Rollini, Art (Arthur Nando), 386, 390, 393, 402n1

Rollini, Cheovolo, 402n7
Rollini, Dixie (Dorothy Van Wagoner Remer), 103, 105, 114, 123, 124, 186, 188, 189, 192, 209, 217, 295, 357, 373, 380, 382, 386, 427n7, 458n56, 470n86
Rollini, Ena (Kelsall), 282, 305, 386
Rollini, Ferdinando, 9–12, 15–18, 21, 189–91, 353, 402n7, 402n11, 403n23
Rollini, Gigia (Luigia), 9, 10, 16
Rollini, Giulia, 9, 10
Rollini, Lorenzo, 402n7
Rollini, Vera (Elvira), 5, 13, 16–18, 354, 384–87, 389
Rollini's instruction book, 335
Rollins, Chuck. *See* Rollini, Vera
Romeo (record label), 240
Roosevelt, Eleanor, 464n68
Roosevelt, Franklin Delano, 248, 294, 295, 344
Rose, Wally (Herman), 151, 430n15
Rosenkrantz, Timme, 303, 308, 458n56
Rossmeissl (shop), 390, 471n25
Roth, Al, 43, 44, 409nn25–26
Roush, Leslie, 396
Ruby, Sam, 121, 129, 131, 136, 139, 141, 142, 150, 162
Rude, John, 275, 276
Rudy, Ernie, 379
Rushton, Joe, 307, 389, 449n4
Russ (band member), 428n30
Russell, Luis, 266, 268, 452n34
Russell, Pee Wee, 159, 160, 162, 173, 212, 279, 292, 293
Russin, Babe, 194, 198, 212, 258, 263, 267, 270, 271
Russin, Jack, 116, 129, 131, 136, 141, 142, 144, 152, 156, 160, 162, 194, 198, 202, 206, 212, 213, 258, 311, 425n53, 440n61, 459n69
Ryker, Doc, 161

Sally and Annette, 358
Samuel, Morey, 299, 396
Samuels, Joseph, 55, 411n34
Sandeman, Harold, 160

Sandow, Teddy, 282, 453n27
Sandro, Joe Della, 384, 469n66
Sanford, Herb, 334, 414n21
Sargeant, Preston, 41, 43
Saturday Night Swing Club/Session, 313, 321, 328, 329, 335, 336, 461n33
Savoy Havana Band, 179, 180, 207, 436n56, 446n7
Savoy Orpheans, 175, 179, 180, 182, 183, 189, 192, 197, 201, 207, 221, 436n56, 437n10, 438n26, 438n30, 439n54, 441n79, 444n43
Sax, Adolphe, 54
Sax, Frank, 278
Sayag, Edmond, 197–99, 440n62
Scanlan, Walter, 278
Schiedt, Duncan, 457n37
Scholl, Dr., 275
Scholl, Warren P., 55, 306
Schubert, Franz, 327
Schutt, Arthur, 94, 147, 154, 156, 165, 174, 210, 268, 280, 433n10, 458n56, 460n17
Schuyler, Sonny, 325, 334
Schwarwanke, Xaver, 12
Scott, Raymond, 326, 327, 461n33, 462n16
Scott-Wood, George, 391
Scranton Sirens, 89, 417n14
Secrets of a Secretary, 256, 395
Seeley, Blossom, 435n43
Selinsky, Wladimir, 300, 330, 396
Sells, Harvey, 379
Selmer (instrument manufacturer), 414n14
Selvin, Ben, 263–65, 269, 329, 330, 400, 413n8, 415n23, 415n34, 417n65, 450n20, 450n22, 461n35
Seven Blue Babies, 274
7th Regimental Band, 424n32
Sexton, Ed, 278
Shafer, Lloyd, 329
Shanahan, Dick, 377
Shanley Brothers, 53, 62, 80, 275, 412n51, 453n10
Shannon, Neil, 23
Sharp, Fred, 355–71, 374, 375, 401n9, 402n24, 465n105

Shaw, Artie, 294, 296, 298, 300, 396, 459n69
Shaw, Georgia, 140
Shearing, George, 377
Shefter, Bert, 326, 327
Sherek, Henry, 222
Sheridan, Ann, 345
Shields, Larry, 409n31
Shilkret, Jack, 314
Shilkret, Nat, 170, 211
Shirley, Eva (Eva Schainbaum), 43–45, 50, 409n18, 409nn25–26, 410n8
Shoobe, Lou, 327
Siday, Eric, 214
Siderious, Sid and Rixie, 469n63
Siebert, Grey, 126, 427n8
Siegel, Al, 296, 360, 409n23, 420n58
Signorelli, Frank, 164–73, 176, 263, 410n32
Sillman, Phil, 286, 296, 301, 313, 320, 321, 422n9, 456n2, 460n10; with Rollini, 5, 16, 17, 28, 302, 305, 319, 384, 385, 401n10, 401n5, 402n2, 402n5, 403n17, 403n23, 403n25, 454n34
Simmons, Hilda, 368
Singing Boys, 211
Sissle, Noble, 197, 198, 454n48
Six Brown Brothers, 49, 55, 58, 69, 74, 404n27, 411n26
Sizzling Syncopators, 267
Sjöström, Frans, 401n2
Sky, George, 381
Small, Abe, 411n35
Smelser, Cornell, 262, 263, 399, 450n15
Smith, Bessie, 68, 85, 401n4, 414n15, 417n4
Smith, Carl, 275, 276, 453n27
Smith, Charles Edward, 434n36
Smith, Chris, 26
Smith, Clara, 68, 86, 91, 414n15, 417n4
Smith, Frederick, 435n40
Smith, George, 439n58
Smith, Joseph C., 415n34
Smith, Kate, 287, 337, 338
Smith, Mamie, 28, 269, 406n24, 414n15
Smith, Steve, 449n3
Smith, Willie "the Lion" (piano), 303, 465n92

Snake and Teddy, 261
Sniffin, Harry (Harrison). *See* Clark, Henry
Snowden, Q. Roscoe, 418n25
Sobol, Louis, 305, 458n46, 458n49
Sohmer (piano factory), 392
Solomon, Sylvan, 43, 45
Song Hits on Parade, 396
Sosnik, Harry, 468n39
Sousa, John Philip, 58, 59
Southern Jubilee Syncopated Orchestra, 41
Sparling, Earl, 241
Spear, Sammy, 298
Specht, Paul, 62, 68, 69, 73, 82, 93, 94, 104, 130, 135, 169, 171, 175, 176, 265, 349, 409n16, 415n34, 417n65, 419n38, 419n42, 419n51, 428n24
Speciale, Mike, 415n23
Spencer, O'Neil, 465n92
Spurrier, Esten, 173, 432n1
St. Cyr, Lily, 468n46
Stanwyck, Barbara, 433n21, 447n39
Star Reporter, 396
Starita, Al, 391
Stauffer, Teddy, 458n47
Stein, Jules, 289
Steinberg, Eddie, 298, 299, 328, 396
Steiner, John, 175, 408n8, 411n40, 433n5, 433n19
Stephens, Bob, 265, 267, 451nn27–28
Stephens, Haig, 322, 323, 327, 330, 396
Sterling (film distributor), 469n57
Sterling, Kay, 468n48
Stern, Hank, 190, 211
Stewart, Rex, 104, 265, 320, 401n1, 421n4
Stock, Tiny, 192, 194, 202, 229, 230, 231
Stokowski, Leopold, 343
Stone, Christopher, 216, 443n36
Stoneburn, Sid, 270, 310, 325
Storey, F. Fabian, 117, 423n28
Strange, Harcourt, 447n44
Strutt, Norman, 434n28
Sudhalter, Richard M., 148, 266, 334, 414n15, 451n26, 451n31
Sugar Step, The, 206, 395, 441n2

Sullivan, Ed, 386
Sullivan, Joe, 273, 292
Sullivan, Maxine, 350, 462n16, 468n29
Superior Jazz Band, 47, 410n32
Suratt, Valeska, 68, 413n4
Susskind, Harry, 281, 453n31
Sutherland, Lt., 424n32
Sutton, Allan, 447n21
Sutton, Ed, 408n9
Suydam, James A., 62, 412n51, 412n53
Sweatman, Wilbur, 217, 408n8
Swezey, Orinda (Peggy), 103, 189, 195, 380
Swing Styles, 397
Synco Jazz Band, 411n27
Syncopating Five, 146, 429n1

Tak, Max, 225, 226, 415n32
Tamburo, Carmela, 153
Tampa Blue Jazz Band, 411n27
Tanner Sisters, 336, 462n19
Tap Room Gang, 309, 310, 313, 459n69
Tarto, Joe, 3, 93, 94, 104, 105, 271, 272
Tatum, Art, 355, 468n29
Taub, Max, 129
Taylor, Harry, 416n51
Taylor, Lena Corinne. *See* Morse, Lee
Teagarden, Charlie, 279
Teagarden, Jack (Weldon Leo), 4, 261, 263, 270, 278–80, 301, 350, 368, 416n58, 449n8
Tenner, Joe, 274
Tennessee Tooters, 429n6
Terres, John, 409n18
Thornhill, Claude, 348
Three Blue Boys, 450n17
Three Eddies, 440n62, 443n35
Three Smoothies, 463n48
Three Suns, 375
Thunen, Tommy, 258
Thurston, Jack, 220
Tice, Larry, 241, 252, 253, 286
Tito and His Swingtette, 397
Tizol, Juan, 327
Tobin, John, 449n9
Torres, Jose, 41

Toscanini, Arturo, 296
Tough, Dave, 198, 217, 377
Treasury Department, 355, 376, 461n38
Tripp, Hugh, 438n35
Troup, George, 117, 129
Troutt, Charlie, 144
Troy, Charles, 397
Trumbauer, Frank (Tram), 147, 154, 159, 167, 171, 173, 175, 193, 259, 268, 333, 420n64, 422n12, 426n65, 432n43, 441n5; with Rollini, 4, 161, 162, 165, 166, 170, 174, 191, 222, 334, 399
Tucholka, Ed, 366
Tucker, Sophie, 62, 296, 406n32, 409n23, 456n3
Tune Twisters, 335
Tunney, Gene, 344, 434n27
Turner, Joe, 310
Turner, Lana, 464n73
Tuttle, Charles H., 248

University Six, 121, 122, 132, 133, 142, 144, 155, 173, 399, 424n33

Vagabonds, 72, 86, 88, 91, 92, 122, 134, 417n10, 418n22
Valentino, Mrs. Rudolph, 73
Vallée, Rudy, 235–37, 251, 264, 289, 296, 297, 436n56, 446nn6–8, 446n15, 447n34
Van & Schenk, 431n29
Van Eps, Fred, 42, 278, 301, 347
Van Eps, George, 347–49, 352
Van Hallberg, Gene, 299, 396
Van Keegan, Benjamin Howe, Jr., 103
Van Nus, Frank, 430n20
Van Steeden, Peter, 161, 167, 172, 175, 435n42
Van Vechten, Carl, 419n36
Vanderhoff, Mildred, 61
Vanderzee, James, 419n36
Vandoren (manufacturer), 388, 441n77
Varsity Eight, 70, 72, 82, 83, 86, 91, 109, 113, 120, 121, 123, 129, 132, 149, 154, 189, 399, 414n20, 418n27, 424n33, 426n62
Varsity Seven, 458n60

494   General Index

Varsity Six, 111, 424n33
Vaughan, Sarah, 377
Venuta, Benay, 396
Venuti, Giacomo, 153
Venuti, Joe (Giuseppe Joseph), 4, 143, 146, 149, 151–54
Verbunt, Emile, 224
Versatile Sextet, 69
Victor (record label), 21, 42, 75, 92, 100, 258, 260, 264, 272, 282, 293, 304, 306, 308, 309, 359, 404n30, 408n8, 420n61, 428n25, 428n28, 435n50, 445n3, 450n21, 451n30, 459n62, 466n112; Goldkette, 160, 165, 167; Himber, 298, 300, 312; Lown, 251–55, 285, 288, 448n47, 448n59, 455n61; Rollini, 170, 174, 187, 257, 258, 310–12, 325–27, 449n5
Victor, Frank (Frank Vigiano), 301, 302, 314, 321–24, 328–30, 332, 338, 340, 347, 348, 365, 396, 397, 457n30, 460n13, 460n17
Victorin, Paul, 417n13
Video Pictures, 469n57
Video Varieties, 371, 397
Vincent Bach Stradivarius, 432n42
Virginians, 69, 410n14, 422n12
Viseur, Gus, 450n16
Vitaphone, 256, 299, 330, 395–97, 448n67, 449n1
Vocalion (record label), 258, 298, 408n9, 416n64, 422n9, 429n6, 450n21; California Ramblers, 40–66 passim, 411n22; Rollini, 300, 335, 343, 345, 359
Voigt Geiger, 337
Volpe, Harry, 323
Voorhees, Don, 176, 259
Votey, Edwin Scott, 20, 21

Wacker, Bob, 335
Wade, Henry, 298
Wagner, Larry, 327
Walker, Edward, 436n56, 445n62
Walker, Frank, 133, 428n25
Walker, Kirby, 303
Wall, Phil, 171, 284, 290, 455n70
Wallace, Ted, 135, 141–43, 149, 152, 154, 278, 280, 311, 453n23, 458n23
Waller, Fats, 4, 167, 261, 279, 303–7, 309, 311, 312, 401n4, 417n4, 451n30, 457n37, 458n59
Waller, Fred, 396
Walters, Eddie, 263, 264, 450n22
Walton, Florence, 89, 418n15
Walton, Greeley, 267
Walton, William, 438n26
Ward, Warwick, 445n61
Waring, Charles, 446n17
Waring, Fred, 94, 197, 440nn62–63, 455n61
Waterman, Neil, 63, 107, 168, 169, 175, 389–91, 412n58, 422n12, 433n4, 433n12, 434n22
Waters, Ethel, 269, 435n43, 451n24
Waters, Fred. *See* Miller, Jack
Watts, Joe, 308, 310, 311
Way of Lost Souls, The, 231
Webb, Chick, 289
Weber, Al, 423n28, 424n33
Weber, Marek, 443n41
Webster, Carl, 434n22
Wechsler, Jack, 275, 276, 278, 280, 453n27
Weems, Ted, 417n65, 448n59
Weil, Herb, 261, 291; California Ramblers, 7, 103–63 passim, 212, 275, 276, 425n48, 428n30, 431n30
Weinstein, Ruby, 396
Weinstock, Manny, 396
Weinstock, Sammy, 395
Weiss, Sam, 309, 311
Weiss, Sid, 307, 309
Wells, Peter, 280, 389, 453n25
Welte, M. and Söhne, 24, 29, 30, 34, 35, 38, 403n15, 406nn19–22, 407n40
Wendling, Pete, 26, 27
West, Bill, 319, 320, 377, 385
West Coast Recorders, 343
Wettling, George, 377, 396
White, Hal, 142
White, Lew, 325
Whiteman, Paul, 43, 44, 58, 66, 69, 70, 73, 75, 77, 82, 85, 92, 105, 135, 139, 159, 164, 187, 190, 211, 226, 246, 251, 252, 274, 285, 86, 288,

313, 320, 323, 327, 335, 355, 362, 388, 405n12, 408n16, 409n20, 410n17, 415n34, 417n1, 420n64, 423n24, 426n65, 428n24, 432n1, 433n6, 433n18, 435n40, 436n4, 437n14, 439n57, 442n17, 442n20, 448n64, 452n5; California Ramblers, 41, 61, 80, 83, 90, 412n45, 422n12; Rollini, 105, 161, 165, 175, 176, 305, 336, 337, 357, 373, 422n11
Whittaker, Charles, 445n61
Wiedoeft, Herb, 178, 436n5
Wiedoeft, Rudy, 69, 73, 74, 85, 101, 145, 226, 415nn30–31, 417n3
Wiener, Jean, 193
Wiggs, Johnny, 449n9
Wilcox, Spiegle, 161
Wild, Harry, 220
Wilkerson, William R., 343
Wilkinson, Jerry, 467nn18–19
Wilkinson family, 378, 386, 469n67
Williams, Clarence, 57, 133, 142, 327, 414n15, 435n48
Williams, Cootie, 422n9
Williams, Fess, 425n58
Williams, Gluyas, 376
Williams, Johnny, 329
Williams, Leona, 409n31
Williams, Mary Lou, 321, 468n29
Williams, "Roll," 417n10
Williams, Roy, 359
Williams, Spencer, 87, 435n48
Williamson, Robert, 369
Wilson, Dallett H., 82
Wilson, Edith, 448n56
Wilson, Frank, 442n10
Wilson, Teddy, 328, 332
Winfield, Herb, 106, 128, 178
Winn, Edith L., 14
Woelber, Frank, 15
Wogan, Terry, 443n42
Wolfe (attorney), 385
Wolfson, Herman "Hymie," 299, 396
Wolverines, 91, 92, 98, 99, 147, 160, 391, 418n27, 420n61, 434n35, 449n7
Woman He Scorned, The, 230, 395

Wooding, Sam, 228, 401n4
WOR, 277, 287, 328, 355, 358, 359, 461n30, 463n40, 466n113, 468n36
World Transcriptions, 376, 379
Worrell, Frankie, 329
Wurlitzer (Rudolph Wurlitzer Company), 389, 417n4, 471n22
Wyllie, Dan, 437n14

Yaner, Milt, 328
Yates, Herbert, 325
Yerba Buena Jazz Band, 430n15
Yerkes, Harry, 55, 69, 75, 297, 415n34, 424n38
Young, Victor, 335

Zadye, Jack, 298
Ziegfield shows, 43, 61, 69, 89, 405n12, 453n12, 453n32
Zildjian (Avedis Zildjian Company), 319
Zir, Isodore (Izzy), 299, 396

INDEX OF LOCATIONS

Adrian's Tap Room, 303–9, 313–15, 458n54, 458n57
Alamac Hotel, 93–94, 101
Apawamis Club, 345

Baker Hotel, 366, 367
Bamberger's store, 328, 461n30
Band Box, 338, 339
Bataclan, 220, 221
Belmont Plaza, 339, 341, 463n36
Biltmore Hotel: Bert Lown, 236–40, 242, 244, 246–49, 251, 252, 255, 257, 269, 271, 285, 446n14, 447n20, 453n8, 454n46, 454n51; Los Angeles, 178, 436n5; Providence, 360, 361
Blue Note, 377
Boardwalk, 358, 432
Bowery, The, 394
Bradford Hotel, 362, 368
Bushwick Theatre, 44

Index of Locations

Cafe de Paris, 41, 432n42
Café Pompeii, 380
California Ramblers Inn, 62–66, 67, 69–71, 77, 79–80, 85–86, 89–90, 93–97, 99, 105, 107–9, 115–17, 129–31, 133, 135, 141, 212, 274, 276, 280, 384. *See also* New California Ramblers Inn
Candlelight Room, 360, 365
Capitol Theatre, 347, 358, 448n47, 464n73
Casino De Luxe, 458n53
Castilian Royal, 280, 281
Chin's, 255, 356, 363
Cinderella Ballroom/Dancing, 92, 160, 168, 178, 432n42
Circus Bar, 335, 336, 338, 343, 365, 371, 373
Circus Room, 357, 368
Ciro's, 365
Clam House, 449n10
Club New Yorker, 164–65, 167–69, 170–73, 175–76, 342, 390, 395, 432n42, 433n4, 433nn19–20, 434n28, 435n40, 454n53
Cocktail Lounge, 345, 349, 353, 360, 394, 465n97
Cocoanut Grove, 286, 287, 352, 454n48, 465n91
Colonial, 255, 349, 412n50
Community Coffee Shop, 376, 378
Community Film Theatre, 412n50
Copacabana, 360
Copley Square Hotel, 352, 465n91
Cotton Club, 105, 146, 258, 290
Cubby Hole, 305

Doc's Cocktail Lounge, 394, 465n97
Driftwood Lodge, 369–81, 386, 467n16, 467n19
Dubonnet Room, 350, 351, 355, 465n88

El Patio, 350, 355, 368
Eliot Lounge, 394
Enduro, 352, 353
Essex Hotel, 297, 300, 323, 327, 328, 331, 335, 336, 456n12, 462n21

Famous Door, 308, 458n53
5 O'Clock Club, 394

Flatbush Theatre (Avenue), 344, 350, 353, 427n15
Fordham, 242, 412n50
Freeport Theater, 344

Green Turtle Inn, 381, 384, 469n63

Half Moon Hotel, 167
Hamid's Million Dollar Pier, 348
Harry's American Bar, 380
Healy's, 410n5
Henry Grady Hotel, 354
Hialeah, 108, 368, 386, 467n19
Hickory House, 307, 315, 320, 329
Hippodrome Theater, 77, 78, 79, 82, 86, 89, 96, 354, 387, 415n46, 419n47
Hollywood Gardens, 274, 280, 453n26
Hotel Astor, 73
Hotel New Yorker, 378, 379, 390
Hotel Knickerbocker, 358, 359, 458n53
Hotel Pennsylvania, 82
House on the Hill, 82
Hunter Island Inn, 244, 275–77, 280, 281, 453n20

Island House Restaurant, 378

James Archer Smith Hospital, 381
Jerry Marsh's New Cafe Lounge, 357, 368

Knickerbocker, 358, 359, 458n53

La Maze, 143
Leon & Eddie's, 338, 349, 463n33
Lido Venice, 129, 130, 139, 140, 427n15, 428n42
Loew-Metro Club, 73
Loew's Capitol, 358
Loew's State, 346, 347, 350, 355, 358, 363, 368, 371, 465n100, 466n112

Macy's, 328, 461n30
Majestic, 48, 209, 365, 394, 435n41
Marymount College, 82
McVan's, 362, 366

Index of Locations

Melton Club, 437n23
Miami Beach Athletic Club, 378
Miami Hotel, 355
Moonlight Ballroom, 107
Monte Carlo, 71–73, 77, 79, 82, 107, 129, 416n50
Music Box, 465n91

New Amsterdam Theatre, 44
New California Ramblers Inn, 280–84, 303, 308, 425n48, 453n31, 454n39
New Mayfair Dance Orchestra, 392
Normandie Restaurant, 369

Onyx Club, 306, 308, 313–15

Palace Theatre, 43, 288, 366
Palladium, 214–17, 220
Park Central, 286, 287, 290, 374, 392, 454nn39–40, 454nn48–49, 455n62, 468n31
Park Sheraton, 374–76, 454n48
Parkway Palace, 43
Pelham Heath Inn, 114, 281, 425n48, 427n20, 453n31
Pell Tree Inn, 62, 64
Persian Terrace, 355
Peter Stuyvesant Room, 347
Piccadilly Hotel, 321, 335, 336, 338, 339, 342–46, 348, 360, 365, 371, 373, 375, 377, 462nn13–14
Plymouth Hotel, 457n41
Poli's Theatre, 44
Post Lodge, 53, 54, 56, 58, 59, 62, 66, 102, 411n22
President Hotel, 303, 306, 348, 373, 457n39, 457n44, 458n52, 462n13
Proctor's, 59, 77, 90, 411n41, 427n4

Rector's, 50, 62, 410n4, 432n42
Reisenweber Restaurant, 40, 456n3
Riley's, 342, 377
Ritz-Carlton Hotel, 82, 297–99, 448n61
RKO Theatre, 349

Roger's Corner, 355, 357, 358, 362, 465n100
Roseland Ballroom, 53, 75, 77, 130, 147, 160, 165, 167, 169, 273, 408n10, 410n15, 418n30, 429n3
Roseland Building, 42, 408n10
Roth's Restaurant, 422n6
Roxy Theatre, 350

Sardi's, 376
Savoy Hotel, 179, 181, 182, 185, 190, 192, 205, 208, 213, 214, 443n31, 446n15
Shanley Inn, 62, 412n52
Shanley's, 53, 62, 64, 410n15
Shea's Buffalo Theatre, 344, 346
Shepherds Bush Pavilion, 218, 443n42
Shubert's, 168, 349
Spotlight Club, 351
Steel Pier, 346
Strand, 89, 90, 96, 107, 172, 176, 342, 418n19, 434n40, 435n44, 437n12

Tap Room, 303–15, 457n41, 458nn54–57
Terrace, 127, 275, 276, 278, 280, 281, 355, 378
Terrace Garden Dance Palace, 62
35 Club, 357
Town House, 373, 374
Towne Room, 377
Triboro Hospital, 379–82, 469n58
Trocadero, 343, 464n57, 464n60
Tuschinsky, 225
"21" Club, 373

Victoria Hotel, 394
Vogue Lounge, 377

Wayside, 394
Whitby Grill, 303, 457n37, 458n56
White Way Music Shop, 315, 317, 322, 338, 346, 375, 377, 385, 460n10
Whiteman's Club, 160, 167, 168, 432n42
Wilber's Supper Club, 369
Winder Stores, 428n30
Windsor Theatre, 347, 350
Wyoming Valley Country Club, 345

INDEX OF TUNE TITLES

"A New Kind of Man," 91
"Aase's Death," 266
"Abide with Me," 419n47
"Accordion Joe," 263
"Admiration," 327, 461n26
"Aeroplane and the Bee, The," 327
"After the Sun Kissed the World Goodbye," 232
"After You've Gone," 150, 154, 155, 179, 261, 270, 429n12, 430n13
"Again," 187, 439n49
"Ain't Misbehavin'," 271, 305
"Ain't She Sweet," 142, 143
"Ain't That a Grand and Glorious Feeling," 152
"Alabamy Bound," 420n53
"Alexander's Ragtime Band," 271, 338
"Alice Blue Gown," 210
"Allah's Holiday," 210
"Alone in a Crowd," 442n8
"Alone with My Dreams," 243
"Amapola," 347
"And Furthermore," 156
"And Then I Forget," 132
"And Then Your Lips Met Mine," 254
"Arcady," 416n48
"Are You Sorry," 120
"Arkansas Blues," 87, 88, 144, 149, 154, 188
"At Dawning," 162
"At the Jazz Band Ball," 171, 434n37
"At the Turn of the Tide," 220
"Au Revoir," 335, 339, 398, 468n42
"Autopsy on Schubert," 327
"Autumn in New York," 312
"Avalon," 246

"Back in Your Own Backyard," 397
"Back Where the Daffodils Grow," 92
"Ballin' the Jack," 271
"Baltimore," 170, 439n49, 439n54
"Bataclan," 220, 221
"Be Bo Bo," 267
"Beale Street Blues," 133, 155
"Beatin' the Dog," 154
"Beautiful Stars Above," 28, 36
"Because I Love You," 425n48
"Because My Baby Don't Mean Maybe Now," 208
"Becky from Babylon," 34, 37
"Beedle-Um-Bo," 144
"Bees Knees," 66, 413n67
"Begin the Beguine," 468n42
"Bei Mir Bist Du Schön," 334
"Beloved," 292
"Bessie Couldn't Help It," 267
"Bill," 333
"Bit by Bit You're Breaking My Heart," 79
"Black and Blue," 261, 271
"Black and Blue Bottom," 153
"Black Horse," 272
"Black Panther," 288
"Bless Your Little Heart," 153
"Blossoms of Broadway," 396
"Blue Baby," 193
"Blue Danube," 397, 467n21
"Blue Hawaii," 350
"Blue Heaven," 184
"Blue Is the Night," 447n31
"Blue Prelude," 291
"Blue River," 161, 162, 166
"Blue Skies," 428n33
"Blue Room, The," 184
"Borneo," 191
"Bouncin' in Rhythm," 309
"Brazil," 468n42
"Broadway Blues," 31, 36
"Broadway Melody, The," 219
"Bugle Call Rag," 325
"Burglar's Revenge," 326
"By the Shalimar," 271
"Bye Bye Blues," 235, 241, 244, 246, 247, 289, 445n3, 447n41, 448nn46–47, 455n66
"Bye-Bye, Pretty Baby," 167

"California Here I Come," 85, 421n80
"Call of the Freaks," 270

Index of Tune Titles

"Calling Me Home," 439n49, 439n54
"Camel Walk, The," 121
"Canadian Capers," 428n33
"Can I Forget You?," 328
"Can't Help Lovin' That Man," 439n55
"Careless Love," 325
"Cariamba, The," 396
"Carolina in the Morning," 271
"Casey Jones," 144, 429n45
"Cat, The," 142
"Chances Are," 279
"Chanson," 192
"Chanson Bohemienne," 396
"Charleston," 99, 421n2
"Charley My Boy," 88
"Charlie's Home," 288, 291
"Charmaine," 184
"Cheese and Crackers," 165
"Chicago," 429n1
"Chime Time," 341, 398
"China Boy," 279
"Chinatown, My Chinatown," 335, 340, 397, 463n52
"Chloe," 233
"Chopinata," 193
"Chopin's Ghost," 326
"Clam House," 261
"Clap Hands, Here Comes Charley," 121
"Clementine," 156, 157, 166, 169, 334
"Coffee in the Morning," 294
"Collegiate Love," 262
"Come Down to Earth, Little Angel," 441n83, 442n8
"Congratulations," 239
"Copenhagen," 91
"Copyin' Louis," 265
"Cornfed," 148
"Cotton," 310
"Could I? I Certainly Could," 122
"Crazy Rhythm," 206, 442n8
"Crazy Words Crazy Tune," 142
"Cross Patch," 396
"Cryin' All Day," 173
"Crying Myself to Sleep," 254

"Daisie," 69, 398
"Dance Little Lady," 192, 193
"Dancing in the Dark," 277
"Dardanella," 372, 450n20, 468n42
"Dark Eyes," 347, 350, 397, 467n21
"Dark Town Strutters Ball, The," 192, 406n32, 429n1
"Davenport Blues," 301
"Daybreak," 442n8
"Dead Man Blues," 431n30
"Deep Blue Sea Blues," 86, 91, 417n4
"Deep Hollow," 392
"Delirium," 155, 156
"Desdemona," 121
"Diane," 186, 187
"Did You Mean It?," 174, 439n49, 439n54
"Did Your Mother Come from Ireland?," 325
"Diga Diga Doo," 324, 343, 397
"Dinah," 246, 328, 428n33
"Dippermouth Blues," 293
"Dismal Dan," 266
"Dixie," 186, 189, 398, 438n35
"Dixie Stomp," 120, 398, 425n58, 438n34
"Doin' the Uptown Lowdown," 292, 293
"Dolly, I Love You," 32, 36
"Donkey Dust," 420n53
"Don't Be Like That," 442n8
"Don't Take Away Those Blues," 28, 36
"Down Georgia Way," 266
"Dreaming Blues," 28, 36
"Dreamy Melody," 81, 416n60
"Driftin'," 322, 398
"Dromedary," 419n41, 426n60
"Dustin' the Donkey," 99, 121, 420n53

"Easy Melody," 71
"Eccentric," 159
"Everybody Loves My Baby," 90, 93
"Ev'rything Is Hotsy Totsy Now," 101

"Fallin' Down," 120
"Falling in Love with You," 442n8
"Farewell Blues," 142, 155, 156, 325
"Feelin' No Pain," 159, 162, 442nn21–22

"Fireworks," 452n40
"First Class Private Mary Brown," 359
"Five Pennies," 148
"Flapper Wife, The," 96
"Flat Foot Floogie," 337
"Follow the Swallow," 90
"For No Reason at All in C," 433n15
"Fra Diavolo Fantasia," 15, 403n19
"Frankie and Johnny," 72
"Free and Easy, The," 243

"Gather Lip Rouge While You May," 298
"Georgia Rose," 43
"Get Goin'," 296
"Get Out and Get Under the Moon," 442n8
"Girl Friend of a Boy Friend of Mine," 272
"Girl of My Dreams," 442n8
"Girl with the Light Blue Hair," 397, 467n21
"Glad Rag Doll," 216
"Gliding Ghost," 334, 398
"God Bless Our President," 364, 376, 398
"Goin' Home Blues," 149
"Gold Digger Stomp," 161
"Good Man Is Hard to Find, A," 173, 174
"Goose Pimples," 173, 435n48
"Got the Jitters," 296
"Gotta Getta Girl," 421
"Grown Up Baby," 206, 442n8
"Guess Who?," 211

"Hallelujah," 184, 260, 350, 463n52
"Happy as the Day Is Long," 290, 291
"Happy Days Are Here Again," 396
"Happy Feet," 391
"Hard to Get Gertie," 122
"Have You Ever Been Lonely?," 284
"Hawaiian Medley," 350
"Heartaches," 254, 448n59
"Heartbreakin' Baby," 149
"Heartbroken Rose," 419n41
"Heebee Jeebies," 132
"Hello Baby," 239
"Hello, Aloha, How Are You?," 431n24
"Here Am I, Broken-Hearted," 439n54

"Here Comes Emily Brown," 271
"Here Comes the Sun," 252
"Here You Come with Love," 288
"Hesitation Blues," 359
"Hey! Young Fella," 285
"Hiawatha's Lullaby," 290
"High-High-High," 428n33
"Holy, Holy, Holy," 419n47
"Honeysuckle Rose," 307, 309, 314, 329
"Honky Tonk Donkey," 364, 398
"Honolulu Blues," 164
"Hot Lips," 327
"How Long Has This Been Going On," 439n54
"Hula Blues, The," 31, 32, 36, 411n26
"Hula Lou," 83
"Humoresque," 342
"Humpty Dumpty," 170, 442nn21–22
"Hustlin' and Bustlin' for Baby," 284
"Hut Sut Song," 368

"I Ain't Got Nobody," 121, 132, 156, 157, 184, 233, 271
"I Call My Girl Revenge," 439n49
"I Can't Escape from You," 396
"I Can't Give You Anything but Love," 233, 441n83, 442n8
"I Cried for You," 325
"I Don't Know Where I'm Going," 326
"I Don't Mind Walking in the Rain," 447n41
"I Found a New Baby," 81
"I Got the Ritz from the One I Love," 279
"I Hear You Calling Me," 407n53
"I Know What It Means," 120, 398
"I Left My Sugar Standing in the Rain," 157
"I Let a Song Go Out of My Heart," 336
"I Like a Little Girl Like That," 447n41
"I Like What You Like," 152, 398, 430n20
"I Lost My Gal from Memphis," 271
"I Love Me," 67, 68
"I Love the College Girls," 141
"I Love You," 336
"I Miss My Swiss," 119, 422n10
"I Must Have Company," 84

Index of Tune Titles

"I Must Have That Man," 442n10
"I Need Lovin'," 133
"I Never Dreamt," 447n31
"I Raised My Hat," 294
"I Think of What You Used to Think of Me," 441n83
"I Told You So," 30, 36
"I Want a Good Man," 269
"I Want to Be Happy," 263
"I Was Made to Love You," 263
"I Wish I Could Shimmy Like My Sister Kate," 47, 57, 133, 142, 409n30, 428n23
"I Wish That I Were Twins," 301
"I Wonder What's Become of Joe," 122
"Ice Cream," 439n54
"I'd Be in a Fairway with You," 246
"I'd Like to Be a Bee in Your Boudoir," 263
"Ida! Sweet as Apple Cider," 159, 160, 228, 263
"If I Had You," 207, 441n8
"I'll Be Blue Just Thinking of You," 248
"I'll Be Lonely," 439n49
"I'll Build a Nest," 288
"I'm Always Stuttering," 58
"I'm Back in Love Again," 144
"I'm Coming, Virginia," 442n20
"I'm Following You," 264
"I'm Going to Dance at Clancy's," 312
"I'm Gonna Charleston Back to Charleston," 120
"I'm Gonna Hang around My Sugar," 121
"I'm Just a Jitterbug," 397
"I'm Just Wild about Harry," 260
"I'm Satisfied beside That Sweetie of Mine," 91
"I'm So Afraid of You," 254
"I'm Somebody's Somebody Now," 152, 430n20
"I'm Sorry, Dear," 279
"I'm Sorry, Sally," 207, 442n8
"I'm Wonderin' Who," 170
"I'm Yours," 252
"Imagination," 162, 442nn21–22
"In a Mist," 220, 320, 433n7, 433n15
"In a Rendez-Vous," 90

"In My Gondola," 113
"In the Dusk," 30, 36
"In the Heart of Dear Old Italy," 34, 37
"In the Ruff," 293
"Indian Cradle Song," 190
"Is She My Girlfriend," 439n49
"Is You Is or Is You Ain't (Ma' Baby)," 359
"Isle of Capri," 307, 314
"Isle of Paradise," 34, 37
"Isn't It Heavenly," 291
"It All Depends on You," 425n48
"It Had to Be You," 301, 397
"It Is the Blessed Easter Morn," 419n47
"It Isn't Fair," 395
"It Takes a Good Woman," 133
"It Was Only a Sun Shower," 164
"It's My Night to Shine," 397
"It's the Talk of the Town," 396, 456n73
"It's the Way You Do It," 30, 36
"I've a Garden in Sweden," 93
"I've Got 'It'," 268
"I've Got the Blues for My Kentucky Home," 32, 37
"I've Got the Girl," 133
"I've Got to Get Up and Go to Work," 292
"Iyone," 438n33

"Japanese Sandman," 246, 260
"Jazz Dance Repertoire, The," 26, 27, 36
"Jazz Me Blues, The," 171, 292, 377, 420n61, 434nn35–37, 446n11, 468n41
"Jazz O'Jazz," 309
"Jeannine," 442n8
"Jelly Roll Blues," 157
"Jig Saw Puzzle Blues," 285
"Jig Time," 395
"Jimtown Blues," 429n4
"Jitters," 322
"Jollity Farm," 441n6
"June," 32, 34, 37
"June Night," 246
"Just a Little Closer," 244
"Just a Little Drink," 426n60
"Just a Little Fond Affection," 441n83

"Just an Hour of Love," 170
"Just Another Day," 184, 439n49
"Just Imagine," 195

"Kaintucky," 79
"Kalua," 350
"Karavan," 260
"Keep It under Your Hat," 67
"Keep On Doin' What You're Doin'," 296
"Kickin' the Cat," 154
"King Porter Stomp," 429n4
"Krazy Kat," 170

"Last Night on the Back Porch," 70, 71
"Laughing Marionette," 206, 392, 442n8
"Lazy Weather," 144, 155
"Leave My Baby Alone," 143
"Let Me Linger Longer in Your Arms," 101
"Let Me Sing and I'm Happy," 264, 265
"Let's Call the Whole Thing Off," 326
"Let's Do It," 219
"Let's Take a Walk around the Block," 299
"'Leven Thirty Saturday Night," 264
"Lies," 279
"Lightly and Politely," 335, 398
"Lili Marlene," 359
"Limehouse Blues," 83, 90, 246, 368, 397, 433n11, 463n52, 468n39
"Little Grey Sweetheart of Mine," 52
"Liza," 376
"Lo the Stone Is Rolled Away," 419n47
"Loch Lomond," 397, 467n21
"Locomotive," 326
"Long Lost Mama," 67
"Looking at the World through Rose Colored Glasses," 132
"Looking at You across the Breakfast Table," 264
"Lord Is Risen, The," 419n47
"Lots of Mama," 82
"Love and Kisses," 153
"Love Bug Will Bite You, The," 326
"Love Is Like a Cigarette," 312
"Love Me Daddy Blues," 120

"Loveless Love," 310
"Lovely Liza Jane," 310
"Lover Come Back to Me," 220
"Loving You the Way I Do," 253
"Lucky Little Devil," 262

"Magnolia," 442n20
"Make My Cot Where the Cot-Cot-Cotton Grows," 174
"Makin' Whoopee," 450n22
"Mama Loves Papa, Papa Loves Mama," 72
"Man from the South, The," 259
"Man I Love, The," 426n65, 439n55
"Maple Leaf Rag," 21
"Marche Funèbre," 156, 431n29
"Marie," 328
"Martha," 353, 397, 467n21
"Marvelous," 160, 442
"Mary Lou," 132
"Maybe It's Love," 448n48
"Me and My Shadow," 437n10
"Me and the Boyfriend," 90, 94
"Me and the Girl Next Door," 264
"Me Too," 132, 428n33
"Mean Blues," 82
"Mean Dog Blues," 150, 154
"Meanest Kind o' Blues," 259
"Meditation," 121
"Mello as a 'Cello," 302, 398
"Memphis Blues," 325
"Merry Widow Waltz," 468n39
"Milenberg Joys," 121, 293, 426n62
"Mindin' My Business," 82
"Minor Gaff," 272, 426n2, 452n39
"Minuet" (by Paderewski), 342
"Minuet in Jazz," 397, 467n21
"Minute Waltz," 15, 397, 403n21, 467n21
"Misery Farm," 207, 442n8
"Mississippi Basin," 291
"Mooche, The," 449n1
"Moon Is Low, The," 264
"Moon of Japan," 439n49
"Moonstruck," 288
"Muddy Water," 143

Index of Tune Titles

"Mug of Ale, A," 165, 166, 433n11
"Music Goes 'Round and 'Round, The," 250, 311, 447n18
"Musical Moonlight," 184
"My Baby Just Cares for Me," 447n41
"My Blackbirds Are Bluebirds Now," 442n10
"My Campfire Dream," 327
"My Castle in Spain Is a Shack in the Rain," 210
"My Cutie's Due at Two-to-Two Today," 132
"My Future Just Passed," 264, 270
"My Gal Sal," 164
"My Gypsy Rhapsody," 291
"My Honey's Loving Arms," 52
"My Kind of a Man," 269
"My Melancholy Baby," 191, 325
"My Missouri Home," 254, 448n58
"My Old Kentucky Home," 409n22
"My Pet," 191–93
"My Sweetie Went Away," 68
"Mysterious Mose," 267
"Mystery," 302

"Nagasaki," 309
"Navy Blues," 262
"Near You," 467n26
"New Twister, The," 164
"Nightingale," 32, 36
"No Wonder I'm Blue," 34, 37
"Nobody but My Baby," 142
"Nobody's Sweetheart," 212, 214, 220
"Nonchalance," 335, 398
"Nothin' Does-Does It Like It Used to Do-Do-Do," 156, 157
"Nothing but Notes," 302, 398

"O, Du Lieber Augustin," 119
"O'er the Billowy Sea," 260
"Oh, Baby! Don't We Get Along," 143
"Oh, Say Can I See You Tonight," 119
"Oh Doris! Where Do You Live?," 162
"Oh Gee! Say Gee!," 30, 36
"Oh! How I Love My Darling!," 93
"Oh! If I Only Had You," 132

"Oh Joe," 70, 414n17
"Oh Lizzie," 142
"On Edge," 335, 398
"On Revival Day," 268
"On the Alamo," 53
"On the Oregon Trail," 99
"One I Love Can't Be Bothered with Me, The," 240
"One Week Ago," 73
"Oodles of Noodles," 443n24
"Operatic Medley," 94, 342, 418n20
"Original Rags," 21
"Out of the Dawn," 442n8
"Oya Negra," 376

"Pack Up Your Sins and Go to the Devil," 407n56
"Pagan Love Song," 397
"Palms, The," 419n47
"Panama," 311
"Parade of the Wooden Soldiers, The," 61
"Pardon the Glove," 143
"Passing Time with Me," 244
"Pastafazoola," 155, 431n29
"Pay-Off, The," 420n70
"Peacock Walk, The," 30, 36
"Penalty of Love, The," 253
"Pensacola," 422n4
"Pianotrope," 220
"Pink Elephants," 285
"Play It Red," 155, 431n27
"Play Me Slow," 419n41
"Playground in the Sky," 439n54
"Please Don't Talk about Me When I'm Gone," 254
"Polly from Hollywood," 428n33
"Poor Richard," 266
"Possibly," 437n10
"Precious Little Thing Called Love, A," 219
"Preparation," 329, 330, 334, 335, 338, 339, 396, 398
"Pretty Kitty Kelly," 30, 36
"Prince of Wails," 420n53

"Put and Take," 268
"Puttin' On the Ritz," 258, 26

"Ragging the Scale," 268
"Rainbow of Love," 434n32
"Rambling Blues, Them," 87, 88
"Readin', Rittin', Rhythm," 272
"Rebound," 322, 329, 398
"Red Hot Henry Brown," 121
"Red Hot Mama," 90
"Remember the Night," 120, 398
"Rememb'ring," 72
"Rhythm Step," 184
"Rising Sun," 439n54
"Riverboat Shuffle," 91, 159, 171, 301
"Roam On My Little Gypsy Sweetheart," 155
"Rocking Chair Blues," 85
"Rolling Around in the Roses," 167
"Rondo Capriccioso," 15
"Room with a View, A," 192
"Rosary, The," 74, 226
"Rose of Washington Square," 25
"Roses of Picardy," 210, 226
"Royal Garden Blues," 171, 173, 434n35, 435n48
"Runnin' Wild," 397
"Running Between the Raindrops," 254

"Sail Along, Silv'ry Moon," 328
"San," 86, 122, 123
"Sarita," 442
"Savage Serenade," 456n77
"Savoy Stomp," 220
"Sax Appeal," 442n21
"Saxema," 74
"Saxophobia," 74
"Sax-O-Phun," 74
"Say Arabella," 119
"Say Hello," 254, 448n58
"Schwarze Augen," 350
"Send Me," 302
"Sensation Rag," 171
"Seventh Heaven," 325
"Shake," 122

"Shake It Down," 452n40
"Shake That Thing," 122
"She Belongs to Me," 132
"She Knows Her Onions," 132
"She Loves Me," 91, 92, 418n26
"Sheik of Araby, The," 43, 81, 270
"She's a Great, Great Girl," 206
"She's Not Too Hot, She's Not Too Cool," 120, 398
"She's One Sweet Show Girl," 219
"Shy Anna," 183, 188
"Side by Side," 143, 442n20
"Sidewalk Blues," 133
"Since My Best Gal Turned Me Down," 173, 174
"Singapore Sorrows," 214, 219
"Singing the Blues," 32, 33, 36, 37, 161, 333
"Sirens Dream," 184
"Sittin' in a Corner," 71, 72
"Sittin' on a Log," 294
"Slap That Bass," 326
"S-L-U-E Foot," 144
"Small Fry," 335, 34
"So Sympathetic," 242
"Sobbin' Blues," 147
"Soliloquy," 259
"Some of These Days," 142, 271, 406n32, 449n1
"Somebody Loves Me," 301
"Somebody Stole My Gal," 191, 192
"Someday Sweetheart," 157
"Someone Is Losin' Susan," 132
"Someone Loves You After All," 405n12
"Sometimes," 442n8
"Sometimes I'm Happy," 260
"Song Is Ended, The," 439n49, 439n54
"Song of Surrender," 294
"Song of the Bayou," 259
"Song of the Islands," 350
"Sorrowful Blues," 85
"Sorry," 173
"S.O.S.," 326
"Sound Your 'A,'" 396
"Southern Rose," 93
"Spread a Little Happiness," 216
"Squeeze Me," 259

"St. James Infirmary," 259, 266
"St. Louis Blues," 270, 330, 396
"Stars and Stripes," 59
"Static Strut," 123
"Steamboat Bill," 144, 429n45
"Streamlined Greta Green," 310
"Stick Out Your Can," 302
"Stockholm Stomp," 133, 141
"Stormy Weather," 290, 452n39
"Strike Up the Band," 271, 447n31
"Stringing the Blues," 153
"Strutting at the Strutters' Ball," 429
"Stumbling," 53, 411n19
"Sugar," 174, 175, 187, 439n54
"Sugar Blues," 328
"Sugar Step, The," 189, 206, 301, 395, 439n54, 441n2
"Swamp Blues," 155
"Swanee," 428n33
"Swanee Blues," 405n16
"Swanee Shore," 155
"Sweeping the Clouds Away," 425n49
"Sweet Georgia Brown," 101, 271, 334, 421n77
"Sweet Lorraine," 292
"Sweet Madness," 293, 456n77
"Sweet Sue," 221, 229, 441n8
"Sweetest Story Ever Told," 333
"Swing Low," 314, 321, 398
"Swingin' 'Em Down," 310

"'T Ain't No Sin," 264
"Take My Heart," 396
"Take Your Finger Out of Your Mouth," 437n10
"Taming the Devil," 327
"Tap Room Blues," 302, 398
"Tap Room Special," 311
"Tap Room Swing," 313, 314, 329, 398
"Tea at the Ritz," 396
"Tea for Two," 90, 263, 450n19
"Teatime," 439n49
"Tech Triumph," 99, 100
"Techland," 99, 421n74
"Teddy Bear Blues," 66, 413n67

"Tell All the Folks in Kentucky," 71
"Tell Her at Twilight," 51
"Tell Me," 260
"Telling It to the Daisies," 268
"Tessie, Stop Teasing Me," 88
"That Old Gal of Mine," 68
"That's a Plenty," 337
"That's All There Is, There Ain't No More," 101
"That's What I Like About You," 279
"Them Rambling Blues," 87, 88
"There Ain't No Land Like Dixieland," 171
"There Ain't No Maybe in My Baby's Eyes," 142
"There's a Cradle in Caroline," 161, 171
"There's a Goldmine in the Sky," 328
"There's a Wah-Wah Girl in Agua Caliente," 268, 452n33
"These Foolish Things," 396
"They Satisfy," 254
"Thinking of You," 428n33
"This Is Heaven," 312
"This Is My True Confession," 396
"This Time It's Love," 456n73
"Those Panama Mamas," 92
"Thou Swell," 191
"Thousand Good Nights, A," 301
"Three Blind Mice," 161
"Three Little Words," 336
"Through," 239
"Tiger Rag," 99, 122, 173, 186, 221, 279, 280, 341, 396, 408n2, 420n53, 420n61
"Tin Roof Blues," 83, 84
"Tired Hands," 439n54
"T.N.T.," 113
"To Whom It May Concern," 254
"Too Tired," 91
"Toot-Toot-Tootsie," 429n1
"Toy Trumpet," 335, 339, 340
"Transportation Blues," 144
"Tripoli," 30, 36
"Trouble with Me Is You, The," 325
"Truckin'," 310
"Two Blue Eyes," 81
"Two Dukes on a Pier," 327

"Under a Texas Moon," 238
"Under the Moon," 152, 186, 442n8
"Under the Sun," 248
"Undercurrent," 336
"Until Love Comes Along," 243
"Until Today," 396
"Up and At 'Em," 132

"Valse Llewellyn," 74
"Valse Vanité," 74
"Vibraphone Interlude," 330
"Vibraphonia," 290, 398
"Vibraphonia No. 2," 302, 398
"Vibrollini," 314, 322, 398
"Vilia," 328
"Virginia," 441n83, 442n8
"Vo-Do-Do-De-O Blues," 144, 149, 154

"Waitin' at the Gate for Katy," 300
"Waitin' for Me," 30
"Waitin' for the Evenin' Mail," 407n56
"Wait'll You See," 132
"Walkin' the Dog," 271
"Wang Wang Blues, The," 144
"Wanna Go Back to Bali," 397
"Was It a Dream?," 441n83
"Was It Rain?," 325
"Way Down Barcellona Way," 27, 36
"Way I Feel Today, The," 269
"Weather Man," 309
"Weeping Willow Blues," 86, 417n4
"We'll Have a Honeymoon Sunday," 288
"What a Man," 122
"What Is This Thing Called Love?," 219
"What-Cha Gonna Do When There Ain't No Jazz," 27, 36
"What-Cha-Ma-Call-It," 132
"What's the Use of Crying?," 267
"What's the Use of Living Without Love?," 244
"When a Woman Loves a Man," 260
"When the Morning Rolls Around," 283
"When You're Feeling Blue," 267
"Where Have You Been All My Life," 442n8
"Where the Shy Little Violets Grow," 442n10

"Where'd You Get Those Eyes?," 123
"Wherever You Are," 195
"Whisper Song, The," 144
"Whispering," 246
"Who?," 271
"Who Walks In When I Walk Out," 296
"Who-Oo? You-Oo, That's Who," 152, 153
"Who's Sorry Now," 67
"Who's That Knocking at My Door," 162, 164
"Wintertime Dreams," 312
"With the Coming of Tomorrow," 34, 37
"Without a Song," 336
"Wonderful One," 81, 416n60
"Worka John," 428n33
"World Is Waiting for the Sunrise, The," 240
"Wringin' and Twistin'," 167

"Yes, She Do, No, She Don't," 144
"Yiddisher Charleston," 391
"Yo San," 29, 36, 39
"You Brought a New Kind of Love to Me," 269
"You Can't Have My Sugar for Tea," 188, 439n49
"You Can't Keep a Good Man Down," 25
"You Can't Pull the Wool over My Eyes," 396
"You Can't Stop Now," 363, 364
"You Darlin'," 244
"You Don't Like It Not Much," 156, 162
"You'll Never Get to Heaven with Those Eyes," 420n61
"You're a Builder Upper," 299
"You're Gonna Get My Letter in the Morning," 372, 373
"You're Simply Delish," 253
"You're the Cream in My Coffee," 442n10
"You're the One I Care For," 248, 253
"You're the Only Girl That Made Me Cry," 28, 36, 39
"You've Got Me Crying Again," 284

"Zulu Wail," 144, 162

ABOUT THE AUTHOR

Credit: Loes van Delden-Posthumus

Ate van Delden (b. 1941, Groningen, The Netherlands) is a music scholar whose writing has appeared in such publications as *Doctor Jazz* and *Vintage Jazz Mart* and in the form of liner notes to several CDs. He is a former board member of the Doctor Jazz Foundation, a Dutch organization for the promotion of classic jazz. He spent his professional career in marketing electronic products. He is happily married to Loes and they have two sons and two grandchildren.

www.ingramcontent.com/pod-product-compliance
Lightning Source LLC
Chambersburg PA
CBHW030559230426
43661CB00053B/1773